The Nature of Creative Development

The Nature of Creative Development

JONATHAN S. FEINSTEIN

Stanford Business Books
An imprint of Stanford University Press
Stanford, California 2006

Stanford University Press

Stanford, California

© 2006 by the Board of Trustees of the Leland Stanford Junior University. All rights reserved.

Printed in the United States of America on acid-free, archival-quality paper

Library of Congress Cataloging-in-Publication Data

Feinstein, Jonathan S., 1960–

The nature of creative development/Jonathan S. Feinstein.

    p. cm.

Includes bibliographical references and index.

ISBN 0-8047-4573-0 (cloth : alk. paper)

1. Creative ability. I. Title.

BF408.F37 2006

153.3'5–dc22

                                                2005032771

Original Printing 2006

Last figure below indicates year of this printing:

15 14 13 12 11 10 09 08 07 06

Special discounts for bulk quantities of Standford Business books are available to corporations, professional associations, and other organizations. For details and discount information, contact the special sales department of Standford University Press. Tel: (650) 736-1783, Fax: (650) 736-1784

In memory of my mother.

For my father, Susan, Leslie, Ariel, and Sara.

Contents

Preface   ix

Acknowledgments   xiv

1 Introduction   1

2 Creative Interests and Conceptions of Creative Interests   36

3 The Development of Creative Interests   62

4 Intrinsic Sources of Interest   107

5 Extrinsic and Strategic Factors in the Development
   of Creative Interests   134

6 Kinds of Creative Interests   160

7 The Distinctiveness and Breadth of Creative Interests   182

8 Resonances and Connections   224

9 Creative Responses   248

10 Exploration of Creative Interests and Creativity Generation;
   Creative Expertise   293

11 The Role of Conceptions of Creative Interests and Associated
   Values and Principles in Guidance; Management of Creative
   Development at the Meta-Level   353

12 Creativity in Projects   388

13 Multiple Interests   425

14 Patterns of Creative Development: Patterns of Projects;
   Projects and Interests   444

viii

15 Patterns of Creative Development: Evolution of Interests
and Sequences of Interests   463

16 Difficulties in Creative Development   505

17 Creative Development and Linkages of Cultural Transmission:
Modeling Cultural Development   522

18 Epilogue: Modeling Individuals in Social Systems   543

Appendix   549

Bibliography   561

Index   562

PREFACE

This book has been many years in the making, with roots extending far back in my development. The path to it has encompassed much, much far from evident in the pages to follow. Here I present some notes about my process of development through which I have come to write it. In my sophomore year in college at Stanford, in my initial engagement with the social sciences, it occurred to me, as a natural framework of analysis, to focus on the way in which individuals are guided by their culture, specifically ideals and information they glean or that is transmitted to them, in their work, through which they come to make the particular contributions to their society that they make. I wrote a number of papers connected with this idea and framework, including one in which I set forth a model in which ideals guide individuals in their work and the cultural development of ideals is in turn driven by individuals' needs in their work and the social evaluation of their work, and another about prehistoric cave painting and possible principles of representation that may have guided prehistoric peoples in their artwork, rooted in their psychological orientation to nature. But I did not move forward in developing the framework in any direct way. Looking back, the framework and viewpoint had, very likely, roots in my earlier development. I read innumerable biographies growing up — of explorers, frontiersmen, presidents, sports heroes, and a wide array of historical figures — surely not especially unusual. In part also my thinking about social science was rooted in my approach to literature. I recall telling a friend of mine in high school that I naturally gravitated, in interpreting literature, to focus on the basic theme of "the individual and society"; I was interested in this theme, for example, in the novels of Thomas Hardy, A *Portrait of the Artist as a Young Man, The Stranger,* and Aristophanes' *The Clouds.* There may have been connections, too, with my interests in mathematical modeling and computer programming. I did a science project in high school measuring air pollutants and was interested in building models combining observations made at different locations to calibrate a regional atmospheric air quality model. However, these links are all rather tentative; the path begins most clearly in my view, looking back, in college, with my first true engagement with social science and my rudimentary conception of individuals guided by their culture in their work and activity.

Lacking a clear sense of how to pursue the approach that seemed intuitive to me for modeling individuals in their culture and society, grasping it only tentatively, and with it seemingly outside of the standard social science models and approaches I was learning, I left it aside. I majored in economics — attracted, I think, by the idea of aggregating individuals to form a market, which resonated with me, and by the formal modeling. In the last years of college and the years following, a number of interests and ideas gained my focus of attention. I wrote my college honors thesis on an idea of individuals embedded in a network — a different focus, but in some way I think connected with my earlier idea. I worked for a firm in law and economics, developing an interest in this field, and also in learning how to forge a direct connection from a theoretical model to its empirical estimation. I pursued a Ph.D. in economics — my dissertation presents an econometric model addressing the problem of incomplete detection of violations of laws and regulations; and accepted a position as an assistant professor at the Stanford University Graduate School of Business.

In the spring of 1990, two and a half years after returning to Stanford, sensing the need to find a new direction, perhaps more aligned with my earlier interests and way of thinking about individuals and culture, I initiated as a loose intellectual activity exploration in the general domain of, as I described it to myself, "technology and values." I spent the second half of the summer and the fall in New Haven on leave. During this period I began to read more widely, especially about conceptions of freedom and liberty, which struck me as the value least integrated into traditional kinds of models in economics. Beginning in the winter of the following year, I embarked upon a wide course of reading, mainly in philosophy at first. This reading continued through that year and the following year, when I was fortunate to have a fellowship at the National Bureau of Economic Research, which enabled me to pursue reading intensively, along with more traditional economics research. My reading expanded into parts of psychology, especially psychological research concerning values and object relations theory. I relocated to the Yale School of Management in 1992. My wife

Leslie and I were married in 1991, and were fortunate to gain positions both at Yale; at Yale I continued to read fairly widely.

Looking back, I realize that during this period I not only learned a great deal — basic concepts, theories, intellectual and cultural history, and different approaches to social theorizing, but also was finding the biographical details about the individuals whose works I read intrinsically interesting. I read biographical details with interest and often sought out details about a person's path of development. However, I did not focus on this — it was in the background. One branch of my reading focused on social activists: I read about abolitionists and reformers of the nineteenth century and, spurred by coteaching a course in environmental management with Sharon Oster, read about environmentalists as well as personal narratives written by environmentalists. Through this period I thought most about modeling ideals and values in a social setting, especially ideals that are or may be useful to individuals in their productive activities. I read and thought about virtues, including wisdom, tolerance, and honesty, and qualities such as creativity and idealism, and how these are and may be used and combined in social systems. I also wrote a note, in December of 1992, on individuals' conceptual inner worlds and the relative "positions" in these worlds of objects they have internalized and built up representations of, a harbinger of things to come. But the pieces did not fit together and I remained unclear as to how to proceed.

I achieved a sort of breakthrough, not so much of ideas as a clear focus, in the summer of 1995. This breakthrough occurred shortly after I read Gananath Obeyesekere's book *Medusa's Hair*. I cannot know definitely the role this book had in my conceiving my idea of the topic to focus on, but the breakthrough seems to me connected with the book. Obeyesekere describes Hindu-Buddhist religious enthusiasts who, in leading their highly individualistic lives, develop personal rituals and symbols that embody and reflect at a personal level fundamental values and beliefs of their religion. The book struck me in showing, for a handful of individuals, how they interpreted and made use of cultural values in their own idiosyncratic, individualized ways. Having wrestled with the question of how to study the ways in which values and ideals are useful to people in their work, through which they come to make contributions to society, it occurred to me to study as a topic how individuals engaged in creative endeavors are guided in their work by cultural values and guiding principles. I chose creativity because in our society we explicitly acknowledge the individuality of each person in the realm of creativity — that creative contributions individuals make are distinctive to them — whereas in other realms this link is less fully acknowledged; and I wanted to study how individuals, drawing on the common cultural pool of values and principles, are guided and function in their work and thereby come to make their distinctive contributions. The link back to my first intuitive response to social science is clear — and was clear to me within a short period of time.

I worked for about a year striving to develop a model describing individuals engaging in creative work, guided by values and principles. My focus, different than in this book, was on creative projects; I focused on how cultural values and principles guide individuals in their choices about which projects to pursue and in defining projects and making revisions to them. I recognized that my focus naturally extended to linkages of cultural transmission, but did not pursue this as much. During this time I also gained more familiarity with the creativity literature. From the beginning I recognized the need to model the creative process as unfolding over time and in stages. But beyond that general insight, which is connected with the description in this book, I did not make much useful progress.

At this point, in the spring of 1996, I decided that as a way to learn more about how individuals go about engaging in creative endeavors I would interview a set of individuals in different fields about their creative development and work. As a practical approach I decided to interview individuals who had recently earned doctorates. I chose two fields initially, literary studies and neuroscience; later I added mathematics and a small group of filmmakers and playwrights, developed a sampling strategy, which I describe in Chapter 1, and embarked upon the series of interviews that form one important empirical basis of the description of creative development in this book. For every individual I interviewed I read their dissertation (for the filmmakers I viewed films they have made, for the playwrights I read plays they have written). I also read relevant background materials; for example, if a literary scholar had focused on a few main literary works, I read those, or relevant parts, before our interview; and gathered additional archival source materials such as dissertation prospectuses. I was on leave from Yale over 1996–97, which was crucial in giving me the time to conduct many interviews and do necessary background work, transcribe the interviews, and begin tentatively to make sense of what I was being told and learning.

At the same time as I engaged in interviewing, and after finishing the bulk of the interviews drawn upon in this book, I read, and continue to read, in the biography literature and source materials of individuals famous for their creative work. I had been familiar with Frederic Holmes's outstanding biography of Hans Krebs, and returned to it as one of the first biographies I read. I also began to read Virginia Woolf's great store of writings — her diaries, published early journals, letters, short stories, essays, and fiction, concentrating, as I have consistently for most individuals, on her work as a young adult and relatively early on in her career, leading to her creative break in late 1919 and early 1920, and her great novels written in the ensuing years. Over time I have read many biographies and primary source materials of many individuals famous for their creative work, gaining steadily a greater store of knowledge; I draw on these biographies and source materials in this book as a second main empirical basis of my description.

Out of and growing from these empirical bases, rooted in them, I have fashioned a theoretical description of creative development. This description has, I believe, the strength of coherence; it provides an integrative framework for thinking about and describing the creative development of individuals in many fields. Without doubt it has also significant flaws and limitations. Some, I am sure, will view it as too sweeping, as seeking for a false generality, some as simply wrongheaded; others will decry it as making only very limited progress. Further, its empirical basis, though broad and in some sense deep, has evident weaknesses and shortcomings. I present it in the belief that its basic structure is sound and the direction in which it points is well worth pursuing, and in the hope that future work, to which it may contribute, will make right its failings and weaknesses, clarify its structure and significance, and overturn it in various aspects, thus going beyond it.

The importance of the description and approach in this book in my view lies not just in its value as a description of creative development. It has also an ideological meaning and value, and importance as a critique. For too long the social sciences have been constructed employing approaches that do not reflect and are not in dialogue with our fundamental cultural value of individualism. Social science models do not describe individuals in their distinctiveness or individuals' unique paths of life and development, at least not in deep ways. And social scientists do not study the significance of individuals' unique paths and distinctiveness for their contributions to society. There has been surprisingly little effort made to grapple with the difficult matter of constructing models of social systems in which individuals, in their distinctiveness and unique paths, are represented and linked together. My purpose here is to take one step, and glimpse further steps ahead, towards the development of such an approach — models of individuals in social systems that reflect and thus support and help sustain us in our culture, with its values of individualism and individual freedom and initiative.

New Haven, CT
December 2004

ACKNOWLEDGMENTS

In the course of my study of creative development and work on this book I have received much help and support.

Michael Iannazzi and Karla Oeler deserve special mention for their assistance, support, and encouragement. Michael's comments at an early stage of work on the manuscript were crucial in helping me recast my approach to writing the book. He also helped me navigate a number of publication issues. Karla was my research assistant during a crucial early phase of work, and had a number of valuable insights about the framework I was developing for structuring narratives of creative development. Karla has also read through much of the manuscript. She has been supportive of my enterprise and overall conception, and has given me valuable general comments as well as many detailed comments, which have been of great use in revising the manuscript.

Many others have also helped. At the end of my work on the book my niece Rachel Hepworth was an enormous help as my editorial assistant on the bibliography and formatting references. Her twin sister Elizabeth also pitched in. I am grateful to them for their help. I had a series of research assistants who helped me in coding the interview transcripts and through whose work my own ideas became clearer: Young Chang, Julia Yun Kim, Rachel Trousdale, and Helen Sullivan. Teaching my creativity class at SOM has been a delight, and I have benefited from conversations with many students, listening to them or reading accounts they have written about their creative development. Especially memorable for their interest and accounts of their development are Robert Bollinger, Josh Chang, Marcy Engler, Robert Enochs, Kevin Frakes, Laurel Grodman, Channing Henry, Kate Ingram, Alice Liu, Markus

Moberg — who also designed my Website, Lauren Stradley, Chad Troutwine, Paula Volent, Ed Woodcock, Frank Wrenn, and Julie Yufe. I owe a great debt to the individuals I have interviewed about their creative development. They were invariably cooperative and helpful, and patient with me as I probed them about their development. It was a joy to get to know them and learn about their development and work. I have been in contact with several in recent years, and continue to follow the development of many; I look forward to continuing to follow their development in the coming years.

In the course of my work I have benefited from many conversations with and comments of colleagues. Sigal Barsade read an early manuscript draft and her thoughtful comments and encouragement were helpful. Robert Shiller also read an early draft and I benefited from his comments about the enterprise of writing a book. Peter Schott read many chapters and made a number of thoughtful and valuable comments; I have benefited from his interest in the topic. Matthew Rabin and I have engaged in a number of conversations that have been valuable to me through the years; through his insights, and general intellectual sensibility, I have gained insight and greater clarity. Joy Amulya shares my interest in creative development and made a number of useful comments to me about my approach. I had useful conversations about the book and the topic of creative development with Jeffrey Alexander, Dave Baron, Erica Dawson, Joel Podolny, and David Stark; each gave me a valuable perspective. Colleagues at SOM have been generally supportive of my work and made useful comments and suggestions to me about it. Ed Kaplan and On Amir are interested in the topic and my approach and have made valuable comments to me about both. Sharon Oster gave me useful comments on a draft of the first two chapters. Other colleagues in the economics group — Barry Nalebuff, Ben Polak, Fiona Scott Morton, Judy Chevalier, Keith Chen, Nat Keohane, and Erin Mansur — have been supportive of my work and several have made useful suggestions. Fiona also arranged for me to meet with Scott Painter. Many others at SOM — Jake Thomas, Rick Antle, Doug Rae, and others — help create a supportive intellectual climate. I am grateful for colleagues I had here at Yale who have since left, especially Joel Demski, Bengt Holmstrom, Paul MacAvoy, Ariel Pakes, and Ivo Welch, who made the intellectual climate a vibrant one.

Family and friends have encouraged me and supported me in my work on this book and for a long time before. My father and I have spoken about the book often over the past years. He has read parts of the manuscript and offered insights and suggestions with his characteristic clarity of mind. His support has meant a good deal and been helpful to me. I also discussed this book often over the phone with my mother before her death. She was steadfast in her certainty I would complete it, and I know she would be proud of my accomplishment.

xvi

My sister Susan has been a support on this project and, even more, throughout my life. My friends Terry Strom and Kevin Kirchoff have been encouraging and have offered thoughtful advice to me at various stages in my development that has often proven timely and has been very helpful. Craig Alexander shares common interests and his knowledge is a valuable source for me. Brian Erard and Chih-Chin Ho have been supportive of my work and followed it with interest. Finally, my wife Leslie has been encouraging and supportive of my work on this project from its inception. She has also offered many valuable practical suggestions along the way.

At Stanford University Press Kenneth MacLeod was my original editor. Ken solicited the initial manuscript for the Press and believed in the project; his untimely death is a sadness, and I am sorry he cannot see the book in print. Alan Harvey, managing director, has worked with me very effectively to resolve issues and get the manuscript set for publication; I am grateful to him for working with me. Judith Hibbard has been excellent as production editor. Martha Cooley, Kate Wahl, and Jared Smith were all helpful. The readers for the Press offered a number of very useful comments and general advice about the book; I am grateful to them for taking the time to read manuscript chapters. I am especially grateful to the main reviewer, who read through multiple drafts; he grasped and appreciated my overall conception, made a number of very valuable suggestions, including suggestions about the format and style of the book, and offered useful references.

I presented material contained in this book in seminars at the Yale School of Management in 1998 and 2004. I made a seminar presentation in the PACE seminar in the Yale Psychology Department in 2002; I am grateful to Robert Sternberg for inviting me. I was invited and gave a seminar presentation at the London School of Economics in 2004; I am grateful to Frank Cowell for arranging the seminar. I made a presentation based on the book at a session at the American Economics Association annual meeting held in association with the ASSA Convention in Philadelphia in January 2005. A number of individuals who attended one of these seminars gave me valuable comments or feedback — I recall in particular statements by Andrew Bernard, Connie Gersick, Nat Keohane, and Stephen Morris.

Libraries and archives and assistance from individuals in academic departments have been crucial for me in my work. I received invaluable assistance from administrators in the Harvard Departments of English and American Literature and Language and Neurobiology, the MIT Department of Mathematics, the NYU Tisch School of the Arts, the Princeton Department of Mathematics, the UC Berkeley Departments of English and Mathematics, the UCSD Graduate Department Program in Neurosciences, the UCSF

Neuroscience Graduate Program, and the Yale Departments of English and Neurobiology, Program in Neuroscience, and School of Drama. I was given an account at Dissertation Express, a service offered by UMI, enabling me to purchase copies of the dissertations of my interview subjects. I also obtained copies of dissertations from MIT and read dissertations on site at UCSF. I have used or obtained copies of theses in the libraries of Dartmouth University, Pennsylvania State University, Princeton University, and Wesleyan University, and in the holdings of the Yale University African Studies Council. I visited and made use of items in the John Maynard Keynes Papers in the Kings College Modern Archives at Cambridge; I am grateful to the staff there for their assistance and making the materials available to me. I have used materials online in the Stanford University Library Making the Macintosh project holdings. Early in my work, while living in the Washington, DC area, I made use of the collections at the Library of Congress; I have also made use of the Hannah Arendt Papers at the Library of Congress available over the Internet. I was put in contact with Roger Hedden by an executive at Lions Gate Entertainment. Last but not least I have made very extensive use of the Yale University libraries during the period of working on this book, consulting and checking out hundreds of volumes; I am grateful for the libraries and to the library staff for help.

The Yale School of Management has provided me with summer support and research support that has been crucial in enabling me to pursue my work over these years and write the book. Beyond this, the environment of the School and Yale University has been a good place for me to pursue my research and write the book. Stan Garstka in particular has my thanks for his crucial role in the administration of the school and for being supportive of my work.

I am, finally, thankful and grateful for my family, Leslie, Ariel, and Sara. This book has been researched and written within our family life, and is a part of it and enriched by it.

The Nature of Creative Development

INTRODUCTION

In this book I describe the nature of creative development of individuals engaged in creative endeavors. I define creative development to be the process of development and creative activities of an individual engaged in a creative endeavor, extending over a period of time, usually several years or longer. Creative development encompasses processes, experiences, and structures that lay the foundation for creativity, as well as the generation of creativity in its myriad forms — including ideas, insights, and discoveries, and the engagement in creative projects, leading to creative contributions.

The organizing principle and central theme of this book is that the creative development of an individual engaged in creative endeavors, across a wide range of fields, has a basic structure, which centers on, is based in, and grows out of his creative interests. More specifically, as I describe it, an individual's creative development is based in, centers on, and grows out of his creative interests, his conceptions of his creative interests, and conceptual structures he builds up in the domains of his interests which guide him in his development, are generative of his creativity, and are the basis for his creative projects, thus a fundamental source and basis of his creative contributions to society. Creative interests, as I describe them, are distinctive domains or topics that individuals define for themselves.

I describe and characterize creative interests and conceptions of creative interests; describe the formation of creative interests; and describe fundamental processes through which individuals develop their interests creatively — processes through which their interests and the conceptual structures they build up in the domains of their interests are generative of their creativity and creative projects, including ways in which they are guided in their development by their conceptions of their interests and associated principles and values. Then I extend my description, describing project work, multiple interests as the basis for creativity, patterns of projects rooted in interests, and longer term processes of creative development, including the evolution of creative interests and conceptions of interests, and sequences of interests. Finally, I discuss difficulties of creative development, and the implications of my description for understanding and modeling cultural development.

Woven through my description I present many examples describing the creative developments of individuals whose developments I have analyzed, illustrating the description and providing evidence in support of it. These include individuals famous for their creative contributions whose creative developments I have analyzed drawing upon biographical and primary sources, including Virginia Woolf, John Maynard Keynes, Charles Darwin, Alexander Calder, Albert Einstein, Thomas Edison, Hannah Arendt, Hans Krebs, Galileo, William Faulkner, Ray Kroc, Tim Berners-Lee, Piet Mondrian, Pierre Omidyar, and others; and individuals drawn from several fields, mainly academic but not only so, whom I interviewed about their development, and for whom I also obtained and have drawn upon source materials. In the examples I describe individuals' creative interests and their conceptions of their interests, as they described them or I reconstruct them, and how their interests, conceptions of interests, and conceptual structures they built up in their interest domains were, and in some cases continue to be, the bases for their creativity and creative contributions. I also describe their formation of their interests and paths of development. I discuss the empirical basis for my description, including sources of information and information about the set of individuals I interviewed, later in this chapter, and list the individuals I interviewed and source materials I have drawn upon in analyzing their developments in the Appendix.

In describing creativity as based in and growing out of a process of development I follow and build on the great tradition of biography. I also follow and build on a smaller but important tradition in the literature on creativity describing and tracing individuals in their creative work over time, describing creativity as rooted in and emerging out of a process of development. What I add to both traditions is a conceptual framework for describing creative development — a theoretical structure that manifests and describes general features of creative development. In turn this enables the developments of different individuals, in different fields, to be described within a common framework.

Descriptions of creativity often focus on peak creative moments of insight, idea generation, and discovery, depicting creativity as a sudden flash of illumination or discovery. This continues to be the common view of creativity and dominant focus in the literature on creativity. Although peak creative moments definitely do occur and are important, they are just one element in a larger process. To focus only on them, and ignore the larger, rich process in which they are embedded and out of which they emerge, skews our understanding of the nature of creativity, specifically its context and conceptual basis. The framework presented in this book delineates specific processes and structures of creative development that are the source and basis of generation of several principal forms of creativity leading to creative contributions. In particular it delineates and thus shows how individuals' ideas, insights, and contributions are rooted in creative interests they form, explore, and strive to develop creatively, including projects they undertake based in their interests, and conceptual structures they build up in the domains of their interests. These roots and bases are by no means evident on the surface: the creative interests that are the basis of individuals' creativity and contributions are often not clearly visible in their contributions, which emerge often through a long process of development, so that the importance of the interests that underlie them is masked. I have as a principal aim to manifest these linkages, to show that creative interests are the basis for creativity generation and creative contributions.

In the conceptual framework presented in this book individuals, through defining their own interests and pursuing the exploration and creative development of their interests, define, at least to a degree, their own paths of creative development. An individual's creative development is thus, at least to some degree, an autonomous activity — an important addendum being the importance of creative collaborations, and another being practical requirements, for example resources. Of course random events and experiences, such as chance encounters, have important roles, which I describe — but within a larger, self-defined, self-guided process. Further, the originality of individuals' contributions is rooted in their interests and the paths they define and follow pursuing their interests, thus in their own self-defined paths of development. As I describe, individuals' creative interests are generally distinctive, even unique — even within a field and a cohort of individuals in a field each individual typically forms a different, distinctive interest; the creative interests I present and describe as examples illustrate this point. In defining a distinctive interest or set of interests, then defining and following a unique path of development pursuing the exploration and creative development of his interests, an individual has a unique set of experiences and encounters, and builds up distinctive conceptual structures in the domains of his interests. These experiences and structures are the basis of his creativity — his ideas, insights, and discoveries, which in turn are the basis of his distinctive, original contributions. Thus an individual's creativity and the originality of his contributions is rooted in the distinctiveness of his interests and the path he follows pursuing their development.

4   The description of creative development in this book includes, as an important facet, channels through which individuals are influenced in their creative development by their culture and the world around them — channels that are not recognized or described in standard accounts of cultural transmission, at least not in the same way. The most distinctive channel of cultural transmission described in the book is that which occurs through individuals' formation of their creative interests. Creative interests originate in individuals' engagement with the world, sparked by specific experiences and elements they encounter. Cultural elements and experiences are the basis for many creative interests, making this a main pathway of cultural transmission and influence. Because these cultural elements and experiences influence an individual at such an early stage in his development, and their influence is transmitted indirectly, by and through his creative interests, their influence, important and pervasive as it is, is nonetheless often not readily apparent in his subsequent projects, ideas, and contributions. To identify these cultural linkages we must trace an individual's development with care, beginning far before his main contributions, at the time when he forms his main creative interests.

Additional channels of cultural transmission and influence I describe arise during exploration and development of interests. Notably, elements and experiences spark creative responses, and individuals build up rich conceptual structures in the domains of their interests out of elements they encounter, that in turn are generative of their ideas and insights.

Beyond describing channels of cultural transmission, the description in this book provides a basis for describing cultural development. Cultural development — the progress of civilization — has its primary source, ultimately, in creative contributions made by people in all walks of life. A well-grounded description of cultural development thus must be based in a description of individual creativity. The description in this book points towards such a description: a model describing cultural development based in individuals' creative developments and creative activities.

AN OVERVIEW OF THE DESCRIPTION OF CREATIVE DEVELOPMENT

The core of creative development consists of three steps: the formation of a creative interest, including a conception of the interest; the process of exploring the interest and developing it creatively; and, in the continuation of this second step, the defining and execution of projects rooted in the interest and growing out of its development, leading to creative works and contributions. I focus on describing the first two steps, then extend my description to include the third step and larger patterns of development. In this section I sketch main

features of my description, providing an overview of creative development   5
as I describe it. At the end of the section I outline the organization of the
book.

Individuals form their creative interests in and through their engagement
with the world around them. In the course of their lives individuals have
many experiences and encounter myriad elements of diverse kinds. They
have many social interactions and personal experiences, witness and learn
about many events, encounter and learn about a great variety of phenomena,
are exposed to and learn or learn about a great multitude of concepts, facts,
ideas, theories, beliefs, experiments and experimental results, methods, styles,
and approaches, and are exposed to, learn about, and study the creative works
and contributions of many people, both in their field and their culture. Out
of the vast numbers of experiences they have and elements they encounter
and learn about, a small number of distinct elements or experiences — or
clusters of interrelated elements or experiences, or, in the case of complex experiences and elements, a particular aspect or a few component elements —
catch their attention and stand out, spark their interest, and spark a response in
them.[1] They form their creative interests in response to and based upon these
experiences and elements.

Individuals are most open to forming interests during periods of their development when they are most open to the world and their experiences. Often
this is just after they enter their chosen field or a new field, when they are
actively learning about the field and encounter many elements in it that are
new to them — they often form creative interests during these periods.

In forming their creative interests, especially in the initial stages responding
to experiences and elements they encounter, individuals generally respond intuitively and spontaneously to what excites and interests them. Their responses
are not rationally planned out, and often they know only a little bit about a
topic or set of elements at the time they form an interest in or based upon
the topic or elements. Interests are primarily rooted in and generated by intrinsic interest: individuals find their interests interesting, exciting, fascinating,
challenging — that is why they form them as interests and wish to pursue
them. I describe a variety of sources of intrinsic interest in Chapter 4. Extrinsic
factors also have a role in the formation of interests, including individuals'
decisions about which interests to pursue. The two main extrinsic factors are
(1) the sense of openness and creative potential — the sense that an interest
holds opportunities for fruitful creative development, and (2) the sense that an

---

[1]Registers of meaning individuals have, based on previous life experiences, often
contribute to the sparking of their interests. I discuss registers of meaning in Chapter 3.

6   interest is potentially important, that contributions generated through pursuing it are likely to be significant and important for one's field and society.

Beginning from their initial interests, individuals form more defined creative interests, which form the basis for their development going forward. A key step in the process of forming a more fully defined creative interest is forming a conception of one's interest. An individual may or may not form a conception of his interest at the time he forms an initial, incipient interest; if he does, it may well be quite rudimentary, or alternatively, as occurs in some cases, he may have a quite clear conception of his interest from early on. Over time, as an individual thinks about his interest, reflects upon it, makes connections among different concepts, ideas, images, works, phenomena, facts, and other elements that fit with it, and imagines it more fully, he develops his interest conceptually, and it becomes clearer, more integrative and more coherent; as part of this process, and generative of it, he forms a fuller conception of it.

In general an individual's conception of his interest develops together with his interest, each developing in stages. There are different patterns of development of interests and conceptions of interests. Thus, in many cases an individual's interest and conception begin as relatively simple and become richer. In some cases an individual's initial interest and conception are narrowly focused, centering on specific elements and experiences, then expand out to define a broader, richer domain; in other cases his interest begins as more general, then he narrows his focus.

Individuals conceive of their creative interests as domains filled with creative possibilities, filled with promise. They desire to learn about them and explore them, and to develop them creatively. They believe or at least hope that through exploring their interests and striving to develop them creatively they will be able to define and pursue creative projects and ultimately make contributions to their field and society. However, individuals do not at the time they form a creative interest have a clear sense for how they will go about developing their interest creatively, or what they will discover, what ideas they will generate, and what contributions they will ultimately come to make through pursuing it and striving to develop it. There are many possibilities, many possible paths of development they may follow; their interest is defined in a relatively open-ended way. Their conceptions reflect this, conveying, as they describe them, a sense of openness.

Creative interests have a striking combination of characteristics. They are distinctive, even unique. Yet they are also broad, broader than individual projects or ideas, defining domains that can be explored and developed in many different ways. These two characteristics, distinctiveness and breadth, are to some degree in tension with one another. The combination of the two is central to defining creative interests as a theoretical construct, in particular defining creative interests as intermediate level conceptual structures; I describe what I mean by this in the next chapter. Distinctiveness and breadth are powerful in combination, and jointly they are integral to the central roles creative interests have in creative development. The many examples of creative interests presented in this book, in particular individuals' descriptions of their conceptions of their interests and my reconstructions of individuals' interests, exhibit distinctiveness and breadth, demonstrating that creative interests possess these characteristics.

My description of creative interests to a degree follows and builds upon the commonplace idea of an interest; however, it also challenges conventional ideas about interests and differs in significant respects from them. It is a commonplace that individuals engaged in creative endeavors have creative interests; indeed individuals engaged in creative endeavors frequently mention their creative interests in discussing their creative activities. The commonplace view of creative interests is valuable as a point of departure, in providing an intuitive sense of creative activity rooted in interests. However, it is also misleading and deficient in some important respects, and I believe as a result can hinder — and has done so — our understanding and appreciation of the true nature of creative interests and their role and significance in creative development.

There are two fundamental ways in which my description is distinct from conventional notions and goes beyond them. One is in the idea of a conception of a creative interest. I do not believe it has been widely understood that individuals form conceptions of their creative interests. In fact individuals do form such conceptions; I present many examples of individuals' descriptions of their conceptions of their interests. Further, their conceptions of their interests are central to their creative development, guiding them in their development, and are conceptual cores around which they form conceptual structures in their interest domains which are vital bases of their creativity generation. The other concerns the nature of interests. Conventionally interests are often viewed as being simple, conventional subjects. This intuition is misleading with regard to creative interests. I define creative interests somewhat differently, as distinctive topics that individuals define for themselves, thus inherently more creative. And I show how important such distinctive interests are as the basis of original ideas, discoveries, insights, and projects, leading to creative contributions; appreciating the distinctiveness of interests is thus critical for appreciating their role in creative development.

Having formed a creative interest or set of creative interests, and conceptions of his interests, an individual explores his interests and strives to develop

8   them creatively. His interests are the focus of his attention, thinking, and creative activity, at the core of his creative development.

Through exploring and learning about a creative interest an individual learns of and about many elements that fit in its domain or are connected with it — for example, creative works, ideas, concepts, theories, facts, phenomena, and images. His attention is drawn by elements, aspects of his experiences, and events that fit and connect with his interest, he notices and focuses on them, and forms internal representations of them. Through these processes of learning, attention, and internalization the individual builds up a conceptual structure in the domain of his interest. His conception of his interest sits at the center of this developing conceptual structure, guides his attention and learning, and is important in providing a core structure around which other elements coalesce, building associations and linkages, creating an integrative conceptual structure.

Individuals' creative interests, specifically the conceptual structures that encode their interests and that they build up in the domains of their interests, are a fundamental basis for their creativity generation. During periods when individuals are engaged in exploring their interests and seeking ways to develop them creatively, these structures are the principal basis for their creativity. A main process through which individuals generate ideas during these periods is through creative responses they make, sparked by specific experiences and elements they encounter that connect with their interests, thus responses mediated by the conceptual structures in their minds associated with their interests. Creative responses spark many important ideas and projects, generating creative opportunities individuals pursue. I present a series of examples of creative responses, including responses by Alexander Calder, Tim Berners-Lee, John Maynard Keynes, and several of the individuals I interviewed.

The conceptual structures that encode creative interests and that individuals build up in their interest domains mediate their creative responses through a combination of two processes. First, they guide individuals' attention, leading them to notice and focus on specific experiences and elements — or particular aspects of them — that connect in some way with one of their interests. Second, they are central for individuals' processing in the wake of an initial response, triggering associations and creative links of thinking leading to further creative ideas and insights. Individuals' creative interests, encoded in their minds, provide unique perspectives, enabling them to recognize and respond in distinctive ways to experiences and elements they encounter, to make creative connections that others fail to make, that are thus original. For example, an individual may recognize the importance of a particular aspect of a phenomenon that others have overlooked, because it connects with one of his interests in an interesting way.

Individuals build up rich conceptual structures in the domains of their interests over time. These rich structures are generative of creativity through a variety of pathways. They are generative of creative responses; for example, Ray Kroc generated a creative response rooted in expertise he had built up over many years of work. They are also the basis for generalizations: noticing and recognizing a general pattern, principle, or relationship among a set of elements in one's interest domain. Charles Darwin's insight that the principle of transmutation of species might be a basis for explaining and modeling patterns of characteristics of allied and related species, and changes in species over time, is a classic example, described in Chapter 10. Finally, rich conceptual structures of creative interests are generative of creative connections among specific elements; a classic example is Samuel Taylor Coleridge's process of creation for his great poems, notably "The Rime of the Ancient Mariner," also described in Chapter 10. I call the rich conceptual reservoirs individuals build up in the domains of their interests creative expertise.

The third phase of creative development is engagement in creative projects. In general individuals develop their projects out of their creative interests. In many cases an individual develops an idea for a project through one of the processes described above. Thus, for example, one common pattern of development is for an individual to generate an idea for a project through a creative response. In some cases an individual develops a project based on an opportunity he uncovers exploring his interest. In other cases an individual is offered a project, for example by a manager or senior colleague, that fits with his interest — or that he modifies to fit with it — which he then pursues. Finally, individuals develop projects in collaboration with one another, in the overlap of their interests; such collaborative projects are often rooted in creative ideas generated through a form of creative response — two individuals encountering one another, their engagement sparking an idea. Making the transition from exploration of interests to projects is crucial and can be difficult, both because of the difficulty in defining a project one wishes to pursue and because in choosing to pursue a project one narrows one's focus and passes over many other possibilities.

Individuals who are actively engaged in projects are generally quite inwardly focused, far more so than in periods when they are forming interests and exploring their interests and seeking ways to develop them — they are focused on tasks and task completion. Thus they are less open to their environment, except insofar as it is useful to them in their projects, for example in solving a problem they confront. Individuals can be extremely creative in project work. I discuss a number of creative processes that are important in project work. One is the generation of creative responses — having a project in mind, then having an experience or encountering an element that has a connection with the project, and triggers an idea for it. Other processes I describe are discovery, creative problem solving, and revisioning. I show by example that in many cases creativity generated through these processes is rooted, at least in part, in the creative interest that is the basis for the project, thus generating a link with the interest.

Projects are crucial to creative work: in the course of pursuing a project an individual is in many cases taken far beyond the interest that was the basis for the project, and beyond his original conception for the project, generating ideas and making discoveries he did not imagine. Yet regardless of how far beyond their interests individuals are led in pursuing their projects, their interests nevertheless are the basis of their projects. Thus, to understand how an individual comes to pursue a given project we must go back further, and identify his creative interest or interests that led him to come upon it or generate the idea for it.

In addition to their creative interests being generative of their creativity and the basis of their projects, individuals' conceptions of their interests are crucial in guiding them in their development. Their conceptions guide them in exploring their interests, and in their decision-making about which projects to undertake and, more broadly, which interests to pursue. Their conceptions also shape the way they conceive and define their projects and are important to their work on projects. Pierre Omidyar's values, connected with his interest in promoting and developing fair systems of exchange, were a vital factor in the way he developed his Internet auction site that became eBay. Piet Mondrian's conception of a new art form, rooted in philosophical ideals and principles, was crucial in guiding him in his artistic development.

In engaging in a creative endeavor an individual undertakes a process of development that is often fraught with uncertainty, following a path that has never been traveled before. To have the best chance of making contributions that fulfill his potential and the potential of his creative interests it is vital in many cases for him to manage his process of development, especially at certain junctures. Management includes decision-making about which interests to pursue and which projects to undertake, as noted above, as well as about when to abandon a line of development or a project. It also includes managing or at least being able to cope with one's emotions along what can be a rocky course.

In managing his development an individual is guided by his conceptions of his creative interests, and values and principles linked to his interests, which provide a context for him to think about his development. This larger context is important in motivating him and giving him a sense of purpose. It is also important in evaluating the course of his development, which is crucial for guidance. A notable feature of creative development is the way individuals, at certain critical junctures, step back and reflect upon their course of development, for example, their interests or the outcomes of a series of projects they have engaged in, from a broader, meta-level perspective. Such meta-level thinking can be very important. For example, an individual may in reflecting upon his development conclude that he has wandered too far from his initial conception of his interest, and decide to engage in a midcourse correction, to steer himself back towards topics that fit better with it; or he may recognize a larger pattern that triggers an idea for a new approach. I provide examples of such thinking, showing its importance, in Chapter 11. In general I argue and show with examples that individuals engaged in creative development think about their development and manage it from a broader, more overarching perspective than has previously been described — specifically, reflect upon their development from the perspective of their interests, guided by their conceptions of their interests as well as associated principles and values.

Every individual who engages in a creative endeavor follows his or her own unique path of creative development. This path may be described most basically by the interests he forms, the projects he undertakes, the ideas he has and discoveries he makes, and the contributions he makes. More richly described, it includes his experiences and encounters, assessments he makes about his development, his decisions and emotions along his path of development, as well as his creative activities, such as exploration and problem solving and the presentation of his ideas and works to others in his field and society.

Patterns of creative development have a variety of forms. For many individuals, over medium spans of time their pattern of development resembles the branching structure of a tree — their core creative interests are like the trunk and their projects are like branches coming off of this trunk. Individuals whose development fits this pattern develop the ideas for their projects in the course of exploring their creative interests. During the time when they are focused on a project they temporarily set their interests aside; but as their project ends their attention returns to their interests, they resume exploration of them, and their new project generally develops out of their interests, not the project they have just ended. In other cases one project leads to the next, forming a chain. Over longer time spans individuals' creative interests change, as they learn and mature; also, their conceptions of their interests often become more sophisticated. These processes of change and maturation create complex, rich patterns of development. I describe two main patterns of this kind: evolution of interests and the formation of a sequence of linked interests over time. Two outstanding cases I present illustrating these patterns are the developments of Hannah Arendt and John Maynard Keynes. Their examples show how through evolution of their interests and forming sequences of linked interests individuals can go far beyond where they begin in their creative development, to make outstanding contributions much later, following a long process of development.

The description in this book naturally extends to developing a description of cultural development. In particular, it provides the basis for describing a core process of cultural development. I sketch this core process here; I discuss development of models of cultural development rooted in the description in this book in Chapter 17.

The elements and experiences that influence individuals in their formation of their creative interests have a deep and pervasive influence on their creative development. Acting by and through their interests, such elements and experiences influence individuals' whole course of development — the paths they follow, what they encounter and learn about, hence the basis for their creativity generation, and the topics, questions, and problems they become interested in and pursue in their projects, leading ultimately to their creative contributions. Among all the different kinds of elements and experiences that influence individuals in forming their creative interests, the contributions and work of other people, especially their predecessors in their field and neighboring fields, are especially important — the main source of their interests in many cases. Individuals in many cases develop their interests out of their reactions to others' work, desiring to extend or apply the work of someone else, to challenge or refute it, or defining their interest in contrast to it, structuring their interest as a topic that is intentionally designed to be different. Even in cases in which an individual's interest develops around other kinds of elements the work of others is likely to have been crucial in exposing him to these elements and helping him recognize their significance; for example, when an individual develops an interest in a particular phenomenon in many cases he first learns about it through a description given by someone else. The adage that individuals "build on the work of their predecessors" is therefore true if it is understood to mean this: "individuals construct their interests and conceptions of interests in and out of their responses to the work of their predecessors."

This link between the contributions one generation makes and the creative interests formed by the next links the creative endeavors of successive generations in a two-step recursive process: the creative contributions made by the members of the preceding generation form the basis for the creative interests of the members of the current generation, who develop their interests creatively, producing their own creative contributions — which in turn become the basis for the creative interests of the members of the following generation.

Thus creative interests and creative contributions form a pair of mutually de- pendent networks, each formed out of the other, a dynamic recursive system.[2]

In the following chapters I focus on each aspect of creative development in turn, describing it; throughout I present many examples, which collectively give broad empirical support to the basic description.

In the first seven chapters I describe creative interests and their development. In Chapter 2 I define and describe creative interests and conceptions of creative interests. In Chapter 3 I describe the development of creative interests and conceptions of creative interests. In Chapters 4 and 5 I describe sources of interests: Chapter 4 focuses on intrinsic sources of interests, Chapter 5 discusses extrinsic and strategic factors in the development of interests. In Chapter 6 I describe kinds of creative interests. In Chapter 7 I discuss the important characteristics of breadth and distinctiveness.

Chapter 8 is a bridge from the first to the second part of the book: I present a series of examples showing that individuals' creative interests and concep- tions of their interests, as they describe them, carry through in many cases and are reflected in their creative contributions. In the following three chap- ters I describe creativity generation and guidance based in creative interests and conceptual structures of interests. In Chapter 9 I describe creative re- sponses mediated by creative interests. In Chapter 10 I describe individuals' processes of exploration, building up conceptual structures in the domains of their interests, and creativity generation rooted in these structures. In Chap- ter 11 I describe guidance, decision-making, and meta-level thinking about creative development, focusing on ways in which individuals are guided by their conceptions of their interests and values and principles associated with their interests.

In the chapters following eleven I round out and extend my description. In Chapter 12 I describe creative project work. In Chapter 13 I describe the generation of creativity rooted in combining and linking elements based in dif- ferent interests. Chapter 14 describes patterns of projects, focusing on patterns of projects rooted in a single core interest. Chapter 15 describes the evolution of creative interests and sequences of linked interests and creativity based in such patterns of development. In Chapter 16 I use the framework of description in the book to describe and analyze difficulties individuals may experience in their creative development. Diagnosing and describing difficulties is not

[2]Other cultural elements and experiences enter into and influence individuals' development during later phases of their development, notably in sparking creative responses and solutions to problems in projects, and as elements in the conceptual structures they build up in the domains of their interests, as described in the preceding text.

my main focus, but the description of creative development provides insight about such difficulties, likely to be of interest for many readers interested in realizing their creative potential or helping others to do so. In Chapter 17 I describe channels of cultural transmission and discuss construction of models of cultural development based in individual creative development.

The book concludes with an Epilogue in which I set forth my further aim, to which this book points: the development of descriptions and models of social systems in which individuals are modeled as distinctive and make contributions to their society rooted in their distinctiveness — an approach reflecting and thus supporting the fundamental principle of individualism and our cultural way of life.

DATA AND SOURCES

The description of creative development in this book is supported throughout by examples drawn from my analysis of the creative development of individuals engaged in creative endeavors. In part the description was developed inductively, based on analysis of the developments of these individuals; and in part it was developed deductively and has gained further support through clearly fitting, as a description, the developments of many individuals in a range of fields. The individuals are two distinct groups. One is individuals famous in history or well known for their creative contributions, drawn from a range of fields and time periods. The other is individuals I interviewed about their creative development who at the time I interviewed them were in an early to middle period in their creative careers. These individuals are not famous, and represent a very different sample; many have achieved some measure of success in their endeavors, producing creative works, having a sense of accomplishment, and achieving a degree of recognition in their field. I present here basic information about the individuals in the two groups and my sources of information about their creative developments.

In choosing individuals famous or well known for their contributions to study I sought for breadth in terms of field, and also, to a more limited degree, time period and nationality. I focused on individuals for whom materials pertaining to their creative development exist and are accessible, including individuals for whom outstanding biographical scholarship exists describing their development. In selecting these individuals I did not follow a systematic sampling process. However, the sample has a good degree of breadth, and in combination with the sample of individuals I interviewed described below I believe it is compelling that the description of creative development I present, fitting with and providing insight about the developments of a relatively broad overall sample of individuals engaged in a broad range of creative endeavors, holds the promise of having general validity.

I list below many of the individuals famous or well known for their contributions whose development I have studied. The list gives a sense of the number and diversity of individuals. Some are very famous, others are not as famous but are well known for their work; all have made outstanding creative contributions.

Hannah Arendt	Paul Barran	Tim Berners-Lee
Ingmar Bergman	Alexander Calder	Rachel Carson
Paul Cezanne	Samuel Taylor Coleridge	Charles Darwin
Walt Disney	Fyodor Dostoevsky	Albert Einstein
Thomas Edison	William Faulkner	Galileo
Robert Irwin	James Joyce	John Maynard Keynes
Hans Krebs	Ray Kroc	Henri Matisse
Piet Mondrian	Isaac Newton	John von Neumann
Pierre Omidyar	Pablo Picasso	Jef Raskin
James Watson	Virginia Woolf	
William Wordsworth	Wilbur Wright	

I have explored the development of many other individuals in a limited manner. Indeed the pool is essentially limitless, which is a challenge and an opportunity in developing a framework for describing creative development.

In researching and analyzing the creative developments of these individuals I have drawn upon two fundamental kinds of sources. One is materials that individuals themselves produce or create; the other is biographical and other scholarly descriptions of individuals' development and creative activities.

Source materials produced by individuals themselves fall into three categories. One is statements individuals make at a relatively early stage in their development, in which they describe creative interests, ideas, plans, or designs they have, as well as beliefs, values, and principles, that turn out to be important for their subsequent development and contributions. Such statements are especially valuable. In being prospective, they avoid any issue of an individual reconstructing beliefs, ideas, interests, plans, or experiences to fit with later beliefs or ideas the individual has or contributions he makes, thus demonstrate especially cleanly the logic and validity of the description of creative development I present. Important sources of this kind that I have drawn upon and incorporate in this book include Virginia Woolf's early journal and Diary, Samuel Taylor Coleridge's notebooks, in particular his "Gutch Notebook," Charles Darwin's *Beagle* Diary and notebooks, Thomas Edison's notebooks, Piet Mondrian's sketchbooks and essay "The New Plastic in Painting," John Maynard Keynes's papers, Hannah Arendt's initial outline for what became *The Origins of Totalitarianism*, and Tim Berners-Lee's original documentation for his Enquire program. I also draw on letters written by individuals early in their development, including letters of Albert Einstein, Henri Matisse, Virginia Woolf, Wilbur Wright, and Coleridge.[3]

A second category is writings, lectures, and creative products produced by individuals relatively early in their development. These do not include direct statements about their development — for example their creative interests — but provide valuable information, indirectly, about their path of development, including in many cases about their developing interests and plans. Examples of such works I have utilized include Virginia Woolf's short stories written prior to her creative break; early writings of Hannah Arendt, including *Love and Saint Augustine*, *Rahel Varnhagen*, and numerous articles; John Maynard Keynes's notes for presentations he made to the Apostles and lectures, as well as early books; Isaac Newton's mathematical papers; Alexander Calder's early sculptures; sequences of paintings and sketches by Henri Matisse, Pablo Picasso, and Piet Mondrian; and Jef Raskin's master's thesis in computer science (Jef is a principal inventor of the Macintosh).

A third category of source materials produced by individuals is descriptions they provide of their creative development retrospectively. Many famous individuals describe their development in autobiographies or memoirs. Such sources are not always reliable, both because individuals often write them late in life when their memory for events and ideas they had when they were younger may be poor, and also because they may shape their account to fit with their later famous contributions and ideas and public persona.[4] However, autobiographies differ markedly — some are candid and very valuable as a source of information. I have drawn upon a number that stand out for their lucidity and seem likely to have a high degree of accuracy. These include Alexander Calder's *Calder, An Autobiography with Pictures*, Ray Kroc's *Grinding It Out*, Albert Einstein's "Autobiographical Notes," and James Watson's *The*

---

[3]Accounts given by other people of statements individuals make, for example, describing interests, plans, or guiding principles they have, are also valuable, and I draw on these in a few cases; as one example I draw on statements made by Fernande Olivier in her journal about Picasso and his attitudes towards her.

[4]There is a large literature on autobiographical writing and the matter of its reliability or lack thereof; see the references later in this section.

Double Helix. Even these are imperfect. Thus Watson's account is at times slanted stylistically; however, there are other sources available to fill in and modify his account. Individuals also make statements describing their development soon after making important contributions, which thus describe relatively recent experiences and thoughts, and are less colored by their later fame, and, for both reasons, are likely in many cases to be accurate. I have drawn upon statements of this kind made by a number of individuals, including notes William Faulkner made, within a few years of his creative break, about the genesis of his work on *Flags in the Dust* and the genesis of *The Sound and the Fury*, and comments by Alexander Calder describing his early abstract sculptural art. Interviews and lectures are a further source of autobiographical information. I have focused on interviews in which individuals speak specifically to their creative development. Interviews and lectures I have drawn upon in this book include interviews with Paul Barran, contributor to the development of the Internet, Jef Raskin, and Ingmar Bergman; and Pierre Omidyar's 2002 Tufts Commencement Address.

The other category of source materials is biographical and scholarly materials. Such materials are a valuable resource; they are also a useful check on my description, for biographers do not have my description in mind or any intent to prove or disprove it in constructing their accounts. For many of the individuals I have studied there is an outstanding biography or body of scholarship that has been invaluable in analyzing their development. Outstanding biographies I have drawn upon include Frederic Holmes's *Hans Krebs: A Scientific Life*, Joseph Blotner's *Faulkner: A Biography*, Elisabeth Young-Bruehl's *Hannah Arendt: For Love of the World*, Hilary Spurling's *The Unknown Matisse*, Tom Crouch's *The Bishop's Boys* biography of the Wright Brothers, and the first two volumes of Robert Skidelsky's biography of John Maynard Keynes, *Hopes Betrayed* and *The Economist as Saviour*. There is extensive and outstanding scholarly work describing the development and work of many of the individuals whose development I have studied that has also been invaluable. John Livingston Lowes gives a brilliant description of Coleridge's process of creation in *The Road to Xanadu: A Study in the Ways of the Imagination*; Kathleen Coburn's and Richard Holmes's insights about Coleridge are also invaluable. There is an extensive body of scholarship on Albert Einstein's creative development; I have found especially valuable John Stachel's contributions, including in *The Collected Papers of Albert Einstein*, and Arthur Miller's *Albert Einstein's Special Theory of Relativity: Emergence (1905) and Early Interpretation (1905–1911)*, which sets Einstein's work developing special relativity theory in context. For Galileo I have drawn upon Alexander Koyré's *Galileo Studies*, Stillman Drake's *Galileo at Work*, and work of William Wallace. Beyond these,

18   much more scholarly work has been invaluable for me in constructing my account of creative development; this work is cited and discussed throughout the body of the book.

The individuals I interviewed about their creative development are a group of gifted young people in a number of fields. Most are drawn from three academic fields: English and American literature; neuroscience; and mathematics. In each of these fields I contacted individuals who had recently graduated from one of the top-ranked doctoral programs in their field, as ranked by the National Research Council.[5] I contacted individuals who had earned a doctorate from one of the top three programs in English and American literature in 1995, one of the top four programs in neuroscience in 1996, and one of the top three programs in mathematics in 1997.[6] In each field I contacted all individuals in the programs who had earned their doctorate in that year, with two exceptions: one English program was substantially larger than the others and I contacted one-half of its graduates; and not all the mathematics doctorates were contacted in order to keep that sample smaller due to the technical difficultness of the work. In both cases those contacted were not selected based on any definite criterion and should be representative of the group as a whole. Nearly everyone I contacted agreed to participate in my study, with the overall participation rate at 90%.[7] I interviewed 22 individuals with doctorates in English and American literature, 19 with doctorates in neuroscience, and 9 with doctorates in mathematics. Several of the literary scholars I interviewed also write fiction, and during our interview we discussed both their literary studies and creative writing. Most of the people I interviewed grew up in the United States and are U.S. citizens. Approximately 10% are Canadian, 10% are European, one is Chinese, one Indian, and one Russian; also, one is deaf. Approximately 50% are women and women are well represented in all three fields.

There are two sampling issues to be noted in regards the groups of individuals contacted and interviewed in these fields. I contacted individuals only at top-rated programs. It is possible that individuals attending lower rated

---

[5]*Research-Doctorate Programs in the United States; Continuity and Change*, ed. Marvin L. Goldberger, Brendan A. Maher, and Pamela Ebert Flattau (Washington, DC: National Academy Press, 1995).

[6]These programs are: Yale, UC-Berkeley, and Harvard in English and American literature; Harvard, Yale, UC-San Francisco, and UC-San Diego in neuroscience; MIT, Princeton, and UC-Berkeley in mathematics.

[7]The percentages of individuals who agreed to participate and were interviewed is 85% in English and American literature, 90% in the neurosciences, and 100% in mathematics.

programs may have systematically different patterns of development.[8] Also, all
the individuals I interviewed completed their programs successfully, earning
a doctorate. Individuals who enter but do not complete their program may be
expected to have at least somewhat different patterns of development. Informal
statistics I gathered speaking with program officers indicate that the great majority of individuals who matriculate in the programs I drew from earn degrees —
at least 75%, and higher for most programs; thus this issue seems not to be a
major concern for my sample.[9]

In addition to the individuals in the fields above I interviewed a small group
of filmmakers and playwrights. I interviewed two playwrights who graduated in
1997 from the Yale School of Drama, one filmmaker who graduated from the
NYU Tisch School of the Arts in the spring of 1997, and one other person who is
a playwright and a filmmaker, whom I gained access to through a contact. The
set of playwrights and filmmakers is small and more haphazard in construction
and cannot be taken to be representative of any well-defined pool of individuals
in these fields. Nonetheless, the interviews I conducted with these individuals
were valuable in providing information about creative development in these
fields.

Before conducting an interview with an individual I familiarized myself
with the main creative products he or she had produced over the preceding
few years. For the individuals who had earned doctorates I read their dissertations, as well as published papers or abstracts. For the playwrights I read plays
they had written, and for the filmmakers I viewed films they had made. In
addition, I familiarized myself with supporting materials that appeared to have
been important for an individual in his work, such as articles and books he analyzed or drew upon in an important way in his work. Having a high degree of
familiarity with an individual's work greatly facilitated our interview discussion,
enabling us to discuss their work, work that in some cases is abstruse and highly
specific, cogently. I believe my obvious familiarity with their work also helped
the individuals I interviewed feel comfortable speaking with me.

A typical interview lasted somewhat more than two hours.[10] Interviews were
conducted by telephone, with the exception of two conducted in person, and

---

[8]One likely difference is that individuals at lower rated programs can be expected to
take longer to complete their degree, in part because of needing to work while attending
school. Beyond this, there may well be differences in the nature of their interests and
patterns of work.

[9]In my sample there are individuals who earned their degree in three or four years and
others who took far longer, thus there was substantial variation in time to completion.

[10]No interviews were shorter than 80 minutes; some were significantly longer and
conducted over two sessions.

were recorded and transcribed. In the interviews I asked individuals to describe their creative development, broadly defined, typically beginning in childhood and college and moving forward to the present, with the main focus on the preceding several years, often beginning in the last year or two in college. I sent individuals a guideline for the interview a few days ahead of time so they would understand the nature of the interview, and many had assembled materials they referred to during our interview. I guided interviews with an open protocol, for the most part going in chronological sequence, dividing the interview into segments. Thus, for example, for individuals who attended graduate school, during the interview segment in which we discussed their graduate school experience we first discussed specific courses, papers, and projects that were important for them during their first year, then discussed their second year, proceeding in sequence. Often we revisited certain topics later in an interview, as the individual recalled further details or I had questions of clarification. The interview transcripts average approximately 17,000 words in length, with variation from as little as 10,000 to more than 28,000 words; the typical length is 35 to 43 single-spaced pages.[11] The majority of words spoken in all interviews were spoken by the individual interviewed — on average, by rough count, close to 70%. I had email correspondence with many individuals after our interview. In addition, I have reinterviewed several individuals, verifying information and earlier statements they made and obtaining information about their path of development since our interview.

In addition to the interviews I collected source materials beyond the basic materials noted above — dissertations, plays, and movies — for the individuals I interviewed. For the vast majority of the literary scholars I obtained a copy of their dissertation prospectus. I also obtained additional materials for many; for several I obtained a copy of their college honors thesis or senior thesis, for a few who wrote a master's thesis I obtained a copy of or examined their thesis, and a few have shared documents with me from early in graduate school, such as papers, orals documents, and reading lists. For many of the neuroscientists I obtained copies of papers or abstracts they published either before entering their doctoral program or early on in their program. For a few I also obtained orals proposals, college materials, such as an honors thesis or class materials they shared with me, and miscellaneous other materials. For the mathematicians, I have located or obtained fewer source documents dating to years prior to our interview but still some: for one a master's thesis, for a second a pair of honors theses, and for a third a set of lecture notes she coauthored. Two of the playwrights sent me documents describing their work and development; I also obtained reviews of movies and plays, and for one transcripts of other

[11] Approximately 90% have length between 28 and 50 single-spaced pages.

interviews. In addition to these materials, pertaining to the period prior to the interviews, I have followed the subsequent development and contributions of many of the individuals — noted articles and books they have published and films they have made, and gathered information about their current interests and projects listed on Websites.

The Appendix provides more detailed information for my interview sample. It lists the names of the individuals interviewed, and source materials, including creative products and other sources of information about their development I have drawn upon.

In addition to the individuals in the fields described above, I have been able to gather information about the creative development of a number of individuals who are entrepreneurs and in business. These include an entrepreneur I interviewed when he visited Yale, and several students in my classes who wrote essays describing their creative development. These individuals are also listed in the Appendix.

I discuss the creative development of many of the individuals I interviewed in the course of this book. For purposes of illustration I introduce here three whose development I discuss — Azad Bonni, Enid Zentelis, and Robert Kaufman. Azad is a neurobiologist who has done important work on neurotrophin signaling pathways and is now head of his own laboratory at the Harvard Medical School. Enid is a talented filmmaker who was awarded the Grand Marnier Award from the Film Society of Lincoln Center, in association with the New York Film Festival, in 1997 for her film *Dog Race*; her first full-length feature film, *Evergreen*, came out in 2004. Robert is a literature scholar, currently a professor at Stanford University, who has developed original theories about the relationship between ideas and beliefs of Keats and Shelley, expressed in their poetry and other writings, and modern Left critical theory.

Throughout the book I describe and discuss the creative development of individuals I interviewed side by side with the development of individuals famous for their creative contributions. This style reflects my belief that my description is general, that it describes the development of both those who achieve great success in creative endeavors and those who achieve more modest success, and that we all have creative potential that can be realized through a process of development of the kind I describe. In a few places I compare and contrast structures, processes, and patterns of development of highly successful and less successful individuals.

I rely in this book on individuals' retrospective statements as one important source of information about their development. The use of retrospective statements raises concerns, for a number of reasons. In this section I discuss potential flaws in retrospective accounts individuals give of their development,

22 and the relevance for my description. I emphasize that in addition to retrospective statements I utilize as well contemporaneous and longitudinal, prospective sources of information. These sources provide important support for the description I provide, and serve as a useful check on many of the retrospective accounts; see my discussion below.

Inevitably retrospective descriptions individuals give of their creative development are highly selective. They may not be able to recall their past thoughts and experiences clearly, or the chronology of their development accurately. In general they are likely to describe main interests, experiences, ideas, and projects they had, especially those that were fruitful or influenced their subsequent development, and to pass over many other experiences and elements that were more minor or they chose not to pursue or were unable to develop, and thus faded in importance. Obviously an individual cannot possibly describe the rich stream of his daily experiences in full. The lack of daily material is not in itself a crucial problem, as my description focuses on creative development over longer periods of time, on more enduring interests, main ideas, pivotal decisions and events, and projects. Individuals recall and describe all of these. However, the record is clearly quite incomplete.[12] In fact, I believe far more detail can be incorporated within the basic framework I present without fundamentally changing its nature. In particular, it can incorporate more detail about development of interests over time and incipient interests, greater complexity and stagewise development of ideas, more decision points, and more details about activities, for example, exploration of interests, learning, and project work.

Psychological studies of memory raise the concern that individuals falsely remember and reconstruct past events or thoughts in some cases. For my description in this book the greatest concern is that individuals may state in a retrospective account that they had an interest at an earlier time that in fact they had not formed at that time. This is a serious concern to be borne in mind. However it is the case that the context of recollection in this book and kinds of memories that are its focus are different than the kinds of memories that seem susceptible of false memory described in the literature. False memories have primarily been identified for traumatic events, for experiences and aspects of experiential memories that do not have high personal relevancy, and, in an experimental context, as individuals "filling in" short narratives they have been told to recall with elements not present in the original story, or falsely

---

[12] In interviews I probed individuals to describe background sources and issues they might not otherwise mention. As one example, I probed for areas of work they did not pursue, and many described interests they chose not to pursue and failed projects. Autobiographies are likely to be more selective than interviews in this regard.

recalling an element that has a close association with an element that is part of a memory, for example, falsely recalling hearing a word having a close association with words in a recited word list. None of these cases fits closely with the recollection of creative interests. Creative interests have high personal relevance, they are not traumatic, nor are they tied to public events, thus subject to scripting, for example by media coverage. Further, while they form part of a larger autobiographical narrative, they do not fit in a tight narrative structure, but on the contrary usually are described as forming, and seem to form, well before critical later events like ideas based in them — thus are not "proximal" causes — not linked closely in time or often narratively to later events, but rather bases for them.[13]

Creative interests as I describe them in this book are relatively stable constructs represented in memory as generic memories. Recalling an interest one

[13]For narrative "filling in" and false recall of words in word lists see M.K. Johnson, S. Hashtroudi, and D.S. Lindsay, "Source monitoring," *Psychological Bulletin* 114 (1993): 3–28. These false memories are of single elements; interests are broader than single elements, and seemingly less likely to arise as the kind of false memory described in this literature, in part because, as noted in the main text, they are not so tightly linked to subsequent events, which is the dynamic that tends to drive false narrative construction in the psychology experimental literature. Research on dramatic public events indicates that memory for such events may be vulnerable to becoming distorted through a combination of shared social memory and lack of personal relevancy; see R. Brown and J. Kulik, "Flashbulb memories," *Cognition* 5 (1977): 73–99; Ulric Neisser and Nicole Harsch, "Phantom flashbulbs: False recollections of hearing the news about *Challenger*," in *Affect and Accuracy in Recall: Studies of "Flashbulb" Memories*, ed. Eugene Winograd and Ulric Neisser (Cambridge: Cambridge University Press, 1992), pp. 9–31. Interests are inherently private, not public, thus not vulnerable to the corruption of a wider social memory interfering with an individual's own memory; and they are personally significant in a way many public events that have been studied are not. It is noteworthy in this regard that public events that have greater personal saliency are remembered far better. A paper by Ulric Neisser, Eugene Winograd, and Mary Weldon (1991), "Remembering the Earthquake: 'What I Experienced' vs. 'How I Heard the News'," reported in Martin Conway, *Flashbulb Memories* (Hillsdale, NJ: Lawrence Erlbaum Associates, 1995), pp. 49–52, 113, reports that individuals who personally experienced the 1989 northern California Earthquake had very accurate recollection of their experience of it eighteen months later, whereas individuals who did not personally experience it but learned about it were significantly less accurate. In his book Conway emphasizes that personal consequentiality is crucial for good memory. False memory has been shown for events or elements in people's environment that were not the focus of their attention; see, for example, the discussion by Daniel Schacter in *The Seven Sins of Memory: How the Mind Forgets and Remembers* (Boston: Houghton Mifflin, 2001). This does not apply to individuals' memories of creative interests: their interests are at the center of their development, thus a focus of their attention.

24   had is like remembering the walk to work one has taken many times — one remembers it as a single generalized event more than as separate instances. Such generic memories are likely to have high general reliability, though with fewer details, as compared with memories of specific events or emotions at a given time, which have detail but are not always reliable. Thus when individuals state interests they had it is likely they did have them, though they most likely will not remember precisely how they thought of their interest at different times.[14] Creative interests have two further characteristics associated with high memory retention: high personal salience, as noted above, and, as I describe them, a high degree of rehearsal, being recalled to mind repeatedly.[15] I note also that individuals' descriptions of their interests are largely self-generated, both in autobiographical contexts and in the interviews I conducted. They do not have to mention having creative interests, especially well before main ideas they had — there is little narrative pressure for them to do so, and certainly they could construct narratives of their creative development without doing so.

I have carefully analyzed the language individuals used to describe creative interests they formed. Overwhelmingly, for those who explicitly describe having an interest (not for those, in particular some of the individuals famous for their contributions, for whom I have reconstructed what I believe their interest to have been) their descriptions are stated in language in which they

---

[14]Generic events are the most basic level of autobiographical memory. See M.A. Conway and D.A. Bekerian, "Organization in autobiographical memory," *Memory and Cognition* 15 (1987): 119–32; Lawrence W. Barsalou, "The content and organization of autobiographical memories," in *Remembering Reconsidered: Ecological and Traditional Approaches to the Study of Memory*, ed. Ulric Neisser and Eugene Winograd (Cambridge: Cambridge University Press, 1988), pp. 193–243; William F. Brewer, "Memory for randomly sampled autobiographical events," in *Remembering Reconsidered*, pp. 21–90; and Martin A. Conway and David C. Rubin, "The structure of autobiographical memory," in *Theories of Memory*, ed. Alan F. Collins, Susan E. Gathercole, Martin A. Conway, and Peter E. Morris (Hillsdale, NJ: Lawrence Erlbaum Associates, 1993), pp. 103–37. For a recent review see D.L. Greenberg and D.C. Rubin, "The neuropsychology of autobiographical memory," *Cortex* 39 (2003): 687–728. It is implicit in much of the literature that generic memories are quite accurate, while memories for details of specific events may be less so.

[15]Ulric Neisser discusses the accuracy of generic memories, and rehearsal, in his study of the memory of John Dean; he argues that Dean's memory of generic facts was very good but his memory for specific events was less accurate. Ulric Neisser, "John Dean's memory: A case study," in *Memory Observed: Remembering in Natural Contexts*, selection and commentary by Ulric Neisser (San Francisco: W.H. Freeman & Company, 1982), pp. 139–59.

unequivocally state that they had the interest at the earlier time. Further, in a considerable number of cases, an individual states that he had a conscious conception of his interest at the time. For my interview subjects I have been able to verify this by explicitly asking them whether they were consciously thinking about their interest at the time — many stated that they were. Thus for individuals to have reconstructed interests falsely they would have had to do so in direct opposition to the language they themselves used to describe their interests.

Overall it seems likely that subjects' descriptions of their creative interests are real. I believe the greatest danger in the retrospective accounts individuals give describing their interests is that they represent their early interests as more coherent than they really were; often an interest begins as more fragmentary and fleeting, then becomes more formed over time, and in a retrospective account an individual may describe it more the way he thought of it later. My description takes this into account: in Chapter 3 I describe the formation of creative interests and emphasize that they are often fragmentary, fleeting thoughts at first, then become more formed later. Further, I describe individuals building up conceptual structures in their interest domains over time.

Contemporaneous materials are very useful in providing a check on what individuals state in retrospective accounts of their development. I have described the contemporaneous sources I rely on for the sample of individuals famous for their creative contributions above. Here I note that contemporaneous materials I collected for my interview sample are very useful in confirming what individuals told me in interviews. These materials both confirm what individuals stated in our interview and in many cases show that an individual had formed his or her main creative interest, as stated in the interview, prior to entering graduate school or early in graduate school. Thus, for example, for the literary scholars their dissertation prospectus generally shows that they had formed their main interest by the time they began work on their dissertation, thus in many cases before they had the main ideas in their dissertation, which they developed after writing their prospectus. For several individuals additional materials, such as a college honors thesis or notes the individual shared with me, confirm what the individual stated in our interview, including specifically about forming a creative interest. A number of individuals had written materials in front of them during our interview, for example notes they had kept or an undergraduate thesis, providing a check on their own memory. Also, a pair of individuals I interviewed mentioned a professor who had direct knowledge about an important phase in their development. In each case this individual confirmed my research subject's account and provided some additional details.

26   I found few discrepancies between archival materials and statements made in interviews.

The main area in which I have found individuals to make mistakes in memory was in dating, usually fairly minor discrepancies, for example, in which term a class was taken. But of course there are many statements individuals make that cannot be checked.[16] For many individuals, as stated above, I have followed their development since our interview. In a number of cases an individual's later contributions and activities show that an interest he had that he described in our interview has been the root of his creative work and contributions since that time, providing further, prospective evidence in support of the description in this book.

The literature on the self suggests that individuals construct autobiographical narratives in light of their present self, their present needs, desires, and attitudes, and self-management.[17] Individuals may be driven to try to create a sense of coherent self-identity through time, in particular in self-narratives of their development. One way conceivably they might do this is through constructing creative interests retrospectively that fit with their later work, or extending interests back further in time beyond when they actually formed them. I believe that the evidence, both linguistic and supporting materials, makes it implausible that the many individuals whose development I studied who described creative interests all or mainly constructed interests they did not have, though they may describe them as more fully formed or more central in their development during an earlier time than they were in reality at that time. As a second possible effect, the drive to construct a coherent self-identity might lead individuals to block out and not describe interests, ideas, and projects not related to the main line of their development and

---

[16] As noted above, I am mainly concerned with accuracy of generic memories. Minor dating mistakes are not a major issue for my description; thus, exactly when someone first formed a creative interest is not crucial. However, if an individual actually formed an interest after other important events that he describes as occurring after forming the interest, such as having ideas or beginning projects that I take as based in the interest, that runs against the description I present. The descriptions individuals gave, many of which are presented in the following chapters, and the archival materials, do not support the view that this was common.

[17] Useful references on self-narratives in general, of which narratives of creative development are a particular kind, include *The Remembering Self: Construction and Accuracy in the Self-narrative*, ed. Ulric Neisser and Robyn Fivush (Cambridge: Cambridge University Press, 1994), *Remembering Reconsidered*, cited above, and Michael Ross and Anne E. Wilson, "Constructing and appraising past selves," in *Memory, Brain, and Belief*, ed. Daniel L. Schacter and Elaine Scarry (Cambridge, MA: Harvard University Press, 2000), pp. 231–58.

current work. Again, I have not found much evidence for this, in particular among my interview subjects, who described many interests, ideas, and projects they did not pursue or that were quite different from their current focus. It may be more of an issue for famous individuals concerned to describe their development in a way fitting their public persona. Interestingly, turning these arguments around, the description in this book is in fact supported by self-psychology arguments. In their drive for coherence individuals will naturally tend to strive to define what their creative interests are, as a way to form a clearer sense of their "creative identity" — and thus will form conceptions of their interests as I describe.

Notwithstanding the potential problems with retrospective accounts of creative development, I note, finally, specifically with regard to the interview sample, that the data collection process employed had definite strengths. Conducting interviews retrospectively as I did within a year after individuals had passed through the end of the period of development we focused on had advantages. The interviews mainly focused on a period that was fresh in individuals' minds — not the distant past, which is the focus in many autobiographical accounts, for which memory is more likely to be poor, but rather the preceding several years. They were given by relatively young individuals whose memory was intact, and focused on topics that were, and in most cases continued to be, at the center of individuals' lives and activity. At the same time, because the interviews were retrospective, individuals were able to reflect upon their development, placing experiences, activities, interests, and ideas in perspective. They were not engrossed in the events they described to the point that it interfered with their ability to describe them clearly. They also were comfortable talking about creative interests they had, which are inherently less sharply focused than ideas or projects. An interview focused on current activities might well lead, through a desire to show the present self in a positive light, to an excessive focus on elements viewed as demonstrating success, definite accomplishments like current ideas and projects, with it being more difficult to gain access to information about inherently more open-ended, less definite interests. Individuals freely shared ideas and interests they had had; I believe their openness was enhanced by the fact that the interviews were focused on the past, not their current ideas.[18]

For individuals famous for their contributions I had far less control over the nature of the data available, including when retrospective accounts were

---

[18]Individuals could speak openly about issues they may have been hesitant to speak about while still in graduate school, such as ideas and interests they had thought of but not yet had the chance to pursue, and their relationship with their advisor.

28   given — many are given very late in life, thus undoubtedly more prone to error and bias. This makes it especially important to gather and use contemporaneous and prospective sources of information for this sample, and to reconstruct individuals' interests using all available information.

This discussion of retrospective accounts of development leads on to one further issue to note with regard to the description in this book: causality. I present the model in this book as a causal structure, using language in which creative interests and conceptual structures in interest domains are described as generative of creativity and guiding individuals in their development. Causality is always an inference. Here the inference is complicated further in cases in which the data are primarily retrospective. Also, it is to be noted that the causal mechanisms I describe are not proximal, but extend over longer time periods. Set against these concerns, the mechanisms are highly intuitive. I put them forward as hypotheses, as mechanisms that generate a coherent description of creative development.

Ultimately, the approach in this book relies on convincing the reader with the weight of the evidence. The reader who approaches the description and cases presented in the following chapters with an open mind, taking note of the many different individuals whose development is described, and the many different forms of evidence and quantity of material presented, will I believe be convinced by the description. There remain significant gaps and many flaws, as I am only too well aware, and future work, with different data, may well modify the description significantly. But I present it in the belief that it will stand in its fundamentals.

RELATED LITERATURES

There are a number of literatures in the field of creativity studies in which aspects of creative development are discussed, in general from perspectives that are somewhat different but complementary to mine in this book. There are also related, relevant literatures on the social environment of creativity and cultural development. In this section I introduce these literatures; they are discussed further where appropriate later. I do not provide a general review of the field of creativity studies.[19]

The fundamental approach in this book is to study creativity as a process of development, unfolding over relatively long periods of time. My description is

[19]For general reviews see *Handbook of Creativity*, ed. Robert J. Sternberg (Cambridge: Cambridge University Press, 1999); Mark A. Runco, *Creativity Research Handbook* (Cresskill, NJ: Hampton Press, 1997); and *Handbook of Creativity*, ed. John Glover, Royce Ronning, and Cecil Reynolds (New York: Plenum Press, 1989).

thus most closely linked with literatures in which creativity is also viewed as based in a process of development. The largest and most diverse literature in which our creativity is viewed in this way is the biographical literature about the lives and creative work of individuals recognized for their creative accomplishments. I draw upon this literature extensively, as discussed above. A second literature in which our creativity is viewed as a process of development is the evolving systems approach, associated with Howard Gruber.[20] The evolving systems approach shares with my approach an emphasis on the distinctiveness of each individual in his process of development, and a careful attention to the rich details of development unfolding over time. Howard Gardner also views creativity as a life developmental process, in *Creating Minds*. He, and Mihaly Csikszentmihalyi in *Creativity: Flow and the Psychology of Discovery and Invention*, focus on the experiential nature of creative work. In their work and the evolving systems literature there is a focus on motivational and affective as well as cognitive processes.[21] What I add to the evolving systems approach and

[20] Howard E. Gruber, *Darwin on Man: A Psychological Study of Scientific Creativity* (Chicago: University of Chicago Press, 1981). See also *Creative People at Work: Twelve Cognitive Case Studies*, ed. Doris B. Wallace and Howard E. Gruber (New York: Oxford University Press, 1989); I note especially the chapter by Margery B. Franklin, "A convergence of streams: Dramatic change in the artistic work of Melissa Zink," pp. 254–77. There was a festschrift and special issue of the *Creativity Research Journal* devoted to Gruber in 2003 (Vol. 15); relevant articles are: J. Vonèche, "The changing structure of Piaget's thinking: Invariance and transformations," pp. 3–9, M.F. Ippolito and R.D. Tweney, "The journey to *Jacob's Room*: The network of enterprise of Virginia Woolf's first experimental novel," pp. 25–43, R. Brower, "Constructive repetition, time, and the evolving systems approach," pp. 61–72, and F. Vidal, "Contextual biography and the evolving systems approach to creativity," pp. 73–82. Joy Amulya has like me engaged in a study of creativity in the doctoral research process; she presents her analysis in *Passionate Curiosity: A Study of Research Process Experience in Doctoral Researchers*, diss., Harvard University, 1998; her approach and findings in a number of ways fit with mine. Frederic Holmes, in his last work, *Investigative Pathways: Patterns and Stages in the Careers of Experimental Scientists* (New Haven, CT: Yale University Press, 2004), presents a general description of experimental scientific work unfolding over long periods of time.

[21] Howard Gardner, *Creating Minds: An Anatomy of Creativity Seen Through the Lives of Freud, Einstein, Picasso, Stravinsky, Eliot, Graham, and Gandhi* (New York: Basic Books, 1993) (see also his *Extraordinary Minds* (New York: Basic Books, 1997)); Mihaly Csikszentmihalyi, *Creativity: Flow and the Psychology of Discovery and Invention* (New York: HarperCollins, 1996). *Creativity and Development*, ed. R. Keith Sawyer, Vera John-Steiner, Seana Moran, Robert J. Sternberg, David Henry Feldman, Jeanne Nakamura, and Mihaly Csikszentmihalyi (New York: Oxford University Press, 2003) contains discussion of creativity as a developmental process. Particularly of interest are Gardner's comments on p. 233, and R. Keith Sawyer's comments in his "Introduction," pp. 3–11, and Chapter 1, "Emergence in creativity and development," pp. 12–60.

30   other descriptions of creativity as a developmental process is a more structured
description, rooted in creative interests, conceptions of interests, the formation and growth of conceptual structures centering on and based in domains
of creative interests, and explicit descriptions of forms of creativity and patterns of development rooted in these structures. A third literature consists of
statistical analyses of creative development, including especially analyses of
rates of production of creative products over the course of creative careers.[22]
Work in this tradition is important, and certainly fits with my description, but
is less closely related to my approach. A fourth literature is psychoanalytically
based and more general approaches viewing creativity as rooted in processes
of transmutation, based largely in the unconscious, whereby individuals trans-
mute their personal experiences into creative products. Such a process is quite
different — or at least is described differently — than the processes I describe.
I discuss the relationship between my description, in particular of the formation
of interests, and theories of transmutation in Chapter 3.

Beyond the literatures discussed above, in which creativity is viewed as an
extended process of development, there are also literatures focusing on creative processes over shorter time periods, on the order of days and weeks. The
most relevant of these for my description is the literature on problems and
problem finding. The importance of problems in motivating creative activity is discussed in many accounts of creativity. For example, obstacles that
individuals encounter in the course of their work are frequently described as
important factors spurring them on to greater creative accomplishments. Problem recognition has been linked with need perception and dissatisfaction with
existing conditions.[23] Problem finding is a more exploratory and constructive
process. Useful references are the classic work of Getzels and Csikszentmihalyi, and *Problem Finding, Problem Solving, and Creativity*.[24] In some respects

[22] Dean Simonton has published the best known work of this kind in modern times;
see his *Scientific Genius: A Psychology of Science* (Cambridge: Cambridge University Press, 1988), and "Creativity from a historiometric perspective," in *Handbook of
Creativity*, ed. Robert J. Sternberg, pp. 116–33.
[23] See Subrata Dasgupta, *Technology and Creativity* (New York: Oxford University
Press, 1996), Chapter 3, "The birth of technological problems," pp. 20–28. This view is
echoed in many accounts.
[24] Jacob W. Getzels and Mihalyi Csikszentmihalyi, "Discovery-oriented behavior
and the originality of creative products: A study with artists," *Journal of Personality
and Social Psychology* 19 (1971): 47–52, and *The Creative Vision: A Longitudinal Study
of Problem Finding in Art* (New York: John Wiley & Sons, 1976); *Problem Finding,
Problem Solving, and Creativity*, ed. Mark A. Runco (Norwood, NJ: Ablex, 1994). Albert
Einstein and many others have emphasized the importance in scientific research of
asking the right question or a good question. For a Gestalt psychology approach see

questions and problems have a similar role in creative development as creative
interests, in defining a creative direction. But there are important differences.
Many problems and questions are relatively briefly defined, and many, especially many problems, are quite specific and involve narrow, precisely defined
goals. In contrast, creative interests and conceptions of interests are broader and
often more richly conceived. They are also inherently open-ended — viewed
as potentially able to be developed creatively in many different ways, defining
rich domains for exploration, and involving goals that are more open-ended.
As described in this book individuals may seek to define problems within interest domains; conversely, beginning from a defined problem they may form
a broader interest centering and growing around it. Thus creative interests
often center on and involve questions and problems, especially ones that have
a degree of breadth and are relatively open-ended. Narrower questions and
problems enter into development separately, for example, in defining projects.
I compare and contrast relatively narrow problems and questions with creative
interests in Chapter 7.

The most widely described form of creativity is making a connection between or combining two elements that have not previously been connected or
combined.[25] A theory of creativity that builds on this principle is the Darwinian
model of random variation and selection, associated with Donald Campbell,
and the basis of many modern accounts of creativity, as well as theories of
cultural innovation.[26] As a theory of creative development this theory has a
minimal structure. Individuals randomly learn many elements, perhaps focused

M. Wertheimer, *Productive Thinking* (New York: Harper & Brothers, 1959). For cognitive
science approaches see Margaret Boden, *The Creative Mind: Myths and Mechanisms*
(London: Routledge, 2004), and *Creativity, Cognition, and Knowledge: An Interaction*,
ed. Terry Dartnall (Westport, CT: Praeger, 2002).

[25] For creative connections see S.A. Mednick, "The associative basis of the creative
process," *Psychological Review* 69 (1962): 220–32. See also Arnold Koestler, *The Act
of Creation* (New York: Macmillan, 1967). For recent work on conceptual combinations see *Creative Thought*, ed. Thomas B. Ward, Steven M. Smith, and Jyotsna Vaid
(Washington: American Psychological Association, 1997). A related process is blend-
ing; see G. Fauconnier and M. Turner, "Conceptual integration networks," *Cognitive
Science* 22 (1998): 133–87.

[26] Donald Campbell, "Blind variation and selective retention in creative thought
as in other knowledge processes," *Psychological Review* 67 (1960): 380–400. An earlier
model, focused on chance configurations as a means of solving problems arising in
creative work, is set forth by Henri Poincaré in "Mathematical creation," in *The Creative
Process*, ed. Brewster Ghiselin (Berkeley: University of California Press, 1952), pp. 33–42;
it was extended by Jacques Hadamard, *An Essay on the Psychology of Invention in the
Mathematical Field* (Princeton, NJ: Princeton University Press, 1945).

in a conventional subject domain; then they randomly make combinations among them, either in their unconscious or more consciously. If a combination they make is a "good" one, that is original and potentially valuable, they retain it and may then develop it further. Thus creativity arises out of a rather general learning process followed by random combinations and selection. In this book I propose a theory in which individuals are significantly more directed in their development; they guide themselves by forming creative interests, distinctive to them, defining distinctive, individualized domains they explore, leading them to build up distinctive conceptual structures in their interest domains which are in turn generative of their creativity. Randomness has a role in my description, for example in random encounters sparking creative responses, but in the context of a self-directed, developmental process. In my view this description fits the facts, biographical and others, better. My description forges a bridge to literatures on self-determination and, in a broader way, the literature on the self as a self-organizing, constructed entity.[27]

Another branch of literature within the field of creativity studies with which my description is connected is the literature concerning the influence of environment on creativity.[28] A wide variety of environmental factors and conditions have been described that may influence creativity, including incentives, feedback, critical reception, mentoring, and organizational and institutional structure and environment. Teresa Amabile has made important contributions

[27]Edward Deci and Richard Ryan, *Intrinsic Motivation and Self-Determination in Human Behavior* (New York: Plenum, 1985), and "The 'what' and 'why' of goal pursuits: Human needs and the self-determination of behavior," *Psychological Inquiry* 11 (2000): 227–68; Richard Ryan, "Agency and organization: Intrinsic motivation, autonomy and the self in psychological development," *Nebraska Symposium on Motivation: Developmental Perspectives on Motivation* 40 (1993): 1–56. On the self see Roy Baumeister, *The Self in Social Psychology* (Philadelphia, PA: Psychology Press (Taylor and Francis), 1999). There is an interesting literature on the self as formed historically and culturally; see Charles Taylor, *Sources of the Self: The Making of the Modern Identity* (Cambridge, MA: Harvard University Press, 1989), and R.F. Baumeister, "How the self became a problem: A psychological review of historical research," *Journal of Personality and Social Psychology* 52 (1987): 163–76. In embedding randomness in a model of development I find some resonance with the work of James H. Austin, *Chase, Chance, and Creativity: The Lucky Art of Novelty* (New York: Columbia University Press, 1976). To the extent I describe individuals managing their development my description also has resonance with the theory of self-regulation of Michael F. Sheier and Charles S. Carver, *On the Self-regulation of Behavior* (Cambridge: Cambridge University Press, 1998).

[28]For an excellent review see the introduction to *Social Creativity*, 1, ed. Alfonso Montuori and Ronald Purser (Cresskill, NJ: Hampton Press, 1999).

in this area in her study of the influence of external reward systems on intrinsic motivation and creativity.[29] There is also much ongoing work studying creativity in the context of organizations. This work is relevant for many of the individuals whose development I describe in this book, but not my focus, though organizational issues and context do arise in places. There is also interesting work on collaborative creativity, mentoring, and more generally, the interpersonal context of creativity. Mentoring and collaborative creativity in particular are relevant for many of the individuals whose development I describe, especially my interview subjects, and enter into my description in places, but again are not my focus.[30]

More directly related to my approach is a growing body of work situating creativity in the field in which it is based and the broader social-cultural environment. Csikszentmihalyi and his collaborators have described what they call the domain-person-field interaction, situating individuals in their creative work in the context of the conceptual or symbolic domain in which they work as well as the interpersonal field of environment of their work. One particular focus is on the collective judgement made in evaluating the value and creativity of individuals' work.[31] Silvano Arieti adapts systems concepts, including the notion of feedback loops, to describe the relationship between individuals engaged in creative endeavors and the social-cultural systems in which they are embedded.[32] Robert Sternberg and collaborators have developed a propulsion theory of creativity focusing on how individuals make decisions and orient their creative activities in relation to their field and their view about how it

[29]Teresa M. Amabile, *Creativity in Context* (Boulder, CO: Westview Press, 1996); see also her review of the literature on motivation and creativity with Mary Ann Collins, "Motivation and creativity," *Handbook of creativity*, ed. Robert J. Sternberg, pp. 297–312.

[30]For recent work on collaborative creativity and relationships in the context of creative work see the references in *Social Creativity*. See also Vera John-Steiner, *Creative Collaboration* (New York: Oxford University Press, 2000); R. Keith Sawyer, *Group Creativity: Music, Theater, Collaboration* (Mahwah, NJ: Lawrence Erlbaum Associates, 2003); and Howard Gardner, *Creating Minds*, especially pp. 43–44. For a discussion of creativity as an organizational activity see Warren Bennis and Patricia Ward Biederman, *Organizing Genius: The Secrets of Creative Collaboration* (Reading, MA: Addison-Wesley, 1997).

[31]Mihaly Csikszentmihalyi, "Society, culture, and person: A systems view of creativity," in *The Nature of Creativity: Contemporary Psychological Perspectives*, ed. Robert J. Sternberg (Cambridge: Cambridge University Press, 1988), pp. 325–39; and David Henry Feldman, Mihaly Csikszentmihalyi, and Howard Gardner, *Changing the World: A Framework for the Study of Creativity* (Westport, CT: Praeger, 1994).

[32]Silvano Arieti, *The Magic Synthesis* (New York: Basic Books, 1992).

34   should develop.[33] My description here has some resonance with these descriptions, but the creative interests and conceptual structures I describe are distinct, and I describe cultural linkages through specific channels of cultural transmission and influence not described in them.

Finally, also relevant for this book is the literature on cultural development. This literature is vast and is not reviewed in detail here; I discuss the literature further in Chapter 17. In fact the study of cultural development has developed almost entirely separately from the study of creativity. Thus traditionally cultural development has been studied mainly from historical, social, and economic perspectives, and, with some exceptions, there has been little emphasis placed on describing the creative development of individuals who have contributed to this development. In one important approach cultural development is described as an evolutionary process. This literature dates back at least as far as the pioneering study by Augustus Henry Lane-Fox Pitt-Rivers, *The Evolution of Culture*, published in 1906.[34] A striking feature of this literature is that the fundamental focus of analysis is not individuals, but cultural forms, such as lineages of weapons, crafts, and tools, and discrete cultural units, often called memes, as defined by Richard Dawkins in *The Selfish Gene*.[35] The evolution

[33] R.J. Sternberg, "A propulsion model of types of creative contributions," *Review of General Psychology* 3 (1999): 83–100, Robert J. Sternberg, James C. Kaufman, and Jean E. Pretz, *The Creativity Conundrum* (New York: Psychology Press, 2002), and Robert J. Sternberg, "The development of creativity as a decision-making process," in *Creativity and Development*, pp. 91–138. These descriptions focus more on individuals directed in their development by a definite sense of the kind of contribution they wish to make, whereas I focus more on individuals forming interests they are intrinsically interested in, with less immediate thought about the ultimate contributions they will make through pursuing them; there is overlap in my discussion of the role of extrinsic and strategic factors in the formation of interests in Chapter 5.

[34] Augustus Henry Lane-Fox Pitt-Rivers, *The Evolution of Culture, and Other Essays*, ed. J.L. Myres (Oxford: Clarendon Press, 1906). He describes the evolution of several different cultural forms among the Australian Aboriginal peoples and other peoples whose cultures were pre-modern at the time. Since his work was published many further studies have been published. George Basalla discusses the literature and gives many references to studies of the evolution of specific technologies in *The Evolution of Technologies* (Cambridge: Cambridge University Press, 1988). Payton Usher provides synopses of the development of several dozen important inventions in *A History of Mechanical Inventions* (Cambridge, MA: Harvard University Press, 1954). There are recent attempts to integrate individual creativity with evolution in design; see C. Eckert and M. Stacey, "Adaptation of sources of inspiration in knitwear design," *Creativity Research Journal* 15 (2003): 355–84.

[35] Richard Dawkins, *The Selfish Gene* (New York: Oxford University Press, 1976). I provide additional references in Chapter 17.

of these forms and units of meaning is described almost as if it happens spontaneously, with the role of individual creativity deemphasized. Sociologists have
in some cases considered the role of individuals in the process of cultural development, but not consistently, and have not developed a comprehensive model
linking individual creativity with cultural development. In his description of
scientific revolutions Thomas Kuhn scarcely mentions processes of individual
creative development. Economists who have discussed technological development have typically focused on forces that transcend individuals, like market
dynamics, demographics, and the evolution of institutions; and when they do
discuss the role of individuals or present models of the generation of innovations, these are highly simplified, with little connection with the literature
on creativity.[36] Even the branch of literature that focuses on the importance
of individual freedom and action, which is one inspiration for my own work,
associated with Friedrich Hayek and with roots extending back to John Stuart
Mill and far further, does not model the individual creative process.[37] The
description in this book, in common with a number of the studies listed in
the paragraph above, situates individuals in their creative development in their
cultural environment. One of my objectives is to contribute, with these studies, to the development of a new approach for studying cultural development,
rooted in a model of individual creativity and creative development.

[36]In a famous passage, Joseph A. Schumpeter describes how capitalism unleashes
a "gale of creative destruction" in which new innovations are continually being introduced into markets, disrupting the established order. See *Capitalism, Socialism, and
Democracy* (New York: Harper & Row Publishers, 1942), Chapter 7. But he does not
discuss the sources of innovation in creative processes. Economists certainly recognize
the importance of technological change for economic development; see, for example, David S. Landes, *The Unbound Prometheus: Technological Change and Industrial
Development in Western Europe from 1750 to the Present* (Cambridge: Cambridge University Press, 1969), and Joel Mokyr, *The Lever of Riches* (New York: Oxford University
Press, 1990). There is a large recent literature on technological innovation, as well as
microeconomic models of the research and development process; but these models are
not linked to the literature on creativity. See my discussion in Chapter 17.
[37]Classic works are Friedrich A. Hayek, *The Constitution of Liberty* (Chicago: University of Chicago Press, 1960) (see also his *Individualism and Economic Order* (Chicago:
University of Chicago Press, 1948)); John Stuart Mill, *On Liberty* (Indianapolis: Hackett
Publishing, 1978 (originally published 1859)); and Alfred Marshall, *Industry and Trade;
A Study of Industrial Technique and Business Organization; and of Their Influences on
the Conditions of Various Classes and Nations* (London: Macmillan, 1919).

2

CREATIVE INTERESTS AND CONCEPTIONS OF CREATIVE INTERESTS

In this chapter I define what a creative interest is and what a conception of a creative interest is. I present a series of examples of individuals' statements describing their creative interests and, more specifically, their conceptions of their interests, outline features of creative interests, sketch main functions of creative interests and conceptions of creative interests in creative development, and note how my account builds on and goes beyond the previous literature in defining creative interests as a theoretical construct.

DEFINITIONS

A "creative interest" is a topic or subject, typically of our own construction, that we find interesting, even fascinating, and are curious about and interested in exploring and learning more about, that we consider worthy to serve as a basis or center for creative activity and in fact would like and usually intend or at least hope to pursue ourself — to try to develop creatively, to employ as the basis or center for creative work. A creative interest may be a substantive topic, or alternatively may center on an approach, a set of principles, or an objective defined in a general way, not in detail. I describe and present examples illustrating different kinds of creative interests throughout the book. We imagine our creative interests to have creative potential, to hold promise as fruitful lines for exploration and development. We do not however generally have a clear idea about where we will be led through pursuing them or even in many cases what lines of development we will pursue — they are not so planned out or specific. Indeed our creative interests are neither very broad nor extremely narrow and specific — they are intermediate, best thought of as medium-sized topics or centers of focus.

A "conception" of our creative interest is a conception we form of our interest, defining it and imagining it. We may form a conception of our interest well after forming the interest, or at the same time as we first form it, essentially defining our interest through our conception. A conception of a creative interest is a mental construct that we form, access, and hold in consciousness, so that we are able to think about it consciously and consciously use it in our thinking process. I note that our conceptions are not, especially at first, necessarily such fixed and solid structures as the definition may be taken to imply. Once we form a conception of a creative interest we do tend to call it to mind often and even dwell on it, especially while actively pursuing it, which lends to it an air of fixedness and permanence in our mind. At first, however, a conception of a creative interest is often more like a passing thought, along the lines of "this is something I find interesting, that I am interested in and would like to explore further and try to develop creatively if I could."

A creative interest and a conception of the interest are distinct and in general different, although closely linked. Both are subjective. In particular, a creative interest is a topic or subject, but one that is essentially constructed in our mind; our interest is encoded in a mental representation or structure that serves to define it and generates our interest, either spontaneously or in response to stimuli in the world or our own mental processes, that call forth a response in us through activating it. However, this representation, although it is lodged in our mind, is by no means necessarily explicit and fully conscious: it may be partly or even mainly unconscious or preconscious, hidden from our internal view, not fully and clearly visible to our mind's eye, not fully accessible in consciousness. In contrast, our conception is fully conscious, a depiction of our interest in consciousness — thus clearly visible to our mind's eye — through which we are able to reflect consciously upon our interest. Typically many elements are incorporated within, and linked to, the structures or representations that encode our creative interest, including for example images, concepts, memories, and feeling states; indeed these structures and representations can be quite large and amorphous. In contrast, our conception of our interest, though in many cases quite rich, is limited and in general does not incorporate all parts or facets of our interest, though it has links to many of them.

When we form or begin to form a creative interest we do not necessarily form a conception of our interest at the same time. This occurs in some cases, in particular in cases in which we form and define an interest through forming a conception of it, but not in all or even most. Rather, more commonly, at first our interest is intuitive, inchoate, not fully conscious, then over time as we think and learn more about it and discuss it with others, we form a clearer, fuller conception of it. Many of our interests in fact form in a piecemeal fashion over time, and some exist in our minds for long periods of time before we form full conceptions of them.

It must of course be admitted, as a possibility, that some of our creative interests never enter into our consciousness, that we never form explicit conceptions of them, yet still they influence our thinking and our creative work, exerting their influence from within our unconscious. But I believe this is highly unusual and not the general pattern of creative development, despite the fact that in certain traditions in the study of creativity, such as the psychoanalytic tradition, a position close to this one is sometimes maintained (though such a position is not really implied or necessary for psychoanalytic theories, since it is possible for us to be motivated by unconscious drives and also to form and pursue conscious conceptions of our interests). I show in this book with many examples that individuals do in fact form conceptions of their interests. Indeed when we consider the fact that our creative development typically extends over many years, and how central our creative work is in our lives, it seems implausible that we would have creative interests and never think about them consciously, indeed mull over them — it seems that inevitably, at certain junctures, we will think about our interests, and when we do we will form conceptions of them. My argument in this book is that in nearly every case in which an individual develops a creative interest he forms a conception of it, typically well before he makes his most important contributions through pursuing it, and further, that his conception is central and crucial for his successful development of it.

Although my description of creative development, including the examples I present, essentially follows and supports this argument, what is truly essential is a more basic point: that rich conceptual structures form in our mind — integrative, with many linkages and associations — that encode and define our creative interests. It is these structures ultimately that matter, that have important functions in our development, guiding us, sparking and mediating our creative responses to elements we encounter, and being the source of our creativity. Forming a conception of a creative interest is valuable primarily because it facilitates the process of such a rich conceptual structure forming in our mind: sitting in the center it links many elements together; and through making our interest accessible to our conscious thinking processes it helps us form a richer, more integrative interest. It is possible such a structure could form without forming a conception of an interest (for example, a series of sensory responses might build up a patterned response that effectively defined an interest, or a person might form an interest in response to a traumatic event and repress his interest but still have a mental representation of it); but it is unlikely given the nature of unconscious processes. These processes are typically more primitive, and a conceptual structure formed strictly through unconscious processing is bound to be less conceptually rich, less defined conceptually, and less integrated, and will most likely function less effectively, for example in guiding exploration and decision-making. Thus my view and conviction is that individuals form conceptions of their creative interests and that forming such a conception facilitates forming a rich conceptual structure encoding and defining one's creative interest in one's mind. But my argument itself rests primarily on the more basic principle that individuals form conceptual structures defining and encoding their creative interests.[1]

In some respects creative interests fit the conventional notion of an interest and resemble ordinary interests; however, in other important respects they are different, hence thinking about them in these conventional terms is misleading. An interest, in customary usage, is a subject or activity that we find interesting, that engages us, and that we enjoy and desire to explore and learn about. Creative interests share these basic properties; they also have a further characteristic, however, which is that they are topics we imagine have creative potential and that we would like and usually intend or hope to try to develop creatively ourselves. In contrast we do not generally believe that our ordinary interests have creative potential, and even if we do believe they have such potential we do not intend to try to develop them creatively ourselves, at least not with the aim of making valued original contributions. In ordinary usage interests are often hobbies or avocations, activities we engage in or subjects we explore purely for our own enjoyment in our leisure time, thus not directly tied to our principal occupation or endeavors. In contrast our creative interests are at the center of our work and our endeavors. However, ordinary interests do influence creative development and work in some cases. In particular, they sometimes form the basis for a creative interest, a good example being a hobby or childhood interest forming the basis for a creative interest.

There is a further, crucial difference between our conventional notion of interests and creative interests, which poses the greatest danger of misleading

[1] I have been led to the notion of individuals forming conceptions of their creative interests also empirically. Many of the individuals I interviewed, and many individuals famous for their creative contributions whose developments I have studied, report forming such conceptions. Thus, they don't typically make a statement such as "at that time I was interested in," or "I was interested in topic X but didn't know it"; rather they state far more directly that at the time they had a conscious thought about their interest, for example, "I realized I was interested in topic X," or "I thought about topic X as something I was interested in pursuing."

us about the true nature of our creative interests. We commonly think of interests as broad conventional subjects that can be described simply, for example, baseball, gardening, modern art, and American politics. Our creative interests however are not like this. They possess breadth, but not so much as broad conventional subjects do; rather they are intermediate in breadth, broad enough to hold mysteries and to explore, but also refined, both defining and providing centers of focus for us in our creative endeavors. And, crucially, they are neither conventional nor simple, but in fact just the opposite — they are distinctive, often unique, and in many cases possess considerable conceptual richness — which is a fundamental source of their distinctiveness and also fundamentally at odds with the commonplace notion of interests as basic subjects described in one or two words. As I show by example later, even two individuals who share a creative interest in the same basic topic almost always conceptualize what they are interested in differently, seeing the topic from different perspectives, focusing on different aspects of it, each noticing subtleties that the other fails to appreciate. The mistaken notion that individuals engaged in creative work form interests in broad, simple, conventional topics masks the true importance of creative interests in our creative development. By blocking us from recognizing the distinctiveness and focus of our creative interests it prevents us from understanding how important our creative interests are in defining our creative identity and being generative of our creativity and originality, even if it is true that that creativity and originality is only fully realized later, in our creative contributions.

SOURCES OF INFORMATION

Because individuals' creative interests and conceptions of interests are mental constructs they are not directly observable by others. This raises the issue of how we can learn about them.

We are able to learn about individuals' interests and in particular their conceptions of their interests in the most direct, cleanest way in those cases in which an individual provides verbal or written descriptions of his interests that we are able to access. Individuals engaged in creative endeavors describe their creative interests and their conceptions of their interests in various ways — in their diaries and notebooks, in their letters, during casual conversations with friends, in stories and reminiscences, in interviews, public speeches, and articles in which they discuss their development, and in their autobiographies and memoirs. These descriptions fall naturally into two groups: those provided by individuals at the time they first form the conceptions they are describing, and those they provide later, looking back on their development and recalling their conceptions. Both sorts are extremely useful, indeed in some respects they are complementary, and I have utilized both in developing my description of creative development. Contemporaneous descriptions have the advantage that individuals have their conceptions fresh in their minds at the time they give them; in addition, contemporaneous descriptions are likely to be free from bias, since at the time individuals give them they do not know what their future paths of development will be, and therefore cannot modify their descriptions to fit later events and their subsequent ideas and contributions. High quality contemporaneous descriptions are relatively uncommon — though there are some and these are of great value; for although individuals think a great deal about their interests, they generally do not carefully record them at the time they first form conceptions of them. In consequence, I rely somewhat more in this book — as we are forced to in many contexts — on retrospective descriptions. One can imagine that retrospective descriptions might be less accurate, especially in cases in which individuals are not able to remember their interests and their conceptions of their interests clearly. They might also suffer from bias, for individuals might modify their descriptions of their earlier interests in order to make them appear more consistent with their later interests, ideas, and contributions; I have discussed these matters in the Introduction. In fact it has been my experience that retrospective descriptions are generally a good source of information; thus, when I have checked individuals' retrospective accounts against documents that they wrote at the time they first formed their interests, like papers and prospectuses, I have found that in general their later accounts match their earlier statements. Further, I have found that individuals are excellent at recalling and describing their interests and their conceptions of their interests retrospectively, most likely because their interests have been so central to their development.[2]

It is also possible for us to learn about individuals' creative interests through analyzing their paths of creative development and creative contributions. Thus in many cases we can learn about an individual's interests by inference

---

[2]Because I have developed my description of creative interests and conceptions of creative interests mainly through analyzing individuals' descriptions of their interests, I have of necessity focused on individuals for whom I have been able to obtain such descriptions. This undoubtedly introduces a bias into my sample of famous creative individuals, though one that seems unavoidable if we are to study creative development from the perspective of individuals' descriptions of their own processes of development. My sample of interview subjects, as described in Chapter 1, was selected in such a way that it should be free from such bias. It is to be noted also that because individuals typically provide retrospective descriptions in settings in which they are able to spend time recollecting and thinking about their interests and their conceptions of their interests, they are able to describe them fairly carefully, providing useful details.

from his choices about what to learn and with whom to work, and the projects he defines and pursues. Often we can also learn something about his interests through analyzing his creative products, though we must recognize in pursuing this line of analysis that, because the paths individuals follow from their initial interests to their ultimate contributions may be long and winding, the relationship between their interests and their contributions may not be evident on the surface. Biographers routinely attempt to reconstruct the creative interests of their subjects from these kinds of information — from details of their subjects' lives and analysis of their creative works. In describing creative interests I draw upon biographers' interpretations in a number of cases, and in other cases present conjectures I have formed myself about an individual's interest and conception of interest based on available evidence about his activities, life, and work.

One further note. The descriptions I rely on in this book are in general linguistic descriptions individuals give of their interests and conceptions of interests. Their conceptions, however, and their interests need not be entirely or even primarily linguistically based; for example, they may be based in images or other sensory elements, or mix different kinds of elements. The example of Alexander Calder's description of his conception of interest below illustrates this.

Examples

In this and subsequent chapters I present descriptions that individuals from many different fields of endeavor have provided of their creative interests, and especially of their conceptions — or parts of their conceptions — of their interests. I hope to convey a sense of the nature of creative interests and conceptions of creative interests, of how fascinating they are, of their range and diversity, of their imaginativeness and distinctiveness. Here I first present descriptions provided by three individuals: Azad Bonni, the neuroscientist introduced in Chapter 1; Henry Chen, a literary scholar I interviewed who worked for many years at Apple; and the sculptor Alexander Calder. Then I present Virginia Woolf's description, in a short story, of her conception describing a literary interest she wished to explore and develop creatively, and briefly sketch her initial breakthrough in developing her interest creatively. Last I present in the manner of a conjecture — recognizing that no definitive evidence exists — a plausible description of a central creative interest of Galileo as he may have conceptualized it.

Azad first formed a conception of his interest during the summer following his first year in college, while he was working in a cardiology lab on a project studying how protein oxidation and reduction affects the development of

tolerance to nitroglycerin, a chemical compound important in the treatment
of heart disease. The orientation in the lab was physiological, but he became
interested in studying the problem from a different perspective. He told me,
"I remember going to the library and reading a lot, and becoming really interested in the intracellular aspect of it. At that point it wasn't even clear if the
nitroglycerin was acting on cells' surface membranes or on molecules inside
the cell, and I remember suggesting experiments to the head of the lab to
distinguish the two." The head of the lab wasn't interested in pursuing Azad's
idea, and thus Azad was not allowed to run the experiments he suggested. But
"that [experience] was really important" nonetheless, Azad told me, *"in that
ever since then really I've always been interested in mechanisms of action —
when a cell is exposed to an agent what happens inside the cell?"* This is a clear
statement of his main scientific interest, an interest he has pursued, in one way
or another, ever since. Reflecting upon the source of his interest he said, "I just
like understanding how things happen, and I thought even at that point that
basically you'd have to look at things at that level in order to understand them."
He also noted that he had been very interested in math and physics, especially
vector calculus and differential equations, topics that are the basis for classical
mechanics. His interest in classical physics seems to have been the source for
the phrase "mechanism of action" that he used to describe his interest to himself, and he suggested to me that his interest in mechanisms of action may have
reflected his interest in math and physics carried over to biology — "I mean it
was sort of the closest that I could make it [biology] to math and physics." Azad
gave two examples of mechanisms of action that interested him: regulation
of gene transcription by outside agents, and promotion of nerve regeneration
by nerve growth factor (NGF), and in both cases he contrasted his interest
in mechanisms with the focus of other researchers. Thus he said about nerve
growth factor, which he first learned about in medical school, "I was always
interested, even at that point, in how it works. But there wasn't really [a lot
on that] — there was a lot of emphasis at that point more on its biology. And
in terms of mechanism of action, it was at the level of the receptor, [because]
people had just found a receptor. . . . But I'd always felt, whenever I read about
it, that it would be really interesting to know what actually happens inside the
cell [when it is exposed to NGF], and there was absolutely nothing on that as
far as I could see."

Henry formed a conception of his interest as he was considering what subject he would like to write about for his college honors thesis. Henry's favorite
authors growing up were Tolkien and Joyce, and his favorite book is *Finnegans
Wake*, which he has loved since he was a youth both for its difficulty and for
its multitude of references to places, many of which are obscure and must

44   be deciphered. Henry grew up in the South Pacific, and his initial interest in *Finnegans Wake* was sparked by his recognizing references to places near where he and his parents lived and imagining he was the first to discover them. He told me: "My parents lived in the Solomon Islands. And all of a sudden I came across Melanesian Pidgin words, and I was like, 'Wow! I bet no one else has ever known that these Melanesian Pidgin words are in here.' Well it turns out I was wrong, that other people actually had known that there's Melanesian Pidgin words." "But I think that was part of my interest in *Finnegans Wake*, this feeling, 'Aha! I've discovered something new that no one else has,' 'these things are in there that I can catch.'" In college Henry took a course taught by V.S. Naipaul, who was visiting his university; he said Naipaul had a profound influence on him. Naipaul talked about how truly original writers "define a landscape" by seeing and describing it in an original way. Dickens, for example, defines Victorian London, and Naipaul himself, at least in Henry's view, has tried to define postcolonial Trinidad. For his thesis Henry decided he wanted to incorporate material on Joyce and *Finnegans Wake* as well as material on Naipaul. Thinking about what Joyce is known for in his great works, his own interest in *Finnegans Wake*, and what Naipaul had talked about, he realized that the common element was a focus on place — "they all tied together about place." In the case of Joyce not only are places central in *Finnegans Wake*, but Joyce is famous for describing Dublin in meticulous detail, and his stated aim in *Ulysses* was to immortalize Dublin as other great cities of Europe have been immortalized in writing. Going back even further, Henry realized that what he had loved about *The Lord of the Rings* trilogy as a child is Tolkien's creation of place, of Middle Earth, in his view more real and richer in detail than the world created by any other fantasy or science fiction writer. "So, thinking about my favorite authors, first Tolkien, then Joyce and Naipaul, [I realized that] there was this weird connection — to me the thread between them was this sense of what I called 'literary geography', that they all created places in a way." (Henry in fact uses the phrase "literary geography" in the title of his college honors thesis.)[3] His conception of this connection thus became his conception of his interest; *he decided then*, he told me, *that he wanted to focus on literary geography, on exploring "how writers create and define places,"* specifically real places, not fantasy.[4]

Alexander Calder had an abiding fascination with the universe, which was his basic theme and inspiration, especially of his most lasting contributions. In

[3]Henry Chen, *A New Map for the Atlas of Literary Geography: V.S. Naipaul's Trinidad Novels*, submitted for honors in English, Wesleyan University, 1981.

[4]In his thesis Henry specifically mentions Tolkien and Joyce as writers who wrote about and defined places. In a note in his thesis (p. 58) he states that he attended Naipaul's class "The Literature of Rebellion" in the winter and spring of 1979.

his *Autobiography* he vividly describes an experience he had in his early twenties on board a ship: "It was early one morning on a calm sea, off Guatemala, when over my couch — a coil of rope — I saw the beginning of a fiery red sunrise on one side and the moon looking like a silver coin on the other. . . . It left me with a lasting sensation of the solar system."[5] He told a reporter, *"The first inspiration I ever had was the cosmos, the planetary system."* And he told an art critic, *"The basis of everything for me is the universe. The simplest forms in the universe are the sphere and the circle. I represent them by discs and then I vary them."* In the introduction to one of his exhibitions he wrote as follows. *"From the beginnings of my abstract work, even when it might not have seemed so, I felt there was no better model for me than the Universe. . . . Spheres of different sizes, densities, colors, and volumes, floating in space, traversing clouds, sprays of water, currents of air, viscosities and odors — of the greatest variety and disparity."*[6] In this passage Calder conveys his conception of his interest wonderfully, in a way that illustrates some general features of conceptions of interests. He begins with an abstract concept, the universe as a model, and then expands upon this with a series of brilliant examples of specific phenomena of the universe, describing them vividly and precisely, imagistically. He imagines his interest as filled with a multiplicity of objects and attributes, teeming with possibilities — an almost boundless variety — waiting to be discovered and created.

Calder was also fascinated by motion and the idea of motion as art. He said he "felt that art was too static to reflect our world of movement," and said that relatively early in his art career, at the time he was living in Paris and possibly even earlier, he became *"interested in the idea of motion as an art form."*[7] Ultimately he connected his interest in the universe with his interest in art in motion, and motion as art, in his invention of the mobile — see Chapter 9.

Alexander Calder's, Azad's, and Henry's interests exemplify creative interests and conceptions of creative interests. Their interests are characteristic in

[5]Alexander Calder and Jean Davidson, *Calder, An Autobiography with Pictures* (New York: Pantheon Books, 1966), pp. 54–55.

[6]Jean Lipman, *Calder's Universe* (New York: Viking Press with the Whitney Museum of Art, 1976), pp. 17–18.

[7]Ibid., p. 263. In his *Autobiography* Calder refers frequently to trains and motion, especially in his recollections of his childhood years. He mentions that at age three his family lived in a house that in back looked out onto a railway yard; and he describes a transcontinental trip the family took from Philadelphia to Arizona: "Hour after hour I stood on the observation platform. I loved it. The *tick-tick* of the wheels made me feel at home." *Calder, An Autobiography with Pictures*, pp. 12–16. He was also apparently fascinated with the mechanisms and motion of the cable cars in San Francisco, where he lived for several years growing up (*Calder's Universe*, p. 17).

46   having breadth, in particular a moderate degree of breadth, yet also being distinctive. Consider Alexander Calder's first interest. He connects the solar system with art in forming his interest — surely unusual, making his interest quite distinctive, especially when one considers the brilliant details of his conception, the specific spatial and physical elements and phenomena of the universe that he imagines representing artistically. At the same time his interest is broad, while also being focused; thus, he could almost certainly develop his interest creatively in many different ways, having many ideas about it, and ultimately producing many different creative products, yet all would fit within the general domain of focus he defines — basic elements and phenomena of the universe arranged in spatial configurations and having any of a wide variety of different kinds of motion or action. Azad's interest in the mechanisms of action through which external molecular agents trigger effects inside cells was also quite distinctive, at least as far as he knew at the time he formed it, as is indicated by his comment that research on NGF (one of the agents most intensively studied) was focused on its receptor biology, not its mechanism of action inside cells, and in fact this seems to have been one reason for his interest, his sense of an opportunity. His interest is distinctive in particular in his focus on characterizing the full pathway of action inside a cell — I discuss this and show its importance in guiding him in his development in later chapters. His interest is also broad, while focused: there are clearly many different agents that influence cells, each involving a specific mechanism of action that might be studied. Further, the pathways through which these agents influence cells are likely each to involve a series of steps or stages, each of which might be studied in depth. Finally, Henry's interest was also quite distinctive. In particular, it was different from the interests of all the other literary scholars I interviewed. And while it seems likely that there would have been other scholars at the time who would also have been interested in how writers create and define places, these other scholars would most likely have approached the topic differently, with a different conception, in relation to a different set of authors and with roots in different personal experiences. His interest was also broad, yet focused — "literary geography" subsumes a range of issues and topics, and may be explored in many different authors and works, in a variety of ways, both thematically and in terms of approach.

In an entry in her diary dated January 26th, 1920, the day after her thirty-eighth birthday, Virginia Woolf wrote of having "this afternoon arrived at some idea of a new form for a new novel." She described her idea referring to three short stories she had written, "The Mark on the Wall," "Kew Gardens," and "An Unwritten Novel." "Suppose one thing should open out of another — as in An Unwritten Novel — only not for 10 pages but 200 or so — doesn't that give the looseness & lightness I want: doesn't that get closer & yet keep form & speed, & enclose everything, everything. My doubt is how far it will (include) enclose the human heart — Am I sufficiently mistress of my dialogue to net it there? For I figure that the approach will be entirely different this time: no scaffolding; scarcely a brick to be seen; all crepuscular, but the heart, the passion, humour, everything as bright as fire in the mist. Then I'll find room for so much — a gaiety — an inconsequence — a light spirited stepping at my sweet will. Whether I'm sufficiently mistress of things — that's the doubt; but conceive mark on the wall, K. G. [Kew Gardens] & unwritten novel taking hands & dancing in unity."[8]

What does she mean? To unravel her meaning we must go back to "The Mark on the Wall," written in 1917, the first of the three stories she mentions, a story that marks a crucial transition in her creative development, the moment when she first formed a clear conception of her literary interest.

The "mark on the wall" is exactly that, a mark on the wall in front of her that she can hardly make out from where she is sitting in her chair — it is vague and unclear, and she cannot determine objectively what it is. She considers what it might be, contemplating the mystery of life, the fact that all our possessions are inevitably lost, that they are accidental and have no deeper meaning, that life is "perpetual waste and repair." Then her focus shifts. She writes, "I want to think quietly, calmly, spaciously, never to be interrupted, never to have to rise from my chair, to slip easily from one thing to another, without any sense of hostility, or obstacle. I want to sink deeper and deeper, away from the surface, with its hard separate facts." Her thoughts shift away from objects, and come to rest on the figure of herself, her internal self-image. The "pleasantest thoughts," she comments, are those "indirectly reflecting credit" upon ourselves, and she describes how we are continually contriving, during our interactions with others, to have these interactions reflect positively upon ourselves. "All the time," she writes, "I am dressing up the figure of myself in my own mind." She notes how carefully she does this, how subtly, protecting her image of

[8]*The Diary of Virginia Woolf*, Vol. 2, ed. Anne Olivier Bell (San Diego: Harcourt Brace and Company, 1978), pp. 13–14. Quentin Bell in his biography quotes from the same passage I quote from and remarks that in it Virginia had envisioned "the whole programme" she would pursue in her fiction "for a decade" to follow; see Quentin Bell, *Virginia Woolf* (New York: Harcourt Brace and Company, 1972) 2, pp. 72–73. Maria Ippolito and Ryan Tweney describe Virginia Woolf's path of development over the period of time I describe, somewhat differently, in "The journey to *Jacob's Room*: The network of enterprise of Virginia Woolf's first experimental novel," cited in Chapter 1.

herself at all costs; and she contemplates how horrible it would be if the image were to dissolve or break apart — "Suppose the looking-glass smashes, the image disappears, and the romantic figure with the green of forest depths all about it is there no longer, but only that shell of a person which is seen by other people — what an airless, shallow, bald, prominent world it becomes! A world not to be lived in." She continues as follows, in the central passage of the story (the italics are mine). "*As we face each other in omnibuses and underground railways we are looking into the mirror; that accounts for the vagueness, the gleam of glassiness, in our eyes. And the novelists in future will realise more and more the importance of these reflections, for of course there is not one reflection but an almost infinite number; those are the depths they will explore, those the phantoms they will pursue, leaving the description of reality more and more out of their stories, taking a knowledge of it for granted, as the Greeks did and Shakespeare perhaps,*" then abruptly concludes "*— but these generalisations are very worthless.*"

Thinking of generalizations brings her back to the world of objective facts, and she recounts a series of facts, with the aim of showing that they can be interpreted in different ways, that there is no true objective knowledge, "nothing is proved, nothing is known." Thus she returns to imagining a world free of sterile objectivity, envisioning a beautiful, peaceful world, lit up by reflections. "Yes, one could imagine a very pleasant world. A quiet spacious world, with the flowers so red and blue in the open fields. A world without professors or specialists or house-keepers with the profiles of policemen, a world which one could slice with one's thoughts as a fish slices the water with his fin, grazing the stems of the water-lilies, hanging suspended over nests of white sea eggs. . . . [ellipses in original text] How peaceful it is down here, rooted in the centre of the world and gazing up through the grey waters, with their sudden gleams of light, and their reflections —. . . ."[9]

It seems clear that Virginia's description, in the passage I set in italics, of what novelists in the future will focus on, though cloaked impersonally, is in reality a statement describing what she herself is interested in exploring in her novels in the future. This statement, together with her beautiful vision, depicts her conception of her literary interest. She is interested in exploring our reflections, specifically the link between self and reflections; in exploring how we see ourselves reflected in the world around us and in the eyes of others — in their expressions, thoughts, and feelings; how we use our reflections to compose,

[9]"The Mark on the Wall," in *The Complete Shorter Fiction of Virginia Woolf*, ed. Susan Dick (San Diego: Harcourt Brace and Company, 1985), pp. 83–89.

bolster, and maintain our self-image, creating the depth of self that makes life worth living; and how we search out our reflections and orchestrate our interactions in such a way that indirectly they shower glory and sympathy upon us. She recognizes that there are many reflections, "an almost infinite number" — indeed this is part of what makes her conception seem so rich with potential. She develops her conception further in her lyrical, imaginative vision, in which she imagines writing from the depths of the self — "rooted in the center of the world," "away from the surface, with its hard separate facts," "gazing up through the grey waters, with their sudden gleams of light, and their reflections" — showing how our inner worlds are illuminated by reflections.

At the end of the passage in "The Mark on the Wall" in which she describes her conception of what novelists will focus on in the future, Virginia writes that "these generalisations" she has made about the aims of literature are "very worthless." Why is she critical? Not because she does not believe in her conception, but rather because for her it is not an end in and of itself — it is abstract speculation, nothing more, and to be made truly meaningful it must be realized artistically, expressed through literature. Her criticism reflects her frustration, for at the time she did not know how to take this step, how to develop her conception of interest creatively.

She began to explore how to develop her conception in "Kew Gardens," the story she wrote next after "The Mark on the Wall." And she hit upon an approach that worked — and recognized immediately that she had done so — in writing "An Unwritten Novel," written in the weeks immediately preceding her diary entry of January 26, 1920. I discuss the series of short stories she wrote, beginning with "Kew Gardens" and culminating in her creative break in "An Unwritten Novel," in Chapter 12.

In "An Unwritten Novel" the narrator describes retrospectively her observations and train of thought traveling in a train car.[10] In the first sentence she tells us that her gaze was drawn to a woman sitting opposite who had a look of misery on her face. A brief digression follows, in which she discusses our knowledge of "life" — how we see this knowledge inscribed on others' faces, though they try to conceal it. Then she informs us that the other travelers soon left the train, leaving her and the woman alone together; she tells us they had a brief, halting exchange, from which she surmised, or believed she surmised, certain facts about the woman's life; then the woman lapsed into silence, making a movement as if there was a spot between her shoulders that "burnt or itched," like a spot of guilt from some crime, then rubbing at a spot on her

[10] Ibid., pp. 112–21.

windowpane, as if she would rub out the guilt. The narrator tells us that she too was impelled to rub, on her window, implying that some communication had taken place between the two; and then she begins to spin a tale, inventing a name for the woman — Minnie Marsh, inventing a life for her, giving her life a definite shape, imagining sundry details.

It is at this point that Virginia Woolf embarks upon a new style. The narrative begins to flow, moving freely, lightly, from one image to the next, one scene to the next, one fragment of life to the next, considering different possible scenarios, inventing a crime for Minnie, imagining her sitting in her room thinking, praying to her god, walking on the street, and sitting at dinner, imagining her thoughts and feelings, inventing a sister-in-law named Hilda, noticing a second passenger who has entered the car and incorporating him into the story as James Moggridge, a friend of the family's, and imagining what Hilda and Moggridge think about Minnie. At places the narrator steps back, taking a more distanced perspective, commenting tongue-in-cheek upon Minnie and her life, and upon life in general, pausing self-consciously to reflect upon the freedom she is taking in inventing a fictitious life for Minnie, while at the same time stopping to consider her options, thereby reminding us that she is inventing the story on the fly. Throughout, the tone is light and playful. The narrative style is mirrored by the train ride itself — incessantly moving, stopping occasionally, passengers coming on and getting off at various times and stops. In fact it seems possible that Virginia imagined the train ride first, a setting she was obviously familiar with, and that the setting in turn helped spark her development of the new style.[11]

Minnie and her life are thus depicted through a series of vignettes, each of which offers us a glimpse of Minnie as she is seen by another character or the narrator — a reflection of her. For example, Hilda's impression of Minnie as Minnie is drawing up to Hilda's home in a cab is described: "'Poor Minnie, more of a grasshopper than ever — old cloak she had last year. Well, well, with two children these days one can't do more.'" Just after, after Minnie has been taken upstairs and left alone in her room, a second description of her is provided, this time from Minnie's own perspective: "Now, Minnie, the door's shut; Hilda heavily descends to the basement; you unstrap the straps of your basket, lay on the bed a meagre nightgown, stand side by side furred felt slippers.... And then the sniff, the sigh, the sitting by the window. Three o'clock

[11]The shift to the supple, freely running narrative is made to seem natural in part because of the context of the train ride. Because we know that the narrator was sitting in a train we are comfortable with the notion that she spent her time concocting a loose-knit story, imagining a life for the stranger sitting opposite her, in an offhand manner.

on a December afternoon; the rain drizzling. . . ." Her mood is reflected in her sniff and sigh, the drizzling rain outside, and late winter afternoon — thus mirrored in the world around her, as it is presented to us. Later, the narrator describes a scene in which James Moggridge is sitting at a table at mealtime with Minnie and others. After describing Moggridge, the narrator's gaze comes to rest on his eyes: "they see something: black, white, dismal." Moggridge thinks, "'Marsh's sister'" — identifying Minnie indirectly, as Hilda's sister — and then remarks to himself, "'wretched, elderly female. . . . [ellipses in original] You should feed your hens. . . . [ellipses in original] God's truth, what's set her twitching? Not what *I* said? Dear, dear, dear! these elderly women. Dear, dear!'" Thus we are shown Minnie through another character's perception of her.

Virginia Woolf later wrote to a friend that in writing "An Unwritten Novel" she had discovered "how I could embody all my deposit of experience in a shape that fitted it."[12] She had discovered a style of writing perfectly suited to her conception of reflections, and it was this remarkable discovery that made her excited, this harmonizing of form and substance that she had in mind when she wrote in her diary that she conceived of the three stories "taking hands & dancing in unity."[13] In the new style she envisions "one thing" will "open out of another" — the reader will be carried along on a swift flowing stream, a stream that in its speed and fluidity will convey a "looseness & lightness" of tone, "a gaiety — an inconsequence," a "light spirited stepping" — and as he is carried along he will glimpse a series of reflections of the characters and their lives, the reflections piling up one after another in his mind, eventually forming a composite whole enclosing "everything, everything." Almost immediately after making this discovery Virginia entered her great creative period, developing the new style and her conception of reflections brilliantly, first in *Jacob's Room* (1922), which she began in April 1920, then in *Mrs. Dalloway* (1925), her masterpiece *To the Lighthouse* (1927), and *The Waves* (1931). I describe the profound resonance of her original conception in "The Mark on the Wall" in *To the Lighthouse* in Chapter 8.

[12]*The Letters of Virginia Woolf*, Vol. 4, ed. Nigel Nicolson and Joanne Trautmann (New York: Harcourt Brace Jovanovich, 1978), p. 231.
[13]Indeed her excitement is reflected at the end of "An Unwritten Novel," when the woman she calls Minnie gets off the train, apparently met by her son, for the narrator is reluctant to let them go, wants to continue spinning her yarn: "And yet the last look of them — he stepping from the kerb and she following him round the edge of the big building brims me with wonder — floods me anew. Mysterious figures! Mother and son. Who are you? Why do you walk down the street? Where tonight will you sleep, and then, tomorrow? Oh, how it whirls and surges — floats me afresh!"

In forming our creative interests, and in particular conceptions of our interests, we, in an imaginative sense, look out at the world around us in all its richness and identify and form conceptions of what we find most interesting and would most like to pursue, explore, and try to develop creatively. The image of Virginia Woolf sitting by the fire daydreaming, forming a conception of her interest, beautifully captures, metaphorically, this process, at least in one form — daydreaming, reflecting, thinking, synthesizing, imagining, doing so freely, without worrying or concerning ourselves overly much with all the constraints and obstacles that might prevent us from pursuing our interest successfully.

The nature of creative development has undoubtedly changed over the centuries, due to cultural evolution, the development of new technologies, and changes in the social order and economic and political systems. For example, the rise of the printing press made it possible to distribute work much more widely and more quickly, and there is evidence that this affected the way in which people in many fields of intellectual endeavor went about their creative work.[14] However, it is my belief — admittedly needing to be substantiated — that throughout human history people living in cultures with developed languages and organized fields of activity who have chosen to pursue creative endeavors have naturally tended to form creative interests and conceptions of their creative interests, around which they have organized their creative development.

Consider as an interesting example Galileo. The available evidence suggests that at the time he became a professor, in his mid-twenties, he had formed as an interest this: *to apply to the study of motion the mathematical approach that Archimedes had developed to study problems of statics.* To paraphrase Alexander Koyré, Galileo set himself the task to "set in motion" the bodies Archimedes had analyzed statically.[15] In forming this interest Galileo was influenced by the texts of Euclid and Archimedes, which were in vogue at the time he was a student, and defined his interest possibly (this is a matter of considerable scholarly debate, and Galileo's views on the scientific schools of thought of the time are not definitely known) in opposition to the medieval tradition, represented by certain branches of Aristotelian medieval thought, perceiving a contrast between these approaches and the mathematical and geometrical

[14]See Elizabeth L. Eisenstein, *The Printing Press As an Agent of Change: Communications and Cultural Transformations in Early Modern Europe* (Cambridge: Cambridge University Press, 1979).

[15]Alexander Koyré, *Galileo Studies*, trans. John Mepham (Atlantic Highlands, NJ: Humanities Press, 1978 (originally published 1939)), p. 38.

approaches of Archimedes and Euclid.[16] In his first published work, 53
La Bilancetta (1586), Galileo demonstrated certain mathematical relationships concerning weights and their distances from the center of a balance,
work solidly in the Archimedean tradition. Slightly later he derived laws of
proportionality describing the degree of immersion of solids of different densities in water and other media, an analysis that he connected methodologically
with an analysis of the relative speeds of fall of bodies of different densities.
At some point it occurred to him to apply these same Archimedean principles
of proportionality to try to derive relationships concerning the relative speeds
with which objects descend along planes inclined at different angles from the
vertical. He presented his early work on motion in *Dialogue on Motion* and
in more complete form in *De Motu*, believed most likely to have been written
around 1589–90 (perhaps begun earlier). He returned to the study of objects
falling along inclined planes around ten years later, his investigations leading
to his discovery of the law of free fall.[17]

[16]The traditional view is that Galileo was vehemently opposed to Aristotle and the
medieval scholastic tradition, and was an empiricist in his methodological approach.
This view is set forth by Stillman Drake; see his account of Galileo's scientific career,
Galileo at Work (Chicago: University of Chicago Press, 1978). Koyré presents Galileo
as more of a "Platonist" and less empirically based; he links Galileo with Descartes,
stressing that they both participated in the revolution in scientific thought of the late sixteenth and early seventeenth centuries that had as its aim the "geometrization of space."
See *Galileo Studies*, Introduction and p. 36. William Wallace argues for more continuity linking Galileo with the Aristotelian tradition; see his Introduction in William
Wallace, *Galileo's Logical Treatises* (Dordrecht: Kluwer Academic Publishers, 1992),
pp. 3–83. He describes Galileo's interest, which he labels his "project," in contrast
with that of Buonamici, one of his teachers, as being (p. 64) "to concentrate on . . .
one motion, essentially that of heavy bodies, and to make a detailed study of that using
mathematical techniques to reveal its true nature." Notwithstanding these differences of
opinion among Galileo scholars, with regard to the specific point with which I am most
concerned — Galileo's conceptualization of what he was interested in studying —
there is reasonable agreement, though some difference as to the relative importance
of different approaches or schools of thought for his conception of what he wished to
pursue.
[17]For Galileo's development see *Galileo at Work*, Chapters 1–5, and *Galileo's Logical
Treatises*, Introduction. Galileo's discussion of speeds along inclined planes is in Chapter 14 of *De Motu* (English translation in *Galileo Galilei, On Motion and On Mechanics*,
trans. I.E. Drabkin (Madison: University of Wisconsin Press, 1960)): "Containing a discussion of the ratios of [the speeds of] the motions of the same body moving over various
inclined planes." He writes in the first sentence of the chapter (p. 63): "The problem we
are now going to discuss has not been taken up by any philosophers, so far as I know."
The phrase is noteworthy; he does not express similar thoughts elsewhere.

54   A FURTHER CHARACTERIZATION: INTERESTS, IDEAS, AND PROJECTS;
THE ROLE OF CREATIVE INTERESTS AND CONCEPTIONS OF
INTERESTS IN CREATIVE DEVELOPMENT

There are a wide variety of different kinds of creative interests and conceptions of creative interests. Some interests are rich conceptions, like Virginia Woolf's profound conception of the reflections of ourselves we see in the world and in the eyes of others that define our sense of ourselves. Others are more simply defined topics or domains, like Azad Bonni's interest in mechanisms of action. Still others are organized around principles or approaches we wish to explore and are guided by in our development. Beyond these, there are several other kinds that are also common, including in the relationship between topics, and in attaining a relatively broadly defined objective or goal or investigating a relatively broadly defined question or set of questions. I describe kinds of interests in Chapter 6.

What links all of these different forms together — what defines creative interests, in light of this diversity? A creative interest is defined essentially by its meaning for the individual for whom it is an interest; it is a topic or subject that he desires to explore and learn more about and would like and usually intends or hopes to try to develop creatively, as defined at the beginning of this chapter. In addition, creative interests and conceptions of creative interests have certain basic characteristics, notably breadth and distinctiveness, discussed in more detail in Chapter 7, and serve certain vital functions in creative development, outlined briefly in Chapter 1 and very briefly below and described and discussed in detail in Chapters 9, 10, and 11.[18] In general, it is best to acknowledge and bear in mind that there are many different kinds of creative interests. It is not my intention to impose limits on their specific form or content, but rather to emphasize that they share certain fundamental features in common, and their commonality in terms of the way they structure creative development — their role in development. It is useful also to note that in general creative interests are not the same as interpretations or unifying themes that we identify in a series of contributions that an individual makes over time, for example in a series of books or films or inventions. These are imposed after the fact and very often by critics and not by the individual himself, and in general they do not represent accurately the nature of the process through which the individual

[18]"Creative interest" and "conception of creative interest" are theoretical constructs, and like any such constructs the range of empirical phenomena that they refer to is defined only approximately and is somewhat diverse. Ultimately, they must be evaluated in terms of their usefulness in describing creative development and helping us understand the process of development.

came to create his body of work; the logic of development is often very different
from the logic of creative products.

In describing creative development it is important to distinguish creative
interests from creative projects and ideas. In general, the distinction between
creative interests and creative projects is that interests involve a greater conceptual breadth and sense of openness than projects. We conceive of our interests
as relatively open-ended — we imagine they hold great possibilities, and we
hope to develop them creatively, but we do not have a clear sense for how or
in what ways we may ultimately do so. Thus, to the extent we define our interests in terms of objectives, these are broad, abstract, not technical, sometimes
visionary, and subject to considerable refinement later; and we recognize that
there may be many different ways in which they can be realized, which generally we cannot even imagine; our intention is to follow out whatever avenues of
inquiry turn out to be interesting. In contrast, we have more definite aims for
our projects. At the time we begin them we envision their end products — in
outline if not in detail — and we have in mind a fairly specific set of activities
we will engage in to produce these products, though we recognize that unexpected events, new information, and new ideas may lead us to change course
midstream. We design our projects to address specific questions or achieve
specific objectives, whereas our creative interests are organized around broad
questions, and often groupings of questions, that can be asked and answered
in many different ways.

Whereas we conceive of our interests as broad and open-ended, our ideas
are sharply defined, complete in themselves — we envision them as discrete
elements that stand out separate from everything else. Our interests are somewhat amorphous domains, filled with mystery, whereas our ideas are clear:
when we have an important idea, we usually recognize rather quickly that it
might be a creative contribution or the basis for a contribution. But note that
when we become interested in exploring an idea and developing it creatively
its category shifts — it now possesses the characteristics of a creative interest,
and we think of it as open-ended and filled with creative possibilities. Teresa
Nick, a neurobiologist I interviewed, is an example of someone interested in
exploring an idea, one that is sweeping in its scope. Discussing her early interest in neuroscience, she said, "I was really into the idea that you can take
behavior to the level of a cell, or even beyond that to the level of a molecule;
and if you alter this molecule then you can alter behavior. Just the idea of
spanning that many levels — the molecules, then the cell, then the tissue,
then the organism, then the behavior, the interaction of that organism with
its environment; being able to control everything from the level of a single

56 molecule." "I like integrating across levels, and trying to see how one level [can affect the others], like how from the [level of the] cell you can affect an animal or how that animal interacts with its environment."

Forming a creative interest and a conception of our interest gives us a domain to explore and a conceptual platform from which and through which to explore it; our creative interests and conceptions of our interests are like way stations or stepping stones, leading us on, enabling us to discover and develop promising ideas and projects. Thus, our projects develop out of our interests. In fact, normally an individual develops an interest in a series of projects over time. Azad's interest in the mechanisms of action or pathways through which molecular agents like NGF influence cells was the basis for his development of a project — his initial dissertation project — studying the regulation of gene transcription by NGF, as well as other projects. Likewise, Alexander Calder developed his interest in the universe as a basis for art in many works. Sometimes we move quickly from interest to project, so that the phase of pursuing our interest is fleeting. In these cases it can be easy to forget we even had such an interest, easy to forget about the period before the project. In other cases we spend years exploring an interest before settling on a project.

There are in fact many different kinds of patterns of development, and many different forms of interrelationship among interests, projects, and ideas; thus, for example, not only do individuals develop interests as projects and ideas, but ideas and discoveries can stimulate new interests and projects. In general, interests, projects, and ideas form complex chains of development; I discuss and give examples of a variety of these chains in Chapters 14 and 15.

Our conceptions of our creative interests are central in the dynamics of our creative development, crucial in enabling us to develop our creative interests successfully. Through envisioning our creative interests and being able to think about them consciously we are able to see and decide how best to go about exploring them and trying to develop them creatively — what to attend to, in which directions to set forth, which projects to pursue. Thus, our conceptions are crucial in helping us navigate the course of our development, in guiding us and helping us envision paths forward. One function they serve, which illustrates their general role, is defining the boundaries of our creative interests — what lies within the scope of our interests and what does not, which is important in deciding what to learn about and which projects to pursue. Many of the neuroscientists I interviewed spoke of choosing which labs to work in and which projects to pursue by thinking about which of these fit best with their conceptions of what they were interested in; an example is Azad, who, once he conceptualized his interest in mechanisms of action, went about learning about it and developing projects that fit with it quite systematically.

Our conceptions are both at the centers of our conceptual worlds and central in our thinking processes. Our conceptions form the centers of and link together hosts of ideas, images, concepts, models, facts, phenomena, cultural works, events, questions, hypotheses, and experiences, forming rich complexes — conceptual webs of associations — in our minds.[19] In turn, our thoughts are carried along these rich webs of associations, leading to — or at least having the potential to lead to — creative insights and ideas, for example, making connections among elements that appear disparate. We organize our knowledge and experiences in terms of our conceptions and interests; they define basic conceptual structures in our minds that define the way we think about our fields and our endeavors, and which can be unusual relative to what is standard in our fields, thus generative of creative insights. A main way our conceptions and the rich webs of associations centering around them lead us to ideas and insights is by guiding and channeling our responses to elements and experiences we encounter, thereby generating creative, original responses. I discuss such creative responses in Chapter 9, and present several examples of cases in which they were crucial in the generation of ideas, including Alexander Calder's invention of the mobile as a modern art form.

Of course our conceptions of our interests are just part of our very rich, complex thought processes during creative development. During the course of our development we think about our creative endeavors incessantly, and many different thoughts concerning them run through our minds, many of which are not related in any obvious way to our conceptions of interests. Nevertheless, without diminishing the importance of these other processes, many of which are undoubtedly quite important for our development, our conceptions of our interests stand out as especially crucial. Forming conceptions of what we are interested in seems to open up vistas for us, enabling us to see ahead and move forward. The story of Virginia Woolf's creative development is a brilliant example of this. Beginning in her twenties, if not before, she spent untold hours engaging in writing and thinking about her writing — dreaming up stories and characters, writing essays about other writers' work, undoubtedly thinking about her own work and ideas in relationship to theirs and thinking broadly about different theories and styles of writing. But she was not able to find her way forward until she formed a conception of what she was interested in and wrote

[19] Indeed forming conceptions of our interests is akin to a process of crystallization, at least at times; ideas, concepts, and facts that were previously disconnected, unconscious, even seemingly chaotic in our minds, become organized at a higher conceptual level and made conscious, as already mentioned. This process of crystallization is one facet of the development of interests and conceptions of interests, which I discuss in the next chapter.

it down in "The Mark on the Wall." It seems that she first had to envision what she wished to do on an abstract conceptual level, before she could push ahead, searching until she found a style of writing that matched her conception.[20]

CREATIVE INTERESTS IN ACCOUNTS OF CREATIVE DEVELOPMENT

People engaged in creative endeavors discuss their interests often, in many contexts; they use the word "interest" frequently in describing their own creative processes. In an interview the playwright Tom Stoppard said he develops intense interests, and that he normally develops an idea for a play out of a confluence of his interests — when several of his interests "plait together."[21] Michel Foucault discussed his childhood and intellectual work in an interview he conducted late in his life. He described living through the rise of the Nazis and the political instability overhanging Europe in the 1930s, and the impact this had on his own development and interests: "The menace of war was our background, our framework of existence. . . . Our private life was really threatened. Maybe that is the reason why I am fascinated by history and the relationship between personal experience and those events of which we are a part."[22] Individuals who have engaged in creative endeavors generally describe their creative interests in their autobiographies, oftentimes portraying them as central to their creative development. For example, in his *Autobiography* Charles Darwin discusses his childhood interest in collecting natural forms; I quote from his description in the next chapter, and describe his development of his more mature interest growing out of this early interest. They also discuss their interests in their journals, diaries, and letters. This is true of Virginia Woolf, Leo Tolstoy, and not only writers but people in many fields, such as Benjamin Franklin, who, shortly after beginning his experiments in electricity, wrote to the individual who had given him the apparatus he was using, "I never was before engaged in any study that so totally engrossed my attention and my time."[23] Individuals interviewed about their creative development — by me or, as the Tom Stoppard example shows, by others — tend naturally to describe their development in terms of their interests and their attempts to develop their interests creatively. The great awareness and concern with creative

[20] Her conception is clearly linked to earlier interests and fragmentary conceptions she had, and therefore seems very much to have been a kind of cystallization; see the next chapter.

[21] Interview with Charlie Rose on PBS, shown in Connecticut on July 15, 2000.

[22] Michel Foucault, *Politics, Philosophy, Culture*, trans. Alan Sheridan and others, ed. Lawrence D. Kritzman (New York: Routledge, 1988), p. 7.

[23] See I. Bernard Cohen, *Benjamin Franklin's Science* (Cambridge, MA: Harvard University Press, 1990), p. 35.

interests shown in all of these cases supports the view that we think about our creative development in terms of our creative interests.

Biographies of people famous for their creative contributions often contain descriptions of their creative interests. Indeed many biographers are interested in connecting a person's interests with his later creative success — tracing, carefully or more loosely, the creative development of his interests, identifying threads of continuity and ways in which earlier statements and interests foreshadow later work and contributions. In Matthew Josephson's biography of Thomas Edison we learn that "The study of sound fascinated Edison — all the more in that he was partially deaf." Josephson links Edison's interest in sound to his early interest in telegraphy, and his later invention of the telephone.[24] He describes several important lifelong interests Edison had, including electricity — he recounts Edison's comment later in life that in his early twenties the "mysteries of electrical force" attracted his great interest, writing that at this time, "all the future potentialities of electricity obsessed him night and day."[25] Many biographers, historians, and critics explicitly use the word "interest." To give two of many examples that could be given, in *Benjamin Franklin's Science* Bernard Cohen writes of "Franklin's interest in the subject of electricity," and in *Matisse on Art* Jack Flam writes that "Matisse had a profound and abiding interest in decoration and decorative art."[26] But the word is used loosely, the meaning that is attached to it is in general somewhat broader and less precise than what I mean by "creative interest" in this book, and in fact somewhat variable; I have as a main purpose to present a more consistent terminology that is theoretically based, more carefully delimited, more coherent and richer.[27] Further, a description of an interest in a biography is often a reconstruction made by the biographer and cannot be attributed definitely to the individual whose creative development is being described, so we cannot be certain

[24]Matthew Josephson, *Edison* (New York: McGraw-Hill, 1959), Chapters 2 and 9. The quote is on p. 159.

[25]*Edison*, p. 54. See also Paul Israel, *Edison; A Life of Invention* (New York: John Wiley & Sons, 1998), who also describes Edison's interests in electricity (for example, p. 308).

[26]*Benjamin Franklin's Science*, p. 35. Henri Matisse, *Matisse on Art*, ed. Jack D. Flam (New York: Phaidon Press, 1990), p. 20.

[27]It is for example somewhat ironic that Cohen's phrase "interest in the subject of electricity" is actually broader and less precise than Franklin's own reference to his interest in the letter I have quoted in the preceding paragraph. Franklin's statement can be read as an interest specifically in electrical experiments, and, linked to this and possibly growing from it, an interest in theoretical explanations of electrical phenomena observed or reproduced in experiments.

whether it was a significant factor in his creative development.[28] Nonetheless, there is no doubt that in the biographical literature interests are depicted as integral to the process of creative development.

Remarkably, despite how prominently creative interests figure in biographical and autobiographical accounts of creative development, and in individuals' discussions of their own development, they are almost entirely absent in theoretical discussions of the creative process, strangely invisible, like forces that without being seen move objects and cause them to be arranged in definite patterns. Creativity is described in terms of chance events, mental operations, illuminations, and surprising discoveries — not in terms of creative interests and their creative development. Surprisingly, even in frameworks in which creativity is described more as a process of development, like the evolving systems approach, interests are not defined, and as a result the process of development is depicted in a manner that makes it seem less structured than it really is. Of course creative interests are sometimes mentioned in analyses of the creative process, but only in passing, and the connection between interests and later creative contributions seems never to be investigated or traced in any detail.

Creative interests and conceptions of creative interests in fact fill a crucial gap in the conventional view of the conceptual universe of individuals who are engaged in creative endeavors. In conventional theories of creativity the conceptual universe contains a large collection of discrete elements, notably ideas, but also facts, hypotheses, problems, images, events, rules, and schemas, as well as representations of creative contributions that have been made by other people, such as articles, experiments, paintings, and designs.[29] It also contains a few very broad concepts, such as paradigms and values, most of

[28]This caveat applies with even greater force to interpretations and analyses of creative works, for example, the elucidation of a theme. Fascinating though these themes may be, they are rarely discussed in the context of the creative development of the artist or writer concerned, and in most cases there is simply no way of knowing if the artist or writer himself conceptualized the theme, and whether it influenced his creative development.

[29]Specific knowledge elements are central in many if not most accounts of creativity, including the model of creativity as based in chance combinations of elements in the mind associated with Donald Campbell, as well as Henri Poincaré; see Chapter 1, footnote 26. Similar conceptions of creativity based in combinations among specific elements are the core of recent descriptions of the creative process from the perspective of cognitive psychology, for example, Ronald A. Finke, Thomas B. Ward, and Steven M. Smith, *Creative Cognition: Theory, Research, and Applications* (Cambridge, MA: MIT Press, 1992), and Thomas B. Ward, Steven M. Smith, and Jyotsna Vaid, eds., *Creative Thought*; see especially Edward J. Wisniewski, "Conceptual combinations: Possibilities and esthetics," pp. 51–81, and James A. Hampton, "Emergent attributes in combined concepts," pp. 83–110.

which are shared in common among many people.[30] But it contains no conceptual structures intermediate between these two extremes, at least none that
is truly general and of first importance for the process of creative development.
(Although correct in a broad sense, this statement is too sweeping; a few important intermediate level structures have been described, such as Howard
Gruber's notion of an "image of wide scope."[31]) Creative interests and conceptions of creative interests are such intermediate level structures. They fit
between the two extremes, occupying the centers of our conceptual worlds.

Descriptions of creative development that do not contain creative interests and conceptions of creative interests seem barren, almost entirely devoid
of conceptual structure. Conversely, through including creative interests and
conceptions of creative interests in our descriptions we are able to depict our
true, rich conceptual worlds, and to see more clearly and fully into them.
We gain a deeper understanding of our creative development, and are able to
describe its basic structure and dynamics more accurately, more clearly and
coherently, and more completely.

[30]The concept of a paradigm is developed by Thomas S. Kuhn in his famous work,
The Structure of Scientific Revolutions (Chicago: University of Chicago Press, 1962).
Related ideas are presented by Norwood Russell Hanson in *Patterns of Discovery: An
Inquiry into the Conceptual Foundations of Science* (Cambridge: University Press, 1958).
Gerald Holton has introduced the concept of themata, which he defines as "fundamental preconceptions of a stable and widely diffused kind," thus broad in application. He
gives as examples the concept of the ether and the belief in the existence of elementary
particles of nature. See Gerald Holton, *Thematic Origins of Scientific Thought: Kepler
to Einstein* (Cambridge, MA: Harvard University Press, 1988), Introduction, pp. 10–24;
the quote is on p. 13.
[31]Howard Gruber defines an "image of wide scope" to be an image that an individual
forms and uses to organize "a wide range of perceptions, actions, ideas." See Howard
Gruber, "Darwin's Tree of Nature and other images of wide scope," in *On Aesthetics in
Science*, ed. Judith Wechsler (Cambridge, MA: MIT Press, 1978), pp. 121–40. Building
on Gruber's work, Jeffrey Osowski has introduced the idea of "ensembles of metaphors";
see "Ensembles of metaphor in the psychology of William James" in *Creative People
at Work*, ed. Doris B. Wallace and Howard E. Gruber, pp. 126–45. In general images
of wide scope and ensembles of metaphors seem to form somewhat later in the course
of development than creative interests, and seem to be more like ideas than interests.
In a recent article, "The role of specificity and abstraction in creative idea generation,"
Creativity Research Journal 16 (2004):1–9, Thomas Ward, Merryl Patterson, and Cynthia
Sifonis describe experiments in which students are asked to generate creative ideas on
a given topic, and show that giving students more abstract statements to guide their
thinking led, in their words, to "more novel creations." Their work seems to suggest the
value of intermediate level guiding principles in creative work; I discuss such principles,
connected with creative interests, in Chapter 11.

The Development of Creative Interests

The processes through which individuals' creative interests and their conceptions of their creative interests develop and are developed by them are both
rich and fascinating. In this chapter I describe these processes of development. In part A I describe kinds of experiences individuals have and elements
they encounter and learn about, including both in their fields and broader
culture, that are important in sparking their creative interests. In part B I
describe patterns of development of creative interests and conceptions of interests, especially paths through which early forms of creative interests and
initial conceptions of interests develop and are developed by individuals into
richer, more mature interests and conceptions. An entire book could be written
about the development of creative interests, for the topic is a large one. My
description is necessarily much briefer than this: I present a basic description
of the development of interests in this chapter, describe sources of interests in
the following two chapters, and discuss evolution of interests and sequences of
interests in Chapter 15.

A. EXPERIENCES, ELEMENTS, AND ENCOUNTERS — THE
SPARKING OF CREATIVE INTERESTS

Our creative interests originate and grow out of our responses to experiences
we have and elements we encounter. These experiences and elements and
our initial responses to them are the seeds, the raw materials out of which we
fashion our interests and our conceptions of our interests.

In the course of our lives we have many experiences and encounter a great
multitude and variety of different elements. We participate in many different

social and cultural activities, engage in a variety of endeavors, have many personal experiences and social interactions, witness many events, encounter an incredible number and variety of phenomena, and are exposed to a great variety of different stimuli; we learn many facts and are exposed to many ideas and concepts, especially in our fields, learn about different theories, methods, approaches, and traditions, and are exposed to and learn about the creative works and contributions of many other people, in both our fields and other fields.

Out of all these experiences and elements, a small number of experiences or elements or groupings of interconnected experiences and elements — or, in the case of complex experiences and elements, a particular aspect or a few component elements — grab our attention and stand out among all the rest, spark our interest, and kindle a response in us. Our responses and interest do not always develop further — sometimes our interest, having been sparked for a moment, fades away and goes no further. But in other cases our interest is held, and develops further — we continue to think about and focus on these experiences and elements, they continue to interest us, and we form conceptions defining or trying to define what interests us about them.

In these initial stages of development in particular, during which our interest is first sparked and we form the first roughhewn conceptions of what we are interested in, the process of formation of our interests is a spontaneous one. We fasten upon and respond to the experiences and elements that become the bases for our interests intuitively, even instinctively. Our responses are not plotted out or rationally planned, at least not to any great degree; rather, we fix our attention on these experiences and elements spontaneously, often in the spur of the moment, in a burst of interest and excitement — and finding them interesting we become absorbed in thinking about them and begin to form interests in and based upon them, often only realizing later, over time, the true depth and extent of our interest. Further, in responding to them and forming incipient interests we act freely, without coercion — at least in ideal conditions; we may be influenced by suggestions or actions of others, but ultimately, our interest flows from our selves, our own senses and responses.

The creative development of Susan Ferguson, a literary scholar I inter-viewed, specifically her formation of an interest that has been the basis of her work in literary analysis, illustrates the way our creative interests are sparked by and grow out of our experiences — or, more correctly, are formed by us out of and in response to our experiences.

Susan lived in Kenya for two years after college, teaching English as a member of the Peace Corps. From the time she arrived in Kenya she found the rich linguistic environment and conversational practices — the variety of spoken languages and intermingling of languages, and the complex patterns of language usage — fascinating. Her experiences engaging in conversations and observing language practices, both in Nairobi and in the rural area where she was stationed, sparked her interest, and, over time, she formed an interest in the way different languages are used in conversation, including the choices speakers make about which language to speak, the social norms governing these choices, and language hybridization.

Kenya is a country of enormous linguistic variety: there are two national languages, English and Swahili, and each ethnic group has its own language — 42 in all, Susan told me. The diversity gives speakers who know more than one language the choice of which language to speak, and Susan found these choices and the flexibility they give speakers fascinating, opening up a dimension of communication and social meaning she had never really been aware of before. "In Kenya I became conscious of that [different languages enabling language choices]," she told me, "[the fact that there were] these different languages, and who spoke which language to whom, and in what circumstances. And I myself was learning to switch among different languages and to use that kind of flexibility — which is not something I had ever done." Susan was interested not only in the patterns of language usage, but also the social norms governing language usage and the ways these norms reflect social status and ethnic identities, thus carry social significance. Speaking of her own situation she said: "There were so many different kinds of people that I would speak to, and in so many different kinds of situations [where I had to decide which was the right language to use]; people that I would speak to in English even though their English wasn't as good and we might have been able to communicate better in something else, but that was really the appropriate language." She was also interested in the phenomenon of language switching, in particular what she called "code switching" — speakers switching languages at a crucial juncture in a conversation to make a point, often one inflected with social significance, in a subtle way that is accessible to insiders but concealed from outsiders. "There was a lot of code switching," she told me, "a lot of people knew at least some words in other languages, so there was a lot of switching around into different languages." It is noteworthy that in describing her interest in norms and patterns of usage Susan did not give me the sense that she felt that she understood the norms and patterns of usage very well at the time — rather that she noticed them and focused on them as interesting elements in her environment.

Susan was very conscious of and interested in the role of English in Kenya. "I became very conscious of English and of the role that English plays in parts of the world where it's not the dominant language, as it is here in the United States, but it's a major language," she told me. "In Kenya they use English very differently than either the British [upon whose language theirs is patterned] or Americans — and that was always very interesting to me." "It's bizarre," she said, "that English has this very important official role in Kenya, and yet is not spoken by a lot of people" — in particular, is spoken by Government officials and on the radio and taught in school, but is not spoken very much in informal settings and is not understood well by most people, especially the older generation; "there are just a lot of strange and interesting nuances to that," she said. She was also fascinated by the borrowing and intermingling of words from different languages — Portuguese, Arabic, and English — into the African base languages, forming hybrid forms. Indeed she went into considerable detail about this during our interview, giving a series of examples, her enthusiasm and interest, even at that time several years later, shining through. "Swahili," she told me, "uses a Bantu grammar and a lot of Bantu vocabulary; but it also has a lot of Portuguese and Arabic words as well, and then English words layered on top of that." "So for instance the word for table is 'meza,' and the word for sugar is 'sukari,' and then in Kipsigis the word for sugar is 'sugarug.' And the word for week is 'wiki,' and weekend is 'wikendi'. . . but the days of the week are Arabic, and so on." She said there are "endless details" like this that she found fascinating.

In summary, Susan's interest was sparked by her experiences and phenomena she encountered in Kenya — a subset from among the vast throng of novel experiences she must have had and novel phenomena she must have encountered. Susan herself is well aware that her experiences in Kenya sparked her interest. She told me in our interview — before I even asked — "that's really where I got my interest in language." The sparking and initial formation of her interest thus fits the description above. Further, also fitting the description, her interest developed spontaneously. She did not go to Africa planning to become interested in patterns of language usage — indeed she went hoping to go on to a career in international development.

Over time Susan formed a more defined interest, defining her interest conceptually as an interest in choices speakers make about which language to speak in in multilingual settings such as Kenya, social norms governing these choices, code switching, and hybrid language forms — with her specific experiences and observations serving as examples within these subtopics, for example, her interest in the way English is used, itself a topic with a host of examples linked to it. Susan certainly did not at the time she formed her interest have any idea how it might relate to literature — she told me at the time she made no connections between them — or any idea about how it could be the basis for a creative project; it was an interest, not more specific or developed than that. In Chapter 9 I describe how it sparked a creative response she had and became the basis for her literary analysis.

Phenomena, Elements, Experiences, Practices, Issues, and People Sparking Creative Interests — Basic Categories

Many different kinds of experiences and elements in our fields and the world around us spark the development of our creative interests. These experiences and elements fall into three broad categories: natural phenomena; cultural and social — including political, economic, and legal — experiences, activities, practices, issues, and events; and experiences, elements, and people in the fields in which we are engaged in creative work. I discuss each in turn.

Natural Phenomena

Natural phenomena spark interests and form the bases for interests in many fields. The notion that scientists' interests are sparked by natural phenomena is commonplace; what is interesting is to trace the way scientists become fascinated by a phenomenon or class of phenomena and form distinctive interests rooted in their fascination, growing out of it. Charles Darwin was fascinated from childhood in life-forms and the diversity of life-forms, interested in classifying them; later, he developed, growing out of and based in this interest, spurred by the incredible fauna and flora he encountered voyaging on the *Beagle*, a conceptually richer, more sophisticated interest (see the end of this chapter). Liz Yoder, a neuroscientist I interviewed, was fascinated by the phenomenon of calcium-based signaling by glial cells, and formed an interest in exploring glial signaling that was the basis for her dissertation research and has influenced the whole course of her development. Jane Minturn, another neuroscientist I interviewed, took a class in college in which she learned about how the development of higher functions and behaviors "coincided with the [evolutionary] development of very specific regions of the brain," which she said "sparked" her interest in anatomical development and how brain evolution is linked to the emergence of new behaviors; later, in graduate school, her interest became more focused and defined on a molecular level (see Chapter 11). Several of the neuroscientists I interviewed were fascinated by the phenomenon of axonal pathfinding, the process of axons traveling and being guided along specific paths to their targets, and developed interests in specific aspects of pathfinding.

Based on my experience it is also quite common for artists to form creative interests that are sparked by and center around or are rooted in natural phenomena. Many painters describe being fascinated by light, by specific qualities it possesses, its reflections or play off objects and surfaces in the world, describing their development in a way that suggests that this fascination was the basis for creative interests they formed. Paul Cezanne, although he left little in the way of an account of his creative development, making any statement or interpretations about his creative interests and conceptions of interests speculative, appears in his mid-thirties, at what turned out to be a crucial juncture in his development, to have become fascinated by the way light illuminates three-dimensional objects and space, in particular the way it affects and mediates our perceptions. Thus he focused, as his creative interest, on the challenge of finding a way to represent these effects in the two-dimensional world of painting. Likewise, one readily imagines sculptors being fascinated by aspects of the human body or other physical forms in the world and developing interests rooted in such fascination.

Cultural and Social Issues, Activities, Practices, Events, and Experiences

Cultural and social — including political, economic, and legal — issues, activities, practices, events, and experiences are all important in sparking interests and form the bases for interests in many fields, most obviously in fields in which they are the primary focus of inquiry and study, as well as in other fields.

William Faulkner formed a literary interest centered on describing in works of fiction the world of the rural South he had grown up in, including its cultural decline and decay and its moral values — not yet finally vanquished or lost he believed — epitomizing the moral essence and courage of man. He described the origins of *Flags in the Dust*, which defined a crucial creative break in his work (together with *Father Abraham*, which he began during the same time but abandoned), when he first formed his mature interest, in a note written two years later. He wrote that he was "speculating idly upon time and death," and began to think about his childhood and the South as he had known it. "All that I really desired was a touchstone simply," he writes, by which to remember that period and time of life — but, being compelled to write, "nothing served but that I try by main strength to recreate between the covers of a book the world as I was already preparing to lose and regret [losing it]. . . ."[1] His statement

---

[1]William Faulkner, *Flags in the Dust* (New York: Random House, 1973), Introduction. My account follows that of Joseph Blotner in *Faulkner: A Biography*, Vol. 1 (New York: Random House, 1974), pp. 531–32.

68   conveys a sense of his nostalgia for his childhood and for the civilization of the South as it had been and he now perceived that it would never be again, that he conceived, as the works he then began to write depict, as steeped in tradition, having a moral rot and decay and overhanging foreboding of doom, together with islands of moral strength, innocence, and resistance. In his initial burst of activity, writing the opening of *Father Abraham* and *Flags in the Dust*, Faulkner later stated, he defined his literary interest and approach: "I discovered that my own little postage stamp of native soil was worth writing about and that I would never live long enough to exhaust it, and that by sublimating the actual into the apocryphal I would have complete liberty to use whatever talent I might have to its absolute top. It opened up a gold mine of other people . . . ."[2] Thus his interest was rooted in the culture and world of his childhood, transformed into the apocryphal to depict evocatively and lyrically the great themes he associated with it and wished to depict through writing about it — decay and moral decadence, yet also moral values not yet lost, still surviving, epitomizing the ceaseless struggle of man and woman to overcome their failings and the flaws of life and this world.

Susan's interest in the uses of different languages in conversation in multilingual cultural settings and the social meanings of different languages is another example of an interest sparked by cultural and social practices, practices that she both observed and participated in.

In many cases individuals' interests are sparked by important and dramatic political, economic, and social events, such as wars, catastrophes, and economic depressions. John Maynard Keynes first formed a clear interest in studying and modeling the impact of monetary policy on economic variables, including output, unemployment, inflation, and interest rates, and the channels through which monetary variables exert their effects, in particular analyzing and modeling the processes through which economic agents form expectations of future prices and economic conditions, at the time of the sharp recession of 1921–1922 in the United Kingdom, his interest forming in part in response to this event and growing out of his belief that the recession was due to the Government's misguided deflationary policy, driven in large part by the desire, wrongheaded in his view, to return to the prewar gold standard.[3] World history and events of all kinds precipitate the formation of interests. Thus, to give one important twentieth century example, the rise to power of the

---

[2] *Faulkner: A Biography*, pp. 526–27.
[3] His interest connected with and was shaped in its conceptual form by his long-standing interest and work on the formation of probability judgements, published in his *Treatise on Probability*. I discuss the links between his early interests and work and later interest in economics in Chapter 15.

Nazi party and the Holocaust caused many individuals in many fields, including intellectuals, artists, and others, to develop creative interests arising out of their feelings of horror and their questioning of how such events could possibly have occurred, that were the bases for subsequent creative work they engaged in and contributions they made. I discuss as one example in this book Hannah Arendt's creative development. Social and political issues and causes — concern about the environment, nuclear arms, abortion, socioeconomic inequalities and other perceived social injustices — and numerous other issues and causes, often controversial, spark interests that are the basis of creative work.

Creative interests are also sparked by cultural, political, and social practices in other countries and cultures. This is intuitive, for the practices of peoples in other countries, their institutions and way of life, stand out and are often quite intriguing in being different from what we know and are used to; as I discuss in the next chapter, novelty is an important source of creative interests.[4] In many cases in which individuals form such interests their interests develop while they are living in these countries, sparked by firsthand experiences and observations. The experience of being immersed in a different culture is very stimulating and conducive to the development of interests; free from our usual surroundings and routines we see and experience the world freshly, and thus naturally tend to develop new interests. For Susan, living in Kenya and experiencing the language practices there firsthand was clearly crucial in drawing her attention to these practices and sparking her interest. Julius Galacki, a playwright I interviewed, went to the Czech Republic in 1989, at the time the Soviet Union was relinquishing control of Eastern Europe, and his interest was sparked by the tensions he perceived there between the pull of traditions and the desire for change, leading him to form an interest in exploring this tension in creative work.

The dividing line between natural phenomena and cultural and social elements, practices, activities, and experiences is not sharp — for the latter can be and often are viewed primarily as phenomena; for example, symbol systems, notably language, are often studied as phenomena. Nonetheless, the distinction is a useful one, for cultural and social systems, experiences, activities, and practices are fundamentally meaning-based, which sets them, as we experience them and in terms of their significance for us, apart from the natural world, in general though not entirely or always. Further, their meaningfulness is a basic factor in our interest in them — even in cases in which we are most interested

---

[4]Similar arguments apply to individuals forming interests sparked by issues and practices of social or regional groups or cultural milieus in their own countries different from their own.

in them as phenomena they are interesting to us as phenomena in large part because of their meaningfulness. Thus, Susan was interested in conversational practices in Kenya as a rich body of phenomena, but a main reason she found them so rich and fascinating as phenomena was because she perceived them as suffused with and carrying social and cultural meaning.

Field-Based Experiences, Elements, and People

Experiences and elements in our primary fields of endeavor, including the creative work of other people in our fields and encounters with people in our fields — engaging with their work and ideas — spark many of our creative interests. Concepts, theories, hypotheses, questions, issues, facts, styles, and methods in our fields that we are exposed to and learn about, experiences, for example learning techniques, and the works, projects, ideas, opinions, beliefs, goals, and visions of other people — all can and do spark creative interests.

We are especially open to, interested in, and influenced by elements circulating in our fields and the creative work and ideas of others in our fields during periods when we are engaged in forming creative interests — working to define an interest for ourself. Such periods of openness and interest formation are especially common when we first enter a field, when we are learning intensively about it and thinking about what creative directions to pursue, as is illustrated by many of the examples of development in this chapter and throughout the book. It is also not uncommon for us to be open to new possibilities later in our development, during critical junctures when we decide we wish to head off in a new direction. In contrast, during periods when we are pursuing projects our attention is more narrowly focused and we are less open to becoming excited about and interested in elements that are not fairly directly connected with our work — though even during these periods at times we do form new interests, in the intervals when we are not working, as we speculate and consider in which direction to head next, after our current project ends.

In the majority of cases our creative interests are sparked by and develop out of positive responses we have to elements we encounter, including positive interactions with other people and excitement about and interest in their ideas and work; thus I emphasize positive responses here. But it is also true that negative reactions spark creative interests, as I discuss in Chapter 5.

Certain kinds of experiences and elements in fields stand out as especially important in sparking creative interests. New developments in our fields — new theories, discoveries, frameworks for analysis, styles, methods, and approaches — are especially important in sparking many interests. This is natural. New developments have a kind of magnetism — they stand out and are at the center of discussion, are "hot topics," exciting and stimulating; we have a natural tendency to get caught up in the excitement they generate and become interested in them, and almost without thinking about it find ourselves imagining the possibilities they offer for further development, forming interests based on them. Mara Dale, a literary scholar I interviewed, described going to graduate school and becoming swept up in the excitement of literary theory movements that were in vogue, especially deconstruction. She described herself as a "playful person" and told me she became especially interested in the playful aspects of deconstruction — theory doubling back on itself and on its subject, turning meanings into their opposites, forming a creative interest in exploring allegory and double meanings in texts, including the two perspectives of male and female. Giedrius Buraças, a neuroscientist I interviewed, told me he was very excited about the breakthroughs in neural networks that occurred in the 1980s. Having worked in a lab in which visual perception is studied, he integrated his interest in neural networks with this research experience and formed an interest in developing neural network style models of visual system processing. It might seem that only those destined to make less-than-stellar original contributions are influenced by new developments in their fields, but this is not so — in fact the greatest of luminaries often form interests rooted in new, revolutionary developments in their fields, which they themselves then develop further, in revolutionary ways. Albert Einstein, in his "Autobiographical Notes," writes, "the most fascinating subject at the time I was a student was Maxwell's theory," describing this as appearing to him at the time as a "revolutionary" shift in physics, from Newton and forces acting at a distance to "fields as fundamental variables" generating waves propagating through space.[5] His fascination with Maxwell's theory sparked and blossomed into an interest in the electrodynamics of moving bodies which he had formed by the age of 16 (see Chapters 5 and 10).

Personal contact and engagement play an important role in the sparking of many creative interests. Listening to and watching people talk about their ideas, work, and beliefs about issues and problems and possibilities in our field, in person, can be very stimulating. Their enthusiasm and interest can be infectious and have a great impact on us, and thus spark our own interest. It is not uncommon for a creative interest we develop to be sparked by a presentation or lecture we attend by someone working in our field. Though we may have

[5]Albert Einstein, "Autobiographical Notes," in *Albert Einstein: Philosopher-Scientist*, ed. and trans. from the German by Paul Arthur Schlipp (New York: Tudor Publishing Company, copyright The Library of Living Philosophers, 1949), pp. 1–95, p. 33. Einstein mentions also the work of Hertz as having interested him in electrodynamics.

some earlier intimation of interest, which indeed may lead us to attend the presentation or lecture in the first place, what we learn and the excitement, enthusiasm, and interest transmitted to us in the presentation or lecture is crucial in sparking our interest.[6] Liz Yoder described her interest in glial cell signaling first being sparked by a class presentation given by another student; she told me he did a "really good job," which helped to catch her attention and highlight the phenomenon for her as exciting and different and potentially important. We are perhaps especially likely to respond to individuals who are charismatic and inspiring — to become swept up in the ideas and visions they present and to form interests linked to these ideas and visions, growing out of them. However, this is not enough; our initial response, no matter how strong, must develop further to become a lasting interest — and this second step depends on our later response, after the event itself, after the speaker has gone and our initial burst of interest has passed. Charisma is not necessary — Liz did not indicate that the student whose presentation sparked her interest was charismatic, though he was clear and a good speaker — but it may be a contributing factor. Teresa Nick is an example of someone whose creative interest was sparked by a charismatic speaker — Eric Kandel, the renowned neurobiologist known for his pioneering work on the neural basis of learning in simple organisms, who gave a presentation at her college on the neural basis of behavior in the slug *Aplysia*. "He is extremely charismatic," she said, "he's a wonderful speaker." "And he gave this talk in which basically what he said was 'it's so simple, everything is so simple; here we have an organism [*Aplysia*] that's so simple, and we take a couple of neurons and we have the behavior, right in these few neurons.' And I was overwhelmed by that." As she described her development, it was evident that his talk was a crucial event in sparking her interest in studying the link between individual neurons and behavior in simple organisms, in particular *Aplysia*. The sparking of Hans Krebs's initial interest in intermediary metabolism, described later in this chapter, is a further example of an interest sparked by a charismatic lecturer.

Our creative interests are also sparked by engaging with teachers and mentors. We naturally tend to look up to them and look to them as influences, in that they are older, have greater experience and a historical sense of our field, and may have achieved what we ourselves hope to achieve; their interests, ideas, beliefs, and visions thus influence us and can be important in sparking our interests. Teresa Faherty, a literary scholar I interviewed, was initially

[6]I do not include in this list general discussions with other people, friends, and colleagues. Such discussions are often crucial later in our development in sparking projects, including ideas for collaborative projects; see my discussion in Chapters 9 and 11. But they seem to be less important in sparking interests.

interested in Dante in college, and formed a strong personal bond with her Dante teacher. During her junior year she switched to Shakespeare as her main focus. She went to speak with her Dante teacher to tell her — "and she was very kind and encouraging," Teresa said, "and she said, 'I love Shakespeare [too], especially the late plays, especially *The Winter's Tale.*'" Teresa, influenced by her teacher, decided to study *The Winter's Tale* and chose it as the topic for her college thesis, forming an enduring interest in it that carried into graduate school and became the base from which her dissertation developed.[7] Sometimes our interests are sparked by visionaries, who can be very charismatic and thus inspire and influence us, sparking us to form an interest linked to their vision. The artist John Peter Russell, with his strong character, fiery independence, and commitment to the primacy of color in painting and individual expression, seems to have been a vital influence on Henri Matisse. Matisse had been trained in the scholastic tradition, under Gustave Moreau, painting with somber, dull color tones. He broke with the tradition and his own previous mode of painting over the course of two summers spent on the coast of Brittany in 1895–96, forming — or beginning to form (he would vacillate back and forth between more and less traditional forms for a number of years) — a creative interest in painting with vibrant primary colors, juxtaposing them in strong contrasts defining shapes and linear contours in paintings, applying them in strong, even brusque strokes. A number of factors influenced him, including his friend Emile Wéry; and the fact that he was staying on the remote coast, far from the pressures and scholastic academy life of Paris, was surely important in making him feel freer and more independent. But Russell seems to have been a crucial influence. Matisse lived next to him during the second summer, on the Isle of Belle-Ile-en-Mer, and it is said he was his pupil. Russell taught Matisse what he himself had distilled under the influence of van Gogh and Monet, and under Russell's influence, his vision, magnetism, and strength of character, Matisse was able to take the first steps toward breaking free from the traditional style he had been taught. The influence of Russell is shown in the fact that Matisse began painting with strong blues and magentas that Russell himself favored; he then formed his own creative interest, based on what he learned from Russell and others, but distinctive to him.[8]

[7]Teresa stated in our interview that she believes it was her teacher's suggestion that led her to focus on the play — "I actually think that's what made me do *The Winter's Tale.*" She added that she also had read *The Winter's Tale* for a Shakespeare class.

[8]See Hilary Spurling, *The Unknown Matisse* (Berkeley: University of California Press, 1998), chap. 4. Matisse said he was influenced by watching Wéry squeeze primary colors right out of paint tubes onto his palette.

Two additional comments are necessary. In fields in which the principle objects of study are cultural works and elements, such as literary and cultural studies and the history of art and the history of science, individuals often form interests sparked by and centering around particular cultural works and elements; but these elements and works belong to a fundamentally different category than the elements and experiences listed and discussed above. They are not elements and works circulating in the field as modes of understanding, describing, or working with primary elements, such as materials, data, or phenomena, that are the center of creative activity in the field — rather, they are themselves such primary elements. And they are not the work of contemporaries in the field, but rather produced by individuals working in the complementary field that produces the objects of study in the field; for example, works produced by creative writers are analyzed in literary studies. And lastly, elements in neighboring fields and encounters with people working in neighboring fields sometimes are important in sparking creative interests — in the interplay, encountering ideas, works, and approaches that are relevant but different, our interest and imagination can be sparked. David Hirsch, a literary scholar, described going to see the film *Dead Ringers* and being struck by its portrayal of brotherhood — which sparked his interest in brotherhood and brotherhood as the basis for community as a theme in literature.

Our creative interests are a vital, central link connecting our creative endeavors with our culture, including our cultural heritage and our fields. The descriptions and examples given above manifest and delineate this linkage — the link is forged through our interests being sparked by, having as their basis, and growing out of cultural elements and experiences, including social experiences through which we are exposed to other people's opinions, ideas, and works, and our responses to these cultural elements and experiences. Looking back, nearly every one of the different kinds of elements and experiences I have listed and described as important in sparking and forming the basis for interests is cultural, either directly so or else a social experience in which we are exposed to cultural elements, culture including in this context both general culture, for example for Susan language practices in Kenya, and the knowledge base in a field, for example for Einstein Maxwell's theory. The only exception to this is the category of natural phenomena; but in fact very often when a natural phenomenon sparks our interest and we form an interest centering on it, the phenomenon first comes to our attention through our encountering descriptions of it made by others who have seen it first. Thus, the phenomenon of glial signaling was first brought to Liz Yoder's attention by another student's presentation. In the case of Charles Darwin, descriptions of nature by others

were important in spurring his interest — most notably, Humboldt's famous
description in his *Personal Narrative* of the South American tropical forests was
important in spurring Darwin's desire to journey to the tropics, contributing
vitally to his decision to join the *Beagle* as naturalist.[9]

Personal Experiences and Personality and Creative Interests

Personal experiences and concerns spark and are the basis of many creative
interests. In this section I describe and give examples illustrating ways in which
they spark and form the basis of interests. I also briefly discuss theories of creativity in which personal experiences and personality structure are viewed as
the basis of creativity, emphasizing that I am describing a different, distinct linkage between personal experiences and creative development, through creative
interests.

It is natural that personal experiences and concerns spark and form the basis
of creative interests, for they have great emotional power, are important, and
absorb us, thus naturally tend to be centers of interest for us and raw materials
out of which we form interests. In addition, they shape our sense of ourselves
and our lives, and through this channel, less immediately but pervasively,
influence our interests. There are many different kinds of experiences and
concerns that are important in sparking and forming the basis of interests:
relationships with parents, illnesses, friendships, love affairs, losses of family
members, friends, or home, memorable and momentous events we witness or
experience, major life events and milestones, and personal issues and beliefs.

The importance of personal experiences and, to a lesser degree, personal
concerns in creative work and creative development is widely acknowledged
and discussed, both within the field of creativity and more generally. Personal
experiences are most widely and clearly recognized as being important for
artists and writers; the notion that art is rooted in experience is ages old. In
modern times it has been in vogue to describe the basis of art in experience
using the term transmutation — to describe artists and writers as transmuting
their personal lives and experiences into art. Thus, a major focus of modern

[9]Charles Darwin, *The Autobiography of Charles Darwin, 1809–1882* (New York:
W. W. Norton & Company, 1958), pp. 67–68. Darwin writes that during his last year in
college he read "with care and profound interest" Alexander von Humboldt's *Personal
Narrative* and John Herschel's *History of Natural Philosophy* (*A Preliminary Discourse
on the Study of Natural Philosophy*) which "stirred up" in him a "burning zeal" to make
his own contribution to natural science; and Humboldt's narrative, with its brilliant
descriptions of the tropics, seems to have inspired a strong desire in him to see the
tropics. For a biographical account of Darwin's early years and development see Janet
Browne, *Charles Darwin*, Vol. 1, *Voyaging* (New York: Alfred A. Knopf, 1995).

biographical studies of artists and writers is trying to identify and describe ways in which they were influenced in their work by their experiences, and, more specifically, ways in which the raw materials of their experiences were transmuted by them into art.

The literature on James Joyce and his process of creation is an excellent example. Central themes are that Joyce's experiences, his family and growing up in Ireland, form the basis for much of his writing, particularly his early writings, and that he transmuted his personal experiences into high art. Richard Ellmann places the "reshaping" of his experiences at the very center of Joyce's literary activity. He states at the beginning of his biography: "The life of an artist, but particularly that of Joyce, differs from the lives of other persons in that its events are becoming artistic sources even as they command his present attention. Instead of allowing each day, pushed back by the next, to lapse into imprecise memory, he shapes again the experiences which have shaped him." He traces the growth of Joyce's own ideas as a reflection of and developing in tandem, however loosely, with his life. He quotes Joyce himself having said, later in life, referring to himself, that his "work and life make one," "are interwoven in the same fabric."[10] It is recognized that Joyce's experiences growing up in Dublin formed the basis for the atmosphere and characters in *Dubliners*; it has been shown that he very accurately and meticulously sticks to local geography and re-creating characters he had known in nearly all of the stories.[11] Joyce's own struggle to break free from tradition, from conventional Catholicism and the Priesthood and traditional life in Ireland, is an essential part of his Stephen Dedalus characters — in his early novel, *Stephen Hero*, and famously in *A Portrait of the Artist as a Young Man*. Of course Joyce's brilliance and originality transcend his personal experiences. Ellmann suggests, citing Joyce's own commentary on the artistic process, and Hugh Kenner argues further, that the early *Stephen Hero* is more autobiographical, and that it was by distancing himself from his own personal experiences and self, while still drawing upon them, that Joyce was able to create his great works beginning with *Portrait*. This fits the description of creative development in this book: Joyce's

[10]Richard Ellmann, *James Joyce* (New York: Oxford University Press, 1982), Introduction, pp. 3, 149. Stanislaus Joyce describes much of his brother's work as "autobiographical" in *My Brother's Keeper: James Joyce's Early Years* (London: Faber & Faber, 1958), preface.

[11]See Don Gifford, *Joyce Annotated: Notes for Dubliners and A Portrait of the Artist as a Young Man* (Berkeley: University of California Press, 1982), and Patricia Hutchins, *James Joyce's World* (London: Methuen and Co., 1957). Quite specific connections are made, for example, linking specific streets near his various boyhood homes to specific urban settings in the stories. Ellmann notes hundreds of specific incidents, people, and scenes from Joyce's life and Dublin re-created in Joyce's fiction.

experiences were the basis for his creative interests — the themes, struggles, and way of life that interested him and that he sought to portray, as well as his notion, and presumably experience, of epiphanies. But in forming his mature literary interest he went beyond his own specific experiences, forming a more abstract, conceptual interest — in, it seems, the growth of the self and its meanings, and the role of epiphanies as generative of revelation and growth within a life setting.[12]

Different connections between creativity and personal experiences as well as between personality and creativity are described in psychoanalytic theory and personality psychology. In these approaches the creative process and in a sense creative development — though meaning by this something rather different than what I mean — are described as emanating from and channeled by basic personality elements, and primary processes — unconscious processing, instinctual drives, and early experiences, particularly infantile and early childhood relationships with parents. Freud introduced the idea of sublimation, in which a basic instinctual drive is diverted from its original aim into a secondary outlet, providing the energy for this secondary activity, and proposed that sublimation is a primary source of the creative impulse.[13] He also put forth the idea, notably in his essay on Leonardo da Vinci, that personality structure, rooted in early experiences, shapes the nature of artistic engagement, including the tendency to focus on particular styles and themes. Both ideas have been developed further in depth psychology approaches to creativity, in which the rich links between personality structure and unconscious desires and creativity are investigated and described.[14] Psychobiography situates these ideas within the individual's social and cultural context — patterns of relationships with parents, adolescent experiences and development, and factors in the larger social and cultural context, for example, social movements and ideologies — and describes the role of such experiences and patterns as drivers that generate creative urges and channel them towards certain outlets and themes.

[12]See *James Joyce*, pp. 144–45, 149, and chap. 18; Hugh Kenner, *Dublin's Joyce* (London: Chatto & Windus, 1955), chaps. 4 and 8. Ellmann discusses Joyce's initial interest in epiphanies and theory of epiphanies (pp. 83–85) and quotes from and discusses Joyce's earliest manuscript of what became *Stephen Hero*, written in January 1904. Unfortunately it is not possible to trace in anything like a coherent, satisfactory way Joyce's conception of interest and development — there is little direct documentary record, as I read the evidence, of his thinking leading up to this manuscript draft.

[13]George Vaillant provides a good discussion of sublimation in Chapter 5 of *The Wisdom of the Ego* (Cambridge, MA: Harvard University Press, 1994).

[14]A classic work is Ernst Kris, *Psychoanalytic Explorations in Art* (New York: International Universities Press, 1952).

As an example, in his study *Young Man Luther*, Erik Erikson describes Luther's creative break with traditional Church dogma and development of a new theology as rooted in his relationship with his father: his resentment and inner anger at his father's harsh punishments meted out while his father himself committed transgressions, combined with his strong emotional bond to his father and an inner voice — the internalization of his father's voice — which formed the center of his superego, censuring his own behavior. He argues that this complex was the root of Luther's rebellion and ultimate development of a new theology, in which man is directly in dialogue with God, and faith comes before justice, rather than justice being viewed as reward or punishment — rewards and punishments seeming poisoned and false to Luther because of how he had been treated by his father. Erikson situates Luther's psychological predicament within the society he inhabited, late medieval northern Europe, showing how Luther's struggle and rebellion mirrored important social, economic, and moral issues and challenges of the time, giving voice to them, to the feelings of struggle of many others in his society.[15]

A second example is studies of the roots of Picasso's art. Mary Matthews Gedo, in her *Picasso: Art as Autobiography*, suggests that Picasso's attitudes towards women, rooted in his relationship with his mother — her difficultness, his ambivalent feelings about her, feeling guilt and concern for her and also repressed anger towards her and by extension all women — linked to what she describes as his "brittle" personality structure, needing constant emotional support, were vital in rooting and channeling his artistic work.[16] A series of interesting and perceptive comments Françoise Gilot makes in *Life with Picasso*, and comments she recalls Picasso making, support this view; her comments are about a time when Picasso was much older, but seem to be about enduring personality traits he had. In her first visit to Picasso's studio Françoise states she was accompanied by her friend Geneviève, a beauty. She states that the pairing of them resonated with a "theme that runs throughout his entire work": "two women together, one fair and the other dark, the one all curves and the other externalizing her internal conflicts, with a personality that goes beyond the pictorial; one, the kind of woman who has a purely aesthetic and plastic life in him [her], the other, the type whose nature is reflected in dramatic expression." She continues: "When he saw the two of us that morning, he saw in Geneviève a version of formal perfection, and in me, who lacked that formal perfection, a quality of unquiet which was actually an echo of his own nature." She remarks that he himself said at the time, "I'm meeting beings I created

[15]Erik H. Erikson, *Young Man Luther: A Study in Psychoanalysis and History* (New York: W.W. Norton, 1958).

[16]Mary Matthews Gedo, *Picasso: Art as Autobiography* (Chicago: University of Chicago Press, 1980).

twenty years ago." It is easy to translate this pairing to a basic ambivalence and tendency towards splitting in his ideation of and feelings towards women, which naturally created discordant feelings. She also states that Picasso, at one point, showing her some prints, stated to her: "Every human being is a whole colony, you know" — again, a comment consistent with contradictory feelings and ambivalence.[17] Fernande Olivier writes, in entries in her journal kept during the time, much earlier, that she was with Picasso, describing his feelings early in their relationship, that "he keeps anything I leave behind as if it were a holy relic," and of how traditional his view of women was, that he did not want her to work, but to be worshiped as a woman, and fully satisfied in her wants. Again, what she writes points to a basic splitting in his attitudes and feelings towards women.[18] Picasso's feelings about women — his creative interest in representing his complex feelings about them for the viewer to experience — were I believe a vital root driving his crucial early break with conventional representation in *Les Demoiselles d'Avignon* (see Chapter 12).[19]

A related but different connection linking personal psychology to creativity, widely discussed and debated, is the connection between madness and creativity. The best documented and described specific connection is between manic-depressive disease and creativity. Kay Jamison provides an excellent survey and discussion of the literature in *Touched with Fire*, supporting the argument that there is a link between the disease and creative achievement in certain fields, in particular poetry and music composition.[20]

Interesting, rich, and deep as these descriptions of the relationship between personal experience and creativity are, they do not directly address or focus on the connection between personal experiences and creative interests, my

[17]Françoise Gilot and Carlton Lake, *Life with Picasso* (New York: McGraw-Hill, 1964), pp. 21, 49, and 81.

[18]Fernande Olivier, *Loving Picasso; The Private Journal of Fernande Olivier*, trans. by Christine Baker and Michael Raeburn (New York: Henry N. Abrams, 2001), p. 140 for the quote and the section "In Love with Picasso," pp. 161–88 for how he treated her.

[19]Later Picasso came to think of his approach as more strictly creating a radical, challenging visual experience, thereby subversive in an aesthetic sense (as Gilot also quotes him stating in *Life with Picasso*, pp. 58–60, 72–73); but at its origins his approach seems to have been rooted, at least in part, in wanting to represent his feelings about women, and by projection their feelings towards men.

[20]Kay Jamison, *Touched with Fire* (New York: Free Press, 1993), chap. 3. See also N. Andreason, "Creativity and mental illness: Prevalence rates in writers and their first-degree relatives," *American Journal of Psychiatry* 144 (1987): 1288–92; her analysis shows a statistically significant link between manic-depressive illness in first-degree relatives and creativity among writers. There is a fundamental tension between the view that creativity is linked to mental illness and the view of Winnicott, Maslow, and many other psychoanalysts and psychologists that creativity is part of healthy, normal experience.

80   focus here. In fact, this link between personal experiences and creative interests is vital: a primary channel through which personal experiences influence
our creative work is through influencing our creative interests. Further, the connection between personal experiences and creative interests is often far more
transparent and direct than the connection between these experiences and
later creative works. Indeed this latter connection often is composed through
two discrete steps — (i) experiences leading to or influencing interests, and
(ii) the pursuit and creative development of interests, leading to creative contributions — and is difficult to trace or see clearly unless these two steps are
separately identified and described.[21]

The influence our personal experiences exert through our interests is especially important because it is exerted at such an early stage of development
and is broad in its scope, potentially affecting the entire course of our development. The linkage between experiences and interests is also extremely variable
and flexible — there are a manifold of different pathways through which personal experiences influence and shape interests, and many different ways in
which individuals integrate and combine personal experiences with other elements in forming interests, creating the potential for enormous variety. This
flexibility and variety is at least somewhat in contrast with the literature, especially the psychoanalytic and personality literatures, for in these literatures
the linkages between experiences and creativity are quite restricted in form
and content, typically involving linking basic personality types to specific,
stereotypical themes and styles in creative work. For example, in his analysis of Joseph Conrad, Bernard Meyer links major themes in Conrad's fiction
to a specific neurotic personality type, bisexuality and voyeurism, which seems
overly limiting.[22] Even Erikson, the most subtle of writers in this tradition, falls
somewhat into this trap. He describes Luther's originality, the root and impetus
of his break from tradition, as rooted in his relationship with his father, later
projected onto or generalized to priests, even God. While this is a valuable

---

[21]A good example of the need to consider these two steps separately is transmutation.
In many cases in which it is argued that an artist or writer forged his creative works
out of personal experiences, the linkage — the specific conceptual and artistic steps
through which he effected this transformation — runs through his creative interests, thus
involves the two fundamental steps, which must each be described separately for the
path to be clearly delineated. Often, however, these two steps are not clearly separated
and described separately.

[22]Bernard Meyer, *Joseph Conrad; A Psychoanalytic Biography* (Princeton, NJ:
Princeton University Press, 1967). Indeed a reviewer of Meyer's book makes just
this point; see Douglas Hewitt review in *Review of English Studies* (Oxford: Oxford
University Press, 1968), pp. 451–53. Nonetheless, psychosexual interpretations of
Conrad's motives and work continue to be widely discussed, for example in *Conradiana*.

perspective, it does not sufficiently describe Luther's creative development as
a broader conceptual process — the way he conceptualized his interest in
the question of what obedience is owed to authority, and to which authority,
the inner voice of conscience, and matters of reward and punishment; thus,
Erikson does not attempt to describe in any real detail Luther's conception of
his interest and how he arrived at it, and how he came to conceptualize his
concerns theologically.

Examples of Personal Experiences Sparking and Forming the Basis of Interests

The best way to gain a sense of the importance of personal experiences in
sparking interests and forming the basis of interests is through examples — these
show the linkages vividly and distinctly. Here I describe the role of personal
experiences in sparking and forming the basis for interests for Virginia Woolf,
Nick Halpern, a poetry critic and creative writer I interviewed, and Hannah
Arendt.

For Virginia Woolf, tragic personal losses shaped her development, her
preoccupations, and her literary interests, profoundly and indelibly. Virginia's
mother died when she was thirteen, her father, after a difficult time, when she
was 22, and her older brother Thoby when she was 24. Psychoanalysts and self-
psychologists describe the importance of our parents and close relationships
in serving as "mirrors" in which we see ourselves reflected and form images
of the selves we would like to be, processes that are crucial for our personal
development.[23] Virginia's parents and brother functioned as her mirrors, making their loss devastating. In her memoir "A Sketch of the Past," she writes
that she was obsessed with both her mother and her father for decades after
their deaths, thinking about them incessantly.[24] She describes her mother as
being at "the very centre" of her childhood world, helping her and others to
"see what they really meant or felt," and describes her death as "the greatest

---

[23]Heinz Kohut discusses the mirroring function; see his books *The Analysis of
the Self* (Madison, CT: International Universities Press, 1971) and *The Restoration of the
Self* (Madison, CT: International Universities Press, 1977). He discusses both the ego-
ideal, our internal representation of the ideal self, and the self-object, our internal
representation of our self.

[24]Virginia Woolf, "A Sketch of the Past," in *Moments of Being*, ed. Jeanne Schulkind
(San Diego: Harcourt Brace & Company, 1985), pp. 64–159, in particular pp. 80–95,
107 on. She also writes of this in a diary entry on November 28, 1928 — *The Diary of
Virginia Woolf*, Vol. 3, 1925–1930, ed. Anne Olivier Bell (San Diego: Harcourt Brace
& Company, 1980), pp. 208–10. See also Hermione Lee, *Virginia Woolf* (New York:
Vintage Books, 1999), chap. 4.

disaster," ushering in a time of "darkness." She writes of the bond she shared with her father — the love of all things literary, of how she mourned the loss of the chance to know him better and for him to know her better as she entered adulthood. As for Thoby, he was a bright light illuminating the path forward to the future, and his death deprived her of that light and guide.[25] The loss of her mother, father, and brother deprived her of the essential mirrors she needed, of her models, and shattered her sense of a safe haven in which to form her self. And in turn this deprivation was almost certainly a vital root of her interest in the self and its reflections; she was able to recognize and express in intellectual form her unfulfilled needs, to form a rich conception based on them, which she could then explore in her creative writing.

Nick Halpern has unique creative interests that are rooted in his family experiences growing up, in particular his relationship and intellectual and emotional response to his parents and their beliefs, especially his father. Nick described his parents as "intensely spiritual" — they converted to new age religious beliefs when he was young and believe in "spiritual transcendence." An enormous influence on Nick has been a book his father began writing in the sixties, growing out of his spiritualism. Nick described his father's book as a "new age" work of philosophy, "written in a very prophetic style." "It's called *The Theory of Transformation in the Personal, Political, and Sacred Realms.*" "It's a big book [1000 pages]. And it has to do with questions of transcendence and what he [my father] calls transformation." "He imagines a trajectory . . . moving from a state of reliance on authority, into a state of incoherence, and from that into a state of transformation; so he imagines this trajectory of liberation — and tells, or thinks he tells, the reader how to do it." "And he's just been working on it forever. So that's always been a presence in my life." It was clear from our interview that Nick views his father as having come to view himself as

[25]"A Sketch of the Past." She describes both her mother and father at length, especially her mother. In a passage beginning on page 80 she writes of how she was obsessed with her mother until the time she came to write *To the Lighthouse*, and that after that time she ceased to be obsessed with her. Regarding her mother's centrality she writes, "I suspect the word 'central' gets closest to the general feeling I had of living so completely in her atmosphere that one never got far enough away from her to see her as a person" (p. 83). She also writes of her mother in "Reminiscences" in *Moments of Being*, pp. 28–59. Quentin Bell discusses her feelings about the loss of her mother, father, and Thoby in *Virginia Woolf: A Biography*; see especially passages on pp. 29, 40, 50–53, and 112. It is certainly noteworthy that Virginia went mad after her mother's death, and again after her father's death. It is also noteworthy that she formed a strong attachment to Violet Dickinson beginning about 1902. Violet, described as patient, moral, and a great sympathizer, may well have been a surrogate mother and mirror.

a kind of prophet figure, and that this has been a major issue for him in his own life.

Nick does not share his parents' beliefs, but he has been profoundly affected by them, and by his father's book, with his own interests and preoccupations formed in counterpoint to them. He is not religious — he told me he is not interested in religious ideas and prophetic messages as far as their content, and in this way is very different from his parents. But his interests are linked to them and their beliefs in a different way: he is interested in "spiritual discourse" — in particular prophecy — in terms of its "style" or form and its relationship to ordinary life. Since college or even earlier his creative interests have centered on prophet figures and the "prophetic voice" in literature — the kinds of voices prophets speak in, their self-presentation, and their strategies of persuasion.

During college Nick was especially interested in the relationship between the prophet in his role as prophet and the prophet's ordinary human self.[26] He told me that the idea that especially interested him was "the idea of prophets as vessels, the idea that a human being would be filled by something else, and would have to be emptied out in order to be filled." This idea seems linked to feelings he had about his father and their relationship.[27] Nick's creative writing is also focused on exploring his interests in the prophet and his ordinary self and the nature of prophetic voices. He told me he "re-creates" and "dramatizes" the voices of prophets, and writes about prophetic figures, the tensions between their prophetic and ordinary selves, and the difficulties they pose for their families, and described a novel he was working on at the time about a prophet figure and his family (see Chapter 14).

Over the years Nick has developed a second, closely linked interest — trying to understand why literature written in the prophetic tone so often fails to be persuasive, and how certain writers are able to make it persuasive. This interest is rooted in a shift in his opinion about his father's book. "I grew up thinking that it was a really interesting book," he told me, "but there's a sense in which I became disillusioned." "The style of a lot of the chapters is very hypnotic and prophetic, and that style has always seemed wrong . . . I've always felt that

[26]"I was interested in the relationship between the personality of the prophet and [his] prophecy," he said, "and in the ordinary day-to-day self of the prophet . . . all these questions having to do with thinking about my parents." Nick wrote his senior thesis on two working class individuals, Joanna Southcott and Richard Brothers, who became known as prophets in late eighteenth century England.

[27]As noted in the footnote above Nick himself realized the connection with his parents even at the time. He told me his interests had to do with "further thinking about both of my parents," and that, "in some ways I was thinking about my father in particular, at the same time as I was thinking about these issues."

somehow something went wrong." Nick came to recognize — in a crucial generalization that transformed his personal doubts about his father's book into a broader literary interest — that it is not only his father who has difficulty writing in the prophetic voice, that in fact it is difficult to write persuasively in this voice, and he became interested in exploring why. In his dissertation prospectus he writes, "I am interested in the strangeness of this voice, the difficulties poets have in producing plausible versions of it, the impediments in its way." Paired with this facet of his interest is a second facet, an interest in successful versions of the prophetic voice — "to try to imagine how someone might be genuinely prophetic, genuinely authoritative [as a prophet]." This facet of his interest is also rooted in his reaction to his father's book: he views his father as having failed to be genuinely persuasive in his prophecy and wants, he told me, to find a way "to save the idea of prophecy."

In some cases personal experiences influence creative development through sparking and forming the basis of an initial interest that in turn leads to a central creative interest. Hannah Arendt's development illustrates this pattern, a story of personal experience intertwining with intellectual development and historical circumstances.

It is now widely accepted that Hannah had a love affair with Martin Heidegger in Marburg in 1925–1926, at the time Heidegger was composing his master work *Being and Time*.[28] After a year she went away, unrequited, with the realization that she would never enjoy Heidegger's undivided love, that their love affair was doomed.[29] During the summer of 1925 she wrote a moving autobiographical essay, "The Shadows," and throughout this time many poems that illuminate her sense of her self and her life at the time and how the love affair affected her. In her biography *Hannah Arendt: For Love of the World*, Elisabeth Young-Bruehl gives translations of several parts of "The Shadows" ("Die Schatten") and several poems, in which Hannah describes living in a state of suspended animation, how she had been awakened by the passionate love affair only to find herself estranged and "homeless," expresses her anguish and despair, and describes coming to terms with her sorrow, forming the belief that in suffering one experiences the truest value and meaning of

---

[28] Elzbieta Ettinger gives an account of their affair based on their letters in *Hannah Arendt/Martin Heidegger* (New Haven, CT: Yale University Press, 1995); she documents their romantic encounters and the depth of their passion for one another. Their letters are now published in Hannah Arendt and Martin Heidegger, *Letters, 1925–1975*, trans. by Andrew Shields (New York: Harcourt Books, 2004).

[29] Ettinger states that Heidegger pressured her to leave; see *Hannah Arendt/Martin Heidegger*, pp. 20–21.

life — "suffering is the point of everything and its reward."[30] The importance of love, and what can be the meaning of life without love, is a central focus of the poems, and thus they seem linked to her dissertation, *The Concept of Love in St. Augustine*, submitted at Heidelberg in 1929. Her dissertation is a work in the history of ideas, focusing on Augustine's description of the route through which man can transcend his mortality, through coming to love — *caritas* — of God; in the final sections she discusses the dictum "love thy neighbor as oneself" in relation to and contrast with this *caritas*. Her work seems to be in dialogue also with Heidegger's thought, especially in probing man's sense of and relation to time, shifting from Heidegger's focus on certain death to memory and the creation of man and his journey towards God.[31]

At Heidelberg Hannah formed an interest in German Romanticism. Young-Bruehl states that she considered writing "an extensive study of German Romanticism when she finished her doctoral dissertation" and undertook "an enormous campaign of reading." This new interest was linked with her interest in Augustine, for she saw him as an original source for the growth of Protestant pietism, viewing him, as Young-Bruehl describes it, as a crucial source for Luther and the basis "for the modern autobiographical novel." With her interest in the self and its quest for meaning it is easy to imagine that she would be drawn to Romanticism. Through her study of Romanticism and interest in autobiography Hannah encountered the figure of Rahel Varnhagen, a German Jew who had lived a hundred years earlier.[32] Encountering Rahel was like seeing herself and her life in a mirror. Like Hannah, in her youth Rahel had been intensely introspective and socially naive; then she had fallen in love with a man who withdrew from her, had continued to love him, had felt despair and hopelessness, and had come to equate life with suffering. Over time, in a way that Hannah must surely have envisioned for herself, she had risen from the ashes of her broken love affairs to forge an identity, a life for herself, entering into social and intellectual life in Berlin. Her flat became

[30] Elisabeth Young-Bruehl, *Hannah Arendt: For Love of the World* (New Haven, CT: Yale University Press, 1982), pp. 50–57.

[31] The German title of the dissertation is "Der Liebesbegriff bei Augustin." The published English translation is *Love and Saint Augustine*, ed. Joanna Vecchiarelli Scott and Judith Chelius Stark (Chicago: University of Chicago Press, 1996).

[32] *For Love of the World*, pp. 68, 81–82. A close friend of Hannah's, Anne Mendelsohn, had acquired the Varnhagen family correspondence, and when Hannah became interested in Rahel, she gave her the materials (p. 56). Hannah dedicated her book *Rahel Varnhagen*, when it was eventually published in the 1950s, to Anne. Hannah may have come upon Rahel in studying Jewish women's involvement in establishing salons in Germany. Another such figure of whom she made a study was Henriette Herz; see Sylvie Courtine-Denamy, *Hannah Arendt* (Paris: Belfond, 1994), pp. 168–69.

86   a popular salon and she herself was at the center of social and intellectual life. Hannah Arendt saw, it seems, her own predicament of life, including her ill-fated love affair, reflected in Rahel's experience, and identified with Rahel; later she called Rahel "my closest friend." And she embarked on a work with the aim to describe Rahel's life as Rahel herself would have done.[33]

Rahel was a Jew, and although she spent much of her life trying to escape from her Jewishness — she did not plan to let it define her life, indeed viewed it as an accidental occurrence to be overcome and did not initially perceive its tenacious grip on her destiny — nonetheless it shaped and defined her life. Regardless of how deep a kinship she felt for Enlightenment and German culture, despite her deepest wish to assimilate, inevitably she was viewed as a Jew, alien and inherently different, and could not escape her Jewishness. Hannah Arendt recognized the fundamental importance of this. Her book on Rahel begins with Rahel's recognition, at the end of her life, that her identity was rooted in this fact, it had made her life what it was: "I was a Jew" — "the thing which all my life seemed to me the greatest shame, which was the misery and misfortune of my life — having been born a Jewess — this I should on no account now wish to have missed."[34] It is doubtful whether Hannah Arendt initially focused on Rahel's Jewishness; her own Jewishness had not been a major concern for her growing up and she did not initially approach any of her intellectual pursuits from that perspective — indeed she came to Rahel first in her study of Romanticism.[35] But over time she came to recognize the importance of Rahel's Jewishness for understanding Rahel's life: the subtitle of her book is *The Life of a Jewess*, and the book is, more than anything else, about how Rahel's life is both unique in its individuality but also reflects her Jewishness which she could not escape. In coming to this view Hannah was

---

[33]The quote is from a letter to Heinrich Blücher, August 12, 1936, in *Within Four Walls; The Correspondence Between Hannah Arendt and Heinrich Blücher, 1936–1968*, ed. Lotte Kohler, trans. by Peter Constantine (New York: Harcourt, 1996), p. 10. In the preface to *Rahel Varnhagen* Hannah writes that her purpose is "to narrate the story of Rahel's life as she herself might have told it," which fits with her attraction to Rahel having been a bond of personal identification.

[34]Hannah Arendt, *Rahel Varnhagen: The Life of a Jewess* (London: East and West Library, Copyright Leo Baeck Institute, 1957), pp. 1, 182–85.

[35]In a letter to Karl Jaspers Hannah writes that she was "naive" and did not understand the significance of Rahel's Jewishness, that she grasped this only with "some difficulty." *Hannah Arendt Karl Jaspers Correspondence, 1926–1969*, ed. Lotte Kohler and Hans Saner (New York: Harcourt Brace Jovanovich, 1992), pp. 196–201. Young-Bruehl gives the text of a television interview Arendt gave in 1964 describing her experience of her Jewishness growing up, summarizing it as "unproblematic" for her; see *For Love of the World*, pp. 11–12.

clearly guided by Rahel's own view of her life, but also by her own experiences and events around her, for at this same time her own Jewishness became visibly central, as increasingly she felt herself viewed as a Jew by others and ostracized, thus forced to view herself as a Jew, and as her political consciousness awakened as the Nazis rose to power and there was an increasing and increasingly hostile focus on the Jews in German public life.[36]

In turn her growing awareness of her Jewishness and the plight of the Jews, which as an intellectual interest began in her study of Rahel, led, under the terrible burden of events in Germany, to her developing an interest in the place of the Jews in German and European society and culture, approached from a historical perspective; see Chapter 15 where I trace her development from this point.

Registers of Meaning

In the preceding sections I have described experiences and elements that spark and are the basis of interests. In fact interests almost always have roots and antecedents: when we investigate the origins of individuals' interests we discover in many cases links with prior experiences and conceptual structures already present in their minds.

We have in our minds registers of meaning, frames through which we "see" the world, including our lives and ourselves, and interpret our experiences. Our registers develop out of the webs of our experiences, including values we internalize, our emotions, and what we learn. They represent and reflect those experiences and those aspects of our experiences that have had the greatest impact on us, as well as what we have distilled from our experiences in the course of reflecting upon and trying to make sense of them.[37]

Our registers of meaning influence, indeed in many situations govern, what we attend to and how we respond to and interpret new experiences and elements we encounter, and through guiding our attention and responses they play a vital role in the formation of our creative interests. When our interest is sparked by particular experiences and elements we encounter, often a crucial factor is that these experiences and elements resonate with certain of our

---

[36]A friend she made, Kurt Blumenfeld, a Zionist, was important in drawing her attention to the "Jewish question" and raising her political consciousness. But Hannah herself had felt the burden of being a Jew even in Marburg, where, even while Heidegger's lover and part of the intellectual community, she was viewed as different, as an outsider, excluded and taunted. See *For Love of the World*, chaps. 1, 2, and 3.

[37]The sense in which I use "register of meaning" resonates with the discussion in Peter Berger and Thomas Luckmann, *The Social Construction of Reality: A Treatise in the Sociology of Knowledge* (Garden City, NY: Anchor Books, 1966).

registers of meaning. They catch our attention because they resonate with these registers — in particular it is because of their resonances with our registers that we are led to perceive them as meaningful and important; and our registers evoke and guide our response to them, and contribute to our developing an interest based in them. The specific source of resonance can take a variety of forms. An experience may call to mind a similar set of experiences we had in the past, evoke feelings tied to previous experiences, and generate an association to a register of meaning in our mind or a fundamental value; or our attention may be drawn by sensory phenomena or data that fit with or stand out as unusual or bizarre compared with past data or facts encoded in a register in our mind.

Many of my subjects, based on my discussions with them, had registers of meaning that were important in triggering the formation of their creative interests. In college Azad was interested in classical mechanics, thus had learned to conceive of physical processes in terms of their mechanisms of action. In turn this made it natural for him later when investigating cellular tolerance to nitroglycerin to consider this question from the perspective of identifying the mechanism of action through which nitroglycerin exerts its effect, which was the genesis of his interest in studying cellular mechanisms of action; as he put it, this was the "closest" he could make biology to classical mechanics. In Susan's case, although it was in Africa that she first developed a clear interest in the use of different languages in conversation, the social meanings of language choices, and the intermingling of languages and language hybridization, in fact she had some familiarity with and an incipient interest in some of these topics beforehand. In particular, in college she wrote her senior thesis about African American women's literature, and she told me she was especially struck by what she called the "theme of language" common to several of the books she read — the importance of learning to speak and articulate one's feelings and perspective. She also said her advisor had drawn her attention to the fact that different people speak in different dialects and that these dialects "have social or cultural meanings."[38] Thus, it seems likely that through her work on her undergraduate thesis a register of meaning formed in her mind around the topic of language, including dialects and their social meanings, and that this register in turn was a factor in her becoming aware of and interested in patterns of language usage in Kenya. Henry also had a register of meaning: he had a personal resonance with the developing world, especially the South Pacific, where he had grown up and his parents lived, which was important

---

[38] She mentioned noticing, for example, the importance of language in *The Color Purple* — "language is so important there, for example, Shug helping Celie learn to speak and be able to say things."

in calling his attention to references to these places in *Finnegans Wake* and in his reaction to and understanding of Naipaul.

Roger Knowles, a neurobiologist I interviewed, is an example of someone for whom an approach for analyzing problems acted as a register of meaning. Roger attended the West Point Military Academy, where he learned military tactics and specialized in ergonomics. After college, while serving his tour of duty, he decided he did not want to remain in the Army, and after exploring a number of fields decided to go into neurobiology. Describing his initial attraction to neurobiology he said, "I liked the idea of thinking about the human brain as this sort of puzzle." "The thing that really intrigued me at first was, 'How is it all put together, how is it all designed?' — in an engineering, building blocks kind of way." From the start Roger was thus interested in studying the "nuts and bolts" of how the brain is put together. As he thought further and learned more about neurobiology he refined this interest, forming a more focused interest and conception of interest: *visualizing neurons developing into their shapes.* "If you think about the neurons as the building blocks in the brain, their shape seems to be very tied to their function," he explained, "and [I thought] how they developed into their shapes would be a fascinating subject [to study]." Roger emphasized that he had a very literal, visual interest: "I really was hoping to be able to get down to the point where I could actually visualize cells in the brain, visualize how the neurons would function as this architectural structure by which the brain is built up." Roger's conception of the brain — as an architectural structure with the neurons its "building blocks" — is striking. During our interview I asked him how he had come to think about the brain this way, and he linked it to his training at West Point: "It's probably something that developed from the way that I was trained at West Point to think of problems. One of the things that you look at in the military in problem solving is visual patterns — that kind of orientation. If you're going to look at how to defend a piece of terrain it's important to understand the shape and the size and the area and how everything's kind of put together. It was important when I was learning how to design pieces of equipment for the human body to think of it in terms of the shape and the size that would be best for performance." He thus thought about the brain by analogy with visual patterns of interlocking elements and the functionality of different shapes, which was crucial in his forming an interest in how the brain is put together and shaped his conception of his interest.

Because our registers are based in our personal history, they often lead us to focus on distinctive or unique aspects of our experiences and elements in our environment, giving us a distinctive perspective, and this distinctive focus is in many cases a main source of the distinctiveness of our interests. This was true to some degree for Roger. I discuss the distinctiveness of his interest in Chapter 7. It was also true for Hannah Arendt. Her love affair with Martin Heidegger and her feelings at its end created an emotionally charged register of meaning in her mind, centering on her personal experience of love with a Gentile and her perspective on herself as a Jew and a woman outsider, which seems to have been vital in her forming an interest in Rahel. In turn this was the basis for her later interest in the place of the Jews in European life and society, one factor leading her to approach this topic — distinctive to her, at least in some respects, as compared with others' approaches — historically.

I note, to conclude this section, that the process I have described is a core process within larger patterns of development. In particular, often our development has a recursive structure; registers of meaning spark our interests, and through our pursuit of our interests new registers form in our mind, which in turn spark our development of new interests. This kind of recursive, multistep process is evident in Susan's development as well as in Hannah Arendt's, and also in John Maynard Keynes's, discussed later.

B. PATTERNS OF DEVELOPMENT OF CREATIVE INTERESTS AND CONCEPTIONS OF CREATIVE INTERESTS

In most cases we form our creative interests and conceptions of our interests in stages and over time. This is true of interests and conceptions of interests separately, and also especially of joint interest-conception pairs — our interest together with our conception of it. In this section I describe common, basic processes through which, over time, we form interests and conceptions of interests. My description is, by design and of necessity, a simplification, and in some cases an oversimplification, of reality; the actual processes involved in the formation of interests and conceptions of interests are often far more complicated than what I describe, involving many intertwined events and many, perhaps hundreds, of discrete mental events, processes, and steps, impossible to describe in full detail.[39]

[39] In general, the processes of development of interests and conceptions of interests cannot be traced exactly, not only because they are often complex, but especially because individuals generally do not keep careful track of the processes through which they come to form their interests and conceptions of interests. They typically recall and describe only the most memorable moments, for example, moments when their interest was initially sparked, and when they came to a sudden realization of it and formed a well-developed conception of it. Alexander Calder's development of his interest is a good example — he describes his memorable experience on board a ship, and his later conception of his interest, but no intervening steps.

At the heart of the process of formation of many of our creative interests and conceptions of interests — and specifically interest-conception pairs — is a fundamental two-stage process. First, our interest is sparked by experiences or elements we encounter, as described in the previous section; during this initial stage we may or may not form a conception of our interest, but if so our conception is typically quite rudimentary. Second, we develop our interest conceptually, through reflecting upon the experiences and elements that have sparked it, analyzing them, working with them conceptually and imaginatively, synthesizing and connecting them with related ideas and perspectives, and thus forming a conception of our interest. Within this basic structure there is substantial individual variation, especially with regard to the second stage, in particular in timing — the interval of time that passes between when our interest is initially sparked and when we first form a genuine conception of it, as well as in the kind of processing we do and the number of distinct stages our conception passes through. There are a number of relatively common patterns based in this basic two-stage process that I describe.

Broadening From a Specific Narrow Base; Conceptual Synthesis

Many interests and conceptions of interests begin from a narrow base and develop through a process of broadening out conceptually. In this pattern an individual's interest is sparked by a specific experience or element — a seed — and is thus initially rather narrowly focused. Over time his interest grows from this seed, broadens, and matures; he builds upon his initial interest, linking it to related experiences and elements and imagining the possibilities it holds, and forms a conception of his interest. An example is Alexander Calder's development of his interest in representing simple forms of the universe, such as discs and spheres, in space and in various kinds of motion in space. His memorable experience on the ship, when he saw a "fiery red sunrise" on one side of the boat and the moon, "looking like a silver coin on the other," was crucial in sparking his interest in the sun and the moon and their positioning in space, and, perhaps more generally, bringing to his attention the artistic possibilities of the solar system. This image was a kind of preconception of an interest, rudimentary in being just a single image, and not really conceptually defined. Over time, he developed a much richer conception of his interest, described by him in the quotes given in Chapter 2, conceiving of a whole family of different shapes, including discs, spheres, and clouds, and imagining them in many different configurations in space and various kinds of motion. Although some of his richest descriptions of his interest were given well after he had made his first important creative breakthroughs, so we cannot be sure that he had similar conceptions in his mind earlier, it seems very plausible that he did. As early as 1932, just after his invention of the mobile, in a catalogue for an exhibit he described art as "coming into being" out of "volumes" and "masses" set in motion in "spaces carved out within the surrounding space, the universe."[40] And, as noted in Chapter 2, he said the universe was the inspiration for his art long before it was apparent and, as quoted, told a reporter that the "first inspiration" he ever had was "the cosmos, the planetary system," which suggests that he thought actively about the solar system while conceptualizing his art.

Another pattern of broadening is a process of conceptual synthesis and integration: an individual's interest is sparked by a set of separate elements and experiences, which he does not originally connect together; then, sometimes significantly later, he recognizes a connection among them and synthesizes or integrates them, forming a conception of interest that encompasses them, typically at a somewhat higher level of abstraction. An example is Henry Chen's development culminating in his formation of his conception defining his interest as "literary geography." At a point of reflection, while considering his literary interests and possibilities for his honors thesis, he realized that what connected his favorite authors together was their rich descriptions of places, the way they created and defined places through their work, through this insight forming a conception defining his interest.

There are many variants of these basic patterns. One example is the development of her main creative interest of Maria Carrig, a literary scholar I interviewed. Maria has been interested since childhood in the shift in philosophical worldview that occurred during the late medieval, Renaissance, and early modern periods, the shift from "ancient to modern" as she described it, centering on revolutionary new theories of knowledge, linked to corresponding developments in ethics and aesthetics and the formation of new systems of thought in many fields, including science and religion. Since college her main academic focus has been Renaissance and early modern drama. In graduate school Maria formed a creative interest by relating these two more general interests to each other. "What began to interest me," she told me, "was finding a way of talking about the revolutionary philosophical shift that started happening around the turn of the seventeenth century, as it might have worked in a drama" — specifically, in the English theater. As she described it she formed this creative interest in a two-step process. Her thinking was sparked

[40]See Alexander Calder, *Calder* (New York: Viking Press, 1971), p. 25. He made similar statements on other occasions.

by a specific event — noticing certain unusual features in the work of the playwright Thomas Middleton, whom she described as the "immediate heir" to Ben Jonson. She said that in "juxtaposing" Middleton to Jonson she was struck by how very different their plays were in their underlying principles and structures. "Jonson was someone who formulates comic theories in his plays that are very much part of the whole tradition of the defense of theater, as both ethically and aesthetically sound." "But Middleton seemed to me to have no such consistency, or to make no attempts at consistency." "As a comic playwright he struck me as nothing short of bizarre, in terms of the radical way he was breaking every ethical rule and structural rule, while at the same time having a kind of conventional veneer." Maria said she thought Middleton was "subversive." And, in a crucial step, she made a conceptual link — she recognized that his subversiveness and radical break from tradition might well be connected with the broader revolution in philosophical worldview that was occurring at roughly the same time, which can also be considered radical and subversive. Thus she broadened out from the initial insight she had about Middleton, connecting it to a larger topic in which she had a longstanding interest, and in this way defined her creative interest.

It is not always easy to know, in cases in which individuals form creative interests through a process of broadening and synthesis, at what stage of their development they first form a well-developed, integrated conception of their interest. Further, as mentioned in Chapter 2, in some cases an individual's interest may exist in a preconscious form, so that, for example, the individual has developed a network of associations and concepts defining her interest and linked to it, but does not have a well-developed conscious conception of it. Susan's development is an example of these points: it is difficult to know exactly how developed her conception of her interest in the uses of different languages in conversation, the norms governing language choice, and language switching was while in Africa. Did she have a fully formed conscious conception, or did she have more of an intuitive awareness that the linguistic experiences and phenomena that had sparked her interest somehow fit together, without having formed a conscious and conceptually integrated conception? Based on my interview with her, I believe the latter is in fact more likely — that her interest was still somewhat inchoate in Africa, and she only formed a fuller conception of it after she had returned to the United States and begun graduate school (the fact that she had a conception of her interest by that point is clear, for she was guided by her interest in looking for and choosing to take a course in anthropology about the cultural development of oral and written language; see Chapter 9).

Narrowing Down, Focusing, and Refining; Reversals

The patterns of development described in the preceding section center around processes of growth, broadening conceptually, synthesizing, and integrating. Processes of narrowing down, focusing, and refining — processes working in the opposite direction, at least with regard to scope and breadth — are important in the development of creative interests as well.

Narrowing, focusing, and refining are especially important and common when we first enter a field and during the ensuing period when we are first intensively exploring and learning about it. We are often first attracted to a field by one or more great questions, themes, and ideas, which define the ultimate objectives and values of people working in the field, and are an important source of motivation for them. As we learn more and become more experienced we move past these great questions, themes, and ideas that first attracted us — indeed find we must do so — because they are not directly accessible to investigation or development, at least not in the form that first attracted us; they are simply too big, too ambitious, too speculative to be useful, at least on a practical level, for organizing our creative development and defining a path forward. Thus we narrow down and form a more refined, focused, specific interest that is linked in some way with the big questions, themes, and ideas that first excited and interested us, or at least some of them, but is more manageable and practical.

Many of the neuroscientists I interviewed described having followed this pattern of development: being drawn to neuroscience by the great questions of the field — what is thinking? what is the basis of memory? how is the brain designed? how does it develop? — questions that are exciting and in many ways define the field, especially to outsiders, but are too big to operationalize; then, as they learned more about the field, forming and pursuing more specific interests, linked to the big questions that first drew them to the field. Roger is an example. He was first drawn to neuroscience by the puzzle of trying to understand how the human brain as a whole is designed and put together — he told me the enormity of this question excited him, the idea of trying to figure out how something so sophisticated — more sophisticated than any piece of equipment ever designed as he described it — is constructed. Then, as he learned more about neuroscience and thought more about it he formed his more specific interest in visualizing neurons as they develop into their shapes, arriving at this interest through envisioning the neurons as the building blocks out of which the brain is constructed. Bruce Peters is another neuroscientist who followed this pattern. Bruce studied computer science and electrical engineering, then switched to neuroscience. He told me that what initially fascinated him was thinking of the brain as a giant computer, and realizing its sheer power, how much it can do that conventional computers can't do. Later, he narrowed his focus dramatically, forming an interest in local circuitry, the electrical functioning of small circuits of interconnected neurons. Explaining the shift, he told me that as he learned more, including how to measure voltages, local circuitry appealed to him as something he could study experimentally with techniques he felt comfortable with given his background in electrical engineering; local circuitry also seems to have resonated with his sense of electrical circuits, whereas the circuitry of the whole brain seemed too big, mind-boggling in its complexity. Chris Callahan is a third neuroscientist I interviewed whose development followed this pattern; I discuss and give his description of his initial fascination with neuroscience, and the interest he formed, in Chapter 8.

In fact in nearly every field there are great questions, themes, values, objectives, and ideas that define the field and the ultimate objectives of people who work in it and are central in attracting people into it. Great questions — that are like mysteries, as Noam Chomsky has described them — are at the core of many fields.[41] Many artists are drawn to fields of artistic expression by the idea that certain conceptions of beauty can be expressed and created through working in them. Many fields are defined and at least in part center around great challenges that draw people into the field and motivate them, at least in an ultimate sense. Thus, many medical fields are defined at least in part by the challenge of finding cures or ways to prevent diseases, and what first excites a person about a field of engineering or technology may be an extraordinary machine or device that people in the field dream about building, like a flying machine, a suspension bridge, or a computer that can think.[42] In all of these fields the pattern of development described above is a common one.

Hans Krebs is an example of an individual who followed the basic pattern of narrowing down from a grand vision to define a more practical, focused

[41]We often feel a sense of awe and wonder about these questions; I discuss these feelings as sources of interest in the next chapter. For Chomsky's views on the mysteries, beyond science, see his comments in the article by Jennifer Rauch in *Temple Times*, "Noted scholar Noam Chomsky explores philosophy of science," 29 (No. 28) (May 6, 1999).

[42]Henry Petroski describes some of the remarkable bridges in the world and how they were built in *Engineers of Dreams* (New York: Alfred A. Knopf, 1995); he conveys a sense for the enthusiasm of the people who built the bridges, and the power of dreams to inspire and motivate.

creative interest; in his case this took some time, and a further period of time passed before he was free to pursue his interest. My account of his development of his interest is based on the description of his development given by Frederic Holmes in his biography, which is based in part on interviews with Krebs in which he described his interest and path of development.

According to his later statements, Hans was inspired as a university student by the grand vision of the field of intermediary metabolism presented by his professor Franz Knoop. Knoop envisioned constructing an "unbroken series of equations" beginning with the foodstuffs an organism takes in and describing the complete chain of chemical reactions or pathways through which these foodstuffs are decomposed to provide energy and synthesized into biochemical compounds for the organism's use, terminating at the final waste products that are excreted by the organism. He described this as being the "true goal of biochemistry."[43] This vision sparked Hans's interest, and stayed with him over the following years — an example of an idealistic, "grand" vision inspiring a young person's interest. But he did not immediately enter the field of intermediary metabolism; instead, he completed his medical education and became involved in a series of research projects unrelated to intermediary metabolism. Several years later, while working as a research apprentice in the laboratory of the well-known scientist Otto Warburg, he formed a more focused interest — in applying novel manometric techniques Warburg had developed to study intermediary metabolism — and forming this conception set his determination to enter the field, which he did several years later. I discuss this phase of his development in Chapters 6 and 12.

A related pattern is having an initial general interest, then forming a narrow specific focus, linked to the general interest, which acts like a toehold, enabling one to move forward in one's development, and then out of this narrow toehold forming a conceptually richer, broader creative interest. An example of an individual who followed this pattern of development is Cheryl Nixon, a literary

---

[43] Frederic Lawrence Holmes, *Hans Krebs: The Formation of a Scientific Life* (New York: Oxford University Press, 1991), pp. 76–79; see also chap. 1, especially pp. 4–5. Additional information is provided in Krebs's memoirs, *Reminiscences and Reflections* (Oxford: Clarendon Press, 1981). Krebs heard Knoop lecture in the summer of 1920; Holmes summarizes Krebs's recollection of what Knoop said in interviews conducted in the 1970s, more than fifty years later. It is striking that Krebs still remembered the visionary statements Knoop had made; in his memoirs Krebs says Knoop made a "lasting impression" on him (p. 19). Holmes also quotes a passage from the text of an inaugural lecture Knoop gave at about the same time that Krebs heard him lecture in which he discusses the central importance of chemical reactions for life and articulates his vision (pp. 76–77).

scholar I interviewed. At the time she entered graduate school Cheryl was
interested in feminism and approaching literature from the perspective of
feminism and the place of women in society. During her first year she took a
class on seventeenth and eighteenth century literature and for her class project
focused on the only woman author the class read, Aphra Behn, who was, Cheryl
told me, the first professional female author in England. She found Aphra
Behn's writings inspiring, especially the way Behn took on important social
issues of her day like slavery and politics. "She wasn't just writing courtship
novels about love," Cheryl said. "She was very much part of larger discussions
of her day — as a woman writer she had this very strong female voice." "It was
mind opening, it spurred me on and made me realize that there are female
writers during the eighteenth century who have interesting things to say." Out
of her excitement and her realization she formed a conception of a broader
interest that became the springboard for her subsequent work: she told me she
went to her professor and told him she was interested in searching for women
writers who came after Aphra Behn and carried on in her wake, writing about
important social issues — Aphra Behn's "literary heirs." She then undertook
an independent study in which she pursued her interest.[44]

A different pattern of development, one that also often involves a narrowing
of focus, is reversal. In this pattern an individual forms an initial interest — often
one that is idealistic, centering on a grand theme in his field — then later, as
he learns and becomes more sophisticated about his field and current trends,
forms a creative interest that is opposite to his initial interest, for example,
questioning of the ideals that first attracted him. To give an example I believe
is fairly common, an appreciation for the beauty of great works of literature or
art is often the source of initial interest in the arts and humanities, but writers,
artists, and scholars who work in the humanities often end up thinking about
literature and art differently, and become interested in topics that seem far
removed from the sense of beauty that first attracted them and inspired their
interest. Ian Baucom, a literary scholar, is an example; see the next chapter.

[44]Behn's most famous novel, actually a novella, is *Oroonoko*, and it was this work that
Cheryl focused on for her class paper. The book is about a woman, writing in the first
person, who visits the British colony of Surinam and meets a black slave, Oroonoko,
who leads a slave rebellion. I spoke with the professor with whom Cheryl took the
class and he confirmed that Cheryl was interested in and excited about searching for
women writers who would have come after Behn and formed a "tradition" or line of
development, having in common with Behn that they wrote about important social
issues. He also confirmed that she did an independent study course with him, pursuing
her interest.

Interests and Conceptions That Develop Over Long Periods of Time

Some creative interests and conceptions of interests develop over long periods of time — years, even decades. This is certainly not always the case or even the predominant pattern — many interests form over relatively short time intervals — but it occurs in some cases.

There are two basic patterns of development for interests and conceptions of interests that develop over long periods of time. One is a gap in development, a long fallow period: an individual forms an incipient interest, then turns away from it, usually without having developed it creatively to any extent; then, much later, often years later, returns to it and pursues it actively. In cases in which the development of an interest follows this pattern the return to the interest may be triggered by specific experiences, for example, that cause a shift in perspective about life and work. A person's conception of his interest when he returns to it is typically different than what it had been before he set it aside — more mature, often more elaborate. This change reflects learning and greater maturity of mind, experiences he has had while his interest lay fallow, sometimes fundamentally new ways of thinking, and may well be rooted in unconscious processes — the incubation of his interest in his unconscious during the fallow period.

Robert Kaufman, introduced in Chapter 1, is an example of someone who had a long gap of this kind in his development. As a youth Robert was interested in the relationship between art and literature and politics, in particular the ways in which artists and writers raise political issues for discussion and thought through their work. He told me he felt there were important political questions that seemed to him to be "most powerfully posed" through literature. He also said that his family has a tradition of Left political and social activism, and that making connections between literature and political and social issues was part of his family environment, for example, making connections linking race and class conscious literature to civil rights demonstrations. In the following decade, during which he attended law school and practiced law, his interest in the relationship between art and literature and politics receded into the background.[45] When, after a time, he grew disenchanted with practicing law, he decided to pursue his first love, literature. As he described it, almost immediately upon beginning in a graduate literature program his original interest

[45] Robert's interest did not disappear entirely during this period. During our interview he recalled seeing many art exhibits and movies during this time and discussing their political and social meaning and implications with friends.

reemerged and became a primary focus for him, in a more historical and rich
critical context (see Chapter 6).

The other pattern is a piecemeal, fragmentary process of development, culminating in the formation of a coherent conception: an individual forms fragmentary conceptions of his interest, but without forming a more integrative conception that can productively guide him in his creative work; then, at a later point, through a process of reflection or sparked by a specific experience or element, he forms a conception of interest that is more coherent and integrates many of the earlier fragments, and then pursues his interest creatively, guided by his conception. When our development of an interest follows this pattern it often is a halting process, sometimes confusing, as we form a series of fragmentary conceptions that don't seem to fit together in any obvious way and don't reveal a clear path forward — until at last, perhaps in a moment of illumination, we form a coherent conception, ushering in a new phase in our creative development, often a highly productive phase.[46]

Virginia Woolf's conception of the self and its reflections developed through a fragmentary, piecemeal process of this kind, culminating in her rich conception in "The Mark on the Wall." A glimmer of her interest first appears in "Phyllis and Rosamond," a short story she wrote in 1906 about two young women who are being brought up in a traditional manner. One night Phyllis and Rosamond go to an avant-garde party in Bloomsbury. Sylvia, one of the hostesses, engages Phyllis in conversation to draw her out. Phyllis tells Sylvia that she feels frightened and foolish, and remarks, "'Yours is such a wonderful life; it is so strange to us.'" Sylvia is interested by Phyllis and engages and probes her, and the narrator remarks, "Sylvia who wrote and had a literary delight in seeing herself reflected in strange looking-glasses, and of holding up her own mirror to the lives of others, settled herself to the task with gusto." Literary enjoyment and sensibility is identified here with viewing literature as a mirror in which we see ourselves reflected through reading about the lives and experiences of other people, who live in strange and different worlds — the looking-glass being "strange" because it is not our own life we see but different lives, yet lives through which we see our own. The mirror concept is applied again in the second phrase, to conversation, in the statement that Sylvia takes delight in "holding up her own mirror to the lives of others" — conversation is a mirror in which we help others see themselves. The conversation that ensues between Phyllis and Sylvia does indeed affect Phyllis's self-image, and

---

[46]This pattern bears a resemblance to the pattern of synthesis described previously; but as compared with that pattern there is more of a sense of catching glimpses of a larger whole without being able to see it fully.

afterwards she feels vulnerable and somehow changed — "in penetrating to her real self Phyllis had let in some chill gust of air to that closely guarded place; what did she really want, she asked herself?"[47] As fascinating as these passages are in foreshadowing Virginia's later conception, her focus in this story remains a traditional one, depicting characters and their transformation, with the notion of reflection essentially an aside — she has not yet conceived a purer form of literature structured entirely around characters seeing their reflections in other characters, with the surface of reality left out.

Virginia's journal written during her trips to Greece and Italy in 1906 and 1908 contains fascinating passages that reveal her developing interest, and insights and conceptions that may well have been important in furthering its development. I discuss two here. In her journal for 1906 she describes her fascination reading *Lettres à une inconnue* by Prosper Mérimée.[48] She writes that the letters present a "mystery" or "puzzle," due to the fact that only Mérimée's letters to his friend, the unknown woman, are presented, while her letters to him are not — "you do not hear her voice once," and thus: "To read the letters intelligently you must construct a reply; they demand it as imperiously as certain notes struck on the piano demand, & seem to imply their harmonies." Virginia finds it fascinating to guess at her replies, to try "to draw forth her notes from his," and discover "what kind of harmony" their two voices made together, and speculates at some length about their relationship. Her fascination with this game of reconstruction, and the insight she gains from it, point to a furthering of her interest in and understanding of reflections in literature. Engaging in the game seems to have helped her recognize how vital characters' replies or reflections are; readers look to the ways in which characters reflect back and forth off each other, relying on these reflections to piece together mental images of the characters and their relationships. Further, recognizing how interesting she herself found this game very likely contributed to her realization — which thus would have begun to form at this time, although she gained a deeper consciousness of it only much later — that interesting literature could be written centering around reflections, leaving the reader to fill in the missing "substance" of the characters by reconstructing it from their reflections.

Virginia's conception of the self and its reflections in "The Mark on the Wall" includes the concept that there are many reflections, "an infinite number," out of which the self-image as a whole is formed. This aspect of her conception has its own history of development, and in particular has an

[47]"Phyllis and Rosamond," in *The Complete Shorter Fiction of Virginia Woolf*, ed. Susan Dick, pp. 17–29.

[48]Virginia Woolf, *A Passionate Apprentice; The Early Journals; 1897–1909*, ed. Mitchell A. Leaska (San Diego: Harcourt Brace Jovanovich, 1990), pp. 341–45.

important precursor in a journal entry she wrote in 1908, while traveling in Italy, sparked by reflecting upon a fresco she had seen painted by the Renaissance painter Perugino. "He saw things grouped," she writes, "[for him] all beauty was contained in the momentary appearance of human beings." There is "not a hint of past or future" in his fresco, "speech, paths leading on, relation of brain to brain, don[']t exist." "Each part has a dependence upon the others; they compose one idea in his mind . . . . They have come together then because their lines & colours are related, & express some view of beauty in his brain." Thinking about his idea of beauty seems to have stimulated her to think about her own, and seemingly in a flash of brilliance she forms a conception of what she strives for. "As for writing — I want to express beauty too — but beauty (symmetry?) of life & the world, in action." "If there is action in painting it is only to exhibit lines; but with the end of beauty in view." "I attain a different kind of beauty, achieve a symmetry by means of infinite discords, showing all the traces of the mind[']s passage through the world; & achieve in the end, some kind of whole made of shivering fragments . . . ."[49] Her conception of a "whole made of shivering fragments" is a conceptual advance, envisioning a form of writing in which the whole is composed entirely out of fragments, alive and discordant, an infinite number — the traditional descriptions of intact "wholes" will be dispensed with, will have no existence beyond the fragments out of which they are composed. Also, the contrast with Perugino's fresco seems to have spurred her to recognize that her focus was the mind in its "passage through the world," not the hard, separate facts that make up the surface of the world, which painters like him focus on; she cares about the mind, the soul, the self.

Despite how remarkable this journal passage is, it is still a considerable distance from her conception in "The Mark on the Wall." Most importantly, it contains no mention of reflections. Thus, to arrive at her later conception she had to make a transposition, replacing "shivering fragments" with "reflections," which required making a connection between the two concepts, which were apparently separate and not directly linked in her mind. She also had to realize that the whole she wished to describe is best described not as the mind's passage through the world, with the complex sense of temporality this implies, but, more simply, as the self, and the self's image. It was fully nine years before she apparently took these conceptual steps, an illustration of how long it can take us to form viable, productive conceptions of interests.

[49] Ibid., pp. 392–93. Interestingly, in journal entries she made during her trip in 1906 to Greece she mentions fragments of sculpture and pottery lying littered about on the ground at the historic sites she visits (pp. 318–19). One wonders if these comments are linked with her later idea of "shivering fragments."

Mature Creative Interests That Develop Out of Childhood Interests

Many of our creative interests develop out of interests we pursue and activities we engage in as children or youths, such as hobbies, games, and political causes. When we develop a creative interest out of a childhood interest or activity, our later interest is generally significantly different from the childhood interest or activity out of which it develops, both in content and form — less activity-based and concrete, more conceptual, often narrower and more refined. Our conception of our interest as a child is usually simple and concrete, typically centering on a basic activity or conventional category, like "stamp collecting," whereas our conception as an adult of our adult interest is more conceptual and complex and often far more distinctive. As children we are not likely to be able to conceive of the rich interests and conceptions of interests we may develop in the future as adults out of our childhood interests and activities, indeed in most cases scarcely stop to give this matter any thought — we simply engage in activities and pursue interests we find interesting and enjoy.

Walt Disney grew up on a farm and from a young age loved animals and had a natural proclivity for personifying them and incorporating them into imaginative play. Later in life he told a story that illustrates the way he personified animals, about a pig named Porker he had taken to riding around the farm, who apparently took great delight in dumping him in the duck pond. Walt got sick and had to stay in bed for a few days and Porker apparently missed him, honking for him incessantly. "When I recovered," Walt said, "Porker practically invited me to climb on her back and stayed as peaceful as pie while I crawled aboard." "I was convinced that I had tamed her," "but I should have known better and guessed that she was only biding her time." "She waded into the pond, stood quite still for a few seconds, and suddenly tossed me like a tadpole into the deepest and slimiest part of the pond. Then she splashed back to her sty, snorting and snickering in triumph. For the rest of the evening, I could hear her honking away between snores — with a smug satisfaction, I suspect." He also loved to draw, and quite naturally loved to draw animals, endowing them with a sense of personality that foreshadows his later famous animated characters. Indeed what is reported to have been his first drawing, unfortunately lost so that we cannot be sure, depicted a "rabbit waving frantically to another rabbit concealed in the grass."[50] His childhood interests in animals and drawing were the root of his desire and interest, formed when he was a young adult, to create animated cartoons featuring animal characters possessing rich,

[50]Leonard Mosley, *Disney's World* (Chelsea, MI: Scarborough House, 1992), pp. 28–31.

vivid personalities — an interest-conception he apparently formed jointly with
Ubbe Iwwerks in discussions they had.[51]

Charles Darwin had interests as a child that were the root of the creative interest he formed in his twenties that was itself the basis out of which he first came to consider the possibility of transmutation of species.

In his *Autobiography* Darwin writes that he possessed a "passion for collecting" beginning as a youth, writing that by the age of eight his "taste for natural history, and especially for collecting, was well developed." "I tried to make out the names of plants, and collected all sorts of things," he writes, mentioning shells, seals, stamps, coins, and minerals, birds' eggs and insects.[52] His greatest pursuit while attending Cambridge was collecting beetles; "no pursuit," he wrote, "was followed with nearly so much eagerness or gave me so much pleasure." He seems to have engaged in close observation of nature even as a young person. In his *Autobiography* he recalled at the age of ten "being very much interested and surprised" during a trip to Wales upon noticing several varieties of insects which were not found near his family's home in England. He described being able, years later, to make fine distinctions among closely allied species or varieties of beetles. Beyond collecting and naming specimens, he also had an interest from an early age in observing the behavior of animals, notably birds.[53]

Darwin formed his creative interest while serving as naturalist on the *Beagle*, journeying around South America, in his mid-twenties. He nowhere states this interest explicitly, thus we cannot know for certain what his conception of it was — indeed it is impossible to know for certain how clear or full a conception he had of it. But based upon numerous notes and descriptions in his *Beagle* Diary and notebooks from the voyage we can roughly phrase it as *an interest in the geographic (and temporal) ranges of extent of species,*

[51]Ibid., pp. 61–63. Mosley states that Ubbe had seen an early cartoon featuring an animated character named "Gertie the Dinosaur" (created by Winsor McCay) who had a defined personality, but his statements indicate Walt never saw it, though he states that Walt had studied the early animations of McCay and Georges Melies.

[52]*The Autobiography of Charles Darwin, 1809–1882*, pp. 22–23, 26, and 45. His love of collecting is alluded to in letters that survive written to him by his brother Erasmus and his sister Emily Catherine. A principal subject of discussion in their letters is obtaining rocks, fossils, and minerals for him. See Charles Darwin, *The Correspondence of Charles Darwin*, Vol. 1, 1821–1836 (Cambridge: Cambridge University Press, 1985), pp. 1–9.

[53]*Autobiography*, pp. 45, 49–51, 62–64. His powers of observation are also apparent in discoveries he made in biology, notably his discovery at Edinburgh University that what had been thought to be ova of the organism *Flustra* were in fact larvae with independent powers of locomotion. See Ibid., pp. 49–51, and Sir Gavin de Beer, *Charles Darwin; Evolution by Natural Selection* (Garden City, NY: Doubleday, 1964), pp. 26–27.

including neighboring ranges of closely allied species and varieties, and similarities and differences in morphology and behaviors of closely allied species and varieties inhabiting different locales and environments, especially neighboring locales, or occupying similar niches in their respective habitats. This later interest clearly grew out of his interests in collecting and classifying species and animal behavior, but was far more conceptually defined and focused, reflecting his intellectual development and development as an acute observer and naturalist.[54]

How did Darwin come to form this conceptually rich interest that was to prove so crucial for his creative development? While ideas circulating in scientific circles at the time undoubtedly were important, what seems to have been most crucial, at least in my view, was his experiences and observations traveling with the *Beagle*. The *Beagle* followed a sweeping path: it first made landfall at South America at Bahia, Brazil, in the tropics, then journeyed south along the eastern coastline, passing out of the tropics into the temperate zone, then traveling to the cold, desolate region of Tierra del Fuego, then returned to the north, via the Falkland Islands, remained in the temperate zone for eight months, then headed south again to Tierra del Fuego, revisited the Falkland Islands, and at last rounded the Cape and headed up the western seaboard, calling as it left the continent at the Galápagos Islands. This path exposed Darwin to a series of dramatic and dramatically different climates and environs, calling his attention to and sparking his interest in the shifts and contrasts in species as one passed from one climatic zone to the next — a clear link with his interest. Indeed based on his written statements in his *Beagle* Diary he was overwhelmed by what he saw, especially by the extremes — the splendor of the tropics, with their incredible richness and diversity of species (see the next chapter) as well as the magnificence and desolation of Tierra del Fuego. I quote from notes he wrote in his diary and notebooks in Chapter 10, showing his interest in the range of scenery and his accumulation of observations about the animal and plant forms and behaviors as he traveled across this great range of climatic zones.

---

[54]In regards Darwin's interest during the voyage in the geographic distribution of species Howard Gruber notes that this is one of a few recurrent themes concerning species in his notebooks; see Howard Gruber, *Darwin on Man*, p. 101. Darwin also had a strong interest in geology, as has been noted by many scholars and biographers. Indeed geology was perhaps the main field in which he envisioned himself making contributions. He thought about geology in terms of the new view of the geologic history of the Earth and was greatly influenced by Charles Lyell's *Principles of Geology*; see *Voyaging*, pp. 186–90.

Of possibly even greater importance for his development of his interest was his coming to notice differences and gradations on a smaller scale, between neighboring locales — between species on the Falkland Islands and the mainland, during overland expeditions he took crossing through locales, and, later, between species from different Galápagos Islands. He records many observations in his notebooks and diary showing his interest in this topic and close observations. To give one example, at the time of the first visit to the Falkland Islands he wrote in his notebook: "It will be interesting to observe difference of species and proportionate Numbers: what also appear characters of different habitations," and wrote many notes about the interesting life-forms he observed.[55] After this, during the *Beagle*'s extended stay along the eastern seaboard he made several overland expeditions, and his notebooks and diary are filled with entries showing his close observations of the subtle changes in species and varieties, both in morphology and behavior. These observations fit with his interest, and suggest that his travels also spurred his formation of it. Indeed his interest seems to have been developing, at least in incipient form, from the time the *Beagle* first arrived in South America. When the ship journeyed from Bahia south to Rio de Janeiro he notes that Rio is clearly different in its life-forms, noting the "brilliant butterflies," writes he has "nowhere seen liliaceous plants" in such plenty, and remarks on four species of hummingbirds, writing a detailed comment about the behavior of one; these comments show he was interested in the differences between allied species at Rio and Bahia, thus already forming his interest.[56] In Chapter 10 I present a series of observations he made in his notebooks and diary demonstrating his interest in some detail. A famous story, noted in a copy of a letter at the time and told in his *Voyage of the Beagle*, illustrates his interest in closely allied species, in the differences between them and in their ranges. He recounts that at Rio Negro he heard settlers describe a rare kind of ostrich, smaller than the common kind; later, further south at Port Desire, his companion shot an ostrich, which, after it had been cooked for dinner, he realized was an example of this second species, later named *Rhea darwinii*. His description, at some length, shows his

[55] For the quote and other notes see *Charles Darwin and the Voyage of the Beagle*, ed. Nora Barlow (London: Pilot Press, 1945), pp. 177–79.

[56] Charles Darwin, *Charles Darwin's Beagle Diary*, ed. Richard Darwin Keynes (Cambridge: Cambridge University Press, 1988), pp. 53–55, 73. Fossils formed another branch of Darwin's interest — he was interested not just in geographic ranges but also temporal ones. He discovered several fossils and his discoveries prompted him to ponder the question of the relationship between earlier life-forms of a region and its current inhabitants.

interest, and he specifically notes that the second species is found in some abundance "about a degree and a half" south of Rio Negro.[57]

In Chapter 10 I build on the brief description here, tracing Darwin's pursuit and development of his interest, and how his observations lead him eventually to consider the possibility of transmutation of species.

[57] *The Beagle Record*, ed. Richard Darwin Keynes (Cambridge: Cambridge University Press, 1979), pp. 175–79; the entry reads "Copy of a letter to my brother Henry," March 19, 1834. Charles Darwin, *Voyage of the Beagle: Charles Darwin's Journal of Researches*, ed. Janet Browne and Michael Neve (London: Penguin Books, 1989), pp. 106–7.

4

Intrinsic Sources of Interest

The preceding chapter describes processes through which our creative interests develop. This chapter and the next describe principal sources of our interests and reasons we form and choose to pursue the creative interests that we do. In this chapter I describe intrinsic sources of interest, and in the next extrinsic and strategic factors that are important to our development of our interests and decisions about whether or not to pursue given interests.

In general the primary source of our creative interests is intrinsic interest: we form the creative interests that we do because we find them intrinsically interesting — no other reason or factor is as important or vital. In forming our interests we are not guided primarily or greatly influenced, in general, by strategic considerations like career concerns, or ulterior motives — we do not in general stop to make careful rational calculations of the long-term implications of forming and pursuing given interests, though we do sometimes. Given how important our choice of interests is it is remarkable how rarely we pause to consider these issues. Intrinsic interest was a central motivation for their development of their creative interests for most of the individuals whose creative developments I describe in this book; other factors may also have played a role, but intrinsic interest was, in many cases, primary. Intrinsic interest was the root of Alexander Calder's interest in the basic shapes of the universe arranged in space as a basis for art, and Henry Chen's interest in literary geography. Intrinsic interest and fascination were the basis of Roger Knowles's interest — he told me he thought that how neurons develop into their shapes "would be a fascinating topic to investigate." Intrinsic interest is the basis of our childhood and youth interests and activities, out of which, as described in the preceding chapter, our mature creative interests often develop. We engage in and pursue interests and activities as children and youths, often in company with others, primarily for the sheer joy of it, and for the challenges they offer, without giving much thought to how our interests in them may evolve or how we may develop them creatively as adults. It is clear, as examples, that both Walt Disney's and Charles Darwin's childhood interests were intrinsically based.

Intrinsic interest is the central driving force in the development of our interests in both their earlier and later stages of development. In the initial stage, when particular experiences and elements catch our attention and spark our interest, our response is in most cases rooted in intrinsic interest — we are drawn to these experiences and elements and respond to them spontaneously and intuitively, driven by our interest. In later stages other factors may play a larger role; I describe the most important of these in the next chapter. But intrinsic interest continues to be a main force driving our development of our interest. We naturally tend to think about experiences, topics, and elements — questions, ideas, theories, phenomena, data — that we find intrinsically interesting, to dwell upon them in our minds and wonder about them, exploring different aspects of them, perhaps imagining them differently, and seek to learn more about them — all of which spurs our interest in them. In turn, through thinking and wondering about them and learning about them our interest in them grows, at least in many cases (in some cases we find we are not especially interested in them and move on to other interests and topics), and we form conceptions of what interests us about them, defining what aspects of them we find especially interesting and would like to explore in greater depth, defining ways we would like to try to develop them creatively, imagining their creative potential — thus our interests evolve from initial stages to fuller conceptions.

Intrinsic interest is in general rooted in specific sources of interest — specific feelings, perceptions, beliefs, and judgements. In the remainder of this chapter I list, discuss, and provide examples of the most common and important of these sources. Any such list is necessarily somewhat arbitrary; further, in most cases there are multiple sources of interest for any particular creative interest, as the examples in this chapter and throughout the book show. Nonetheless, I believe such a list and description of intrinsic sources is useful.

A final introductory note: we do not in the ordinary course of events necessarily recognize clearly the intrinsic sources of our interests — we are not necessarily prone to such introspection. Further, knowing the sources of our interest is not necessarily likely to help us in our creative development of it, thus we have no strong motivation to try to determine what its sources are.

Nonetheless I believe identifying main sources of interests is useful for developing a deeper understanding of creative development.

RICHNESS

A fundamental source of intrinsic interest is the sense of richness, the sense
that a domain is filled with riches — teeming with interesting, fascinating
elements — a large number and variety of elements, possibly organized and
arranged in subtle or complex ways. The sense that a domain is rich, imagining
its riches, is exciting and both sparks and spurs our interest. We are excited to
explore the domain and discover its riches — indeed there is often a sense of
mystery and adventure about exploring it. We want to explore and try to uncover
its laws of organization and dynamics and understand its deeper meanings, and
to develop it, in its richness, creatively, though we don't generally initially have
a very clear idea how we will go about doing so. Thinking about the domain and
its rich possibilities creates a rich ferment of ideas, wonderings, and possibilities
in our mind which is a rich seedbed out of which we form a conception of what
our interest is, defining our interest more precisely and often conceptually in
ways that go beyond the way we think about the domain at first, when our
interest is first sparked.

Susan Ferguson and Charles Darwin both formed interests in rich domains,
and in both of their cases a sense of the richness of the domain that interested
them seems to have been vital in sparking their interest and in their developing
a lasting interest in the domain. Susan perceived the linguistic environment in
Kenya to be extraordinarily rich, and it is clear from the way she described her
interest that its richness as a domain was a major factor in her fascination and
interest. As discussed in the last chapter, she described being fascinated by the
incredible diversity of languages and rich commingling of languages — she
could, she told me, go into "endless details" on this topic, conveying her sense
of its richness as a domain. In describing patterns of language usage she told
me, "there were so many different kinds of people that I would speak to, and in
so many different kinds of situations" — a phrase that suggests a multiplication
table pairing different people with different situations, generating the potential
for an enormous variety of encounters — a rich set of possibilities, each with
its own rules of engagement, some quite subtle. And, as noted also in the last
chapter, she was fascinated by the use of English in Kenya. Here again she told
me there are "endless details" to be explored about the way it is used, and "a lot
of strange and interesting nuances," again giving the sense of a rich domain.
Darwin found the incredible richness and variety of life-forms fascinating; his
sense of their richness and variety, of the myriads of species and the subtleties

of similarities and differences across species, was a prime source driving his interest in collecting and natural history. Amassing collections, including his vast collection of beetles, and spending time examining and classifying them clearly deepened his sense for the rich diversity of forms; and the very activity of collecting undoubtedly gave him the sense that there are always more kinds, more species beyond those already named and known waiting to be discovered, spurring his interest. His fascination and sheer delight at the richness and variety of life-forms reached almost a fever pitch when he first came to South America. In his *Beagle* Diary he describes walking in the Brazilian tropical forests in a state of rapture, experiencing "transports of pleasure," his senses and mind overwhelmed with the rich luxuriance of the vegetation, the beautiful flowers and trees, the vast, uncountable numbers of species of insects and plants — he describes his mind as a "chaos of delight."[1] His fascination with the richness and rich variety of life extended beyond an interest in the diversity of life-forms to a fascination with the incredibly subtle and diverse ways in which these life-forms are adapted to their environment. In his *Autobiography*, discussing the origins of his theory of evolution by natural selection, he writes that he "had always been much struck" by the "innumerable cases in which organisms of every kind are beautifully adapted to their conditions of life" — thus again his language illuminates a rich domain.[2] Darwin formed a conceptually more defined interest over time, as described in the last chapter, fitting the description above — fashioning a conceptually defined and structured interest out of the richness of a domain.

It is noteworthy that Darwin often employs metaphors of mineral riches and treasure in his diary and letters to describe the riches of nature. For example, he writes in his diary, "a forest is a gold mine to a Naturalist & yesterday's [collections] a very rich one," and in a letter to a fellow beetle hunter in England writes that "the brilliancy of the Scenery throws one into a delirium

[1] His most vivid descriptions and feelings of rapture are associated with his first few days in South America, walking in the forests around Bahia, the *Beagle's* first port of call in South America. On the day of his arrival he wrote: "The delight one experiences in such times bewilders the mind. If the eye attempts to follow the flight of a gaudy butter-fly, it is arrested by some strange tree or fruit; if watching an insect one forgets it in the strange flower it is crawling over. — if turning to admire the splendour of the scenery, the individual character of the foreground fixes the attention. The mind is a chaos of delight, out of which a world of future & more quiet pleasure will arise." He continued in a similar vein on succeeding days. For these quotes and his description of his first days in the forests and South America see Charles Darwin, *Charles Darwin's Beagle Diary*, pp. 42–44.
[2] Charles Darwin, *The Autobiography of Charles Darwin*, p. 119.

of delight and a Beetle hunter is not likely soon to awaken from it, when whichever way he turns fresh treasures meet his eye."[3] In my experience this kind of language is quite common among individuals who are motivated in their interest by the sense of richness. Thus Cheryl Nixon, describing her quest to find rare eighteenth-century books by female authors, told me she perceived "the library as having all of these riches" that if she could "unlock" would reveal "all sorts of interesting materials." Also William Faulkner described finding or imagining a "gold mine" of characters he could write about in developing his interest in depicting in literature the world of his youth.

There are different kinds of rich domains that are the basis of creative interests. Many rich domains that spark and are the basis of interests are domains of real phenomena, as was the case for Susan Ferguson and Charles Darwin. Others are largely imaginary.[4] For example, the domain that interested Alexander Calder, basic shapes of the universe arranged in space and in different kinds of motion, is, while based on real phenomena, in terms of his conception fundamentally imaginary. Other domains are conceptual — domains of ideas, theories, and conceptual possibilities. Of course all domains of interest are to a degree conceptual, but some are more directly so. An example is Virginia Woolf's conception of our reflections and a world defined by such reflections. As she conceived it this seems to have been a rich domain for development by writers — "those are the depths they will explore, those the phantoms they will pursue," she writes, conveying her sense of a rich domain to be explored.

Many rich domains of interest are field based. For such field-based domains knowledge of the field is generally crucial for appreciating the richness of the domain. Thus, for individuals who form interests in field-based domains that they perceive to be rich, their sense of the richness of the domain is generally rooted in their knowledge about their field, and individuals outside the field would typically not perceive the domain as so rich. Hans Krebs's sense of the many possibilities open to him applying manometric techniques to study intermediary metabolism (see Chapter 6) is shown in a statement he made describing his perception when he first set up his own independent lab to pursue his interest: "[there were] so many pebbles on the beach," he said — so many possible reactions to investigate and experiments to choose among. It is doubtful people outside chemistry would have perceived this domain

---

[3]*Charles Darwin's Beagle Diary*, p. 74, and Darwin to Frederick Watkins, 18 August 1832, in Charles Darwin, *The Correspondence of Charles Darwin*, 1, pp. 260–61.

[4]Of course even individuals with interests in real domains, like Susan and Darwin, exercise their imagination in imagining the domain of their interest.

to have been so rich; indeed, even other individuals working in biological chemistry and allied fields at the time probably did not fully share his sense of the richness of possibilities opened up in applying quantitative techniques in this area, which contributed to making his interest pioneering.[5]

CURIOSITY AND WONDER

A second fundamental source of intrinsic interest is curiosity. If we are curious about something then it follows that we are interested in it at some level — for if we were not we would not have any curiosity about it, would simply ignore it. To form a creative interest requires more than just passing curiosity of course; to form an interest our curiosity must endure and grow, so that we continue to think about the issue or element — for example, phenomenon, puzzle, model, or idea — that sparks our curiosity, and form an interest based on it, that we want to explore and pursue.

Curiosity is an important source of interests in most fields of creative endeavor. It is classically important in fields in which the primary objective is to gain understanding and knowledge, including the sciences, social sciences, and philosophy, as well as other fields. Many of the neuroscientists I interviewed described an important source of their initial interest in neuroscience being curiosity about the answers to the great questions that define neuroscience as a field, questions like those presented in the last chapter: How does the brain work? What is the basis of memory? How is the brain designed? How does it develop? Curiosity about such questions is what first drew Roger Knowles to neuroscience. He told me he "liked the idea of thinking about the human brain as this sort of puzzle," and that what "intrigued" him at first was wondering how the brain is designed and put together. A number of the neuroscientists also described their more specific creative interests in ways that indicate curiosity was an important source of their interest. Thus for Sophia Colamarino, whose development and conception of her interest I describe below, curiosity was a main source of her fascination with axon growth cones. She described watching growth cones grow and wondering what makes them grow, and said as she studied she kept wondering why and how they are guided along the intricate paths they travel to reach their targets. Albert Einstein stated that what set him apart was that he was "intensely curious" about certain questions. Curiosity is also an important source of interests in the arts; see the discussion of conceptual artist Robert Irwin's development below.

[5]Frederic Holmes, *Hans Krebs: The Formation of a Scientific Life*, p. 248. Actually, like many scientists, Krebs focused less on the domain of phenomena itself, and more on the domain of potential experiments and connected hypotheses concerning metabolic processes he might investigate; see my discussion in Chapter 6.

Curiosity is linked to questions. When we are curious about something our curiosity normally can be framed, and is framed by us, at least in part, in terms of questions. Thus interests rooted in curiosity often center on and are constructed around questions. Questions are generally recognized as important for creativity. In the standard model of creative development as problem finding questions are central — in this depiction of creative development an individual finds a question or problem to focus on, then works to solve it creatively.[6] There is a fundamental element of truth in this in a fair number of cases. But it is fundamentally incorrect in describing too narrow a base for our development. Questions and problems often are an important source and driver of our development of our interests, in grabbing our attention and sparking our interest through sparking our curiosity. Quite often, even typically in such cases, however, these initial questions serve as seeds out of or on the basis of which an individual forms a creative interest. Thus, in many cases an individual's curiosity and interest is sparked initially by a relatively narrowly focused question or problem; then, as he explores this question or problem, thinks and learns about it, he discovers or formulates additional questions, problems, issues, and topics related to it, as well as new ways of thinking about and approaching it, and he forms a conceptually broader and richer interest that is the basis for his development going forward. This was the case for Albert Einstein: Beginning from a paradox he hit upon he formed a richer interest expanding and branching out from it; see the end of the next chapter and in particular the discussion in Chapter 10.

In my experience it is also common for individuals to conceptualize their interests not as a single question but as a set of interrelated questions, again giving their interests a breadth that transcends a single question, defining a richer domain of interest.[7] Nick Halpern described having "all these questions" about prophets, their voices, and their relationship with their ordinary selves and their family that defined his creative interest. Charles Darwin formed an interest in a set of questions that he seems to have seen as interconnected: thus he was curious about the geographic extent of species, the temporal extent of species, and the relationships between neighboring species and varieties that appeared to be related. Robert Kaufman also described his literary interest as involving a number of interrelated questions.

Curiosity often continues to be important through much of a person's development, with the focus of his curiosity evolving as he matures in his

[6] In fact the drive to solve a problem is in many cases rooted not so much in curiosity but equally or more in the sense of challenge, discussed in the next section.

[7] Sometimes our interests emerge through our sensing intuitively that questions that had seemed disparate are in fact linked.

development. In a documentary film about his creative development entitled *The Beauty of Questions*, conceptual artist Robert Irwin describes following a pattern of development asking a series of questions, broadening out. Originally, in his twenties, he painted in the style of abstract expressionism; but, as he describes it, he had a sudden realization that his work was not good, that many of the elements in it were superfluous, and this triggered his embarking on a long journey of discovery and development. From this point on his development, again as he describes it, was organized around questions. He began by focusing on basic, specific questions, such as "What is the simplest, least evoking kind of mark" one can use in a painting? which he decided was the straight line, thus he painted only with lines for a period of time.[8] Over time, his questions and approach opened up to a broader, more conceptually based interest, rooted in broader questioning — wondering and trying to define what is the essence of the artistic experience, leading him to explore philosophy and conceptual approaches to art, which led eventually to his becoming a pioneer in the development of conceptual art. I note as a somewhat opposite, related process of development, illustrated by some of the neuroscientists and discussed in slightly different guise in the preceding chapter, being curious about and interested initially in a "big" question, then narrowing down and focusing on a narrower topic or set of questions that are based in or linked with this big question.

The importance of curiosity in sparking creative interests, and the process of broadening out, is illustrated in an account Douglas Hofstadter has given of the origins of his interest in integer sequence patterns, an interest that led him eventually, in combination with other interests, to the ideas at the heart of his acclaimed book *Gödel, Escher, Bach*.[9]

Hofstadter writes that at the age of 16 he became curious about "the relationship between the triangular numbers and the squares — in particular how they interleave along the number line." The squares are the numbers 1, 4, 9, 16, 25, ..., and the triangular numbers are 1, 3, 6, 10, 15, 21, ..., the nth triangular number being defined as the sum of the first n integers, for example, the 5th triangular number is $1 + 2 + 3 + 4 + 5 = 15$. Combining the two

---

[8]This quote and the description are from the documentary: Robert Irwin, *The Beauty of Questions*, produced by Leonard Feinstein; catalog #38407 (Berkeley, CA: UC Extension Center for Media and Independent Learning, 1997).

[9]See Douglas R. Hofstadter and the Fluid Analogies Research Group, *Fluid Concepts and Creative Analogies: Computer Models of the Fundamental Mechanisms of Thought* (New York: Basic Books, 1995), pp. 7, 13–25. My account simplifies somewhat the sequence of steps he describes having gone through, without however altering the essence of his description.

sequences, with their terms placed in order of increasing magnitude, produces the sequence

1, 1, 3, **4**, 6, **9**, 10, 15, **16**, 21, **25**, 28, **36**, 36, 45, **49**, 55, **64**, 66, 78, **81**, ... ,

with the squares set in boldface.[10] To investigate the pattern of interleaving Douglas counted the number of triangular numbers between each successive pair of squares, generating a derived sequence — 2, 1, 2, 1, 1, 2, 1, 2 — for the initial segment above, which suggests that the number of intervening triangular numbers is consistently either one or two, but does not show a clear pattern beyond this.

Tantalized by this sequence, Douglas was driven to explore it further. Believing that the derived sequence must have a hidden pattern, that there is a rule that determines the number of 1's between each successive pair of 2's, he became focused on figuring out what this rule is. He writes that he computed hundreds of squares and triangular numbers, placing them in sequence, then counting the number of triangular numbers between each pair of squares to compute the derivative sequence, the first segment of which, starting with the initial fragment above and extending significantly farther out, is

2, 1, 2, 1, 1, 2, 1, 2, 1, 2, 1, 1, 2, 1, 2, 1, 1, 2, 1, 2, 1, 2, 1, 2, 1, 1, 2, 1, 2, 1, 2, 1, 1, 2, 1, 2, 1,

1, 2, 1, 2, 1, 2, 1, 1, 2, ...   (A)

The basic structure of this sequence is that the 2's always occur as singletons, while the 1's occur either as singletons or doubletons. This structure made it seem promising that the sequence has a simple pattern, but Douglas was unable to discover a rule that correctly predicts where in the sequence the 1's occur as doubletons. Eventually, it occurred to him to count the number of 1's between each successive pair of 2's and write these numbers down as a new sequence, which he hoped would show a clearer pattern. The first term of this new sequence is 1, because there is a single 1 between the first and second 2 in A, the second term is 2, and, calculated as far out as A is calculated above, the sequence is

1, 2, 1, 1, 2, 1, 2, 1, 1, 2, 1, 2, 1, 2, 1, 1, 2, ...   (B)

B is similar to A in that it contains 1's and 2's, with the 2's always occurring as singletons and the 1's occurring either as singletons or doubletons, a resemblance Douglas found intriguing; but it is not identical to A, and Douglas could not

---

[10] Some numbers, including 1 and 36, appear in both sequences; in these cases Hofstadter placed them in the combined sequence twice, assigning the first number of each such pair to the squares and the second to the triangular numbers.

discover any simple relationship between the two sequences. It occurred to him to try applying the same operation to B that he had applied to A, so he counted the number of 1's between successive pairs of 2's (omitting the first 1, which is not, strictly speaking, between two 2's), and placed them in sequence:

$$2, 1, 2, 1, 1, 2, \ldots \qquad (C)$$

These six terms are exactly the same as the first six terms of A. Douglas, finding this remarkable and exciting, computed more terms, and discovered that C is in fact identical to A. The rule describing the pattern of interleaving is thus recursive: the pattern of interleaving in the original sequence of squares and triangular numbers, given by A, itself has a pattern of interleaving, given by B, which in turn has a pattern of interleaving given by C. Since C is identical to A, it must have the same pattern of interleaving, given by B, and hence the pair (A, B) repeats itself forever. Further, because the rule is recursive the pattern cannot be periodic — that is, it can never repeat itself, no matter how many terms in the sequence are computed. To see why, suppose that in fact A did repeat after some number of terms, say, after 100 terms. Then sequence C, since it is derived from A through condensation (in the sequences shown above, for example, 42 terms of A condense to 6 terms of C), would begin repeating sooner than 100 terms, and that would mean that A also must begin to repeat after this fewer number of terms since C and A are identical, contradicting the original assumption that A begins to repeat only after 100 terms.

Describing how he felt at the time he made this discovery, Douglas writes that the recursive rule seemed to him "mysterious," that in discovering that the pattern never repeats he felt he had uncovered something "complex and elusive, something much harder to pin down than mere repetition."[11] He clearly had been somewhat curious about mathematical sequences before this, as is evident by the fact that he was curious about the relationship between the triangular numbers and the squares. But the discovery marked a watershed in his development. In its wake, his conception of the nature of sequences altered; he saw that their rules are far more complex, subtle, and interesting than he had imagined, and gained confidence that with enough effort and ingenuity it was possible to figure out the rules governing them, even for complex, seemingly patternless sequences. His curiosity and interest in discovering the rules governing integer sequences blossomed, and investigating sequences became a central intellectual activity for him — a creative interest; and over the next few years, he writes, he investigated hundreds. Thus curiosity led him to investigate a given problem, which he solved, finding a solution deeper and more interesting than he had expected. And spurred on by this solution and

[11] Ibid., pp. 23–24.

his experience working and solving the problem he formed a broader interest
which he pursued.

The sense of wonder is another source of intrinsic interest. Wonder is in-spired in us by experiences, works, phenomena, events, and ideas that amaze and astonish us, that we marvel at. The objects of our wonder seem extraor-dinary; often they have an air of mystery about them, sometimes a grandeur. Wonder is a natural source of creative interests: we are naturally drawn to want to learn more about an object of our wonder and to explore it. Like the great questions and themes of fields, objects of our wonder are often too large and far-off to be suitable in and of themselves for creative interests, but they inspire and are the basis of creative interests.

Wonder is linked with curiosity in that when we experience wonder we are also normally curious to know and understand more about the object of our wonder, including how and why it has come to pass or come into being or how it functions. But wonder includes feelings and attitudes that distinguish it from curiosity. In particular, when we experience wonder we not only have a sense of curiosity but also experience feelings of awe, and possibly reverence, for the object of our wonder and its maker or the forces that have brought it into being. Wonder is also linked to novelty — novel experiences, ideas, events and phenomena are especially likely to strike us as unusual and out of the ordinary and thus to inspire wonder in us.[12] However, experiences, events, and elements that are not novel certainly can and do inspire wonder in us — we can feel a sense of wonder about love even after having experienced it many times, and the mysteries of life and the universe continue to inspire wonder in us long after we first learn about them.

Wonder was an important source or factor in the development of their cre-ative interests for a number of the neuroscientists I interviewed. To give one example here, feelings of wonder, joined with curiosity, awe, reverence, and a sense of beauty, were fundamental sources of the interest Sophia Colamarino formed, which became her main creative interest, in the processes through

[12]In his essay "The Principles which lead and direct Philosophical Enquiries: illus-trated by the History of Astronomy" Adam Smith writes that we experience wonder when we encounter a novel element that does not fit naturally into one of our cus-tomary categories or is an unusual case, or when events occur in a manner that does not fit into our preexisting theories about either their customary relationship to one another or their natural order of succession, and he argues that feelings of wonder are a principal source of our interest in philosophy and the sciences. His essay is in *Adam Smith, Essays on Philosophical Subjects*, Vol. 3 of the Works and Correspondence of Adam Smith, ed. W.P.D. Wightman and J.C. Bryce (Indianapolis, IN: Liberty Classics, 1980), pp. 33–105; for wonder see the Introduction and Sections I and II, pp. 33–47.

which axons growth cones grow and are guided along their intricate, complex paths to reach their targets. Sophia's interest originated during her senior year in college in a class in which she was introduced to neuroanatomy. She described being amazed — as she is still to this day — at the complexity of our neuroanatomy, especially the complexity of the paths axons follow, and wondering how axons know where to go — what guides them to their targets. "It's so complicated, I think that's what makes it so incredibly cool to me." "The fact that cranial nerve seven grows around the nucleus of cranial nerve six before it exits, and all these little loops and dips and contrasts. As I studied I just kept thinking, 'Why the heck does it do that, why?'"[13] Sophia's sense of wonder and her interest grew in graduate school. Sophia chose to study under a scientist who studied pathfinding, and at the time of our interview she vividly remembered sitting with him, watching axon growth cones grow through a microscope. "We'd sit there together, late at night, passing the microscope back and forth, pointing out incredible growth cones to each other. The beauty of them. Again the wonderment — what is it that they know that we don't know? It's almost like they have a mind. . . . [I sat there and wondered] what is making these things grow? why are they growing?" Sophia's sense of "wonderment" beautifully expresses the idea of wonder as a source of interest and shows the way wonder includes or involves a mixture of curiosity and amazement. Sophia also described her awe and reverence at the remarkably complicated paths nerves are able to trace and the incredible architecture of the nervous system. "It's so amazing. And I'm not terribly religious, but it makes you think that there is a God. How do we work? Why does this [the nervous system] do this, how does this ever come together and make us work? It's amazing that it does."[14]

Wonder was vital for Rachel Carson in her belief system and creative development. She believed, and wrote, that wonder is crucial in sparking our interest in the natural world. She also referred frequently to her feeling of reverence for nature in her writings, a feeling that seems to have been closely connected in her mind with the sense of wonder, and which was important for her in justifying and explaining her strong feelings about and feeling of connection with nature and her interest in preserving it. Early letters and essays she wrote, as well as anecdotal evidence, indicate that her own early interest in the sea,

[13] Sophia shared with me some of her notes from the class, her exam, and grade sheet. Her notes show very detailed note-taking, a sign of her interest. Sophia scored extremely well on the exam and earned a high grade, also a sign of her interest.

[14] There were also other factors that contributed to Sophia's interest. In particular a second facet of her interest was an interest in axon regeneration following trauma and injury; see Chapter 5.

her first love in nature, was rooted in her sense of its mystery, mystique, and
power — feelings linked to feelings of awe and wonder.[15]

CHALLENGE AND DIFFICULTNESS

A third source of intrinsic interest is the desire to take on or respond to a
challenge. Challenges are inherently interesting — they represent something
or some achievement or work or state that has not yet been achieved, generally
not even fully thought out, and it is exciting to imagine achieving or creating
them — hence are a natural basis for interests we form and pursue. Intrinsically
we want to challenge ourselves in choosing interests to pursue.

When individuals form an interest in a challenge often they focus on a
particular aspect of it or a particular way of approaching it. Thus they define
their interest more specifically than simply the challenge itself, focusing in
terms of what they wish to explore and pursue, viewing themselves in many
cases not as likely to achieve it fully themselves but rather contributing to a
larger effort to achieve it. A good example of this is Wilbur Wright's view of
what he hoped to accomplish at the time he first formed an interest in flight,
described below. Delimiting our interest in this way, and being comfortable
doing so — recognizing and being comfortable with the idea that what we
achieve may be limited — is crucial, at least in some cases, for while challenges
are interesting, they also can be daunting. Indeed our response to a challenge
that sparks our interest in most cases takes one of two opposite forms: in some
cases a challenge that attracts our interest motivates us to form and pursue some
aspect of it or way of approaching it as an interest; but in other cases, although
we find a challenge interesting, we find it too daunting and unlikely ever to be
able to be achieved through our efforts, and we turn away from it, despite our
interest, to pursue other interests. As a further, related point, it typically takes
a degree of knowledge to truly appreciate a challenge; thus we are especially
likely to form an interest in a challenge at a point in our development when
we have attained enough knowledge to appreciate it.

Many challenges take the form of a question or set of questions to try to
answer, a problem or set of problems to try to solve, or a goal or set of goals to

[15]Rachel wrote about the importance of our sense of wonder in *The Sense of Wonder*
(New York: Harper & Row, 1956). Neighbors of the Carsons told the story that, as a child,
Rachel discovered a fossilized shell and this sparked her own curiosity and wonder about
the sea; see Linda Lear, *Rachel Carson: Witness for Nature* (New York: Henry Holt and
Company, 1997), pp. 7–8. Her later mature interest in the sea was more scientifically
based and based in the reality of experience of the sea and seashore, which she had not
experienced growing up inland, in Pennsylvania. Even so it undoubtedly had roots and
flowed from her early romantic sense of wonder and mystery about the sea.

try to attain. The sense of challenge indeed is one of the main factors or sources generating interests in questions, problems, and goals — the desire to meet the challenge offered, both to be challenged and to respond to the challenge, are often crucial factors in triggering our interest in these cases and leading us to pursue our interest. Douglas Hofstadter was clearly attracted to investigating the pattern of overlap between the squares and triangular numbers in part because it was a challenging problem. Posing a challenge is not enough, of course — we must also find the subject matter inherently interesting, but, given that, the sense of a challenge is often vital in drawing us in and generating the drive to engage with the subject. Indeed so long as we are free to form whatever interests we wish, and are influenced and guided primarily by our sense of what is intrinsically interesting, not by ulterior motives, it seems likely that we will become truly interested only in questions, problems, and goals that pose a challenge of some kind; for those that don't pose a challenge will inevitably seem boring and will not hold our interest.

There are two basic patterns of development for interests for which challenge is a main source of the interest. In some cases the pattern follows the description above: a person focuses his interest on specific aspects or elements of a larger challenge. One form of this is for a person's interest to be sparked by a challenge that seems essentially impossible to attain in the foreseeable future, much like the great questions that define fields, and then, through a process of narrowing down, for the person to form a more practical, specific interest linked to the challenge and its ultimate attainment. In other cases a person's interest is sparked by a relatively narrowly defined challenge, such as a specific problem or question, then his focus broadens and he forms a broader creative interest growing from it, as happened for Douglas Hofstadter.

Among the individuals I interviewed, challenge was clearly important as a source of interest for a number of the mathematicians. It was, for example, a primary motivation driving Victoria Rayskin — as she described her own development — in the formation and pursuit of the interest that was the center of focus for her in her work through graduate school. Victoria was given a difficult problem in analysis for her thesis by her advisor in college, which she was able to solve following an approach he outlined for her. She enjoyed the process of working on the problem, including the challenge of it and the feeling that she could successfully meet the challenge, and upon entering graduate school she told me she wanted to continue to work on more difficult versions of it. "I wanted to solve that problem," she said, and it was clear from our interview that she was attracted by the challenge of it. I describe how she was led to reformulate it in a broader, conceptually more sophisticated form, thus into more of a true interest, in Chapter 7. Challenge has also been important for Colin Ingalls, another mathematician I interviewed, in the development of his interests (see below).

Beyond mathematics, the desire to take on a challenge is important as a source of interest in fields of invention, including engineering, and medicine and business. Individuals working in these fields often develop creative interests that are sparked by and center around doing something that has never been done before or designing and creating something that has never been made or designed before. Many factors contribute to such interests, including curiosity and the extrinsic factors of hoped for rewards and fame; but the desire to take on the challenge of achieving what has never been achieved before — even what others say is impossible — is in many cases central. Wilbur Wright's interest in flight, described below, is an outstanding example of an interest in a field of invention sparked by, rooted in, and spurred on by the sense of a challenge.

It is often said that "necessity is the mother of invention," meaning that we are spurred to be creative — especially in fields of invention and practical fields like business — by obstacles and problems we must overcome and needs we are driven to find a way to satisfy. Necessity is in some cases the basis for creative interests we form. More commonly, however, necessity comes into play later in our development, after we have formed interests, either when a need arises or is brought to our attention that fits with one of our interests and that we believe we have the expertise to address, or when we are engaged in a project and encounter a problem or obstacle.[16] Challenges thus seem to be more important in sparking our interests than needs and obstacles that block our path forward. Further, they affect us very differently — we engage with challenges and form interests based in them because we want to, of our own free will, because we find them intrinsically interesting, not because we feel driven to out of necessity. However, necessity and challenge are not mutually exclusive; necessity can spur a sense of challenge.

Difficultness is another related source of interests. Complex, difficult subjects, such as abstruse theories and complex phenomena, pose a challenge of understanding, and the desire to rise to the challenge is often an important source of interests we form in them and based on them — important in both spurring and holding our interest. Even beyond the challenge they pose, their very difficulty is itself attracting and draws us, similar to the way the sense of richness is a source of interest. Imagining grappling with such difficult and

[16]Subrata Dasgupta discusses necessity as an important source of problems in engineering and technology and provides examples in *Technology and Creativity*, chap. 3. In all of the cases he describes it is almost certainly the case that the individuals involved had formed interests prior to the episode he describes that were important in leading them to recognize and decide to pursue the problems they worked on.

complex subjects can be daunting, of course, and in some cases this discourages us and damps our interest. But in other cases we are drawn to a theory, topic, body of phenomena, issue, or work precisely because of its difficulty and complexity, become deeply engrossed in it, and develop an interest based in it. Jeffrey Shoulson, a literary scholar I interviewed, is an example of someone who was drawn to a work — *Paradise Lost*, known for its difficultness — by its difficulty. Describing his first encounter with it, as a freshman in college, Jeffrey told me he "was attracted to it, more than anything else, by its difficulty," by how "resistant" it seemed to be to any "simple reading and immediate comprehension." Drawn to it by its difficulty, by the challenge of understanding it and developing his own interpretation of its meaning, he developed an interest in it — specifically focusing on its connection or resemblance to rabbinic literature — that was at the center of his creative work for more than a decade.[17] Colin Ingalls is drawn to subjects of great complexity and with many details. He told me he gets very "into" them and forms interests in them that become the focus of his work. For example, he was drawn to abstract algebra, which he began to learn independently, by its difficulty and the challenge and great undertaking of understanding it and working creatively in it as a field. At the time I interviewed him he was taking on the challenge of learning Japanese.

For Wilbur Wright a deep personal desire for a challenge seems to have been crucial in leading him to form and pursue an interest in flight. In his biography *The Bishop's Boys* Tom Crouch writes that Wilbur had "longed for a challenge; a measure of himself," and describes how Wilbur came to the realization, in the winter of 1899, that flight — working towards the construction of a flying machine — was the challenge he had been searching for, forming the decision, then or soon thereafter, to pursue flight as an active interest.

Wilbur's turn to flight came after many years during which he seems to have felt that he had failed to realize his potential and utilize his abilities to the fullest, had failed to find his true calling. Wilbur had been an outstanding student with

---

[17] Jeffrey is Jewish and attended a Jewish day high school. As a result he was steeped in Jewish literature and lore, including the Midrash; this was a register of meaning for him, which was important in sparking his interest in *Paradise Lost*. He told me that an important factor in his becoming interested in it was that it struck him as "uncannily familiar" — reminded him in some way of Midrash — and this became the basis for his creative interest. For more on his development see Chapters 11 and 14. Jeffrey's first book, reflecting his interest and development of it over a number of years, is *Milton and the Rabbis: Hebraism, Hellenism, and Christianity* (New York: Columbia University Press, 2001).

a promising future. But in the winter of 1885 he was hit in the face by a bat and suffered a severe illness. This seems to have produced a deep depression in him and he became a recluse, withdrawn and inactive. Four years after the accident he emerged from his withdrawn state and began collaborating with Orville, who was four years younger, first in building and running a printing press and publishing a local paper, and later, beginning in 1892, in running a bicycle shop.[18] Orville and Wilbur achieved modest success in their business and became known locally for their mechanical prowess and ingenuity. But it seems, based on the limited evidence that exists, that Wilbur felt unfulfilled. He wrote a letter to his father in 1894 in which he stated that he was considering taking a college course, and, explaining his motives, wrote, "I do not think I am specially fitted for success in any commercial pursuit," suggesting his unhappiness in his current occupation. He also wrote, "intellectual effort is a pleasure to me" — a phrase that rings of his desire for a challenge worthy of his intellect and ability.[19] His father offered Wilbur money for college, but Wilbur did not accept it and did not pursue his education. Instead he and Orville expanded their bicycle business and began building their own bicycles. But Wilbur seems to have continued to feel unfulfilled. His feelings about himself, that he had failed to realize his potential, are revealed in a letter to his sister-in-law about her plans for her son, written in the spring of 1901, two years after he and Orville had begun to pursue flight, but revealing of feelings and assessments about himself that had dogged him by this time for many years. He writes that her son, like Wilbur and his brothers, possesses "talent sufficient to make him really great." But neither Wilbur nor his brothers had achieved success to match their talents, they had failed to find a calling to match their talents: "None of us has as yet made particular use of the talent in which he excels other men, that is why our success has been very moderate" — and her son is in danger of the same fate. And in a remark that has great poignancy, he writes, in reference to his sister-in-law's son, "if left to himself he will not find out what he would like to be until his chance to attain his wish is past" — a comment that almost certainly refers to his view of his own life. Even though he and Orville had already begun to pursue flight, he feared, at the age of 34, that although he had finally found a challenge worthy of his talents it might

[18]See Tom D. Crouch, *The Bishop's Boys* (New York: W.W. Norton & Company, 1989), chaps. 5-8.

[19]The letter is in *Miracle at Kitty Hawk: The Letters of Wilbur and Orville Wright*, ed. Fred C. Kelly (New York: Farrar, Straus and Young, 1951); dated Sep. 12, 1894, pp. 8–11. For relevant portions and discussion see Harry Combs (with Martin Caidin), *Kill Devil Hill* (New York: Houghton Mifflin Company, 1979), p. 38. For Wilbur's mental state see *The Bishop's Boys*, pp. 104, 129–31, and 164.

be too late, that he would not be able to achieve all that would be possible if he were younger.[20]

According to a deposition he later gave, Wilbur first became interested in aeronautics in the late summer of 1896, his interest sparked by newspaper reports of the death of Otto Lilienthal, the German aeronautical pioneer, in a gliding accident.[21] Over the next few years his interest simmered — thus he delayed pursuing it, as Hans Krebs was delayed (prevented) from pursuing his interest; during this time his interest may have been shared by Orville, but that is not certain. Then, in the winter and spring of 1899, it emerged full-fledged, kindled by a book he and Orville read about animal locomotion and aeronautics — most likely *Animal Locomotion or Walking, Swimming, and Flying, with a Dissertation on Aëronautics* by J. Bell Pettigrew, of which well over half is devoted to flight and aeronautics — and by the conclusion he had come to that human flight was possible — that if birds and insects and other creatures could fly, so could people.[22] Wilbur wrote to the Smithsonian in May

[20]For the relevant portions of the letter and a discussion of what it reveals about Wilbur's psychological state see *The Bishop's Boys*, pp. 129–31. At the time the brothers had not yet achieved much success in their attack on the problem of flight, which undoubtedly contributed to Wilbur's tone in the letter. According to Tom Crouch it was Adrian Kinnane who first called attention to this letter for what it reveals about Wilbur's psychological state at the time in "The Crucible of Flight" (unpublished manuscript). Ironically, Wilbur's self-awareness of his inability thus far in his life to find a creative outlet for his talents was probably important in pushing him to find such an outlet.

[21]The deposition is cited in Wilbur and Orville Wright, *The Papers of Wilbur and Orville Wright*, ed. Marvin W. McFarland (New York: McGraw-Hill, 1953) in the footnotes on pp. 6–7. He also said this in the lecture he delivered to the Western Society of Engineers in Chicago on September 18, 1901; see *Papers of Wilbur and Orville Wright*, p. 103. In a rudimentary form Wilbur's interest went back to childhood; he is reported to have been an avid kite flyer when young. In addition, the brothers had known about Lilienthal and his exploits for some time. An article about Lilienthal had appeared in the weekly *McLure's* in the summer of 1994, and although it is not certain that Wilbur and Orville saw it they did regularly read *McLure's*. Even earlier, in 1890, Wilbur had picked up a report circulated by the news service they subscribed to describing Lilienthal's success lifting himself into the air with wings, writing about it humorously in their newspaper; see *The Bishop's Boys*, p. 159.

[22]J. Bell Pettigrew, *Animal Locomotion or Walking, Swimming, and Flying, with a Dissertation on Aëronautics* (New York: D. Appleton & Company, 1874). It is not certain this is the book the Wright brothers read, but it is suggested that it is the book by Crouch, who argues that the book would have been accessible to them; see *The Bishop's Boys*, p. 160. Pettigrew presents a detailed discourse on flight, including discussion of different kinds of animal wingforms. Lore has it that at the time Wilbur first began to be interested in flight he spent many hours watching buzzards and other large birds

of that year requesting whatever papers the Smithsonian had published on the subject of flight, as well as a list of other works in print in English. In his letter he writes that he is firmly convinced that "human flight is possible and practical," and that he would like to "add" his "mite" towards the ultimate achievement of this goal. Thus at the time he seems to have considered human flight far-off and not likely to be attained by his generation, but ultimately attainable. This pairing is in fact characteristic of challenges that form the basis of creative interests. Such challenges are lofty, difficult to attain, and worthy of pursuit, but we must also perceive them as at least remotely possible and have the sense that our work, even if it does not itself meet the challenge, will contribute to progress towards meeting it eventually.[23]

Wilbur's development shows the drive for self-fulfillment as a vital force in creative development, and shows the desire or need to find or construct a challenge to take on and pursue driving the formation of an interest. From the start, it is noteworthy, Wilbur approached the problem of flight from a particular perspective — specifically, focusing on issues of stability and control, including turning, clearly linked to his expertise in bicycling — setting his interest apart from the focuses of interest of others pursuing flight.

NOVELTY

Novelty is another important source of intrinsic interest. Novel experiences and phenomena, facts, and ideas stand out and tend to draw our attention, because they jar with our preconceived notions of what the world is like and our expectations about what we will encounter; and for exactly this reason

circling in the air. He may first have become convinced that human flight was a real possibility watching these birds. Observing them he came to recognize that there are two different kinds of flight — flight sustained by flapping wings and gliding flight with fixed wings — and saw that, while it would not be possible to build a device strong enough to sustain flight by flapping wings, it might be possible to build a machine that would use wings for stability and control, the way large birds do, with a separate power source.

[23]For the letter see *Papers of Wilbur and Orville Wright*, pp. 4–5. Tom Crouch gives a useful discussion of Wilbur's developing interest in *The Bishop's Boys*, pp. 159–64. As he discusses, from several details, including the fact that the letter to the Smithsonian was written in the first-person singular, not plural, it seems very likely that Orville was significantly less interested than Wilbur in flight at this point. But Orville liked a challenge, too, and once he became involved his enthusiasm and energy and mechanical ingenuity were crucial. Historically, of course, flight had been viewed as one of the ultimate challenges for man, and for those individuals who pursued it as a serious interest there is little question that the challenge it posed was important in sparking their interest and spurring them on.

they are exciting and interesting. When we truly notice novel elements and experiences the effect on our development can be dramatic and drastic. They can cause a dramatic shift in our worldview and spark us to form new creative interests, thus dramatically altering the course of our development. However, precisely because they go against our preconceptions we often do not notice them — they are screened out by our preconceptions, which act like filters shaping our perceptions. Even in cases in which we do notice them often it is just in passing, and instead of dwelling on them we continue on the path we have been following, preoccupied with preexisting concerns.[24]

By definition novel experiences and elements are experiences and elements that we have never experienced or encountered before, that strike us as unusual and do not seem to fit into any conventional categories. Sometimes experiences and elements catch our attention and spark our interest because they are novel in this sense, but often when they do so it is not just because they are novel in this sense but because they seem radical — to break established conventions and rules, challenge prevailing beliefs, or cross conventional boundaries. Thus, what struck Maria Carrig about Thomas Middleton and sparked her interest in his work was his radicalness and subversiveness as a playwright, the way he seemed to break long-standing structural conventions of the theater and challenge conventional morality, a radicalness that stood out especially sharply because she juxtaposed his plays with those of his predecessor, Ben Jonson, who was far less radical.

Liz Yoder is an example of someone whose interest was sparked by a novel phenomenon that challenges established beliefs in her field, dramatically affecting the course of her development. Liz became interested in neuroscience during her last two years of college. Her initial interest was in the area of learning and memory, and she told me that on her applications to graduate programs in neuroscience, during the fall of her senior year, she wrote that she wanted to study the cellular basis of memory. But in the winter of her senior year, the winter of 1990, her attention was captured by a novel phenomenon completely unlike anything she had learned about previously, a calcium-based form of signaling by glial cells in the brain. Glial calcium signaling was reported in a paper published in *Science* that January, and a synopsis of the paper appeared in *Science News*. Liz told me she read *Science News* every week and saw the synopsis, but "didn't think anything about it" until another student made a presentation about the *Science* paper in one of her classes; I describe this event in the previous chapter, as the critical event that sparked her interest. Liz said, describing her reaction, "I was just flabbergasted. Because here I had been

---

[24]Sometimes we pass over them when we first encounter them, but later our thoughts return to them and we see their significance and become interested in them.

taking all these neuroscience classes, and I had never heard anything about these cells." It is not surprising that the glial cells had not been discussed in her classes, for historically they have been considered much less important than neurons and consequently have been investigated and discussed much less. And it was precisely because they hadn't been discussed in her classes that they caught her attention, for they were completely novel to her.[25] More than the glia themselves, however, it was the glial calcium signaling that she found fascinating and exciting, because it demonstrated the existence of a new form of signaling in the brain, which might potentially be a new form of communication among brain cells. She described the calcium indicator dyes used to detect calcium activity as providing "a whole new way of looking at nervous system function."

From the start Liz viewed glial signaling as radical, in the sense that it poses a fundamental challenge to the conventional view in neuroscience about how the brain works, which is that essentially all cognitive processing is performed by the neurons, with the glia serving merely as support cells. In fact she seems to have been attracted not only by the scientific radicalness of the glial signaling, but also by the fact that it seemed to be radical in the sense of a challenge to authority in the field. Indeed she seems to have believed that there was a kind of conspiracy and cover-up — that the neuroscience establishment was intentionally not teaching students about the glial cells and glial signaling, which provoked her and made her even more determined to find out about them. "[It was] very interesting to me," she told me, "that you could have these cells out there that I had heard nothing about in all of my courses. And the more I looked into it the more [I realized] 'Wow! They're there, they're doing these things, and they're not telling us anything about them.' Yeah, the fact that they weren't telling us anything about them made me want to find out more about them."[26]

[25]Liz sent me copies of both the *Science* article and the write-up in *Science Express*; the *Science* article is: A.H. Cornell-Bell, S.M. Finkbeiner, M.S. Cooper, and S.J. Smith, "Glutamate induces calcium waves in cultured astrocytes: Long-range glial signaling," *Science* 247 (1990): 470–73. It is interesting to note that Liz didn't pay much attention to the glial signaling the first time she encountered a description of it, in *Science News*, but only the second time, when it was the focus of a class presentation.

[26]It is interesting to note in this regard that the professor in her class was not planning to discuss glial signaling, and that she first learned about it in class from a fellow student. She said, however, that the professor did provide some background information about the glia and the history of research on them after the student's presentation. Discussing how biased the teaching was against discussing the glia she commented, "In grad school in my neurochemistry class there was a lecture on neurons and glia, and here's how it started: 'The glia are the packaging peanuts of the brain; now for the neurons.' And then the rest of the two hours was on the neurons. That's how extreme it was."

A fifth source of intrinsic interest is beauty. We are naturally drawn to phenomena, works, and ideas that we perceive as beautiful. They inspire us, we
enjoy thinking about them, want to learn more about them, and like imagining
ourselves pursuing endeavors and projects that concern them or are somehow
connected to them, in part because it creates the feeling that we ourselves
are connected with them and will create works that are beautiful like them.
Thus we have a natural tendency to form interests in and based on elements
of beauty.

Beauty was mentioned as a source of interest by several of the individuals I
interviewed. Sophia referred to the beauty of axon growth cones. Andreas Walz,
another neuroscientist I interviewed who was also interested in axon pathfinding, did as well; describing looking at growth cones as they were growing, he
said, "it was just aesthetically beautiful to watch them." Many of the literary
scholars I interviewed described first being attracted to literature for its beauty.
For example, Ian Baucom, now a professor of English at Duke University, told
me that his first love in literature was Romantic and lyric poetry, which he
loved for its beauty and the beautiful, poignant emotions it inspires. Karen
Kebarle, another literary scholar I interviewed, told me she has always been attracted to beautiful "transcendent" passages in literature, which was important
in sparking her interest in Willa Cather; see my synopsis of her development
in Chapter 13.

What strikes us as beautiful when we first enter a field and begin to learn
about it may be quite different from what we perceive as beautiful later, when
our understanding and knowledge are deeper and our perceptual sense more
developed and refined, and these shifts in what we consider beautiful may
parallel or even contribute to corresponding shifts in our interests. Further, in
studying paths of creative development I have found that beauty seems to be
more important in sparking early interests than later interests. Ian's experience
is an example of this pattern: beauty was crucial in sparking his initial interest
in literature, but his later, more mature interest, that has been the basis for
his creative work was not inspired by beauty — rather, his interest has been in
exploring the way political issues and ideals, specifically related to the British
empire and Britain's postimperial relationship with its former colonies, are
described, embodied, and reflected in literature.

Allied with interests rooted in the sense of beauty are interests rooted in
aesthetic valuation or appreciation — interests based in wanting to study a
body of phenomena, theory, or other topic because it seems to embody or
reflect aesthetic values we care about and appreciate, wanting to employ a

particular approach because it resonates with aesthetic values or principles that inspire and motivate us. Aesthetic valuation and appreciation is important in literary studies, art, mathematics, design, and many other fields. Many of the mathematicians I interviewed described being attracted to mathematics and certain subfields of mathematics for their beauty and elegance. David Metzler told me he had originally been interested in both theoretical physics and mathematics, but decided to go into mathematics because it seemed far more beautiful to him, as a deductive system working from first principles, in comparison with physics, which seemed "messier" and more inductive. During our two-and-one-half hour interview he used the words "beautiful" and "pretty" fifteen times when describing certain kinds of mathematics and specific results. He also contrasted what he views as beautiful math with what he considers "grungy" math and physics problems. It was clear from our interview that he is drawn to subfields and problems — forms interests in topics — that he considers beautiful and able to be approached and likely solved using "beautiful" mathematics.[27]

DESIRE FOR UNDERSTANDING, TRUTH, AND ENLIGHTENMENT; PHILOSOPHICAL BASES OF INTERESTS

Another source of intrinsic interest, the last I discuss, is the desire to attain understanding, truth, or enlightenment. It is not necessarily easy to disentangle the desire for truth and understanding as sources of interest from other sources — curiosity, wonder, and the desire to take on a challenge; many scientists, for example, would describe their interests as having as their source a combination of these. Nonetheless I believe the distinction is valid and useful. As compared with curiosity, the desire to attain truth and understanding is defined more in terms of the perspective of eternal, unattainable ideal objects, states, or objectives. Thus, whereas interests rooted in curiosity typically center on a set of questions that it is believed or hoped can be answered, in some finite time and with a degree of success, interests rooted in the desire to attain truth and understanding center on questions and aims that are never likely to be fully answered or attained, have about them the sense of infinite development, are framed in ways suggesting they can be investigated, contemplated, and sought after, in new and different ways, unfolding, without exhaustion. Many great

---

[27]For a discussion of the role of beauty and aesthetic appreciation in science see S. Chandrasekhar, *Truth and Beauty; Aesthetics and Motivations in Science* (Chicago: University of Chicago Press, 1987), especially "Beauty and the quest for beauty in science," pp. 59–73.

scientists, thinkers, leaders, and artists — Einstein, Cezanne, Michelangelo — seem to have the sense of ultimate truth, creation, understanding, or enlightenment as both beyond them and yet as framing their conceptions of their work, shaping their interests — convinced that to seek after these is the true aim and end. Wonder is naturally linked to the desire to attain truth, understanding, and enlightenment, but the focus is slightly different — more on the visceral sense of astonishment and amazement.

One form of the desire to attain truth or understanding is the desire to create a work or product that will approach closer to truth than previous works or products. This is an important source of interest in the sciences and philosophy, and also in the arts. For example, Cezanne seems to have been driven by the desire to represent light and space in painting more accurately, to approach more closely to capturing and replicating in a two-dimensional painting the nature of human perception of three-dimensional objects and scenes.

Distinct from the desire for truth and understanding, the desire for enlightenment has the aim of enlightenment of the self. I have not encountered many individuals driven by the quest for enlightenment in their formation of their interests; Hannah Arendt, in her desire to understand the meaning of her life and her place in German society, is perhaps one person whose interests have such a quest as their source. However my failure to find many cases of such a quest driving the formation of interests is undoubtedly in part because I have focused on certain fields in which the quest for enlightenment is not, at least overtly, central — it is likely to be very important in certain fields, especially fields of spiritual inquiry and experience and certain experiential art forms.[28]

In cases in which the source of our interest is our desire to attain or approach certain understandings or truths we naturally organize our interests and our conceptions of our interests around our conceptions of these understandings or truths. Our conceptions of such ultimate truths and understandings are inherently abstract and sketchy, giving our interests a sense of abstractness, openness, and, in many cases, universality. Beyond the ultimate objectives and aims, our interests and our conceptions of our interests often center on approaches for how we hope or intend to go about trying to achieve these aims and objectives. Having an approach that we believe may enable us to attain an understanding or truth — often an understanding or truth that we have been interested in for some time but have not known how to approach, and that others before us have also been interested in but possibly unable to find a way to approach successfully — gives us a way forward, driving our pursuit of our interest.

[28]Transcendent experiences are included; they may be a source of creative interests in certain fields.

Philosophical principles, ideas, and ideals are linked to and the basis for an individual's quest for understanding, truth, or enlightenment in many cases — they ground our quest for truth, understanding, and enlightenment. Consistent with this, they are often conceptual bases for individuals who form interests rooted in the quest for truth, understanding, or enlightenment, grounding and shaping their conceptions of their interests.

Piet Mondrian is an example of an individual who formed and pursued a creative interest, the quest for a new art to reflect the modern age, grounded in a philosophical belief system. Mondrian believed in the basic duality of spirit and matter, in the principle that they can and do form a unity, that life evolves towards greater spiritual consciousness over time, and that art can help society in its spiritual development. In forming these ideas Mondrian was influenced by the Theosophical movement prominent in the Netherlands in the early 1900s, and his beliefs clearly reflect the views of individuals in that movement. What is especially interesting is the way his beliefs shaped and guided his conception of art, specifically his conception of his artistic aims and principles of artistic composition, which guided him in his artistic development.

Mondrian's conception, in its formative early stages, is set forth, though in a somewhat fragmentary manner, in a series of remarks in two sketchbooks he kept over the years 1912 to 1914. Outlining basic principles, he writes as follows (in Book II, which was in fact composed first): "The focus of consciousness is being transferred from without to within. This process is a continuing one, because consciousness is Evolving. As consciousness turns away from the surface, the latter is also less imitated in the art of painting." "By turning from the surface, one comes closer to the inner laws of matter, which are also the laws of the spirit. Hence, the two things (finally) converge." "As a result these laws are becoming the principal concern of art. They are harmony, balance. . . . These will be expressed in painting through: Spirit [Force] and matter: a Unity."[29] He continues, specifically linking art with religion: "All religions have the same fundamental content; they differ only in form. The *form* is the external manifestation of this content, and is thus an indispensable vehicle for the

[29]Robert P. Welsh and J.M. Joosten, *Two Mondrian Sketchbooks, 1912-1914*, trans. Robert P. Welsh (Amsterdam: Meulenhoff, 1969). The dating is not certain; see the discussion in the Introduction. The quotes are on pp. 70 and 69 (Book II is composed in reverse page order). Mondrian's belief in philosophy as the basis of art and of conscious spiritual awareness as important for artistic creation is shown as early as a letter of 1909 to the art critic Israël Querido. "It seems to me," Mondrian writes, "that you too recognise the important relationship between philosophy and art, and it is exactly this relationship which most painters deny. The great masters grasp it unconsciously, but I believe that a painter's conscious spiritual knowledge will have a much greater influence upon his art...." The letter was published by Querido on October 29, 1909 in the magazine *De Controleur*. See *Two Mondrian Sketchbooks*, Introduction.

expression of the primal principles." "It is precisely form which is of critical importance. To be sure the inner is the main thing, but the inner can be known only through the form." He then links artistic form — specifically "primary forms" — to the path towards evolving consciousness and spiritual development. "Art transcends reality — it has no direct rapport with reality. . . . In order to approach the spiritual in art, one employs reality as little as possible because reality is the polar opposite of the spiritual. This explains logically why primary forms are employed." The artistic forms he envisions are abstract, nonmaterialistic, yet precise in showing a vision of enlightenment: "Since these forms are abstract, an abstract art comes into being. Art must transcend reality — Art must transcend humanity. Otherwise it would be of no value to man. This transcendent character appears *vague* and dreamy to the materialist, but for the spiritual person it is precisely positive and clear."[30]

In Book I, written slightly later, Mondrian restates this conception and extends it to a theory of artistic evolution. "The spiritual is expressed firstly in physical form, but also in other intermediate forms [which we do not see]. If one conceives these intermediate forms as increasingly simple and pure, commencing with the physical visible forms of appearance, then one passes through a world of forms ascending from reality to abstraction. In this manner one approaches Spirit, or purity itself."[31] He then goes a step further, forming a clearer conception of how to realize spiritual development, the representation formally of the unity of spirit and matter, in art, through combining vertical (male) and horizontal (female) elements. He outlines basic dualities of male and female, spirit and matter, defining a series of pairings (p. 16):

> *Female*: static, preserving, obstructing element.
> *Male*: kinetic, creative, expressive, progressing element.
> Woman: matter-element
> Man: spirit-element
> Woman: horizontal line
> Man: vertical line.

He expands on the link of the male element with the vertical line and the female element with the horizontal line in a later, lyrical entry: "Since the male principle is the vertical line, a man shall recognize this element in the ascending trees of a forest; he sees his complement in the horizontal line of the sea. The woman, with the horizontal line as characteristic element, recognizes herself in the recumbent lines of the sea and sees herself complemented in the vertical lines of the forest [which represent the male element]. Thus the

---

[30] Ibid., pp. 52–53, 59, 62.
[31] Ibid., pp. 37–38.

impression differs. In art it is unified because the artist is sexless. Since the 133 artist accordingly represents the female and male principle, and not nature directly, a work of art transcends nature."[32] Finally, he also develops an artistic, formal principle: "In order to express in form the power which emanates from nature, lines generally must be made much blacker in the plastic arts than one ordinarily sees them in nature."[33]

In these passages we see Mondrian spelling out and defining a set of elements and principles he then explored and sought to develop creatively artistically, working to embody them in art over the ensuing years. He went further later in his conception of principles, forming a richer conception that guided him in his art, going further in his artistic development; see Chapter 11.

[32] Ibid., p. 22.
[33] Ibid., p. 23.

5

EXTRINSIC AND STRATEGIC FACTORS IN THE DEVELOPMENT OF CREATIVE INTERESTS

In addition to intrinsic interest, we are also influenced by extrinsic and strategic factors in the development of our interests. Such factors fall into two categories: (1) those that relate to creative potential; and (2) those that relate to strategic positioning or a desire to create works that will define and defend a certain position with respect to one's field or society. In this chapter I outline what I believe to be the most important factors in each category.

In most cases our interests have multiple sources, both intrinsic and extrinsic. I discuss multiple sources in the last section.

CREATIVE POTENTIAL

The creative potential of a creative interest or potential topic of interest is the potential it has, through being pursued and developed creatively, to generate valued creative contributions. The potential of an interest is determined by the number of contributions it may lead to, together with the potential value or importance of these contributions. Our assessment of the creative potential of an interest is the extrinsic factor that most commonly and strongly influences us in our coming to form it as an interest and our decision about whether or not to pursue it actively. Imagining and believing that an interest or potential topic of interest has creative potential spurs our interest, makes us excited at the prospect of learning more about it and trying to develop it creatively. In many cases our sense that a topic has creative potential is crucial in turning a passing interest into something deeper and more lasting; conversely and equally importantly, if we sense that a topic does not have creative potential we may choose not to pursue it and our interest in it may wane.

There are two key characteristics associated with interests and the creative contributions we make through pursuing interests that are fundamental in assessing the creative potential of a creative interest or topic that may form the basis for an interest: importance and opportunity. I discuss each in turn, focusing on how we form judgements about it and providing examples illustrating the role of assessments about it in the formation of creative interests.

Importance

The importance of a creative interest is defined to be the potential importance of the contributions that conceivably can be and are likely to be made through its exploration and creative development — how significant these contributions will, if they come about, be considered to be by ourselves and others whose opinions concern us, including the degree to which they will influence the future course of development of our field and society. There are three basic kinds of important creative contributions: important discoveries and advances in understanding; important creative works, like works of art and inventions; and creative contributions that attain important objectives or make their attainment possible or more likely. When we judge a creative interest or potential topic of interest to be important our judgement is in general linked to one of these three. We believe that through exploring the interest and developing it creatively we will (1) discover important phenomena, or come to understand or contribute to understanding an important phenomenon or group of phenomena or theoretical construct more deeply, (2) create or contribute to the creation of important and valuable works, that is, works valuable in and of themselves, or (3) attain or contribute to progress towards attaining important objectives.

Importance was an important factor for many of the individuals I interviewed in influencing their formation of their creative interests: recognizing the importance of topics that had caught their attention and sparked their interest contributed to their forming interests in or based upon them. A main reason why Roger was interested in studying how neurons develop into their shapes was because he believed that their shapes are "very tied to their function," thus likely to be important for the working of the brain. Liz viewed glial signaling as potentially very important in brain functioning, indeed believed it poses a radical challenge to the conventional neuroscience view that the neurons are the basis for all important mental processing; her sense of its potential importance was clearly a principal reason she found it so exciting. Azad thought mechanisms of action were important, as is indicated by his statement that he "thought it would be necessary to understand things at that level" — in terms of how these mechanisms operate — in order to understand how external agents exert their effects on cells.

For many of the individuals I interviewed believing in the importance of their interests was also important in spurring them to strive to develop their interests creatively. Thus, Liz was driven to pursue glial signaling for her dissertation research because of how important she viewed it — she hoped to contribute to correcting what she viewed as a gross imbalance in neuroscience, overemphasizing neurons and underemphasizing glia. Discussing his interest in exploring how English national identity has been represented and defined in British colonial and postcolonial literature over the past two centuries, Ian Baucom told me he thought it was "intellectually important" to explore the ways in which representations of identity have been intertwined historically with British imperial culture and imperialism — to explore and make manifest what he called "the long history of England's collaborative identity." Enid Zentelis, the filmmaker, is interested in portraying the lives of individuals who are poor and oppressed and views her interest and her films as important ideologically, as a way to increase social awareness of the lives of the poor and oppressed and thus contribute towards eventual social change. Note that in the examples given here the first and third kinds of importance are represented; Roger, Liz, Azad, and Ian believed that through exploring their interests they would contribute towards a deeper understanding of important phenomena, and Ian and Enid believed that through developing their interests creatively they would contribute towards the attainment of important ideological and social objectives.

Importance has been a significant factor historically for many individuals who have made famous creative contributions: they have achieved success through pursuing interests they believed were important, possessing an uncanny ability to identify interests that turn out to lead to important contributions. James Watson's development and pursuit of an interest in DNA, specifically in determining its structure, is an outstanding example of an individual forming an interest in a topic he recognized was potentially important, to great result. As Watson described it later, his interest in DNA derived from a more basic interest in the gene, formed in college. Describing his intellectual development he wrote, "Population genetics originally intrigued me, but from the moment I read Schrödinger's *What is Life?* I became polarized towards finding out the secret of the gene."[1] He believed, with Schrödinger, that the gene is the key to life, and was drawn at this early stage of his development, as we so often are at this stage, to a "big" topic that appeared to be truly important — that held the promise of a revolution in our understanding of life. At the time, however, in college, he knew little if anything about DNA, indeed may not even have heard of it. It was in graduate school at Indiana University that he became focused on DNA. At Indiana he joined the "phage group," a group of geneticists who studied phages, viruses which were thought to be "naked genes" and thus offered what seemed to be a promising avenue of investigation for determining what the gene is and how genetic replication occurs.[2] Phages are part DNA and part protein, and either part could in principle have contained the basic genetic information. But the experimental results of Oswald Avery and his colleagues published in 1944 seemed to show clearly that DNA was the basis for hereditary transmission in bacteria; and this, as Watson describes it in his autobiographical account of the discovery of the double helix structure of DNA, *The Double Helix,* "made it smell" like DNA "was the essential genetic material."[3] Following this idea to its logical implication with a clarity of mind that seems to have been characteristic of him, he reached the conclusion that was the basis of his interest: "so working out DNA's chemical structure might be the essential step in learning how genes duplicated."[4] Thus his attention was drawn to DNA and its chemical structure, his interest sparked by how central it seemed to be for understanding the gene and genetic transmission. I describe the subsequent phase of his development, leading to his collaboration with

[1]"Growing up in the phage group," in *Phage and the Origins of Molecular Biology* (Cold Spring Harbor, NY: Cold Spring Harbor Laboratory, 1966), pp. 239–45. Robert Ortnoy raises questions about how seriously Watson was committed to studying the gene at this time, noting that he continued to be known as a "bird-watcher" interested in natural history. See his comments in Robert Ortnoy, *The Path to the Double Helix* (Seattle, WA: University of Washington Press, 1974), chap. 18. On balance I believe it is best to accept Watson's statements as the most reliable indications of his own mental states, though remaining aware of the possibility that he may overstate the case.

[2]He discusses his graduate school experience and development in "Growing up in the phage group."

[3]James D. Watson, *The Double Helix: A Personal Account of the Discovery of the Structure of DNA* (New York: Atheneum Publishers, 1968), p. 23.

[4]Ibid. Robert Ortnoy questions Watson's account here as well; see *The Path to the Double Helix,* chap. 18. It is interesting to note that, according to Ortnoy, Watson took a course on the chemistry of proteins and nucleic acids taught by Felix Haurowitz, in which Haurowitz apparently told the students he believed proteins were the basic genetic material, not DNA — thus Watson's opinions were clearly formed independently.

Francis Crick studying DNA's structure using X-ray diffraction techniques, in Chapter 9.

For Hannah Arendt, the importance of understanding how the political situation in Germany could have developed to the point at which the Nazis gained power with anti-Semitic propaganda at the center of their political rhetoric was a crucial event driving her interest in understanding the roots of anti-Semitism in European history, linked, as she came to understand it, to a host of other factors. Albert Einstein had an intuitive sense for the importance of the paradox he had discovered regarding traveling behind a light beam, his description of which is given below, which in turn drove his development of his broader interest in understanding conceptions of space and time in physics and philosophy, which I describe in Chapter 10. Many further examples could be given, such as John von Neumann's interest in computational methods for solving certain classes of applied mathematics problems, and Rachel Carson's interest in conservation of nature and harm to nature caused by man's activities and pesticides.

Judgements of importance are inherently difficult to make, since it is impossible for us to know ahead of time what we will discover or create or attain through pursuing given interests. We do make such judgements, instinctively and intuitively, and they often have an important influence on the course of our development. However, relative to the ideal of how they should be formed, the way in which we actually form such judgements is generally more narrowly based, less fully thought out, and rooted more in simple extrapolation. Specifically, when we form the opinion that an interest or potential area of interest is important we commonly base our opinion on just a handful of potential contributions or kinds of contributions that we imagine may come to be made through its pursuit, often mainly on just a few outstanding contributions, for it is these that come to mind, that we fantasize about and find exciting. Thus we do not generally do a good job of considering or attempting to gauge the full range of possible outcomes in terms of contributions and levels of success we might achieve. This is a failing widely observed in decision-making involving uncertain outcomes, the heuristic of availability — that in evaluating decisions with uncertain outcomes people tend to consider just a few scenarios that come to mind.[5] It is exacerbated in this context by the fact that at the time we form our judgements we have often only just begun to learn about the area we are interested in and thus do not have a deep understanding of the subtleties and potential pitfalls involved in trying to develop it creatively.

[5]Availability is presented as a heuristic by Amos Tversky and Daniel Kahneman in their classic article "Judgment under uncertainty: Heuristics and biases," *Science* 185 (1974): 1124–31.

We often form the opinion that a potential area of interest is important through a process of extrapolation. We are drawn to an interest area by ideas, questions, problems, phenomena, and works that are widely regarded as important and strike us also as important, and, extrapolating in a natural way, form the belief that interests we form based upon them will also be important. Although this is natural, it can introduce biases into our judgements. In particular, we do not always distinguish as clearly as we should between important contributions that have already been made in an area and the potential importance of future contributions that might be made through pursuing interests based on these past contributions, which might not be as great. This relates to a bias frequently described in the literature on decision-making under uncertainty, imagining and placing too high probability weight on extreme potential outcomes, in this context focusing excessively on especially outstanding outcomes or contributions that might be made through pursuing an interest.[6] Further, we do not always distinguish clearly between the contributions we ourselves may be capable of making, taking into account our own unique constellation of abilities and opportunities, through pursuing a particular interest, and contributions that may be made by others with different abilities pursuing related but distinct interests.

Three additional characteristics of our judgements of importance are worthy of note. First, while ideas, facts, and concepts in our field and the opinions and beliefs of people working in the field are important factors in our judgements, our judgements are often influenced just as much by personal factors, such as personal registers of meaning. Thus, we judge interests to be important in relationship to our fields, but very often the reason why we perceive them to be important is because they resonate with registers of meaning, beliefs, and values we hold to and believe are important. An example is Roger's judgement of the importance of neurons developing into their shapes as a topic. He believed the shapes of neurons are likely to be important for the architecture and functioning of the brain — subjects that are obviously of fundamental importance in neuroscience — which is why he believed visualizing neurons developing into their shapes would be an important topic to research. And it was because of his unique personal background — his military training — that these shapes caught his attention and he recognized their potential importance. Further, because personal factors matter, it is not unusual for a person to form

---

[6]This bias relates to the "probability weighting function" introduced by Kahneman and Tversky in "Prospect Theory," *Econometrica* 47 (1979): 263–91. It is also consistent with the idea that forming interests and conceptions of interests has something in common with daydreaming, imagining paths of development that we believe will lead us to success in our endeavors.

an interest that he believes is important, yet for his interest to be distinctive, or even unique, with others not perceiving its importance. Most neuroscientists do not recognize the shapes of neurons to be as important a research topic as Roger considered it to be. Out of the 19 I interviewed, just one other, Bruce Peters, had an interest that in any way concerned the shapes of neurons, and his interest was actually very different — as mentioned in Chapter 3, he has a background in electrical engineering, and is interested in how the shapes of neurons are important for their electrical functioning, not for their physical fitting together. Importance is so often a matter of point-of-view; though Jim Watson saw clearly how important the structure of DNA was and how important it was to pursue figuring it out as an interest, far fewer biologists shared this view at the time than one might expect given how important DNA turned out to be — an interesting example I return to in Chapter 7.

Second, sometimes the main reason why we view an interest as meaningful and important is because we perceive it to be connected with a broader social or intellectual movement. Cheryl, for example, told me that she sensed that in pursuing her interest in "the literary heirs of Aphra Behn" she was participating in a larger movement spearheaded by younger scholars that was "redefining" eighteenth-century studies by shifting the focus in the field to noncanonical writers, including women, and this feeling of participating in a larger intellectual movement gave her a much firmer sense of the potential importance of her work than she would have had if she had thought she was pursuing her interest in isolation.[7]

Third, not all the topics we believe are important and worthy of being pursued because of their importance are topics we view as fun or pleasant to pursue. Some are the opposite, important and engrossing because of the threats they pose or the unhappiness and difficulties they involve. Feeling this way about a topic can make it more difficult to feel motivated to pursue it, but nonetheless we do pursue such topics if we view them as being important enough. Rachel Carson, filled with the wonder of nature, developed an interest, beginning in the late 1930s, in the conservation of nature from the threat of development and destruction, especially coastline, and in the harm man was doing to the natural environment and humanity through the use of pesticides. This was hardly a pleasant topic, but it was one that she came to see as of the utmost importance. Her interest led her eventually, nearly twenty years later,

[7]Cheryl mentioned in particular a book published at that time that she read, *The New Eighteenth Century: Theory, Politics, English Literature*, ed. Felicity Nussbaum and Laura Brown (New York: Methuen, 1987). Another book which she may or may not have seen at the time is Angeline Goreau, *Reconstructing Aphra: A Social Biography of Aphra Behn* (Oxford: Oxford University Press, 1980).

to focus on pesticides and their destructive powers, and to agree to write a book about it. "Nothing I could do would be more important," she said about her decision to work on pesticides, she would "have no peace," if she did not pursue the topic and bring it to public attention. Thus she pursued it even though it was very different from her earlier writing projects, all of which were rooted in her love of nature and interest in explaining nature and nature science to lay readers.[8]

Opportunity

The second key characteristic associated with interests that is crucial in assessing their creative potential is opportunity. For a creative interest, opportunity means offering good prospects of being able to be developed creatively in interesting and original ways — of leading to opportunities to engage in novel and original creative projects that will be fulfilling and, with luck, will lead to valued creative contributions.

Our judgements of the opportunities for creative development afforded by an interest depend principally on our assessment of two factors. One is the degree to which the interest is a relatively unexplored domain. It is significant that even if a topic or area has been worked on extensively, it is still possible for us to view it as providing opportunities for further creative development, because we may believe it can be approached in a new way, for example, using newly developed methods or techniques. The other factor is the degree to which the interest contains rich creative possibilities. Richness of creative possibilities calls to mind richness as an intrinsic source of interest; however, the two concepts, although related, are distinct. Being intrinsically interested in a domain for its richness means imagining it to be filled with fascinating elements, but does not necessarily imply thinking or imagining that it affords rich possibilities for creative development. In contrast richness as a source of creative potential refers specifically to having a sense of rich creative possibilities that one may be able to realize. Finally, in addition to these two factors, our judgement of the opportunity an interest affords for creative development also depends on our assessment of the match between our own abilities and what we imagine it will take to pursue the interest successfully — how feasible

[8] See Linda Lear, *Rachel Carson: Witness for Nature*, pp. 92, 118–119, 310–11, chap. 14; and Paul Brooks, *The House of Life: Rachel Carson at Work* (Boston: Houghton Mifflin, 1972), chap. 16. Brooks quotes Rachel as saying, in describing her motivation to pursue the subject, that she felt "there would be no peace for me if I kept silent," and that "the time had come when it must be written . . . [and] knowing the facts as I did, I could not rest until I had brought them to public attention" (p. 228).

it will be for us to pursue the interest and develop it successfully in light of our own specific experiences, constellation of abilities, and developmental path. Wilbur Wright developed an active interest in flight only when he realized flight should be possible for humans — if birds and insects could fly, man should also be able to do so.[9]

Opportunity was an important factor in the development of their interests for many of the individuals I interviewed, as well as in their decisions about which interests to pursue. Indeed more individuals mentioned opportunity in discussing the factors that influenced them in these phases of development than mentioned any other extrinsic factor. Azad said he had the perception at the time he developed his interest that not much was known about the mechanisms through which molecular agents act inside cells, and that current research was focused on the biology of these agents and their receptors, not on their mechanisms of action. During our interview he recalled going to a conference while he was in medical school, looking for current research related to his interest. "And I remember there were a lot of posters on NGF and neurotrophins," he told me, "and I looked in particular for posters on the mechanism of action downstream of the receptor, and I didn't find any at all." "So it made it clear to me that that was something that would be really interesting to do because it hadn't been done yet." Stephen Shapiro, a literary scholar I interviewed, is another example of someone for whom opportunity was important. As a graduate student Stephen chose to focus on American literature of the early 1790s through the 1820s. Partly this was because he found the literature of this period exciting. But an additional reason why he was attracted to the period was because it seemed relatively under-studied and hence open for development — he described it as falling between the Puritans and the American literary Renaissance of the 1840s (Hawthorne, Melville, and Poe are three of the defining writers of the Renaissance), which are two of the defining poles of early American culture, and told me that whereas these two periods had been overworked, in contrast, "one of the attractions of working on the period between them was that not that much had been written on it."

Historically sensing opportunity has been very important in their development of their creative interests for many individuals who are famous for their creative contributions. Highly creative, ambitious people, including many of those who turn out to be extremely productive, are naturally attracted to areas that they perceive to be unexplored and promising, and are excited and

[9]Initially, as discussed in the preceding chapter, he does not seem to have considered it likely that flight would be achieved by him or even necessarily in his lifetime, writing in his letter to the Smithsonian only that he would like to add his "mite" towards progress towards the ultimate goal.

energized by the prospect of exploring them and developing them creatively. They attack their interests in these areas, fired by a buoyant optimism and having great fecundity, often initiating many projects and making many contributions, large and small.

Thomas Edison is a classic example of an ambitious, optimistic, creative person who had the sense of great opportunities for creative success — invention — through pursuit of his interests. At the time he set up his laboratory in Menlo Park, Edison stated that he intended it to be "an invention factory" where he would produce "a minor invention every ten days and a big thing every six months or so." Indeed the act of setting up an independent lab devoted to invention itself shows his optimism and his confidence that he would be able to produce a stream of successful inventions. Edison began his career as an inventor focusing on improvements to the telegraph, with a special focus on the problem of multiplexing. But his interests expanded from this point outwards; in particular he formed an interest in peripheral devices linked to telegraphy, specifically writing and recording devices and, more broadly, electromechanical systems. Over time he formed further, interrelated interests, in chemistry and electrochemical devices, including batteries, and in acoustic transmission, building up a constellation of interests. As he began working exploring an interest he would conceive dozens of ideas for potential inventions, jotting them down in his notebooks, and pursue many different ideas and approaches, dozens of leads — resilient in the face of failure, not allowing failure in any one approach to dampen his enthusiasm or lessen his confidence that he would achieve success through a different approach, optimistic about the opportunity the area offered for inventions. His various interests fed off one another and his sense of innumerable ways of combining them contributed to his sense of great opportunity; and ultimately he did combine his interests, brilliantly, notably in his invention of the phonograph — I describe this in Chapter 13 — and electric lightbulb.[10]

Judgements of opportunity are generally somewhat easier to make and more reliable than judgements of importance, but still difficult and subject to biases and limitations. We are usually capable of gauging with some degree of

[10] For further information see Paul Israel, *Edison: A Life of Invention*, chaps. 8–9. Israel discusses Edison's laboratory and its operation in some detail. The quote is from p. 120. Part of the quote, and the general portrait, is drawn from Matthew Josephson, *Edison: A Biography*, pp. 133–37. Edison's notebooks show the fecundity of his thought and way of pursuing many leads and approaches. See Thomas A. Edison, *The Papers of Thomas A. Edison*; Vol. 3, Menlo Park: The Early Years, April 1876-December 1877, ed. Robert A. Rosenberg, Paul B. Israel, Keith A. Nier, and Martha J. King (Baltimore, MD: Johns Hopkins University Press, 1994).

144 accuracy how much creative work has been done in an area, and thus can sense if the area has been overworked, leaving little room for new development, or, conversely, if it is relatively free and open for development. However, we do not always assess how much work has been done as accurately as we might, in theory, be able to. Swept up in the excitement of an exciting discovery or work that has sparked our interest, and imagining that it opens up a new area for development, we do not always search as carefully as we might to see what else has been done in the area or on related topics, with the result that we often discover later that more has been done than we realized at the time we formed our interest. Further, often we do not pause to consider the possibility that some of our contemporaries will form interests similar to our own, with the result that they will end up working in the same general area as us, and possibly on similar topics, so that even if the area or topic we are interested in was previously relatively open and free for development, it will now become crowded. Liz is an example: at the time she began pursuing her interest in glial signaling it was her impression that very few other researchers were pursuing related interests, and later when she began work on a specific project investigating calcium-activated signaling in Schwann cells (the glial cells of the peripheral nervous system) she believed this was a project unique to her. As it turned out, however, another researcher at a different university began studying calcium activity in Schwann cells at the same time, unbeknownst to her.[11]

Judging the creative opportunities of an interest, although somewhat easier than judging its potential importance, is still quite difficult, and for the same basic reason — it is difficult to guess what we will discover or create through exploring the interest and trying to develop it creatively. In fact most of us are more comfortable and better at judging creative opportunities than at judging importance. In part this is because judging importance is extraordinarily difficult because it requires making conjectures about outliers — major discoveries and creative breakthroughs, outcomes which are extremely difficult to foresee, whereas assessing potential requires imagining some subset of possibilities, which we can more readily do. In addition, we are typically somewhat flexible with regard to creative opportunities, willing to consider moving in a variety of directions so long as we can pursue projects we find interesting, and as a result are reasonably good at spotting and assessing different kinds of opportunities. However, we have an inherent tendency to be optimistic in our judgements of opportunity: because we find our interests genuinely interesting

[11]As it turned out Liz and the other researcher focused on the effects of different compounds on Schwann cells. See Chapter 13.

and exciting, we naturally imagine that we are bound to find interesting and creative projects to work on through pursuing them, and bound to make a contribution that, even if it is not of the first importance, will nonetheless be valuable and afford us satisfaction. Being optimistic, in fact overly optimistic, we tend to overestimate the creative opportunities our interests or potential interests offer, just as we tend to overstate their importance. And just as we generally do not consider as wide a range of scenarios as we should in judging importance, and tend to extrapolate more than is warranted from important contributions that have already been made, similarly we typically do not consider as wide a range of factors or scenarios as we should in forming judgements of opportunity — having learned about one or two discoveries or inventions or creative works, typically quite recent, in an area, we extrapolate too freely and leap to the conclusion that there must be much more to be found or created, without having solid grounds for thinking so.

Perceptions of lack of opportunity — judging that an interest or area of potential interest is not open, but rather crowded, with little room for further development — are also important in creative development, especially in influencing our decisions about which interests to pursue. Sensing a lack of openness and opportunity can cause us to choose not to pursue an interest that we otherwise would pursue. A number of the individuals I interviewed described becoming interested in a topic, but then, upon investigating it or discussing it with others, learned how much had been done on it and decided ultimately not to pursue it. Anne Mette Pedersen, who is interested in the intersection of literature and philosophy, told me she originally intended to explore phenomenological themes in the work of Gertrude Stein for her dissertation, but was discouraged when she discovered how much was written on Stein, and found that much less had been written, especially from a literary perspective, on George Santayana, whose work she found she could also analyze from a phenomenological perspective. "Gertrude Stein was very, very popular at that time," she told me, "[whereas] people had not written a lot about Santayana, and what had been written was written mainly by philosophers... nobody in an English department had really sat down and written about him." So she decided to switch to Santayana, thinking that he offered more opportunities, that focusing on his work would make her own "a little bit more original." Likewise, Liz Yoder told me that one factor in her decision to pursue glial signaling instead of learning and memory, which had been her first interest in neuroscience, was that learning and memory seemed to be a field in which, in her words, "if I didn't do it someone else would do it in two months — it was saturated," whereas, in contrast, glial signaling "looked like it was completely wide open," "unexplored territory."

A theme of my discussion of the development of creative interests is that our interests often grow out of our responses to elements in our fields — ideas, issues, phenomena, theories, beliefs, works, facts, styles, approaches, in some cases broader currents of thought. Much of the time the elements that spark our interests act primarily as points of departure for us. We fashion our interests and our conceptions of our interests out of them or starting from them, but our interests are not specifically about trying to respond to them or produce work that will stand in a particular position in relationship to them — for example, proving or disproving them. Sometimes, however, our interests are centrally about responding to elements we have encountered. Stimulated or provoked, annoyed, angered or inspired, we desire to produce a body of work that will carve out a position in relation to specific elements, and form an interest defining how we wish to go about doing this, for example, avenues or approaches we desire to explore and develop in contrast with or opposition to specific elements. This kind of interest is strategically based, at least to some extent, because we are thinking consciously about how the works we will produce or desire to produce through pursuing it will fit or stand in relation to what other people have done or are doing in our fields or culture. It is not, however, necessarily extrinsically motivated in the same way that some interests are motivated or inspired by importance and opportunity, in that we are not necessarily thinking about the creative potential of the interest or how successful we may be if we pursue it.

Negativity

A form of response that commonly forms the basis for a creative interest is negativity, believing that a theory, argument, set of assumptions, or approach that we have encountered is wrong, and wanting to pursue a line of inquiry or approach opposed to it, to produce work that negates it. An example of negativity is Alexander Calder's feeling that art was "too static to reflect our world of movement" and his desire to redress this imbalance by making motion itself an art form and introducing motion into traditionally static forms of art.

Calder's negative conception was broad, a sweeping statement about art in general. A second pattern is for our feelings of negativity to be fairly narrowly focused initially, for example, on a specific assumption or interpretation we disagree with or a work we feel discontented by — starting from which, over time we develop a broader interest and conception. A number of the literary scholars I interviewed formed interests in this way that turned out to be central for their development. An example is Celia Carlson, one of the scholars

I interviewed. Having been taught the conventional interpretation of the poetry of William Carlos Williams in an American literature class, Celia read some of his poems and was struck by a different, opposite meaning. The conventional interpretation, as she paraphrased it, is that Williams "presents things directly as they are," objectively and innocently, in a "transparent," "natural" way, without any ulterior motives.[12] But the poems struck her as not being objective and innocent, but rather embodying a latent sexuality and expressing it in a veiled way, under cover of a pretended objectivity that is meant to create an aura of authority. "I remember having the idea," she told me, "looking at the poem 'Nantucket,' thinking, 'this isn't transparent, there's something here.'" "And so I wrote a paper about this poem that was ostensibly objective and said it's not really. It's not purely objective, it has an embedded narrative that's affirming an illicit sexuality, presenting it in an objective, veiled way. It's not a transparent poem really, it's a veiled argument on behalf of this illicit sexuality, and the presentation is attempting to naturalize it." Sensing that she was on to something interesting, that her ideas had an "edge" to them, she explored them further, forming an interest centering on them. She described her interest as exploring the way poets cloak sexuality and sexual claims under veils of authority, thus concealing their true motives, and at the same time draw upon this sexual energy to supply the energy for their poems. Thus her interest had a twofold negativity — she was out both to unmask the poets themselves and to argue against conventional criticism, which in her view had read certain poems naively and in a fundamentally misleading way.[13] Her development is an example of a pattern that is common for interests formed on the basis of negativity, first having an idea, which then opens up into a broader interest.

Celia's case is an example of negativity based in dissatisfaction with a theory or explanation of something, driving one to form an interest in exploring and developing arguments against it and to try to come up with something better. Another related form of negativity is recognizing the flaws in an existing product, invention, method, or approach, and believing one can do better; again, this negativity is often initially narrowly targeted, then grows into a broader interest. Jef Raskin, principal inventor of the Apple Macintosh, traced

[12]Celia mentioned in particular the interpretation of J. Hillis Miller, which is well known in the field. See J. Hillis Miller, "Introduction," in *William Carlos Williams: A Collection of Critical Essays*, ed. J. Hillis Miller (Englewood Cliffs, NJ: Prentice-Hall, 1966), pp. 1–14.

[13]Examples of poems that interest her, containing — in her view — these dynamics are Williams's famous "little girl" poems, and the poems of Sharon Olds, a contemporary poet (Celia did not specify which poems of Olds she was referring to and they are not referred to in her dissertation, which is just about Williams's work).

148   the emergence of his interest in designing computers "from the user-interface out" to experiences he had as a graduate student in the mid 1960s trying to teach novice users how to use a graphics package, that made him aware that the approach to computer design standard at the time, focusing on hardware capability and technical ingenuity, was flawed. "Working with graduate students and faculty from the humanities and arts, I began to realize how badly our computers were designed. Whereas most of the other people who were in Computer Science or were graduate assistants helping people using the computer said 'Oh, those people just don't have the right technical background,' I suddenly realized it was the bad design of the computers that was hindering them. What they were trying to do was very simple — we just had these arcane systems to do it. So that was moving from helping people use software to recognizing that the problem was the design, not the people." His 1967 master's thesis that presents his "Quick-Draw Graphics System" shows his concern for designing software that is easy to use by people of all backgrounds. He writes that the advantages his system has are "a function of the design and implementation philosophy which demanded generality and human usability over execution speed and efficiency" — showing his interest in opposition to the dominant focus. At the end of his thesis he presents a manual written for general users. His system, he writes, "is aimed at the computer user whose interests lie in his specialty, and who has already spent too much time away from his real purpose learning FORTRAN and attende[a]nt details." And he provides as an example of its range of application a graphical display of a line of music by Beethoven. Jef brought this same basic interest and orientation — his interest being essentially a certain approach to personal computer design — to the Macintosh project more than ten years later, describing his goal as being to help Apple make the switch "to being user interface oriented, rather than hardware oriented," a view which he described as at that time still "completely alien" to most people in the industry.[14]

Negativity tends, at the level of a field, to produce dynamics of development in which each new movement or wave of progress, for example, new style or paradigm, triggers a counterreaction, as individuals who have not been part of the movement, perhaps entering the field after it has become established,

[14]Jef Raskin interview with Alex Pang; original recording in the Stanford University Library Special Collections. The interview transcript is accessible at http://library.stanford.edu/mac/primary/interviews/raskin/trans.html. Jef's master's thesis is: Jeffrey F. Raskin, *A Hardware Independent Computer Drawing System Using List Structured Modeling: The Quick-Draw Graphics System*, Pennsylvania State University, 1967. The first quote is from the Introduction, pp. 4–5; the manual is presented in the Appendix and is entitled "Primer on the Quick-Draw Graphics System (QDGS)." The music example is described on p. 82 and presented on p. 84.

recognize and focus on its flaws and limitations, hoping thereby either to re-dress them so as to advance the movement, or perhaps to destroy the movement entirely. These dynamics fit with the first part of Hegel's famous theory of the dialectic — a positive thesis is put forward and becomes established, which then triggers the recognition and development of its antithesis or negation. In Hegel's theory this process of splitting is followed by synthesis — the thesis and antithesis are resolved in a synthesis, which combines them at a higher level of consciousness or development, and becomes the ground for the next thesis, triggering the next spiral of development. I have in fact encountered relatively few cases of individuals forming creative interests based on the idea of searching for a synthesis of opposing or seemingly contradictory approaches, paradigms, or models; thus I believe this is a less common basis for interests than negativity — though to the extent synthesis does occur it may well (though it need not) grow out of work by individuals who have formed interests of this kind. Among the individuals I interviewed I encountered only one person, Karen Hadley, a literary scholar, who wanted to explore differences between competing paradigms or approaches and potentially synthesize them. Karen was interested in comparing and contrasting the very different approaches to "the meaning of language" she was being taught in linguistics and literary studies. There are certainly famous cases in which the drive for synthesis is considered likely to have formed the basis for interests and creative work. For example, St. Thomas Aquinas is viewed as having worked through his scholarly career to reconcile and reach an accommodation between (not exactly synthesize) reason and philosophy with faith (or revelation as an alternative mode of acquiring knowledge) and theology. I do not describe his story or any similar cases in this book, but it would be interesting to investigate some, as a way to explore how the dialectic is generated at the level of individual creative development.

Notwithstanding the importance of negativity as a source of interests, my analysis of the creative developments of many individuals and my theoretical description do not in general support the notion that dialectical processes are the main source of creative interests. There are in fact many sources of interests and patterns of development of interests, as I document, for example, the richness of phenomena, curiosity, the sense of wonder, personal experiences, and the desire to apply or extend current work in one's field.

The Desire to Do or Produce Something Different

A second form of response to previous and current work in a field that often forms the basis for a creative interest is the desire to do something different from what has been done before or produce something that has not previously been produced. This is an interest rooted not in the desire to negate what has gone before, at least not directly and not primarily, but rather in the desire to set off in a different direction, to explore a new domain, or perhaps a new facet of an old domain, or a new approach, and produce a body of work that will not necessarily contradict what has gone before, but stand apart from it and contrast with it. Individuals who form interests rooted in the desire to produce something different generally define their interests and aims at least in part by differentiating them from what has been done in the past, using what has been done in the past as a negative model to define what approaches or topics or directions not to pursue. In some cases individuals in this situation, though driven and wishing to be creative, do not have any clear topic in mind to pursue at first, and search and experiment, sometimes for a considerable period of time, before defining a more focused interest they wish to pursue.

In some cases individuals have definite reasons for wishing to pursue a different direction than what has been customary in their field in the past. For example, individuals sometimes hope through their work to further certain ideological or aesthetic principles that are not widely accepted and have not been developed or expressed in the work that has been done in their field in the past. Tina Brooks, a literary scholar I interviewed, is committed to fighting the widespread use — and unthinking acceptance — of social categories like race and gender to label people and segregate them into groups, and a guiding principle for her in her work is to try to structure her analysis in such a way as to break down these categories. She told me that although she respects both feminist literary theory, which has traditionally tended to focus on white women writers, and the evolving separate tradition of African American women's fiction, she has wanted to do "a more integrated analysis." "I was committed [in my dissertation] to doing a cross-racial analysis," she said. In her dissertation she analyzes women writers of the turn of the twentieth century of different races, including mixed races, emphasizing their commonalities in terms of basic themes, such as identity and the struggle for personal independence. Crossing categories thus formed part of her literary interest, and it has also been a source of creativity for her, for in analyzing together works that have traditionally been kept separate, like Edith Wharton's *The House of Mirth* and Pauline Hopkins's *Contending Forces*, she has arrived at fresh insights; see Chapter 12 for a creative link she made between the main female characters of these works, seeing connections that have not previously been recognized among books written by women of very different backgrounds. It is well to note that, as with many of the sources of our interests, our initial hopes, at the time we form an interest, for what we may accomplish through pursuing it in terms of raising consciousness or contributing to changing the world are often quite

idealistic and not necessarily very accurate: in actually pursuing our interest
we may be led in directions we did not initially anticipate and, further, the
actual impact our work will ultimately have is highly uncertain.

Oftentimes when we form an interest rooted in the desire to produce something different from what has been done in the past or do something different the main reason is simply our desire to be different, to do something
different — to leave our unique, individual mark on the world. William
Faulkner expressed this sentiment well. In his Nobel Prize address he stated
that the purpose of his work was "to create out of the materials of the human
spirit something which did not exist before." And he stated on other occasions
that he believed the root of the artist's impulse is the elemental human desire
to leave his mark on the walls of the cave of human experience, "that final
oblivion beyond which he will have to pass" — to carve "Kilroy was here," as
he phrased it, meaning, as I interpret him, to try to tell the truth as the artist
has uniquely experienced it, though he will never be able to do so completely
or perfectly, in a way that will endure over the ages.[15] Of course this motivation
does not preclude the desire to raise consciousness or change the world as a
motivation for forming an interest; Faulkner himself remarked on the value of
art in helping man "endure and prevail" "by lifting his heart, by reminding him
of the courage and honor and hope and pride and compassion and pity and
sacrifice which have been the glory of his past," and it seems clear that a desire
to do just this lay behind the literary interest he formed, described in Chapter 3.

MULTIPLE SOURCES AND FACTORS

In this and the previous chapter I have discussed intrinsic sources of interest
and extrinsic and strategic factors that influence us in the development of
our interests, focusing on each in turn separately from the others. This is
the best approach for describing these different factors and sources and helps
to distinguish them from one another. But it is not — and is not meant to
be — a portrayal of the typical process of development of our creative interests.

[15]The text of his Nobel Address is in *Essays, Speeches, & Public Letters*, ed. James B.
Meriwether (New York: Random House, 1965), pp. 119–21. His remark about the artist's
impulse and the phrase "Kilroy was here" may be found in his acceptance speech
for the National Book Award, in the same book, pp. 143–45, and is discussed at greater
length in an interview he gave in Japan; see *Lion in the Garden: Interviews with William
Faulkner*, ed. James B. Meriwether and Michael Millgate (New York: Random House,
1968), pp. 106–7. It is also referred to by him in his class conferences at the University of
Virginia; see *Faulkner in the University*, ed. Frederick L. Gwynn and Joseph L. Blotner
(New York: Random House, 1959), entry for March 13, 1957, p. 61.

To the contrary, our interests very commonly develop through the confluence of multiple sources and factors, their combined effects reinforcing one another, heightening our interest and making it more likely that it will grow beyond a momentary fascination to become an enduring interest.

Many creative interests seem to have multiple intrinsic sources, as described in Chapter 4. Jeffrey Shoulson's interest in *Paradise Lost* was based in its intrinsic difficultness as well as, I believe, his sense of its richness, its rich potential for interpretation and exploration of its sources and linkages. Douglas Hofstadter's interest in rules of generation of integer sequences was rooted in curiosity and challenge and a sense of richness, as discussed earlier. Challenge and curiosity led him to investigate the interleaving of the triangular numbers and the squares, but had he not discovered that this sequence has the interesting feature that it never repeats his interest might never have developed further — this discovery convinced him that integer sequences have deep structural rules that it is possible to discover, which was crucial in spurring him on to explore other sequences.

More fundamentally, many creative interests grow out of a combination of intrinsic sources and extrinsic factors. Sophia's interest in growth cones was rooted in a sense of wonder and fascination at the intricate paths growth cones follow and the fact that they somehow know to follow the correct paths, in basic curiosity and a fascination with processes that were complex and rich as a domain of study. In addition, she described a second facet of her interest that was more extrinsically based — she was interested in axon regeneration and regrowth following nervous system trauma and injury. This facet of her interest was spurred partly by an accident a friend had in college, and by research another woman was pursuing in the lab in which she worked in college studying nerve regrowth following trauma. "That really interested me," she told me, "trauma and nerve death and saving nerve death and how we can get nerves to [re]grow." This facet of her interest is tied to a belief that the topic is important for helping people and developing a medical treatment for nerve trauma and injury.[16] Virginia Woolf combined an intrinsic interest in reflections of the self, going back many years, and in developing her conception of a world of reflections in literary form with what seems to have been a belief that if she could develop her conception successfully it would lead to a new kind of literature, that would take its place in the great literary tradition. We may infer she believed this, though it is by no means clear how seriously or strongly,

---

[16] In a follow-up interview, Sophia again stated that this is an important interest she has had from early on.

from her references to Shakespeare and the ancient Greeks linked with the statement of her conception in "The Mark on the Wall."[17] Albert Einstein is an example of an individual who was intrinsically interested in and formed interests in, centering around, and growing out of topics and problems that were important for his field and that he intuitively sensed were important; see the end of this chapter.

In many cases individuals assess the potential importance of a topic and the opportunities it affords for development at the time they become interested in it, pursuing it as an interest only if it seems sufficiently important and offers sufficient opportunity. Azad, for example, recognized intuitively from when he first became interested in mechanisms of action that these mechanisms are likely to be important, even though at the time he knew very little neurobiology to back up his intuition, and his sense that they are important clearly contributed to his interest. Another pattern is to form an intrinsic interest in a topic, and then in the course of beginning to explore and learn about it to form an assessment about its importance and the opportunities it affords for creative development, pursuing it if these factors seem favorable, dropping it if they do not. Many of my interview subjects seem to have followed this pattern of development. Liz was struck initially by the novelty of glial signaling, finding it surprising and fascinating, different from everything she had been taught about the brain. Her interest piqued, she investigated further and discovered that not much was known about glial signaling, that it seemed to be "wide open territory," in sharp contrast to learning and memory, the far more conventional topic that she had been interested in initially, which seemed saturated. In turn, this contrast and her belief that glial signaling was an open field ripe for development were important factors in her decision to pursue glial signaling as her main research interest. Cheryl's interest began with a fascination with the literary figure of Aphra Behn, with her "strong female voice." While researching Behn she discovered that not much had been written about her, which spurred her on, and, her curiosity roused, she shifted and expanded her focus, becoming interested in identifying and studying novels written by women who came after Behn, her "literary heirs." She discovered that these later women had also not been written about much, which contributed to her excitement,

---

[17]Also, in commenting, on seeing the Perugino fresco, that she will show life in a different way in her art she reveals perhaps some sense of personal destiny, that her own mature work would stand with the great masters of the past, different but equal. There is not, however, a great deal of evidence to support the view that she thought this — though she may well have — in her diary or letters over the period of her development I discuss in this book.

giving her the sense that she was discovering works that had been buried for years. Her excitement and sense that she was doing important original work intensified when she realized that other scholars were just beginning to explore these kinds of noncanonical works as well.

It is also possible for the sequence of development to be reversed — to be attracted to a topic initially because it seems to be important or to offer opportunities for development, then begin to explore it and either find it intrinsically interesting and decide to pursue it or find it uninteresting and abandon it. But this pattern is rarer in my experience.

Sources of Interests of Individuals Who Achieve Success

Individuals who achieve success and fame through their creative work very often owe their success to the fact that they form interests in what turn out to be "good" topics to explore and develop at that time — topics that turn out to be important in the development of their fields. Often they form such interests well before others in their fields become interested in similar topics; indeed in some cases it is only after they make their initial important contributions, revealing the importance of the topics, that others become interested in similar or related topics themselves. Given their success, it is natural to wonder why they form the interests that they do, in particular, which has the primary role in their development of their interests, intrinsic interest or extrinsic factors and strategic considerations, and how aware they are of the potential importance and creative potential of their interests at the time they form them.

In my view, based on studying the patterns of creative development of a fair number of such individuals, including statements they have made describing their own development and interests, although their individual patterns of development obviously vary, the key to their success is that they are intrinsically interested in topics that turn out to be important and to lead to important creative contributions. They do not force themselves to be interested in these topics and to form interests based on them — they do not choose to be interested in topics just because they seem important — they generally are not that strategic. Rather, they form interests in these topics because they find them intrinsically interesting; in fact they are often distinguished by the intensity and depth of their interest, which manifests itself in a high degree of focus, concentration, commitment, and perseverance. This is not to say that a sense of importance and creative potential is not also important for these individuals in their formation of their interests, for in many cases it is. In particular, as noted above for Virginia Woolf and Albert Einstein, many individuals who make important contributions through pursuing particular creative interests sense intuitively the importance and potential of these interests, which can enhance their interest, making them more excited and motivated and determined to pursue them. Indeed for some individuals who make important contributions the process seems to work somewhat in reverse: they possess an uncanny ability to sense intuitively which topics in their fields will turn out to be truly important and possess great creative potential, and their interest is naturally drawn to these topics because of their importance and potential; the case of James Watson, presented below, is an example of this. Indeed becoming interested in a topic that seems important or to hold creative potential is so natural that it can be difficult to disentangle intrinsic interest and importance as independent causal factors.[18]

Intrinsic interest, however, is in general central in the creative process regardless; individuals may recognize the importance and potential of their interests, but their awareness of this tends to slip into the background and be of secondary importance during periods when they are actively working to explore their interests and develop them creatively.[19] Indeed it is hard to imagine individuals being sufficiently motivated, curious, and engaged to pursue interests they do not find intrinsically interesting, at least for long enough stretches of time to make substantial progress in developing them — it seems that inevitably in such cases an individual's attention will drift away to some other topic or pursuit. Thus, without intrinsic interest in a topic an individual will likely not be able to develop it successfully, no matter how much potential it has — finding it not intrinsically interesting he will not pursue it with the same intensity.

Certainly, as noted above, there are cases in which individuals are drawn to topics and develop and pursue them as interests in large part because of their importance, and achieve success, making important contributions. James Watson seems to have had a remarkably clear sense that solving the structure of DNA was important, the most important topic he could possibly work on, which was the primary reason he focused on it, why he was so interested and determined to find a way to solve its structure. His iron firmness in never losing

[18]It is also true that many individuals, including many who are very talented, form interests in topics that are not of broad significance or importance, for example, topics that were important in the past but turn out not to be important for the future development of their fields, which greatly reduces their chances of making an important contribution.

[19]This primacy of intrinsic interest over extrinsic factors fits with research in social psychology supporting the view that extrinsic rewards are less central and effective in motivating and guiding creative activity than intrinsic motivation, indeed in certain circumstances can actually retard creativity. Teresa Amabile is best known for this viewpoint; see her work cited in Chapter 1, foonote 29. However, this view is controversial.

sight of its importance, and not allowing himself to be deflected to alternative topics, is indeed what stands out the most in *The Double Helix*. He notes there how other very talented and better equipped scientists, like Linus Pauling, and even Francis Crick, seemed to be less focused and allowed themselves to become distracted by other problems even though these were evidently (in his view) less important. In fact Watson doesn't really seem to have been interested in DNA for its own sake, but because of its connection with the gene, which he was convinced held the secret of life — that was his true interest, and he was interested in solving the structure of DNA because he was convinced that DNA is the basic constituent of the gene, thus that solving its structure would reveal the secret of the gene and thus the secret of life. John Maynard Keynes clearly was motivated by a sense of importance in forming and pursuing his interest in exploring the channels through which monetary policy and expectations affect economic decisions and output. Even in these cases, however, and others like them, intrinsic interest is important. Thus, even Watson, who is unusual in having been so aware of the issue of potential importance, writes of how it was great "fun" talking to Francis Crick, and this sense of fun, the sheer interest and enjoyment of the collaboration, was clearly important in the two of them forming a working relationship and beginning to work seriously on trying to construct models of the structure of DNA and in carrying Watson forward in learning about X-ray diffraction analysis.

In fact many individuals who make important contributions seem to have little or no notion of the importance of their interests, at least at the time they initially form them — they pursue their interests simply because they find them intrinsically interesting, and find themselves led serendipitously — often to their surprise and amazement — to a point at which they are capable of making important contributions. Charles Darwin's youthful interest in collecting natural forms and in the diversity of forms was certainly intrinsic — collecting was an end in itself, and he clearly had no idea his interest would lead where it eventually did. And intrinsic fascination at the diversity of life-forms and the relationships among them seems to have been the fundamental source of the more conceptual interest he formed during the first part of his time in South America, described in Chapter 3, in the spatial and temporal ranges of extent of species and the similarities and differences in morphology and behaviors between allied species inhabiting neighboring habitats or that appear to fill similar niches in their environments. In particular, at the time he first became interested in these patterns and began recording information about them in his *Beagle* Diary and notebooks he did not recognize their full import, that they held the key to understanding the origin of species — that awareness only dawned on him later, perhaps towards the end of his stay on mainland South America, most likely after his visit to the Galápagos Islands during the voyage home (see Chapter 10).

The evidence that exists in letters and recollections indicates that Henri Matisse began painting with strong vibrant colors and experimenting with color contrasts, juxtaposing colors and using them to create and define object and spatial boundaries, because he found this mode of painting exciting and had a sense of liberation, breaking free from his conventional, conservative training, and perhaps also because it resonated with his cultural roots growing up in Bohain, renowned for the rich colors and luxuriousness of its textile products — not because he had any immediate sense that pursuing this interest would lead him to such pathbreaking contributions as it did. Over the ensuing few years he seems to have been intrinsically driven to pursue his interest and radical approach. He remarked on "the misery of not painting like all the others," speaking almost fatalistically about the path he followed, somehow compelled; he seems to have been driven, like so many highly creative individuals are, to pursue his independent path for internal, intrinsic reasons, because it resonated with his internal sense of what he wished to express through his art, and also because it seemed to be a new path forward, enabling experimentation, thus affording opportunity for creative development.[20]

There is no better example of an individual deeply, intrinsically interested in topics and problems that turn out to be of great importance than Albert Einstein. Einstein's intensity of concentration and interest is renowned, and he himself told a friend that what distinguished him was simply that he was "intensely curious" about certain questions and problems. His development, as I interpret it and as it fits in the framework of creative development, is a fascinating case of the recognition of a paradox — combining intrinsic interest with an intuitive sense of its importance — leading to the formation of a rich creative interest that in turn led, after many years, to great creative insight.

As described in Chapter 3, Einstein formed an interest in Maxwell's theory of electromagnetic radiation as a youth. He seems to have been especially interested in the passage of light, electromagnetic radiation, through space, or, as he then understood it, through the ether, which would naturally have led to

[20] See Hilary Spurling, *The Unknown Matisse*, chaps. 5–10; quote on p. 140. Another account of his development that focuses more on interpretation of his development based on his artistic production over this period is given by Alfred H. Barr, Jr. in *Matisse: His Art and His Public* (New York: The Museum of Modern Art, 1951).

his being interested in and exploring current work on working out formulas describing electromagnetic radiation by moving bodies. In a memo written (most likely) at the age of sixteen Einstein refers to "the marvelous experiments of Hertz" that have "elucidated the dynamic nature" of electromagnetic phenomena, their "propagation in space." He goes on to describe experiments he has devised to measure the "deformation" of the ether caused by a magnetic field induced by an electric current, which he believed held the potential energy of the magnetic field.[21]

In his "Autobiographical Notes" written late in life and noteworthy for its clarity Einstein states that at the age of sixteen (the same age at which he wrote the memo) he hit upon the following paradox. "If I pursue a beam of light with the velocity c (velocity of light in a vacuum) [that is, travel just behind the beam at the same velocity it is moving] I should observe such a beam of light as a spatially oscillatory electromagnetic field at rest [since he will be moving at the same speed as the beam it will, according to classical physics, not appear to be moving from his perspective, thus will be at rest]. However, there seems to be no such thing, whether on the basis of experience or according to Maxwell's equations."[22]

The basic problem of adapting Maxwell's equations to bodies in motion relative to one another — light beams emanating from moving sources — was recognized not only by Einstein, but also by others, including Lorentz and Poincaré. What I believe distinguishes Einstein, apart from how young he was at the time he formulated his paradox, was the way in which, over the ensuing years, he defined an interest branching out from the paradox in two directions, one focusing on the physics of electrodynamics of moving bodies, the other conceptual foundations and ultimately philosophical conceptions of space and time — with the paradox at the center linking these two branches, shaping his interest and his pursuit of it. Einstein described the decade after he identified the paradox and formed his initial interest in electromagnetic radiation of moving bodies as "years of groping" — conveying the sense of his exploration of his interest and preoccupation — through which and at the

---

[21]In reference to the experiment he proposes he writes, "I believe that it would be of great importance for the understanding of the electromagnetic phenomena also to undertake a comprehensive experimental investigation of the potential states of the ether in magnetic fields of all kinds, or, in other words, to measure the elastic deformations and the acting deforming forces." The memo is in *The Collected Papers of Albert Einstein*, Vol. 1; The Early Years: 1879–1902; Anna Beck, trans. (Princeton, NJ: Princeton University Press, 1987), pp. 4–6.

[22]Albert Einstein, "Autobiographical Notes," in *Albert Einstein: Philosopher-Scientist*, p. 53.

end of which insight came.[23] I describe his path of development leading to his insight in Chapter 10.

[23]"Fundamental Ideas and Methods of the Theory of Relativity, Presented in Their Development," in *The Collected Papers of Albert Einstein*, Vol. 7; The Berlin Years: Writings, 1918–1921; English translation of selected texts; trans. by Alfred Engel (Princeton, NJ: Princeton University Press, 2002), p. 135, the footnote.

6

Kinds of Creative Interests

Many of our conceptions of our creative interests have a relatively simple underlying form. Our creative interests center and are constructed around our conceptions and thus many of them also have or appear to have a relatively simple core conceptual form — the reason for the qualification being that our interests are typically not fully accessible to us, which makes it difficult to determine their form. Even rich, elaborate conceptions and interests often have relatively simple cores — are constructed upon simple underlying conceptual structures, elaborating on them.

There are a number of especially common conceptual cores of creative interests and conceptions of interests. In this chapter I describe and present examples of the most important of these, showing with examples how interests and especially conceptions of interests are constructed based upon them. The set of core forms I describe provides the beginnings of a taxonomy of creative interests.

Describing common conceptual cores draws attention to the similarities in conceptual structure among creative interests, in particular interests and conceptions that share the same basic core. While calling attention to these commonalities and describing them is valuable, it is important that we not be distracted from recognizing and appreciating the great variety and distinctiveness of creative interests. In particular, form and content as I employ them here are distinct — interests that share the same core conceptual form in general have completely different, unrelated content. Indeed the conceptual cores I describe are cores of interests in many different fields, interests which thus differ enormously from one another in terms of content, although it is also true that certain kinds of cores seem to be more common in certain fields. Further, creative interests and conceptions of creative interests in many cases have additional structures and elements woven around or constructed upon their cores — conceptual elaborations and refinements; see the examples and the next chapter.[1] It's natural to wonder whether particular conceptual forms of creative interests and conceptions of creative interests are associated with particular patterns of creative development, and also whether certain conceptual forms are more likely to lead to highly valued contributions than others. It is my belief that both conjectures are most likely true; however, my data and analysis are not sufficient to reach definite conclusions about them. In any event I leave them aside in this chapter; I take them up, to a very limited degree, in later chapters.

Two further points should be noted. I do not discuss here separately interests that are "simple" topics, for example, Alexander Calder's interest in motion as an art form and setting art in motion; even simple topics have a conceptual and logical structure that could be explored in more depth.[2] Also, I do not separately discuss questions, problems, and goals as they enter into creative interests. These are of course central to many creative interests and conceptions of interests and it would in principle be possible to define these as distinct conceptual forms. But that seems to me artificial because they are pervasive in all forms of interests, and also because the forms thus defined would be, I believe, less interesting than the forms on which I focus.

[1]The conceptions of creative interests I focus on analyzing are mainly described linguistically (see the discussion in Chapter 2). A number of approaches may be useful for analyzing descriptions of conceptions of creative interests, viewed as linguistic structures revealing conceptual structures in the mind. One is semantics, especially structural modeling linking syntax to meaning; a good example is Ray Jackendoff, *Semantic Structures* (Cambridge, MA: MIT Press, 1990). Another is cognitive linguistics, in which there is a focus on the use of metaphors and mental models and developing a taxonomy of basic kinds of categories, structures, and models. A key reference is George Lakoff, *Women, Fire, and Dangerous Things: What Categories Reveal About the Mind* (Chicago: University of Chicago Press, 1987). See also *Cognitive Linguistics in the Redwoods: The Expansion of a New Paradigm in Linguistics*, ed. Eugene H. Casad (Berlin: Mouton de Gruyter, 1996). I do not attempt to forge an explicit link to these approaches in this book — such links would be a useful direction to explore.

[2]Some creative interests appear to have conceptual structures that do not readily match any common core, at least none of the cores I describe. But it is not clear how truly irregular or idiosyncratic they are without a full taxonomy of interests, which I have not developed.

A basic form of creative interest is an interest in a domain. A domain is a category containing elements, defined by a set of properties that identify or define implicitly which elements or kinds of elements are contained within the domain, delimiting its scope. A domain that is a creative interest has about it a sense of mystery — we do not know what all of its elements are, or its properties, but rather imagine them, conjecture about them — much of the attraction is the sense of the unknown, the quest of exploration. The domains in which we form creative interests are, in many if not most cases, not conventional; rather they are domains we define for ourselves, and are thus original, or at least unusual, both in the way we define them and the sets of elements they contain — or, more accurately, that we imagine they contain (see the next chapter, in which I discuss distinctiveness of interests). They are also of medium breadth in most cases, not as broad as most conventional domains.

The set of potential domains that might be defined and form the basis for a creative interest is essentially limitless. Domains can be defined in almost any field or practice and area of knowledge or experience, and there are many different kinds of elements that may and do form the bases for domains for creative interests — physical entities and phenomena, words, concepts, images, people and other kinds of living creatures, cultural works, processes, models, problems, approaches, movements, and structural forms. Further, a myriad of different domains can be defined over a given class of elements, each defined differently and thus circumscribing a different, unique set of elements.

Many of the creative interests introduced in the preceding chapters are domains. Cheryl Nixon's interest, the "literary heirs" of Aphra Behn, is a domain — a group of women writers whom Cheryl imagined and believed existed (though she did not know for certain) in the eighteenth century, who carried on in Aphra Behn's wake, writing about important social issues.[3] It is noteworthy that Cheryl defined this domain herself. Douglas Hofstadter's interest, rules of generation for integer sequences, is likewise a domain. The fundamental elements of this domain are best thought of as pairs, each element consisting of an integer sequence together with its rule of generation; Douglas was in particular interested in sequences with nonobvious rules of generation, rules that can be discovered only with difficulty and that he imagined to be mysterious and beautiful. A characteristic of a domain that is a creative interest is that it has many elements, not just a few. Thus, had Douglas been focused on one or two specific sequences it would not be correct to call his interest

---

[3]Cheryl actually was primarily interested not in the women themselves, but their writing — a domain of literary works.

a domain. But in fact he explored hundreds of sequences, and clearly conceived of his interest as a vast pool of sequences generated by an enormous variety of different rules. Stephen Shapiro's interest, American literature from the early 1790s through the 1820s, is likewise a domain.[4] Many of Thomas Edison's interests were, as he conceived them, domains, filled with many elements and possibilities. An example is his interest in electromechanical devices: he imagined all sorts of such devices, making notes about them in his sketchbooks, and undoubtedly imagined that there were many more possibilities beyond those he had thought of at any time, that he felt optimistic he would eventually discover or invent. This in fact is a general point: when we form a creative interest we incorporate into our conception of our interest elements we imagine as well as a sense of those we cannot explicitly imagine but nevertheless believe or hope are present. Other examples of domain interests are Samuel Taylor Coleridge's interests, described in Chapters 10 and 13, and Hannah Arendt's interest mentioned below and described in Chapter 15.

In defining a domain-based creative interest individuals in some cases begin from a base domain, then define a second, conceptually richer domain, the elements of which are based upon the elements of the base domain, with this second domain being the focus of interest. For example, for Charles Darwin his childhood interest in life-forms, in collecting specimens of different species and varieties, established a base domain which later, during the voyage of the *Beagle*, served as a basis for defining a second, more conceptual domain, focusing on geographic (and temporal) ranges of extent of allied species and varieties and similarities and differences in characteristics between members of allied species inhabiting neighboring locales or similar niches in their environments.

As a related point, in many cases when we form a creative interest that is based upon and defined in terms of a base domain, but goes beyond it, our interest is in discovering, defining, and characterizing general laws, properties, or themes of the base domain, in particular discovering underlying properties of its elements, identifying commonalities among sets of elements, and making connections among elements and sets of elements, thus identifying general, overarching patterns and structures — in short, discovering general truths about the domain. In her twenties and early thirties Hannah Arendt pursued an interest in the history of anti-Semitism, initially exploring its history

---

[4]Stephen told me that as he explored this period more closely he eventually realized that it is best thought of as two distinct periods or domains: the literature of the 1790s, which he considers forward-looking, imagining social improvements and experimentation, influenced by the French Revolution; and the literature from the early 1800s on, which he came to see as more escapist in tone, more somber, withdrawing from risky social experimentation, emphasizing clandestine themes and activities.

164 in Germany, then, after she fled to Paris, in France, building up an extensive historical knowledge base.[5] During World War II, as the extent of the Nazis' atrocities and the true nature of their terrible rule began to be apparent, Hannah, now living in America, formed an interest in trying to understand the historical and theoretical linkages connecting the history of both anti-Semitism and public debates about the place of Jews in Germany and European society with the rise of the Nazis and Fascistic political movements, expanding her inquiry to incorporate the rise of imperialism. Thus she came to focus on identifying the roots, currents, interconnections, events and ideologies out of which emerged or, in her term, "crystallized" political extremism linked to extreme forms of anti-Semitism, racism, and imperialism, the rise of Nazi Germany with its concomitant terror of concentration camps, the Holocaust, and global war — what she later came to recognize and so brilliantly describe as a distinctive political form, totalitarianism. Thus her interest was rooted in a base of historical knowledge but focused not on this knowledge base itself, but on using it to identify critical historical and theoretical relationships, linkages, and processes of emergence of extreme political ideas and movements. Susan Ferguson's language experiences in Kenya provided a rich domain of phenomena out of which she formed an interest in the norms governing language choice, the social meanings of using different languages, language and code switching, and language hybridization. Thus her interest — not necessarily initially, but as it developed — focused not just on the rich domain of phenomena, though this remained important for her, but also on a more abstract level on rules and practices of language usage and their social meanings. Similarly, many scientists and mathematicians have as their ultimate creative interest when they form an interest in a domain to discover general laws and properties of the domain, thus to go beyond specific phenomena and cases to discover more general truths.

There are it appears two different patterns in cases in which interests are defined as domains formed over base domains. Sometimes the domain of interest has more elements, hence is denser or richer than the base domain. This for example was the case for Matisse, whose domain of interest had as one of its main kind of elements combinations of base domain elements — basic color dots, patches, and lines. More commonly, particularly in the case of interests focused on general properties, characteristics, and themes of base domains, the second domain is conceptualized as having fewer but far more complex elements.

[5]*For Love of the World*, chaps. 3–5, especially pp. 142 and 147–48, also pp. 81–82, 86, 89, 91–95, 108–10, and 121–22. Hannah's studies of anti-Semitism were the basis for a series of articles she published; I discuss her development in Chapter 15.

A second kind of creative interest is an interest in the relationship between two — or, rarely, more than two — topics, subjects, or approaches. There are two main forms of relationship interest: an interest in exploring and seeking to understand the relationship between two topics, subjects, or approaches, for example, by comparing and contrasting them; and an interest focused on forging a relationship between two topics, subjects, or approaches that have not previously been connected, at least not in the way envisioned. For such interests often the base topics, subjects, or approaches are at least somewhat conventional, and the true distinctiveness of the interest is the relationship between them that is imagined.

In the course of studying creative development I have come across two main types of relationship interests, that mirror these two forms but are more specific. I describe each in turn.

One form of relationship interest that seems relatively common is an interest in applying a methodology or framework of analysis that has previously been developed and utilized in one area to the exploration and development of a different area that has traditionally been studied in other ways. Based on the sample of individuals whose developments I have studied this type of interest seems often to be fruitful and to lead to valued creative contributions. I present two examples of this type of interest here, the main creative interests of Takao Hensch, a neurobiologist I interviewed, and Hans Krebs. For each of Takao and Hans I describe in brief his development of his interest and present his conception of interest. Hans Krebs achieved great success through pursuing his interest, making fundamental contributions, pursuing a path that led to work for which he won a Nobel Prize. Takao, although certainly not having achieved such great success as that, has also been quite successful — his research pursuing his interest has generated a series of papers in *Science*. Another example of this type of relationship interest is Galileo's interest in applying the methods of Archimedean analysis to study the physics of motion, described in Chapter 2; Galileo of course achieved fame in history for the discoveries he made through pursuing his interest.

Takao became interested in neurobiology in college. From the start he was interested in neural circuitry and especially synaptic plasticity, the cellular processes through which the strength of synaptic connections between neurons is altered, which is believed to be important in brain development and learning and memory. "I was interested in circuits in the brain," he told me, mentioning in particular the visual system and the cerebellum as systems he found interesting — "plasticity, long-term potentiation and depression, the idea that you could change circuits that had been laid down in development, that was interesting to me." He said that one of the most interesting topics he learned about in college was the pioneering work of Hubel and Wiesel on ocular dominance columns — the organization of the visual cortex into columns such that all the neurons in a column receive their primary inputs from the same eye, and adjacent columns alternate eyes.

After college Takao spent two years in Japan working with a well-known neurobiologist who studied long-term depression in the cerebellum; he described his work in Japan as "the first step for me into synaptic plasticity." While in Japan he formed a conception of what has been his main creative interest. "I was reading quite a bit about plasticity at this point," he told me, "and about the visual cortex, especially the [formation of the] columnar organization of the visual cortex and the fact that it can be perturbed by alterations of visual experience." "And by now it was 1989 and the cellular mechanisms of long-term potentiation had started to be worked out in other areas like the hippocampus." It became clear to him, Takao told me, that the developing visual cortex would be an excellent system in which to study these kinds of cellular mechanisms of plasticity, because the formation of the ocular dominance columns "is a clearly very strong plasticity that is observed in young animals but disappears with age." Further, he saw an opportunity: for although scientists were beginning to explore the cellular mechanisms of plasticity in the cerebellum and the hippocampus, very little work had been done exploring these mechanisms in the developing visual cortex. In particular, as he told me, visual cortical plasticity was still thought about in terms of abstract theoretical, computational models, rather than more explicit molecular mechanisms — "visual cortical plasticity was discussed at a level of, two eyes' inputs are competing for cortical space, whatever that means, competing for some reward factor possibly... these terms were used that have come down to us from computational scientists, theoretical neuroscience."[6] "And the field was sorely lacking any kind of cellular or molecular underpinnings." Thus Takao was interested in *applying the molecular and cellular techniques that had been developed for studying plasticity in the cerebellum and other parts of the brain to study plasticity in the developing visual system.* This clearly has the form of a relationship interest of the type defined above. Takao was interested in borrowing and adapting techniques that have been developed and applied in other

[6]In his famous book *The Organization of Behavior: A Neuropsychological Theory* (New York: Wiley, 1949), Donald Hebb put forward the hypothesis that when two neurons are connected and fire synchronously (e.g., in response to the same stimuli), the connection between them will tend to become stronger, and if they fire asynchronously the connection between them will tend to become weaker. These are the kinds of ideas/ models Takao was referring to.

areas to address questions and study phenomena in a different area that have traditionally been studied using different methods. As natural as his interest seems, Takao's interest was in fact distinctive, as I discuss in the next chapter.

Going forward, Takao's conception of his interest guided him in his development. In particular, he organized his doctoral research program around his interest; I describe a set of projects he developed based on his interest in Chapter 14.

As described in Chapter 3, Hans Krebs was inspired as a student by the vision of his teacher, Franz Knoop, of "an unbroken series of equations" beginning with the foodstuffs an organism takes in and describing the complete chain of chemical reactions through which these foodstuffs are decomposed by the organism, providing energy and basic materials for the synthesis of biochemicals, terminating with the final waste products that are excreted. This vision excited his interest in the field of "intermediary metabolism," the study of the component processes of this chain, with emphasis on elucidating its intermediate steps.

Though his interest had been sparked, Hans did not immediately begin to work in this field, as noted in Chapter 3. After university he went to medical school. One of his teachers, and the teacher's assistant, lectured on metabolic diseases, furthering his interest in metabolic processes; but other than that he focused on other subjects and his medical training.[7] During these years he conducted research in several labs, under the supervision of physicians, in the area of physical and colloid chemistry.[8]

In January 1926, Hans began working in the lab of Otto Warburg, the eminent biochemist. Warburg had developed a general manometric technique for measuring rates of biological oxidation and a method for preparing thin tissue slices, preserving cells in the slices intact, then measuring their rates of metabolic activity (the manometric method could be used to measure both oxidative respiration (aerobic metabolism) and glycolysis (anaerobic metabolism), the two phases of metabolic activity). During his first ten months in the lab Hans learned the basic manometric technique, working on a project he was assigned investigating rates of oxidation of sugars in alkali solutions, and measuring the increase in rates of oxidation caused by the introduction of metal ions, which Warburg believed act as catalysts in the oxidation reactions. After completing this project he learned the tissue slice method and employed it on a second project, investigating rates of metabolism in cancer tissue and normal tissue.[9]

---

[7] Frederic Holmes, *Hans Krebs: The Formation of a Scientific Life*, pp. 91–93.
[8] Ibid., chap. 3, part IV, chap. 4, and the beginning of chap. 5, through part I.
[9] Ibid., chap. 5, from part II on, and chap. 6.

Around the time he completed work on this second project, seventeen months after entering the Warburg lab, Hans formed a conception of an interest that he believed would be fruitful to pursue and desired to pursue himself. He described his conception and what he believed, looking back, to be its origin, in interviews with his biographer Frederic Holmes.[10] He said (the quotations in this and the following paragraphs are restatements by Holmes of statements Hans made during their interviews) that during the time he worked on the second project "he came to appreciate and admire the power of the methods Warburg had devised" for studying metabolic processes; he especially recognized their value in allowing quantitative calculation of rates of metabolism and "how quickly and easily one could test a variety of ideas or examine the effects of diverse conditions on a given process." Warburg was focused on a particular set of issues — measuring rates of oxidative respiration and glycolysis quantitatively under various conditions, and comparing rates between cancerous and normal cells. But Hans imagined that the methods Warburg had developed "might be applicable to many processes beyond those with which Warburg was presently concerned." In particular, it occurred to him that it would be possible *to apply the manometric tissue slice method as the basis for experimental investigations in the field of intermediary metabolism.* Further, he "thought that he would like to explore such possibilities" in his own research, and that such investigations might potentially be of "general significance," that is, lead to important discoveries and advances. Thus he formed a conception defining a creative interest he wished to pursue. His interest was a relationship interest — specifically, an interest in applying methods that had been developed and utilized in one area to address questions and investigate processes in a second, related area.

Discussing the formation of his interest Hans said that what enabled him to "envision" the possibility and appreciate the potential importance of applying the methods Warburg had developed to study intermediary metabolism was the vision he "had absorbed from Knoop" so many years earlier.[11] The process of formation of his interest thus followed the pattern of narrowing down from a broad idealistic vision to a more specific topic of interest, as described in Chapter 3. Another factor in his development of his interest may have been his investigation, as part of his work on the second lab project, of a lactic

        [10] Ibid; the discussion in this and the next two paragraphs, including all quotations, comes from pp. 178–79. Holmes's biographical approach here is a model for biography of creative persons, in eliciting vital information from a subject about his conception of interest.
        [11] Krebs also noted that his interest in intermediary metabolism had been reinforced by the lectures he had heard as a medical student about metabolic diseases.

acid cycle that had recently been proposed by a well-known biochemist at his institute. The idea of the cycle was that in certain conditions, for example, muscle metabolism, lactic acid is produced in the first stage of respiration, glycolysis, while simultaneously being used up as an input in the synthesis of a sugar in the second stage, oxidative respiration, with the implication that it will be observed as a final product only if its rate of formation in the first process exceeds its rate of reuptake in the second. This was actually a specific example of a general point about the formation of intermediaries in metabolic processes — any chemical compound that serves as an intermediary and does not accumulate in the body as an end product must be reutilized at a rate equal to its rate of formation. Hans may have come to realize through investigating the lactic acid cycle using the manometric method that this method was in fact well suited to address the formation of intermediaries, since it could in theory enable a precise quantitative comparison of two rates and therefore allow determination of whether a given compound could in fact be an intermediary product.[12] Notwithstanding the possibility that investigating the lactic acid cycle may have played a role in the sparking of his interest, he did not specially have this cycle in mind when he formed his conception of his interest. To the contrary, he said that at the time he formed his interest, not having studied intermediary metabolism in any depth since he heard Knoop lecture about it, he did not have any specific reaction or pathway in mind to study — he had not "fixed his attention on any concrete set of problems within the field." Thus, although more specific than the grand vision of Knoop, his conception had breadth, a fundamental characteristic of creative interests, as discussed in Chapter 2 and the next chapter — his conception defined an interest he wished to pursue, not a specific problem or project.

During one of the interviews with Holmes during which they discussed this phase of his development Hans said that one day soon after forming his conception of interest he went to Warburg and told him that "in his opinion the tissue slice [manometric] method 'is a useful tool for studying intermediary metabolism,' and that he would like to study [such] metabolic processes with the techniques that Warburg had developed."[13] He described being rebuffed by Warburg: He said Warburg told him that "such experiments would be of no interest to him" — Warburg was in fact disdainful of studying the intermediate steps in metabolic processes and in his own work focused exclusively on measuring metabolic rates from initial inputs to final end products,

---

[12]Ibid., pp. 170–75.
[13]The middle passage in single quotes is a verbatim statement by Krebs, the remaining parts of the quote a restatement of what he said by Holmes. Ibid., p. 179 for this and following quotes.

ignoring intervening steps and products — and that "there was no room" in his lab for individuals to pursue their own ideas. Having essentially no choice in the matter, Krebs said, he gave up his idea for the time being and stuck to projects that Warburg gave him to pursue, that were in line with Warburg's own research program. But, as Holmes describes it, using words Hans himself surely used, "the vista that had opened up to him seemed compelling," and "he clung to the idea that when he was in an independent position he would do something about it." As I describe in Chapter 11, he in fact did take up his interest and pursue it several years later, when he left Warburg's lab to set up his own independent lab and thus was free to do so.

The second form of relationship interest is an interest in exploring the relationship between two topics, subjects, or approaches, between which no such relationship has previously been discussed, at least not from the same perspective. The focus may be on exploring causal linkages between two topics or subjects, exploring ways to synthesize two topics, subjects, or approaches to create a new form, for example, combining two different styles, or comparing and contrasting two topics, subjects, or approaches, for example, comparing two systems of thought.

Robert Kaufman is an example of an individual who formed a relationship interest of this type that he pursued as his main creative interest. As described in Chapter 3, Robert grew up in a politically Left family and early on formed an interest in the relationship between literature and politics. He told me that as a youth he read widely in modern world literature and also formed an interest in modern art and aesthetics. After a long gap, during which he went to law school and practiced law, as described in Chapter 3, Robert decided to make a career switch and pursue literary studies, and matriculated in a graduate program in English and American literature. Almost immediately upon entering graduate school, he formed — or perhaps it is better to say he recognized — his central creative interest. "Almost immediately it became evident to me that my great interests were in the period starting with the later eighteenth century, the French Revolution and/or its impact all the way through modernism," he told me. "It was increasingly clear to me that the problems of modern art [including literature] started there. They weren't the same exactly, but they were in many senses, their genesis was there."[14] Robert said he "immediately

[14]Robert's interests were in fact slightly more complex than this. He continued: "It also seemed to me, in terms of literary study as a whole, that that period, roughly Romanticism, is poised right between the world of the Renaissance, looking back towards it and in a certain sense doing a modern re-creation of it, and poised in the other way equally towards what becomes modernism, even postmodernism." During his graduate career Robert worked on two projects that together reflect these dual interests.

became very interested" in Keats and Shelley, Shelley being well known for his radical political views. "I recognized right away that they were on the verge in various aspects of what in just a couple of decades would become attempts at putting together various kinds of Left or Marxist aesthetics, that with hardly a detour lead straight to the modern period, modernism and twentieth-century literature." "And it seemed to me a really fascinating thing to burrow into something like, at least a provisionally founding moment of what would become so many issues and problems for modern poetry and aesthetics." "Thus I was pretty certain by the end of that first year that I was interested in Romanticism and modernism and modern aesthetics and the way those three things circled around one another. In particular, I was thinking about it in terms of the genesis of something like a tradition and history of Left poetics and aesthetics and criticism."

Modern Left poetry, criticism, and aesthetics focuses on the relationship of literature and art with its political, economic, social, and historical context, with linkages of influence running in both directions. In speaking of wanting to burrow into the "founding moment" of "issues and problems" of modern poetry and aesthetics it was this relationship that Robert said he meant. Specifically, he was interested in the history and development of Left critical thought about the possible impact of literature and art on political consciousness and, ultimately, political action — as he described it, "questions of what is or can be the relationship of poetic activity, and the aesthetic experience of the reader, to political thought and activity" — thus linked to his youthful interest. His interest thus had a twofold relationship structure: he was interested in (1) the relationship across two historical periods, the Romantic and modern, of (2) Left critical ideas and debates about the relationship between literary activity and political consciousness and action — in exploring the genesis of ideas and debates about this relationship in the Romantic period and ways in which these ideas and debates were reconstituted and developed further in the modern period.

INTERESTS IN ASPECTS OF BROAD, CONVENTIONAL TOPICS

A third kind of creative interest is an interest in a particular aspect or subtopic of a broad general topic. There are three basic types of interests of this kind: (1) an interest in a particular aspect or feature — or subset of features — of a broad topic; (2) an interest in a subtopic of a broad topic; and (3) an interest in approaching a broad topic from a particular perspective. These three types are not necessarily sharply differentiated. The broad topic is in most cases fairly conventional, often a topic that other people in the same field also form interests based upon. Hence what makes a creative interest of this kind distinctive in most cases is the particular aspect, feature, or subtopic of the broad topic that is focused upon, or particular perspective from which it is approached.

Interests of this kind are most common and most natural in fields in which principal objects of study or focuses are complex and multifaceted. Examples are scientific fields in which main objects of study are complex phenomena, areas of the humanities in which the main objects of study are complex works, fields of engineering centering on relatively complex devices and processes, and areas of study in the social sciences that focus on complex human practices and behaviors.

Hannah Arendt approached the topic of anti-Semitism and debates about the place of the Jews in European society from a historical perspective; this was due in part to the fact that her interest grew out of or developed at about the same time or just after her study of Rahel Varnhagen, and also to her training. Her historical perspective and the historical knowledge base she built up shaped her approach when she came to make an intensive study of the origins of Fascism, the rise to power of the Nazis, and their mode of wielding power. She focused on the historical roots of Fascistic political ideas, reaching back into the nineteenth century. It is noteworthy that her perspective was distinctive, different from that of others who analyzed the rise to power of the Nazis and Fascists — most other analyses of the time focused either on much shorter term historical events, such as the German hyperinflation and the failure of the moderates in the 1920s, or psychological characteristics that may lead individuals to be attracted to Fascist and authoritarian ideologies. Thus the distinctive focus of her interest carried through and is reflected in the distinctiveness and depth of her work.[15]

Sophia Colamarino, whose development and conception of her interest is described in Chapter 4, and Chris Callahan, another neurobiologist I interviewed, both developed interests in axonal pathfinding, the process through which neurons grow to their targets. Axonal pathfinding is a central process in the formation of neural connectivity, hence for the formation of neural

[15] Hannah's approach, in *The Origins of Totalitarianism*, especially parts I and II, with its relatively long-term historical perspective, stands in marked contrast to the approach taken by others in their analyses of the rise of the Nazis and Fascist movements. These include the well-known work on personality structures that lead people to be attracted to Fascistic ideologies, notably Erich Fromm's *Escape from Freedom* (New York: Holt, Rinehart and Winston, 1941), and Theodore W. Adorno, Else Frenkel-Brunswik, Daniel J. Levinson, and R. Nevitt Sanford, *The Authoritarian Personality* (New York: Harper, 1950), as well as biographical studies of Adolf Hitler and studies of short-term historical forces that led to the Nazis rise to power, such as the German hyperinflation, the reparations payments, and other political and economic events following World War I.

circuits, thus a central topic in the field of neurobiology. It is also important for axon regeneration following nerve injury, studied in this context both in neuroscience and medicine. It is a relatively broad topic — a complex, multifaceted phenomenon, important developmentally for the brain and nervous system, and studied from several different disciplinary bases, including molecular biology, genetics, neurodevelopment, and comparative anatomy. Thus it has many different aspects and subtopics and is studied in different ways, with a variety of approaches. Consistent with its breadth and importance, pathfinding is — and was also at the time Sophia and Chris formed their interests — relatively intensively studied. In the *Abstracts* for the Society for Neuroscience 1991 Annual Meeting, which occurred around the time Sophia and Chris formed their interests, there are four listed sessions on axon guidance mechanisms and pathways, with 59 abstracts published for posters presented. There are also a number of other abstracts for posters concerning pathfinding listed in other sessions, including in sessions on process outgrowth, growth cones and sprouting, and regeneration.[16]

Given how important a topic pathfinding is, and that there is ongoing research on it, it is to be expected, based upon the description of creative interests set forth in this book, that individuals who become interested in the general topic of pathfinding will form interests and conceptions of interests focusing on particular aspects or subtopics of pathfinding — their interests will have a more specific focus. This was in fact the case for Sophia and Chris: each focused on a particular aspect of pathfinding. Further, they focused on very different aspects, highlighting how a broad conventional topic can be the basis for many different interests, each centering on a different aspect of the topic. In chapter 8 I present their descriptions of the aspects of pathfinding that interested them and their conceptions of their interests, showing that they were interested in very different aspects of pathfinding.

When we form an interest in a particular aspect or subtopic of a broad topic, or in approaching a broad topic from a distinctive perspective, it is frequently the case that the particular, distinctive focus of our interest is rooted in or connected with a second topic that we have prior interest or expertise in.[17]

John von Neumann developed an interest of this kind that illustrates its form. As a mathematician von Neumann had a long-standing interest in nonlinear

---

[16]This is out of a total of 639 listed sessions and about 10,000 posters. The meaning of creative interests being distinctive is shown here: each researcher (or research team) pursuing his own distinctive interest, generating a series of research results that is distinct from, albeit at times overlapping with, others'.

[17]This prior interest may thus serve as a register of meaning.

partial differential equations — he was interested in them theoretically, and was also appreciative of their great practical importance in many fields, including hydrodynamics, aerodynamics, and meteorology, interested in their application and development in these fields. He was also well aware of how limited progress had been towards developing general methods for solving such problems using traditional mathematical techniques, how intractable they had been, as he in fact wrote later.[18] During World War II he became involved in developing methods for the mathematical analysis of bomb detonation charges to deduce charge configurations yielding optimum explosive power, a problem of particular importance for the design of nuclear bombs, for which a satisfactory analysis requires solving nonlinear partial differential equations. This wartime work intensified his sense of the importance of developing practical methods for solving such problems.[19]

It was during and just after the war that von Neumann developed a new interest, connected to his interest in developing general methods for solving nonlinear differential equations. This new interest, sparked by his learning about computers, was, as we may state it: *designing computers and developing computational methods for solving nonlinear partial differential equations and related problems in applied mathematics.* Von Neumann learned about computers in 1943, and rapidly developed knowledge about them. He seems to have grasped very quickly that computers had enormous potential for solving nonlinear partial differential equations and related kinds of problems — indeed given his extensive experience with these kinds of problems he probably grasped this as or more deeply than anyone else at the time. In turn, this sparked his interest in using computers to solve such problems — an interest clearly rooted in his previous experience, including extensive practical experience trying to solve problems of this kind, and his awareness of how intractable they are to general analytic solutions.[20] His interest was not just academic but also hands-on; thus,

---

[18]Von Neumann and a colleague wrote in 1945-46 that "the advance of analysis is, at this moment, stagnant along the entire front of nonlinear problems," and that even though "the main mathematical difficulties in fluid dynamics" had been known for many years, "yet no decisive progress has been made against them." This was written in the context of justifying the need to develop computers and computational methods for solving such problems. See William Aspray, *John von Neumann and the Origins of Modern Computing* (Cambridge, MA: MIT Press, 1990), p. 59.

[19]Ibid., chap. 2, pp. 25–39 and 47–48. See also Richard Rhodes, *The Making of the Atomic Bomb* (New York: Simon & Schuster, 1986), pp. 479–80, 540–42, 544–45.

[20]*John von Neumann and the Origins of Modern Computing*, chap. 2, pp. 27–39, 47, and chap. 3, pp. 52–53 and 59–63. Von Neumann was also aware of, though less concerned with, the possibility of using computers to solve large-scale linear systems; see Ibid., pp. 97–104.

he became interested in and probed in depth engineering details of computer design, and, not immediately but within a year or two, wanted and hoped to build a computer himself, to his own design and specification.

Von Neumann thus formed an interest focusing on a particular subtopic of a broad topic — the broad topic being computers, their design and the development of computational methods, and his specific focus being the design of computers and development of computational methods for a certain kind of purpose, to solve a general class of problems. His focus on designing and using computers to solve such equations is shown by the fact that in lectures he gave and papers he wrote with collaborators during the mid-forties about the design and development of advanced computers, first in association with a working group at the University of Pennsylvania in proposals for the EDVAC computer and then at the Institute for Advanced Study, nonlinear partial differential equations are consistently pointed to as paradigms of the kinds of problems the computers should be able to solve and will be used to study, and are referred to — their great practical importance pointed out — in motivating the need to build such advanced computers.[21] His interest can be viewed as both an interest in a particular subtopic of a broader topic and also as an interest in linking a technology or solution approach with a class of problems, thus as a relationship interest.

APPROACHES

Some creative interests center on an approach, such as a methodology, style, or technique. An individual who forms an interest centering on an approach is interested in exploring the approach and developing and applying it creatively, thus organizes his development, at least in part, around learning about it and developing and applying it as the basis for creative work. In many cases he is wedded more to the approach than to any specific substantive topic or area. An interest that centers on an approach resembles a domain interest — the different variants or forms of the approach, and different potential applications

[21] See "First Draft of a Report on the EDVAC," in *Papers of John von Neumann on Computing and Computer Theory*, ed. William Aspray and Arthur Burks (Cambridge, MA: MIT Press; and Los Angeles: Tomash Publishers, 1987), pp. 19–20 and 56–57; and "Preliminary Discussion of the Logical Design of an Electronic Computing Instrument" (with Arthur Burks and Herman Goldstine), Ibid., pp. 98–99, 102, and 136. The focus on solving problems like nonlinear partial differential equations permeates many aspects of design discussion in both documents. See William Aspray, *John von Neumann and the Origins of Modern Computing*, pp. 34–41, 52–53; and for the use of examples for design specifications and decisions see pp. 36–39, 52–53, 60–72, and chap. 4.

being the elements of its domain. As a variant of this basic form, in some cases we form an interest in employing a particular approach to explore and develop a particular topic or area — wedding an approach to a topic, thus forming a kind of relationship interest; Takao's and Hans Krebs's interests are examples.

Enid Zentelis, the filmmaker I interviewed, is an example of someone whose creative work centers around a particular approach, what is really a philosophy of filmmaking. She is interested in depicting the details of individuals' everyday lives in film, as a way to raise consciousness about larger social issues and conditions of life. "Details — the fabric of people's lives. The more people I met and the more places I went the more I realized how ignorant people are of certain things and that it is the 'little things' that can really tell somebody how somebody else's world is. And not only that, but also maybe [raise the issue], 'Is this the way that things should be?'" Enid believes it is the everyday details that grab an audience's attention and communicate what a person's life is really like, and that this is the most effective way to raise political and social consciousness. "My philosophy [on] how to change things is that if you are overt and [direct], that those messages never come through. Whereas, someone will be fascinated by the way someone else brushes their teeth. And I happen to believe . . . that in observing the way a person brushes their teeth you are going to learn about how they live their life and why they live their life that way, and all the things that influence how their life is lived." Enid has searched for subjects that fit with this approach, and each time she has taken up a social issue in a film she has done so through depicting an individual life in its details. Describing the origins of her film *Dog Race* about the plight of working-class single moms, who had come under attack for having babies and being on welfare, she said, "I thought, 'someone has to experience what it's like'. . . . there was an unending stream of political debate and controversy without anyone ever really living those lives. So I wanted to show something — make a film that showed something that you couldn't refute — that you couldn't stick a finger in and say 'that's not true' — so that at the end of the day I have made my point in a way that is indelible."[22]

Karen Hadley, a literary scholar, is interested, as an approach to literary analysis, in doing close, linguistically based readings of specific passages of literature, for example analyzing the tense and aspect of verbs, as a way to probe for the meaning of a passage and larger work. As a last example, Tina Brooks

---

[22] Enid's first film project, which she worked on in her last year and a half in college, was about her grandmother, a Holocaust survivor; she told me she approached this first film — recollecting the project in hindsight — from the perspective of depicting "each and every detail" of her grandmother's life, thinking that was the most effective way to "inform the viewer of what an experience such as the Holocaust is, or experiences [like that] of great suffering."

is interested in doing cross-racial, cross-gender analyses of literature, crossing conventional boundaries; this is also an approach — very different from
Karen's — for doing literary analysis.

HOLISTIC CONCEPTIONS; THE ROLE OF METAPHORS
IN CONCEPTIONS OF INTERESTS

A fifth kind of creative interest is an interest defined by a holistic conception —
a conception or vision of a complex whole or world, containing multiple elements that are imagined to fit together in some fashion, and conceived as
self-contained, at least to a degree. There are two basic types of interests of this
kind, differing in the nature of the holistic conceptions that define them, and
especially in the ways in which these conceptions relate to the interests they
define and are employed by the individuals who form and pursue the interests they define. One is an interest in the creative development of a holistic
conception — in developing the conception itself creatively. In this case the
holistic conception is imagined as being able to be given creative form: an
individual who forms and pursues an interest of this type hopes and intends
to bring her holistic conception to life — to realize its creative potential in
or through creative products. The other type is an interest in a topic, oftentimes a domain, that one conceptualizes in terms of a holistic conception. In
this case the holistic conception is not itself intended to be developed creatively or even necessarily able to be so developed — rather, it is a tool for
thinking, to help conceptualize, think about, explore, and develop the topic
or domain of interest creatively. An individual who pursues an interest of this
type is guided by his holistic conception, thinks in terms of it, and generates
ideas and projects through exploring it mentally and using it to think about
and explore his interest.

Holistic conceptions that define a creative interest are typically coherent,
at least to a degree, organized and cohering around a central theme or vision,
thus having a sense of wholeness. Most also have breadth of vision, at least
to a degree. In addition most, though not all, involve many elements that fit
together, for example into a system, which makes them inherently somewhat
complex, and contributes to their sense of richness. All of these qualities carry
over at least to a degree to the creative interests they define.

Holistic conceptions that define a creative interest resemble the conventional notion of a vision in several respects, in particular in their sense of
wholeness and richness. They do not, however, fit the notion of a vision as a
clear picture of a future state or event that will or may come about. In particular, they are not so definite as to serve as an outline defining creative projects

and products and describing where projects are headed, with just the details left to be filled in — they are not and are not intended to be nearly so specific as this nor able to be directly implemented — they are not blueprints. Rather, they are thematic and abstract, often somewhat idealistic. Further, they do not generally have the same form as the creative products they inspire or are the basis for — again, they are not directly applicable in that sense, but imaginary, conceptual guides for thinking and for generating ideas and possibilities. They must thus be transformed, through being generative of ideas and projects, for their creative potential to be realized — they must be developed creatively, not merely mechanically.

Virginia Woolf's conception of us looking into the mirror as we face one another, seeing reflections of ourselves, and of our internal representations of ourselves being constructed out of and sustained by these reflections, is an example of a holistic conception defining a creative interest. It is a conception of the first type — she desired to develop her conception creatively, to find a way to give it expression and realize it creatively in literary form. Her conception is truly holistic — it is a vision of the human world, of the human condition, the self as constituted and sustained by its reflections in social interactions and the world around us. This holistic sense is emphasized by her statement that there is "an almost infinite number" of reflections — thus the generation of reflections is an ongoing, productive process, generating selves and the human world. Her own view of her conception — that she viewed it as holistic in the sense of a constituting experience of the human condition — is shown by her statement that our reflections "are the depths novelists in future will explore, leaving ordinary reality more and more out of account." There are two planes of existence, each holistic, and the plane of reflections is the deeper, more interesting one in her view, the basis of human identity. This is shown further by her linking her conception to the literature of the Greeks and Shakespeare, the most profound literary masters she knows of, whom she views as having also focused on these depths.

Tim Berners-Lee, principal original inventor of the World Wide Web, was inspired and guided by a conception of a web of ideas and information, created on a computer or, as he later envisioned it, by linking many computers together. Tim describes his conception and development of it in his book *Weaving the Web*, describing what he remembers as his initial conception, important stages and episodes in the evolution of his conception, and his pursuit of its practical development and realization. Here I give just his description of his initial conception, leaving a description of his further development to later chapters.

Tim writes that he was first drawn to the idea of creating a web of information when he was in high school. Both his parents programmed computers, and he recalls coming home from school one day and finding his father reading books about the brain, musing over how to program computers to enable them to be able to make the kinds of intuitive connections between apparently unrelated pieces of data or ideas that people are able to make but computers at the time could not, and discussing the matter with him. The idea, Tim writes, "stayed with him" that "computers could become much more powerful" if a way could be found to program them to link together information not readily linked in conventional data structures like hierarchies. It remained "in the background of his mind" as a challenge, a topic he hoped to pursue one day, thus a creative interest, albeit one he did not pursue immediately.[23] His conception at the time seems to have been of developing a computer program, and perhaps also designing a computer, that would make it possible *to make links between arbitrary elements of information stored on or accessible by a computer — to create and represent any possible pattern of interconnections, thus opening up new ways to organize information, making it possible to explore new kinds of linkages between ideas and bits of information, generating creativity rivaling that of the human mind.* His conception was holistic in envisioning a whole encompassing structure or web linking ideas and information of all kinds.

Tim developed his conception initially in a program called Enquire he wrote while working at CERN as a consultant in 1980. I describe this program and his subsequent development, including his development of a more re-fined conception of a web of information created through linking computers, growing out of his work on Enquire, in Chapters 9 and 15.

A striking feature of many holistic conceptions that define creative interests is that they are a metaphor or based upon metaphor. Metaphor is in fact central to many conceptions of creative interests; for example, "literary geography," the phrase Henry Chen coined describing his interest, is a metaphor. Metaphor is also important in the development of many interests and conceptions of interests. For Roger Knowles, conceiving of the brain as like an engineering construction, with the neurons as "building blocks," was crucial in enabling him to identify and conceptualize his interest in visualizing neurons develop-ing into their shapes. In the case of holistic conceptions that define creative interests, often the very essence of the conception is a metaphor; further, being

[23]Tim Berners-Lee, *Weaving the Web: The Original Design and Ultimate Destiny of the World Wide Web by Its Inventor*; with Mark Fischetti (San Francisco: HarperSan-Francisco, 1999), pp. 3–4.

a metaphor, or being based upon or bolstered by a metaphor, is often what gives a holistic conception its power to inspire and guide the process of creative development. Virginia Woolf's conception of reflections is a metaphor: we are not literally "looking into the mirror" when we face each other — that is a metaphor for social interaction, and the "reflections" we see of ourselves are not literal reflections (in the sense of reflected light) but looks, gestures, and verbal expressions by others communicating their thoughts and feelings about us and themselves, which activate, shape, and bolster our internal self-representations. Her beautiful vision of living in a "quiet spacious world," "rooted in the centre of the world and gazing up through the grey waters, with their sudden gleams of light, and their reflections," is a rich metaphor in its vivid visual details.

The theory of metaphor describes metaphor in terms of a source domain, which is the domain that the metaphor directly refers to or describes, and the target domain, which is what the metaphor is "about," what it is meant to communicate information, beliefs, or feelings about.[24] Many metaphors employed in holistic conceptions defining creative interests have a highly imaginative source domain — Virginia's being an illustration — with the gap and hence distinction between the source and target domains being thus quite evident. In contrast, the metaphors used by individuals in defining other kinds of creative interests do not necessarily have such an imaginative source domain or such a dramatic gap between source and target.

Kelly Overly, a neurobiologist I interviewed, is an example of someone who defined her main creative interest through a holistic, imaginative conception rooted in a metaphor — a metaphoric vision of the neuron.

Kelly formed her conception during the summer following her first year in graduate school while working in a lab studying nerve regeneration. Kelly had been interested in the cell biology of the neuron since her senior year in college — her interest was sparked through working in a lab studying tau, a protein that is thought to be important in the formation of the amyloid plaques characteristic of Alzheimer's disease and is a key component of the cytoskeleton, which both creates the physical structure of the cell and is also the main cellular transport system. She said her work in the lab gave her "an appreciation for the complexity of a single cell." After college she worked for a biotechnology company growing cells in culture. She told me she enjoyed the

[24]On metaphor see George Lakoff and Mark Johnson, *Metaphors We Live By* (Chicago: University of Chicago Press, 1980) and Andrew Ortony, ed., *Metaphor and Thought* (Cambridge: Cambridge University Press, 1993). See also the Website www.metaresolution.com/Metaphor/web_axonfiles/sourcetarget.htm.

"day-to-day" routine of taking care of the cells, for example feeding them. The experience deepened her appreciation for the cell as a complex living entity; in addition, in growing neurons she noticed many interesting differences between axons and dendrites.

Working in the lab on nerve regeneration, Kelly found herself wondering how the different parts of the neuron communicate. "I don't think that before that time I had thought about how signals were carried within the cell, how one part of the cell knows that something else is going on," she told me, for example, "how the cell body knows that the tip of the nerve cell has been injured." Pondering these issues spurred her thinking about the neuron as a complex entity with different parts that need to communicate and coordinate their activities, and she formed a rich metaphoric conception of the neuron as a cell. "[I started thinking about] the fact that the cell [neuron] itself is a very complex system," "and how there are these different parts of the cell [neuron] and that somehow there has to be communication between the different parts, but also each part has different needs because it's different." "So, I was thinking about activities occurring throughout the cell as part of the cell's sort of way of life." It is conventional to view the neuron as a complex system; but Kelly goes beyond this, personifying its different parts. She imagines that the different parts have "different needs" and that they must have a way to "communicate" so that each part "knows" about events occurring elsewhere. And she describes thinking about the "activities" going on in the neuron as part of its "way of life" — a beautiful phrase showing that she was imagining the neuron as a kind of living community, with its daily routine of work and activity. Her conception is thus a rich, holistic metaphor. It is also distinctive as a way of thinking about the neuron — others do not conceptualize the neuron so literally as being like a community. Going forward, Kelly formed interests based on her conception — in communication among the different parts of a neuron, and in the transport mechanisms that "shuttle" biochemicals around the cell — both flowing naturally from her conception. I discuss the project she developed out of these interests, and its resonance with and clear basis in her conception, in Chapter 8.

THE DISTINCTIVENESS AND BREADTH
OF CREATIVE INTERESTS

Creative interests are striking in being distinctive, even unique, while also possessing breadth, in particular being intermediate in breadth. In this chapter I define distinctiveness and breadth with regard to creative interests, describe the features of creative interests and conceptions of creative interests that make them distinctive and give them breadth, and give examples showing that they possess these characteristics.

These two qualities, distinctiveness and breadth, in combination are what make our creative interests so powerful and central in our creative development — cores out of and from which we develop ideas and projects, and central in guiding us along our paths of development. I describe central functions of creative interests in creative development in following chapters. I raise the issue here because it is a principal motivation for this chapter — characterizing and demonstrating the distinctiveness and breadth of creative interests is crucial for understanding and appreciating their central functions in creative development.

With regard to these functions, in particular those functions rooted in distinctiveness and breadth, what is crucial is that the conceptual structure that an individual forms and builds up in the domain of an interest is distinctive and has a degree of breadth, for it is these conceptual structures that are in general generative of creativity, as I describe in Chapters 9 and 10. Regarding distinctiveness (and to a lesser extent breadth) there are in fact two factors that are important in making the conceptual structure associated with an interest distinctive. One is the distinctiveness of the underlying interest; the other is the distinctiveness of the path the individual follows exploring his interest and more generally, through which he has particular experiences and is exposed to and internalizes a given set of elements in the domain of his interest. Charles Darwin formed a distinctive creative interest; he also had a distinctive experience, voyaging on the *Beagle*, giving him the opportunity to observe a remarkable, rich collection of life-forms, which was crucial for the distinctive conceptual structure he built up in the domain of his interest. The distinctiveness of his interest was crucial — no one else on the *Beagle* or traveling in South America built up the same conceptual structure — but so was his remarkable set of experiences. While both factors thus are important, in this chapter I focus on describing the distinctiveness and breadth of creative interests. The importance of experiences and the paths individuals follow in sparking their creativity and as the basis for their building up conceptual structures in interest domains is described in later chapters.

The fact that creative interests are distinctive yet also possess breadth is or at least may be surprising, for it would seem on the face of it that narrower topics are more likely to be unusual or idiosyncratic and hence distinctive, and broader topics are more likely to be shared in common with others and hence less likely to be distinctive. That is, there is an inherent tension between these two characteristics. This makes it all the more important to describe both characteristics and give examples showing that interests possess both. A further reason to describe these characteristics in detail is that, as discussed in Chapter 2, the fact that creative interests are distinctive and possess an intermediate degree of breadth runs counter to the conventional notion that interests are simple, conventional, broad topics.

In the final section of this chapter I discuss narrow interests — interests in narrow topics and interests that center on problems, questions, and goals. I emphasize and show with examples that such narrow interests nonetheless still possess a degree of breadth and open-endedness, thus fit the basic profile of interests, at least to a degree. Also I discuss the conventional view of the creative process as centering on the effort to solve specific problems, answer specific questions, and attain specific objectives. I argue that the conventional view is misleading in portraying problems, questions, and goals that are at the center of creative work as overly rigidly defined, that in fact such problems, questions, and goals are often broader and more open-ended, thus more similar to interests.

A final introductory note: In this chapter I discuss distinctiveness and breadth primarily as discrete characteristics; degree of distinctiveness and breadth is discussed, but only in a limited way. Developing a methodology for assessing degrees of distinctiveness and breadth more systematically is left to the future.

As noted above, what is most essential for creativity generation is the distinctiveness of the conceptual structure an individual forms in the domain of his interest, and this distinctiveness is created through the combination of the distinctiveness of his interest and the distinctiveness of his experiences along the path he follows. I focus here on describing distinctiveness of interests, not of individuals' paths. I do this for two reasons. One, the distinctiveness of creative interests is I believe not widely appreciated, whereas the distinctiveness of an individual's path of life is more widely recognized. Two, an individual is guided by his creative interest and conception of interest along the path he follows; thus the distinctiveness of his interest and conception of interest is a crucial factor in making the path he follows distinctive. As noted above, distinctiveness of paths is discussed in later chapters.

For a creative interest to be distinctive means that it is distinctive, as a creative interest, in the field in which it is defined, held by just one individual or perhaps a few, but not by many people in the field. A second condition, which is not logically necessary but in fact is satisfied by essentially all creative interests that are distinctive, and is useful for describing what makes creative interests distinctive and judging their distinctiveness, is that a creative interest that is distinctive is not a standard topic in its field. This second condition is the basis for my main analysis; I come back to the first condition at the end of the section.

There is in every field a hierarchy of established, generally accepted concepts and categories, that develops over time, that defines the knowledge structure in the field and is used to classify activity in the field. This hierarchy includes and defines the set of standard or conventional topics in the field: topics that are widely known in the field, have generally accepted meanings, are generally recognized as defining established areas of research, and are used to classify work, in organizing teaching, to set agendas for meetings, and for resource allocation decisions.[1] Most creative interests that are not distinctive are a standard or conventional topic in their field, more precisely, a standard or conventional topic that is viewed by a significant number of individuals in the field as an important, potentially fruitful topic for development and that at least a moderate number of individuals are interested in pursuing creatively.[2] We are most likely to form such nondistinctive interests when we first enter a

[1] At any given time there is likely to be reasonable agreement among most individuals working in the field about the hierarchy and what many of the standard topics in the field are, though invariably with significant individual differences.

[2] The reverse does not apply: there are many standard or conventional topics that are part of the established conceptual hierarchy but are not widely held creative interests — not viewed as potentially fruitful topics for development.

field; in particular it is quite common to be first attracted to a field by a "hot" topic — a conventional topic that is a main focus of current research or creative work in the field and about which there is a general feeling of excitement and a widespread belief that major creative breakthroughs are occurring or about to occur.[3] Thus several of the neuroscientists I interviewed, including Liz and Takao, told me that learning and memory — specifically, synaptic plasticity as the basis for learning and memory — a hot topic at the time — was the first neuroscience topic they became interested in, and was important in attracting them to neuroscience.

A creative interest that is distinctive is, in general, not a standard or conventional topic in its field. This statement must be qualified, as I have done, for it is possible for a creative interest in a standard or conventional topic to be distinctive — this happens if someone has an interest in a conventional topic that no one else is interested in — but such cases are uncommon, at least in my experience. Azad's interest in mechanisms of action is perhaps an example of such an interest, but even in his case this is not exactly a correct interpretation. Though this topic may have been a standard topic in cell biology at the time he formed it, it was not such a standard topic in neuroscience. His focus on mechanisms of action for neurons, in particular triggered by neurotrophins, was distinctive, as shown by the fact that he did not discover any posters or articles when he searched for research about it.[4] Further, there were nonstandard conceptual aspects to his conception: the way he linked the biologic phenomenon he was interested in to math and classical physics; and the fact that he was specifically interested in characterizing the pathways through which external agents exert their effects in totality, not just receptors or specific biochemicals involved. A creative interest that is distinctive is thus not in general part of the established hierarchy of concepts and topics in the field in which it is defined.[5] Other people have generally not thought of it

[3] In Chapter 3 I describe a different, related pattern of development — being attracted to a field initially by one or more of its big questions, themes, or ideas. Such big questions, themes, and ideas are generally conventional, but do not typically satisfy the conditions for being a nondistinctive creative interest — in particular are typically not viewed as suitable topics to pursue seriously as creative interests because they are not directly accessible to investigation or development.

[4] By the time he began his own research, around 1991, there was some ongoing research. In the *Abstracts* for the 1991 Society for Neuroscience meeting, in the sessions on nerve growth factor (seven sessions) there are a few abstracts for posters describing research on aspects of the intracellular pathways of action of neurotrophins.

[5] It would seem that interests in conventional topics are most likely to be distinctive in fields in which the degree of knowledge is so vast and detailed that there are many conventional topics as compared with the number of individuals working in the field. As a possible example, an individual working in biology might develop an interest in

independently themselves, or at least have never focused on it or considered it as a topic to pursue seriously and try to develop creatively, and it is not a topic that is regularly coming up for discussion.

This discussion of knowledge hierarchies and standard topics, and definition describing the distinctiveness of creative interests in a negative sense, in terms of what they are not, provides the basis for describing the distinctiveness of creative interests in a positive sense. For even though creative interests that are distinctive are in general not part of the established knowledge hierarchy and not a standard topic in the field in which they are defined, most, as it turns out, involve or employ conventional concepts and categories based in this hierarchy, and many are constructed around or based upon standard topics in their field. There are distinctive interests that are not linked to or based upon conventional concepts and topics in their field, but these are relatively rare. For interests and conceptions of interests that do involve or employ conventional concepts and categories, or are constructed based upon standard topics, the analysis of their distinctiveness is rooted in and begins from the established knowledge hierarchy in their field. Understanding and defining their distinctiveness involves identifying the conventional concepts and standard topics that they are based on, then the ways that these conventional concepts and topics are built upon, extended, modified, challenged or opposed, departed from, and combined with nonstandard concepts and topics to form novel conceptual combinations and define novel topics. I describe the main forms and sources of distinctiveness of these kinds of interests below; first, I discuss the distinctiveness of interests that are not directly linked to or based upon the knowledge hierarchy or standard topics in their field.

Interests Not Directly Linked to or Based upon the Conventional Knowledge Hierarchy

Personal experiences are the source of distinctiveness of many distinctive creative interests individuals form; these are not in general linked with or based upon standard topics or the conventional knowledge hierarchy in their field. Creative writers often have highly distinctive creative interests that do not fit within established literary hierarchies, in particular do not fit in conventional topic, theme, or plot categories; and many of these interests are rooted in personal experiences. The example of William Faulkner given below is an illustration. As a second example, Jennifer Nelson, a literary scholar I interviewed, is deaf, and formed an interest in the portrayal of deafness and individuals who

a certain family of species. This family is a well-defined category that fits within the standard classification system, but it is certainly possible that no one else is interested in it, in which case his interest is distinctive.

are deaf in literature. Personal experiences that spark distinctive interests are not always deeply rooted like hers — in some cases particular events or experiences, for whatever reason — perhaps because they resonate with personal registers of meaning — catch our attention and spark our interest. Alexander Calder's experience early one morning on a boat off the coast of Guatemala, when he saw "a fiery red sunrise on one side" of the boat and "the moon looking like a silver coin on the other," seems to have been crucial in sparking his interest in creating art with basic shapes of the universe and solar system set in space, and the seed of his rich conception of his interest; his interest and conception were certainly distinctive, and were not tied directly to conventional conceptual categories or styles of art.

The other main type of distinctive creative interest that does not fit in the established hierarchy of concepts in a field is interests in or based upon topics that are conventional in other fields or settings. These fall into three main categories: topics that are standard and part of the conventional hierarchy in another field; hobbies; and topics of general interest, like politics or sports. People who have such interests, especially hobbies or interests in general interest topics, generally don't expect them to play an important part in their creative development, and often they don't — they remain separate interests; but sometimes they turn out to be important. Ross Hamilton, a literary scholar I interviewed, has an interest in gardening, through which he became interested in botany. Ross's field of specialty is eighteenth-century studies, and his interest in botany created a natural connection to Rousseau, who was also interested in botany, in particular to his last work, *The Reveries of the Solitary Walker*; as it happened, reading the "Second Walk" sparked an idea Ross had that was the seed of his dissertation (see Chapter 9). Susan's interest in conversational practices in multilingual settings is an interest that would be quite conventional in sociolinguistics or even anthropology; it is a topic that forms part of the standard hierarchy of topics in those fields. But in the context of literary studies it is unusual.[6] These examples are all individuals who work in the arts and humanities; interests of this type may be less common in the sciences and engineering and certain other fields, but that is uncertain.

Forging Distinctiveness: Combining Conventional and Distinctive Elements

Many of the most creative interests individuals form, and specifically their conceptions defining their interests, involve concepts that are standard in their field, part of the conventional knowledge hierarchy in the field. What is striking

[6]Susan's interest was of course sparked by a personal experience, her time in Kenya.

is the fact that their interests, even while based on conventional elements and topics, are yet distinctive. Thus the question to be addressed is: What makes creative interests and conceptions of interests distinctive even while they are constructed based upon, out of, and around conventional elements and topics?

For many creative interests and conceptions of creative interests this question is most fruitfully approached structurally: identifying the elements and topics — some of which are likely to be conventional, but not all — that are contained in an interest or are its basis, then studying how these elements and topics are combined or linked. There are a few main forms of combination and linkage. Many creative interests and conceptions of creative interests that are distinctive are rooted in or center around a conventional topic and add distinctive elements to it — either elaborating upon and extending it conceptually and imaginatively, or else refining and modifying it, for example, focusing on a particular aspect of it. Others have a distinctive topic at their core and add conventional elements to it. Many interests, including especially relationship-based interests, combine or link conventional elements or both distinctive and conventional elements together, forming novel conceptual combinations. Finally, some interests and conceptions of interests cut conceptually across conventional categories or topics; still others are rooted in negativity, defined in opposition to a conventional topic. These different forms are not mutually exclusive — a creative interest can involve more than one.

Alternatively, for some creative interests the question of the basis of their distinctiveness is best approached through tracing and analyzing their development. Here, too, there are a few basic patterns: in some cases an individual forms a creative interest beginning from conventional elements and then either adds distinctive elements or synthesizes the conventional elements creatively; in other cases an individual's interest begins from a distinctive element or topic and then, as she thinks about her interest in relation to her field and learns more, she adds conventional elements to it. With this approach we trace the stages of development of an individual's conception of interest, observing how it becomes richer and often more distinctive over time.

Visualizing neurons developing into their shapes, Roger's interest, more precisely his conception of his interest, is a good example of a distinctive interest that is rooted in a conventional topic and adds distinctive elements to it. The topic at the root of his interest is "the shapes of neurons." This topic itself is rooted in and derives from the even more basic concept "the neuron," which is one of the fundamental, central elements in the field of neuroscience and a main subject of study. The neuron in fact is a super-topic that encompasses and is the basis of many other topics. Neurons have many different features, parts, characteristics, and functions in the nervous system, are associated with and integral to many different processes of brain development and function, and there are different kinds of neurons — and each of these different topics is or potentially can be the basis for creative interests. The shapes of neurons is one such topic, shape being a central, distinguishing feature of neurons. Viewed as a topic, "the shapes of neurons" is fairly conventional: certainly not the most widely discussed and well studied of topics based on the neuron, but nonetheless a generally recognized topic. Historically neuroscientists have considered the shapes of neurons to be interesting and worthy of study both because their shapes are so distinctive — the basic shape of the neuron, a cell body with an elongated axon and many dendritic brushes sticking out in variegated patterns, is striking and distinctive, and neurons have a great variety of specific shapes — and, more importantly, because their shape seems to be important for their functioning, specifically in creating the circuitry of the brain and the rest of the nervous system. Indeed this second reason is the main reason Roger gave for why he became interested in studying the shapes of neurons: "If you think about the neurons as the building blocks that are within the brain, their shape seems to be very tied to their function." "The shapes of neurons," however, while a recognizable topic, is not an especially widely discussed or popular one — only a small percentage of contemporary neuroscientists have interests in studying this topic. Among the eighteen other neuroscientists I interviewed, just one, Bruce Peters, was also interested in it. It is thus best characterized as a moderately conventional topic, falling somewhere between highly conventional and unusual.

Roger's conception of his interest, however, elaborates upon "the shapes of neurons," refines and focuses it, which makes his interest far more distinctive. Specifically, his conception adds two distinct conceptual elements. The first is the idea of development: he is interested in the processes through which neurons develop into their shapes — he said he thought "how neurons develop into their shapes" "would be a fascinating subject" to investigate. This focus fits with and grows out of his conception of the brain and his interest in the way its structure is built up out of neurons. It makes his interest significantly more distinctive, for most neuroscientists who become interested in the shapes of neurons are interested in how these shapes are related to and affect the functioning of neurons, not in processes through which neurons develop into their shapes. Bruce, for example, became interested in how subtle variations in the shapes of neurons influence the propagation of electromagnetic input signals through them and the summation of these signals in their cell bodies, a process which is thought to govern the generation of impulse responses; his focus was thus quite different from Roger's. While Roger's focus on development thus makes his interest distinctive, it does not make it unique — there are other researchers interested in processes through which neurons develop into their shapes, including a neuroscientist at the university where Roger attended graduate school whose lab Roger ended up working in for his dissertation. But Roger adds one additional element to his conception, which makes his interest quite distinctive: the idea of wanting to visualize neurons as they develop into their shapes. He told me he "was hoping to be able to get down to the point where" he "could actually visualize" neurons in the brain developing into their shapes, watch them grow and see how "they develop into the architectural structure" of the brain. The distinctiveness of Roger's focus on visualization is illustrated by the fact that the faculty member in his department who shares his interest in studying the processes through which neurons develop their shapes had never been interested in visualizing neurons as they are developing into their shapes before speaking with Roger — he was focused on identifying genetic and molecular factors associated with cells developing the distinctive features of neurons, not observing their physical development. This does not mean that Roger's interest was unique. In particular, there were other neuroscientists at the time using video techniques to visualize axons growing, and they may have shared a similar interest. However, there were just a few of them by my accounting, and they seem, based on looking at abstracts of a number of papers and posters, to have been interested in other topics, thus more likely viewed visualization as a tool and not as central to their interest as it was for Roger.[7] Regardless, it is clear that Roger's interest was quite distinctive and unique in his university setting.

In addition to Roger's interest a number of the other creative interests I present in this book have the basic form of being rooted in or centering around a conventional topic and adding distinctive elements to it. Charles Darwin's interest in the geographic (and temporal) ranges of species, differences in

---

[7]I have examined abstracts for the Society for Neuroscience annual meetings for these years, and a number of abstracts for published papers. Video techniques were in wide use, at least by the time Roger began his own doctoral research, and specifically used to study axon growth processes by a number of researchers. But they were used within projects typically focused on specific biologic processes, for example midbrain crossings or retinal ganglion nerve growth. It seems likely that the individuals engaged in this research would have described their interests differently than Roger described his.

morphology and behavior among members of the same species inhabiting different habitats, and similarities and differences between closely allied species in neighboring locales or inhabiting similar niches in different habitats (his conception of his interest as I have reconstructed it based on his *Beagle* Diary and notebooks) has this form. His interest is rooted in a conventional topic, the variety of species (and varieties) and their variations in form and behavior, as well as the commonplace observation that there are different species in different locales and regions. In his conception of his interest as I construe it Darwin elaborated upon this topic by imposing a conceptual structure or grid on it, conceptualizing variations among species and varieties in terms of spatial (and temporal) patterns and comparisons of related species inhabiting neighboring as well as distinct habitats. Other naturalists at the time also were interested in the geographic locations and ranges of species, but in a looser way, for example in terms of the set of species in a given region of the world or specific location. Darwin's conception is thus distinctive in its focus on neighboring and overlapping geographic ranges and the correlations of similarities and differences in physical characteristics and behaviors of related species and varieties across domains — other naturalists would not generally have taken this step, but rather defined their interests differently.

Thomas Edison's interest in developing electromechanical, and later, electrochemical, peripheral devices to connect to telegraphic equipment, for input and output of information — his focus being writing and recording output — also has this form. His interest was rooted in telegraphy, one of the most exciting, widespread topics of interest in America in the mid-nineteenth century; but in focusing on peripheral devices and on combining telegraphic technology with other kinds of electromechanical and electrochemical devices he added distinctive elements, thus making his interest distinctive, which was an important factor in the commercial success he achieved with a number of devices he invented through pursuing his interest, notably the stock ticker and electric pens.

The converse form, also relatively common, is an interest that is rooted or based in a distinctive topic and adds conventional elements to it. An interest that is viewed by the individual who forms it as radical, as going against the conventional creed in her field, is oftentimes rooted in a nonconventional, hence distinctive topic. For example, Liz Yoder viewed signaling by glial cells as a radical topic, and it was certainly a nonconventional one at the time. Radical here means being in opposition to a conventional topic or view; Liz's interest was radical, as she viewed it, because it focused on the glia and glial signaling instead of on neurons and neuronal signaling, thus challenging the conventional focus on neurons. Thus this kind of interest has a distinctive, nonconventional topic at its core, with the conventional topic or view that it challenges included as a less central element of contrast or opposition.

Many interests that are rooted or based in a distinctive topic and add conventional elements to it develop in stages — the distinctive core interest forms first, then the conventional elements are added, sometimes years later. Nick Halpern's main creative interest is an example. As described in Chapter 3, Nick has had an interest since childhood and young adulthood in prophetic figures and the prophetic voice in literature. This interest is quite distinctive. In particular, it does not fit naturally into the conventional knowledge hierarchy in literary studies, which focuses more on structural and theoretical topics and principles or schools or genres. Though it is connected with certain conventional topics, such as the study of biblical literature, it is distinct from them in its focus on the prophetic voice, not the content of prophecy, and on the relationship between the prophet and his ordinary self and family life. In graduate school Nick added a second conceptual component to his interest, the voice of the everyday, ordinary human world, thus forming an interest in the tension, balance, contrast, and interrelationship between the prophetic voice and the voice of the everyday in literature; in Chapter 15 I describe his path of development and formation of this richer, more mature interest. Nick told me that his attention was drawn to the everyday human world in part because at the time this topic was in vogue in literary studies, was thus conventional or at least somewhat conventional; thus he formed his interest by adding a conventional element to his distinctive core interest.

As a different pattern, many creative interests and conceptions of creative interests combine and link conventional and distinctive elements together from early on. An example is William Faulkner's creative interest conceived at the time he began writing *Flags in the Dust* and *Father Abraham*.[8] His interest focused on his own particular local Southern milieu, his "little postage stamp of native soil," on drawing upon it as a source of material. This cultural milieu is clearly distinctive, being so local and specific. But there was also a second aspect to his focus: based on the description he later gave of "speculating idly upon time and death" and of how this train of thought lead to the genesis of *Flags in the Dust*, and the sequence of short stories he wrote just after he formed his interest, it seems he wished to focus on certain aspects and themes

---

[8]See Chapter 3. In developing an understanding of Faulkner's interest and conception of interest I have drawn on Joseph Blotner's *Faulkner: A Biography*, I, especially pp. 526–31 and 565–69.

of life within this local milieu or society — patterns of family life over the generations, time and destiny and his sense of irretrievable loss, the society's moral basis and values and moral decay and breakdown, over time, with the continuing existence of a few having virtue, innocence, and courage. These are classical themes that resonate with the greatest literary works, including the Bible — the conflict of good and evil, innocence and innocence lost, purity, courage, loyalty, and other virtues, and, conversely, greed, corruption, injustice, and moral decay, as well as man's efforts to overcome these, to improve the imperfect world he lives in. They are hence basically conventional elements. Faulkner's conception and desire to explore and develop classical themes in his unique cultural world is reflected in his statement that he thought that in pursuing his interest creatively he would sublimate "the actual into the apocryphal" — the word apocryphal having a biblical connotation, suggesting he would rework biblical themes using his own material, on his own terms.[9] This combination of universal themes with distinctive settings would seem to be a natural form of creative interest for creative writers.

Faulkner's mature style, which he developed over the same period of time he was beginning to pursue his thematic interest, also combined distinctive and conventional elements. He had developed distinctive stylistic elements in his poetry and first novels and stories. He now more clearly brought in as conventional elements influences from modernism — most obvious to me are influences from T.S. Eliot, and there are others. An especially distinctive element of his style as he developed it was his use of very long sentences; in this there is a tie with his thematic focus on time and history — he remarked that the purpose of his very long sentences was to gather up the past with the present and future, in the same way a man always carries his past with him.[10]

[9]Faulkner said repeatedly later in life that it is the goal of the writer to express universal truths of the human condition through his writing, in his own particular way, thus to wed the universal to the particular. The importance of the sense of history for Faulkner has been discussed by many critics; see, for example, Carl E. Rollyson, Jr., *Uses of the Past in the Novels of William Faulkner* (San Francisco: International Scholars Publications, 1998). On Faulkner's wide reading of and use of the classics, see Joan M. Serafin, *Faulkner's Uses of the Classics* (Ann Arbor, MI: UMI Research Press, 1983).

[10]*Faulkner in the University*, ed. Frederick L. Gwynn and Joseph L. Blotner, p. 84. He may have come to this exploring his interest stylistically. However, overall it is unclear to what degree he had an independent style-based interest that he actively explored. Faulkner made the important innovation of telling the story from different points-of-view, an idea which he seems to have invented for himself (though it certainly has precursors in modernist literature) as he began writing *The Sound and the Fury*; see Chapter 12.

Novel conceptual combinations are the principal source of distinctiveness of many creative interests and conceptions of interests. Such interests combine or relate elements that no one has previously connected or related; more precisely, no one has previously defined and pursued a creative interest centering on the relationship or connection. The elements themselves may be wholly conventional, or some may be conventional and some distinctive, rarely are all distinctive; in some cases they are drawn from two or more fields or subfields. The distinctiveness of relationship-based interests nearly always lies in the relationship defined between topics — the topics themselves are often quite conventional, but they have not previously been related or connected together, or, even if they have been casually, no one has previously defined and pursued a creative interest centering on exploring and developing the relationship between them. Takao's interest in employing molecular and cellular techniques to study plasticity in the developing visual cortex is an example. The techniques he was interested in using, and plasticity in the developing visual cortex, especially the role of plasticity in the formation of ocular dominance columns, were standard topics at the time he formed his interest — but no one up to that time had formed an interest based on relating them, or at any rate formed such an interest and actively pursued it. Hans Krebs's interest is another example. The study of metabolic pathways in the body and the techniques Warburg had developed were both known topics at the time (though Warburg's methodology was not entirely standard); the insight Krebs had that made his interest distinctive was the idea to use these techniques to study metabolic pathway reactions. Another example is Robert Kaufman's interest, which is distinctive in its twofold relationship structure, creating a rich, distinctive interest based in relatively — though not entirely — conventional ideas and topics.

For creative interests that focus on a specific aspect of a broad topic, generally the main source of their distinctiveness is the distinctiveness of the specific aspect on which they focus. Thus, in most such cases the broad topic itself is conventional, and what makes the interest distinctive is the fact that it focuses on an aspect of this standard topic that other people have not focused on, which has thus never before or rarely ever served as the basis for a creative interest. The broad topic in which Roger's interest is rooted, "the shapes of neurons," is quite conventional (and is itself an aspect of the fundamental topic "the neuron"); what makes his interest distinctive is its focus on a particular aspect of this topic, neurons developing into their shapes, and a particular approach for studying this process, visualization in real time. Sophia's interest in axonal pathfinding was distinctive in her focus on turning processes and the idiosyncrasies of individual paths nerves travel (see Chapter 8 for more).

The distinctiveness of John von Neumann's interest in designing computers and developing computational methods for solving nonlinear partial differential equations and related problems lies in the fact that he was focused on a particular cluster of problems within the wide field of possible applications of computers.

Crossing Conventional Categories — Distinctiveness of Conceptions

Some creative interests and in particular conceptions of creative interests that are distinctive are related to conventional topics in their field obliquely — they cut across or overlay a conventional category or topic or set of categories or topics in an original, unusual way, defining a novel, distinctive topic; or alternatively, they envision a conventional topic in a distinctive, imaginative way. The "literary heirs" of Aphra Behn, Cheryl's conception of her creative interest, is an example of a creative interest that defines such an idiosyncratic, distinctive topic. The standard subfield within which Cheryl's conception is defined is eighteenth-century women writers — to be sure not a heavily studied topic at the time, but nonetheless a recognized field of study.[11] Within this subfield Cheryl defined a group of women writers that is not standard and generally recognized as a group, for example a recognized school, but rather is original to her in the way she defined it — the "literary heirs" of Aphra Behn — a group of women who carried on in Behn's wake, writing, as she did, about the larger issues of the day, in a strong female voice. This group does not fit into the conventional hierarchy of literary categories; it defines an imagined group of writers cutting across conventional categories like genre and locale.

A holistic conception that forms the basis for a creative interest in many cases centers on envisioning a conventional topic in a novel way. One way this is done is through transforming a conventional topic or theme. This is essentially what Virginia Woolf did: her conception of a literature that focuses on and explores the reflections of ourselves we see in the eyes and attitudes of other people and the world around us, that build up and sustain our self-image,

---

[11]Cheryl mentioned a few books that had been written relatively recently at the time she formed her interest focusing on eighteenth-century women writers, helping to define it as a field of study. One was Dale Spender, *Mothers of the Novel: 100 Good Women Writers before Jane Austen* (London: Pandora, 1986). Another was Nancy Armstrong, *Desire and Domestic Fiction: A Political History of the Novel* (New York: Oxford University Press, 1987).

is rooted in conventional notions of literature as a mirror of the world, but goes far beyond these, and is meant to challenge and counter conventional notions, especially of nineteenth-century literature. Another way is through imagining a topic in a new way, often through an extended metaphor that has never before been used to think about and imagine the topic. Kelly's conception of the neuron as being like a community is an example.

The Emergence of Distinctiveness — Development

To trace the emergence of distinctiveness, the path of development through which an individual comes to form a distinctive creative interest and conception of interest, is fascinating, all the more so because the process of forming a distinctive creative interest is so crucial in developing original ideas and projects leading to creative contributions. Virginia Woolf's creative development is a wonderful example for which we are able to witness the process, at least to a limited degree, as it is revealed in her stories, journal, Diary, and letters. Her conception in "The Mark on the Wall" of a new form of literature composed entirely out of reflections was rooted in and grew out of the conventional notion that literature is a mirror, both in the sense that a writer reveals herself through her writing and, even more conventional, the idea that in literature we are shown strange and different worlds. This conventional idea lies behind the narrator's comment in "Phyllis and Rosamond" that Sylvia "had a literary delight in seeing herself reflected in strange looking-glasses, and of holding up her own mirror to the lives of others," and Phyllis's remark to Sylvia that her life is "a wonderful life; it is so strange to us," thus a life the sisters are very interested to learn more about in conversation or as a story.[12] The loss of her mother, father, and elder brother Thoby, depriving her of the people who were the mirrors she needed to form a full, coherent sense of self, made it natural for Virginia to be drawn to the idea that literature is a mirror and to wish to explore mirroring within literature as a way to learn more about the mirroring function, and perhaps also in the hope, probably largely unconscious, that it might help her find mirrors and contribute to her own self-coherence. Virginia moved beyond convention in a series of conceptual leaps. She made a conceptual shift from the conventional view of mirroring as occurring between writer and reader to a different, novel conception, sparked perhaps in part by her reading of Mérimée's *Lettres à une inconnue* (or it may

---

[12]It is a commonplace, old view that a play presents a picture of the world, thus is its mirror. Such ideas are in Shakespeare, whose plays were performed at the famous Globe Theatre.

be she had already begun to form this idea and that is why his *Lettres* so interested her) — the idea of characters in a literary work casting reflections
back and forth off each other, so that the mirroring is internal to the work.
Then, in a break from the conventional form of the nineteenth-century novel,
she developed the idea of showing "the mind's passage through the world" in
literature, showing a life not as a single chronologically continuous sequence
of reflections but rather as a series of disconnected, scattered reflections, discrete fragments that, in aggregate, form a composite whole.[13] Finally, in "The
Mark on the Wall" she connected these ideas together; indeed she went a step
further, taking the idea of showing characters through a series of reflections to
an extreme, imagining a new form of literature composed entirely out of such
reflections.

The pattern of development Virginia followed, beginning from a conventional idea or topic then making conceptual leaps or connections leading to a
distinctive conception and creative interest is in many cases followed by individuals who develop a distinctive relationship-based interest, and by individuals
who form an interest based in negativity or consciously trying to depart from
convention — though their creative leaps and connections are not generally so
brilliant as hers. The opposite pattern also occurs, as for example in Nick's case.

Distinctiveness as Being Unique or Unusual

In the previous section I have described the distinctiveness of creative interests
in terms of the distinctiveness of their conceptual elements and structure.
This is often the most direct way to analyze their distinctiveness. It is not,
however, the basic criterion for distinctiveness; rather, distinctiveness is based
on comparing a creative interest to the interests of others working in the same
field. A creative interest is distinctive to the degree it is unique or unusual as
an interest in the field in which it is defined relative to the interests of other
individuals actively working in the field.

To determine the distinctiveness of a creative interest based on this criterion
requires an exhaustive data collection process — in principle one would have
to determine the creative interests of all individuals working in the same field.
I have not attempted an exhaustive analysis of this kind. I have, however, done
a partial survey of this kind: in the fields of English and American literature and

---

[13]The fact that she mentions this idea in response to what she sees in Perugino's
fresco suggests she may well have developed the idea in opposition to conventional
forms in which all elements are shown and explicitly linked together, as a reaction
against them, in which case her thinking followed a negativity line.

the neurosciences (and to a quite lesser extent mathematics) I interviewed and identified the main creative interests of nearly every individual who graduated in a given year from one of the top programs in the field. Thus I have been able to identify nearly the full set of creative interests for this one-year cohort of graduates from top programs. I have not collected information about the interests of older individuals working in these fields or about individuals close in age but a year or two ahead or behind the cohort I studied — thus my dataset is quite incomplete. Nonetheless, it is a striking fact that there is little overlap, and no direct overlap, among the individuals I interviewed in each field in their creative interests. This is evident from the descriptions of these individuals' interests presented through the course of the book — I mention the interests of many of the individuals I interviewed and their interests are in general all distinct. Even interests of my subjects that do overlap to some degree are in general quite distinct, especially in their details. A good example of this is the interests of neuroscientists Sophia Colamarino and Chris Callahan. I present their descriptions of their conceptions of their interests, and compare and contrast them, in the next chapter.[14]

For creative interests that are distinctive there are two main possible reasons why others do not share them as interests or have similar interests. One is originality — some creative interests that individuals form are truly original conceptions that others haven't thought of, especially in all their richness. Interests that individuals form that reflect their unique backgrounds and personal experiences, their unique sensibilities, are especially likely to be original in this way. Examples are Matisse's interest in painting with vivid colors in patches and color-delineated boundaries, setting up strong contrasts and interrelationships — an interest which, as Hilary Spurling describes, reflected his Flemish heritage and background, a cultural heritage of weaving and "decorative art"; Faulkner's interest in re-creating the world of his youth, transforming the real into the apocryphal — most other writers simply did not share his cultural background, not just Southern but rooted in a particular rural locale and Southern tradition, especially not coupled with his distinctive artistic sensibility for telling gothic tales of doom and destiny, of moral decay and striving; and Roger's interest in visualizing neurons developing into their

---

[14]In contrast to the distinctiveness of their creative interests individuals are far more likely to share similar initial interests — to be drawn into their field by the same big questions, topics, or themes. The fact that individuals enter a field sharing a fascination with the same big topics is not surprising, for in most fields there are just a few of these at any time; it shows that distinctiveness generally emerges somewhat later, in the formation of more focused creative interests.

shapes, which reflected and was based in his training in military tactics — inherently spatial and visual — at West Point. The other explanation is lack of interest on the part of others — some creative interests are distinctive because other people are simply not interested in pursuing them. An example is Takao's interest in bringing the approaches and techniques that had been developed to study the cellular basis of plasticity in other parts of the brain to bear to study plasticity in the developing visual system. This idea surely must have occurred to other vision researchers, for as Takao told me there was clear evidence of "very strong plasticity" in the developing visual cortex, and vision researchers were surely aware that the cellular mechanisms of plasticity were being studied intensively in other brain systems — thus the idea of adapting these techniques to explore plasticity in the developing visual system must have occurred at least to some of them. But for whatever reason — perhaps because of commitments to ongoing research projects and established methodologies, perhaps due to lack of technical expertise — the topic was not being actively pursued by other vision researchers at the time, and that made his interest distinctive.

In retrospect it can often be surprising, in light of the important contributions that an individual or group of individuals has made through pursuing a particular creative interest or cluster of interests, that their interests were as distinctive as they appear to have been — that more people were not pursuing similar interests. This is true, for example, of James Watson's interest in elucidating the structure of DNA to show how it functions as the basis for genetic transmission, which led to his discovery with Francis Crick of the DNA double helix structure: there were at most a very few other individuals pursuing similar interests. There are two main explanations for this lack of substantial numbers of individuals pursuing interests that turn out to lead to important contributions. One is that although we can see in retrospect how evidently important an interest was, at the time its importance may be much less clear. In an interview that Horace Judson quotes from in *The Eighth Day of Creation* Max Delbrück, a founding member of a group of biologists who studied the mode of action of phages in the hope of understanding genes and their mode of transmission and action, stated that he and others were well aware of Oswald Avery's results published in 1944 seemingly demonstrating that DNA is the crucial genetic material, but felt at the time that it was still highly uncertain what the role of DNA actually is, that they were not certain DNA actually was the genetic material, and even if it was it might in fact not be the key to understanding the gene, but rather just a simple switch that turns on certain proteins in the cell. Thus DNA's remarkable function in transmitting information, which seems so evident now that we know its structure of sequential base pairings, was not obvious at the time.[15] The second explanation is inertia, an inability or unwillingness on the part of individuals to stop pursuing interests they have been pursuing, abandon ongoing projects, and make a radical shift to pursue novel interests. This kind of inertia is familiar in many areas of decision-making and studies of commitment, and individuals engaged in creative work are not immune from it — to the contrary such problems may be severe for those pursuing creative endeavors due to their intense commitment and strong identification with their work and also because it often requires a great deal of learning, for example of new skills, to pursue a new creative interest. Inertia was undoubtedly one of the factors that prevented established vision researchers from pursuing interests similar to Takao's. It was also undoubtedly an important reason why many established researchers in genetics and chemistry did not pursue the structure of DNA. In *The Double Helix* James Watson writes that Salvador Luria, his advisor at Indiana, though he suspected that determining the structure of DNA would be key to unlocking the secret of the gene, "could never bring himself to learn" the necessary chemistry and other skills he would need to pursue such a line of research, preferring to stay with techniques and an approach he was used to and continue pursuing research on phages. Watson writes — and his view is confirmed by Maurice Wilkins — that even Francis Crick was not "prepared to jump into the DNA world" himself but rather, if left to his own devices, would have remained studying proteins, which he found intellectually challenging.[16] Other individuals who did have the requisite training in structural determination and were

[15]Horace Judson, *The Eighth Day of Creation: Makers of the Revolution in Biology* (New York: Simon & Schuster, 1979), pp. 57–60. See also James Watson's account in "Growing up in the phage group," cited in Chapter 5, footnote 1.

[16]James Watson, *The Double Helix*, pp. 23, 19. Crick, in his account in *What Mad Pursuit: A Personal Account of Scientific Discovery* (New York: Basic Books, 1988), does not really dispute this. He states that, at the time Watson came to Cambridge, "I was working on a Ph.D. thesis about the X-ray diffraction of proteins. Jim Watson, a visiting American, then age twenty-three, was determined to discover what genes were and hoped that solving the structure of DNA might help" (p. 64). At a later point he states that both he and Watson were interested in solving the mystery of the gene, but on p. 74 states, tongue-in-cheek, "If Jim had been killed by a tennis ball, I am reasonably sure I would not have solved the structure alone. . . ." Overall his account of his career to that point does not suggest the same overriding focus as Watson had. Maurice Wilkins, in his autobiography *The Third Man of the Double Helix* (Oxford: Oxford University Press, 2003), recalls meeting Crick on a number of occasions in the later 1940s. He states (p. 110): "He [Crick] thought I was wasting my time on DNA, and he told me one day, as we sat by the Thames in the Embankment Gardens just outside King's, that he could not understand why I did not concentrate on something useful such as proteins."

working with analytic X-ray methods, including J.D. Bernal, Max Perutz, and John Kendrew, were pursuing other interests, notably the determination of the molecular structures and spatial configurations of proteins like hemoglobin, and were unwilling to shift to a focus on DNA. Linus Pauling did make an attempt to work out the structure of DNA but did not pursue the problem with the kind of single-minded intensity Watson brought to bear, wrapped up as he was in pursuing other research interests; he told Horace Judson he and Robert Corey "weren't working very hard at it."[17]

BREADTH

The breadth of a creative interest is defined primarily by the breadth of its creative potential — the range, number, and variety of different ways in which it may be able to be developed creatively, including the different approaches that may be used to develop it — the opportunities it seems to offer for creative development: our sense or imagining of the set of potential projects, discoveries, problems, ideas, and creative works that may be generated, discovered, and created through developing it creatively — their number, diversity, and importance.

Our creative interests have a significant degree of breadth, both in an objective sense — to the extent we can measure their breadth objectively — and, centrally for their role in creative development, in a subjective sense. They can be and we imagine them as able to be developed in a variety of different ways and directions, having the potential to spark a range of different projects and ideas, leading to different contributions; they contain and we imagine them as containing a range of creative possibilities. Individuals' conceptions of their interests both define and reflect their sense of the breadth of their interests. They conceive their interests in an open-ended manner, broadly and imaginatively, in general not particularly systematically or methodically, their conceptions colored by their hopes and dreams of what they will create and accomplish through pursuing their interests. Indeed it is hard to imagine how we could conceive our interests otherwise than in this way — in broad outline,

[17] Pauling and Corey published a paper in early 1953 proposing a triple helix structure that had several evident flaws — L. Pauling and R.B. Corey, "A proposed structure for the nucleic acids," *Proceedings of the National Academy of Sciences* 39 (1953): 84–97. Their work on DNA grew out of Pauling's discovery of the alpha-helix structural form for polypeptides; see Franklin H. Portugal and Jack S. Cohen, *A Century of DNA: A History of the Discovery of the Structure and Function of the Genetic Substance* (Cambridge, MA: MIT Press, 1977), pp. 221–22. Pauling's comment to Judson is on p. 91 of *The Eighth Day of Creation*. On Pauling focusing mainly elsewhere, see also *The Double Helix*, p. 93.

in imaginative and even speculative terms — for the creative potential of a creative interest can be realized only in the future, in future discoveries and ideas and works that we cannot fully imagine, certainly not with any real degree of accuracy or coherency, at the time we form the interest and a conception of it.

Individuals do often have specific examples linked to their conception of interest, as for example Alexander Calder had the image of the sun and the moon in the sky on opposite sides of the boat linked to his conception of the universe as the basis for art. This use of examples is consistent with the general finding in psychology that individuals use exemplars in defining basic categories.[18] But individuals are not narrowly fixated on these examples, thus are not narrowly focused in thinking about their interests, but rather open to different possibilities and directions, as Calder was.

An individual's creative interest and conception of interest are built up out of two kinds of elements: those that he knows — works others have created, facts, concepts, approaches, and ideas; and those he imagines — including elements he imagines waiting to be discovered in the domain of his interest and works that have not yet been created that he imagines may be created. The known elements are essential in defining interests — they are basic materials out of which we form conceptions of our interests, and are also crucial in sparking our interests. The imagined elements are likewise essential. For having a creative interest means not only being interested in and intrigued by what we have learned about the interest, but also believing that there is more to discover and learn about it, beyond what is currently known, that it can be understood and appreciated and developed in new ways and spawn further creative ideas, discoveries, and creative works. Imagining the creative possibilities an interest

---

[18]Work in psychology focuses on how individuals define and think of conventional categories, like "birds" or "chairs," and shows that we typically have an exemplar or paradigm in mind when we think of such a category, a typical case that illustrates the category — for example, for bird a typical exemplar we might think of is a robin. See E. Rosch and C.B. Mervis, "Family resemblances: Studies in the internal structure of categories," *Cognitive Psychology* 7 (1975): 573–605; E. Rosch, C.B. Mervis, W.D. Gray, D.M. Johnson, and P. Boyes-Braem, "Basic objects in natural categories," *Cognitive Psychology* 8 (1976): 382–439; and E. Rosch, "Cognitive representations of semantic categories," *Journal of Experimental Psychology: General* 104 (1975): 192–233. See also George Lakoff, *Women, Fire, and Dangerous Things*. Our creative interests are not conventional categories but categories we define for ourselves; but still it seems we rely on examples, together with general descriptions, to conceptualize them. A related form of spontaneous category generation is Lawrence Barsalou's discussion of how we define impromptu categories. The example he gives is our definition of "what things to take from our house in a fire" which we define when there is a fire; see L.W. Barsalou, "Ad hoc categories," *Memory & Cognition* 11 (1983): 211–27.

holds is what generates and supports this belief in its potential; the elements and possibilities we imagine are thus vital in defining the interest and forming a conception of it and its creative potential.

Individuals' conceptions of their interests often center and are organized around links they conceptualize from known elements to imagined ones. Such linkages are a kind of imaginative extrapolation; they are speculative, but nonetheless central to conceptions of interests, to imagining the creative possibilities of an interest. Cheryl's interest in the "literary heirs" of Aphra Behn is a good example of the process of imaginative extrapolation linking known elements to imagined ones. Beginning from Aphra Behn and her writings, a writer and body of work that is well known and that sparked her interest, she extrapolated to a group of writers that she was not certain actually existed, but imagined — Behn's "literary heirs," women writing later in the eighteenth century who took up important social and public issues in their writing as she did, following in her footsteps. Linkages from known elements to imagined and unknown possibilities are the source of much of the breadth of creative interests. This is clearly the case for Cheryl's interest: she imagines a whole group of women writers, linked to Behn in their outlook, to be discovered, and this is the basic source of breadth of her interest.

In general our creative interests and conceptions of our creative interests have the quality of multiplicity — as domains we imagine that they contain many elements and possibilities, and in general they do. This is true of many of the interests described in this book, for example Charles Darwin's interest: there were many species and varieties and patterns of overlap and similarities and contrasts in morphology and behavior among allied species and varieties he could investigate, so that his interest contained potentially an enormous number of elements or cases to note and investigate. Likewise for Susan's interest in the use of different languages in conversation and norms governing language use there are a very large, essentially boundless number of conversational settings and patterns of usage that fit in the domain of her interest. The same holds for other interests, such as Douglas Hofstadter's and William Faulkner's — indeed for most, if imagined in sufficient detail.

Many creative interests also have a sense of structure: we imagine that there are interconnections and larger patterns and groupings among the elements contained in them. Imagining and wondering if we can discover such structure is often an important aspect of our interest, as it obviously was for Darwin, Hofstadter, and Susan. One structural characteristic of many interests is that the unknown elements or elements yet to be created — the creative possibilities — are, we imagine, "connected" to the known elements — able to be reached or generated from them. Thus, in Cheryl's interest in the "literary heirs" of Aphra

Behn Behn's "literary heirs" is an imagined group of writers whom we imagine as being linked to Behn, in terms of the kinds of themes and topics they would have written about, as well as in being the succeeding generation of female writers. The sense of structure is often linked to a sense of importance — a sense that we can find a larger pattern or truth or synthesize elements to generate an important discovery or work.

The multiplicity and structure of interests are main sources of their breadth. The sense of multiplicity generates a sense of multiplicity of possibilities, and the sense of structure generates a sense of the possibility of exploring a multitude of patterns, interrelationships, and complexities, potentially leading to general discoveries or insights, or a larger synthesis of elements.

It is important to recognize that even creative interests and conceptions of interests that appear to be focused on narrow, simple topics contain, as domains, both known and imagined elements, and possess multiplicity and usually some degree of structure — thus possess breadth. Suppose, for example, I say that I am interested in a specific painting or idea as a creative interest. It follows that I must not be thinking of it as a simple and fully revealed and understood entity, with just a handful of elements, all of which are known and have been well explored, and no complexity of structure beyond what is already known about it. For if I were thinking of it in this way then although I might consider it beautiful, strange, and important, and might even wish to continue reflecting upon it — for example, to continue to enjoy contemplating its beauty, I could not consider it a creative interest, for I would not be thinking that there was anything further of importance to discover or understand about it — there would be no sense of mystery about it leading me to want to explore it further, no sense of its having the potential for generating new ideas, new interpretations, new ways of being developed creatively. I must rather be thinking about it or imagining it differently, as containing elements that are not known and have never been described, most likely many such elements, and as having depths of structure and meaning that have not yet been fully plumbed.

It is because we imagine they contain a multiplicity of elements and typically that there is some structure among these elements, larger patterns and relationships and groupings, that it is so natural to think of many creative interests as domains. A domain is a connected space or set of elements that are related, connected, or in some way seem to fit or belong together; it is an integrated, holistic sphere of knowledge, thought, and activity. Many creative interests fit this definition — they contain concepts, facts, phenomena, and works that are related or connected to one another and that form or we imagine form or can be grouped into larger structural units, for example, clusters of related phenomena or similar works, and, beyond this, we imagine

them as whole realms for exploration and creative development. Such interests are naturally broad, and individuals with such interests conceive them
broadly, imagining their interest spawning many different possible projects, insights, discoveries, and ideas. I have presented several examples of interests that
are naturally thought of as domain interests in previous chapters — Charles
Darwin's interest, both his childhood interest and his later, mature interest,
Susan Ferguson's interest, and the interests of Douglas Hofstadter, William
Faulkner, and Cheryl Nixon. Many other interests also can be thought of this
way, including Hannah Arendt's interest in the history of discussions of the
place of the Jews in Germany and Europe, naturally containing many specific
historical episodes and incidents, and Thomas Edison's interest in peripheral
devices for telegraphy.

Factors Important in Generating and Determining Breadth; Judgements of Breadth

The breadth of a creative interest is in general generated by four main attributes:
(1) the multiplicity and variety of elements, including in particular imagined
creative possibilities, and potential for generating or identifying larger patterns
and structural relationships among elements; (2) degree of importance; (3) the
breadth of the goals the individual who forms it as an interest has for developing
it creatively; and (4), when applicable, the range of approaches that might
potentially be employed for exploring and developing it creatively. In this
section I discuss each of these characteristics in turn, discuss how they generate
and contribute to breadth, as well as how we assess them and form judgements
of breadth.

The characteristics I describe are intuitive, and I believe individuals assess
them intuitively in judging the breadths of creative interests and prospective
interests they are considering pursuing. However, these intuitive assessments
are subject to potential biases — I describe a few such biases below — thus
I intend my discussion not only to describe how individuals make such assessments but also to outline a framework for making them more systematically
and accurately. Judgements of breadth are inevitably subjective, because the
breadth of an interest is defined largely by its future creative potential, which
cannot be known with any certainty and may well be assessed differently by
different people; thus an individual may judge the breadth of his own interest
differently than others judge it. Understanding this, and how individuals judge
breadth, is valuable for understanding why they make the choices they do,
pursuing certain interests rather than others.

Multiplicity, Range, and Structure

Our assessment of the degree of multiplicity and variety of elements, including creative possibilities, of a creative interest is often central in the informal, intuitive judgement we make of the breadth or creative potential of an interest or potential interest we are considering pursuing. Indeed a sense of multiplicity and variety of possibilities is often a main source of the excitement we feel about a creative interest. Alexander Calder's description of his conception of his interest, presented in Chapter 2, is an outstanding example of a conception that captures and reflects this excitement; Susan Ferguson's description of her interest given in Chapter 3 is another example. As described in the previous section our creative interests and our conceptions of our interests are built up out of both known and imagined elements; in assessing multiplicity and variety we must judge and take into account both kinds of elements, with our assessment resting especially on our assessment of the multiplicity and variety of imagined elements, which are so crucial in defining the creative possibilities an interest holds. Assessments of multiplicity and variety of known elements within the scope of an interest can for the most part be expected to be governed by knowledge — the more knowledgeable a person is about the domain and general field of an interest the more known elements he is likely to think of.[19] The factors that determine assessments of imagined elements and creative possibilities are more idiosyncratic and harder to predict; but in general we expect that people who are the most excited by an interest, most especially the individual whose interest it is, are likely to imagine more elements and thus gauge the breadth of the interest — its creative potential — as greater. Our intuitive assessments of multiplicity, range, and variety are neither exhaustive nor systematic — as with nearly all of our assessments of characteristics of interests we typically make them heuristically and quite nonsystematically, based on whatever sets of elements come to mind and the imaginative extrapolations we make from these elements. Nonetheless they are certainly often quite rich, and we tend to have a good intuitive grasp of these qualities, especially multiplicity. To assess these characteristics more systematically and exhaustively we must try to imagine the full range of elements and possibilities, which means thinking beyond a few key examples, searching systematically in our mind over the full domain of the interest.

[19] For this reason the specialist often views a topic as broader than does someone less familiar with the field in which the interest is defined; however, the reverse is also possible — greater knowledge may reduce assessment of breadth — in particular if an expert believes the domain in which an interest is defined is crowded, in that he knows many contributions that have already been made in it, he may view its creative possibilities as limited.

The sense of interrelationships, patterns, and groupings is also important for judging the breadth of many interests — the possibility of identifying or creating larger meaningful groupings of elements, for example discovering interesting patterns or linking elements to generate new ideas or forms. Structure is not always paramount; for example, it was not central in Alexander Calder's conception of his interest. But often it is critical, driving a person's interest in a topic and his sense of its creative possibilities. Henri Matisse's interest, as I have reconstructed it, in juxtapositions and contrasts among basic color elements and the relationship of color blocks and boundaries with form and composition, generates, we can imagine — and can imagine him imagining as well — rich possibilities for interrelating color combinations with forms. As this example illustrates, imagining that an interest has rich structural connections and patterns within it does not necessarily mean believing one is searching for a single unifying pattern; rather often our interest is in exploring a multiplicity and variety of connections, patterns, and relationships. The assessment of potential structure, including gauging how another person conceives the structure and structural possibilities of his interest, can be difficult. A person's sense of potential structural relationships and the structure-building potential of an interest is quite fuzzy at the time he forms the interest, and difficult to conceptualize. Tim Berners-Lee clearly had a strong interest in patterns of interconnections among sets of elements from a young age, especially in the idea of going beyond standard hierarchical structures, but it is not clear to what degree he articulated to himself early in his development a sense of the variety of patterns and forms of interconnection.[20] In the case of Matisse it is simply not possible for us to know the full richness of his conception, to reconstruct in detail how he conceived color and the prospects of juxtaposing and contrasting different colors, and the overlapping and interrelationship between color and form, especially early in his exploration of color in the late 1890s, for we have only a few letters, early paintings, and limited other biographical information to go on; thus it is difficult for us to gauge his assessment of the breadth of creative possibilities open before him.

An example of an interest for which breadth is generated by both multiplicity and structure is Charles Darwin's interest. Darwin recognized the incredible number and variety of different species and varieties, as shown by his rapturous descriptions of the tropics, and his sense of this multiplicity obviously

---

[20] In *Weaving the Web* Tim does not provide a clear enough sense of his conception of his interest at this time for us to be able to gauge very accurately how he was thinking about the breadth of structural possibilities it held. An interview, especially one done at the time or within a few years afterwards, might well have provided richer information about his conception of his interest.

208   contributed to his sense of the breadth of his interest. But his sense of his interest transcended this. His *Beagle* Diary and notebook entries, quoted from and discussed in Chapter 10, show that from early on he was actively thinking about and searching for patterns and relationships among species and ranges of extent of species, for example, wondering why the extent of one species stops at a certain point and that of another begins, and noticing differences in behavior of allied species and varieties in different habitats. His sense of the variety and richness of these patterns and relationships was I believe central both to his conception of his interest and to his sense of its creative possibilities, hence breadth.

An important source of breadth for certain creative interests is that they are constructed or defined via a twofold conceptualization — as an interest in exploring or creating relationships or connections between two topics that are themselves each richly conceived and broad. Such twofold conceptualization generates multiplicity and structural connectedness through the possibility of pairing, relating, combining, and connecting elements from the two domains. Most relationship-based interests have the form of a twofold conceptualization — each topic is a relatively rich domain and the interest is in relating these domains, forming or exploring rich combinations, connections, and relationships between their elements. Takao's interest is an example: he had learned about a whole collection of molecular and cell biology techniques that he could use to study plasticity — this was one rich domain; and he had in mind not one fixed pathway or circuit in the developing visual cortex or hypothesis or question concerning visual cortical development to study, but many — this was the other. A second example is Robert's interest, with its potential for generating a rich variety of interconnections and interrelationships, across time periods, Romantic and modern, concerning relationships between the literary and political realms.

Importance

In Chapter 5 I discuss importance as a characteristic of creative interests linked to their creative potential, and discuss judgements of importance. Here I describe channels linking judgements of importance to judgements of breadth, specifically four characteristics of importance, or linked to the sense of importance as it pertains to creative interests, that generate a sense of breadth. Importance is distinct from breadth, and an interest may be important without having much breadth, as for example James Watson's interest in elucidating the structure of DNA. But there are natural links between the two.

In our cognitive world, which is composed of cognitive maps we construct and use to make sense of and describe the world, there is a fundamental connection between importance and conceptual density and richness: The more important we view a topic, subject, or issue to be, the richer is the conceptual "field" — the set of conceptual structures — with which we define and describe it, for example, the more subcategories, individual cases, and relationships among its parts or objects we define and incorporate into our cognitive map. This connection defines a channel through which importance generates a sense of breadth for a creative interest. The more important we view an interest as being the denser and richer we conceptualize its internal conceptual structure to be, and the greater we assess its structural complexity and richness, including its multiplicity, to be — hence the broader it seems. An example showing the link from importance to conceptual density and richness, hence to breadth, is the shift that took place in the minds of many Americans after the 9–11 attacks, including individuals working in fields in which terrorism and response to terrorism are topics of study — the attacks made early warning and defense against terrorism seem far more important, and for most of us our cognitive maps of this topic became far richer, making interests in this area seem broader than they had before the attacks.

Our assessment of the importance of the projects an interest may spawn also influences our judgement of the breadth of the interest. In general the more important we imagine a project to be, the "bigger" it seems to us, and hence the broader we tend to judge it to be — for we tend to think that big, important projects are more likely to be approached in a variety of different ways, to have more parts and involve more time and effort, with more details to be ironed out, and are more likely to give rise to subprojects and spawn further developments, including refinements. In turn, thinking of the projects an interest will spawn as relatively big naturally leads us to judge the interest itself as relatively broader than we would if we thought its projects would be relatively small. An example might be Hannah Arendt's interest in European debates about the role of the Jews in European society and the Jews' own view of their place in society. In viewing this topic as so vitally important she undoubtedly imagined that projects she would pursue would require great attention and work, and felt she would need to delve deeply and thoroughly into historical materials to be sure she understood each historical vignette or epoch well, thus enhancing her sense of the breadth of her interest as a topic.

A third factor that influences our assessment of the breadth of an interest is our assessment of the likely importance or impact of the contributions that will be made through its pursuit. Believing that the contributions an interest generates will have impact means believing these contributions will be useful to many people and spawn further projects; and to the extent these further projects and activities are subsumed within the interest, imagined as its further reaches, this increases our assessment of its breadth. Potential impact does not always make an individual's creative interest broad; for it to do so initial contributions must be imagined as leading on to further projects and possibilities that fit within the domain of the interest. John Maynard Keynes's interest in the role of expectations about future economic variables in economic decisions and outcomes may not seem especially broad, but imagining the many economic models and policy issues it might give rise to or impact (especially for us looking back knowing the many projects and issues it actually has spawned and impacted) makes it seem quite broad.

Finally, a fourth channel through which importance generates breadth is through increasing our assessment of the number of projects an interest will spawn that will turn out to be worthy of pursuit. Holding fixed the total number of projects an interest may generate, the higher the percentage of projects that will turn out to be sufficiently important to warrant pursuing the greater the number of projects likely actually to be pursued — hence the more real possibilities the interest holds, and thus the broader it is. Azad not only had the sense that there are many potential projects investigating mechanisms of action that might be pursued, but also believed implicitly that because these mechanisms are important a high proportion of these projects would be worthy of pursuit, contributing to his sense of the breadth of his interest. Our assessment of the fraction of projects that will turn out to be worth pursuing is often based upon the fraction of projects others have undertaken in the same general area that have been successful. While this is sensible, it makes us prone to being overly influenced by past results — prone to a bias of overextrapolation in which we assume that the degree of success achieved in the past predicts success in the future more exactly than is actually the case.

Goals and Questions

Goals an individual has for the development of his interest often contribute to defining its breadth. Goals are important for breadth in two ways. One, linked to the discussion above, is as a factor contributing to defining the importance of an interest — a person's goals for the development of her interest both define and also reflect and embody the contributions she envisions making if the projects she pursues turn out as she hopes, including the breadth of impact and impor- tance she hopes and imagines these contributions will have. The other way goals contribute to breadth is through their open-endedness. A person's goals for the development of her interest are open-ended to the extent she imagines her interest as not having a fixed set of endpoints, but rather having the potential to continue to unfold, as an ongoing process, each wave of ideas, projects, and contributions being followed by and sparking a further wave; in general her interest is broader the more open-ended are her goals for its development. In most cases our goals for our interests are open-ended, at least to some degree; indeed many people have as their main goal, especially when they first form an interest, simply to explore and learn about it, and thus approach its creative development in a quite open-ended manner. When our goals are open-ended we may continue to develop our interest for years. Roger's goals for developing his interest were open-ended, and he was led, in the course of a decade, in directions he did not originally envision — for example, investigating the role of pathological shapes of neurons in the formation of amyloid plaques that characterize Alzheimer's disease. Tim Berners-Lee's vision of large-scale net-works that would connect people and computers in open network structures, connecting and enabling creative connections to be made among all different kinds of information and data, was broad, even grand, thus defined broad, far-reaching, almost utopian goals, making it far more open-ended than it would have been had his initial vision and hence goals been narrower and more specific, so that it transcended the specific, relatively narrow initial projects he first worked on, such as Enquire (see Chapter 9). Similarly, William Faulkner's goals seem to have been quite open-ended — to develop his interest creatively exploring its different facets. Indeed for most of the interests presented in this book the goals the individual has or had for its development were open-ended. This is true even when it might not seem so. Thus, for example, for Wilbur Wright, at the time when he first formed a serious interest in flight — in pursu-ing it as an interest — the overarching goal of achieving flight seemed to him far-off and not attainable in his lifetime, and thus he seems to have thought more in terms of aiming at a series of smaller subgoals; hence his interest had a sense of unfolding, of going on from each accomplishment he (and Orville) might achieve to the next stage of development.

Individuals often define their interests around questions they hope to answer or at least probe, explore, and ponder, and in such cases the questions are central in defining the breadth of their interest. The broader and more open-ended the questions that define an interest, in general the broader the interest; and conversely, if the questions are narrow the interest is typically also narrow. In general when we employ questions in defining an interest our questions are in fact quite broad and multifaceted and open-ended — we are quite open about what sorts of answers to them we will find or arrive at, and how we will try to answer or address them. Robert's questions that defined his interest are an example — his questions were broad and profound, not given to easy or short answers, but opening up to a lifetime of work. Often our interests contain or unfold into clusters of questions, some of which we conceptualize initially, others that are incipient in our initial conceptions and we define fully later, others that we are led to and form in the course of pursuing our interests — contributing to the open-endedness of our interests. Nick, for example, told me he had "many questions" about prophets and the prophetic voice in literature, some of which he began with, such as, What is the relationship between a prophet and his family and ordinary self?; and others that he formulated and explored later, such as, What makes the prophetic voice successful or unsuccessful?

There is a natural link between questions and goals: when we define our interest through questions our goal in pursuing our interest, at least one principal goal, is to find or construct answers to our questions, and thus the breadth and open-endedness of our questions is central in defining the breadth and open-endedness of our goals.

Approaches

In general an individual develops a creative interest via a definite approach or set of approaches; by approach I mean both the perspective from which he approaches his interest and the methodology, style, or technique he uses in developing it, in projects. In some cases, in particular in some fields during certain times, there is one basic approach employed; but in many cases there are a variety of possible approaches, and individuals make choices about which ones to use. The approach or variety of approaches that an individual intends or imagines potentially using or, as we view it, might potentially use to develop his interest contributes to defining the breadth of his interest, in some cases centrally; thus it is important that we take planned and potential approaches into account in judging breadth.

The set of approaches that can or might potentially be used to develop an interest is distinct in general from the substantive topics the interest is "about", thus defines a second dimension of the interest. Hence the breadth of an interest is determined by the combination of the breadths of these two dimensions. For example, the breadth of Virginia Woolf's interest in developing literary forms depicting a world of reflections was generated and defined by the breadth of her conception — its richness and abstraction in suggesting whole worlds, characters and situations that might be explored, portrayed, and created — together with the breadth of approaches or literary styles we imagine — and she imagined — she might invent, explore, and employ for portraying these worlds. In fact, exploring different approaches or styles was central to her development of her interest; I discuss this phase of her development in Chapter 12.

For interests centering on applying an approach, the breadth of the approach is central to defining the breadth of the interest. In general the breadth of an approach is governed by two factors: the range of topics or projects for which the approach can conceivably be used, and the number and diversity of specific, often technically defined approaches within the general approach, including possible new forms or variants that may be developed in the future. Both factors are important and contribute to defining the breadth of the approach, and thus of an interest based in it or developed using it. As an example, the approach of depicting everyday details of individual lives at the center of Enid's interest and philosophy of filmmaking is broad in both factors: her approach contains many specific elements and aspects — in our interview we discussed factors like location, actor characteristics, and camera placement; and there are obviously many potential venues of application in which she can use it — diverse lives she can film focusing on the details of everyday existence. Both Takao's and Hans Krebs's interests were broad due to breadth on the first dimension. Though the techniques they were interested in applying were fairly specific, particularly Hans Krebs's, limiting breadth on the second dimension, each had the sense that with the approach he wished to employ there were many projects he could take on, many discoveries and contributions to be made, thus making his interest quite broad.

Judgements of Breadth: Subjectivity, Biases, Influences

It is difficult to judge the breadth of an interest accurately, for its breadth is defined by the full range of its creative possibilities, and it is very difficult if not impossible to imagine this full range of possibilities with any real degree of accuracy. Not surprisingly given this inherent difficulty our judgements are prone to error, and specifically to a variety of potential biases. Also not surprisingly they tend to be quite subjective — so that often different individuals judge the breadth of the same interest differently. Here I describe a few key sources of subjectivity and potential biases.

Knowledge is central to judgements of breadth: what we know — and don't know — about an interest and related topics has a crucial impact on our assessment of its breadth. Our knowledge base is fundamental to our assessment of the multiplicity — both elements and creative possibilities — of an interest. Consider, for example, Cheryl's interest in the "literary heirs" of Aphra Behn. The multiplicity of her interest is determined primarily by two factors: the number of women writing in the eighteenth century whom we would consider "literary heirs" of Behn, who wrote about the larger public and social issues of their day as she did; and the variety and richness of the social and public issues they wrote about, including the thematic richness of their development of these topics. Considering these factors it is clear that our judgement of multiplicity will be influenced by what and how much we know about eighteenth-century literature, especially women writers of that period, and the main social and public issues under discussion in the eighteenth century, especially issues pertinent to women. This applies to Cheryl's judgement as well. At the time Cheryl first formed her interest she did not know very much about eighteenth-century women writers, but in her enthusiasm and in the wake of reading Aphra Behn she imagined that there were potentially many women who had carried on after Behn writing about larger social and public issues. In hindsight, knowing what Cheryl herself knows now but didn't know then, we can see that she may have overestimated the breadth of materials she would find; although there were many women who wrote during this time, many of these wrote about love and family or domestic matters, not larger public issues. Cheryl in fact discovered this for herself in reading many works by women authors, and it influenced her as she pursued her interest.

The details of our conception of an interest, such as specific images and concepts, as well as the associations that come to mind, have a strong influence on our judgement of its breadth. The dependence on details, while a strength in that such details are a rich basis for imagining the creative possibilities of the interest, introduces a subjective element into judgements of breadth. For the details of our conception are generally neither systematically generated nor comprehensive, but rather somewhat arbitrary and limited, thus do not in general provide a good basis for accurately judging the full breadth of possibilities the interest offers. For example, in judging the breadth of Alexander Calder's interest, in particular its multiplicity and range of possibilities, we are guided by our conception of it, which is shaped by his conception as he describes it; and the specific images that come to mind are central to our assessment. Thus we imagine — guided by what he describes — "Spheres of different sizes, densities, colors, and volumes, floating in space," moving through space in orbits or other simple repetitive or sporadic motions. Because he mentions the universe, mental images of the universe — stars and galaxies and our solar system as we have seen them depicted — may well come to mind. The second part of his description, "traversing clouds, sprays of water, currents of air, viscosities and odors — of the greatest variety and disparity," leads us to add further elements to our conception, making our conception richer and adding additional kinds of sensory elements we imagine. Although we are guided by Calder's description it is evident that each of us will form a somewhat different conception — different images and impressions integrated into a unique whole conception — and thus have a different basis on which we judge the breadth of creative possibilities of his interest.[21]

An important limitation and source of bias in judgements of future outcomes documented in the field of judgement and decision-making is the phenomenon of availability: when we judge the possibilities or range of outcomes for a decision or future event we do so based on the images and scenarios that come to mind and thus are "available" to us mentally, and this is generally a quite limited set, so that we fail to think of and grasp the full range and number of possibilities, which is often much larger.[22] I believe availability impacts judgements of the creative possibilities and hence the breadth of an interest in many cases. The conception we form of a creative interest, on which our judgement of breadth is based, is quite limited — comprised of a relatively small set of elements and associations, a handful of scenarios of possible paths of development, which tend to center around the specific wording and imagery with which the interest is conceptualized or described. It is difficult for us to move beyond this to envision further possibilities — they are less immediately available, and tend to be crowded out by the images, concepts, and scenarios we initially focus on — thus our judgement of breadth is susceptible to the availability bias. An interesting example is the difference in what comes to mind in judging the breadth of Roger's interest in "visualizing neurons developing into their shapes" as compared with what comes to mind in judging the breadth of "the shapes of neurons." When we think about "the shapes of neurons" we think about the standard shape of a mature neuron, with a long axon and many dendrites extending out in complex patterns from the cell body. We also think about the great varieties and intricacies of dendrite patterns and, depending on how much we know, the wide variety of shapes of different kinds of neurons. These sources of variety and complexity are major factors that enter into our judgement of breadth. In contrast, when we think about Roger's interest we visualize a neuron developing, growing an axon and dendrites, the axon reaching and connecting to a target and the neuron in turn receiving contacts on some of its dendrites. Our sense of multiplicity and possibilities is thus based primarily on the variety of possible scenarios of development we imagine, and

---

[21]This is especially true for our conception corresponding to the second half of his description. Images of spheres and discs and the solar system are fairly standard and our conceptions of these are likely to share much in common, though even here there will be individual variation; but the parts of our conceptions based on the second half of his description are likely to be highly subjective, based on our own personal experiences and imagination. Also, elements and features he does not mention are less likely to come to mind, limiting our conception of his interest.

[22]For the availability heuristic see Chapter 5, footnote 5.

less on the diversity of mature, final shapes. Our thinking about creative possibilities is also quite divergent between the two topics. In the case of Roger's
interest we are likely to think about exploring the rates at which neurons grow
and develop into their shapes, which parts develop first, different patterns of
growth, and the ways in which neurons interconnect as they develop, building up the brain — Roger's original source of fascination. In contrast, when
we think about the creative possibilities of "the shapes of neurons" we tend
to think about exploring the diversity of shapes, perhaps creating a taxonomy
of shapes, investigating new kinds of shapes or overlooked details of shapes,
and exploring functions related to shapes that are not yet fully understood, for
example how the shapes of mature neurons influence their electrochemical
behavior and thus, possibly, memory and cognition. What is noteworthy is how
different these lists are, how much we are influenced in our imagining by what
each conception of interest leads us to focus on.

Assessments of both goals and importance are subjective and may be difficult to make accurately. With regard to goals, learning about a person's goals
for the development of his interest helps us determine how open-ended he
is in approaching the exploration and development of his interest, an important factor in judging its breadth (of course his goals may change over time
as he explores and learns about his interest). Importance is subjective because
different individuals may value different kinds of contributions and assess importance based on different factors or weighting factors differently. A factor
that often influences our assessment of the importance of an interest is the
degree of importance others attach to the interest. Cheryl's assessment of the
potential significance of contributions she might make through pursuing her
interest was influenced by her realization that other scholars were becoming
interested in similar topics and were starting to "redefine" the eighteenth century, in particular focusing on noncanonical materials, making her believe
that whatever she discovered might fit with a larger scholarly movement, thus
enhancing its significance. This jointness of assessments can potentially lead
to all or most of the individuals working in a field jointly over- or undervaluing
certain interests, thus can influence overall field development.

I believe it happens fairly often that an individual judges the breadth of his
creative interest greater than others who do not share his interest judge it or
would judge it if it were described to them. There are two reasons why this is
natural. First, in the excitement of forming a creative interest it is natural for
us to imagine it has great creative potential. Second, because an individual
thinks in greater detail, both more deeply and more extensively, about his
interest than others do, it seems natural that he will appreciate its potential

more — thus will estimate it as having greater potential and hence as broader. Of course in making a decision about whether or not to pursue a given interest it is an individual's subjective assessment of breadth that guides him — if an individual conceives his interest as broad then it possesses this attribute in terms of its role in his development, even if it might turn out not to be as broad as he imagines it to be.

Narrow Interests and Problems

Some creative interests are relatively narrow. Since creative interests are defined as possessing at least some degree of breadth and open-endedness, narrow interests must be examined closely to see if they fit the definition — they are an important test case. In fact I believe narrow interests do not contradict the basic definition, though they do define its limit — even relatively narrow interests possess a degree of breadth and open-endedness. Narrow interests fall into two main categories: (1) an interest in a narrow topic, and (2) an interest centering around the desire and endeavor to solve a problem, answer a question, or attain a defined goal. I describe each kind in turn, to show that interests of the given kind possess a degree of breadth and open-endedness, and provide examples illustrating the nature of such interests. I also note, placing the discussion in this section in context, that a focus on a specific problem or question is in general rooted in a broader interest.

Interests in a Narrow Topic

In general, having an interest in a narrow topic means viewing it not as fixed and fully revealed, completely known and described, but rather as open-ended, containing many elements, aspects, or structures not yet discovered or created, thus as holding creative potential. It means viewing it not in one fixed way, not having one fixed way to develop it already in mind, but being open to exploring it, to discovering new things about it and developing further ideas beyond those we start with. Thus an interest in a narrow topic, though its object of focus might appear narrow, is not itself extremely narrow, at least not in the sense that is important for creative development — rather it possesses the sense of openness and exploration that is characteristic of creative interests, and at least a degree of breadth as measured by our sense of its creative possibilities. In fact the appearance of narrowness is in many cases an illusion: when we look at a narrow topic such as a specific creative work or idea at close range, as a person who is interested in it does, we see a degree of complexity and richness, and possibly multiplicity, which from a distance is not apparent, thus are able to see and appreciate its creative potential. The example discussed above of what it would mean to have an interest in a specific painting or idea is a good illustration of this.

Teresa Faherty's interest in *The Winter's Tale* is an example of an interest in a narrow topic, a play, that possessed breadth. *The Winter's Tale* is a rich text capable of being analyzed in many different ways, for example in terms of language, structure, themes, the portrayal of different characters, and culturally and historically. It has many different characters, five acts, and many scenes that may be the focus of analysis. Thus, although it may be narrow it has nevertheless a degree of multiplicity and richness and hence breadth; this is further shown by the fact that there is a considerable scholarly literature on it.[23] Teresa's interest reflects this. Her interest was an enduring one, extending over a number of years, and over that time she did not remain attached to or focus on just one idea or interpretation of the play or one specific part of the play, but rather approached the play in a more open-ended, flexibe manner, thus giving her interest breadth in terms of the possible ways in which she might develop it. For her college honors thesis Teresa developed a novel interpretation of King Leontes's speech in Act I, in which he accuses those around him of treachery, interpreting his speech as a descent into madness in which he has what she described in our interview as a "psychotic break," and developing a reading of the play in which "the rest of the play, all the characters, were just figures in his own mind." Due to personal circumstances she never completed her thesis, and she told me that she left college feeling that she had "unfinished business" with *The Winter's Tale*. Thus, feeling a lack of closure, the play remained on her mind, her interest in it enduring into graduate school. When I asked her whether the play remained "central" for her she agreed with me that it did and told me that she continued to think about it a lot. But she did not remain focused on her original interpretation, or the figure of Leontes or his speech in Act I — rather it was the play in its totality, a complex whole, that continued to hold her interest. Thus, as she learned different theoretical approaches and matured as a literary scholar it is clear she thought about the play differently and in different ways. The breadth of her approach to the play is shown by the fact that when she did have a further insight about it it was about the "flowers" scene in Act IV, a completely different part of the play than she had originally focused on; I describe her insight in Chapter 9.

[23]There is a fairly extensive literature about the play. See, for example, Charles Frey, *Shakespeare's Vast Romance: A Study of The Winter's Tale* (Columbia, MO: University of Missouri Press, 1980), David Laird, "Competing discourses in *The Winter's Tale*," *Connotations* 4.1–2 (1994–95): 25–43, and the references cited therein, and *The Winter's Tale: Critical Essays*, ed. Maurice Hunt (New York: Garland, 1995), among many others.

Jeffrey Shoulson's original interest in *Paradise Lost* was likewise quite open-
ended and hence broad, especially initially. He told me that he was first attracted to *Paradise Lost* in his freshman year in college by its complexity and
sheer difficulty, and said that he didn't initially have any specific "take" on
it, thus did not have a fixed thesis or way of approaching it in mind; rather
he was open to its rich possibilities — indeed was attracted by the fact that it
was "resistant" to simple interpretation — interested in exploring and learning
more about it.

Interests in Solving a Problem, Answering a Question, or Attaining a Goal

Some interests center on the quest to solve a problem, answer a question, or
attain a goal. If the problem, question, or goal in such a case were very narrow
we might imagine that the interest would likewise be narrow, and somewhat
closed, thus would violate the basic definition of a creative interest as possessing
a degree of breadth and open-endedness. In such a case an individual would
be best described as following the conventional model of problem finding
described in Chapter 1: he enters his chosen field, learns about it in a general
way, then jumps directly to a focus on a specific problem, question, or goal,
never forming a creative interest as described in this book. The creative process
is in fact often described, implicitly, in this way.

In general I believe that in cases in which a problem, question, or goal
is a center of focus for an individual in his development, particularly over an
extended period of time, he does not conceive it as narrow and fixed, but rather
more broadly and in an open-ended manner, fitting the description of a creative
interest. In essentially every case I have investigated in which an individual
focused on a problem, question, or goal and organized his creative development
around the quest to solve, answer, or attain it, I have found that he did not
conceive it as narrow, fixed, and rigidly defined, or, in the case of a goal, did not
have narrowly defined, fixed objectives for what he hoped to attain, but rather
conceived it in a more open-ended, less rigid manner, often as a complex having
many subparts, thus conceptually richly — in short, like an interest, possessing
a degree of breadth and open-endedness. I give two examples below, focuses
of interest James Watson and Wilbur Wright had, illustrating this. Individuals
are also in general open to redefining a problem or question or goal in the
course of their development, as their thinking evolves and they learn more, and
to exploring different ways of approaching it. Such fluidity of definition and
conceptualization and openness to different approaches contributes further
to the sense of breadth and open-endedness. An example illustrating this is

the case of Victoria Rayskin, described below, who focused on a problem and whose conceptualization of it and approach and context of thinking about it shifted in the course of her development.

There is a second way in which conventional descriptions that focus on problems, questions, and goals are misleading and flawed. A question, problem, or goal on which an individual chooses to focus is in general rooted in a preexisting creative interest he has that he is engaged in pursuing. It is through their interests, through exploring them and learning about them, that individuals discover, identify, and formulate questions, problems, and goals they then pursue. Likewise — a mirror image pattern of development — individuals often construct a broader, richer interest rooted in a particular problem or question, that the problem or question opens up into. Thus there is in this case again a breadth to their focus of interest, fitting with the description of creative development in this book. This happened in the case of Albert Einstein, as noted in Chapter 5 and discussed in some detail in Chapter 10. Thus, in general a focus on a specific problem, question, or goal is and should be described as embedded in a larger context of development.

As described in Chapter 5, from the end of his time in college James Watson was focused, as he describes it, on discovering how DNA transmits genetic information, the secret of life. It may seem at first glance that he was focused on a fixed, narrowly defined goal or problem and thus did not form a creative interest as defined in this book. But in fact I think a conventional view depicts his focus and conception of his objective too narrowly, with too little sense of openness and fluidity of development. Watson's conception of what DNA is and what he hoped to discover about it was in fact quite vague at the time he formed the intent to pursue it, hence substantially open-ended. DNA was almost completely mysterious to him: he knew little — and in general little was known — about its chemical and especially biologic properties; in particular, little was known about how it might transmit genetic information or what its role might be in some larger process, for example whether it interfaces with other biochemicals or changes its physical state. Thus it was simply not possible for him to have a clear sense of what aspects of DNA he should focus on or what approaches he should use to study it. He thus approached his task quite open as to what path and possibilities he would pursue, and did not initially tie himself to one approach or specific aspect of DNA, but rather thought more freely, letting himself be guided by what he learned and discovered — in a sense floating—open to pursuing whatever directions seemed promising. He first studied phage genetic replication, then went to Denmark to study with a specialist in nucleic acid chemistry, then abruptly shifted direction when he attended Maurice Wilkins's presentation and suddenly became aware of the potential of structural X-ray crystallography for solving the mystery of DNA (see Chapter 9). Thus, while Watson had an ultimate objective, it was fairly broadly and loosely defined, thus resembled a domain filled with alternative approaches and possibilities for exploration. As he explored it he identified specific opportunities, specific techniques and problems, to focus on — thus its role in his development fits the description in this book of the role of creative interests in creative development.

Looking back at the Wright brothers' creative development in light of their accomplishment building the first truly functional flying machine, it is easy to imagine that from the start they were focused on building such a machine, thus had a fixed objective. But in fact this was not the case as far as is known. In the crucial period in 1899 when Wilbur decided to focus on flight as a challenge to devote his energies to, he seems to have viewed building a working flying machine as beyond his reach, as a goal not likely to be reached in his or his brother's lifetime. His statements at the time suggest he viewed flight as a complex problem involving a host of specific issues and subproblems; he himself expected and hoped to tackle perhaps a few of these, and thus contribute his "mite" to the ultimate achievement of flight, as he wrote in his letter to the Smithsonian.[24] Thus, while we cannot know for certain how he was thinking about flight at the time, it seems likely that to him it was a rich domain, directed towards an ultimate objective to be sure, but filled with many challenging, fascinating, and difficult problems that he might investigate and try to solve, as well as interesting phenomena like the different mechanisms of flight of different kinds of birds — thus was like an interest in many ways.[25]

Victoria Rayskin, the mathematician I interviewed, is someone whose development fits the conventional view of the creative process as centering around the effort to solve a problem to a degree; but even in her case there are significant differences. In particular she reconceptualized her problem, the context in which she viewed it shifted and broadened, and she explored and considered alternative formulations for it. For her college thesis Victoria was given a problem to work on by a well-known professor at her university in Russia. The problem

---

[24]See Tom D. Crouch, *The Bishop's Boys*, chap. 12. I cite the source for the letter and discuss Wilbur's development up to this point in Chapter 4.

[25]It is also doubtful whether Wilbur knew at the start exactly which problems he would focus on, although approaching the topic with his expertise in bicycles he may well have been drawn to issues of control, turning, balance, and stability from early on, for example watching birds. But recognizing the need to solve these in an integrated manner surely was an insight that came later.

was to determine for a particular type of ordinary differential equation with unbounded singularities the conditions under which its solution is smooth. Victoria solved the problem following a general approach her professor outlined for her.[26] This problem remained a focus of interest for her as she went on in her education, matriculating in a U.S. doctoral program in mathematics. She told me she learned a lot, but, she said, "I wanted to continue to work on something related to my thesis, because that problem was really really interesting to me." During her second year in her doctoral program she contacted a professor in her department who works on related problems, and met with him and described her thesis project. "The next day," she told me, "I received a message from him stating that he thinks my problem can be reformulated." "So I met with him and he explained to me that this problem of higher order dimensions [of singularity] can be reformulated; and in that new formulation there are lots of references" (the problem thus reformulated is connected with chaos theory). Victoria told me a higher order singularity of an equation is called a resonance, and the reformulation of her original problem is this: Given an equation with a resonance, define an operator such that the fixed point of the operator corresponds to the point of resonance, and determine the bound for the degree of smoothness of the linearization of the operator around its fixed point.[27] "I started to read papers related to this reformulated problem," Victoria said, "and I realized that there is some bound for linearization which is not sharp [had not been fully worked out in the literature]. So I became interested in the question, How good could be the smoothness of a resonance map [linearization around a resonance]?"

The very fact that Victoria states that her advisor stated — and there evidently are — lots of references on the problem shows that it has breadth as a topic, even if more limited than for many interests. Further, the fact that she found that the "bound" for linearization is "not sharp" shows that she was thinking about and exploring different ways of formulating and approaching the question of the bound, again showing breadth. Under the impetus of her professor Victoria fundamentally reconceptualized her problem, in terms of how she thought about it and the context within which she thought about it. This indicates that the problem can be thought about in different terms and contexts, again showing its breadth as a topic. It is noteworthy that Victoria may not initially have thought about the problem as having breadth in terms of different ways of being formulated and approached and having different contexts, and that her

[26]Victoria Rayskin, B.S. thesis, *Multidimensional Differential Equations with Unbounded Discontinuities*, Kharkov University, 1989.

[27]Victoria explained to me that usually there is only one such operator, although it may be able to be expressed in a number of different ways.

professor, having more experience and breadth of knowledge, was able to help
her see this — thus appreciate its breadth and importance. Overall, Victoria's
problem had breadth and fluidity in terms of both formulation and context,
and thus fits, at least to a reasonable degree, the definition of a creative interest.
Indeed had it not had these characteristics it is doubtful whether she would
have continued to focus on it and pursued a form of it for a main part of her
doctoral research, which she did (see Chapter 12).

8

RESONANCES AND CONNECTIONS

Individuals' creative interests and conceptions of creative interests — more generally, the conceptual structures that encode and define their interests — are the basis out of and from which their creative projects and ideas develop, leading to their creative contributions. We see evidence of this when we compare their creative interests and specifically their descriptions of their conceptions of interests with their later projects, ideas, and contributions: we see striking resonances and connections between their interests and descriptions of conceptions of interests and projects they pursued, ideas they had, and contributions they made.

These resonances and connections are remarkable in being so well defined and clear. Especially remarkable is the way in which so often the distinctiveness of an individual's interest and conception of interest is reflected in his subsequent projects, ideas, and contributions — in many cases with a clarity and exactitude of correspondence that is stunning. It is not just that Virginia Woolf and William Faulkner were interested in creative writing and went on to write great novels — rather what is striking is the way for each the distinctiveness of their conception defining their literary interest is reflected, so evidently and with such striking resonance, in their great works. Similarly, when we juxtapose Alexander Calder's early abstract sculptures with his conception of his interest in the universe as the basis for art, the correspondence and resonance is stunning. This is not to say that knowing someone's creative interest and conception of interest we can predict what projects he will pursue, what ideas will occur to him, what discoveries he will make, what his ultimate contributions will be. Creativity is inherently uncertain and unpredictable, and an individual's path

of development cannot be predicted with such exactness. Individuals themselves do not and cannot know at the time they form their interests how they will
develop them, what their future projects, ideas, and contributions will be — an
essential feature of creative development is not knowing this, developing one's
interest freely, in unexpected ways, not being able to imagine fully at the time
one forms one's interest exactly how and in what ways one will develop and
realize it. What it is to say is that the specificity inherent in individuals' creative
interests and conceptions of their interests carries through in their subsequent
development — that through exploring their interests and developing them
creatively they generate ideas and projects, leading to contributions, that have
clear, striking resonances with their interests and conceptions of interests.

In this chapter I present a series of examples showing clear, striking resonances between an individual's description of his conception of his interest and
a project he undertook or creative work he produced. My approach is to juxtapose an individual's description of his conception of interest with his project
or work, manifesting the resonances and connections between them. My purpose is to show that such resonances and connections exist. I do not attempt to
demonstrate either how they come about or, more generally, a causal role for
creative interests and conceptions of creative interests in generating ideas and
projects. These matters are taken up in the following chapters; thus this chapter is a bridge to these chapters. In order to keep the chapter relatively short —
in the spirit of a bridge — I present a limited number of examples, enough to
make the basic point. There are further examples in following chapters.

It is not my intention to suggest, and I do not in fact believe, that individuals engaged in creative endeavors are necessarily aware of or think about
resonances and connections between their interests and conceptions of interests and their subsequent projects, ideas, and contributions. To the contrary, in
my experience individuals often are not aware of such resonances and connections, though once they are pointed out to them they typically do recognize and
validate them. I have had a number of experiences interviewing individuals
when I pointed out a connection between their conception of their interest
and a later idea they had or project they engaged in that they themselves do
not seem to have been aware of, though once I pointed it out to them they
recognized it and appreciated its significance. Indeed identifying such resonances and connections, and more generally helping individuals recognize
connections and patterns in their development, is a way in which interviewing
them about their creative development can be useful to them.

Many of the examples in this chapter are based on retrospective accounts
individuals have given of their creative development. This raises an important
caveat: it is possible that individuals who describe forming a creative interest

and conception of their interest at an early point in their development may in fact have formed their interest or conception later, looking back at their development, perhaps trying, unconsciously, to give it continuity and coherence. This possibility is noted in Chapter 1. I mention it here because of its relevance for this chapter. If individuals construct their interest and conception of interest later than they say, in particular after having had the ideas, undertaken the projects, and made the contributions that I describe as having resonances and connections with their interest and conception, then these resonances and connections are based on after-the-fact constructions and cannot be taken to demonstrate interests and conceptions of interests foreshadowing subsequent projects, ideas, and contributions as I interpret them to. I believe it is reasonable to proceed on the view that individuals are by and large accurate in their descriptions, but with an awareness that because their descriptions are retrospective they may in some cases make mistakes in describing their early interests and conceptions of interests, raising the possibility of false or misleading interpretations in certain cases.

I note that a considerable number of the examples in this chapter and elsewhere in the book are based on descriptions of conceptions of interests individuals gave prior to the projects and creative works having resonances and connections with their descriptions, thus are not subject to this caveat; these include the examples for Virginia Woolf, Piet Mondrian, John Maynard Keynes, Samuel Taylor Coleridge, and for individuals I interviewed who engaged in projects after I interviewed them, including Enid Zentelis and Roger Knowles. Further, for several of the examples there is supporting information, either archival documentation or another person's independent account of an individual's development, confirming a description of an interest; this includes the examples for Chris Callahan, Liz Yoder, Tim Berners-Lee, Hans Krebs, and Jef Raskin.

RESONANCES AND CONNECTIONS IN PROJECTS; REALIZATIONS OF ABSTRACT CONCEPTIONS

A fundamental kind of resonance or connection between an individual's creative interest and conception of interest and his subsequent creative work is a resonance or connection in which his interest and conception of interest carries through and is embodied and reflected in subsequent projects he defines and pursues, leading to contributions he makes. These resonances and connections are in many cases very clear and direct — indeed strikingly so.

In many cases an individual is directly guided by his conception of interest in defining or choosing which projects to undertake, or his interest is important in developing ideas for projects that fit with his interest. This pattern is very common among the scientists whose developments I have studied. Thus, when Hans Krebs established his own independent lab he set out to define and pursue projects fitting with his interest — applying the manometric tissue slice method to study processes of intermediary metabolism. After exploring in a limited way a number of such processes, he settled on the investigation of the formation of urea — a project clearly fitting with his conception and in the domain of his interest. I describe this phase of his development in Chapters 11 and 12.

Roger Knowles has engaged in a series of projects directly rooted in his interest in "visualizing neurons developing into their shapes." In his graduate program Roger chose to work with a faculty member who had developed a hybrid cell line in which the cells grow axon-like extensions. The cells are not neurons, but physically they embody a key feature of neurons that is central to Roger's interest, for it is through their axons that neurons make connections with other neurons, thus building up the brain. Indeed the faculty member shares Roger's interest in studying how neurons develop into their shapes, which was presumably the basis for his development of the cell line, which is what attracted Roger to work with him — though he had not, before meeting Roger, been interested in visualizing this process, making Roger's interest distinctive, as discussed in the previous chapter. When he entered the lab Roger undertook as his project to set up a video microscopy system and watch and record the development of the axon-like extensions, and investigate the rate and pattern of development of these extensions.[1] It is noteworthy that recording and observing the development of these cells visually and in real time is something no one else in the lab had thought of doing; Roger's approach was thus distinctive, reflecting — embodying — the distinctiveness of his interest. Roger told me that working on the project, which turned out successfully, was fulfilling to him because it fit his conception of his interest: "I finally [after engaging in other, less satisfying projects] felt like I was doing what I had envisioned." Somewhat later Roger undertook a second project, in collaboration with a post-doc in the lab, visually recording in neurons, again in real time, the process of resources being transported from the cell body to peripheral growth sites where dendritic extensions were forming, and using the visual recording to determine the timing of these transport movements in relation to subsequent growth spurts. Thus visualization of the process of neurons developing into their shapes was again central, though in this project Roger moved one step beyond his original conception of interest, studying the flow of resources needed for growth. Since I interviewed him Roger has worked on a further

[1]These cells were not neurons but "acted like" neurons in growing extensions; watching them develop thus fit Roger's interest fairly closely, though not perfectly.

project, investigating the shapes of neurons in Alzheimer's disease, that also reflects and has grown out of his interest (see Chapter 14 and the Appendix for references), showing the continuity of his interest and its role in his work over many years.

Many of the other neuroscientists I interviewed also pursued dissertation projects that clearly reflect their interests, that they essentially defined through their conceptions of their interests. These include Sophia Colamarino and Chris Callahan, for whom the connections between their conceptions and their initial dissertation projects are described below; Azad Bonni, who has pursued a series of projects that directly reflect his interest, described in Chapters 12, 13, and 15; and Takao Hensch, who developed a portfolio of projects applying molecular and cellular techniques to study the developing visual cortex, reflecting and embodying his conception of interest, described in Chapter 14.

A second fundamental way in which interests and specifically conceptions of interests are reflected and embodied in subsequent creative work is through an individual realizing an abstract conception of interest in a creative product, thus giving his conception creative form. In an abstract conception of interest an individual defines what he is interested in pursuing and trying to develop creatively in abstract terms, thematically, often somewhat idealistically. Holistic conceptions are one example of a kind of conception that is often abstract and idealized. When we compare, for individuals who form such abstract conceptions of interest, their conceptions with their later creative works, we see clear, often striking resonances, ways in which their works realize, in concrete form, or as definite ideas, their conceptions. The example of Alexander Calder realizing his conception of the universe as the basis for art in his abstract sculptures is a brilliant example. Seeing his early sculptures, shown in Figure 2, the resonance with his abstract, thematic conception is striking — he realizes his conception in his art through simple objects, reminiscent of the basic objects of the universe, set in space, like the planets orbiting the sun, often set in opposition to one another, as the sun and moon were opposite one another in the sky when he saw them early one morning on the boat off the coast of Guatemala.

The idea of a creative work realizing an individual's conception or vision is standard. However, in general what is meant is a conception or vision that is quite specific and directly tied to the specific work in which it is realized — an artist, for example, who has a vision for a painting, then works to realize his vision in the painting. That is not the kind of conception and linkage I am describing. Rather, I am describing links from conceptions of interests to creative works — thus links from conceptions that are not so fixed or specific, are not tied to a specific work, but rather are broader and more open-ended, as described in earlier chapters. A marker of the difference is that the links I describe often extend over long periods of time, in many cases years, whereas in conventional accounts of realizations of visions the length of time from vision to realization is generally shorter, often much shorter. Indeed length of time span is integral to the linkages and resonances I am describing, part of what makes them so fascinating — they span long times of development, thus by implication, at least in many cases, manifest and reflect deeper, richer developmental processes. During this long period of development, trying to realize their interests creatively, individuals often engage in a sequence of projects and in experimentation and exploration, and in some cases refine their conception and develop it; Piet Mondrian, Virginia Woolf, and Tim Berners-Lee are three such individuals. I describe such patterns of development in later chapters.

Virginia Woolf's conception of reflections, as she describes it and I interpret it in "The Mark on the Wall," is abstract, indeed so conceptual as to be in the manner of a philosophical statement about the human condition. Her conception is realized, strikingly — beautifully and profoundly — in her great novels beginning with *Jacob's Room*. I discuss here its realization in *To the Lighthouse*, for in this book it is realized most richly, fully and profoundly, on many levels.[2]

Its most basic realization in *To the Lighthouse* is in the definition of the characters: they are defined, and define themselves, through their reflections of each other, including reflections they provide, knowingly in many cases, sustaining one another's sense of self. They provide reflections to each other in their conversations with one another; and they also gossip incessantly, judging and commenting on the qualities of the others. Their thoughts, which are a central element of the book, concentrate, strikingly, on reflecting on the other characters — reflecting on their qualities, empathizing with them, articulating to themselves feelings they have about them — disgust, love, hate, apathy. In this way characters are thus shown to the reader indirectly, via the thoughts and feelings other characters have about them. In addition, the characters imagine the way others view them — manifesting their selves being built up out of these imagined reflections.

At the center of this world of reflections is Mrs. Ramsay. She is essential in reflecting the other characters' selves back to them. Further, she is a vital source of reflections for us as readers: the other characters think about her and

[2]All references are to Virginia Woolf, *To the Lighthouse* (San Diego: Harcourt Brace & Company, 1981).

imagine her, showing her to us indirectly; and she thinks about them, showing them to us indirectly. Mrs. Ramsay's powers of reflection are especially evident for the men. To give one example, in an early scene in the book she walks with Charles Tanley into town, and the experience, her reflection of him back to himself, has a deep effect on his view of himself. "She made him feel better pleased with himself than he had done yet, and he would have liked, had they taken a cab, for example, to have paid for it. As for her little bag, might he not carry that? No, no, she said, she always carried *that* herself. She did too. Yes, he felt that in her. He felt many things, something in particular that excited him and disturbed him for reasons which he could not give. He would like her to see him, gowned and hooded, walking in a procession. A fellowship, a professorship, he felt capable of anything and saw himself" — here his thoughts break off as she stops to look at a man pasting up an advertisement for a circus, casting an ironic reflection on his self-imagining. As their walk continues, he describes himself and his life to her, we hear his description through her, thus by reflection — she scarcely follows much of what he says, and has a running internal commentary that is quite scathing at times. By the end of their walk he feels buoyed with self-confidence, feels "an extraordinary pride" walking beside her, basking in her attention. Meanwhile, her view of him and feelings towards him vacillate, and are far different than his view of himself and the way he imagines she views him. Before the walk, thinking about what her children think of him, she thinks him "a miserable specimen," at intervals during the walk she feels "warmly" towards him, and afterwards she again turns cold, thinks him "an odious little man" for telling James they will not go to the lighthouse the next day.[3] There is thus a rich layering of reflections — his view of himself, his imagining of her image of him, including the image of her looking at him "gowned and hooded," juxtaposed with her far different, fluctuating views of him — all reflections we see of him. Mrs. Ramsay is most centrally and most dramatically a reflecting element for Mr. Ramsay — he has a need for her to provide positive reflections of himself and thereby restore his self that erupts, with urgency, at certain moments. Thus, he comes to her at one point, "his satisfaction in his own splendour" "shattered, destroyed" — and she rises to the occasion, by her sympathy and by conveying her sense of his worth restores and renews him, restoring his self-confidence.[4] We feel his need most acutely at her death and afterwards — without her presence his self

[3]*To the Lighthouse*, "The Window," sections I and II, pp. 7–15.
[4]Section VII of "The Window." Mrs. Ramsay is sitting with James, and James is intensely angry at his father for absorbing her attention and exhausting her. There is another occurrence of a breakdown of Mr. Ramsay's confidence during the dinner party, pp. 107–8.

is unable to be sustained as it was, cannot be kept whole, intact.[5] James's need matches his, intense and possessive, if less conscious.

Mrs. Ramsay herself has a very rich character that is both defined by reflections and also transcends them. The other characters give her shape in their thinking about her. The men and children see her as the incarnation of beauty, idealizing her. Lily has contradictory thoughts and feelings; on the one hand she is "in love with" the Ramsays and their life, which she recognizes Mrs. Ramsay is vital in creating; on the other she views Mrs. Ramsay critically — suspicious that her beauty is a façade that is inherently deceiving, that there is no deeper meaning within matching the beauty on the surface. For her part, Mrs. Ramsay is aware that others idealize her, see her as the embodiment of beauty. Thus (p. 41): "She bore about with her, she could not help knowing it, the torch of her beauty. Men, and women too, letting go the multiplicity of things, had allowed themselves with her the relief of simplicity." There is a striking resonance in the second sentence with the phrasing in "The Mark on the Wall" — "to sink deeper and deeper, away from the surface, with its hard separate facts" — the implication being she is the center of the world of reflections that lies beneath the surface of reality. But this is not the primary element in her view of herself — her own view is questioning of her character and her life, complex — an amalgamation of others' reflections of her self and her own thoughts and feelings. She is doubtful she deserves idolatry, feels that her true self is not equal to others' views of her — thus, her reaction to the feelings her daughter Rose has for her is a feeling of not measuring up: "Like all feelings felt for oneself, Mrs. Ramsay thought, it made one sad. It was so inadequate, what one could give in return; and what Rose felt was quite out of proportion to anything she actually was." And she herself needs to see reflections, and knows she does, most notably from her husband — his deep sense of truth and truthfulness and courage reassure her sense of the solidity of the world and help her to define her place in it. Thus, in the last scene in the first part of the book she is depicted as feeling the need for her husband's reflections on her and life, his sense of critical awareness and reality, to bolster her own. She enters the room where he is sitting, reading (p. 117): "Of course, she said to herself, coming into the room, she had to come here to get something she wanted." We see her here reflecting upon herself. A short time later she tells him that Paul and Minta are engaged, then waits, desperate for him to reply. And at last he does (p. 123): "'You won't finish that stocking tonight,'

[5]Mr. Ramsay has additional qualities beyond his need of Mrs. Ramsay's reflection. In particular he has a solidity about him — a sure drive for the truth, a truthfulness and a courage, a zest of life, that is in fact an important source of reflections for Mrs. Ramsay; see below in the main text.

he said, pointing to her stocking. That was what she wanted — the asperity in his voice reproving her. If he says it's wrong to be pessimistic probably it is wrong; she thought; the marriage will turn out all right." The scene concludes with her looking at him, giving him the love he needs in return. Thus they are shown providing reflections to one another — the essence of relationships in the book. Beyond all of this Mrs. Ramsay has a philosophical depth that goes beneath — ranges beyond — the world of reflections, that itself is linked to Virginia Woolf's conception in "The Mark on the Wall"; I describe this at the end of the chapter.

The conception of reflections is realized in *To the Lighthouse* not only in the characters' definitions but also in the book's structure and plot, thematically and stylistically. The book has a three-part structure. In "The Window" we are shown the world of reflections — Mrs. Ramsay is present and at the center, and we are shown the characters defined and defining themselves through reflections, in a loose-knit sequence of scenes. In "Time Passes" Mrs. Ramsay dies, and the impersonal narrative shows us how with her death the human world cannot sustain itself, is overwhelmed by the inhuman — without reflections human selves are not able to be constituted or sustained. Finally, in "The lighthouse" we observe Mr. Ramsay, James, Cam, and Lily as they struggle to cope with Mrs. Ramsay's absence, attempt to pick up the pieces and carry on, to find other sources of reflections and reconstitute their selves, thus the human world: James, Cam, and Mr. Ramsay on their journey to the lighthouse, at first disconnected and dysfunctional, by the end achieving at least a degree of community, symbolized, for example, in Cam's thinking about James's satisfaction when his father compliments his steering, at last reaching the lighthouse rock; Lily, for whom art is a substitute for the reflections of human relationships and a way of representing life by reflection, working on her painting, thinking about Mrs. Ramsay and the old times, at last, exhausted, finishing it.[6] We thus are shown the world of reflections, constituting the basis of the human world, first as it is or can be, then fallen apart, destroyed by the loss of its central source of reflections, finally reconstituted, imperfectly, by the survivors — conveying as a theme that reflections are vital in constituting the human self, which is the center of human intercourse and existence, hence in creating human community. Stylistically, the book is a series of reflections, each reflection — each thought, each conversation, each scene — giving way to the next, loosely knit together, making the whole out of the composite, with

[6]The lighthouse serves as an alternative source of reflections, as is shown most clearly in James's satisfaction with the lighthouse in its being similar to and thus a mirror of himself. It is also a symbol of the ideal, showing us how the ideal and elements in the world that have symbolic meaning can help us, as a source of reflection, achieve community.

few facts or definite plot elements intervening — thus flows in the style of "An Unwritten Novel."

In focusing on describing the realization of Virginia Woolf's conception of reflections in *To the lighthouse* I do not mean to suggest that this is all *To the lighthouse* is. It contains important elements and themes not contained in her description of her conception in "The Mark on the Wall." In particular, in having a central figure, and a family structure, it adds important structural elements not in the conception, goes beyond it in constructing a fictional family-based world of reflections. And it has richness and depths of meaning not anticipated in the earlier conception, one such important depth being as elegy.[7] Nevertheless, the book is very much a realization of the conception, the conception is its conceptual basis.

Tim Berners-Lee and Walt Disney are two further examples of individuals who formed abstract conceptions of interests, and realized their conceptions in creative works that reflect and embody their conceptions. Walt Disney's conception of developing animated cartoons featuring animal characters possessing vivid, memorable personalities, human-like characters, is abstract. In particular, it does not define any specific animal character or even kind of animal, and might be realized through many personality traits. It thus needs to be realized through specific characters who display rich personalities, making them memorable.[8] His conception is first truly realized, in an animated cartoon, in *Oswald the Lucky Rabbit* — indeed according to Leonard Mosley's account, after the first film, *Poor Papa*, was rejected by Universal he was consciously guided by his conception, resolving to make Oswald a true personality — "a real character with a personality you could love or hate or despise but never ignore." Following Oswald it is realized, with a success that is historical, in Mickey Mouse — a character who has bravado, is impudent, gallant, brash, with courage greater than his muscles, mischievous, constantly getting into trouble, but resourceful, always coming out all right in the end, thus a rich personality.[9]

[7]The book is clearly about Virginia's own experience — the death of her mother and its effect on her father, on her, and on the entire family. In the book Virginia is identified with the female children and also, very clearly, with Lily as the artist. Indeed the ending of the book, when Lily, exhausted, completes her painting (pp. 208–9) — "Yes, she thought, laying down her brush in extreme fatigue, I have had my vision" — seems clearly to reflect Virginia's own sense of realization of her vision, of laying to rest her difficulties in coming to terms with the death of her mother and its impact on her family.

[8]Disney was also concerned from early on about technical quality, recognizing that a cartoon must have sufficient quality and detail to convey richness of personality.

[9]See Leonard Mosley, *Disney's World*, pp. 62–63, 92–95, 100–16.

Tim Berners-Lee's conception of a data structure that would allow any possible pattern of interconnections among elements, creating a web of information and ideas that would be generative of creative connections, was, at the time he formed it in high school, abstract, and essentially thematic — he did not have in mind any particular design or even general approach to realize it. Later, after college, working at CERN, Tim wrote a program, Enquire, that realized his conception in a limited form. Enquire was a program for representing a system with nodes and arbitrary links among nodes — thus enabling the formation of a web of interconnected elements, though one not nearly so rich in terms of the kinds of elements and connections, and the generation of novel connections among elements, as imagined in his conception. Tim realized his conception more fully later, returning to CERN, when he took the crucial step, now possible with knowledge he had gained about hypertext and the development of the Internet, of enabling information stored on different computers to be linked, thus generating the potential to create a truly expansive web, which he named the WorldWideWeb — a name recalling his initial conception in its scope and ambition.

As described in Chapter 4 Piet Mondrian formed a philosophically based, abstract conception of a modern art form that was central in his creative development. His initial conception, as he describes it in his sketchbooks, is almost wholly abstract: it is summarized in his guiding statement "Spirit [Force] and matter: a Unity." He believes this new art form will attain the expression of, thus make manifest, the universal — both reflecting and enabling the evolution of human consciousness to a higher plane. Over the next years he developed his conception further, and it became both richer and more definite. He developed the idea of the male and the female, embodying spirit and matter, represented in art through the vertical and the horizontal line, as described in Chapter 4; then formed a conception of the primary colors balanced in "equilibrated relationship" in rectangular color planes — I present his description of his conception of the use of colors and discuss his later development in Chapter 11. His art developed in parallel with his conception, in stages — thus his conception and art evolved together, with his conception in fact leading his artistic development it appears, at least at some stages.[10] Thus his whole

[10] However, the following cautionary statement attributed to Mondrian is given by Harry Holtzman in Piet Mondrian, *The New Art — The New Life; The Collected Writings of Piet Mondrian*, ed. and trans. Harry Holtzman and Martin S. James (Boston: G.K. Hall & Co., 1986), p. 1 and must be noted. "His writings and his theories, Mondrian repeatedly cautioned, 'always came later,' after his paintings, as their consequence. The paintings are the result of 'pure intuition,' . . . the writings were his efforts to fulfill the constant demand for verbal rationalization." In interpreting this statement we must

artistic development was guided by and centered around his striving to realize   235
his abstract conception of modern art, linked to the evolution of human consciousness. He was able to realize his conception, famously, in his paintings
beginning in 1920–21; see Figure 3(viii), *Composition with Large Blue Plane,
Red, Black, Yellow, and Gray.*

RESONANCES AND LINKAGES OF SPECIFIC ELEMENTS
IN CONCEPTIONS OF INTERESTS

In some cases specific elements in individuals' conceptions of their interests —
in their descriptions of their conceptions, for example, specific words or
images — carry through and are reflected or incorporated in later projects
they undertake and contributions they make. Thus, at least in some cases the
specific details in individuals' conceptions of interests are significant for their
subsequent development: their conceptions capture and reflect their intuitive
understanding of their interests, down to the level of specific details.

There are a number of examples among the individuals whose developments
I have studied of specific elements in their conceptions being reflected or
incorporated in later projects they undertook and contributions they made.
For Alexander Calder, the image of the sun on one side of the sky and the
moon "looking like a silver coin on the other," an example that was both
formative of and an example within his conception of art inspired and based
on the universe, is a fundamental element of his earliest abstract sculptures —
many have two objects, often discs or spheres, set on opposite sides of a center
origin or plane (see Figure 2).[11] In several of the early mobiles, spheres or discs

distinguish between a conception Mondrian may have had in his mind, and a conceptual structure that he formed earlier — and letters and his sketchbooks corroborate he
formed conceptions prior to surviving artistic compositions that realize them — which
thus guided him, and later attempts to define his art and write down and elaborate
upon his conception formally, in essays. Further, in writing down his conception at
one stage it surely influenced his thinking and conception going forward so that, for
example, his essay "The New Plastic in Painting," published in 1917 and written in the
preceding years, surely influenced his thinking going forward, leading to his creative
breakthrough of 1920–21.

[11] In many of these early sculptures and mobiles spheres are supported with circular
wires that seemingly represent their orbits. In some wooden mobiles Calder created
slightly after the first wire mobiles, two spheres center around a wooden slab that can be
taken, in one interpretation, to be an abstract representation of a boat. See Alexander
Calder and Jean Davidson, *Calder, An Autobiography with Pictures*, pp. 127–29, and
Alexander Calder, *Calder*, plates 18, 37, 20, 21.

are shown in relation to a horizontal plane, either above — high in the sky — or at a lower height like the sun or moon at the horizon. There are striking resonances between the cartoon animal characters Walt Disney invented and his childhood drawings and personifications of animals as he later recalled and described them. Thus perhaps his first drawing, he later recalled, was a drawing of a rabbit "waving frantically" to another — and, strikingly, his first successful animation of a rich animal character, Oswald, was also a rabbit. Though he was not the one who first thought of making a cartoon with a rabbit as the main character, he responded eagerly when it was suggested to him, reportedly going over to his table and drawing a series of sketches, inventing Oswald on the spot.[12] This same sense of personification and personality features are the essence of his cartoon characters, for example, Mickey Mouse — full of bravado, cheeky, mischievous, fun, good at heart, chivalrous — a creature with whom we sympathize in his plights and escapades. It is interesting that he didn't pick dogs or cats for his first animal characters, traditional pets, but rather animals more associated with life on the farm, thus linked with his own childhood experience living on a farm for four years.

In describing specific elements in interests carrying through in creative development I wish to be clear, reflecting my larger view of creative development, that specific elements are not carried through as isolated elements, but rather are defined, exist in our minds, and carry through in our developments as elements embedded within rich conceptual structures that encode our interests — are remembered, accessed, and used as elements embedded in these structures. Thus, Calder's image of the sun and moon on opposite sides of the sky I believe fit within a rich conceptual structure in his mind, defining and encoding his interest — basic objects of the universe arranged in space, in different spatial positions, having a variety of forms of motion. It was as part of this conceptual structure that the image had meaning for him and was encoded in his memory. It is important, as a related matter, to clarify that my description and viewpoint is thus opposite to theories that describe cultural transmission as occurring at the level of isolated specific elements — that argue that culture is made up of discrete units, say "memes," that individuals are exposed to, retain, then use and transmit as discrete elements, distinct from richer conceptual structures. At least in the context of creative development and creative work, this is, I believe, a false description of cultural linkages. Rather, we form rich conceptual structures of interest that have specific elements embedded within them; and these elements thus are carried, take their meanings from,

[12]*Disney's World*, pp. 28, 92–94.

and exert influence over our development, linking to and resonating with subsequent ideas, projects, and contributions, from their base embedded within these structures. See Chapter 17 for more on this subject.

FOCUS ON A SPECIFIC ASPECT OR APPROACH IN A CREATIVE INTEREST: LINKAGES WITH SUBSEQUENT PROJECTS AND CONTRIBUTIONS

When an individual forms a creative interest focusing on a specific aspect of a broad topic or an approach for developing a broad topic creatively, very often the aspect or approach she focuses on is a central, defining feature of subsequent projects she undertakes and contributions she makes, and in many cases a main source of their distinctiveness. A useful approach to see and gain an appreciation for this kind of linkage is to consider a pair of individuals with interests that focus on different aspects of or ways of approaching the same broad topic, and set side by side and compare their interests, projects, and contributions — in the comparison we see the differences in their focuses in sharp relief, and how these differences are reflected in and define fundamental differences in their projects and contributions. I follow this approach in this section: I describe the creative interests and initial dissertation projects of Sophia and Chris, two neuroscientists introduced in earlier chapters, who both formed interests in axonal pathfinding, but were fascinated by and focused on different aspects of pathfinding, showing the clear, direct link that exists for each between the aspect of pathfinding that was the focus of their interest and their initial dissertation project idea, and how the differences in their focuses of interest carry through and are reflected in fundamental differences between their projects.

Sophia's interest in pathfinding was sparked during her senior year in college in a class in which she was introduced to neuroanatomy, as mentioned in Chapter 4. She was struck and amazed by the complexity of our neuroanatomy. In particular, she was amazed and fascinated by the complexities of the paths axons travel to reach their targets, their intricacies and idiosyncracies, especially the fact that axons do not travel along simple straight lines, but rather make many turns and changes of direction, circumventing obstacles to reach their targets. "The thought that we are so complicated and yet we work, it just blows me away," she told me. "The fact that cranial nerve seven grows around the nucleus of cranial nerve six before it exits, and all these little loops and dips and contrasts." Her phrasing "loops and dips and contrasts" is distinctive and, together with the example she gives of cranial nerve seven circumventing cranial nerve six, shows that her interest focused especially on turns and the idiosyncracies and complexities of individual paths.[13]

In the beginning of her first year in graduate school Sophia attended an orientation meeting in which research of the neuroscience faculty was described. Her interest was sparked by the description of work by a new faculty recruit who hadn't arrived yet, who was studying the role of chemoattractants in guiding axons during neurodevelopment. "Because he was this hot new recruit," she told me, "they highlighted his research." "They drew little pictures of axons turning towards pieces of floor plate [that contain the chemoattractants]." "And I remember sitting there thinking, 'wow, this is really cool.'" "It's very graphic, it's impressionable — if you see the picture, it tells you a thousand words." "It was just this incredibly cool thing to think that you could get something to turn and follow you around a dish." The resonance with her interest is clear: the intricacies of axon paths, and especially the turns axons make following paths. A new element has also been introduced, the idea of influencing the direction an axon takes, causing it "to turn and follow you around."

When the new faculty recruit arrived Sophia did a rotation with him. As described in Chapter 4, she still remembers them sitting together late at night, "passing the microscope back and forth, pointing out incredible growth cones to each other," watching them grow, struck by their beauty, amazed at how they know where to go. Thus her fascination and interest in axon pathfinding continued and grew, and she continued to focus on individual axons, watching them grow and travel along their paths. A short time later Sophia joined the lab of this faculty member and he became her advisor.

Sophia developed an idea for a dissertation project in discussions with her advisor. "I was going to make a chemotaxis chamber where you could vary all the parameters and basically create an artificial gradient of chemoattractant and then watch axons turn and look at all the parameters involved in their turning," she said. "How they steer in a gradient, how they detect a gradient, what are the parameters of the gradient." "Basically the cell biology of turning." Sophia's Orals Proposal, which she shared with me, is entitled "Characterization of growth cone response to chemoattractants." In the first part of her proposal, "Specific Aims," she lists two main aims: "(1) *Documentation of growth cone behavior during chemotaxis through a cellular environment.* The navigation of

[13]As an illustration of the distinctiveness of her interest, in the 1991 *Abstracts* for the Society for Neuroscience annual meeting, though there are a fair number of abstracts for posters on pathfinding (see Chapter 7 above), I found only two specifically making reference to studying turning processes — out of approximately 10,000 published abstracts. Neither mentions the complexity of paths.

individual growth cones in response to a nearby source of chemoattractant will be followed using real-time imaging of labeled axons in tissue explants. (2) *Determination of how axons respond on a cellular level to the presence of the molecule.* Development of a chemotaxis chamber will allow dissociated neurons to be placed in a controlled gradient of chemoattractant, thus recreating the orientation response in a cell-free, optically favorable environment." She lists as primary issues to investigate under (2): "a) sensitivity; b)strategy; c) steering; and d) mechanism of response."[14]

What is remarkable about Sophia's project is how it centers on and so precisely reflects the aspect of pathfinding at the center of her interest — turning, specifically the mechanics of turning, through which axon growth cones navigate their complex, winding paths, and the factors and parameters that govern turning. Indeed she devotes several pages of her proposal to discussing how she will study navigation and turning. Her plan to "watch axons turn" using "real-time imaging" fits with her excitement watching growth cones. Her focus on constructing an artificial gradient to control or influence the turning process fits with and reflects her fascination at the possibility of getting an axon to "turn and follow you around a dish."

Later Sophia added a second, related project: to image axons turning *in situ*, in live tissue; and through pursuing this approach she eventually came to focus on very specific turning processes and chemoattractants, leading to an important finding that was published in *Cell*.[15] Thus her focus of interest carried through in a series of projects leading to distinctive contributions.

Interestingly, Sophia's interest was also the basis for her post-doctoral research, conducted after our first interview, which she described to me in a follow-up interview — showing how enduring her interest was over these years.[16] She told me that in thinking about a suitable topic she returned to her core interest in axon pathfinding, in particular to her interest in axon regeneration following trauma or injury — how to make axons regrow. She thus

[14]Sophia Colamarino, Orals Proposal, "Characterization of growth cone response to chemoattractants," p. 1. Sophia told me about several previous projects by other researchers that informed her own study design. Chemotaxis chambers had been successfully constructed for peptides, bacteria, and other organisms, but never before for nerve cells; she drew on these chambers for other biologic systems in designing her chamber.

[15]S.A. Colamarino and M. Tessier-Lavigne, "The axonal chemoattractant netrin-1 is also a chemorepellent for trochlear motor axons," *Cell* 81 (1995): 621–29.

[16]The fact that this research was conducted after our initial interview also provides prospective data showing links between a person's interest and subsequent creative projects and path of development.

240   accepted a position working in a lab having a focus on stem cells, which provide one important approach for generating axon regeneration.

Chris became interested in neuroscience, in particular in the development of the nervous system, during his junior year in college. Like Sophia, he is filled with awe and amazed at the complexity of the nervous system and the fact that neurons are able to grow to their targets. In contrast to her focus on the paths individual axons travel, however, his fascination and focus is at the level of the whole system — how the system as a whole is "wired up." What amazes and fascinates him is the fact that billions of neurons all find their way to their correct targets, and, especially, that they do it all at once without getting confused. "You have this hugely complex circuit," he said, "and [what I was interested in was] how does it all come together, developmentally?" "How do these billions and billions of neurons in our brains all get connected, at the same time, and what are the molecular mechanisms that control that?" Linked to this difference in focus, he conceptualizes pathfinding differently than Sophia, more as a choice process, and as an aggregate process, akin to a problem of traffic flow. "If you look at a particular neuron, that specific neuron will take exactly the same path, make exactly the same pathway choices during its development [in every developing embryo of a particular species]. There have to be these signposts, there have to be these signals that tell it how to do it." "And it's something that fascinated me because it seems incredibly sophisticated, because it's not just happening for one neuron — it's happening to billions of neurons with millions of targets, all at the same time." Chris envisions the developing nervous system as a world filled with alternative pathways and targets that a neuron must choose among, in which "billions of neurons with millions of targets" all make their choices "at the same time," sharing common pathways while traveling to their respective targets. It is the fact that neurons are able to choose correctly in the face of this confusing multiplicity that he finds remarkable — how is a neuron able to distinguish its correct path and target from among the many alternatives? His answer is that there must be signals and signal detection processes that tell neurons where to go, the signals arranged like "signposts" along the paths, with the array of signals sufficiently rich to enable each neuron to distinguish its own path from all the other potential paths it might follow. He thus has a rich conception of the process through which the brain becomes wired, which defines his interest.

In graduate school Chris chose to focus on the genetic regulation of pathfinding. This was a natural choice for him in light of his interest in pathfinding as a system level process and his focus on signals and pathway and target choices, for genetic regulation is central to these aspects of pathfinding: the products pathfinding genes express regulate signal detection and thereby pathway and target choices. For his dissertation he joined a lab in which genetic techniques are used to study the molecular mechanisms of axonal pathfinding in *Drosophila*, with the principal investigator as his advisor.

The idea for Chris's dissertation project was based on a new reporter called *kinesin-beta-gal-lacz* that Chris and his advisor learned about. A reporter is a DNA sequence that includes a gene and a promoter that turns the gene on and off, controlling expression of the gene's product; linked to the reporter is a trigger molecule that causes the promoter to turn the gene on, and a method of detecting the gene's product, thus identifying when the reporter has been turned on. Reporters are used to learn about expression patterns of genes, as a way to help determine what a gene does or what its product is. A reporter is linked to a gene by being placed adjacent to it in the genome, so that the reporter can be turned on by its trigger only when the gene is being expressed; then, when the organism is exposed to the trigger, if the gene is being expressed in a cell the reporter is also expressed in the cell and its product can be detected, thus revealing that the gene it is linked to is being expressed.[17] The products expressed by traditional reporters, for example the *beta-gal-lacz* reporter, are present in neurons' cell bodies, nuclei, and axon tips, but not throughout the lengths of their axons; thus they do not reveal the full lengths of axons, hence which cell bodies are connected with which axon tips, thus do not identify which neurons project to which targets. The *kinesin-beta-gal-lacz* reporter was designed to overcome this limitation. Kinesin is a molecule that shuttles other molecules back and forth along axons. Thus, fusing it (its gene) to *beta-gal-lacz* creates a reporter the product of which taxis back and forth throughout the length of a neuron's axon, hence is designed to reveal the axon in full, from cell body to tip. Chris and his advisor had the idea to construct what is known as an enhancer trap screen using the *kinesin-beta-gal-lacz* reporter to search for genes that regulate axonal pathfinding.[18] An enhancer trap screen works in three steps. First, a system is developed for springing the reporter randomly into the genome of the host organism (here *Drosophila*), so that it lands adjacent to different genes in different embryos. Second, the embryos are grown into distinct cell lines. Third, each cell line is exposed to the trigger, revealing the expression pattern for the gene the reporter is adjacent to in that line. Most cell lines do not show interesting expression patterns, but with luck a few will, and these are then investigated further. Their idea was that the

[17]The product of the gene the reporter is adjacent to is either unknown or cannot directly be detected, and is thus revealed indirectly, by the expression of the reporter.

[18]Chris told me, "What we were going to do was to be one of the first people to do an enhancer trap screen with it."

242 *kinesin-beta-gal-lacz* reporter would show the full lengths of axons in which it is expressed, thus making it possible to identify genes involved in important pathway and target choices.[19]

In discussing the project Chris made it clear that he was primarily interested in expression patterns in which a group of neurons that express the reporter all choose a common pathway or project to a common target — for this indicates that they all are expressing a gene linked to the reporter that may be leading them to make the same choice. "Say you had three neurons," he said, "[all expressing the reporter], and all those neurons projected onto the same pathway, or they all projected to the same muscle, something like that. And that gene, as suggested by the expression pattern of the reporter, comes on exactly when or just before those axons either reach their target or reach that common pathway that they take. That would be something that would be intriguing because [it would be] tied to the choosing of a common pathway or common target." Identifying a common pathway or target is key — without that it is much less likely any of the genes next to the reporter in this cell line are pathfinding genes.[20] Once a pathfinding gene is identified, if the reporter can be localized in the genome the gene can be identified and sequenced.

The enhancer trap screen project fits with Chris's conception of the process through which the brain is wired, and centers on elucidating the basis of exactly the aspect of pathfinding he finds fascinating. Fundamentally Chris's conception is of a network process — billions of neurons traveling along a network, all at the same time, to their targets, guided by signals arrayed along the network paths. Central to this conception is the idea of neurons sharing signals and pathways in common.[21] Signal sharing is indeed a basic feature of pathfinding — there are not many distinct chemical signals relative to the vast number of neurons, thus many neurons respond to each signal, though in varying ways and degrees depending on other factors, including the presence or absence of other signals and their stage of development.[22] The detection of

[19]In fact when they tried out this reporter it did not work and this led Chris on a search to develop a reporter that would work; see Chapter 12.

[20]Thus Chris told me, "If you're interested in genes involved in axonal pathfinding, you are going to be much more intrigued by an expression pattern where [a bunch of] seemingly unrelated neurons all happen to project to the same target [or along a common pathway] [than a pattern in which they project different places]."

[21]Chris did not explicitly use these words in his description of his conception, though he did in describing his project (see main text); but the idea of common pathways and signals and targets is central to the logic of his conception.

[22]In general it is simply not feasible for each neuron to have its own unique signal, for there are far too many neurons compared to the number of signals. Rather, each neuron is guided by a particular combination of signals depending on its gene expression

and response to a particular signal is typically controlled by a specific gene or set of genes; in this way genes control the "traffic flow" of neurons along the network. The enhancer trap screen is designed to identify such genes: when a pattern is identified in which a group of neurons all express the reporter and also all choose the same pathway or share a common target it points to the gene adjacent to the reporter as being a gene that controls this choice. In turn, mapping out such pathfinding genes is central to decoding the network flow patterns, thereby unraveling the mystery of how the brain is wired which is at the heart of Chris's interest.

In addition to sharing signals, neurons also share common pathways — a network. The sharing of pathways is also basic to Chris's conception and his fascination with the process of wiring the brain. What fascinates him is the fact that neurons don't get confused, and if each neuron followed a path that only it travels the fact that it doesn't get confused would be a lot less remarkable, for along its path there would be signs only for it. What is amazing is that neurons traveling common paths, that are lined with many "signposts," are able to pick out only the ones meant for them, ignoring all the others, making their way through a confusing maze of alternatives. Chris's idea was to use the enhancer trap screen to identify genes that govern common pathway choices; by building up an inventory of such genes one can map out the set of signals and signal responses that govern network flow. This is thus another way the project links with his interest.

Beyond specific patterns, the enhancer trap screen project fits with Chris's conception in its approach. It casts a wide net: it is not focused on one kind of neuron or signal or pathway; rather, many genes are screened, searching over large numbers of neurons, in the hopes of discovering, randomly, as many of the genes involved in pathfinding as possible. Thus it is a system level focus that fits with his focus on the wiring of the system as a whole, on signaling and signal detection mechanisms integral to the functioning of the network as a whole.

pattern, its location, and the signals it encounters. Of course if the detection of each signal were controlled by a specific combination of a relatively large number of genes it might be possible to form many such combinations and thus have different signals for each neuron. But the evidence does not show this, or at least did not suggest this as an avenue of research that Chris wished to pursue at the time. I discussed further work on identifying genes that govern axonal pathfinding in *Drosophila*, since Chris completed his dissertation, with his advisor in a brief conversation in 2004. He said that a number of such genes have been identified, including one Chris identified, and that individual genes do control pathfinding — or critical stages of pathfinding — for identifiable groups of neurons.

Chris and Sophia share a common general interest in pathfinding, but the focuses of their respective interests — what they find most fascinating — and their conceptions defining their interests are strikingly different. The idea of neurons sharing a common pathway or target, which is central to Chris's conception, is never mentioned by Sophia; likewise, the complexity of individual paths and turning processes, which so fascinate Sophia, are not mentioned by Chris. What is striking — what I have tried to show — is the way these differences, and the richness and distinctiveness of their conceptions, are reflected — directly and clearly — in their respective projects. As a different way of seeing how their projects match their conceptions, if we consider each project matched with the conception of the other person we see how poor the fit would be. Thus, the enhancer trap screen would not be appropriate for studying idiosyncracies of individual paths, the phenomenon that Sophia finds most interesting, since these idiosyncracies are unlikely to be tied to the expression of a single gene, and are specifically not common across neurons. Similarly, the chemotaxis chamber Sophia wanted to build is not designed, at least not primarily, to study the kinds of network patterns that Chris finds most interesting, such as common pathways, and also is not designed to search for the genes that govern such pathfinding patterns, but rather is focused on the mechanics of turning, which Chris is less interested in.

RESONANCES AND LINKAGES OF CONCEPTUAL ELEMENTS LINKED TO CONCEPTIONS OF INTERESTS

In some cases there are resonances and connections of conceptual elements and general concepts that are naturally linked to an individual's conception of interest with her subsequent projects and contributions. These are subtle, not necessarily obvious at first glance; it requires understanding and thinking about an individual's conception of interest to see them. But they can be equally rich and significant in illuminating an individual's path of development as other, more evident resonances and connections, and oftentimes show a person's great creativity rooted in her conception.

Kelly Overly, whose rich conception of interest is presented in Chapter 6, is an individual for whom a concept naturally linked to and implicitly part of her conception came to the fore and was central to her subsequent creative development, generating a link from her conception to her dissertation project. As described in Chapter 6, Kelly defined her creative interest through the rich conception she formed of the neuron, imagining it as being like a community, with a "way of life" and a day-to-day routine of "activities occurring throughout" its different parts. Rooted in this conception, she developed interests in how the different parts of the neuron communicate with one another and in cellular transport — "how things are shuttled around" the neuron — her use of the word "shuttled" creating the impression of frequent, routine trips back and forth across the cell, fitting with her focus on routine activities of daily life.

In the course of her doctoral research Kelly developed a novel idea for a project, in collaboration with her advisor: to study waste disposal in neurons, specifically the endosomal-lysosomal waste disposal system. This became a main focus of her research, and she and her advisor made a significant contribution to the understanding of how this system works, first developing a method for measuring pH levels in endocytic organelles that sort, transport, and help to break down and recycle cell products, which is useful for understanding how the endocytic system is organized in neurons and its pattern of operation; then using the method to measure pH levels in different regions and constituent bodies of axons.[23]

Although the endosomal-lysosomal system is an important and well-defined area of study in cell biology, it had been neglected by neurobiologists. Kelly told me that at the time she and her advisor took it up "people knew virtually nothing about" how it works in neurons and just assumed that it works similarly to the way it works in other cells.[24] Neurobiologists have traditionally been far more interested in studying how neurons develop, form synapses and circuits, and generate impulse responses — the bases of brain development and cognitive function — than in studying routine day-to-day maintenance functions of neurons like waste disposal, which are a lot less glamorous. Kelly, however, her interest flowing from and defined by her conception, was an exception. She was very much interested in the daily life and activities of neurons, thus it was natural for her attention to be drawn to the waste disposal system and for her to desire to study it. Waste disposal is a quintessential activity of daily life, a part of the "way of life" of every community, and thus is linked implicitly to

[23]C.C. Overly, K.D. Lee, E. Berthiaume, and P.J. Hollenbeck, "Quantitative measurement of intraorganelle pH in the endosomal lysosomal pathway in neurons by using ratiometric imaging with pyranine," *Proceedings of the National Academy of Sciences* 92 (1995): 3156–60; and C.C. Overly and P.J. Hollenbeck, "Dynamic organization of endocytic pathways in axons of cultured sympathetic neurons," *Journal of Neuroscience* 16 (1996): 6056–64.

[24]As an example, in a recent survey book, *Endocytosis*, ed. Mark Marsh (Oxford: Oxford University Press, 2001), published five years after Kelly earned her degree, of eleven chapters there is just one about neurons, and it focuses on synaptic vesicle recycling, not intracellular transport systems, and exclusively on axon pathways, with no discussion of transport in dendrites. Further, it is a very short chapter — just 14 pages, the shortest chapter in the book, with the average length of the other ten chapters being just over 26 pages; and it contains relatively few references, suggesting limited recent work on endocytosis in neurons.

her conception. Further, it involves moving or "shuttling" products from one part of a cell to another — this is a critical aspect of waste disposal systems, especially in neurons, in which waste products must be transported through the length of the axon back to the cell body, which links it both to her conception as well as to her interest in transport.[25] Though she was not necessarily thinking specifically about waste disposal at the time she formed her conception and initial interest, nonetheless waste disposal is implicitly connected with her conception, an integral part of the cell's day-to-day life, thus a natural topic for her to have become interested in studying given her conception. Indeed I think it is striking how Kelly's work on waste disposal so clearly resonates with her conception — flows so naturally, in its distinctiveness, from her distinctive conception.

This kind of resonance or connection of a linked conceptual element is, I believe, likely to be fairly common among individuals who, like Kelly, form holistic conceptions defining their interests. Such conceptions invariably have a host of associated conceptual elements, and often a rich conceptual orientation, that often foreshadows or may directly lead to later ideas and works. Also, such conceptions are often, as Kelly's was, rooted in metaphor, which may be a rich source spawning ideas and projects.

A last kind of linkage is one based in conceptual transformation, in which a conceptual element that is part of an individual's conception of interest, or closely linked to it, is transformed by her and incorporated or reflected in a later creative project or contribution as this transformed element. Such conceptual transformations can be highly creative and carry an individual far beyond where she began with her original conception.

A beautiful example of such a transformation is Virginia Woolf's development of a conception of the self that goes beyond her conception of the self as defined and sustained by reflections, in the character of Mrs. Ramsay in *To the Lighthouse*. In her portrayal she adds to the conception of the self as constructed out of and sustained by reflections the opposite: a part of the self that is not visible through reflection, that escapes the penetrating gaze of others, living in a subterranean world. This part of Mrs. Ramsay runs through the first part of the book. It is particularly striking in the following passage. Mrs. Ramsay is by herself, having finally sent James to bed:

> No, she thought, putting together some of the pictures he had cut out — a refrigerator, a mowing machine, a gentleman in evening dress — children never forget.

[25] Waste disposal also links with Kelly's earlier feeling of enjoyment taking care of cells in culture, the "day-to-day" routine she enjoyed, including feeding them, et cetera; waste disposal fits naturally into this routine.

For this reason, it was so important what one said, and what one did, and it was
a relief when they went to bed. For now she need not think about anybody. She
could be herself, by herself. And that was what now she often felt the need of — to
think; well, not even to think. To be silent; to be alone. All the being and the doing,
expansive, glittering, vocal, evaporated; and one shrunk, with a sense of solemnity,
to being oneself, a wedge-shaped core of darkness, something invisible to others.[26]

Mrs. Ramsay's self thus has two distinct parts, uneasily joined: the self of reflections, and this other, private self. Note how carefully it is portrayed as thick
and dark, thus invisible to reflection, exactly the antithesis of the reflected self,
the pair generating a richer, mature, holistic conception of the self.[27]

[26]*To the Lighthouse*, p. 62.

[27]There are antecedents for what Virginia does with Mrs. Ramsay in her description
in "The Mark on the Wall" of the self under water "gazing up through the grey waters," in
the silent core of Rachel in *The Voyage Out*, and in what is visible and invisible to others
as a basic theme of *Night and Day*. There are also various related comments she makes
in letters and her diary about the self that is hidden and below the surface — indeed
this theme is recurrent in her work, as has been noted by critics.

9

CREATIVE RESPONSES

In the previous chapter I describe as a general feature of creative development and depict for a few specific cases clear, striking resonances and connections between individuals' creative interests and conceptions of interests and subsequent projects they undertook and creative works they produced. These resonances and connections are suggestive that individuals' creative interests are generative of ideas they have and projects they define and pursue, leading to creative contributions. But they do not, in and of themselves, demonstrate this. In particular, they do not define or manifest specific mechanisms through which interests and the conceptual structures individuals build up in the domains of their interests are generative of their ideas and projects.

In this chapter and the next I describe such mechanisms: fundamental processes through which individuals' creative interests and conceptual structures they form in interest domains are generative of ideas they have, which in turn are the basis for their projects and contributions. I illustrate these processes with numerous examples, showing that these processes are central to the creativity of many people, including, among the presented examples, Alexander Calder, Susan Ferguson, Charles Darwin, Albert Einstein, Cheryl Nixon, Tim Berners-Lee, Ray Kroc, Robert Kaufman, Ian Baucom, James Watson, Samuel Taylor Coleridge, and Chris Callahan. These processes are the springs of action by which individuals move from creative interests to specific ideas and projects, setting them forth on paths that lead to their main creative contributions. They are critical to my argument in this book, showing processes through which creative interests are generative of creativity and creative contributions — for if they did not exist, or were not important for individuals in their development, creative interests would be far less important, since they would have no causal link to ideas and projects, and thus to creative contributions.

In this chapter I describe creativity generated via mediated creative responses: the generation of a creative response by an individual, sparked by an experience he has or element he encounters, mediated by a creative interest he has, generating a creative idea or insight. Such responses are a fundamental source of creativity, in particular during phases of development when individuals are exploring their interests, including the source of ideas for many of the projects they pursue, thus a main pathway through which their ideas and projects are generated by and develop out of their creative interests.

Creative responses are the element in the overall description of creative development in this book that fits best with the classic view of creativity as sudden illumination, ideas and insights that occur suddenly, in a flash or at least over a short time period. They are, however, distinctive in two regards that fit with and reflect the basic orientation and description in the book. Conventional models and descriptions, with some exceptions, view creativity as generated within the individual; thus they depict individuals generating possibilities and associations and puzzling over problems, leading to creative ideas and insights — with the environment in the background, playing little or no direct role. Such a portrayal is characteristic of psychodynamic as well as cognitive processing and search models; indeed the basic idea of a conceptual combination as the essence of creativity has this flavor — the combination occurs inside the mind, independently of the world outside. In contrast, in creative responses creativity is generated by and flows out of individuals' engagement with the world, specifically their responses to specific experiences and elements they encounter. While the conventional view clearly has merit — for creativity is in general based in the mind — its portrayal of the creative process, in particular during the phase of development centering on the exploration of creative interests, is both inaccurate and incomplete. I demonstrate this point in this chapter with many diverse examples, showing the important, direct role of experiences and encountered elements in sparking individuals' ideas and insights.

Mediated creative responses are also distinctive in the way they are rooted in individuals' creative interests and the conceptual structures, centering around their conceptions of their interests, that encode their interests. Because creative interests, including conceptions of interests and conceptual structures that encode interests, have not been the focus of creativity research, their importance in the generation of ideas and insights has not been recognized. The description I present here in contrast shows how our creativity, especially during periods of open-ended exploration, when we are not focused on projects, is rooted in and generated out of our interests.

I divide this chapter into two main parts: in part A I set forth the basic description of creative responses; in part B, which is the bulk of the chapter, I present a series of examples illustrating creative responses, demonstrating how central they are in the generation of creativity. At the end of the chapter I present some additional remarks.

A. BASIC DESCRIPTION

The Stream of Experience and Our Limited Focus of Attention

In the course of our creative development, of our lives, we have many experiences and encounter a great multitude and variety of different elements. We are especially open to engagement with the world during periods of our development when we are forming creative interests, as discussed in Chapter 3. We are also open to the world in later phases of development, especially when we are exploring and thinking about creative interests we have formed, when we are not inwardly focused as we are, for example, when concentrating on projects.

It is well established in neuropsychology and cognitive psychology that human attention is very limited in scope. As a consequence, it is simply not possible for us to attend closely to most of the experiences we have and elements we encounter — there are simply too many, of too great complexity, and the vast majority pass us by. Thus we attend to and focus on just a small fraction, a limited number of discrete elements or experiences, or sequence or small group of elements, embedded in the stream of sensory data.[1] Further, when an element or experience does draw our attention in most cases our attention is fleeting and we generate no significant response to it — either none at all, or else a fleeting response that does not lead to a larger, more integrated response, but peters out, as our focus of attention shifts to something else. Only a very few experiences and elements trigger a significant, lasting response in us that influences us. I note that a constellation of processes influence and guide our attention, focus, and responses, including perceptual processes, central to attention, and cognitive, affective, and motivational processes.[2]

[1] See, for example, Daniel Kahneman, *Attention and Effort* (Englewood Cliffs, NJ: Prentice-Hall, 1973), Michael I. Posner and Oscar S.M. Marin, eds., *Attention and Performance XI* (Hillsdale, NJ: Lawrence Erlbaum Associates, 1985).

[2] Attention and focus are well-studied topics; see, for example, the discussions by Kahneman and in the Posner and Marin edited volume. Responses, as I define and use them in my description, are a particular form of mental process that is important in cognitive psychology and related fields, but I believe less well studied and described.

*The Role of Creative Interests in Guiding Attention
and Generating Responses*

During creative development our creative interests, specifically the conceptual structures in our mind that encode our interests, are central in guiding
our attention and sparking and mediating our responses to experiences and
elements we encounter. Once we form a creative interest and a conceptual
structure defining and encoding our interest forms in our mind, this structure
acts like a filter, sifting through our experiences and elements we encounter,
picking out and calling our attention and focus to select experiences and
elements — or particular aspects of complex experiences or elements — that
fit with or call forth an association in our mind to our interest. This act of
recognition and connection is itself often creative. Moreover, in many cases
it triggers a further response, again mediated by the conceptual structure encoding our interest, that goes beyond the initial response, generating a further,
sometimes even more creative idea or insight.

To summarize, we are more likely to attend to and focus on an experience
or element we encounter if it connects in some way with one of our creative
interests, and we tend to respond to it from the perspective of our interest —
through links to elements within the conceptual structure that encodes the
interest. Our mode of engagement with the world once we form a creative
interest is thus fundamentally different than what it is before we have defined
an interest, in being mediated by the conceptual structure in our mind that
encodes the interest.

Creative interests are not the only factor that governs attention and responses
of course. For example, a person's attention may be drawn to a particular
element because it is unusual, or because others are focusing on it, and, in
drawing his attention, such an element may in turn spark a response in him.
Nevertheless, creative interests have a fundamental role in mediating creative
responses during creative development. As my purpose is to show their role
I focus here on describing the way in which they mediate responses; I note
other factors in the course of my description.

The process through which experiences and elements trigger creative responses has a clear resonance with the process of experiences and elements
sparking creative interests described in Chapter 3. Creative development in this
regard thus has something of a recursive structure: experiences and elements
spark creative interests; conceptual structures form over time encoding these
interests; and experiences and elements in combination with these structures
spark creative responses. The resemblance extends, to a degree, to mediation:
creative responses are mediated by conceptual structures that encode creative
interests, and the formation of an interest is often mediated by a register of

meaning. However, the resemblance is not at all exact. The conceptual structures encoding interests are qualitatively different from registers of meaning, being more articulated and defined; further, creative responses are the basis of original ideas and insights.

Sources of Resonances and Connections

The source of a resonance or connection between an experience or element, or set of experiences or elements, and elements in the conceptual structure of a creative interest is generally an overlapping of some kind or a close link. Overlapping is often conceptual: a shared concept or conceptual schema that links the experience or element with the interest. Thus, for Chris Callahan the idea of the reporter he heard described at a talk — to light up the entire length of axons — overlapped with his interest in tracing axon paths — sparking the idea for his dissertation project. The way dialogue is shown as spoken in many languages, each language having its own social meaning, in *Kim* overlapped with Susan Ferguson's interest in multilingual conversational practices, and maybe with memories she had of such conversations in Kenya.

A resonance or connection may be primarily linguistically based, a specific phrase or word that sparks a connection or association with an interest. Alternatively, it may be a shared approach or technique or stylistic resonance, perhaps seeing something — thus a visual overlap — that has a stylistic resonance with a creative interest one has. Or it may be emotional, for example a personal experience an individual has may resonate with an emotion associated with an interest he has, sparking a response in him.

Experiences and elements that trigger creative responses often stand out in being highly salient or stimulating — features that in general tend to draw our attention. Often highly salient experiences or elements that spark responses stand out in a way that highlights their connection with the interest with which they connect. Mondrian's studio was famous for its simply shaped art works arranged on the walls, which, as I argue further below, seems to have been important in triggering a creative response in Alexander Calder, through enabling him to see a clear connection with his own interest in basic shapes of the universe arranged in space as the basis for art. CERN stands out among organizations for its loose, nonhierarchical organizational structure, and it seems likely this was important in leading Tim Berners-Lee to focus on it and its connection with his interest in such kinds of structures. The idea of different languages being used in conversation, and language switching, is highlighted in *Kim*, as I document below, which seems to have been important in drawing Susan's attention to this aspect of the book.

Highly stimulating experiences are more likely to spark creative responses. Mondrian's studio was visually highly stimulating. As a second example Bruce Peters had an inspiration while sitting in class looking at a slide on which were displayed pictures of many kinds of neurons, showing their distinctive shapes and dendritic branching patterns — Bruce called them "stunning" — which brought his attention to the distinctiveness and intricacies of their shapes. Presentations and direct face-to-face communication are often stimulating and generate high attention. Thus, in such settings if something comes up that overlaps or links with an interest we have, we are relatively likely to recognize the connection, and this may spark an idea or insight. Two examples given below are James Watson's coming to an awareness of the power of using X-ray diffraction methods to investigate the structure of DNA, spurred by a talk he attended, and Chris Callahan's development of the idea for his dissertation project. A new acquaintance or colleague can be highly stimulating, as Francis Crick was for James Watson, and ideas often are born in the overlap and synergy of the partners' mutual interests and the different perspectives they bring to bear on shared topics of interest. An example given below is Roger's conversation with a faculty member who shared his interest in the shapes of neurons, that sparked the idea for his initial dissertation project. Finally, intense experiences that link to interests seem more likely to trigger creative responses than ordinary experiences and events. An example is Hannah Arendt's idea to write a book describing the historical roots of the racist-imperialist, Fascist political movement and its nature as a political organizational form, clearly sparked by the horrible, deeply affecting events of her time.

Creative Responses: Basic Forms

There are two main forms of creative response I have identified in my analysis of creative development. These forms, as I describe them here, fit standard models of creativity in some respects — in particular the first is linked with models of insight rooted in perceptual processes, and the second with idea generation through creative connections and chains of associations. The responses I describe set these processes in the context of creative development, and show that during development, in particular during periods of exploration of interests, these forms of creativity are based in creative interests.

The most immediate, direct form of creative response is a response that is perceptually based. There are two basic forms of this response: noticing or recognizing something, for example a phenomenon or an aspect of a complex work, that has never been noticed or recognized, at least not focused on, before; and seeing or thinking about an experience or element, for example a phenomenon, event, or model, in a new way — from a different perspective or in terms of a novel frame of reference. In the context of creative development such responses are in many — even most — cases mediated by a creative interest, and I focus on this kind of response here.

For such perceptually based responses the perceptual recognition that triggers and is the basis of the response is based in a creative interest, specifically, the conceptual structure that encodes the interest. Thus, one comes to notice and focus on an experience or element — or aspect of a complex element or experience — through a resonance or connection it has with one's interest, or sees an experience or element from the perspective of one's interest or in the context of one's interest. In both cases the originality of the response is in general rooted in or at least connected to the distinctiveness of the interest in which it is based. This type of response is somewhat like a response generated out of the adherence to a paradigm — the paradigm leads one to focus on certain specific experiences or elements or aspects of experiences or elements, viewing them from the perspective of the conceptual frame of the paradigm. However, there is a fundamental difference: paradigms are shared, whereas creative interests are distinctive, even unique — and as a result the kind of response described here is far less likely to be seen or noticed by others, and thus far more likely to be novel and thus a basis of originality.[3]

An example of this kind of perceptually based creative response that I describe below is Susan Ferguson's recognition of the importance of the different dialects and languages that are spoken — as indicated by the narrator — in the dialogue scenes of Rudyard Kipling's novel *Kim*. A second example, also described below, is Ross Hamilton's noticing the literary centrality of the accident Rousseau describes in the "Second Walk" in *The Reveries of the Solitary Walker*, being knocked over by a Great Dane, which connected with Ross's interest in comic accidents. A third example, which I do not discuss further here, is an insight Bruce Peters had: that the shapes of neurons, in particular the idiosyncratic details of their branching patterns, is important for their integration of incoming electrical signals. Bruce's insight was sparked sitting in class looking at a slide showing the distinctive shapes and branching patterns of

---

[3]Applying a paradigm in a new way or to a new set of elements — forming an interest, for example, in applying a paradigm from one field in a different venue — may lead to the kind of creative response I describe. A creative response that sparks a new paradigm also fits my description. But the application of preexisting paradigms to experiences and elements they are conventionally applied to does not. The idea of conceptual frameworks governing how we see is central in Gestalt psychology; it is discussed by Norwood Russell Hanson in *Patterns of Discovery*, and by Thomas Kuhn in *The Structure of Scientific Revolutions*.

different kinds of neurons, and was rooted in his interest in the electrical properties of small circuits of interconnected neurons. Often a perceptually based
creative response is based in rich knowledge of an interest domain — creative
expertise — that cues a recognition or way of seeing a particular experience
or set of data or facts. Examples are the creative response of Azad Bonni described in Chapter 13 and the creative response of Ray Kroc described in the
next chapter.

A second form of creative response is making a creative connection, sparked
by an experience or encounter, through connecting the experience or element
with a creative interest one has, specifically elements in the conceptual structure encoding the interest. The most basic form of this response is making a
creative connection between an element or aspect of an experience or set of
elements one encounters and an element or cluster of elements contained
in the conceptual structure that encodes and is associated with one's interest.
Two other, related forms of this response are (1) making a connection between
two elements in the domain of one's interest that one has never previously
connected or related, the connection spurred and mediated by an experience
or element or set of elements one encounters, and (2) making a connection
between two experiences or elements or sets of elements one has encountered,
the connection mediated by one's interest, which enables one to make the
connection.

In general, for this form of response the first step in the response is, like for
the first form of response, noticing and focusing on a particular experience or
element or set of related experiences and elements — or particular aspect of
a complex experience or element — that one senses, possibly unconsciously,
has a connection with a creative interest one has. This initial act of recognition
is not the main response in this case however — rather it triggers or leads to a
further response, triggering a creative association or connection to a conceptual element or structure within the conceptual structure that encodes and is
associated with one's interest, generating an idea or insight. Notwithstanding
this distinction, I note that the second form of response is not sharply distinguished from the first form; it does, however, often involve more mental steps
and take longer.

I have identified many cases of this form of creative response analyzing
the creative developments of individuals, across a range of fields. A brilliant
example described below is Alexander Calder's shift to making sculptures in a
new style, leading to his invention of the mobile in modern art. His response
was triggered, as he describes it, by his visit to Mondrian's studio: the simple
shapes, many in red, connected with his interest in and conception of simple
shapes of the universe arranged in space as the basis for art, most likely through

associations to specific images in his mind, and also connected with his interest in motion as an art form and setting art in motion. A second example, also described below, is Tim Berners-Lee's idea for Enquire: he developed the idea for this program, the forerunner of his idea for the World Wide Web, after he began working at CERN, as he describes it through making a creative association between the CERN organizational structure and his interest in nonhierarchical structures. A third example is Pierre Omidyar's development of a Website for buying and selling used items through auction, which was sparked by the request of a friend; I discuss Pierre's development in Chapter 11. A fourth example is John Maynard Keynes's initial insight about the process of forming probability-based judgements, sparked by G.E. Moore's *Principia Ethica*; I describe this episode in the context of describing his development in Chapter 15. Among my interview subjects examples of this form of response include Chris's idea for his dissertation project — sparked through going to a talk and hearing about a new reporter that held the promise of depicting the entire length of an axon, which connected to his interest in identifying genes that control signals that guide axon pathfinding; Teresa Faherty's insight that a model of pastoral as language contest that she learned about in a class applies to a main scene and theme in *The Winter's Tale*; and a creative insight Henry Chen had about James Joyce's *Ulysses* sparked by statements in a book he read about Dante, described in Chapter 15. Many other interview subjects also described creative responses of this basic form, some of which are also described in the book.

The basic process of idea generation for this form of response — a conceptual connection linking elements that have not previously been connected or related — fits the classic, standard model of creativity. Further, also fitting the standard model, these responses, as individuals describe them and as they appear examining accounts of creative development, seem often to be sudden, dramatic moments or illuminations that stand out and are striking for their clarity and creativity. However, whereas in standard views such sudden, dramatic creativity is often viewed as striking out of the blue as it were — not rooted in any clearly defined preexisting structure, these responses, and the ideas and insights generated, are clearly rooted in the rich conceptual structures that define and encode interests: this is a fundamental difference between my account and standard models. Indeed it is fascinating, in tracing and describing these creative responses, to see how clearly the ideas and insights individuals generate are rooted in their creative interests — fitting and illustrating the description in Chapter 8. The ideas and insights generated through these responses reveal, often in a striking manner, the creative potential of a domain of interest which previously was only latent. Indeed they often seem, once we see them (though we would not have been able to imagine or form them beforehand), a natural, evident implication or development of the interest.

Responses of this second form are generated in many cases not through a single conceptual association or link, as may be implied by the description above, but through a chain of associations and links. In such cases an initial connection, linking an experience or element with an element or substructure in the conceptual structure of a creative interest, sets in motion a chain of further associations and links — a chain of thought — leading to and culminating in a creative idea or insight. The chains of thought may be a series of conceptual steps, as an individual works from a first intuitive response to a further, deeper, more grounded insight. It may involve free associations, driven by unconscious processing based in the conceptual structure of a creative interest; this has occurred, for example, for Enid Zentelis — as an example, the mundane event of waiting on a food line triggered her idea for a film showing individuals waiting on such a line, linked to other images and topics, for example the provision of food — often of poor quality — to poor people. I believe that most creative responses, if we are able to break them down and analyze them in sufficient detail, will in fact be seen to be generated through a chain or sequence of steps. Thus, Calder's invention of the mobile was not really one simple step, but a sequence, as I describe below, linking certain images he saw to other images, and also to motion, and combining these links to form a novel art form.

Many creative responses, in particular of the second form, are socially mediated — triggered through conversations, or through two or more individuals interacting in a collaborative way, generating ideas and insights through the overlapping of their interests, making connections between them. Roger Knowles's two main dissertation projects were sparked through this kind of collaborative interaction; and a number of the other neuroscientists I interviewed also described collaborative interactions as important to the origins of their projects. Another example is the initial idea for working to solve the structure of DNA that James Watson and Francis Crick developed together, that grew out of the excitement and sparks of their initial engagement with each other. I do not focus in this book on collaborative creativity, but it is an essential form of creativity in many fields, including popular music and jazz, science, technology and design, and business, and creative responses sparked by social interactions are a vital source of creativity.[4]

[4]See Chapter 1, footnote 30 for references to works on collaborative creativity. See also Chapter 17.

Timing

Many creative responses seem to occur quickly — during or soon after the precipitating experience or encounter that sparks them. This is not always true; some responses are described as occurring after longer time lags. For example, one pattern is for a current experience or encounter to trigger an association to an earlier experience or element already known. But in my experience rapid response is the more commonly described case. Much of the evidence in fact for how rapidly creative responses occur is based on descriptions individuals give retrospectively. In general they tend to describe creative responses — which often stand out in their minds as highly creative — as sudden illuminations that occurred immediately or soon after the experiences or encounters that sparked them. For example, James Watson describes his response upon hearing Maurice Wilkins's talk at a conference he attended in Naples, which I describe in context below, in a way that emphasizes its rapidity. He describes Maurice putting a picture on the screen at the end of his talk and remarking that it could be construed to arise from a crystalline structure, emphasizing immediate perceptual recognition of this. He then begins the following paragraph with the phrase "Suddenly I was excited about chemistry," the next sentence begins with the word "Now," and the following sentence begins with "Immediately." The rhetorical flourish is remarkable, the three words "suddenly", "now", and "immediately" conveying the sense of a sudden illumination.[5] While Watson's writing style is distinctive, in my experience creative responses are typically described in terms like his. The individuals I interviewed, who reconstructed their creative developments in a much more unpolished way, also described many of their responses as sudden illuminations. For example, Susan depicted her insight about dialogue in novels, which came to her while reading *Kim*, as relatively sudden. Likewise Ross and Azad, among others, described key creative responses they made as sudden, dramatic illuminations, at least to a degree.

In fact, while creative responses may well often be quite sudden and dramatic, I believe their degree of suddenness and drama is probably overstated. Two main factors contribute to this: one is telescoping — individuals tend, in recollecting crucial creative moments, to compress the timescale of events; the other is the desire to give a sense of drama to one's development — creative responses are among the most dramatic moments in creative development,

---

[5] James Watson, *The Double Helix*, pp. 27–28. He does the same in describing the beginnings of his collaboration with Francis Crick (p. 37): "From my first day in the lab [at Cambridge]", he writes, "I immediately discovered the fun of talking to Francis Crick."

and it is natural for individuals to overstate the drama, as a way to make their creative development seem more dramatic and exciting. ·

The Originality of Creative Responses

The originality of a creative response is rooted in the interplay of the specific experience or element or set of experiences or elements that spark it and the creative interest that mediates it, generating the creative idea or insight.

In some cases the primary source of originality of a response is that the experience or element that sparks the response is itself quite unusual, rarely experienced or encountered. A person's creative interest, specifically his conception of interest, may be important in guiding him along a distinctive path leading him to have an unusual experience or encounter an unusual element; alternatively, having the experience or encountering the element may be more a matter of luck.

In the remaining cases, which I believe are the majority, other people do have similar experiences or encounter the same element or set of elements as the individual who makes the creative response, but they do not make the same response. There are two main reasons for this. The first reason, which I believe applies in many cases, is that others who have the same or a similar experience or encounter the same element do not notice or focus on it or the particular aspect of it that the individual who makes the creative response notices and focuses on. Among the group of people for whom this reason applies, there are two subgroups: some fail to notice the experience or element entirely; others do notice it, but quickly discard it from their minds as unimportant or meaningless, thus do not focus on it, never giving themselves the chance to respond creatively to it. The second reason is that individuals who do notice and focus on the experience or element the individual who makes the creative response focuses on, even on the same aspect, think about it in a different way, thus generating and following a different chain of thought than he did, generating a different response, which may be original also, but more commonly is not. Crucially, in both cases the fundamental reason for the lack of a similar response is the lack of a conceptual connection with a like creative interest, specifically, with a conceptual structure equivalent to the conceptual structure that the individual who makes the response has in his mind, which mediates his response. Thus others, not sharing this individual's same creative interest, are not guided by the same conceptual structure, and, even if they do happen to focus on the experience or element or set of elements the individual who makes the response focuses on, even the same aspect, they do not have in their minds conceptual structures that can generate an equivalent response. The examples presented next and in following chapters illustrate these reasons as the basis of the originality of responses, as well as the crucial role of interests in both mediating responses and generating creative, original responses.

B. EXAMPLES

Alexander Calder's Visit to Mondrian's Studio and Invention of His Abstract Mobiles

For Alexander Calder a visit to Piet Mondrian's studio was a defining event that sparked a vital creative response in him. Here I provide a brief background description of his development, his description of the experience of visiting Mondrian's studio and its aftermath, a description of Mondrian's studio, then describe Calder's creative response to his visit, which unfolded over a period of days and months.

From childhood Calder had a flair for and interest in fabrication, making objects out of wood and wire. He became interested in art after college, and pursued it seriously beginning about one year after his experience on the boat off the coast of Guatemala.[6] In 1926, turning twenty-eight, he went to Paris. Around this time he began building up his famous circus — starting from a toy circus set, he added embellishments and actions of various kinds, and began exhibiting his circus in performances to friends.[7] He also began working systematically in wire, fashioning people and animals, and had several shows of his work.

Calder shuttled back and forth between the United States and Paris several times over the ensuing years. Returning to Paris in the spring of 1930, he met an architect who knew Mondrian and a circle of artists and art critics.[8] Calder put on circus performances for this group, with an American friend helping him. This friend went to visit Mondrian at his studio and, as Calder describes it, "recounted marvels" of what he had seen there. Thus enticed, Calder went with him to visit Mondrian at his studio at 26 rue du Départ.

---

[6] Alexander Calder and Jean Davidson, *Calder, An Autobiography with Pictures*, first part up to page 73. It is of note that his father, Alexander Stirling Calder, was a sculptor.

[7] He had gone on assignment to the Ringling Brothers Circus for two weeks, he recounts, while working for the *National Police Gazette* in New York. Ibid., pp. 67–75. He describes starting from the toy circus on page 80, and mentions circus performances on ensuing pages.

[8] Ibid., pp. 85–112.

Calder described Mondrian's studio, and its transforming effect on him, this way:

> It was a very exciting room. Light came in from the left and from the right, and on the solid wall between the windows there were experimental stunts with colored rectangles of cardboard tacked on. Even the [V]ictrola, which had been some muddy color, was painted red.
>
> I suggested to Mondrian that perhaps it would be fun to make these rectangles oscillate. And he, with a very serious countenance, said:
>
> "No, it is not necessary, my painting is already very fast."
>
> This visit gave me a shock. A bigger shock, even, than eight years earlier, when off Guatemala I saw the beginning of a fiery red sunrise on one side and the moon looking like a silver coin on the other.
>
> This one visit gave me a shock that started things.
>
> Though I had heard the word "modern" before, I did not consciously know or feel the term "abstract." So now, at thirty-two, I wanted to paint and work in the abstract. And for two weeks or so, I painted very modest abstractions. At the end of this, I reverted to plastic work [sculpture; wire] which was still abstract.[9]

In *The New Art — The New Life; Collected Writings of Piet Mondrian* Harry Holtzman describes Mondrian's New York studio and presents photos of it. He writes that Mondrian took incredible care in its spatial organization and wall compositions. "The sole painting displayed in the studio," he writes, "was the *Victory Boogie Woogie* on his easel at right angles to the largest wall work, the long east wall." On the walls there were a set of *Wall Works* "composed with rectangular cards of red, yellow, blue, gray, and white, tacked to the off-white (*not white*) walls with small nails."[10] Admittedly Mondrian's New York studio was not identical to what Calder would have observed in Mondrian's Paris studio a dozen or more years earlier; nonetheless it is clear from descriptions that they were similar aesthetically and in many details. A comment by de Kooning, quoted by Holtzman, conveys a sense of the experience of being in the studio — it was "like walking around inside one of Mondrian's paintings."

Figures 1a and 1b show photographs of the Paris studio at around the time of Calder's visit. Figures 1c and 1d present photos of reconstructions of the studio created by Frans Postma and his workgroup; they give a sense for the vivid colors and the effect of being in the room. As conveyed in the photos, Mondrian sought to transform his studio space into an artistic composition, with rectangular colored cut-outs arranged on the walls and few cluttering, nonessential objects. Mondrian viewed his studio as a critical laboratory, an

[9]Ibid., pp. 112–13.
[10]Piet Mondrian, *The New Art — The New Life; Collected Writings of Piet Mondrian*, p. 9.

262 essential part of his creative effort and aim. In one of his last articles he states that we are at the end of *"art as a thing separated from our surrounding environment,"* and at the beginning of "the unification of architecture, sculpture and painting," creating "a new plastic reality. Painting and sculpture will not manifest themselves as separate objects, not as 'mural art' which destroys architecture itself, nor as 'applied art,' but *being purely constructive* will aid the creation of a surrounding not merely utilitarian or rational but also pure and complete in its beauty."[11] It is befitting of this statement that Mondrian's studios were of enormous importance to him and that he expended great effort in creating them, to great effect. They were, Holtzman states, his "only opportunity to partially concretize his radical ideas toward the total environment," "to explore his conception in environmental scale," and take on the challenge of designing a holistic living environment.

It seems no accident that Mondrian's studios had such great impact — they are in fact viewed as having been important for the development of modern art and architecture. And consistent with this, it is not surprising that they would have sparked creative responses as the Paris studio did for Calder. They truly stood out as stimuli of heightened intensity — and such stimuli tend to spark responses, as noted above.

Calder stated that his visit to Mondrian's studio gave him a "shock that started things," sparking the desire in him to begin working in "the abstract," in the way of modern abstract art. Out of this shock he generated, over the following weeks and year, a creative response — creating new forms of sculptures and inventing the mobile as a modern art form. Calder did not describe explicitly the conceptual linkages and associations he made through which he generated his creative response. In fact I believe his response was generated through a connection he made with his interest in the basic objects of the universe and the solar system arranged in space as a basis for art, and through a further connection, that he made subsequently, with his interest in setting art in motion and creating art having motion as an integral element. He had not pursued his interests artistically up to this point, at least not directly or in a major way, but they were present in his mind, encoded in conceptual structures — and the visit to Mondrian's studio, through stimulating his imagination and thinking, led to his finding and forging a way to develop them creatively. His response is thus a classic illustration of a creative response mediated by a creative interest — in his case two linked interests. Here I offer a reconstruction, based on and consistent with his account and the record of what he produced, substantiating

[11] "The Necessity for a New Teaching in Art, Architecture, and Industry," in *The New Art — The New Life*, pp. 310–17; the italics are in the original.

this view — sketching what I believe were the crucial linkages through which
his response was generated.

The distinguishing feature of Mondrian's studio was the colored cut-out rectangles tacked on the walls — the *Wall Works* — and the objects painted and designed to fit with them — creating a powerful, unified overall impression or sensibility, coherent and forceful in its simplicity. In fact the *Wall Works*, and their effect within the overall design of the studio, made the studio a natural to catch Calder's attention and spark a response in him, given his interest in the basic shapes of the universe and the solar system as a basis for art — there were clear resonances and links with his interest. The rectangles of the *Wall Works* were not parts of paintings — it is a basic feature of traditional paintings that the edges of the canvas demarcate boundaries cutting off the painting, as a work of art, from the surrounding environment, but the *Wall Works* were arranged directly on the walls that encased and were integral to defining the studio as a three-dimensional space and environment, hence were integral to defining the experience of being in the studio. The same holds true of the objects in the studio — all were integral to defining the studio as a space and an experience. With its simple colored shapes and objects on various walls and in various locations, surrounding a person, the studio, as both a space and an experience, resonates and connects with Calder's conception of and interest in the shapes of the universe and the solar system as a basis for art. His conception is fundamentally similar in having simple shapes (admittedly not rectangles but rather discs and spheres) set in space, not disjoint from the surrounding space as traditional art is but part of it, having a three-dimensional configuration, creating a rich spatial sense, a rich surrounding visual field — as the moon and the sun had done so memorably for him early in the morning on the boat off the coast of Guatemala. Indeed the very idea of the universe as a basis for art implies an art that fills and defines a whole spatial environment, fitting with the way Mondrian approached and crafted his studio as a holistic environment. It is also noteworthy that not only were the cut-out rectangles Mondrian used simple shapes, connecting quite directly with Calder's conception, but many were red, and the studio as a whole had a lot of red — a color that was Calder's favorite, as he stated on many occasions, enhancing the likelihood of drawing his attention and thus sparking a connection.

While Calder writes that the experience of visiting Mondrian's studio gave him a "shock" — triggered an immediate response in him, he does not appear to have forged a connection to his interest in the universe as the basis for art immediately. He writes that he went home and for the next two weeks painted "modest abstractions" — which suggests that the idea of shapes set in space as art hadn't yet occurred to him, though the idea of simple, colored shapes as the basis for art presumably had. The fact that the shapes he saw were rectangles, not discs, and that they were set on two-dimensional planes, not in space, may well have contributed to this delay — the stimulus was two steps away from his conception, near it conceptually but not quite overlapping it. But, after two weeks of painting, he writes that he "reverted" to sculpture, mainly wire-working, which he was used to and expert in. It was following this shift back to sculpture — an inherently spatial art — that he made a direct connection with his interest in simple shapes of the universe or the solar system arranged in space, in different configurations, as the basis for art (this at least is the interpretation that fits well with the record, although it may be that making the connection in fact triggered or influenced his decision to shift back to sculpture). In turn this connection triggered a creative burst — within a few months he executed a series of wire sculptures, realizing his conception of the universe as the basis for art in abstract form, with simple abstract shapes and wire connections, his objects based in wire with some wood and metal — the beginnings of his invention of a new art form. Figure 2 shows a set of sculptures he exhibited at a show at Galerie Percier in Paris the following April. Calder describes two of these sculptures in *Calder, An Autobiography with Pictures*, which stand out as showing the new art form: the sculpture on the far left, which he describes as "a more or less horizontal rod with a square sheet of tin on one end and an ebony counterweight on the other," and the sculpture on the center right (fourth from the right), which he describes as "an almost vertical rod, slightly inclined, about a yard long with at the top a little wire loop with a counterweight at its far end, and another little piece, with another counterweight — there were three elements," which he especially liked; he writes of these that they "swayed in the breeze."[12] The first, with the square, shows the link to Mondrian's studio and the *Wall Works*, that lies behind his own original creations. For the square is of course Mondrian's shape, and, further, it is a shape Calder did not frequently use in his later work, that was not natural to him — he said he did not like it because of its sense of closure, preferring triangles, because they seemed to him to open up and connect naturally with other elements. All the sculptures have an incredible resonance with his interest that is plain to see.

In describing his visit to Mondrian's studio and his response Calder explicitly refers back to his experience on the ship off the coast of Guatemala. He thus links the two experiences in his narrative account of his creative development — views them as connected, two critical junctures in his development, the first sparking a conception of a creative interest, the second triggering

---

[12] *Calder, An Autobiography with Pictures*, p. 118.

a response that linked to this conception, pointing to a way to realize it artistically. The link he makes between the two supports the interpretation that his creative response, following his visit to Mondrian's studio, was generated by linking his experience and what he had seen to his interest — specifically, to the conceptual structure in his mind encoding this interest, within which his image-memory of the experience on the boat fit as a central, vivid element. It took him eight years to make the creative step from this initial event on the boat and formation of an incipient interest to the development of an art form realizing his interest-conception artistically, the crucial step sparked by a visit to the studio of a man who was himself a master of modern art and had created a studio highlighting the idea of art as integral to and transforming the environment.[13]

Calder did not invent his famous mobiles immediately. His initial abstractions had only limited movement — they moved the way objects on wire do, as indeed some of his earlier wire sculptures do, but movement was not a major feature.[14] The fact that movement was not initially paramount supports the view that the initial connection he made was with his interest in shapes of the universe arranged in space as a basis for art, not his interest in setting art in motion and making art with motion as an integral element. Once he began to design wire art objects set in space, however, the further association and link to his interest in creating art with motion as an integral element followed: given his interest in the solar system the idea to set objects in orbit (so to speak) or motion would have followed naturally, and did. Calder himself describes focusing on motion later, in the winter of 1932, thus more than a year after he had fashioned his initial abstract works, designing motor-driven objects. It was one of these that Marcel Duchamp saw — and when Calder asked him what name he could give his objects, Duchamp replied: "Mobile." Thus was the modern art mobile christened.[15]

[13] It should be noted that we do not know how much Calder thought about his interest in the universe as the basis for art in the intervening years, and how richly he articulated his conception of his interest. He may have formed a rich conception early on — or his conception may only have truly blossomed later, after his visit to Mondrian's studio or during or after his initial creative burst.

[14] Calder describes the movement of the initial objects by saying they "swayed in the breeze" — thus he recognized movement as a feature, but it was not a central feature. *Calder, An Autobiography with Pictures*, p. 118.

[15] Ibid., pp. 126–27. Calder had much experience with simple motions in his circus — though there the motion always served a purpose, whereas the motion he developed for his mobiles was in terms of art in space. Robert Weisberg also discusses Calder's invention of his mobiles in *Creativity: Beyond the Myth of Genius* (New York: W.H. Freeman & Co., 1993), pp. 13–18. While I share his interest in Calder's process of invention, I am not in accord with his description. He nowhere mentions Calder's

Susan Ferguson's Creative Response to Kim: The Scene of Dialogue

Susan Ferguson had a creative response sparked by reading Kipling's classic novel *Kim*, linked to and mediated by her interest in the use of different languages in conversation, the social meanings of different languages, the norms governing language choice, and language switching.

After living in Kenya for two years Susan returned to the United States and matriculated in a graduate English program. It is noteworthy that at the time she entered graduate school she had not made any direct connection between her interest and literature.[16] From the start in graduate school Susan focused on novels of colonial and postcolonial societies, picking up on her experience in Kenya and general interest in the developing world. During her first year she took a course on the modern English novel and wrote a paper about *A House for Mr. Biswas* by V.S. Naipaul — she chose it, she told me, because it was the only novel set in a postcolonial society the class read. Initially she focused on the different generations and forms of education portrayed in the book, and the movement from more traditional education to — for the youngest generation — a modern British education. Her professor suggested that she explore, in relation to this theme, the shift from oral to written forms of language portrayed in the book, the traditional education being more oral and based on oral transmission and the modern English education that is replacing it being based more on writing. He also recommended several essays for her to read about this topic.[17]

The following year in the fall Susan took a course in the Anthropology Department about oral and written forms of language, their cultural development, and the relationship between them. She told me she had been looking

interest in the shapes of the universe arranged in space as a basis for art as important in his development of the mobile despite the fact that Calder himself states that it was central to his art from early on. Further, he suggests that Calder created his motorized mobiles directly after his visit to Mondrian's studio, e.g., very early or as a first step (he incorrectly dates Calder's visit to Mondrian's studio as 1931, not 1930), and does not discuss Calder's "first generation" abstract sculptures, in which movement was secondary.

[16] I asked her specifically about this, and we discussed it. She said that in Kenya she read "for the plot" and sheer enjoyment, and had not made any connection she was aware of.

[17] Two of the essays in particular had a great impact on her, she said — one by Claude Levi-Strauss and the other by Jacques Derrida, about language as a vehicle for power. Derrida's essay is in *On Grammatology*, trans. by Gayatri Chakravorty Spivak (Baltimore, MD: Johns Hopkins University Press, 1974). I have not found the reference for the Levi-Strauss article.

for courses to take in a few other departments and this course stood out for her because it picked up on the paper she had written about *A House for Mr. Biswas* and the reading she had done for it, and resonated with her interest in language and conversational practices.[18] The fact that Susan was looking at course listings in Anthropology is unusual — based on the graduate students with whom I have spoken it is fairly uncommon for a literature student to take courses, or even look at course listings, in an anthropology department. It seems clear that it was her distinctive interest that led her to the course and led her to take it, thus guided her — a process I describe in the next chapter. Through the course Susan built up a base of knowledge about the relationship between oral and written language, and in particular the representation of speech in written form, which proved to be important for her.

Susan's creative breakthrough came during the next term, when she read *Kim*. "I read it on my own," she told me, "because it was something I knew I wanted to get to, because of my interest in colonial and postcolonial literature — it's a classic in that field." In the course of reading the book she had a realization connecting the dialogue scenes in the book with her interest.

> I was incredibly struck in reading the novel — and I think this was really the first time I had been struck this way by something — by the fact that nobody in the novel was speaking in English. The whole novel was in English, but nobody in the plot was supposed to be speaking English. And Kipling had all these different ways of changing the English in the speech to try to indicate what language was being spoken. And he did this in a much more complicated way than just throwing in "My Gott" or "Herr" [the way] that somebody might do to try to suggest "Germanness" — he did much more complicated kinds of things. So — for really the first time — I really got into looking specifically at dialogue.

The force of Susan's insight — and its link to her interest — is that she saw that in *Kim* a multilingual world of conversation is depicted strikingly reminiscent of the world of conversation in Kenya she found so fascinating. The use of different languages, and the subtle social meanings associated with these choices, are highlighted in the book, as I illustrate with a passage from the book below. Indeed there is a connection with her interest in multiple facets: speakers use a variety of different languages, and there is a stress on the social meanings of different languages and the norms governing language choice. While we cannot know for certain through what process Susan first recognized

[18]The course also resonated with her experience in Kenya teaching English — she told me that experience made her "very conscious" of the distinction between oral and written language, in particular that English is not phonetic and thus you cannot pronounce words the way they are written, a big issue for nonnative speakers trying to learn to speak the language.

268 and became aware of the way that Kipling is representing different languages in *Kim*, it is a sensible interpretation that conceptual structures encoding her interest in her mind were crucial in drawing her attention to this aspect of the novel and sparking her realization — thus mediated her response. Indeed specific scenes may well have resonated with specific recollections she had of Kenya, though this is speculative.

As Susan described it, her focus on the dialogue in *Kim* was a new focus for her, the first time she "really got into" looking at dialogue in a novel.[19] Her focus on dialogue and her realization about the way Kipling is representing different languages being spoken seems not only rooted in her interest but also clearly linked to — and very possibly was made possible by — what she had learned in the Anthropology class about the representation of speech in written form: dialogue is the written representation of conversation, thus her experience in the class undoubtedly sensitized her to noticing and focusing on dialogue.[20] As I discuss further at the end of this discussion her focus on the dialogue in *Kim* is distinctive, different from what other critics have focused on — thus her case shows by example how a distinctive interest generates a distinctive focus.

Although evident in retrospect, it definitely required an act of creativity for Susan to make the connection between her interest and the dialogue scenes in *Kim*, for the simple reason that *Kim*, like most novels, is written in one language — multiple languages are not actually employed in the dialogue, creating a step of separation from her interest and experiences in Kenya.[21] Based on our interview discussion it seems fairly certain that Susan had not read a novel in which conversations are presented literally taking place in multiple languages. Thus making the connection between her interest and literature was challenging, not transparent — a creative insight. Further, Susan's interest had been sparked and was rooted in her experience of actual conversations — thus a link to literature had to be forged, it was not present from the start.

[19]She had previously focused on language as a theme, notably in her class paper on *A House for Mr. Biswas* and her undergraduate thesis, but not on dialogue, the representation of actual conversation in a novel.

[20]Of course it was her interest in conversational practices and language that led her to take the class — thus the knowledge structure she built up with regard to speech and writing was generated through her pursuit of her interest.

[21]It is a basic feature of novels, and certainly the classic novels of the nineteenth century and early to mid-twentieth century Susan was reading like *Kim*, that they are written in one language — there may be some passages in a second language, but in general authors do not make their novels truly multilingual. There are of course inevitably exceptions to the rule. One important case is the use of nonstandard dialect; dialect in fact turned out to be a main focus for Susan.

And the theories about the relationship between speech and written language she studied in her Anthropology class were linguistic and anthropological, not literary, thus did not forge a direct connection to literature and dialogue.

Central to Susan's initial insight was seeing that Kipling uses a host of literary techniques to convey and depict the different languages being spoken. Going forward, she focused on the way the narrator in the book functions as a kind of translator, conveying to the reader which language is being spoken, and, even more, helping the reader understand the social meanings of language choices and language switching and alluding, typically indirectly, to the norms governing these choices. She had a further insight as she pursued this topic, that translation has a major role at large in the book, including in the plot, and she wrote her class paper about this.

> What I got interested in was this way that the narrator in a sense in the novel was like a translator in a very prominent way. And how in the plot as well there were many instances of translation. So... [I had] this mediacy idea — it wasn't as if somebody could just talk and then the other person would just get it, there was a real highlight in the book on what happens in between, which is how there are miscommunications or potential misunderstandings and so on between people. And that middle part is highlighted in the book by the fact that there was often a third party [either the narrator or another character] involved who was actually translating, or mistranslating in many cases, what was being said; or [in other cases] somebody was overhearing what was happening.

This idea again connects with Susan's interest, specifically her interest in "code switching" and what she called "language games" — situations where insiders say things having subtle, often double meanings that novices — outsiders — do not understand. In fact there are two kinds of outsiders in the world of *Kim*: the narrator treats the reader as an outsider, explaining and interpreting for him; and various characters are outsiders in particular contexts and scenes, in that they do not know critical pieces of information. The need for translation follows from the insider/outsider distinction: outsiders need what is being said to be translated for them; and in *Kim*, as Susan saw, the mechanics of translation, and mistranslation, are made prominent. The emphasis on the insider/outsider distinction, with the resulting need for translation and possibility of mistranslation and misunderstanding, resonates with Susan's experience in Kenya — she surely felt like an outsider there, and was very attentive to difficulties in communication, including reading subtle conversational signals — indicated in her statement that she was "learning to use" different languages, and by implication hardly expert at it.

I present here a scene from *Kim*, which is illustrative of many scenes in the book, that manifests the connection between the dialogue scenes in the book and Susan's interest in the use of different languages in conversation, the social meanings of using particular languages, and code switching and language games.[22] It also demonstrates the validity of Susan's insight about the role of the narrator in telling the reader or indicating indirectly what language is being spoken and explaining or, more commonly, providing hints to the reader why — thus functioning as a translator, helping the reader understand the true meaning of the exchange.

The scene is in part one. Kim and the Tibetan lama (a holy man) with whom he is traveling encounter the Afghan horse trader Mahbub Ali in a crowded bazaar. Mahbub speaks first:

> "Allah! A lama! A Red Lama! It is far from Lahore to the Passes. What dost thou do here?"
>
> The lama held out the begging-bowl mechanically.
>
> "God's curse on all unbelievers!" said Mahbub. "I do not give to a lousy Tibetan; but ask my Baltis over yonder behind the camels. They may value your blessings. Oh, horseboys, here is a countryman of yours. See if he be hungry."
>
> A shaven, crouching Balti who had come down with the horses and who was nominally some sort of degraded Buddhist, fawned upon the priest, and in thick gutturals besought the Holy One to sit at the horse-boys' fire.
>
> "Go!" said Kim, pushing him lightly, and the lama strode away, leaving Kim at the edge of the cloister.
>
> "Go!" said Mahbub Ali, returning to his hookah. "Little Hindu, run away. God's curse on all unbelievers! Beg from those of my tail who are of thy faith."
>
> "Maharaj," whined Kim, using the Hindu form of address, and thoroughly enjoying the situation; "my father is dead — my mother is dead — my stomach is empty."
>
> "Beg from my men among the horses, I say. There must be some Hindus in my tail."
>
> "Oh, Mahbub Ali, but am *I* a Hindu?" said Kim in English.
>
> The trader gave no sign of astonishment, but looked under shaggy eyebrows. "Little friend of all the World," said he, "what is this?"[23]

This scene truly has a richness of diversity — diverse ethnic and religious identities and a diversity of languages spoken. The characters' different ethnic and religious identities are referred to by the narrator as well as one another, emphasizing the distinctions. Thus Mahbub starts the exchange by exclaiming "Allah!" establishing his Islamic identity, and cries out "God's curse on all unbelievers!" twice — a stock phrase through which he emphasizes to Kim and the holy man his identity and difference from them. The main language is implied to be the Indian vernacular; but there are several significant departures

---

[22] All quotes are from Rudyard Kipling, *Kim* (London: Macmillan and Co., 1920).
[23] *Kim*, pp. 26–27.

from this that are indicated either by a change in syntax or by the narrator. Thus, Mahbub's stock phrases are implied as spoken in Arabic, while the Balti is described as speaking to the lama in "thick gutturals" by which the narrator is indicating that he is speaking in a non-Indian Asiatic language. Kim makes two switches out of the vernacular, each clearly deliberate and designed to communicate something specific to Mahbub, and in each case the narrator, serving as a translator or guide, informs the reader of the switch. Thus, we are told Kim switches to the "Hindu form of address" in asking for assistance — he does this to feign supplication to Mahbub, and the narration emphasizes his tone by describing him as having "whined," thereby helping the reader read his intention. Just after this we are told Kim switches to English in response to Mahbub's casual suggestion that he join the other Hindus. Kim's shift to English is intended to remind Mahbub of the multiplicity of his identity — that he is not an ordinary Hindu or Indian. The narrator tells us that Mahbub expresses "no sign of astonishment" in response to Kim speaking in English — this is consistent with Mahbub's character, and also reveals to us — who have already learned that Kim is of Irish descent — that Mahbub too is familiar with Kim's mixed identity. The diversity of languages and language switching have a definite resonance with Susan's interest and her descriptions of her conversational experiences in Kenya. Each of the languages depicted in the book in fact has specific social meanings and usage patterns, as depicted in this scene — a further resonance with her interest. It is noteworthy that most of the other books Susan was reading — classic English novels — would not have such clear resonances; it was no accident that *Kim* was the book through which she first recognized a connection between her interest and literature.

The scene also shows the importance of the narrator in serving as a translator, very much as Susan says, in some cases telling the reader directly what language is being used, in others employing techniques to indicate a particular language, for example using a descriptive phrase like "thick gutturals." Indeed the narrator has a larger role than this: for the world of *Kim* is a world in which language and communication is subtle and tricky, in which there is often something being concealed, there are coded messages and double meanings — messages are not always what they seem; and the narrator is the reader's primary source of information and guide. Thus it is important for the narrator to inform the reader not only what language is being spoken, but also why, and what the implications are. The world of *Kim* is very much a game — Kim thinks of it this way and of himself as a player, as shown in the scene above in which he is described as "thoroughly enjoying the situation" sparring with Mahbub, and Mahbub is depicted as a player in a game, strategic and savvy in his interactions. This is how the narrator approaches matters also. Thus he does not always or even often explain why an individual chooses to speak in a certain language — as in the scene above he does not explicitly state why Kim switches to English or tell us explicitly that Mahbub knows Kim is not Indian; rather, he drops hints, reveals bits of information along the way.[24] In this regard Susan's idea about the narrator's role truly is an insight — the techniques he employs to depict why a given language is being used are subtle and indirect, not obvious on a first, casual reading.

Messages in code are central to the plot of *Kim*, as Susan says — there are many instances in which a message is in code and at least some characters don't know what it means, and there is a premium on decoding messages thought to contain valuable information. This further highlights, as she says, the act of translation, or, as it sometimes turns out, mistranslation, and the nontransparent nature of communication.

A coded message, and Kim's degree of understanding of it, is at the center of the latter part of the scene between Kim and Mahbub. Kim informs Mahbub that he and the lama are setting forth on a pilgrimage and asks Mahbub for money. Mahbub interrogates Kim and the lama to try to determine if Kim is being truthful, then raises the possibility of a transaction in which Kim will deliver a coded message for him in return for money.

> "And if thou wilt carry a message for me as far as Umballa, I will give thee money. It concerns a horse — a white stallion which I have sold to an officer upon the last time I returned from the Passes. But then — stand nearer and hold up hands as begging — the pedigree of the white stallion was not fully established, and that officer, who is now at Umballa, bade me make it clear." (Mahbub here described the horse and the appearance of the officer.) "So the message to that officer will be: 'The pedigree of the white stallion is fully established.' By this he will know that thou comest from me. He will then say 'What proof hast thou?' and thou wilt answer: 'Mahbub Ali has given me the proof.'"

He then gives Kim a roll of bread wrapped in oilskin and tissue paper, concealed inside which Kim finds money. Kim goes to where the lama is lying down and prepares to go to sleep. The narrator, depicting Kim's awareness that the message is in code, remarks, "not for one little minute did he believe the tale of the stallion's pedigree." He continues:

> But Kim did not suspect that Mahbub Ali, known as one of the best horse-dealers in the Punjab.... was registered in one of the locked books of the Indian Survey Department as C.25.1B. Twice or thrice yearly C.25 would send in a little story, baldy

---

[24]Many of the major characters in *Kim* are in fact linked through participation in the "Great Game" of mapping out the territorial boundaries of British India.

told but most interesting, and generally — it was checked by the statements of R.17
and M.4 — quite true.[25]

This passage shows how the narrator, acting as an informed insider, provides necessary information to the reader — in Susan's terms translates for him, and conveys a sense of the layers of hidden meaning that pervade the book.[26]

Susan's focus on the way the narrator in *Kim* depicts different languages being spoken and her insight about the importance of translation and mediacy in the book is a good example of noticing and generating a creative response to a particular aspect — here two related aspects — of a complex, multifaceted phenomenon. *Kim* surely qualifies as complex — it contains more than one hundred thousand words and dozens of scenes, plumbs the circumstances, thoughts, and feelings of a handful of major characters, sketches the lives and personalities of numerous minor figures, is set in the midst of a rich culture and complex society, and recounts a lengthy tale. It is quite striking — and characteristic of the way we respond to complex experiences and stimuli — that among all these rich possibilities Susan forged a sharp focus on a small set of tightly bound aspects of the book, her focus rooted in and linked to her interest.

Susan's focus and insights are striking in being distinctive, indeed I believe original — different from those of other critics who have written about *Kim*, who focus on different aspects of the book and present very different insights about it, in many cases broader interpretations. Through the years *Kim* has been considered from a variety of perspectives. The book is famous for its portrayal of Kim, a character of mixed identity journeying along life's path, part of two worlds—the British and the indigenous Indian; and Kim's identity and life path are a main focus in much criticism, for example Ian Baucom's described below. *Kim* is viewed as a classic of colonial and postcolonial literature, as Susan said, known for its representation of the complexities

---

[25]The narrator continues, telling the reader that "five confederated Kings, who had no business to confederate, had been informed by a kindly Northern Power that there was a leakage of news from their territory into British India" — namely Mahbub, whom they have tried to kill, and explaining that the tissue paper conveys a secret message in code — five microscopic pinholes in one corner, that betrays the five Kings. To give another example of a coded message, in the first part of the book Kim is searching for the fulfillment and meaning of his father's prophecy: "I go to look for — for a bull — a Red Bull on a green field who shall help me" — which turns out to be the flag of an Irish military regiment, the Mavericks.

[26]Another related element that complicates communications and makes them more like a game is that individuals may and do lie if it serves their purpose, and this is recognized by the other characters. There is as a result a preoccupation and a great deal of game playing around lying and truthfulness.

of identity, in particular, Kim's complex, multilayered identity, and a colonial state struggling to govern a stratified multicultural society.[27] It has also been analyzed — and criticized — as a novel of imperialism, reflecting Western views of superiority over the Orient and more generally other races and cultures.[28] Earlier scholarship focuses on *Kim*'s portrayal of an exotic world of adventure and different life paths — the lama's striving for transcendence, the other characters spending their lives playing the "Great Game."[29] It truly is striking, in contrast with these critical perspectives and interpretations, how different Susan's focus and insight are. Her focus on the dialogue, the diversity of spoken languages, and the techniques through which the narrator depicts different languages is fundamentally different than that of other critics. Many of them mention in passing the diversity of languages in *Kim*, typically to support statements about the book's depiction of a multiethnic, multicultural society — but they do not focus on the actual dialogue the way she does. Also, although others have noted the importance of secret messages in code, no one prior to her, as far as I know, has focused specifically on the idea of translation and mediacy.[30] Her case illustrates the distinctiveness and originality of a creative response, and the way this distinctiveness and originality is rooted in and flows out of the distinctiveness of the interest that sparks and mediates it: her interest in the use

[27] See, for example, the discussion in Thomas Richards, *The Imperial Archive: Knowledge and the Fantasy of Empire* (London: Verso, 1993). For a recent collection of critical perspectives see Rudyard Kipling, *Kim: Authoritative Text, Backgrounds, Criticism*, ed. Zohreh T. Sullivan (New York: W.W. Norton, 2002). In general, the analyses in this book focus on issues of identity, imperialism, cultural and national development, and multiculturalism as portrayed in the book; Ian Baucom, who approaches the book in this way, is the author of one section.

[28] See Edward Said's comments in his introduction to *Kim*, ed. and with intro. by Edward W. Said (London: Penguin Books, 1987). A phrase used by a number of critics to describe *Kim* is "imperial discourse."

[29] Edmund Wilson has a well-known critical discussion along these lines in *The Wound and the Bow: Seven Studies in Literature* (Oxford: Oxford University Press, 1947). In the statement by the Nobel Prize Committee on the awarding of The Nobel Prize for literature to Kipling in 1907 there is one paragraph on *Kim*, singling it out for its "delineation of the Buddhist priest" on his pilgrimage as well as the endearing "little rascal Kim." Nobel Prize Committee, "The Nobel Prize for Literature, 1907."

[30] In focusing on translation and mediacy Susan takes a linguistic perspective on the secret coded messages, linking them to the narrator's role more generally in the book in describing and explaining the different languages; this is at least to a degree original to her. I am grateful to Rachel Trousdale for sharing with me a document that surveys a significant portion of the critical literature, which has aided me in my own understanding and confidence in the originality of Susan's focus and insights.

of different languages in conversation was clearly the root of the distinctiveness and originality of her focus and insights.

An example illustrating these points that reinforces them is provided by the contrast between Susan's focus and insights about *Kim* and Ian Baucom's reading of the book, which forms part of his dissertation. As described in Chapter 4, Ian formed an interest in the way the political ideals and values of the British Empire and imperial rule are described, embodied, and reflected in literature. In reading novels set in the British Empire, including *Kim*, he noticed a general theme, which I describe in the next chapter — "that at a very real, literal level imperialism was about not just the conquest of space but the organization of space." The central insight Ian had about *Kim* is that there is a correspondence between two spaces that the empire wishes to organize — the space of India which is to be organized through mapmaking by the Survey of India, and the space of Kim himself, whose identity is to be refashioned as English. In his dissertation Ian writes how at a certain point in the book, when Kim has been claimed by the English, "the narrative of Kim's life joins the narrative of imperial cartography. Kim. . . can be redeemed for orderliness, Kipling discovers, by his enlistment in the mathematization [surveying] of the continent."[31] He describes the Survey of India, then makes the interpretation that there is a correspondence between the Survey and Kim: "In joining Kim to this band of wandering mapmakers, Kipling identifies the problem of refashioning Kim's identity with the dilemma of India's. . . cartographers."[32] Nowhere does he mention the scenes of dialogue in *Kim*, the fact that different languages are being spoken, or the importance of translation in the book. Thus the aspects of the novel that he considers are essentially disjoint from those that Susan focused on.

Kim was a watershed in Susan's creative development, opening up a path forward for her, the origins and root of her doctoral work. I describe her development going forward and dissertation work in Chapter 15.

More Examples

In this section and the next I present a series of further examples of creative responses. These show that creative responses are a central mode of creativity generation for individuals across a range of fields — indeed by my count half or more of the individuals whose creative developments I have studied have reported at least one insight or realization based on a creative response that has

[31] Ian Bernard Baucom, *Locating Identity: Topographies of Englishness and Empire*, diss., Yale University, 1995, p. 112 and surrounding.
[32] Ibid., p. 113.

been important in their development. The examples also illustrate a variety of kinds of stimuli sparking responses.

For Tim Berners-Lee, a work environment — the organizational environment at CERN — sparked a creative response. This response was his generation of the idea for the Enquire program, leading to his writing the program, which was his first clearly delineated venture on the path leading to the development of the World Wide Web.

As described in Chapter 6, Tim formed an interest growing up in non-hierarchical, nonstandard data structures and systems and how to create and model such structures and systems. He writes in *Weaving the Web* (p. 4) that his interest stayed with him, but in the back of his mind, through college and for several years thereafter while he worked in software engineering. Then, in 1980, he took a consulting job at CERN.

CERN is, as Tim describes, an unusual organization — indeed not an organization in the classical sense at all, rather, as he aptly describes it, "an extended community," loosely organized and nonhierarchical. Researchers and teams from different countries and speaking different languages come to work at CERN for limited time periods. CERN has many ongoing collaborative projects, with teams sharing hardware and software; and researchers work with a multitude of different software programs, administrative units, and hardware and computer systems.[33] The fluidity of the workforce and organizational teams makes it difficult, as Tim describes, to gain the requisite knowledge about who is in charge of software programs and hardware devices, who or which team uses which programs and devices, who has worked on which projects, and who is linked with whom in terms of both research and administrative responsibility.[34] The work environment is thus quite unusual and distinctive.[35] What is striking with regard to Tim and his creative development is the way the distinctive features of the environment resonate with his interest. In particular, the organization is nonhierarchical, and there are fluid, webbed interrelationships and highly diverse patterns of overlapping interconnections and interdependencies among people, projects, administrative units, hardware devices, and software programs. The highly dynamic nature of the organization further calls attention to these features: because the organization is so dynamic people do not maintain accurate representations of the structure as it changes, which

[33]This continues to be the situation at CERN as far as I know; see the description at www.cern.org.
[34]*Weaving the Web*, pp. 7–9.
[35]It was especially so at the time. Today there is more discussion of such open and flexible organizational forms than there was at that time, and perhaps more of such organizations as well.

tends to call attention to its structure, at least for newcomers like Tim, because it is difficult for them to find people who can describe it and tell them what they need to know — a difficulty exacerbated by the nonhierarchical form, having no clear lines of command. Further, standard fixed representations like organizational charts become inaccurate over time, calling attention to the need to build a more sophisticated representation that can be modified, building in new connections, fitting with Tim's interest in systems in which new connections can be created.

Tim thus found himself, at CERN, immersed in and needing to navigate an organizational context that resonated and connected with his interest in non-hierarchical systems — indeed in which the features of this context resonant with his interest were highly salient for him. This resonance and connection stimulated him and sparked a creative response in him (at least this is a clear, straightforward interpretation of the basis of his response, that fits the model in this chapter and his own account). Drawn by the link to his interest, he was curious — more so it seems than most people at CERN — about the organization and its complex interconnections, and sought out information about it. And at some point — we don't know exactly how soon after he got to CERN — the idea occurred to him to build a computer program to represent the organization and organizational relationships in a nonhierarchical, flexible form.[36] Motivated — the connection with his interest was surely crucial here as well — he took up the challenge and began working in his spare time writing the program, which he called Enquire.[37]

Tim wrote a manual describing Enquire at the same time he wrote the program.[38] In the manual he describes the purpose of Enquire: "ENQUIRE

[36]Ibid., pp. 9–11. Tim did not necessarily recognize the connection with his interest consciously prior to having the idea to write the program — nothing in his account, as I read it, indicates whether he recalls recognizing it consciously or not; that may have come later. But he did have or had at one time formed a conception of his interest, which, in its role in the formation of a conceptual structure in his mind encoding his interest, was very likely important in the generation of his response.

[37]It is noteworthy that no one else at CERN undertook a project to write such a program — at least I can find no record of anyone having written such a program, surfing the Internet, and Tim does not mention anyone else having done so. This is further evidence for the importance of his interest in the generation of his response: other researchers, not sharing his interest, were undoubtedly not as interested as he was in the organizational structure, nor were they motivated as he was by his interest to write a program about it, not as a formal job assignment, but in his free time, for no compensation.

[38]Tim Berners-Lee, *The Enquire System; Short Description. Manual.* V1.1, 1980. Hypertext rendition by Sean B. Palmer at: http://infomesh.net/2001/enquire/manual/.

is a method of documenting a system. It concentrates on the way the system is composed of parts, and how these parts are interrelated." "The primary objective" he writes, "is to store and retrieve information about the structure of a system." The basic assumption is that the system "can be broken up into modules." He refers to the modules as "nodes, because of the role they take in the network of interrelationships within the system." Further, crucially, "No assumptions are made about how the breaking up is done — ENQUIRE imposes no constraints on the high level design." These statements show that Tim was thinking about the program as a methodology for representing an arbitrary, nonhierarchical system — showing clearly the link with his interest.[39] Further, a key feature, described in the manual, is that the user can add a node, and can create new relationships between nodes that were not previously connected, thus giving the program great flexibility and again resonating with his interest.

It is noteworthy that in his account in *Weaving the Web*, retrospective but meant to describe how he felt at the time, Tim writes: "I liked Enquire and made good use of it because it stored information without using structures like matrices or trees." Thus he himself makes an explicit connection with his interest, supporting the interpretation that the Enquire program was rooted in his interest.[40]

Ross Hamilton, the literary scholar introduced in Chapter 7, has had an interest since youth in comic accidents. Describing his interest he said, "I think my interest in accidents stems from the fact that I've always found accidents — [I mean] comic accidents — hilarious, and wondered, why are they so funny?" His interest in comic accidents sparked a creative insight he had that became the basis for his dissertation.

Ross went to France to study after his third year in graduate school. In France he studied with Louis Marin, the noted art historian. During the latter part of his time in France he became interested in Rousseau — he said that in part this was due to the influence of Marin, who was interested in Rousseau's *Confessions*. Reading a number of works by Rousseau he turned at some point to Rousseau's last work, *The Reveries of the Solitary Walker*, less well known than many of his others. When I asked him why he read the *Reveries* he said, "because a friend of mind had it in his library, and I was interested in botany, and I liked the idea of Rousseau walking around looking at plants" — thus

---

[39]*Enquire Manual*, pp. 2–4. There are several different kinds of nodes and several different kinds of relationships between nodes.

[40]*Weaving the Web*, p. 10. Given, however, that his account is retrospective we cannot be sure whether he made such an explicit connection with his interest at the time.

the connection with his interest in botany guided him in part to it. (Rousseau had an interest in botany and natural landscapes, as Ross apparently knew, which formed one of the bases for the *Reveries*, being a source of his interest and enjoyment in country walks.) Reading the "Second Walk" in the *Reveries* turned out to be a crucial event for him, sparking his insight.

In the "Second Walk" Rousseau describes a walk in the countryside and an accident that befell him and its aftermath. In the initial segment of his account he describes wandering over meadowlands, recognizing several rare plants, then contemplating the landscape. He describes how this evoked an emotional response in him, it being late fall with "winter approaching" — causing him to think about his old age and reflect upon his life.[41] On his return journey home, he writes, people walking ahead of him swerved aside and, he writes, "I saw a Great Dane rushing down upon me." The dog knocked him over, and the next thing he recalls is regaining consciousness in the arms of several people. He writes that his state on awakening was "unusual" and describes it: "Night was coming on. I perceived the sky, some stars, and a little greenery. This first sensation was a delicious moment. I still had no feeling of myself except as being 'over there.' I was born into life at that instant, and it seemed to me that I filled all the objects I perceived with my frail existence."[42]

Ross described his response reading Rousseau's account: "I read the second reverie [Walk] and I thought it was fascinating and hilarious that he's out botanizing and gets knocked down by a Great Dane. And [that] he writes about it. And I thought, 'Well how interesting that this accident is this site of interpretation, and experience.'" "It's just so central — it's about his self. And then it's the paradox, which I recognized at the very beginning, of the literary accident, which is narrated as something unexpected, surprising, that ruptures the everyday, and yet is thematically central, and so operates literarily exactly counter to the way it should operate, as a surprising and unexpected event. I recognized that as something that was interesting." Rousseau actually refers to the accident twice before he comes to describe it, foreshadowing it in a way which is, as Ross says, in direct contrast to the event itself, which presumably happened unexpectedly. Thus the "paradox" that Ross recognizes in his insight — that the accident is made thematically central — is highlighted. Also, it is noteworthy that the dog described as being a Great Dane is part of

[41] His discussion of plants and the landscape links to Ross's interest in botany, and is particularly apparent in his account of this walk, which may well have drawn Ross to it and heightened his attentiveness while reading it.

[42] Jean-Jacques Rousseau, *The Reveries of the Solitary Walker*, trans. by Charles E. Butterworth (New York: New York University Press, 1979), chap. 2, pp. 12–26; the Great Dane incident is on pp. 15–16.

what made the accident so comic to Ross, sparking his interest, as shown by his statement that he thought it hilarious that Rousseau "gets knocked down by a Great Dane" — not any dog, but this specific kind of dog. The reason for this is the obvious allusion to Hamlet — the idea being that Rousseau is knocked down by Hamlet as it were — the connection made even stronger by the fact that the state Rousseau describes awakening in matches Hamlet's — an intense subjectivity and detachment from ordinary self.[43]

Thus Ross's interest in botany lead him to the *Reveries,* and his interest in comic accidents sparked a creative insight. This is an instance of two interests working in tandem in the generation of a creative response.[44]

The Creative Work of Others and Social Interactions as Stimuli of Creative Responses

The creative work of other people is extremely important as a stimulus in sparking creative responses. Among the individuals whose creative developments I have analyzed, I have found that their creative responses were sparked by the work of other people in a significant fraction of cases, most frequently by the work of someone in their field.

There are a variety of different channels through which the work of others sparks creative responses individuals have. In some cases an individual recognizes a link of a particular aspect of another person's work with an interest he has, sparking an idea. In other cases the work of another person sparks an idea for a way to apply the work in relation to an interest he has — a new application which the other person may well not have thought of. In some cases others' work serves as a point of departure — guided by his interest, an individual sees a way to take their ideas further. Finally, encountering another person's work sometimes sparks an idea in opposition to it: an individual has a creative interest that leads him to perceive flaws in the work or a way to approach the same topic or a related topic from a different perspective or employing a different approach.

The work of others in our field — very commonly a source sparking a creative response — is especially important in helping us forge a connection linking our interests with ideas and currents of thought in our field, which is

[43]Ross did not say that he caught the allusion to Hamlet initially — though the way he phrased his initial response to me suggests he did. He discusses the connection to Hamlet in his dissertation, *"And Nothing Pleaseth But Rare Accidents": A Literary History of Accident,* diss., Yale University, 1995.

[44]Ross pursued his idea of literary accidents, exploring accidents and their place in literature and art for his dissertation; two examples he discusses in his dissertation are Wordsworth's descriptions of the "spots of time" in *The Prelude* and Bruegel's painting "Landscape with the Fall of Icarus."

often important in developing our interests creatively. Recent work is especially important, in exposing us to new topics, ideas, and directions. In my experience, analyzing the developments of individuals, encountering an exciting new topic or idea is often pivotal — through forging a connection with their interest, thus linking their interest to an exciting new idea or topic, individuals generate ideas, including project ideas, that they feel excited about and pursue.

Social interactions — conversations, discussions, meetings, group activities, and forums in which people present their work in person, such as seminars — are also important in sparking creative responses. Such interactions are highly stimulating, and at least a good part of the time when individuals are in such settings they are quite alert, which increases the likelihood they will notice a connection with an interest they have and generate a creative response.

Chris Callahan's idea for his dissertation project is an example of an idea sparked by the work of someone else, through a talk. Chris said that when he first joined the lab he chose for his doctoral work his advisor gave him the option of working with a post-doc, carving out a project from one of the larger research projects underway in the lab, but he chose not to do this. "The other option," he said, "was one where I could kind of do my own thing. And that's the thing I get the biggest charge from — creating my own project. . . . And so that's what we did." His approach fits a guiding principle of this book, creative development as self-directed: defining one's interests for oneself — interests that are in general at least somewhat distinctive — then striving to develop them creatively.

At this point, Chris said, he and his advisor "were trying to figure out what I should do. And we had just recently gone to a really neat talk by a guy who was a post-doc. He gave a talk about a neat reporter that he had devised called *kinesin-lacz*. What he did was he fused *kinesin* to *beta-gal* very cleverly and so [was going to use] the kinesin to taxi the beta-gal [up and down the axon]."[45] I described the idea for this reporter in the last chapter. Starting from this reporter Chris and his advisor took a further creative step, defining a project for Chris: "What we were going to do was to be one of the first people to do an enhancer trap screen with it." Their idea, as described in the last chapter, was to construct an enhancer trap screen to search for genes involved in axonal

[45]The individual who had developed the reporter is Ed Giniger. His reporter is described in E. Giniger, W. Wells, L.Y. Jan, and Y.N. Jan, "Tracing neurons with a kinesin-beta-galactosidase fusion protein," *Rouxs Archives of Developmental Biology* 202 (2) (1993): 112–22. When I spoke with Chris's advisor he recalled the reporter and he and Chris having asked for it and being sent it. He did not recall definitely whether Ed Giniger gave a talk they attended, but said it was certainly quite possible.

pathfinding, and analyze any genes they identified. Their creative response is an example of a creative application of someone else's work, extending it. Of course the post-doc himself may well have had the same idea; but for whatever reason — because he had different interests, and was busy with other projects — he did not pursue such a project. Thus Chris's project was distinctive and, as it turned out, led to significant contributions. I describe his further work on the project, the difficulty with the *kinesin-lacz* reporter and his solution, developing a different reporter, in Chapter 12.

For James Watson, a presentation Maurice Wilkins gave describing his work on X-ray diffraction analysis of DNA was critical in sparking his realization illuminating a path forward for pursuing his interest in deducing the structure of DNA.

Watson had gone to Europe after finishing his dissertation to learn nucleic acid chemistry from a Danish chemist whom his advisor Salvador Luria knew, hoping that he would learn the chemistry he needed to crack the structure of DNA and learn the "secret of the gene." However, he later wrote, this plan was a "flop" — he did not feel stimulated or interested by the work, did not see its relevance. "I could not see why the type of problem on which he was then working (the metabolism of nucleotides) would lead to anything of immediate interest to genetics" — or, more specifically, to him in his pursuit of the structure of DNA, revealing its role in genetic transmission.[46]

Then, in the spring of 1951, Watson went to a meeting in Italy and attended the talk given by Maurice Wilkins.[47] The highlight of Maurice's talk, as Watson describes it in *The Double Helix*, came at the end, when Maurice showed an

---

[46]James Watson, *The Double Helix*, p. 24. In Denmark Watson worked on a phage project that, while it concerned nucleic acids, did not involve any attempt to consider or try to make progress towards determining their structure. He writes that he dreamed of solving the structure of DNA and achieving fame; but he had no concrete plan for how to approach his task, how to proceed.

[47]Maurice Wilkins was at that time Assistant Director of the Biophysics Research Unit established by the Medical Research Council in the U.K., stationed at King's College in London. See his account in Maurice Wilkins, *The Third Man of the Double Helix*, chap. 4, "Randall's Circus." His superior was John Randall, famous for his role in the development of a cavity magnetron that greatly improved radar. Randall was listed to attend the meeting and give the talk, but decided to send Wilkins instead. Watson writes that "made no difference" to him since he knew neither. He also writes that he had been anticipating the talk, which was listed as being about the structural analysis of nucleic acids, hoping he might learn something about these techniques, which he knew little about. He was aware of X-ray diffraction techniques for studying the structures of large molecules, but had found it difficult to follow written accounts describing these techniques and was hoping an oral presentation would be easier to follow. The fact that he was anticipating the talk certainly may have primed his attention.

X-ray diffraction picture of DNA and stated "that the picture showed much more detail than previous pictures and could, in fact, be considered as arising from a crystalline substance." Maurice then stated, as Watson recalled it, that "when the structure of DNA was known, we might be in a better position to understand how genes work" — exactly the kind of statement that would resonate with Watson's interest. Watson writes that he was excited: the picture Maurice showed and his interpretation made it clear to him that DNA must really have a solvable structure. "Before Maurice's talk I had worried about the possibility that the gene might be fantastically irregular. Now, however, I knew that genes could crystallize; hence they must have a regular structure that could be solved in a straightforward fashion."[48] Further, it suggested an approach he could pursue to solve its structure — the application of X-ray diffraction analysis. Jim had been aware of X-ray diffraction analysis, as it was discussed in many articles in the literature, but had not really considered it likely to yield important insights, and thus had not invested in learning about it. Now he suddenly saw its potential. Thus he defined a path to follow going forward: he decided to find a lab in which he could learn X-ray diffraction methods of analysis, with the aim of using them to investigate the structure of DNA.[49]

The plan Watson formed, to use X-ray diffraction methods to deduce the structure of DNA, was not in itself original, at least not in basic outline. Notably, John Randall, Maurice Wilkins, and their associates at the Biophysics Research Unit of the Medical Research Council in the United Kingdom developed a similar program of research, beginning in the 1940s.[50] Nonetheless, Watson's approach — I believe from the time he first conceived it — had an element of

[48]*The Double Helix*, p. 22 and chap. 4. The quotations attributed to Maurice Wilkins are Watson's restatement of what he recalls Wilkins saying. In *The Third Man* Wilkins corroborates much of Watson's account. In particular he states that he went to the conference and delivered a lecture, and that in his recollection, "the high point" of the talk "was showing the first really clear crystalline X-ray pattern of DNA" that he and his associate Raymond Gosling had obtained (p. 137). He also recalls meeting Watson. It should be borne in mind that his account was written after Watson published his account in *The Double Helix* and may have been colored by that.

[49]He writes that his conviction that it was the right technique for solving the structure of DNA was strengthened when he learned that Linus Pauling had announced a breakthrough discovery — the alpha-helix structure of proteins — which was also based on X-ray diffraction analysis; see *The Double Helix*, pp. 30–32.

[50]Wilkins describes the work of the Research Unit in *The Third Man*. Rosalind Franklin began working in the Research Unit in 1950 and made important contributions to their technical work. Wilkins discusses her and his relationship with her in his book. A description of her life and contribution is provided by Brenda Maddox in *Rosalind Franklin: The Dark Lady of DNA* (New York: HarperCollins, 2002). See also Anne Sayre, *Rosalind Franklin and DNA* (New York: W.W. Norton, 1975).

distinctiveness, rooted in his distinctive interest. At Cambridge he and Francis Crick formulated a plan for how to proceed: build models, use deductive principles to compare alternative structures, and guess the structure of DNA by reasoning, based on X-ray data. Their approach was, as Watson notes, modeled more on Linus Pauling's than on the approach taken by Wilkins and Rosalind Franklin at the Biophysics Research Unit. But it was distinct even from Pauling: Watson and Crick were not wedded to the particular alpha-helix structure Pauling had been working with; and Watson, given his training, seems to have had a greater focus on the genetic functionality required than Pauling — he was guided, more it seems than others, by the search for a structure that would fit the function of DNA as central in genetic transmission, as for example in phages.[51] Thus they followed different leads and considered different models, leading ultimately — only after Watson saw a crucial X-ray picture Rosalind Franklin had taken, shown him by Wilkins — to success.[52]

Several mathematicians I interviewed described having a crucial creative response sparked by a paper they read written by another mathematician, generally sparking an idea for a project, thus enabling them to define a way to try to develop an interest they had formed; this is likely a common pattern in this field. Anna Gilbert formed an interest in college in classical analysis and its application to solve differential equations describing physical processes. In graduate school her mentor suggested she read several recent papers that develop a new approach for solving certain classes of differential equations, called multiresolution. Anna read the papers and they sparked an idea for a project: to compare the new method with the classical method for solving such equations, in which she was well-versed — she told me she thought the comparison wasn't clear and said "it was just something that I thought should be done." Performing the comparison for a specific type of differential equation

[51]*The Double Helix*, Chapter 7 for their initial idea of an approach. The collaboration itself was an event of happenstance to some degree, of course. Also, Crick's interests and approach must also be recognized as important in their formulation of their workplan and their approach. In particular, he liked model building and knew far more about X-ray methods and physical chemistry principles.

[52]The story of Watson seeing these pictures Rosalind had taken, of the so-called "B" form of DNA, has been told and interpreted in various ways. Watson describes the matter, from his point of view, in Chapter 23 of *The Double Helix*, writing that Maurice Wilkins showed it to him. Wilkins provides his account in *The Third Man of the Double Helix*, pp. 197–98. He states he was handed the photo by Raymond Gosling and had the understanding that it was being given to him by Rosalind, whom he had heard was to leave the lab. He states he showed it to Watson a few days later. This occurred in January 1953.

she determined that the two methods do not generate the same result, and that the multiresolution approach generates more accurate answers for a range of parameter values. These findings were original — thus she made a contribution, and the project was the origin of her dissertation.[53] Victoria Rayskin also initiated a project based on a paper she read; I describe this phase of her development in Chapter 12.

Literary scholars also described creative responses sparked by the work of others, though less commonly. One for whom such a response was crucial is Gregg Crane. Gregg left graduate school part way through to go to law school. He grew disillusioned practicing law, realized he wanted to pursue literature, and returned to graduate school. Returning, he told me he wanted to find a way to draw upon his legal training and, in his words, "incorporate" it into his literary work. Thus he defined a creative interest: to try to link his training as a lawyer with literature — to find a way to "interrelate" law and literature. During his second term back he took a class on race in American literature. His professor had written an article on Homer Plessy — who brought a lawsuit, *Plessy v. Ferguson*, which was decided against him by the U.S. Supreme Court in a decision pivotal in establishing the "separate but equal" doctrine — and Mark Twain, and the cultural conditions of the 1890s. Recognizing from the title that it "related law to literature" Gregg decided to read it.[54] Reading the article was crucial for him. Spurred on by it he read Twain's *Pudd'nhead Wilson*, then the Supreme Court decision in *Plessy v. Ferguson*, focusing on the dissent written by Justice Harlan, who writes that the white race is superior, but then goes against the majority opinion, placing, in Gregg's interpretation, his allegiance to the rule of law above racial arguments. Reading this dissent, seeing it in relation to Twain's writing, Gregg had an insight which became the basis for a paper: that the 1890s was a time when law was leading literature, rather than the reverse, which is the more common view, at least as Gregg understood it at the time. "[Twain] is extremely pessimistic at this moment, is in his nadir in his feelings about the direction the country is taking, feeling like law is always just a tool of the will of the majority — law is just power," he told me. "And I wanted to show that in Harlan's dissent in Plessy... he used the rule of law... to check his racist views, to check himself in effect. And that that was actually more optimistic and forward-looking [as an] approach." "That comparison would challenge the usual take on law and literature, which is that literature

[53] Anna Gilbert, *Multiresolution Homogenization Schemes for Differential Equations and Applications*, diss., Princeton University, 1997. Anna goes through the comparison and results of this project in Chapter 2.

[54] The citation is Eric J. Sundquist, "Twain, Mark and Plessy, Homer," *Representations* 24 (1988): 102–28.

286   leads law, is always in advance of law," "that law is the work of conservative representatives of the status quo, so is always lagging behind." Gregg's insight was the starting point for his dissertation, and a book he published based on it.[55]

Inventors also often have creative responses sparked by the work of other people — often by another inventor's invention. An example is Thomas Edison being spurred to begin working on designing an acoustic telegraphy system. This project grew out of his longstanding interest in telegraphy and his linked interests in electrochemistry and electromechanical devices. It seems to have been sparked by Elisha Gray's innovative acoustic telegraphy system, in which reeds or tuning forks were used to transmit multiple frequencies over a wire. Gray's system posed a threat to Western Union's existing telegraph business, which was one factor in spurring Edison to undertake the project — Edison seems to have been prompted in part to work on acoustic telegraphy by William Orton, whom Paul Israel describes as "concerned" about Gray's new system. In addition, Edison may well have seen Gray exhibit his system in New York — Israel states he probably did see it, and this likely spurred his interest.[56]

Conversations are another source of creative responses that are generative of ideas — especially ideas initiating collaborative projects. Conversations and social interactions are in general — at least many of them — free-flowing; and in moving fluidly from topic to topic with a partner we generate creative links and ideas, especially in the region of overlap of our interests — combining and interrelating our interests.

For Roger Knowles, conversations were key in developing his interest in visualizing neurons developing into their shapes in projects. It was through a conversation with a classmate that Roger learned about the faculty member who became his advisor, Ken Kosik. Roger explained his interest to her, and she told him that Ken, whom she knew from college, had overlapping interests. Based on what she said Roger signed up to do a rotation with Ken. As Roger described it, his initial project for his dissertation was born in a conversation he and Ken had at the start of his rotation. Ken is interested in the genes and cellular processes that control the growth of axons in neurons. At the time Roger came into his lab he had devised a cell system in which he exposed insect cells to a baculovirus containing the *tau* gene, causing the cells to grow axon-like extensions. He had apparently not thought about directly observing the actual growth process of the cells, the approach at the core of Roger's interest — thus

---

[55]Gregg Crane, *Fiat Justitia: American Literature and the Jurisprudence of Rights, Power, and Community*, diss., UC-Berkeley, 1995, and *Race, Citizenship, and Law in American Literature* (New York: Cambridge University Press, 2002).

[56]See Paul Israel, *Edison: A Life of Invention*, pp. 108–10.

there was a natural opportunity in the overlap of their interests. Roger told me he explained his interest to Ken, and Ken responded very favorably, and together they decided on a project for Roger: to set up a video microscopy system in the lab and use it to make a video recording of the cells growing in real time. Roger did so, learned a great deal, and was able to record the cells successfully. The project was successful and resulted in a journal article publication.[57] Roger's second project for his dissertation was a collaborative one that also grew out of conversation, and out of the expertise Roger had developed with videomicroscopy — I noted this project in Chapter 8 and discuss it further in Chapter 14. Conversations with their advisors also seem to have been critical for Kelly Overly and Chris Callahan in developing main ideas for their dissertation research.

Conversations, often around first meetings, have been important historically in sparking many famous collaborations. In *The Double Helix* Watson describes the excitement of meeting Francis Crick, the two realizing they had a shared interest in DNA, and how they developed their idea for how to approach solving the structure of DNA, initiating their project, in the course of their highly stimulating conversations. Likewise, this was the case for psychologists Daniel Kahneman and Amos Tversky; Kahneman recalled them talking a great deal the summer they met, generating ideas, initiating their pioneering work on judgement and decision-making.[58]

Reflection and the Generation of Creative Responses

The descriptions and examples in the previous sections may give the impression that creative responses are always generated immediately in direct response to experiences or stimuli, with no gap of time or period of reflection intervening. In fact the available evidence indicates that this is not the case — processes of reflection are central to the generation of many creative responses. Individuals generate many responses in the course of recalling, reimagining, and reflecting upon experiences they have had and elements they have encountered, in particular thinking about them in the context of and together with their interests, making connections.

[57] R.B. Knowles, N. Leclerc, and K.S. Kosik, "Organization of actin and microtubules during process formation in tau-expressing SF9 cells," *Cell Motility and the Cytoskeleton* 28 (1994): 256–64.

[58] This was stated in a *New York Times* interview with Kahneman — I have not located the date. First encounters would seem to be important in many fields in sparking ideas and collaborative projects.

All creative responses involve some linkages generated in the mind. Here, however, I am calling attention to a basic distinction between responses that occur more or less in the heat of the moment, in the midst of the experience or encounter that sparks the response, thus with minimal chains of thought inter-mediating between the experience or stimulus and the response, and responses that occur later, apart from the intensity of immediate experience and direct engagement, in conditions that we may label conditions of reflection — think-ing back over experiences, events, phenomena, works and contributions of others, following out chains of thought, making vital links with one's interests, imagining, and experiencing feelings called forth through thinking and imag-ining, which may in turn spark further associations. Calder's initial response while in Mondrian's studio — becoming excited, suddenly thinking about and realizing he would like to create abstract art similar to what he was seeing — is an example of the first form of response — a response that occurred to him in the midst of direct engagement with the stimulus. His later creative response, the flowering of his creativity, developing abstract sculpture art and later his mobiles, was generated through imagining, thinking, and working, forging a powerful link with his interests.

Many of my interview subjects in literature described insights they had about works of literature in a way that strongly suggests that the insights occurred to them while they were thinking or reflecting — not while first reading the works, thus not in the first blush of engagement with them. Teresa Faherty, who left college with an interest in *The Winter's Tale*, learned in a class in graduate school a model of pastoral as a language or singing contest in which two individuals compete to see who can outperform the other in classical allusions and wit and paying tribute to Ovid. Teresa was of course very familiar with *The Winter's Tale*, and at a certain point, some time after learning the model of pastoral, she recognized a connection with Act IV, Scene IV of the play: she realized that Perdita and Florizel can be viewed as engaging in just such a pastoral contest, and that Perdita's famous "flowers" speech is part of this contest, through which Perdita shows herself superior to Florizel. As Teresa described it her insight was very much a sudden and dramatic event, that did not occur while she was reading the play but at large, spontaneously. Knowing the play so well, she could call to mind any of its different parts fluidly, and through such a process, seeing the part with more clarity as a unit, and more compactly, than if she were actually reading it, make a creative connection with another element—as it turned out, a theoretical model.

For many writers it seems likely that their ideas for stories emerge in the course of reflecting, as certain experiences come to mind guided by and connecting with their creative interests. This is an interpretation of William Faulkner's process of developing the initial kernels of the stories that became the bases for *Flags in the Dust* and *The Sound and the Fury* that is consistent with his own later accounts. See the discussion in Chapter 12 of the origins of *The Sound and the Fury*, based on Faulkner's own later statements and Joseph Blotner's reconstruction.

There are two distinct ways in which creative responses generated in reflection are generally separated from the stimuli and experiences that spark them. One is in time — creative responses generated in reflection generally occur after the experience or stimulus that sparks them has occurred or been encountered, through recollecting the experience or stimulus. There is great variation in the time that elapses between experience or encounter and response — ranging from a few minutes or hours to days, months, or years. When the time interval is relatively large a great deal of mental activity can and normally does go on between the experience or encounter and the response, and this is in some cases crucial in building up conceptual structures and paths of association central in generating the response.

The other separation is context — responses generated in reflection typically occur in settings distinct from the experiences and stimuli that spark them, often in more tranquil settings or amidst the routines of daily life.[59] Lulls in ordinary activity are conducive to reflection, and at least for some people are important in providing opportunities for reflection that are generative of creative responses. Lulls can occur in any setting, but perhaps are especially likely in conditions of relative tranquility. It is reported that Albert Einstein loved to sail — a classic example of an activity conducive to periods of reflection — when the wind was down he would think and write notes, when it sprang up again he would sail, undoubtedly continuing to think.[60] It must be noted that we do not know what activities he was engaged in when his main ideas, such as, notably, the founding principle of the special theory of relativity, occurred to him; he described a conversation with his friend Michele Besso in which he began the thinking that led to his insight, and this conversation may thus have had a part in prompting the chain of thinking that led him to the insight, but he did

[59]The issue of the environment in which creativity occurs is discussed by Mihaly Csikszentmihalyi in *Creativity: Flow and the Psychology of Discovery and Invention*, notably in Chapter 6, "Creative Surroundings," also somewhat in Chapter 5, "The Flow of Creativity."

[60]This is reported by Ronald Clark in his biography, *Einstein; The Life and Times* (New York: Avon Books, 1984), p. 50.

not describe any immediate external stimulus sparking his idea. I discuss his development leading up to this insight in the next chapter.[61]

Responses Cumulating Over Time; The Stream of Experiences and Encounters

In this chapter I have focused on describing creative responses sparked by a single experience or stimulus or set of linked stimuli encountered more or less as a group. In fact many creative responses are triggered by the cumulative effect of a series of experiences and encounters. Experiences occurring one by one over time, or elements encountered and internalized one by one, have a cumulating effect: the groundwork for the response is laid over time, with each experience or element fitting into an emerging conceptual structure, perhaps also triggering a realization or response that contributes to the development of this structure, with the main creative response generated, at a certain point, out of this structure.

Analyzing Matisse's paintings and letters and comments describing his development beginning from his stays on Belle-Ile-en-Mer it appears such a process was central for him in his path of development. In particular, we see how specific steps he took in his artistic development seem to have been sparked by summer sojourns at specific places in the south, the vivid colors and distinctive scenes sparking creative responses in him. Over time, through these responses, and through his encounters with schools and specific works of art, notably Cezanne's *Three Bathers*, which he studied day after day, his sensibility in terms of the application of color and juxtapositions of colors grew. For example, we see him spurred, his creativity sparked, during his summer at Saint-Tropez, under the influence of the intensity of the summer light and his engagement with Neo-Impressionism, the Divisionism of two more senior painters, Paul Signac and Henri-Edmond Cross, leading to his experimental, powerful *Luxe, calme et volupté*. This series of creative steps culminated in his creative breakthrough a year later, in the summer of 1905, at Collioure, which was in an immediate sense sparked by specific scenes, but is best interpreted as the culmination of many discrete jumps forward he had made in approach, technique, in his grasp of color, color juxtaposition, and overall

[61]Albert Einstein, "How I Created the Theory of Relativity," trans. by Yoshimasa A. Ono (translation of a lecture given in Kyoto on 14 December, 1922) *Physics Today* 35, 8 (1982): 45–47.

composition with color.[62] As a second example, Hannah Arendt's idea to write a book presenting an analysis of the historical and ideological roots of what she at the time called racial imperialism, of its emergence and crystallization as a political movement and its organizational structure and use and abuse of power and false authority, grew out of the cumulative impact on her of a series of events, that sparked a response in her that grew and formed over a period of time. I describe her development over this time period in Chapter 15.

Our Limited Understanding of Processes of Creative Responses; Developing a Framework of Analysis

It is well to conclude this chapter with the recognition that our understanding of creative responses, especially the processes through which conceptual structures encoding creative interests mediate responses, is very imperfect. My description of these processes should be taken as a working model, a sketch, that should and is meant to be developed further.

There are two main deficiencies in the description I have presented. One is the lack of direct neuropsychological information about the processes generating creative responses. It is not my approach, nor is it possible with available brain imaging technology, to image brains with the precision required to see the specific perceptual and attentional processes and conceptual linkages that occur. Further, since these processes happen spontaneously, out in the world, in the midst or aftermath of experiences and encounters, it seems doubtful we will have the research technology to observe them in real time in the foreseeable future.

The other deficiency is the lack of a more precisely specified representation of response processes and the conceptual structures associated with interests that mediate them. This deficiency I believe can be addressed through development of a suitable framework. A fundamental requirement for such a framework is representing experiences and elements in the world together with conceptual structures that encode creative interests and the mental processes through which responses are generated in a common, unified framework. In my view a natural candidate that can satisfy this requirement and fits the description of creative development in this book is a framework based in knowledge representation as, for example, set forth by John Sowa in *Conceptual Structures:*

[62]This period in Matisse's development is beautifully described by Hilary Spurling in *The Unknown Matisse*. Of course each discrete step forward he took, for example at Saint-Tropez, was itself undoubtedly the product of many smaller events, ideas, and responses.

Information Processing in Mind and Machine (Reading, MA: Addison-Wesley, 1984) (see also his *Knowledge Representation; Logical, Philosophical, and Computational Foundations* (Pacific Grove, CA: Brooks/Cole, 2000)). In such a representation experiences and elements can be described as conceptual elements and relations, that interface with conceptual elements and structures in individuals' conceptual worlds, and are able to be internalized into these conceptual structures. Obviously many elements are highly complex, comprised of thousands of discrete elements — for example, a book or complex visual phenomena — thus simplification, focusing on main elements and subunits, seems essential in developing a representation for experiences and elements. Further, the simplifications should track individuals' own perceptual and cognitive processes.

Such a framework can be used to describe the building up of the conceptual worlds of individuals engaged in creative development, including, in particular, the conceptual structures that define and encode their creative interests. As is evident from this statement, this is not specific just to the description of creative responses, but more generally is a basis for describing and modeling creative development. The framework can then be used for describing creative responses. Here there are two distinct processes that must be described. The first is the guidance of perception and attention, leading to a focus on particular experiences and elements, and particular aspects of complex experiences and elements. A model of such guidance will work through searching for conceptual resonances and connections linking specific experiences and elements an individual encounters — or aspects of experiences and elements — with elements and structures in her conceptual world, specifically elements and structures that are part of the conceptual structures that encode her creative interests. The second process is describing processes of response — chains of thinking — conceptual linkages and associations and other mental processes that generate creative ideas and insights.

I believe a framework along these lines can be developed and provide a further basis for describing creative development.

10

Exploration of Creative Interests and Creativity Generation; Creative Expertise

In this chapter I describe patterns of exploration of creative interests and forms of creativity based in exploration and the rich conceptual structures individuals build up in the domains of their interests through exploring and learning about them. I describe how individuals are guided by their interests and their conceptions of interests along paths of exploration, building up conceptual structures and networks of associations in the domains of their interests, and fundamental creative processes through which they generate ideas and insights based in these conceptual structures and networks and what they learn exploring their interests. Fundamental to my description is the idea that through pursuing distinctive interests individuals follow distinctive, unique paths of exploration, exploring domains that are distinctive, building up rich, unique conceptual structures and networks, which are the basis of their ideas and insights. Thus I show how the distinctiveness of individuals' interests, in defining distinctive domains for exploration, is the source and basis of their creativity and originality. I present many examples illustrating the processes I describe, demonstrating that for many individuals these processes are central to their development and generation of important ideas and insights; individuals for whom I describe their pattern of exploration of their interests and ideas they generated rooted in conceptual structures they built up exploring their interests include Albert Einstein, Samuel Taylor Coleridge, Charles Darwin, Ray Kroc, Robert Kaufman, Maria Carrig, Cheryl Nixon, and Ian Baucom.

The chapter is divided into three sections. In the first section I describe patterns of exploration of interests. Then I describe processes through which individuals generate ideas and insights rooted in conceptual structures and networks they build up following paths exploring their interests. In the second section I describe three forms of creativity generation: making creative connections; creativity based in rich webs of associations and networks; and generalization and pattern recognition. In the third, brief section I describe creative expertise.

EXPLORATION IN DOMAINS OF INTERESTS

As described in Chapter 7, creative interests possess breadth, in particular define domains of intermediate breadth, and thus provide room for exploration. Once an individual forms a creative interest he naturally focuses on exploring the domain it defines. The drive to explore an interest arises both out of intrinsic interest and curiosity — to learn about the interest, its different elements and facets, and also the desire to discover and generate creative opportunities in its domain. Susan was seeking to explore her interest in taking the Anthropology class on oral and written forms of language. Charles Darwin explored his interest in the geographic ranges of extent of species and the comparison and contrasts, in both morphology and behavior, between allied species and varieties in neighboring locales in his travels in and around South America; below I present notes from his *Beagle* Diary and notebooks that show this. Albert Einstein, motivated by the desire to resolve the paradox he had hit upon at the age of sixteen, explored the interest he formed, growing out of and around this paradox, reaching into philosophy; I sketch an outline of his path of exploration, as reconstructed, below. Maria Carrig explored her interest, searching for a philosophical basis for the radical shift in English comic drama she had observed, exploring Renaissance and early modern currents of thought.

There are four basic patterns of exploration in interest domains that I have identified analyzing the creative developments of individuals across a range of fields.[1] A first, very common pattern is exploration in discrete forays — exploring distinct elements or subregions of an interest with no strongly defined link from one element and focus of attention to the next, a root with branches pattern. A second, very common pattern is following an unfolding path of exploration, in which each element one encounters sparks an association or link, mediated

[1]My analysis is based on individuals' descriptions of their exploratory activities in interviews or written documents as well as interpretation of their exploratory activities apparent in records documenting their development.

by one's interest, to another element, which in turn sparks a link to another, generating a connected path consisting of a series of elements in the domain of one's interest. In general in this pattern the links are generated spontaneously — in engaging with an element one spontaneously encounters a link to another element or makes an association to another element; the path is often quite original, generating a novel set of connections among elements. A third pattern is exploration of defined sequences of elements, in many cases planned or arranged as a sequence of encounters in advance, at least to some degree, or at least expected to be encountered as a sequence. Such a path is not so spontaneously generated as sequences generated through the second pattern, but powerful in being highly structured — to the extent the sequence reflects a deep, valuable intuition, the series of elements and interconnections may be the source of great creativity. I describe these three patterns in greater detail and present examples illustrating them in the following sections. A fourth pattern of exploration is exploration interwoven with project work, project outcomes sparking new phases of exploration. This pattern fits more naturally in Chapter 14, in which I describe patterns of projects, thus I do not discuss it here, rather it forms part of my description in that chapter.

The processes of exploration I describe are distinctive in a number of ways from the way exploration and search are described in the creativity literature. In descriptions in the literature the domain of search or exploration is typically left rather vague — it is assumed to be broad and is often not explicitly defined. In contrast, for the processes I describe the domain is crucial: individuals explore in the domain of their interest, thus in a domain they define for themselves, that is distinctive and often richly articulated in the way they think about it. Further, this domain, in its distinctiveness, shapes in an essential way their process of exploration: they explore within the domain, guided by their conception of interest and the conceptual structure that encodes their interest — which itself evolves and grows as they explore and learn and encounter elements. The creativity they generate later, rooted in what they learn and discover through exploring, is thus clearly based in the distinctive domain in which they search, thus in their interest. This is a basis for creativity not described — scarcely mentioned — in conventional descriptions. The case of Albert Einstein's exploration in the domain of his interest illustrates this: led by his interest he took one crucial step beyond the domain contemporaries in physics were focused on, to explore philosophical conceptions of space and time, and in particular to read David Hume, which was crucial for his development of the theory of relativity.

A second difference between the processes of exploration I describe and conventional descriptions of search and exploration is in breadth of focus of exploratory activity, especially in terms of its objective. Most descriptions in the literature focus on search as directly generative of ideas, problems, and solutions, in particular search with a narrowly defined objective, for example, to find a solution to a problem or identify a problem on which to focus. In contrast, the exploratory processes I describe are focused on exploring a domain of interest more broadly. In standard descriptions, because the domain is generally (often implicitly) taken to be a whole field, such exploration is really just general learning. Such general learning is important (though it has not been a focus in the creativity field) but different from what I describe. I describe exploration in a domain that is more refined and narrower than a field — that is defined by a creative interest, thus of intermediate breadth, fitting with the basic definition of a creative interest as an intermediate level conceptual category or structure. Thus the processes I describe are intermediate between a narrow focus on problems and general learning. They are processes of exploration and learning tailored to a creative interest, occurring in a domain that is distinctive and idiosyncratic and intermediate in breadth.[2]

Exploration of Interest Domains in Forays

A basic form of exploration in an interest domain is exploration in discrete forays, exploring in different parts of the domain. In this pattern elements encountered do not trigger links to further elements. Rather, an element in the domain is sought out or encountered, focused on, and learned about, perhaps triggering an idea or being developed creatively to a limited degree, then the search moves on, to seek out and find or encounter another element — with no direct connection from one element to the next. Individuals engaged in this form of exploration are guided by their interest, often their conception of interest. Their interest defines the domain in which they search, guides them in choosing what kinds of elements to look for and focus on, for example what books to read, what facts to explore, and what techniques to learn about, and

[2]There are of course useful insights about search and exploration in the literature. See for examples David Perkins, "Insight in minds and genes," in *The Nature of Insight*, ed. Robert J. Sternberg and Janet E. Davidson (Cambridge, MA: MIT Press, 1995), chap. 15, pp. 495–533 — he describes search spaces in which the payoff function is nonlinear; Pat Langley, Herbert A. Simon, Gary L. Bradshaw, and Jan M. Zytkow, *Scientific Discovery: Computational Explorations of the Creative Process* (Cambridge, MA: MIT Press, 1987), in which search algorithms are described; and the model of dual search spaces — a space of hypotheses and a space of experiments to test given hypotheses — presented by David Klahr and Keith Dunbar, in "Dual space search during scientific reasoning," *Cognitive Science* 12 (1988): 1–48. In general these and other models focus on searching for a solution to a problem, or for a problem or hypothesis, not on exploration of an articulated domain of interest.

guides their attention, governing which elements among those they encounter they focus on. They are not pursuing a specific path or chain of associations or ideas, but rather exploring throughout the domain of their interest, so that after focusing on a given element they return to their interest at large, from that point deciding where to search and what to focus on next. Thus individuals follow this pattern of exploration who seek to learn about a domain of interest broadly and extensively.

This pattern of exploration is generative of creativity through three main processes. One is the discovery of a specific element during a foray that is itself a creative discovery or sparks an idea or insight that becomes the basis for a creative contribution. A second is the generation of an insight based in identifying a commonality among a set of elements encountered and learned about in the course of different forays throughout the domain of an interest. Classic examples of this are generalization and pattern recognition. A third is making creative connections between divergent elements in the domain of an interest, encountered on different forays.

Several of the literary scholars I interviewed described processes of exploration and gathering of source materials fitting the pattern of exploration in discrete forays. Cheryl Nixon explored her interest in the "literary heirs" of Aphra Behn by searching for names of female authors from the eighteenth century, using the card catalogue in her library and a few guidebooks that list English women authors of this time period. She described doing archival library research, finding novels that are not available in modern editions in her university library's rare book collection. It is notable that, as Cheryl described it, she did not follow a connected path in exploring her interest — it was not generally the case that reading a book triggered a link to another. Rather she explored by searching for and reading works by many different authors that she found in the card catalogue or lists, seemingly consciously striving to span the domain of her interest, to gain a sense for the range of themes, plots, and approaches to be found in eighteenth-century novels by English women authors. In fact she incorporated her lists of books in her oral exams — this is shown by her orals document, which she shared with me, which lists authors and books to be discussed.[3]

Gregg Crane said that in his first year back in graduate school after leaving law to return to school to pursue a doctorate in literature he explored various approaches that relate law and literature, hoping to find a way to incorporate his legal training and the aspects of law he values — its practicality, and its

[3]Cheryl's orals document lists, as best I can determine, 22 female English authors of the late seventeenth and eighteenth centuries, and 32 texts written by them.

role in American society and in sustaining the American way of life — into his studies. "I was looking around, trying to figure out a way to incorporate law [my legal training]. And so, outside of class, without any particular class guiding this, I bought some books that were readers in law and literature, and I read them during the first year I was back in grad school, trying to find a model — trying to find something that would suggest a way that I could interrelate these things [law and literature]." His approach was thus to explore a spectrum of approaches to linking and interrelating law and literature. Hence he followed a process of searching over the range of his interest in discrete forays.

Another example of a literary scholar I interviewed who described exploring in the domain of his interest in a way fitting this general pattern is Ian Baucom. I describe his exploratory activity and an insight he came to through reading widely in the domain of his interest — a generalization across a number of specific works — later in this chapter.

In fact many individuals across a wide variety of fields, especially fields in which the building up of knowledge and specific cases is important for generating ideas and insights, explore their interest domains through broad-based and at times extensive exploration in discrete forays. Liz Yoder, having become interested in glial signaling, described exploring literature on this phenomenon comprehensively, searching for and reading articles and reports from labs around the world describing observations of glial signaling. David Johnson, a neuroscientist I interviewed, described building up a knowledge base about acetylcholine receptors, his focus of interest, consistently attentive to new articles and findings reported at conferences. Hannah Arendt seems to have engaged in this kind of exploration in building up materials and knowledge in the domain of her interest, exploring the history of debates about the role of the Jews in Germany and, after moving to France, in France, extensively and in great depth, seemingly not pursuing a connected path so much as investigating exhaustively discrete episodes and topics. Evidence for this is articles she published in the 1940s — these evidence great learning on several topics which, though lying in a common interest domain, are discrete.[4] She was in fact famous for her exhaustive knowledge, and it seems likely — is intuitive — that she gained this through innumerable discrete forays of investigation and learning. In fact exploration in discrete forays is I believe a natural, common pattern for individuals who build up expertise in the domains of their interests.

The basic pattern of development described here is exploring in a series of forays in a domain of interest prior to embarking on a major project in

---

[4]However, I do not claim that we know with any assurance what her actual pattern of exploration was; I am not aware of materials documenting it.

the domain. A second pattern, subsumed within the basic pattern, is exploration in discrete forays alternating with project work. See Chapter 14 for discussion of this and other patterns of projects and interests.

Connected Paths of Exploration in Interest Domains

A second pattern of exploration in a domain of interest is exploring along a connected path, each element along the path triggering an association or link to the next. This is a natural pattern of exploration. In particular, in exploring in a domain we are naturally led from one element to the next: an element or subtopic we discover, investigate, and learn about naturally sparks ideas and triggers associations and links to others, which we naturally are curious about, track down, and learn about; in turn this generates links to further elements, and so on. For example, reading an article we come upon references to related articles that strike us as interesting, and seek them out and read them, and they in turn contain references to yet other articles that seem potentially interesting, which we seek out. Individuals often follow a modified form of this pattern: after following a path through several links they return to the original source element from which their path began and pursue a different path. Thus they explore a series of paths that are linked at their common point of origin but define distinct lines of inquiry.

I have stated that individuals are guided along paths of exploration in interest domains by their interest. In following a given path an individual moves from one specific element to the next; thus his path forward is defined at the level of linkages between specific, discrete elements, not at the broader level of his interest. This may seem to imply that his interest does not have a major role in guiding him, thus in defining his path. But in fact this is incorrect: for the elements he explores in general have many potential links and associations, dozens or even hundreds, and his interest is key in guiding him in choosing which among these links to follow up. In particular, he pursues, at least predominantly, links that fit with his interest — it is these that he notices and that catch his interest.[5] Thus, guided by our interest, we generally remain within and close to its domain, not pursuing links that would carry us far afield. Beyond their role in guidance, our interests are also crucial in calling our attention to elements that initiate our paths of exploration; for example, encountering a book or phenomenon and recognizing a connection with our interest we may decide to explore and learn more about it, which may in turn generate leads to further elements.

[5]Paths do sometimes stray outside the strict domain of an individual's interest. But the farther a path strays I believe the more likely it is that the individual will abandon it to return to the domain of his interest.

A fundamental feature of the paths individuals follow exploring interest domains is that they are not standard paths that others commonly traverse, but rather distinctive, in many cases unique. The sequences of elements they encounter, investigate, and learn about have in general never before been explored as a grouping, almost never in the same sequence, defining the same set of linkages. This is illustrated, stunningly, by the paths Samuel Taylor Coleridge followed exploring his interests, described later in this chapter. But it is true quite generally — our paths are almost always distinctive, both in their sequence of elements and in certain specific elements they include.

The distinctiveness of individuals' paths exploring their interests is in fact crucial for their creativity generation. A basic feature of exploring along a connected path is that an individual builds up in his mind a network of associations that mirrors the links that define his path. Thus he internalizes not only specific elements he encounters along the path, but also the links connecting elements — for we naturally tend to remember events and elements in the sequence in which we encounter them, creating links in our mind connecting the events and elements corresponding to this sequence. This web of associations is in general distinctive, mirroring the distinctiveness of his path. It is also generally interconnected with the conceptual structure that encodes the individual's interest, creating a further set of associations. In turn, this web is the basis for generation of creative connections among elements the individual has encountered on his paths of exploration, as well as elements on the paths linked to elements in the conceptual structure associated with his interest. I describe these processes of creativity generation and provide examples illustrating them in the second part of this chapter. Samuel Taylor Coleridge's poetic associations and combinations are wonderful examples of them, as described by John Livingston Lowes. I draw on his account below, describing associations Coleridge seems to have built up in his mind exploring along paths in interest domains, and the way these were, or so it seems, generative of novel, striking juxtapositions of elements in "The Rime of the Ancient Mariner."

Following a path of exploration in an interest domain is somewhat akin to surfing the World Wide Web, traveling from Website to Website. But the paths individuals follow exploring their interests are in general quite distinctive to them — self-defined paths they follow guided by their distinctive interests — whereas so much of the time when we surf the Web we are either quite narrowly focused, for example searching for a given product, or allow ourselves to be guided by links strategically placed by advertisers or Webmasters, thus lose much of our autonomy.

Maria Carrig explored an interest domain following a path, exploring a series of subtopics, each leading to the next, leading ultimately to a creative connection she made. As described in Chapter 3, Maria formed an interest in exploring how the revolutionary shift in worldview in philosophy in the Renaissance and early modern period influenced and was reflected in English theater, specifically comic drama. Beginning to pursue the topic after her oral exams Maria found it difficult to move forward. She decided to take a break from graduate school and went to Italy for a year.

While in Italy Maria became interested in Machiavelli and his influence on English comic theater, and when she returned to the United States she explored his influence. Beginning from this point she followed a connected path of exploration. She described the path she followed this way. "Through Machiavelli I started to read earlier humanists' dialogues. Machiavelli was also a comic writer as well as a philosopher, so I started to think about English humanists who were [also] interested in the intersection between comedy and philosophy. And that took me back a little bit earlier, into the sixteenth century, and I started looking at Erasmus and More." "Erasmus and More wrote a bunch of dialogues, and I found those; and I discovered that the dialogue was a very popular rhetorical form. And I started to think maybe the dialogue might be a good place to try to find a link between drama and philosophy. Then I discovered this vast body of Lucianic dialogues [rooted in the ideas of the skeptical philosopher Lucian], and I realized the popularity they had in the Renaissance; and so I started thinking maybe that would be a direction I would take." Thus, as she described it, she was led from one topic to the next, leading well beyond where she began. As it turned out, the Lucianic dialogues provided a key linkage, generative of the idea that was the basis for her dissertation.

In many cases other people provide us with important contacts and leads to pursue, thus have an important role in defining the paths we follow. We may, for example, describe a creative interest to a mentor who is likely to be more knowledgeable about certain aspects or subdomains of our interest, and our mentor may suggest elements or directions to explore which we then pursue. Victoria Rayskin is an example of someone for whom this was the case. As described in Chapter 7, during her second year in graduate school Victoria met with a faculty person who has interests related to hers and described to him the problem she had worked on for her college thesis in Russia. The next day he contacted her, they met, and he described how her problem could be recast in a way that reveals its connection to an important class of problems in dynamical systems theory — a connection she had not previously been aware of. Through this interaction Victoria was led to reconceptualize her focus and it became more of a true interest, encompassing different ways of formulating the general problem she was interested in and different contexts in which it is relevant. Victoria told me that the professor also "stated that there is a large literature" on the problem as he recast it, "and gave me the references." She then began to read these references, and through them was led to a specific paper, in which she discovered an error. It appears she found this paper on her own, thus through a path of exploration, beginning from the references her professor gave her. In turn, finding the error led her to formulate the problem in the paper differently — essentially a creative response — and this reformulated problem became the basis for her dissertation work. I describe her revised formulation in Chapter 12.

Critical Steps

In many cases individuals follow relatively short paths of exploration, consisting of just one or two main steps, moving from an initial element or subdomain to a second, and perhaps from the second being led to a third. Importantly, paths of this kind, though having just one or two main steps, can be highly distinctive, even unique, exposing individuals to a distinctive, unique set of elements. Through following such paths individuals thus build up distinctive networks of elements, which may enable them to generate highly creative ideas and insights. Even one step of exploration from a base point in an unusual direction, different from the direction others starting from a similar base have taken, can be important, exposing an individual to an unusual juxtaposition or set of elements, sparking an original idea or insight.

Individuals' creative interests are crucial in guiding them on their paths of exploration, in leading them to take a step in an unusual direction, to explore elements that others starting from a similar base point do not explore. Thus the distinctiveness of a person's interest is crucial in making the path he follows distinctive, leading him to explore specific elements and subtopics that others, even those who share the same general interest but whose interests differ from his in specific details and perspective, thus do not wholly overlap with his, do not explore. In other cases taking an unusual step of exploration may be more the result of happenstance; or it may be a result of an individual being in an unusual environment, exposing him to elements connected with his interest that are unusual, that others are not exposed to.

Mette Pedersen is an example of someone who took one critical step in the domain of an interest. As stated in Chapter 5, Mette is interested in the intersection of literature and philosophy; even before she came to graduate school she was interested in phenomenology applied to literature. In graduate school Mette formed a more focused interest centering on what she called the idea of "the dissolution of the self": the idea that the subject, the "poetic eye," in the act of reading or contemplating art projects itself and becomes "immersed in" its object, so that the classical subject/object dichotomy breaks down. Mette described this idea as phenomenological; it lies at the intersection of literature and philosophy, thus fits with her underlying, broader interest. Mette wrote an initial paper exploring some of her ideas analyzing the dissolution of the self in the poetry of Wallace Stevens.[6]

Mette planned to write her dissertation originally on Gertrude Stein. Then, in a class on modernism, she read an article in which the author discusses the works of Stein, Wallace, and George Santayana from a phenomenological perspective, thus in a way that fit with her interest. She told me the article caught her attention and sparked a response in her: to explore the writings of Santayana, to see if his writings fit with her interest and ideas.[7] She thus read *The Sense of Beauty*, his most famous work. It was this step she took that was unusual, for Santayana is written about and discussed far less in literary studies than either Gertrude Stein or Wallace Stevens. Indeed he is best known as a philosopher, but in fact authored both philosophical and literary works — thus his work lies on the border between the two fields, where Mette's interest also lies, which seems to have been a main reason why she chose to follow the link from the article and read his work, something that most literature students, not having interests on the boundary with philosophy and particularly phenomenology, would not have done. Mette found that her ideas did in fact fit with and provide a way to interpret *The Sense of Beauty*, and further seemed to be somewhat original as an interpretation of his work. And she decided, as described in Chapter 5, to write her dissertation about him, having found that whereas a large amount had been written on Gertrude Stein not much had been written on him from a literary perspective.

Albert Einstein's Distinctive Interest and Path of Learning

Albert Einstein formed a distinctive creative interest, which took him a critical step beyond the standard world of nineteenth-century physics into philosophy, specifically epistemology, following a path of development that was, by his own

---

[6]Mette described the ideas as rooted in ideas developed by Michel Foucault in *The Order of Things: An Archaeology of the Human Sciences* (New York: Vintage Books, 1971), and Paul Fry, in particular his article "Non-construction: History, structure, and the occasion of the literary," *Yale Journal of Criticism* 1 (2) (1988): 45–64.

[7]The article is Lisa Ruddick, "Fluid symbols in American modernism: William James, Gertrude Stein, George Santayana, and Wallace Stevens," in *Allegory, Myth, and Symbol*, ed. Morton W. Bloomfield (Cambridge, MA: Harvard University Press, 1981), pp. 335–53. The fact that Santayana is included in this article shows that some literary scholars do discuss his work; Mette made it clear, however, that this is relatively rare.

304   account, crucial for the revolutionary step he took in formulating the principle of relativity.

As described in Chapter 5, Einstein hit upon a paradox at the age of sixteen: If one could follow along just behind a beam of light, moving at the speed of light, one would apparently observe a "spatially oscillatory electromagnetic field at rest" — but "there seems to be no such thing, whether on the basis of experience or according to Maxwell's equations." Over the course of the ensuing years Einstein pursued an interest growing out of and broadening from this insight. His interest had two branches. One was the physics of the electrodynamics of moving bodies, a topic at the intersection of mechanics and electromagnetism, and that expanded out to include a number of central topics of physics, that he viewed — more so over time it appears — as interconnected. The other was definitional issues and philosophical ideas about conceptions of space, time, and motion. This twofold development of his interest is clear from his "Autobiographical Notes" as well as other statements he made and supporting materials. Einstein's interest was distinctive, especially in his focus on the paradox and the way he conceived the two branches as linked, especially (though not necessarily only) via the paradox. This shaped his conception of what specific elements he chose to seek out, focus on, learn about, and think about, shaping his path of exploration, leading him to follow a distinctive path, that led him to philosophical ideas that proved crucial in helping him resolve the paradox.

There is a voluminous literature on Einstein's development and development of the relativity theory. My account here — focusing on Einstein's interest and the path he followed — distinctive to him — exploring it, giving him exposure to ideas crucial in resolving the paradox and developing the theory of relativity, is broadly consistent with John Stachel's in "'What Song the Syrens Sang': How Did Einstein Discover Special Relativity?" and, in parts, Arthur Miller's in *Albert Einstein's Special Theory of Relativity: Emergence (1905) and Early Interpretation (1905–1911)* — though in details, including my specification of Einstein's interest, and interpretation it is distinctive.[8]

During his years as a student Einstein read many standard German works in contemporary physics, in mechanics, electromagnetism, thermodynamics,

[8]John Stachel, "'What song the Syrens sang': How did Einstein discover special relativity?" *Einstein From 'B' to 'Z'*, ed. John Stachel (Boston: Birkhäuser, 2002), pp. 157–69. Originally published in Italian. Arthur I. Miller, *Albert Einstein's Special Theory of Relativity: Emergence (1905) and Early Interpretation (1905–1911)* (Reading, MA: Addison-Wesley, 1981). See also Robert Rynasiewicz, "The construction of the Special Theory: Some queries and considerations," in *Einstein: The Formative Years, 1879–1909*, ed. Don Howard and John Stachel (Boston: Birkhäuser, 2000), pp. 159–201.

the physics of emission and radiation, and the physics of metals. He read major works by the major figures in German physics of this period — including very likely (all titles are English translations) Hertz's *Electric Waves* and *The Principles of Mechanics*, and printed lectures by Gustav Kirchhoff and Ludwig Boltzmann. Gerald Holton points to him having read as a basic text Föppl's *Introduction to Maxwell's Theory of Electricity*. And he read in the major journals in the field.[9] Thus Einstein read widely, though he was not necessarily conversant with all recent work. As an example showing his knowledge, Arthur Miller calls attention to a note by Joseph Sauter, a colleague of Einstein's at the Swiss Patent Office, in which he recollects a conversation in which he and Einstein discussed attempts to provide a mechanical foundation for Maxwell's equation, an approach being pursued at the time, for example by Boltzmann — as he recounts it Einstein was quite familiar with this line of inquiry, which in fact he viewed as wrong-headed.[10]

Einstein writes in his "Autobiographical Notes" that "from the very beginning" he recognized that the basic Galilean principle of relativity should apply to whatever theoretical model was developed for describing electrodynamics — that the same laws of physics would apply to an observer at rest relative to a light beam and an observer in motion. Thus, from the beginning he approached the search for a way to resolve the paradox in a way linking it with concepts of classical physics, in particular the principle of relativity which is fundamental to and a basic constraint on transforming equations across different inertial frames in uniform motion with respect to one another. Another set of foundational concepts for classical physics is Newton's conception of absolute space and time, which we can presume Einstein studied as well. Newton states in the *Principia* (English translation): "Absolute, true, and mathematical time, in and of itself and of its own nature, without reference to anything external, flows uniformly and by another name is called duration. Relative, apparent, and common time is any sensible and external measure (precise or imprecise) of duration by means of motion; such a measure — for example, an hour, a day, a month, a year — is commonly used instead of true time." He gives a

[9]See the bibliography and annotations to *The Collected Papers of Albert Einstein*, Vol. 1, *The Early Years, 1879–1902*, ed. John Stachel (Princeton, NJ: Princeton University Press, 1987). Arthur Miller provides a guide to the texts Einstein is likely to have read in *Albert Einstein's Special Theory of Relativity*, pp. 126–27. Gerald Holton makes his case for Einstein having read and been influenced by Föppl in *Thematic Origins of Scientific Thought; Kepler to Einstein*, chap. 6. Philipp Frank, who wrote an early biography of Einstein, describes him, as Miller notes, "devouring" physics texts in college (*Albert Einstein's Special Theory of Relativity*, p. 126). For further background on Einstein's early development see the essays in *Einstein: The Formative Years, 1879–1909*.

[10]*Albert Einstein's Special Theory of Relativity*, p. 126.

similar definition for absolute space, and also for absolute motion, which he distinguishes from relative motion. He also discusses the difficulty of measuring absolute time. "It is possible that there is no uniform motion by which time may have an exact measure. All motions can be accelerated and retarded [thus made not uniform], but the flow of absolute time cannot be changed."[11]

In fact Einstein does not appear to have engaged with these definitions of space and time and the principle of relativity at first. Rather, his initial focus was grappling with the concept of the ether. Initially Einstein definitely seems to have believed in the existence of an ether and its importance for the propagation of electromagnetic radiation. This is shown by the memo he wrote at age sixteen, in which he describes experiments he has devised to measure the "deformation" of the ether caused by a magnetic field. Later, however, he renounced his belief in the ether — possibly in stages — coming to believe in the idea of electromagnetic radiation as propagating through empty space. A letter to Mileva Marić dated 1899 contains statements showing the shift to this view: "The introduction of the term 'ether' into the theories of electricity led to the notion of a medium of whose motion one can speak without being able, I believe, to associate a physical meaning with this statement. I think that the electric forces can be directly defined only for empty space, also emphasized by Hertz." He continues, further on: "Electrodynamics would then be the theory of the motion of moving electricities and magnetisms in empty space: . . ."[12] Einstein continued to have some interest in experiments to detect the effect of the ether on light propagation.[13] But gradually he seems to have lost interest in the ether and given it up entirely, and his attention shifted to different conceptual issues — including a focus on epistemology.

Einstein is reported to have read and been absorbed by Kant's *Critique of Pure Reason* when he was thirteen, thus had an early interest in epistemology, which may have been a factor in his now returning to it. In going back to it he was influenced, especially early on in his thinking, by the ideas of Ernst Mach, who was well known for his critique of assumptions of classical physics, notably the ideas of absolute space and time, which he viewed as "metaphysical" nonempirical concepts that should have no role in physical theory, which must be based on phenomena and states accessible by the senses, such as relative motion. In his "Autobiographical Notes" Einstein writes: "It was Ernst Mach who, in his *History of Mechanics* [*Science of Mechanics*] shook this

[11] Isaac Newton, *The Principia; Mathematical Principles of Natural Philosophy*, trans. by I. Bernard Cohen and Anne Whitman (Berkeley, CA: University of California Press, 1999), pp. 408–10.
[12] *Collected Papers of Albert Einstein*, trans. by Anna Beck, 1, pp. 130–31.
[13] Ibid., p. 224.

[my] dogmatic faith [in classical mechanics as the basis of physics]; this book exercised a profound influence on me in this regard when I was a student."[14]

At Bern, while working at the Swiss Patent Office, Einstein went further, exploring further in philosophy and epistemology. We know some of what he read from records kept of books he and a group of friends read in their Olympia Academy — a reading and discussion group they formed. Their reading included Plato, Spinoza's *Ethics*, John Stuart Mill's *System of Logic*, David Hume's *A Treatise of Human Nature*, Richard Avenarius's *Critique of Pure Experience*, and Henri Poincaré's *Science and Hypothesis*.[15] This is a reading list that would hardly be surprising for a college student engaged in a general course of studies. But for Einstein, now in his twenties, working, and at an advanced level in his understanding of modern physics, it is striking. It is hard to imagine many other young physicists of his age group reading a similar set of works. Striking especially are the non-German philosophers, seemingly unusual reading for a young German scientist at the time. It seems very likely that in moving to explore more deeply in philosophy and epistemology Einstein was led by his interest and conception of interest, by the paradox and his awareness of its twin roots, not just in physics, but also in conceptions of space, time, and motion. Having recognized from the start the importance of preserving the principle of relativity, he was led, intuitively, to explore more deeply conceptions of space and time that are integral to and a foundation for defining this principle.

Einstein thus followed a path of exploration that was clearly unusual, guided by his interest — and it turned out to be crucial for his intellectual development. In particular he was led to the work of David Hume — and Hume, with but also beyond the others, seems to have been critical for his thinking. Einstein writes

[14]Albert Einstein, "Autobiographical Notes," in *Albert Einstein: Philosopher-Scientist*, p. 21. For Mach see the second revised and enlarged edition English translation of 1902, most likely similar to the edition Einstein would have read: Ernst Mach, *The Science of Mechanics; A Critical and Historical Account of its Principles*, trans. by Thomas J. McCormack (Chicago: Open Court Publishing Co., 1902). Mach presents Newton's definitions of absolute time and space and motion and his view that they have no empirical meaning in chapter II, section vi, "Newton's Views of Time, Space, and Motion." He presents some further thoughts in chapter IV, section ii, "Theological, Animistic, and Mystical Points of View in Mechanics." Einstein writes that he sees Mach's "greatness in his incorruptible skepticism and independence"; it seems, at least from one interpretation, that Mach helped him, by example, gain a sense of the possibility of making a radical critique of existing theory.

[15]A list of many works they read and description of the group is in *The Collected Papers of Albert Einstein*, Vol. 2; *The Swiss Years: Writings, 1900–1909*, ed. John Stachel (Princeton, NJ: Princeton University Press, 1989), pp. xxiv–xxv.

in his "Autobiographical Notes" (p. 53) that his "critical reasoning" about time and simultaneity was "decisively furthered" "by the reading of David Hume's and Ernst Mach's philosophical writings." In two other statements he made he assigns a greater role to Hume, stating that reading Hume had the greatest direct influence on his thinking. In a letter to Michele Besso in 1948 he states: "As for the influence of Mach on my thinking, it has certainly been very great. I remember very well how, during my early years as a student, you directed my attention to his treatise on mechanics and to his theory of heat, and how these two works made a deep impression on me. Frankly, however, I cannot clearly see to what extent they affected my own work. So far as I can recall, David Hume had a greater direct influence on me; . . ."[16] Much earlier, in a letter in 1915, discussing the influence of positivism on his thought, he writes that it had "a great influence on" his efforts, then writes of this influence: "E. Mach, and even more so Hume, whose *Treatise of Human Nature* I had studied avidly and with admiration shortly before discovering the theory of relativity. It is very possible that without these philosophical studies I would not have arrived at the solution."[17]

Einstein did not state the exact path through which he was led to read Hume's *Treatise*. There are in fact a number of possibilities. Mach mentions Hume in several places, though strictly with regard to Hume's critique of our notion of causality, and this may have led Einstein to Hume. As an alternative path Karl Pearson cites Hume specifically on conceptions of space and time in his chapter on "Space and Time" in *The Grammar of Science*, a book also listed as having been read by Einstein and his group. Avenarius also cites Hume, but

[16] Albert Einstein and Michele Besso, *Correspondance; 1903–1955*, Traduction, Pierre Speziali (Paris: Hermann, 1972), Einstein to Besso, January 6, 1948, pp. 390–92.

[17] Letter to Moritz Schlick, 14 December 1915, printed in *Albert Einstein: Collected Papers*, Vol. 8, *The Berlin Years, Correspondence, 1914–1918*; English translation of selected texts; trans. by Ann M. Hentschel (Princeton, NJ: Princeton University Press, 1998), pp. 161–62. Not all scholars credit Hume as having been crucial for Einstein, despite what Einstein himself said. In part this seems to be because they associate Hume with his famous critique of causality, whereas as I discuss in the main text it seems far more likely that when Einstein stated that Hume had a "direct influence" on him it was through his description of our conceptions of time, and possibly space. John Stachel does call attention to Hume, noting that Einstein "was engaged in a careful reading of Hume" around the time he developed the theory of relativity — "'What song the Syrens sang'," p. 166. Also, John Norton, in "How Hume and Mach Helped Einstein Find Special Relativity," manuscript, 2004, discusses the importance of Hume and his conceptions of space and time for Einstein.

just once, towards the end of his two-part work.[18] Einstein may have been led to Hume not specifically through seeking to learn about Hume's conceptions of space and time, but by Hume's general reputation as a skeptical philosopher, possibly by his famous critique of the idea of causality noted by Mach. But when he read Hume it was Hume's description of our conception of time that most influenced him — at least that is my reading of his development in the relativity paper (see below). He was, in any event, led to Hume through following a distinctive path, exploring his distinctive interest, venturing well outside the ordinary domain of exploration for most physicists.[19]

Einstein never stated, as far as I know, what specific sections and arguments of Hume's *Treatise* had the deepest impact on him and most directly influenced his thinking leading to the relativity theory. I believe we can surmise, however, that it was Hume's discussion of the concept of time, which is conjoined with his discussion of space in "Of the ideas of space and time" in Book I, Part II, that had a direct, critical influence on his thinking. Hume focuses in this section on the basis of our conceptions of space and time. He argues that we have no direct sense knowledge of space and time as abstractions, but rather conceive space only through our sense perceptions of objects and time only through sequences of events and changes in state.

Hume first discusses our conception of space, arguing that our knowledge of space comes only through our knowledge of objects that we see and touch. Then he turns to our sense of time, arguing that though the "idea of time" is "an abstract idea," "yet [it] is represented in the fancy by some particular individual idea of a determinate quantity and quality." "As 'tis from the disposition of visible and tangible objects we receive the idea of space, so from the succession of ideas and impressions we form the idea of time, nor is it possible for time alone ever to make its appearance, or be taken notice of by the mind." Thus, time "is always discover'd by some *perceivable* succession of changeable objects." He argues that we cannot form any conception of time apart from a definite sequence of events — that time has no independent meaning separate from such a sequence:

[18] Karl Pearson, *The Grammar of Science* (Gloucester, MA: Peter Smith, 1969 (first published 1892)). Pearson mentions Hume several times in "Space and Time" and cites him in his list of relevant literature at the end of the chapter. Richard Avenarius, *Kritik der Reinen Erfahrung* (Leipzig: part (i), Fues's Verlag (R. Reisland), 1888, part (ii), O.R. Reisland, 1890), ii, p. 243.

[19] In reading Plato and Spinoza Einstein and his friends were clearly exploring somewhat broadly in philosophy. But it is still noteworthy he was led to Hume and his work in epistemology — showing the guidance of his interest.

310   The idea of time is not deriv'd from a particular impression mixed up with others, and plainly distinguishable from them; but arises altogether from the manner, in which impressions appear to the mind, without making one of the number. Five notes play'd on a flute give us the impression and idea of time; tho' time be not a sixth impression, which presents itself to the hearing or any other of the senses. Nor is it a sixth impression, which the mind by reflection finds in itself. . . . . [T]he mind only takes notice of the *manner*, in which the different sounds make their appearance [i.e., their sequence]; and that it may afterwards consider without considering these particular sounds, but may conjoin it with any other objects. The ideas of some objects certainly it must have, nor is it possible for it without these ideas ever to arrive at any conception of time; which since it appears not as any primary distinct impression, can plainly be nothing but different ideas, or impressions, or objects dispos'd in a certain manner, that is, succeeding each other.[20]

It follows by the same argument that the "idea of duration is always deriv'd from a succession of changeable objects," of events or changes of state, and has no definition apart from its measurement in terms of such a sequence, so that if there is no change of state or sequence of events there is no sense of duration, of time passing.[21]

Hume focuses on describing how we define time and duration concretely through sequences of definite impressions, either events or changes of state, and argues that we have no sense of time outside of this. One can find brief similar accounts of defining time in terms of sequences of events in both Mach's *Science of Mechanics* and Poincaré's *Science and Hypothesis* and "The Measure of Time," which Einstein may also have read. However, in these works the emphasis is in general more on criticism and less on a constructive definition of time, and certainly at least in my view less clear than Hume, especially about how to define time.[22] Einstein might have gained awareness of a constructive

[20]David Hume, A *Treatise of Human Nature* (Penguin Books: London, 1984 (first published 1739–40)), pp. 83–88, 113–14.
    [21]Hume also argues that our sense of duration is subjective, dependent on our state, for example whether we are asleep or awake.
    [22]Mach makes the point that we measure time by the changes in state of objects, but he does so only in brief, and his reasoning is less clear; in particular, it is entangled with his idea that "all things in the world are connected with one another and depend on one another," and the idea that time is measured by the connection between our memory and sense impressions, a more psychological approach — neither directly relevant for Einstein it seems to me. See *The Science of Mechanics*, pp. 223–38. Poincaré discusses time measurement in "The Measure of Time," included in the English translation of *The Value of Science*, in *The Foundations of Science*, trans. by George Bruce Halsted (Lancaster, PA: The Science Press, 1946), Chapter VIII. Peter Galison states that a large excerpt from the work was appended to the German translation of *Science and Hypothesis* and thus may have been available to Einstein; Peter Galison, *Einstein's*

approach for defining time from either, but because they do not focus on it and are not as clear as Hume it was less natural for him to do so. In any event, based on his own account it seems that he did not, but rather gained such awareness from Hume.[23]

In stating that Hume had the greatest "direct" influence on him in his development of the special theory of relativity I believe Einstein means that he gained from Hume an awareness and appreciation that time and space exist only in being constructively defined — leading to a focus on a constructive approach to define them. This is the viewpoint he himself adopts in his special relativity paper — indeed it is the basis of the crucial first step he takes, defining time in inertial frames, through a system of measurement in which clocks in a frame are placed at different locations and light beam signals are sent from one clock to another to synchronize them. This in turn opens the way to time being measured differently by different observers, a possibility Hume does not consider, but which fits naturally with his description. (Poincaré also focuses attention on measurement in *Science and Hypothesis*, for example in his chapter "Experience and Geometry.")[24]

Several other arguments Hume makes may well also have appealed to Einstein, contributing to Hume's influence on his thinking. Hume argues that our conceptions of space and time are not infinitely divisible, but rather there must be some finite limit of divisibility beyond which we cannot go. This is likely to have resonated with Einstein, for it fits with Planck's idea of energy quanta, which Einstein stated that he recognized as revolutionary in

Clocks, Poincaré's Maps: Empires of Time (New York: W. W. Norton & Company, 2003), pp. 238–39. Poincaré's approach is more pragmatic and never directly questions the existence of an absolute time, just our ability to measure it.

[23]Of course it may also have been a question of timing; he read Hume later it appears, and perhaps at a time when he was receptive to this approach.

[24]There were other accounts describing a constructive approach to time measurement given before Einstein's that are important to note. Emil Cohn gave the suggestion to use clocks to define time in an article published in 1904 (see Olivier Darrigol, *Electrodynamics from Ampère to Einstein* (Oxford: Oxford University Press, 2000), pp. 366–69, 382). There is no clear evidence Einstein was aware of his work before developing his theory. Poincaré, in his essay for a volume in honor of Lorentz published in 1900, gives a definition of simultaneity defined by observers in an inertial frame moving with respect to the ether sending light signals back and forth, ignoring their motion with respect to the ether, assuming the light beams travel at the same velocity in both directions, using these measurements to define the local time in their coordinate system. In Poincaré's worldview, holding on to the concept of absolute time, they thus make a small error in their definition of time (see *Electrodynamics from Ampère to Einstein*, pp. 358–60). While some believe that Einstein may have read Poincaré's essay prior to his breakthrough he himself did not say so.

312   its implications from when he first learned about it, shortly after Planck published his papers on the quantum theory in 1900–01.[25] Hume also discusses the
inherent limitation of measurement, our inability to measure duration and
length precisely. This viewpoint also may have resonated with Einstein as he
went back to his paradox. He stated later that he believed that the principle
of relativity was not apparent to humans previously because we live in a world
in which all relative speeds are low compared with the velocity of light, so
that for all practical purposes light signals travel "instantly" from one place to
another — so that we have no direct experience of the very high relative speeds
at which relativistic effects become important.[26]

Einstein thus followed a distinctive path of intellectual development guided
by and exploring his interest: studying epistemology — reaching so far as the
philosophy of Hume — concurrently with electromagnetism and electrodynamics, as well as a host of other physics topics, all of which he viewed, in part
at least, as interrelated, including Planck's quantum theory, thermodynamics, radiation, and molecular motion. It follows logically, and is a plausible
reconstruction of his development, that as a result a paired set of cognitive
structures built up in his mind. One contained ideas, theories, assumptions,
and experimental results in physics, the other philosophical ideas, focused on
epistemology and conceptions of space and time, including Hume's approach
to defining time and space. At the center of his interest, critically, was the
paradox — which, as he described his development, remained on his mind
throughout these years. The paradox was not only a focus of his thinking, but

[25] I hasten to add that Einstein never made any comment on Hume's discussion
that space and time are not infinitely divisible. Einstein's statement that he recognized
Planck's work to be revolutionary from the start is in "Autobiographical Notes," p. 45.

[26] *A Treatise of Human Nature*, part II, section iv, pp. 88–102; see also section v,
pp. 102–14. In evaluating Hume's influence on Einstein it is important to distinguish
Einstein's philosophical views when he was young and wrestling with the puzzle of
electrodynamics and related matters from his views later in life. Later Einstein articulated a philosophy of the formulation of scientific theories as based on conceptions we
are able to form freely in the mind, that are based on empirical data but not directly
tied to them. He describes this view, for example, in his "Reply to Criticisms" in *Albert Einstein: Philosopher-Scientist*, pp. 678–79. There he links his approach to Kant.
We should not identify this mature position as describing his mindset earlier. Indeed
Einstein himself never states that his early position was similar to his later view — to
the contrary, at one point in his reply, responding to an individual who suggested that
he was a follower of Kant from early on, Einstein comments, "I did not grow up in the
Kantian tradition, but came to understand the truly valuable which is to be found in his
doctrine, alongside of errors which today are quite obvious, only quite late" (p. 680).
This is at least consistent with the view that around 1905 Einstein was perhaps close to
the position of Hume, more so than later.

also the crucial, central point of interconnection of the two conceptual structures. This nexus — the paradox and the set of elements linked with it, especially philosophical conceptions of space and time — was distinctive to him. Below I describe — based on his own description and interpretation of his description and special relativity paper — the path that it seems most likely he followed, drawing on this nexus as the crucial basis, in developing the theory of relativity.

Einstein's particular interest and the way he pursued it — the path he followed, the works he read, and concepts and problems he had in his mind as he pursued it — were different from the interests and paths, thus conceptual development, of other physicists of the time working on electromagnetic theory. Hendrik Lorentz, whose equations of transformation from one inertial system to another are fundamental to Einstein's theory, focused on developing a model based on a theory of ions as the carriers of electric charge and basis of electromagnetic phenomena. He developed the idea of a "local" time and his transformation enabled calculation of physical processes in different inertial frames in motion relative to one another. Lorentz focused entirely on physical phenomena and theories and seems to have been markedly less interested in philosophy, thus does not appear to have explored philosophical ideas, notably conceptions of space and time.[27] His lack of interest in the philosophical basis for Einstein's theory is shown by his comment several years after Einstein published his theory, as Miller paraphrases it, "that the two theories were equivalent both mathematically and in their empirical predictions; consequently the choice between them, [continuing in Lorentz's own words] 'and especially the question of true time can be handed over to the theory of knowledge.'"[28] He remained wedded to the notion of the ether and the Newtonian conception of absolute space and time, even as he developed extremely innovative physical-mathematical theories. His failure to be interested in and explore philosophy likely contributed to his being unable to overcome this conservatism and consider alternative conceptions of space and time, thus preventing him from moving to reexpress his theory directly in terms of time and space measurement.

A number of physicists focused on building atomic or microscopic foundations for electromagnetic theory, thus on development of theories different in kind from the one Einstein ultimately worked out, in general in a more technical way less rooted in philosophical concepts; their work is reviewed by

[27]I have found no record indicating he read Hume. His *Collected Papers* evince a focus entirely on physics.

[28]*Albert Einstein's Special Theory of Relativity*, pp. 255–56. The wording implies that the choice lies outside the province of physics and his own interests and expertise.

Olivier Darrigol in *Electrodynamics from Ampère to Einstein*. To give one example, Max Abraham developed a mathematical model of the electron linked to a theory of electromagnetic phenomena in the years just after 1900. His work exhibits technical grasp and knowledge of the physics literature and physical phenomena as then understood, with the possible exception, as Darrigol describes it, of not taking Planck's revolutionary quantum theory into account. It is fundamentally different in approach than the approach Einstein pursued, not directly concerned with conceptions of space and time, not grappling with the meaning of these concepts. Others, including Mach and Hertz, were from an older generation and were not active (Hertz died in 1894) at a time when the accumulated evidence and conceptual development made it most feasible to develop the theory of relativity.[29]

Henri Poincaré is generally considered to be the individual other than Einstein who came closest to developing the theory of relativity. In fact he articulated a principle of relativity; but he did not develop the theory of relativity that Einstein did. Poincaré remained wedded to the notion of the ether. And, while he recognized the puzzles of measurement of simultaneity, and his parables of alternative geometric systems clearly show his grasp of the possibility of different systems for describing reality, it does not seem he gave up the notion of absolute time and space.[30] His personality, stature at the time, and being of an earlier generation all may have had a role in why he did not give up conventional notions and develop relativity more in its full, radical implications. Two additional factors, rooted in the difference between his interests and that of Einstein, seem also to have been important — to have influenced his path of exploration, the kinds of problems he chose to work on, how he thought

[29]Mach was concerned with the epistemological foundations of scientific theories. But he remained wedded to the ether, and his approach to integrating philosophical reasoning with physics was more critical, his concern with the psychology of perception made his views more complex, and he was less given to the simple, daring constructive approach Einstein pursued. Emil Cohn developed a theory of electrodynamics that was field-based. His theory, however, as Darrigol describes it, continued to assume an absolute space and time, relevant for mechanical processes. See *Electrodynamics from Ampère to Einstein*, pp. 366–69.

[30]Poincaré describes parables and alternative geometries in *Science and Hypothesis* (New York: Dover Publications, 1952), part II, chaps. III, IV, and V. He discusses the principle of relativity and introduces an approach of using light beams to measure time at different places and communicate in *The Value of Science*, chap. VIII. He explicitly states that when two points are in relative motion their time measurements will differ, then makes clear he still believes in a true time separate from this "local" time measurement: "The watches adjusted in that way will not mark, therefore, the true time; they will mark what may be called the *local time*, so that one of them will be slow of the other" (pp. 305–7).

about and tried to solve problems, and his beliefs. One is that he was far more pragmatic in his approach than Einstein.[31] Poincaré, in the context of physics and practical problems, seems to have adopted the view that there are always a multitude of alternative theories available, and one should choose to work with the one that is most useful for problems at hand. Thus he did not explore foundational concepts in philosophy with an eye towards their influencing theory construction the way Einstein ultimately seems to have used Hume's fundamental conceptualization. This practical bent is probably an important reason why Poincaré never saw the need to abandon absolute time and space; as long as theory could be used practically he saw no need to do so, or, more fundamentally, to explore the meaning of doing so. The other difference is that, though interested in time and space measurement, Poincaré did not have the paradox in mind that Einstein had hit on, and thus his interest in time and space was not as closely linked to electrodynamics, but rather more separate, more of a distinct interest domain.[32]

Sequences of Experiences and Encounters

A third pattern of exploration is exploring a domain of interest through structured sequences. Such sequences do not unfold, like connected paths do, one element leading to the next. Rather, they are constructed or coalesce as a whole. They come about in two main ways. One is through an individual arranging a sequence of encounters or experiences in advance, guided by his conception of his interest, that he believes is likely to be fruitful in advancing his learning and generative of ways to develop his interest creatively. Robert Kaufman is an example of someone who arranged such a sequence, as described below. The other is less planned out: an individual does not plan out a sequence of experiences or encounters so deliberately, but a sequence of experiences and encounters he has, for example guided by his interest, naturally coalesces. Charles Darwin is an example of someone who followed this pattern in the sequences of experiences he had and observations he made journeying about South America.

As described in Chapter 6 Robert formed an interest in Romanticism, in particular the works of Keats and Shelley, as the genesis of modern Left critical

[31] Peter Galison's discussion of Poincaré's training at the École Polytechnique and career in *Einstein's Clocks, Poincaré's Maps* makes this evident.

[32] It is noteworthy in this regard that Poincaré's discussion of alternative geometries is in part II of *Science and Hypothesis*, while his discussion of electromagnetism and optics is at the end of the book in part IV, thus the two discussions are quite separate. Similarly, his discussion of "The Measure of Time" in *The Value of Science* (*Foundations*, pp. 205–355), is in part I, "The Mathematical Sciences," whereas his discussion of physics, including relativity and local time, is in part II, "The Physical Sciences."

thought, and in the origins and evolution of Left critical thought about the relationship between artistic and literary experience and the development of political consciousness. Robert seems to have recognized intuitively that a powerful way for him to pursue his interest was to follow an approach to learning that would enable him readily to juxtapose and thus relate ideas and works from the Romantic and modern time periods. He told me that from "early on" it was "very clear" to him that "thinking about the [two] periods together worked very well." Tracing his path of development over the following several years it is clear that he in fact pursued such a strategy, deliberately, and in part through force of circumstances.

Based on his description, his learning process during these years consisted of three successive phases. Initially, he read widely in modern Left critical thought. His initial reading was broad, gaining familiarity with a range of thinkers; he mentioned in particular Frederic Jameson, who is himself quite wide-ranging. From what he told me it appears that, following his interest, he was especially cognizant of and learned about alternative theories and beliefs about the relationship between literary activity and political consciousness.

The second phase of Robert's learning was the period leading up to his oral exams. During this time he focused on reading poetry. He set as one of his orals topics the work of Shelley, and told me he concentrated his time on this.[33] Describing why he chose Shelley he said he knew Shelley had been an influence on Marx, DuBois, and Left modernism — thus guided by his interest he was thinking about Shelley and Romanticism as an influence on later Left critical thought. As it turned out, in studying for orals Robert focused also on Keats, the natural partner with Shelley, with whose work he had been less familiar. As he read Keats and Shelley, Robert compared their ideas about art and literature and their potential influence on political consciousness, and compared his interpretation of their conceptions of this relationship with the way their conceptions are portrayed in later criticism. These comparisons sparked a pair of creative insights which I describe in the next section.

The third phase of Robert's learning process happened after his oral exams. During this phase his focus shifted back to the modern period. Guided both by his interest and the ideas he had formed in phase two, he said he focused on differences in viewpoint and debate among members of the Frankfurt School about the relationship between literary and artistic activity and political consciousness and action. During this period he had a further insight, linking this debate within the Frankfurt School back to a similar difference in viewpoint

[33]Robert's two other orals topics were Romanticism and modernism — thus again he structured his learning process so as to juxtapose works from the two periods. But he seems to have spent less time preparing for these two topics.

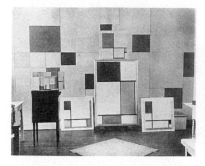

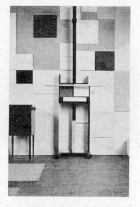

FIGURE 1A Photo of Mondrian's studio, 26 rue du Départ, Paris. Shown in the photo are (on left) the maquette for *L'Ephémère est éternel*, 1926, and four paintings (from left) *Composition with Red, Yellow, and Blue*, 1929, Stedelijk Museum, Amsterdam, *Composition with Red, Blue, and Yellow*, 1928, private collection, *Composition No. I*, and (above) *Composition No. II*, to be sent to the A.S.B. exhibition in Amsterdam in November, 1929. Photograph presumably by Charles Karsten. ©2006 Mondrian/Holtzman Trust c/o HCR International, Warrenton, VA.

FIGURE 1B Photo of Mondrian's studio, 26 rue du Départ. Photograph by unknown photographer. Published in *Das Kunstblatt* of March, 1930. ©2006 Mondrian/ Holtzman Trust c/o HCR International, Warrenton, VA.

FIGURE 1C   Photograph of reconstruction of Mondrian's studio created by a work group led by Frans Postma; not dated (late 1980s–mid-1990s). ©Frans Postma.

FIGURE 1D   Second photograph of reconstruction of Mondrian's studio created by the work group led by Frans Postma; not dated (late 1980s–mid-1990s). ©Frans Postma.

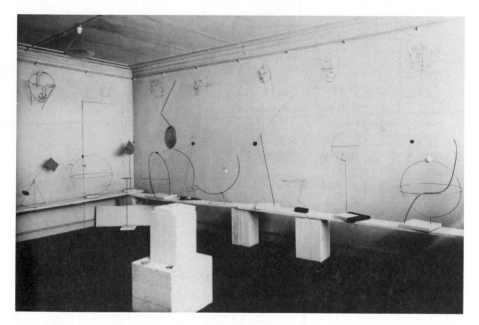

FIGURE 2   Photograph of Calder's April 1931 exhibit at Galerie Percier, Paris. Reproduced by courtesy of the Estate of Alexander Calder.

FIGURE 3   Series of paintings by Piet Mondrian showing his development in painting style over the period 1914–1921.*

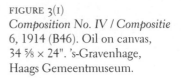

FIGURE 3(I)
Composition No. IV / Compositie
6, 1914 (B46). Oil on canvas,
34 ⅝ × 24". 's-Gravenhage,
Haags Gemeentmuseum.

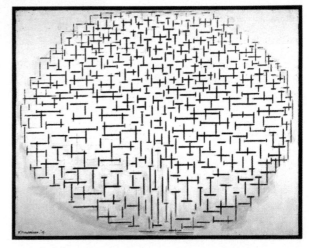

FIGURE 3(II)
Compositie 10 in Zwart
Wit (*Composition 10 in*
Black and White), 1915
(B79). Oil on canvas,
33 ½ × 42 ½". Otterlo,
Kröller-Müller Museum.

FIGURE 3(III)
Composition, 1916 (B80). Oil
on canvas, 46 ⅞ × 29 ⅝". New
York, Solomon R. Guggenheim
Museum.

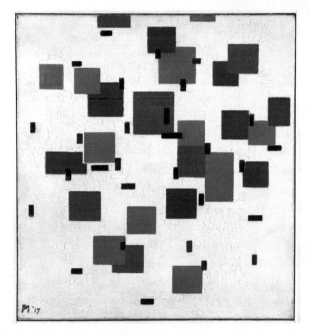

FIGURE 3(IV)
Composition in Color
A, 1917 (B84). Oil on
canvas, 19 ⅞ × 17 ⅞".
Otterlo, Kröller-Müller
Museum.

FIGURE 3(V)   *Composition with Color Planes 2*, 1917 (B88). Oil on canvas, 18 ⅞ × 24 ¼". Rotterdam, Museum Boijmans Van Beuningen.

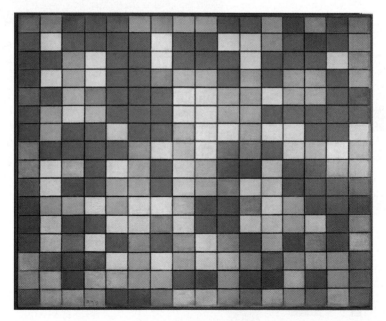

FIGURE 3(VI)   *Composition with Grid 9: Checkerboard Composition in Light Colors*, 1919 (B103). Oil on canvas, 33 ⅞ × 41 ¾". 's-Gravenhage, Haags Gemeentmuseum.

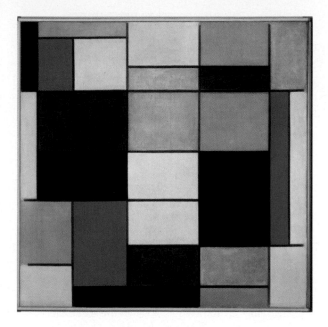

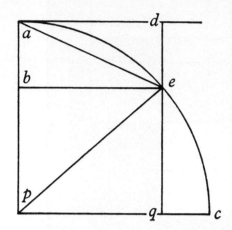

FIGURE 4A   Diagram depicting Newton's method for computing the inverse sine function. Angle *ape* is computed by determining the area of the pie-shaped wedge *ape* lying inside the circle and comparing this area to the area for a 90° angle. The area of the pie-shaped wedge is determined by subtraction: it equals the area under the circle integrated from *p* to *q*, thus area *aeqp*, minus the area of triangle *peq*. The area of triangle *peq* is given by the length of *pq*, which is *x*, multiplied times the height *qe*, given by $\sqrt{1-x^2}$ (from the formula for a circle), divided by 2. Reproduced from *The Mathematical Papers of Isaac Newton*, Volume I, 1664–1666, ed. D.T. Whiteside, Cambridge: Cambridge University Press, 1967, p. 108.

1st. $+x$ ×1.	1.	1.	1.	1.	1.	1.	1.	1.	1.	1.	1.	1.	
2d. $-\dfrac{x^3}{3}$ ×0.	$\dfrac{1}{2}$.	1.	$\dfrac{3}{2}$.	2.	$\dfrac{5}{2}$.	3.	$\dfrac{7}{2}$.	4.	$\dfrac{9}{2}$.	5.	$\dfrac{11}{2}$.	6.	
3d. $+\dfrac{1}{5}x^5$ ×0.	$-\dfrac{1}{8}$.	0.	$\dfrac{3}{8}$.	1.	$\dfrac{15}{8}$.	3.	$\dfrac{35}{8}$.	6.	$\dfrac{63}{8}$.	10.	$\dfrac{99}{8}$.	15.	
4. $-\dfrac{1}{7}x^7$ ×0.	$+\dfrac{1}{16}$.	0.	$-\dfrac{1}{16}$.	0.	$\dfrac{5}{16}$.	1.	$\dfrac{35}{16}$.	4.	$\dfrac{105}{16}$.	10.	$\dfrac{231}{16}$.	20.	
5. $+\dfrac{1}{9}x^9$ ×0.	$-\dfrac{3}{128}$.	0.	$\dfrac{3}{128}$.	0.	$\dfrac{-5}{128}$.	0.	$\dfrac{35}{128}$.	1.	$\dfrac{315}{128}$.	5.	$\dfrac{1155}{128}$.	15.	
6. $-\dfrac{1}{11}x^{11}$ ×0.	$\dfrac{7}{256}$.	0.	$\dfrac{-3}{256}$.	0.	$\dfrac{3}{256}$.	0.	$\dfrac{-7}{256}$.	0.	$\dfrac{63}{256}$.	1.	$\dfrac{693}{256}$.	6.	
7. $\dfrac{1}{13}x^{13}$ ×0.	$\dfrac{-21}{1024}$.	0.	$\dfrac{7}{1024}$.	0.	$\dfrac{-5}{1024}$.	0.	$\dfrac{7}{1024}$.	0.	$\dfrac{-21}{1024}$.	0.	$\dfrac{231}{1024}$.	1.	$\dfrac{3003}{1024}$.

FIGURE 4B   Depiction of one of the tables Newton drew to compute the area under the circle, the basis of his discovery of the binomial theorem. The rows are defined by odd powers of *x*, specifically, a row is defined by x^n/n with signs alternating, as shown. The columns define the function being integrated: $\int_0^x (1-t^2)^r\, dt$. In alternating columns, the table includes both integer values of *r*, for which the pattern of coefficients fits Pascal's Triangle, and half powers of *r*: thus the columns represent (as powers of *r*) 0, ½, 1, ¾, 2, and so on. Newton is interested in the coefficients for *r* = ½. Reproduced from *The Mathematical Papers of Isaac Newton*, I, p. 107.

he had identified between Keats and Shelley in phase two — I describe this as well in the next section.

Robert's program of study led him to focus on the different subdomains of his interest in turn — first, modern Left criticism broadly, then the poetry of Keats and Shelley, then modern Left critical thought with a more specific focus — a pattern which was conducive to generating the creative insights he had.

Charles Darwin's pattern of travel in and around South America generated a sequence of experiences he had and observations he made that mirrored his interest in the geographic extent of species and the similarities and differences in characteristics and behaviors between members of closely allied species and varieties having neighboring ranges of extent or inhabiting similar niches in their environments. Indeed this sequence was almost certainly vital in spurring his interest, as described in Chapter 3, driving him to think about and conceptualize it and explore it.

Darwin's sequence of experiences and observations was determined principally by the path the *Beagle* followed as it circumnavigated South America, as noted already in Chapter 3. This path was remarkable in exposing him both to great extremes of climate and life-forms and a series of juxtapositions of neighboring climatic zones. The *Beagle* first made landfall at Bahia, Brazil, in the tropics, which were stunning to him for their incredible richness and diversity of life-forms and sheer novelty. From there, the ship journeyed south to Rio de Janeiro — still tropical, but, he notes, clearly different in its life-forms from Bahia, as noted in Chapter 3.[34] From Rio the *Beagle* journeyed south again, to more temperate zones — to Monte Video, where he remarked on seeing an animal with two "small hind legs or rather fins" that "marks the passage by which Nature joins the Lizards to the Snakes" — noting the transition between kinds. Then it voyaged on to Buenos Aires and Baía Blanca, then back to Monte Video and Buenos Aires — with the result that the different life-forms he saw in these different places naturally would have been juxtaposed in his mind. The ship then journeyed south along the coast of Patagonia to Tierra del Fuego. The climate here was similar to England, but Darwin notes on his very first visit to shore, "the little I then saw showed how different this country is from the corresponding zone in the Northern Hemisphere," with a "thick wood of evergreen," so that again he made comparisons. He was moved by the awe-inspiring vistas, the gloom, what he describes as a "savage Magnificence," and the comparison with the tropics. It is clear that going from the tropics to

[34]Charles Darwin, *Charles Darwin's Beagle Diary*, pp. 41–80. All the while he worked busily making collections of specimens, which he arranged on board the *Beagle*, which surely furthered his focus on differences between allied, related species and varieties.

this cold, twilight landscape in the space of just eight months was a profound experience for him.[35] The ship then visited the Falkland Islands, where, as I have noted in Chapter 3, Darwin's notes clearly show how interested he was in the differences in species from the mainland.

The *Beagle* then returned to the north, to Maldonado, remaining in the temperate zone on the eastern seaboard for eight months. During this period of time Darwin took a series of overland trips, during which he gained an appreciation for gradations of life-forms on a much finer scale, observing how species subtly altered both in physical characteristics and behaviors from one local habitat to the next, and how one species would be replaced by another, slightly different one. He wrote notes describing features and behaviors of birds. For example, he writes, "Flycatcher with red wings — iris yellow — eyelid blackish; base of lower mandible especially yellow"; "King fisher continually elevates its tail." "Alecturus [*Alecturus*] . . . appear very curious in flight, first feather is very curiously excised." "The white and grey shrike fly in circles and alight again, more so than the long-tailed one, which feeds more amongst the bushes." Wandering around Rio Negro, several hundred miles south of Maldonado, he was struck by the differences in the birds, including in particular between closely allied species. He notes, "Ornithology different [from Maldonado]. Only small Icterus [*Icterus*] not so very tame; some pidgeons; different parrots; different partridge."[36]

Darwin traveled north on an expedition from Rio Negro to Buenos Aires, and as he crossed through different terrains he noticed the stepwise changes in plants and animals. Describing crossing to the north side of the Colorado River he writes, "the country had a different appearance from that South of the Colorado; there were many different plants & grasses & not nearly so many spiny bushes, & these gradually became less frequent; until a little to the North there is not a bush." Further on he observed a long-tailed shrike, and notes that it had "different habits" than the ones he had seen in Maldonado: "Much wilder, Tranesia sits differently on twig; alights on summit of branches — does not use its tail so much. Song infinitely sweeter." As he continued he made notes about several other birds, contrasting them with their counterparts at Maldonado, and making notes about the geographic limits of species; for example, he notes, "Molina does not go South of Tandil."[37] He has many notes in a similar vein about plants. For example, he describes a variety of wild artichoke as very common around Monte Video and the Uruguay River, and writes, "I certainly

[35]Ibid., pp. 120–27.
[36]*Charles Darwin and the Voyage of the Beagle*, ed. Nora Barlow, pp. 183, 185–86.
[37]*Beagle Diary*, p. 172. Notebook entries from *Charles Darwin and the Voyage of the Beagle*, pp. 188, 191–92, 198, See also excerpt from his notebook on p. 164 of *Beagle Diary*. I have not been able to identify the bird he refers to as "Tranesia".

never saw it South of R. Salado; . . ." In the same passage he discusses the range of the "true thistle."[38] Thus he was extremely attuned to geographic range and differences between allied species in different habitats, and his journeying was conducive to his making observations within this focus of interest.

In December 1833, the *Beagle* set sail again, heading south, passing through Port Desire and Port St. Julian, and on to the Straits of Magellan and Port Famine. Traveling down the coast Darwin recognized transitions in kinds of species. Thus, describing the country around Port Famine he writes, "The country, in this neighborhood, may be called an intermixture of Patagonia & Tierra del Fuego; here we have many plants of the two countries; the nature of the climate being intermediate."[39] He thus noticed changes in life-forms accompanying the change in climate, seeing these changes as systematic, as showing patterns of relationship and intermingling. The *Beagle* next revisited the Falkland Islands, and Darwin's interest in the differences in life-forms and behaviors from the mainland is evident in his notes — he observes that many common mainland species are absent, for example that there are no snakes, and conversely that there are species on the Islands distinct from those on the mainland. Crossing back to the mainland highlighted these differences further, and he made a further series of notes concerning geographic limits of birds.[40]

After heading north again briefly the *Beagle* at last passed through the Straits of Magellan to the western side of South America and headed up the western coast. As he traveled on the western side of the continent Darwin was struck by the fact that the life-forms were essentially distinct from those of the eastern side; he describes encountering many different species having different characteristics. At Valparaíso he writes, "The vegetation here has a peculiar aspect; this is owing to the number & variety of bushes which seem to supply the place of plants." At Chiloé, later, he writes in his notebook of "3 distinct noises" of a bird species he called "Chucao", which turned out (it is not clear when he learned this) to be three distinct kinds of birds, all new to him. Hiking a mountain near Chiloé with Captain FitzRoy they encountered thick wooded growths, with some specimens familiar to him and others "the names of which I did not know." They came upon rather stunted specimens of the Tierra del Fuego beech tree, and he writes of these trees: "This must be, I apprehend

---

[38] *Beagle Diary*, p. 190. It is in this paragraph that he makes a comment that a farmer told him he saw the common artichoke degenerate into the wild form in his garden, perhaps a harbinger of his later thinking.

[39] Ibid., p. 218. He mentions this transition again on pp. 221–22.

[40] *Charles Darwin and the Voyage of the Beagle*, pp. 217–19. Darwin seems to have become more and more attuned to the principle that particular species are found in particular geographic regions and habitats, a principle also held by Lyell in *Principles of Geology*, which Darwin read.

from their appearance, nearly their Northern limit."[41] Darwin was especially struck when he hiked up to the crest of the Andes, crossed the continental divide, and then traveled partially down their eastern slope by the differences in vegetation between the two sides, even though they are separated by only a relatively short distance. He writes, "I was surprised by the general difference of the vegetation in the valleys on this side & those of the other; & still more so with the close identity in the greater part of all the living productions [on the eastern side] with Patagonia."[42] Six months later, as the *Beagle* had begun sailing across the Pacific, heading for home, it stopped at the Galápagos Islands. Though Darwin had anticipated being mainly interested by their geology, in fact his attention was drawn to the life-forms, and he made sure to collect as many specimens as he could, noting which islands they came from, guided by his interest in the geography and range of species.[43]

Darwin did not plan out this remarkable travel sequence; rather it unfolded fortuitously out of the path the *Beagle* followed, together with his taking advantage of opportunities to go on overland expeditions. He had as a result the opportunity to make a sequence of observations remarkable for its variety and juxtapositions of related species and varieties, in its details clearly unique. What is especially remarkable and of note is the way the sequence mirrored his interest; thus it likely spurred his interest. At the same time, having his interest in mind clearly guided his observations and notes, helping him create a remarkably rich repository of observations in the domain of his interest. One could hardly imagine a sequence better suited to pursuing the interest he had formed: with its sequences of local regions, encountered one after another, enabling him to make observations of allied species in neighboring regions and readily compare them — indeed encouraging such comparisons; with its incredible sweep, through which he experienced firsthand the vast differences ranging from the tropics with vivid colors and teeming life-forms to the cold and forbidding southern regions; with its visits to islands, through which he was naturally led to think about the differences between islands in a given chain and between islands and neighboring regions on the mainland; and finally, in its coverage

[41]*Beagle Diary*, pp. 250, 273; *Charles Darwin and the Voyage of the Beagle*, p. 229.

[42]*Beagle Diary*, pp. 250, 272–73, 292. Regarding the differences in species between the eastern and western slopes of the Andes he makes a somewhat stronger statement in the *Voyage of the Beagle* (Charles Darwin, *Voyage of the Beagle: Charles Darwin's Journal of Researches*, ed. by Janet Browne and Michael Neve), writing (p. 249), "I was very much struck with the marked difference between the vegetation of the eastern valleys and that of the opposite side: yet the climate, as well as the kind of soil, is nearly identical, and the difference of longitude very trifling."

[43]In a letter to Henslow written a few months later he writes that he industriously collected all the species he could find; Charles Darwin, *Correspondence of Charles Darwin*, 1, p. 485.

of both the eastern and western sides of the Continent, enabling him to appreciate the striking differences in their life-forms. The rich, unique database of observations Darwin built up in the domain of his interest was — at least so it appears and is a sensible interpretation — the seedbed out of which he came to the idea of the possibility of the transmutation of species and was led to focus on it; I describe this crucial insight and transition in his development below.

CREATIVITY GENERATION BASED IN CONCEPTUAL STRUCTURES IN INTEREST DOMAINS

In this section I describe how the conceptual structures individuals build up exploring their interests are generative of creativity. I describe a few basic forms of creativity and present examples illustrating them. Certain patterns of exploration tend naturally to be associated with certain forms of creativity generation, as illustrated by the examples.

Creative Connections

Through exploring their creative interests individuals build up rich conceptual structures in the domains of their interests, containing many elements and webs of interconnections among these elements, for example associations among conceptually linked elements and elements encountered in sequence. In turn, this opens up rich possibilities to make original creative connections and combinations among these elements. The distinctiveness of creative interests is fundamental for this form of creativity, for a distinctive interest defines a distinctive domain, and an individual, in exploring the distinctive domain of his interest, encounters a distinctive set of elements and builds up a distinctive, indeed unique conceptual structure in his mind, containing a unique set of elements and potential interconnections — which is then the basis for his making novel connections. In particular, the elements an individual connects have never before all been in someone else's mind, especially not as elements in a common, integrative conceptual structure, the way they are in his mind, with such rich potential for making interconnections among them.

There are two main variants of creativity generation through making connections between elements contained in a conceptual structure in an interest domain. One is making a single important connection, generating a central idea or insight. Examples of this are connecting a theory with a new class of applications or problems; adopting a style or technique to a new medium; combining two styles or themes together, generating a new, hybrid form; and linking a model with a new assumption or perspective, leading to a fundamental change in orientation. The other variant is making a set of smaller creative connections that form a larger whole — a larger creative work that is synthesized out of them and possibly other elements. Examples of this are generating a set of creative elements forming a larger work of art which is built up out of them; inventions built out of a set of insights and innovations; and scholarly works, for example a work of philosophy or a mathematical proof, in which many smaller insights are synthesized in the creation of a whole argument. The examples following illustrate both variants.

Albert Einstein's Development of the Special Theory of Relativity

Above I describe Albert Einstein's creative interest, spanning both the physics of electrodynamics and a set of related topics and philosophy, in particular conceptions of space and time, carrying him, as he explored it, to the work of David Hume; at the center of his interest was the paradox he had hit upon at sixteen. Einstein appears to have forged the way of thinking that led to his development of the theory of relativity through creatively linking elements from the two main subdomains of his interest, which were implicitly integrated in the conceptual structure of his interest, so that it was within his conceptual reach to connect them.

Later statements Einstein made about his development of the theory of relativity indicate that he was led to develop the theory through grappling with two physics problems. One was the paradox he had hit upon at sixteen. The other was the problem of electromagnetic induction, specifically the analysis of the situation in which a magnet and a wire conduction loop are in relative motion. In such a system current flows in the wire, and in conventional accounts at the time different physical processes were described as occurring and being the source of generation of the current depending on which reference system was taken as fixed, that of the wire loop (with the magnet in motion) or that of the magnet (the wire in motion). Einstein found this dissatisfying, wanting a common physical basis for the current regardless of which reference frame was taken as fixed.[44]

While we certainly do not know the exact thought path Einstein followed in developing his theory, the wording he used in his later statements describing his thinking, as well as the nature of the breakthrough he achieved and its roots in what he had learned exploring his interest, indicate that it was very likely the paradox that was primary in sparking his initial realization that led

[44]He discusses this in "Fundamental Ideas and Methods of the Theory of Relativity, Presented in Their Development" (1919), cited in Chapter 5, footnote 23, on p. 135. In the first case it was thought that an electric field generated by the magnet's motion generated the current, in the second a magnetic field, through the lines of which the loop cuts as it moves. Miller provides an excellent discussion; see *Albert Einstein's Special Theory of Relativity*, pp. 144–49.

to his development of the theory. In his "Autobiographical Notes," describing arriving at the formulation of the fundamental principle that is the foundation of the theory, he writes: "After ten years of reflection such a principle resulted from a [the] paradox upon which I had already hit at the age of sixteen." Here he gives priority to the paradox as the source of the basic insight of the theory of relativity. Further, the fundamental problem that is resolved by the theory — the incompatibility of the constancy of the velocity of light with the standard Galilean transformation of coordinate systems and the assumption of absolute time and space — is posed especially starkly in the paradox, so that the paradox seems especially likely to have been the basis for his solution.[45]

[45]Einstein made a similar statement in his 1922 Kyoto lecture, "How I Created the Theory of Relativity," cited in Chapter 9, footnote 61. However, he made different statements on other occasions. This makes it difficult to know for certain that the path he followed had as the crucial seed of the theory the resolution of the paradox. But the wording he used in other statements is ambiguous and I believe consistent with this view. In "Fundamental Ideas and Methods of the Theory of Relativity," describing the role of the problem of induction, he writes (p. 135): "The idea that these two cases should essentially be different was unbearable for me. According to my conviction, the difference between the two could only lie in the choice of the point of view, but not in a real difference.... This phenomenon of the magneto-electric induction forced me to postulate the principle of (special) relativity." He writes in a footnote to this: "The difficulty to be overcome was originally in the constancy of the speed of light in a vacuum which, initially, I thought I would have to abandon. Only after years of groping did I realize that the difficulty rested on the arbitrariness of the basic concepts of kinematics." The wording in this passage — in particular taking the footnote into account — does not support the view that he developed the basic idea of the theory through resolving the induction problem; rather it suggests that once he had arrived at the idea — through resolving the paradox — he realized it would also solve the induction problem.

In an account given by Shankland Einstein is reported to have stated, much later: "What led me more or less directly to the special theory of relativity was the conviction that the electromotive force acting on a body in motion in a magnetic field was nothing else but an electric field." See Robert S. Shankland, "Conversations with Albert Einstein," *American Journal of Physics* 31 (1963): 47–57. This wording seems to give somewhat greater priority to the role of the induction problem in his development of the theory. However, it is not a direct statement by him but a recollection by someone else; also, he inserts the qualifying phrase "more or less," suggesting there may have been something else involved. Further, he uses the word "conviction" — the wording seems to lay stress on the induction problem motivating him, because of its obvious empirical importance, rather than necessarily being the source of creative insight. I note that Miller does not necessarily share my view that the paradox was primary; rather he traces possible paths of development of the theory through resolving either the paradox or the induction problem, though weakly suggesting the "technical route" may have lain through resolving the paradox. See *Albert Einstein's Special Theory of Relativity*, chaps. 3 and 4.

324   What path then did Einstein travel in his thinking, what concepts did he link together, generating the insight that led to his development of the theory? Einstein stated in "How I Created the Theory of Relativity" that he was speaking with Michele Besso, his close friend in Bern, about electrodynamics, apparently about the paradox: "Then suddenly I understood where the key to this problem lay. Next day I came back to him again and said to him, without even saying hello, 'Thank you. I've completely solved the problem.' An analysis of the concept of time was my solution. Time cannot be absolutely defined, and there is an inseparable relation between time and signal velocity." Einstein was at this time committed to the hypothesis that the velocity of light is constant (in a vacuum) — the velocity of a light beam, no matter whether we emit it or it is emitted by someone else traveling towards or away from us, is always measured by us as the value c. Thus the paradox as he would have been thinking of it is this: From the perspective of an observer in a frame of reference which may be taken to be at rest, if a second observer is moving nearly at c relative to this rest frame, and a light beam is emitted by the first observer, it would appear, applying the standard Galilean transformation, subtracting velocities, that from the second observer's perspective the light beam would be moving at just a tiny fraction of c — which violates the hypothesis that he must also calculate the light beam to be moving at c relative to his frame of reference. To be consistent with the hypothesis it is necessary to assume that each observer calculates the light beam as moving at velocity c relative to his frame of reference — but then the two calculations appear to contradict each other. Einstein's statement indicates that he had the realization that the way to resolve this apparent contradiction was to allow each observer to define time and space measurements with respect to his own frame of reference, so that their measurements, specifically of time, might differ.[46]

Einstein's description of his thought process in his "Autobiographical Notes" (p. 53) suggests that the key to his recognizing this point was essentially philosophical and conceptual, not technical. "Today everyone knows, of course, that all attempts to clarify this paradox satisfactorily were condemned to failure as long as the axiom of the absolute character of time, viz., of simultaneity, unrecognizedly was anchored in the unconscious. Clearly to recognize this axiom and its arbitrary character really implies already the solution of the problem. The type of critical reasoning which was required for the discovery of this

[46] In trying to resolve the paradox there were only so many possibilities. After long thinking Einstein may have come to recognize that if the velocity of light is held to be the same in every inertial frame of reference, then simple Galilean addition of velocities being ruled out, the one element left that could be adjusted to enable consistency across frames is time and, linked to time, space.

central point was decisively furthered, in my case, especially by the reading of David Hume's and Ernst Mach's philosophical writings." He thus links his recognition of the key to resolving the paradox to his philosophical explorations, specifically of Mach's and Hume's works. His comments indicate that the key breakthrough enabling him to see a way to resolve the paradox was with regard to time, shifting away from assuming it to be absolute, and instead focusing on how observers define time, specifically, as he developed his theory, observers in different inertial frames. His wording manifests his view that he was able to arrive at this insight through his philosophical exploration and reading — for these had unchained his mind from being wedded to the assumption of absolute time, which, in his elegant phrasing, "unrecognizedly was anchored in the unconscious" — making it difficult to break free of without the conscious work engendered by a philosophical perspective and philosophical reflection.[47]

Realizing that the definition of time was crucial, Einstein formed the idea of constructing definitions of time and space for observers in an inertial frame. From what he states in his "Autobiographical Notes" it seems that his basic realization about the definition of time went hand in hand with the recognition that it was necessary to conceptualize a system for measuring time and length in an inertial frame, and that he thus turned his mind to the formulation of a concrete, constructive method for doing so. In the first section of the next paragraph he writes: "One had to understand clearly what the spatial co-ordinates and the temporal duration of events meant in physics. The physical interpretation of the spatial co-ordinates presupposed a fixed body of reference, which, moreover, had to be in a more or less definite state of motion (inertial system). In a given inertial system the co-ordinates meant the results of certain measurements with rigid (stationary) rods." He continues, in the next paragraph: "If, then, one tries to interpret the time of an event analogously, one needs a means for the measurement of the difference in time." "A clock at rest relative to the system of inertia defines a local time. The local time of all space points taken together are the 'time,' which belongs to the selected system of inertia, if a means is given to 'set' these clocks relative to each other. One sees that *a priori* it is not at all necessary that the 'times' thus defined in different inertial systems agree with one another." He then restates the paradox in this way: under the

---

[47]Put slightly differently, taking the step Einstein took required a cognitive awareness that time is not absolute but subject to definition, an awareness he had gained through reading Mach and Hume especially. Conversely, if one believed unconsciously that time was absolute, as nearly everyone did — even Poincaré it would appear clung to this — one could not reach the realization that time may be defined differently in different frames. This is also stressed by Stachel in "'What song the Syrens sang'," p. 166.

transformation of space coordinates and time measurement between inertial frames used in classical physics, "the two assumptions of (1) the constancy of the velocity of light (2) the independence of the laws (thus specially also of the law of the constancy of the light velocity) of the choice of the inertial system (the principle of special relativity) are mutually incompatible (despite the fact that both taken separately are based on experience)."[48]

At this point in his "Autobiographical Notes" Einstein makes the connection with the Lorentz transform: "The insight which is fundamental for the special theory of relativity is this: The assumptions (1) and (2) are compatible if relations of a new type ('Lorentz-transformation') are postulated for the conversion of co-ordinates and the times of events." Based on the sequence of this account it thus seems that he first conceptualized the need for a constructive means for defining space and especially time, and began working out the details in terms of measuring rods and a system for setting clocks, then realized as he was working out this measurement system that the Lorentz transform exactly fit his problem and resolved the paradox. This is not the only route his thinking might have followed. The Lorentz transformation describes precisely the relationship between space and time measurements made in two frames of reference that resolves the paradox. Einstein knew Lorentz's equations, thus it may have been the case that he saw intuitively that applied to the moving frame they would resolve the paradox first. Indeed the form of the transform, with the $\sqrt{1-(v/c)^2}$ in the denominator, seems to mesh with the paradox — for in the limit, as v approaches c, the transform slows time measurement down to an extreme degree, and Einstein may have realized that this offered a route to resolving the paradox. But his own statements do not support this view — they suggest he began to move towards constructing measures of space and time first, with rods and clocks, then realized that the relationship between the measures of length and elapsed time in different frames fit the Lorentz transform.[49]

[48]"Autobiographical Notes," pp. 55, 57, for this paragraph and the quote in the following one.

[49]Indeed he may have worked out the transformation himself, following the line of presentation in his special relativity paper, then recognized that it was the same as the Lorentz transform, with a few additional steps. Another clue to a possible path Einstein might have followed is provided by the relativity paper itself, written just six weeks or so after his reported realization: "Zur Elektrodynamik bewegter Körper" ("The Electrodynamics of Moving Bodies"), Annalen der Physik 17 (1905): 891–921. There he writes at the beginning of section 2 that "$velocity = \frac{light\ path}{time\ interval}$." In the paradox, if the velocity was going to be held constant in the two frames, then something had to give. Writing this formula for the velocity suggests that perhaps Einstein, working from this definition of velocity, realized that a way out was if the distance and time interval measures differed in the two frames; again this is only a conjecture.

Thus, in his train of thinking Einstein seems to have moved from recognizing the need to abandon absolute time to developing a constructive system for measuring length and elapsed time, spelling out in some detail a system for doing so using rigid rods, clocks, and light beams as signals sent between observers at different locations. He sets this system forth in his special relativity paper, then works out the calculations for observers in different inertial frames, moving relative to one another, and shows that their measures of time and length will be different and that the relationship between them is given by the Lorentz transformation. He thus follows, in spirit, Hume's approach — defining time via definite sequences of events, clocks, and space measurement with physical objects, rigid rods. It seems, then, as a plausible interpretation, that in his taking this step, designing a physical system for defining time and space measurement, Hume was a main philosophical guide, perhaps pointing him towards this step. Einstein may have gotten ideas for some of these specifics, in particular the idea of synchronizing clocks, from either Cohn or Poincaré; but he never stated that he had.[50] Certainly his system in its details and purpose goes far beyond Hume. But based on his own statements a sensible interpretation is that reading Hume was crucial in giving him ideas and tools for going forward, showing him the possibility of using a concrete system, definite tools of measurement, to define space and time measures — thus crucial for his taking this crucial step and developing his theory.[51]

[50]Darrigol describes these possible sources in *Electrodynamics from Ampère to Einstein*, chap. 9. Though Einstein may have seen these works I am doubtful that he was as fully aware of all the literature being published as later historians, themselves very aware of the literature through their excellent researches, may imagine. Miller discusses Einstein's possible sources on pp. 86–92 of *Albert Einstein's Special Theory of Relativity*. I read him as conservative about whether Einstein knew of Cohn's and Poincaré's most recent work as of the spring of 1905. From what he writes, summarizing various sources, it is clear that by 1906–07 Einstein did have a full grasp of the earlier literature, but it is less certain he had such a full grasp in the winter and spring of 1905, though there were some works he did know, notably Lorentz's 1895 treatise and Poincaré's *Science and Hypothesis*. Einstein stated he had not, when he worked out his theory, seen Lorentz's 1904 paper in which Lorentz works out equations, using his transformation, to resolve the problem of induction — though he may have been aware of it indirectly, as Miller notes, notably through the work of Abrams.

[51]It is also noteworthy that Einstein had, by the time he resolved the paradox and developed the special theory of relativity, worked out his theory of light quanta as the explanation for black body radiation, and thus was perhaps convinced even more by Planck's example of the value of breaking from accepted principles and focusing on discovering "a universal formal principle" for grounding electrodynamics, which may have spurred him to address the paradox yet again, apparently soon after reading Hume, and seek to resolve it at a fundamental conceptual level.

The path Einstein followed, based on his own testimony and the limited available additional documentation, is a brilliant illustration of the argument in this chapter. Einstein learned and internalized a unique set of conceptual elements through exploring a creative interest which was distinctive in its scope, carrying him beyond the world of late nineteenth and early twentieth-century physics into the realm of philosophy, especially conceptions of time and space, to the work of David Hume. Through linking ideas and the approach inherent in this philosophy, both the skeptical deconstruction of absolute time and the constructive approach to defining space and time, to the paradox he had hit on at sixteen, linked also with the great knowledge of physics he built up — which gave him a deep appreciation of the significance of the paradox and a reservoir of knowledge, most notably of the Lorentz transformation and the induction problem — Einstein generated his creative insight resolving the paradox that was the basis for the theory of relativity.[52]

At the beginning of the book I state that my description of creative development describes individuals pursuing paths of their own definition — through defining and pursuing distinctive creative interests — and that their creativity is rooted in their interests — generated out of and through exploring their interests and striving to develop them creatively. Einstein's development of his theory illustrates this at the highest level.

Creative Connections — More Examples

Maria Carrig had an insight that became the basis for her dissertation that is a second example of a creative connection linking elements encountered through exploring a creative interest. Her ideas and contribution do not have the radicalness or importance for her field that Albert Einstein's did — as is of course true of most of the contributions most of us make. Leaving this aside, her path of development and creative process illustrate this form of creativity.

As described above, in exploring possible philosophical sources for early modern British comic drama Maria discovered the Lucianic dialogues of the Renaissance and early modern period, which she believed might have been a source for the radical shift she had identified in early modern English comedy.

[52]My interpretation of Einstein's path of thought leading to his development of the theory is certainly not the only one possible, as my previous comments in the main text and footnotes reflect. Darrigol, for example, describes Einstein's breakthrough as epistemological, hence rooted in philosophical outlook as I do, but he mentions Einstein's reading of Hume and statements about Hume only in passing, placing more emphasis on Einstein having gained his critical epistemological perspective from the German tradition of Hertz and Mach; see *Electrodynamics from Ampère to Einstein*, pp. 376, 382–83.

The most famous Northern European early modern work in the tradition of Lucian is Erasmus's *The Praise of Folly* (a monologue). Maria read this and many dialogues, as well as the writings of Lucian. As a result of what she learned she was able to make a creative connection with the shift she had identified in English comic drama, through the idea of perspectivism.

In her dissertation Maria defines skepticism, in its early modern meaning, to be: "a philosophical system that espouses both radical doubt as to the possibility of knowledge and suspension of all judgment, and that grounds its position in the rhetorical method of disproving any argument through multiple counter-arguments or 'perspectivism.'" She writes that the "rise of realism on the stage" — the radical doubt and breaking of convention she had noticed in the works of Thomas Middleton — "shows the influence of skepticism in its use of multiple interpretive perspectives, particularly in its self-consciousness of the shifting interpretive authority between playwright, character, and audience." She thus links perspectivism as a rhetorical device in philosophical argumentation with the idea of multiple perspectives in English early modern comic theater, arguing that they are historically as well as conceptually linked. She argues that the deliberate taking of multiple perspectives in the comedies, not privileging any one perspective or character as inherently true, acts to break down conventionally accepted truths, including the traditional view that truth comes to light through the dramatic performance.[53] Maria presents a quote from Lucian's *Icaromenippus, An Aerial Expedition* (a view of life on earth as seen from the perspective of sailing above the earth) at the start of her Chapter 2, which illustrates on several levels the connection she is making. The quote concludes with Lucian's comment looking down on the theater and human life on earth: "But there in the playhouse itself, full of variety and shifting spectacles, everything that took place was truly laughable."[54]

Maria thus made a creative connection between two different uses of perspective in two distinct cultural traditions. What enabled her to make this connection was exploring her interest through a series of steps — she thus encountered Lucianic dialogues and skeptical philosophy, and recognized the resonance with the radical shift she had identified in English comic drama.

[53] Maria Carrig, *Skepticism and the Rhetoric of Renaissance Comedy*, diss., Yale University, 1995, Abstract. In our interview Maria said the link she found was "through theory" — Italian comic theory and the Lucianic tradition influenced English comic theory, and through that route influenced English comic drama.

[54] Ibid., p. 66. See also *Icaromenippus, An Aerial Expedition*, in *Works of Lucian of Samosata*, trans. by H.W. Fowler and F.G. Fowler (Oxford: Clarendon Press, 1965), pp. 126–44, 136 (I note that Maria's translation is significantly different from the translation in this edition).

Robert Kaufman is a third example of an individual who made creative connections between elements he had learned about in the course of exploring his interest. As described above, Robert planned and pursued a three part sequence of learning that reflected and to some extent was generated by the structure of his interest — reading in modern Left critical theory widely, then focusing on the poetry of Keats and Shelley in preparation for his oral exams, then returning to a focus on certain currents of thought in modern Left critical theory. His creative insights were rooted in this structural sequence.

In his first phase of learning Robert read modern Left criticism discussing Keats's and Shelley's views about the link between art and revolutionary political consciousness. He described this criticism as portraying Keats and Shelley as having been quite naive in their thinking — believing poetry and literature with revolutionary sentiments could engender revolutionary consciousness and thereby directly contribute to revolutionary ferment. When he focused on their poetry in his second phase of learning, studying for orals, he came to a different conclusion:

> I felt that in looking at Keats and Shelley on the one hand, and some of the concerns in modernism on the other, that I saw far more of a critical awareness [in them] . . . than I thought I had seen them being given credit for by the later modern [criticism]. . . . I began to think that what I was seeing [in their poetry] were structural and imagistic reflections on what is inherently going to be problematic about mixing the political and the literary, or the aesthetic, rather than what seemed like, for understandable reasons, just a naive faith that they might have had in art, that often seems to be the theme of quite a lot of [later] criticism.

This insight was linked with a parallel shift in his own thinking. Robert said that prior to this time he had viewed the relation between art and literature and politics as a "direct connection" — the ability of art directly to inspire political action. This view that art can exert a direct "positive" influence on political activity, for example by sparking emotions and ideas that inspire political revolt, is the one that, in his view, most modern critics have attributed to Keats and Shelley. Now, however, he came to appreciate that the relationship of art and literature to political activity may be less direct — that art may not be able directly to influence political activity but do so only indirectly and with difficulty, if at all, by fostering the development of critical thinking skills that are crucial for grasping the true import of political rhetoric and action. He said he now saw this "negative" perspective in the poetry of Keats and Shelley — "a distancing from the naïveté, and a sort of darkness about [the] possibility [of art directly influencing political activity]." And he began to appreciate that there are differences between Keats and Shelley in terms of how the relationship between art and political activity is conceptualized. "I began to see that it [the idea of art influencing political consciousness indirectly, through fostering the development of critical thinking skills] had a much more ornate, a more formalized structure in Keats . . . and I also thought I saw intellectual and conceptual and thematic reflection on it inside that structure in Keats. And this seemed to me somewhat present in Shelley, but not nearly so intensely." That is, as he described it, Keats contains elaborate reflection on the idea that the influence of art on political activity must follow an indirect "negative" route, whereas Shelley elaborates this position less while also conveying the contrasting idea that art can exert a direct "positive" influence.

After his orals, in his third phase of learning, Robert again focused on modern Left critical thought. He described reading about the "dispute in the modern period among wings of the Frankfurt School, notably Adorno on one side and on the other Brecht and Benjamin," about whether the influence of art on political activity is more effectively channeled in a direct positive way or indirectly through a "negative" influence. He realized, in a creative insight, that this dispute resonated with the distinction he had recognized between Keats and Shelley — that the distinction he had noticed between them foreshadows this later debate. "I started to feel that what I was seeing, although it was all pitched towards modern and postmodern debates, related back to a set of Romantic problems." "I can specifically remember reading some work about the debates between either Adorno or Horkheimer on one side and Benjamin or Kracauer on the other, the debates being about a certain kind of surrealist or avant-garde or very palpable art on the one hand [arguing for a direct influence of art on political activity], and a more distanced and critically reflective art that Adorno and Horkheimer were defending on the other, and all of a sudden feeling 'oh my goodness, there's something in this in Keats and Shelley already.'" Robert said that he felt from the start that his insight was original, that "no one . . . had talked before about the possibility of locating the earliest version of such a debate within Romanticism." He also said he thought it was potentially important historically. He pursued it and it became the core of his dissertation and several articles he has published.

Thus Robert's insights, in particular the first and last, were rooted in his sequence of learning, which naturally juxtaposed in his mind modern Left critical works and the poetry of Keats and Shelley, spurring him to make connections between them.[55]

---

[55]It is interesting to note that Robert has been interested in the relationship between art and literature and political and social issues since youth, as noted in Chapter 3.

Samuel Taylor Coleridge: A Rich Web Generative of Creativity

Samuel Taylor Coleridge is a fascinating example of an individual who built up rich conceptual structures in his mind through exploring a distinctive set of interests, which were in turn generative of creative combinations and connections he made in composing his poetry, at the level of specific words, phrasings, and created images.

In his fascinating book *The Road to Xanadu: A Study in the Ways of the Imagination* (Boston: Houghton Mifflin, 1927) John Livingston Lowes documents Coleridge's mode of exploration of his interests, describing how this created rich webs of associations in his mind, and shows how these webs were the basis of many creative combinations he made in his poetic compositions. Here I follow and draw upon his account, as well as other descriptions of Coleridge's interests and sources of information: I present Coleridge as an example of an individual who made many smaller creative connections and combinations between elements in conceptual structures he built up through exploring interests, illustrating this form of creativity generation. I focus on Coleridge's exploration of interests in relation to his composition of "The Rime of the Ancient Mariner," the poem most richly textured out of many diverse elements interwoven and imaginatively fused. In Chapter 13 I describe the way a unique constellation of interests Coleridge had plaited together to create the basic plot and structure of the poem.

Coleridge formed a set of intellectual interests as a young man that he pursued with zeal, reading omnivorously in each. A central interest he had, crucial for his composition of "The Rime," was descriptions of exotic regions of the earth, only recently discovered and still to some degree unknown — the polar regions, the oceans, and, to a lesser degree, the equatorial zones. Linked to this was an interest he had in phenomena of nature, in particular descriptions of sensory phenomena — light, colors, sounds, and extreme events such as storms, volcanic eruptions, and earthquakes. His interest stretched to the edges of scientific comprehension, fusing with another interest he had, in mysticism and the occult, including accounts of supernatural beings, daemons and angels. Coleridge had other interests as well, notably in politics and religion; I discuss a number of these further in Chapter 13. Here I focus on the first two interests — on his exploration of them and his poetic composition based in descriptions he encountered exploring them.

Coleridge had, at least as a young man, a remarkable memory, and also an abiding interest in synthesis. He believed the rich diversity of the world is in fact a unity, and was driven to search for commonalities and interconnections among diverse elements to manifest this unity. He described his memory as "tenacious and systematizing" — thus attributing to himself both retention and the drive to synthesize and interconnect elements, creating organic structures and wholes, qualities that were naturally conducive to building up rich integrative conceptual structures in the domains of his interests.[56]

Driven by curiosity, an innate drive to read, and a voracious appetite for knowledge, Coleridge explored his interests intensively through reading. He borrowed many books from friends and libraries, from the time he was a boarding student and later in Bristol, and purchased books. He annotated his copies of books, and jotted facts and opinions from books and comments about books in his notebooks.[57] Through his extensive reading, having an excellent memory, Coleridge must have, we can surmise, built up rich knowledge structures in his interest domains.

A defining feature of Coleridge's exploration of his interests was the way he read. Lowes shows in detail that Coleridge regularly followed references from one work to another, and, in reading an article in a journal or section of a book that fit with an interest he was exploring, would often peruse and read adjacent pages or articles that caught his attention because they fit with the interest also or fit with another of his interests.[58] Through following leads in this way and reading adjacent materials that caught his eye Coleridge built up knowledge structures in the domains of his interests that were both extensive and distinctive, incorporating elements not only from the most obvious sources, but from less common secondary and tertiary sources he hunted down or happened to encounter. His pattern of exploration fits two of the models described above — exploration in discrete forays, and exploring along connected paths, following links. Coleridge was clearly guided by his interests, including in particular his

[56]Lowes gives this quote on p. 43 of *The Road to Xanadu*. College friends recalled Coleridge quoting verbatim whole passages from political pamphlets he had read. For more on Coleridge's belief in the unity underlying the diversity of appearances and phenomena see *Coleridge's Notebooks: A Selection*, ed. Seamus Perry (Oxford: Oxford University Press, 2002), pp. vii–viii.

[57]George Whalley provides a record of Coleridge's borrowings from the Bristol Library, which occurred during the critical period before and during his composition of "The Rime": "The Bristol Library Borrowings of Southey and Coleridge, 1793–8," *Library*, third series, 4 (1950): 114–32. Coleridge was not just a reader, it should be noted — he was also a keen observer, a point made by Kathleen Coburn and Richard Holmes; see Chapter 13.

[58]*The Road to Xanadu*, especially Chapter II, "The Falcon's Eye." Lowes writes as follows at the end of the chapter (p. 37), summarizing: "*[he (Coleridge)] habitually passed from any given book he read to the books to which that book referred*" (italics in original text). I show Lowes's method in the text following.

334   conceptions of them, in choosing which books and articles to read, and especially in choosing which references and links to pursue from among, in many cases, dozens or hundreds of possibilities.

Lowes's argument, which he supports with detailed analysis, is that through his extensive reading and pattern of reading Coleridge encountered and internalized a multitude of elements — facts, ideas, particularly vivid descriptions of natural phenomena — in a way that generated a rich pattern of associations among them, and that working from these associations Coleridge generated new creative combinations which are central in his poetic composition. In tracing Coleridge's reading Lowes focuses on Coleridge's first extant notebook, known as the "Gutch Notebook," in which he wrote over the period 1794–98, thus before and during the time of his initial composition of "The Rime of the Ancient Mariner." He also draws upon evidence in Coleridge's letters, his known library borrowings, annotations Coleridge made in books, and books Coleridge almost certainly read that were well known at the time and fell within the purview of his interests.[59]

Through tracing Coleridge's sources Lowes identifies, for a great number of cases, specific descriptions Coleridge encountered and read (or at least is likely to have read) in one source having close associations with material in other sources. He links these clusters of associated elements to specific phrases and passages in Coleridge's poetry, showing stunning correspondences. Thus he argues that the source of many of Coleridge's phrasings is creative combinations he forged based on associations among source elements, concatenating words and images from different sources.[60]

An example showing this process and its role in Coleridge's process of poetic composition, traced by Lowes in detail, is Coleridge's process of creation of the beautiful lines in "The Rime of the Ancient Mariner" describing the shadow of the ship in the water and the play of the water snakes. The lines are these:[61]

> . . .where the ship's huge shadow lay,
> The charméd water burnt alway
> A still and awful red.

[59]Lowes's general description of the notebook is Chapter I in *The Road to Xanadu*, "Chaos."

[60]Lowes's view is that Coleridge made these creative connections and combinations largely unconsciously. This seems sensible, but we cannot know for sure; Coleridge may also have recalled descriptions in a more deliberate way.

[61]*Samuel Taylor Coleridge: The Major Works*, ed. H.J. Jackson (Oxford: Oxford University Press, 1985), p. 57.

Beyond the shadow of the ship,
I watched the water-snakes:
They moved in tracks of shining white,
And when they reared, the elfish light
Fell off in hoary flakes.

Within the shadow of the ship
I watched their rich attire:
Blue, glossy green, and velvet black,
They coiled and swam; and every track
Was a flash of golden fire.

One might think that Coleridge created these lines through a process of sheer imaginative construction, with no specific sources for the images and phrasings. But that is not the case, as Lowes shows quite convincingly. He identifies sources for nearly every word and phrase in these lines, including the most creative and striking, showing how key words and images link the sources to one another, creating associations among them. Thus as he describes it Coleridge created much of these lines through associations, creatively combining words and images from different sources.

Lowes first shows that an entry on the first page of Coleridge's notebook is a reference to an item in Joseph Priestley's book on optics.[62] In his book, Lowes notes, Priestley has a chapter on "Light from Putrescent Substances" containing a passage describing fish that "in swimming, left so luminous a track behind them, that both their size and species might be distinguished by it." Priestley has a footnote to this passage referencing a letter by a Father Bourzes, "Luminous Appearances in the Wakes of Ships in the Sea," in the *Philosophical Transactions of the Royal Society (Abridged)*.[63] Father Bourzes writes:

> In my voyage to the Indies . . . when the Ship ran apace, we often observed a great Light in the Wake of the Ship . . . . The Wake seemed then like a River of Milk . . . . on the 12th of June, the Wake of the Vessel was full of large Vortices of Light . . . the Vortices appeared and disappeared . . . like Flashes of Lightning. Not only the Wake of a Ship produces this Light, but Fishes also in swimming leave behind 'em a luminous Track . . . . I have sometimes seen a great many Fishes playing in the Sea, which have made a kind of artificial Fire in the Water, that was very pleasant to look on.

[62]*Road to Xanadu*, p. 38. Joseph Priestley, *History and Present State of Discoveries relating to Vision, Light, and Colours* (London: Printed for J. Johnson, 1772). Priestley was something of a hero to Coleridge, and this work fits with Coleridge's interest in descriptions of natural phenomena; thus it is not surprising Coleridge would have read it.

[63]*Road to Xanadu*, p. 40. Lowes states that the letter is stated as from *Letters of the Missionary Jesuits*. My quotation follows Lowes (p. 45) with some omissions.

Several words and phrases in this passage have associations with Coleridge's lines of poetry: the notion of fish leaving a "track"; the description of the track as luminous and resembling the wake of the ship, which is depicted as a "River of milk," hence white — in the poem the track is "shining white"; and the "Flashes" of lightning and "artificial Fire," which resonate with the phrase "a flash of golden fire." As to whether Coleridge had read Priestley's passage on the luminous tracks of fish and tracked down the reference to Father Bourzes, Lowes notes that later in his letter Father Bourzes writes about "Marine Rainbows" he observed during a "Tempest" off the Cape of Good Hope: "the Tops of the Waves made a kind of Rain, in which the Rays of the Sun painted the Colours of a Rain-bow." He notes that this matches an entry in Coleridge's notebook — "Sun paints rainbows on the vast waves during snow storms in the Cape."[64] There is a striking agreement in wording, specifically "Sun paints" with "Sun painted" — phrasing too unusual to be due to chance, indicating that Coleridge did read the letter — an example of how he would go from one source to another referenced by it.

Lowes describes a number of exploration books Coleridge almost certainly read that contain passages that are likely sources for specific words and phrases in the passage quoted above, that mesh with Bourzes's account. Coleridge most surely read Captain Cook's famous *Voyage to the Pacific*. In that book there is a description that fits with Coleridge's lines:

> During a calm, on the morning of the 2d, some parts of the sea seemed covered with a kind of slime; and some small sea animals were swimming about.... that had a white, or shining appearance, and were very numerous. Some of these last were taken up, and put into a glass cup.... When they began to swim about...they emitted the brightest colours of the most precious gems...tints of blue...which were frequently mixed with a ruby, or opaline redness.... with candle light, the colour was, chiefly, a beautiful, pale green, tinged with a burnished gloss; and, in the dark, it had a faint appearance of glowing fire. They proved to be...probably, an animal which has a share in producing some sorts of that lucid appearance, often observed near ships at sea, in the night.[65]

Here is Lowes's commentary:

> There, then, is another account of luminous creatures swimming about, like Father Bourzes's fishes, beside a ship, and like them producing the effect of fire in the

[64]*The Road to Xanadu*, pp. 40–41.

[65]James Cook, A *Voyage to the Pacific Ocean, Undertaken by the Command of His Majesty, for Making Discoveries in the Northern Hemisphere. Performed Under the Direction of Captains Cook, Clerke, and Gore, in His Majesty's Ships the Resolution and Discovery, in the Years 1776, 1777, 1778, 1779, and 1780. Three Volumes.* (London: H. Hughs, 1785), Vol. 2. p. 257.

waters of a slimy sea. It needs no elaborate reasoning to show that the two accounts are peculiarly adapted to recall each other. But... there is a significant increment. Captain Cook's animalculae are described as '*shining*' white, and blue, and '*glossy*' green. And those are precisely the colours which in the poem are associated with the water-snakes.[66]

Cook is thus a possible source for the colors blue and "glossy green" in the poem. Lowes in his description implies that in thinking of Father Bourzes's letter, with its reference to the track left by the fish as "luminous," and creating an "artificial Fire" and with the word white and reference to milk, also white, Coleridge was led to think of Cook's description, which also contains the word "luminous," sea creatures that are depicted as white, and the reference to "glowing fire" — generating an association in his mind between two works he had read pursuing his interest, combining their accounts.

Is there a source for the phrase "velvet black"? Lowes identifies a source for this as well — William Bartram's *Travels Through North and South Carolina*. Amidst a cluster of descriptions in this book that Coleridge made notes about is Bartram's description of the sun fish: "The whole fish is of a pale gold (or burnished brass) colour... the scales are... powdered with red, russet, silver, blue and green specks," and at the gills is an area "encircled with silver, and velvet black."[67] The words "burnished" and "pale" and the colors red, blue, and green all mesh with Captain Cook's account, suggesting that Coleridge may have formed an amalgamation of the descriptions, commingling them.

All of these accounts describe fish, leaving the question of how Coleridge developed the idea for the creatures in the water to be water snakes. Lowes identifies a number of sources for this. One is Samuel Purchas's *Purchas His Pilgrimage*, which Coleridge knew well, which contains this description in a chapter on the "Canibal Islands" taken from *Observations of Sir Richard Hawkins, Knight, in his Voyage into the South Sea*: "At the Asores many moneths becalmed... [the ship's men saw] seuerall sorts of gellies and formes of Serpents, Adders, and Snakes, Greene, Yellow, Blacke, White...." The colors in this account form a natural association with colors in Cook's, Bourzes's, and Bartram's accounts. In addition Cook's description also refers to a calm and to "gelatinous" life-forms, analogous to the "gellies" referred to. Another source for the water snakes identified by Lowes is Captain William Dampier's *New Voyage round the World*, which Coleridge knew and made references

---

[66]*The Road to Xanadu*, p. 46.

[67]William Bartram, *Travels Through North and South Carolina, Georgia, East & West Florida, The Cherokee Country, The Extensive Territories of the Muscogulges, or Creek Confederacy, and the Country of the Chactaws*, intro. by James Dickey (New York: Penguin, 1988 (first published 1791)), pp. 140–41.

to, including a note on file in the British Library containing observations on snakes from Dampier. Lowes identifies a set of additional references Coleridge may well have seen. He also gives sources for the idea of fish and snakes coiling and rearing, as Coleridge describes his water snakes doing.[68]

To trace a different chain of associations, in his notebook entry beginning "Sun paints Rainbows" Coleridge has the word "snow" which Father Bourzes makes no mention of in his description of marine rainbows. Lowes argues that the source for this is another description of rainbows, by Frederick Martens in his *Voyage into Spitzbergen and Greenland*, which is included in a volume Wordsworth owned that Coleridge surely knew about and would have read given his interests.[69] Martens describes rainbows seen during snow storms: "We see in these falling Needles [of snow] a Bow like a Rain-bow of two colours, white and a pale yellow, like the Sun . . . . [We also see] an other Bow, which I call a Sea-bow. This is seen . . . not in the great Waves, but in the Atmosphere . . . ." Father Bourzes, in the second part of his description of the rainbows, writes, "we could distinguish only two Colours, viz. a dark Yellow on that side next the Sun, and a pale Green on the opposite side." Thus the two accounts of rainbows share a string of elements in common — the color yellow, the Sun, the word "pale," the concept of great waves as in a storm — and Coleridge seems to have fused them in his notebook entry.[70]

Martens appears to have a further influence, identified by Lowes, in the way the stanzas I have quoted are framed. Martens continues: "Commonly we see this [Bow] before the Ship, and sometimes also behind . . . where the Shadow of the Sail falleth. . . . A Bow sheweth itself in the Shadow of the Sail." This image of the shadow of the sail, or ship, is the central image in the three lines that frame the passage from "The Rime" quoted.

Thus, in summary, there are a rich collection of sources for Coleridge's beautiful, richly descriptive lines, with many associations among them. The rich set of sources reflects Coleridge's interests, and, reflecting the distinctiveness of his interests and the way he read broadly in them, is distinctive in its range — ranging from standard travel and adventure books like Cook and Purchas to less common books of discovery like Martens, to scientific works, Priestley's book on optics and the *Philosophical Transactions of the Royal Society*. Not many

[68]*The Road to Xanadu*, pp. 48–50. Lowes notes that Purchas has an account in his book of a sea "all red as if it had beene mixed with bloud," one possible source for the "still and awful red" of the sea in Coleridge's poem.

[69]Ibid., pp. 481–82 for citation.

[70]Ibid., pp. 67–68. Lowes quotes a further passage from Martens showing that he meant snow by the phrase "falling Needles." He notes that Coleridge used the phrase "drizzled needle-points of frost" in his play *Osorio* completed just a short time before "The Rime" was begun.

poets, we can be sure, would have read so deeply in this diverse set of works! Thus Coleridge's interests, guiding his reading, were crucial in his building up unique sets of elements, out of which he created his wonderful poetry.

This same pattern of generation, creatively combining elements from a rich array of sources having many associative links, is the basis of many other stanzas of "The Rime of the Ancient Mariner." I give just one more example here, drawn from Lowes. A number of lines previous to the passage above is this one (*Samuel Taylor Coleridge: The Major Works*, p. 53):

> Yea, slimy things did crawl with legs
> Upon the slimy sea.

> About, about, in reel and rout
> The death-fires danced at night;
> The water, like a witch's oils,
> Burnt green, and blue, and white.

The last line, with its vivid colors, calls to mind the passage from Captain Cook quoted above; the first two lines have an association with this passage too, through Cook's phrase "the sea seemed covered with a kind of slime."[71] Even more interesting are the possible sources for the analogy of the sea like "witch's oils" and the "death-fires" dancing. Lowes identifies an article in the same issue of the *Transactions* as Father Bourzes's letter — indeed immediately preceding it, ending on the page on which it begins, thus natural for Coleridge to read — that gives an account of an island being raised out of the sea, a violent, cataclysmic event, just the kind to catch Coleridge's interest. In the article the sea is described as like oil bubbling — "the Sea was seen to emit Smoak.... The Water of the Sea looked like Oil, and seemed to rise up and bubble."[72] The idea of the sea burning has many sources, was a standard observation at the time.[73] The death-fires seem an amalgamation of two elements: the *corpo santo* or play of light around a ship and ship's mast, which was widely reported in many accounts Coleridge read; and the belief that light is emitted by decaying human bodies, thus explaining lights seen in cemeteries, which Priestley, for example, describes in his book close to the passage quoted above.

These descriptions of natural phenomena are wedded with a very different source: *Macbeth*. "About, about" derives from this passage in the play:[74]

---

[71]Another source Lowes identifies for the slimy things and slimy sea is Martens, who has an entire chapter about slimy creatures, entitled "Slime-Fishes." *The Road to Xanadu*, pp. 81, 88–89.

[72]Ibid., pp. 82–83 and footnotes.

[73]Ibid., pp. 83–84.

[74]William Shakespeare, *Macbeth*, ed. Kenneth Muir (London: Methuen and Co., 1955), Act I, Scene iii, p. 14.

> The weird sisters, hand in hand,
> Posters of the sea and land,
> Thus do go about, about.

From *Macbeth* Coleridge got the association to witches, hence "witch's oils." The whole passage, in fact, with the dancing fires in "reel and rout," calls to mind the image of the Witches dancing round their cauldron.[75]

Lowes identifies sources for many other details of "The Rime," including the albatross, the images of sun and moon, the sounds, and the overall pattern of the voyage.[76] In sum, it is clear that Coleridge did not simply invent the images and phrases and phenomena of his poem without recourse to sources, nor did he draw mainly on fictional sources. Rather, the evidence supports as the model of his creative process, fitting the model in this chapter, that through exploring his interests in voyages of exploration and descriptions of natural phenomena he read many descriptions of real phenomena, with vivid specifics, and formed associations among them and wove them together creatively. This does not make his achievement less creative, but it does show his process of creation to be rooted in the conceptual structures he had built up through extensive explorations of his interests.

Generalization and Pattern Recognition

A second creative process rooted in knowledge structures built up through exploration of interest domains is generalization and pattern recognition: recognizing a common unity, pattern, theme, principle, characteristic, structure, or causal mechanism among a collection of elements. Such insights may be and are in some cases significant contributions in their own right. In addition they may trigger theoretical development leading to further significant contributions, through the drive to construct theories that explain, predict, or make use of the general pattern, principle, theme, characteristic, structure, or causal mechanism that has been identified.

Generalization and pattern recognition is widely recognized as an important form of creativity. My purpose is to place this form of creativity in the context of my description in this chapter and the book as a whole. In particular I describe generalization and pattern recognition as based in a conceptual structure built

[75]There are many resonances with *Macbeth* in the poem. As Lowes notes, the First Witch has just before the lines quoted uttered a curse that seems to echo the curse under which the Mariner falls.

[76]See Chapters VI, VIII, IX, X, and XI in *The Road to Xanadu*. The number of sources Lowes identifies is very impressive — a testament both to Coleridge's knowledge base and his own excellent scholarship.

up through exploration of a distinctive interest. In exploring their interests individuals build up rich conceptual structures — databases and groupings of elements — in their interest domains that are unique to them. They thus put themselves in an ideal position to identify general patterns among elements within these structures that have never before been recognized.

Charles Darwin first seems to have articulated to himself as a serious idea the possibility of the mutability of species through a generalization he made rooted in the knowledge he had built up in the domain of his interest through his travels and observations.

Darwin's initial insight and reflections are documented in a note he wrote during the voyage of the *Beagle* across the Pacific, most likely ten to eleven months after visiting the Galápagos Islands, in the summer of 1836. He writes first about the mockingbirds he observed on the Galápagos Islands: "These birds are closely allied in appearance to the Thenca [*Thenca*] of Chile," and describes various similar behaviors they exhibit; but then writes: "I imagined, however, its note or cry was rather different from the Thenca of Chile—." He recognizes that the species are closely allied but distinct, an observation which is clearly linked in his mind to the fact that one is from the mainland, the others from islands off the coast. He notes about the mockingbird specimens he collected, "I have specimens from four of the larger Islands; the specimens from Chatham & Albemarle Isd. appear to be the same, but the other two are different. In each Isd. each kind is exclusively found; habits of all are indistinguishable." He continues, adding to this observation, then in the last sentence makes his striking generalization:

> When I recollect the fact, that from the form of the body, shape of scales and general size, the Spaniards can at once pronounce from which Isd. any tortoise may have been brought: — when I see these Islands in sight of each other and possessed of but a scanty stock of animals, tenanted by these birds but slightly differing in structure and filling the same place in Nature, I must suspect they are only varieties. The only fact of a similar kind of which I am aware is the constant asserted difference between the wolf-like Fox of East and West Falkland Isds. — If there is the slightest foundation for these remarks, the Zoology of Archipelagoes will be well worth examining; for such facts would undermine the stability of species.[77]

In putting forth this idea as a possibility Darwin was, I believe, drawing upon the great body of his accumulated knowledge of geographic ranges of species

[77]These quotes are from notes Darwin wrote on the voyage. See *Charles Darwin and the Voyage of the Beagle*, pp. 246–47. Frank Sulloway has given a careful dating for the notes in "Darwin's conversion: The *Beagle* voyage and its aftermath," *Journal of the History of Biology* 15 (1982): 325–96.

and patterns of shadings of morphology and behavior moving from one locale to another in closely allied species that he had built up, whether consciously or more unconsciously. The select facts he writes out may have stood out, but they were linked in his mind with the multiplicity of observations he had made throughout the course of his travels — traveling on the east coast of South America, down to the tip of the continent, with the progression of changes in life-forms, noting the differences between the animals of the Falkland Islands and the adjacent mainland, which mirror his observations about the Galápagos Islands, the striking difference in life-forms between the eastern and western slopes of the Andes, and the fossils he had collected.

This broader base for his thinking comes to the fore in a more extensive note he wrote to himself slightly later, on the voyage home to England. He writes first: "Go steadily through all the [geographic] limits of birds and animals in S. America." His aim evidently is to identify general patterns that might suggest a suitable theoretical model, perhaps species change, by sorting through the many observations he had made pursuing his interest in the geographic ranges of extent of species. He then writes a series of notes about different species, raising possibilities. "Zorilla; wide limit of waders;" "Speculate on neutral ground for 2 Ostriches: bigger one encroaches on smaller; — change not progressive; produced at one blow, if one species altered." He notes the contrast between the two slopes of the Andes: "Great contrast of two sides of Cordillera; where climate similar. I do not know botanically — but picturesquely." He then writes down a creationist idea: "Should urge that extinct Llama owed its death not to change of circumstances; . . . . Tempted to believe animals created for definite time: — not extinguished by change of circumstances."[78] This comment and others show that Darwin was most probably not firmly convinced of the correctness of the hypothesis of instability of species, or, as he would later call it, transmutation of species, at this time. Rather, he is groping, searching for a general theory to clarify and explain the diversity of species, their interrelatedness and geographic distributions, and the replacement of species by other species in time and space — thus puts forward and considers a variety of alternative hypotheses. The next note shows this drive to identify general principles: "The same kind of relation that common ostrich bears to Petisse [the smaller kind] — and difft. kinds of extinct Guanaco to recent. In former case position [geographic], in latter time . . . ." He continues: "not *gradual* change or degeneration from circumstances, if one species does change into another it must be per saltum — or species may perish. This representation of species important, each its own limit and represented. Chiloe creeper; Fournarius [*Fournarius*], Calandria [*Calandria*]. Inosculation alone shows not gradation."[79]

[78] *Charles Darwin and the Voyage of the Beagle*, p. 263.
[79] Ibid., p. 263.

Darwin continues in the next paragraph: "Propagation, whether ordinary
hermaphrodite, or by cutting an animal in two (gemmiparous by nature or by
accident) we see an individual divided either at one moment or through lapse
of ages. Therefore we are not so much surprised at seeing Zoophite producing distinct animals, still partly united, & egg which becomes quite separate.
Considering all individuals of all species as each one individual divided by
different methods, associated life only adds one other method, where the division is not perfect." "Dogs, Cats, Horses, Cattle, Goat, Asses, have all run
wild and bred, no doubt with perfect success. Showing how creation does not
bear upon solely adaptation of animals. Extinction in same manner may not
depend. There is no more wonder in extinction of species than of individual.
When we see Avestruz [the smaller Ostrich] two species certainly different, not
insensible change; yet one is urged to look to common parent? Why should two
of the most closely allied species occur in same country?"[80] Darwin is focusing
on differences between closely allied species, thinking of this as analogous to
differences between individuals of the same species, imagining, perhaps, these
differences to emerge through processes of division like the way young issue
from their parents.

It thus seems that Darwin had many examples in mind, including many
from the large pool of observations he had made during the course of the
voyage, in writing this second set of notes. There is no way to know with any
certainty to what degree this large pool formed a basis for his thinking at the
time he wrote the first note. But it is plausible, and seems natural, that it lay
behind his initial insight about instability of species — that the body of his
accumulated observations, the many notes he had written and specimens he
had collected and labeled, his experiences traveling in the different parts of
South America, seeing different species, including members of closely allied
species he observed in adjacent locales, all attuned him to this possibility. It is
certainly possible that some of his many observations and cases he was aware
of flitted through his mind at the time he was writing the first note, but, for
whatever reason he chose not to write them down. They may have seemed
less clear than the examples he chose to focus on — this would explain why
slightly later he wrote a note to himself to go back and sort through them
more carefully. If this view is correct it strengthens the interpretation that
his original insight was the product of a relatively large-scale generalization,
larger scale than his brief note records, rooted in the database of cases he had
built up exploring his interest, attending to observations fitting with it. It is
noteworthy that Nora Barlow expresses a similar view in her annotations to
Darwin's notes. Describing his thinking process she describes him puzzling

[80]Ibid., pp. 263–64.

over his observations, searching to generalize. "The natural limitations in time and space of Natural Species had haunted him; he had watched the changes of each species with its change of geographical range. Now he must generalize from all this accumulation of fact."[81] Of course it is also possible Darwin did not have the larger pool in mind at first, but only began to think back over his many observations afterwards, thinking about supporting evidence. Even if he did not have it in mind consciously, however, it was present in his unconscious, a reservoir of elements pertaining to the idea of gradations of differences among closely allied species in adjacent locales, providing a supporting basis for his initial insight.

Going forward, Darwin's conviction of transmutation of species became strong on his return to England, under the weight of the evidence shown him by naturalists, including John Gould's careful classification of his birds, including the famous finches. His process of groping for a theoretical model would continue for some time until he forged a coherent theory; see Chapter 12 for a brief synopsis of this later phase of his development.

A number of my interview subjects made creative generalizations based in interest domains. While these obviously do not have the historical importance of the generalization made by Darwin, they are further illustrations of the process.

Cheryl told me that in analyzing eighteenth-century women's novels she found in the library, exploring her interest, she focused on identifying common plots, themes, and structural elements — thus generalization was the guiding principle of her approach. She said she "noticed" "several patterns," which she discussed in her oral exams, including suicide of the heroine, and enclosure of the heroine in a confined place (these topics are listed in her orals document). Another pattern she identified was guardianship: "I started to see a repeating pattern revolving around the issue of guardianship," she said. "I noticed it enough that, in studying for my oral exams — it's funny how I can remember this — I took a little sheet of paper and said, 'Oh, isn't this funny that out of these eight novels I've just read by women five of them are talking about guardianship.' So I jotted down the names of the texts." Receiving encouragement from advisors and friends, and spurred by the link with her interest in social issues, Cheryl pursued the topic of guardianship for her dissertation.

Ian, pursuing his interest in English colonial and postcolonial literature, and specifically the portrayal of British identity in this literature, read widely in this literature. He said, "as I took notes I felt that I just kept seeing a pattern." The pattern he saw was that the culturally defined spaces that characters are

[81]Ibid., pp. 262–63.

depicted inhabiting and moving through, such as public squares and buildings, houses, gardens, and temples, are important to the formation of their identity. "I kept seeing this in the various works," he said. "That empire organizes space," "that from the second half of the nineteenth century onwards there is a sort of marriage of politics and aesthetics, which begins to read [define] personality and identity within a constructivist paradigm, and pays attention to the ways in which the literal organization of cultural spaces has an impact on the identities of the subjects who inhabit those spaces." "For example in *A Passage To India*, that book is organized... into three sections, and the section headings are 'Mosque,' 'Caves,' and 'Temple.' When I was reading it I was thinking about what the relationship is between these sort of banner headings... and the narrative they contain." Ian realized, as he described it, that there seems to be a connection implied between the place or places in which the action is centered in each section and the story and its meaning. Ian identified this same pattern in other texts, including *Beyond the Boundary*, in which he saw that cricket, and in a literal sense the cricket field, is shown to be formative of English character, *Kim*, discussed in Chapter 9, in which Kim's identity is linked to cartography and the map of India, and *The Satanic Verses*, in which Ian recognized that culturally defined spaces, notably certain kinds of urban settings, shape characters' cultural identities. Thus, seeing a general pattern, he formulated his idea — that "at a very real, very literal level imperialism was about not just the conquests of space [territory] but the organization of [lived] space" — as a way to define the identities of its subjects.

Ian's insight was original in linking identity to culturally defined, inhabited spaces in a more literal, more direct manner than previous work, which often makes the connection in a more theoretical or metaphoric way, not focusing on actual spaces like temples, cricket fields, and houses. It was the starting point for his dissertation, that was the basis for his book *Out of Place: Englishness, Empire, and the Locations of Identity* (Princeton, NJ: Princeton University Press, 1999).

CREATIVE EXPERTISE

A useful concept for describing many patterns of development and creative processes described in this chapter and the last is *creative expertise*, which I define to be *expertise an individual builds up through exploring, learning about and working in an interest domain, that is in some way distinctive to him*. For individuals who build up such creative expertise, it is a powerful basis for generating ideas and insights.

Creative expertise is rooted in, but also somewhat different from, the conventional notion of expertise. Conventional expertise, as defined and studied

346   in psychology, refers to attaining a high level of performance and skill in a field or practice, supported, in most cases, by an extensive knowledge base in the field, typically knowledge that is primarily practical. Two examples that are widely mentioned and studied in the literature and illustrate the standard meaning of expertise are expertise in chess and the expertise of radiologists in reading and interpreting X-ray films.[82]

The fundamental difference between creative expertise and conventional expertise is that creative expertise is expertise that is distinctive in its knowledge base. The knowledge structures individuals build up through exploring intensively and extensively in the domains of their interests are similar to the extensive knowledge bases experts build up in their fields, but with the crucial difference that they are not standard, as are the knowledge bases built up by experts in conventional fields, which are shared in common by a pool of experts, but rather are distinctive. The logic is straightforward: creative interests are distinctive and often unique, hence the domains they define are also distinctive and unique, hence the knowledge structures individuals build up through exploring their interest domains are also distinctive and unique. Indeed the knowledge structures individuals build up exploring their interests are doubly distinctive: the domains in which they are built up are distinctive; and individuals follow unique paths of exploration exploring their interests, as many of the examples above demonstrate, such as Charles Darwin's path voyaging on the *Beagle*, hence have a unique series of experiences and encounter a unique set of elements. This path uniqueness holds more for creative expertise than for conventional expertise, for in working to acquire conventional expertise in a field or practice individuals generally follow paths that are relatively standard for their field, for example learning a set of standard cases and engaging in standard training exercises.

There are several main ways in which creative expertise is generative of creativity that mirror the forms of creativity described in this and the last chapter. One is through being generative of creative connections. A rich, distinctive knowledge structure in a domain, containing many elements and many interconnections among elements — classic for expert knowledge — is a fertile source for generating connections, including connections that have never been made before. Samuel Taylor Coleridge's process of creation for "The Rime of

---

[82] For work in the psychology of expertise see *The Nature of Expertise*, ed. Michelene T.H. Chi, Robert Glaser, and Marshall J. Farr (Hillsdale, NJ: Lawrence Erlbaum, 1988). See Robert Proctor and Addie Dutta, *Skill Acquisition and Human Performance* (Thousand Oaks, CA: Sage Publications, 1995) on the development of expertise. A classic work on how experts reason and make decisions using "chunks" is H.A. Simon and W.G. Chase, "Skill in chess," *American Scientist*, 61 (4) (July, 1973): 394–403.

the Ancient Mariner" is an outstanding illustration. Robert's insight that there is a difference in viewpoint between Keats and Shelley concerning the relationship between art and political consciousness that foreshadows the later debate, between analogous viewpoints, in modern critical theory, is a second example. His insight was based on a creative connection he made between the two domains of his interest, Romantic poetry and modern Left criticism, which he had explored jointly, thus building up a knowledge base that was distinctive in the way it spanned and juxtaposed the two domains.

Creative expertise is also generative of creative responses. A number of the individuals I interviewed described insights rooted in creative expertise they had developed. The most creative insight Azad Bonni had as a graduate student, at least in his view looking back, was seeing the structure of a recently characterized interferon receptor in an article in *Science* and recognizing that it bears a resemblance to the ciliary neurotrophic factor (CNTF) receptor, leading him to form the conjecture that the two share a common signaling pathway. His insight was rooted in twin expertises he had developed, in mechanisms of action and CNTF and nerve regeneration. I describe his insight and the path through which he came to it in Chapter 13. David Johnson's creative response, described in the next chapter, is another example.

A third way in which creative expertise is generative of creativity is through being the basis for generalizations. This is intuitive: rich knowledge structures that are the basis and result of developing expertise in an interest domain are a fertile source for identifying general patterns and insights. Richer conceptual reservoirs of knowledge allow more scope for generalization, and make it more likely that any potential generalization in a domain is in fact identified. The examples of Cheryl Nixon, Ian Baucom, and Charles Darwin illustrate generalization rooted in knowledge built up in an interest domain. Of the three, Darwin's knowledge was by far the most extensive in the domain of his interest, built up over the longest time — and he of course made by far the most important creative generalization.

In general individuals build up creative expertise in domains of their interests in the natural course of exploring and learning about their interests, not so much by design but rather more as a by-product. They find their interests intrinsically interesting and fascinating, thus naturally are led to learn a great deal about them. They do not typically have a clear idea about what use they will put their expertise to — how it may be generative of creativity or what specific kinds of ideas, insights, projects, and contributions will flow from it. Of course this is true generally of creative interests — we do not know what we will find or what creative work and contributions exploration of our interests may lead to. But it is especially true for the building up of creative

348 expertise, because this expertise, like other forms of expertise, is often built up over relatively long periods of time. This was the case, for example, for Charles Darwin, Hannah Arendt, Azad Bonni, and for Ray Kroc, whose development of expertise leading to a creative insight is described below.

Hannah Arendt is an example of someone who developed an enormous body of knowledge in the domain of her interest, investigating in breadth and depth the history of anti-Semitism and discussions about the place of the Jews in Germany and Europe, and, as her interest evolved and expanded, imperialism and the development of the modern nation state. In turn she developed many of her central insights about the origins of totalitarianism through drawing upon and synthesizing elements from this body of knowledge. It is clear in retrospect that when she began pursuing her interest she did not envision as an end product *The Origins of Totalitarianism* — in particular did not appreciate the scope of the argument she would make, the set of interconnections she eventually came to identify, or the description of totalitarianism as a form of political and social control she developed.

There is a further pattern of development based in creative expertise. Individuals often form and pursue interests they do not expect or plan to develop creatively, interests they pursue for the pure joy or interest of it. Such an interest may be an ordinary interest like a hobby, or an interest they form as part of their work — such interests being most commonly formed in practical fields like business and professions. Such interests, while not strictly creative interests, may nonetheless be quite distinctive. Over time an individual who pursues an interest of this kind may develop considerable expertise in its domain, expertise which, to the degree his interest is distinctive, is distinctive to him. It happens in some cases that the individual's expertise is the source of a creative insight he has that becomes the basis for a creative contribution.

Ray Kroc followed this pattern of development, to great success. Ray describes his path of development in *Grinding It Out*.[83] He states that he began work in the food services industry as a salesman selling paper cups in 1922, at age 20. He describes thinking of paper cups as having great potential — hygienic and modern, "part of the way that America was headed." He describes also thinking up various ways to increase sales — for example, selling drinks to people who would take their drinks outside, instead of sitting at a fountain as was customary at the time.[84] Based in Chicago, Ray was impressed by a new

---

[83]Ray Kroc, *Grinding It Out* (New York: St. Martin's Paperbacks, 1987) (first published 1977, Henry Regnery (Contemporary Books)); I also draw on John F. Love, *McDonald's: Behind the Arches* (New York: Bantam Books, 1995).

[84]*Grinding It Out*, p. 23, chap. 4.

ice cream parlor chain that opened up, Prince Castle. One of his paper cup buyers invented an ice-milk shake which he thought had potential, and he brought the owners of Prince Castle to see it. They were impressed also and began making ice-milk shakes in their stores. Soon after, Earl Prince, one of the owners, invented a multimixer — a blender with multiple spindles that made it possible to produce ice cream shakes in larger volume. Believing the multimixer had great potential, Ray formed his own company that was the national sales distributor for Earl Prince and his multimixer.

During these years as a salesman Ray developed a strong interest in commercial grade kitchens — in their operation, including workflow patterns, physical layout, efficiency, and hygiene. As a salesman selling kitchen products he would have seen many such kitchens, as well as bars, in which he made sales calls. He undoubtedly visited many more kitchens than a typical restaurant owner, who would be familiar mainly with his own kitchens and perhaps a handful of others. Thus he was in an ideal position to gain enormous expertise in the domain of his interest, and it is evident that he did. "I considered myself a connoisseur of kitchens; after all, selling multimixers took me into thousands of them," he writes. "I prided myself on being able to tell which operations would appeal to the public and which would fail." John Love writes that Ray had "an appreciation of technical improvements" in food service delivery systems, "accompanied by a remarkably keen eye for inefficiency and an intense interest in making things work better." Ray was also interested in changing lifestyles and new consumer trends and their implications for the food services industry. Selling multimixers to corner drugstores with fountains, he was made intensely aware of the flight to the suburbs because it took away business from the drugstores. He also tracked the shift to carry-out and car-access restaurants, exemplified by the success of *Dairy Queen*. Summarizing all Ray Kroc knew, John Love writes: "He had never run a restaurant, never served a hamburger, and never sold a milk shake, but by the end of that period [by the early 1950s] he knew more about the trend toward convenience foods than did most food service professionals." Thus Ray, with an interest that was both somewhat distinctive and distinctive in its intensity, built up a distinctive expertise.[85]

It was these interests and the expertise he had built up in them that enabled Ray to recognize a remarkable opportunity when it appeared. In 1954 he made a trip to the McDonald brothers' restaurant in San Bernardino. He had heard about their restaurant, investigated, and learned they had bought eight or more multimixers, the most of any restaurant. His interest piqued, he decided

[85]*Grinding It Out*, p. 63; *McDonald's: Behind the Arches*, pp. 32–33.

to make a visit. In *Grinding It Out* he describes his visit and how amazed he was by what he found — by the McDonald brothers' operation in its efficiency, mass production style, simplicity, cleanliness, and quality of prepared food. His visit sparked an epiphany in him that launched him into business operating McDonald's restaurants.

He writes that he drove to the building — a low-slung octagonal shape — in the morning, and initially was not impressed. But then things starting happening.

> I parked my car and watched the helpers begin to show up — all men, dressed in spiffy white shirts and trousers and white paper hats. I liked that. They began to move supplies . . . into the octagonal building. . . . Then the cars began to arrive, and the lines started to form. Soon the parking lot was full and people were marching up to the windows and back to their cars with bags full of hamburgers.

> It was a hot day, but I noticed that there were no flies swarming around the place. The men in the white suits were keeping everything neat and clean as they worked. That impressed the hell out of me, because I've always been impatient with poor housekeeping, especially in restaurants. I observed that even the parking lot was kept free of litter.[86]

Ray and the McDonald brothers had dinner together that night and the brothers described their operation to him. "I was fascinated by the simplicity and effectiveness of the system they described," writes Ray. "Each step in producing the limited menu was stripped down to its essence and accomplished with a minimum of effort." They produced just hamburgers, french fries, and beverages, on an assembly line basis. In Ray's view the key to their success was quality: "the simplicity of the procedure allowed the McDonald brothers to concentrate on quality in every step, and that was the trick."[87]

The next day Ray went back to the restaurant.

> I was on the scene when McDonald's windows opened for business. What followed was pretty much a repeat of the scenario that had played the previous day, but I watched it with undiminished fascination. I observed some things a lot more closely, though, and with more awareness, thanks to my conversation with the McDonald brothers. I noted how the griddleman handled his job; how he slapped the patties of meat down when he turned them, and how he kept the sizzling griddle surface scraped. But I paid particular attention to the french-fry operation.

> The McDonald brothers kept their potatoes . . . piled in bins in their back warehouse building. . . . [T]he walls of the bins were of two layers of small-mesh chicken wire.

[86]*Grinding It Out*, pp. 7–8.
[87]Ibid., pp. 9, 71.

This kept the critters out and allowed fresh air to circulate . . . . [The potatoes] were carefully peeled, leaving a tiny proportion of skin on, and then they were cut into long sections and dumped into large sinks of cold water. The french-fry man, with his sleeves rolled up to the shoulders, would plunge his arms into the floating schools of potatoes and gently stir them. I could see the water turning white with starch. This was drained off and the residual starch was rinsed . . . with a flexible spray hose. Then the potatoes went into wire baskets . . . . A common problem with french fries is that they're fried in oil that has been used for chicken or for some other cooking. . . . There was no adulteration of the oil for cooking french fries by the McDonald brothers. Of course, they weren't tempted. They had nothing else to cook in it.[88]

He also describes observing their kitchen layout and equipment more closely, observing how well designed it was: "They had a specially fabricated aluminum griddle . . . and the set-up of all the rest of the equipment was in a very precise, step-saving pattern." Love describes the set-up this way: everything sparkling clean, the kitchen open to clear view behind glass, with, in Dick McDonald's words, "a spotless grill, and all that shining stainless steel," as well as customized equipment designed by a local machine craftsman, including a rigid spatula and special pump dispensers for ketchup and mustard, and a precise operating routine, with individuals staffing each function — grill, shakes, et cetera — that was highly efficient.[89]

As Ray describes it he had the vision of opening a chain of McDonald's restaurants throughout the country — for he was convinced this was a remarkable business opportunity, perhaps the great opportunity of his life. This was his creative insight — recognizing how remarkable their restaurant in its operation and quality was, and seeing in it the prototype for a chain of restaurants. His insight was in fact rooted in the expertise he had built up through years of visiting restaurants and observing closely their operations, efficiency, quality, cleanliness, and general appeal. This expertise enabled him to see, more than others, the unique features, and hence opportunity, of the McDonald brothers' restaurant — it stood out among all the restaurants he had seen as remarkable and having great potential. Many other people had been aware of the success of the McDonald brothers and tried to imitate it. But these others saw only that — their success; they didn't see with the acuity Ray did why the McDonald brothers' operation was successful, its unique, intrinsically appealing features of very high quality food preparation coupled with customized kitchen design and highly efficient operations. Not appreciating the overall workings they did not replicate it — tended to miss details and tinker with it, in the process de-

[88]Ibid., pp. 10–11.
[89]Ibid., p. 72; *Behind the Arches*, pp. 16–18.

352   stroying, without even realizing it, the very values and system they sought to copy.[90]

Later on the second day, after the lunch rush was over, Ray approached the McDonald brothers and described how impressed he was with their operation and his idea to open a chain of restaurants. They made it clear they enjoyed the life they had and were not interested. But he persisted and suggested they get someone else to run them, and when they asked who, he writes, "I sat there feeling a sense of certitude begin to envelope me. Then I leaned forward and said, 'Well, what about me?'"[91]

[90]Love describes the many other efforts to replicate the McDonald brothers' restaurant in *Behind the Arches*, chap. 1, and the tinkering others did, that Ray Kroc did not do, on pp. 41–42. As he notes, the McDonald brothers' restaurant was well known — Ray Kroc did not discover it in that sense; but he appreciated it and was able to replicate it on a large scale in a way no one else did.

[91]*Grinding It Out*, pp. 11–12, 71–72. Love states that he broached the possibility after having flown home to Chicago — *Behind the Arches*, p. 40.

The Role of Conceptions of Creative Interests and Associated Values and Principles in Guidance; Management of Creative Development at the Meta-Level

In this chapter I describe the role of creative interests and conceptions of interests in guiding decision-making and in serving as touchstones for individuals in reflecting upon the course of their development and managing or attempting to manage it. I endeavor to show that individuals make decisions and think about their course of development from the perspective of their interests and conceptions of interests; and also that they attempt to manage their development in a broader sense — at a meta-level — in terms of its overall course, guided by their conceptions of interests, arguing and showing with examples that such thinking is crucial for some individuals. I describe how values and principles individuals have that are integral or linked to their creative interests are often important in motivating and sustaining them and guiding them in their work.

In describing ways in which individuals manage or attempt to manage and guide their creative development I do not mean to imply that creative development is predictable or easy to guide and manage. There is, of course, a great deal that is unpredictable, and a good deal of randomness that is important, such as random events that spark creative responses and the randomness of project outcomes. Nonetheless, it is clear to me, based on the individuals I have studied, and shown by the many examples I present in this chapter that

354 many individuals do attempt to manage and guide their development, and do so in ways that are important in influencing their path of development and outcomes.

DECISION-MAKING

In the course of our creative development we confront and make many decisions that shape the course of our development and thus are important in shaping the nature of our contributions, directly and indirectly. On the broadest, most far-reaching level we make decisions about what fields to work in, and, within our chosen field, about which interests to pursue; we also make decisions about which organizations to join, and other career decisions. We make many kinds of decisions that are intermediate in their scope of impact — including decisions about which individuals to collaborate with, whether or not to pursue particular pathways of exploration, for example paths in a given interest domain, and about which projects to undertake and abandon. Finally, we make many decisions that are narrow in scope — decisions about what elements to learn about in exploring an interest, and many decisions about projects.

In making these decisions, in particular those of broad and intermediate scope, we are guided principally, though not exclusively, by our creative interests and in particular by our conceptions of our interests. We are also guided by practical considerations like the likelihood of success and that the contributions we might make if we pursue a certain path will be important. But interests are primary: individuals in general pursue ideas and projects that fit with their interests — that they find exciting, are interested and excited to explore and develop creatively. As a result, it is not unusual for individuals to pursue ideas and projects that turn out to be somewhat impractical or that fit with their interests but that they themselves recognize may be less important, in the larger scheme of things, than other topics they could pursue.

My interview subjects described many kinds of decisions they made in which it was clear they were guided by their conception of interest or, if they had not formed a well-defined conception at that stage of their development, their general sense of their interest. Many described choosing which doctoral program to attend based on identifying faculty members who appeared to share some commonality of interest. Jeffrey Shoulson, who had an interest in *Paradise Lost* and was interested in exploring its relationship with rabbinical interpretation, and more broadly the similarities between literary criticism and rabbinic interpretation, said: "I chose to go to [my program] because I knew that there would be people there whom I could work with, who were uniquely capable and qualified to advise me in the kind of diversities of rabbinic and

Judaic studies on the one hand, and literary studies on the other hand. There are relatively few places, I think, in the country where I could have gone that would have given me that contact with people who had those similar interests." Azad Bonni described his interests and a possible idea for a project to a faculty member at the school where he was doing his residency training in neurology and this individual mentioned several names of possible researchers at other schools where he might go for his doctoral work and to pursue his ideas. Azad contacted several of these, and made a positive connection with one — and on this basis chose to enter the doctoral program in this individual's university. Teresa Nick chose the doctoral program she attended largely because there was an individual on the faculty who had worked with Eric Kandel on classical conditioning models of learning, work that had inspired her own interest in studying neural circuitry and behavior in simple organisms like *Aplysia*.

My subjects also described many decisions they made about their program of study in which they were guided by their interests and conceptions of interests. Those in literary studies and mathematics mentioned most frequently decisions about what classes to take and whom to choose as their advisor. Jeffrey Shoulson did an independent study with a professor on rabbinic interpretation and literature; he said that the professor, who became his advisor, was sympathetic to his interest and helpful to him in pursuing it. As described in Chapter 9 Susan was looking outside her department for classes that fit with her interest. She discovered the class in Anthropology about written and spoken forms of language, recognized it fit with her interest, and took it. Ian Baucom chose as his advisor an individual who shares his interest in British colonial and post-colonial literature and its cultural meanings. Several of the mathematicians chose as their advisor an individual they had been led to through pursuing their interests. Victoria chose her advisor upon finding that he had at least a broadly similar interest in analysis and initiating a dialogue with him about her college thesis problem, about which he made a very useful suggestion, as described in Chapter 7. Daniel Upper, who has an interest in time series prediction, was led through a colleague's suggestion to approach an individual outside the main mathematics department at his university who shared his interest.

The neuroscientists described making decisions about both their advisor and connected with this what lab to work in for their doctoral research — their main advisor usually being the principal investigator in the lab in which they worked. Jane Minturn, building on her earlier interest in development, noted in Chapter 3, developed an interest in changes in the constellation of proteins expressed by cells during development. She formed this interest while doing a rotation working in a lab in which she was studying protein expression in glial cells. At this same time her focus of interest shifted from glial cells to neurons.

356   She thus switched to a lab that fit specifically with her interest in studying protein expression during development in neurons. "There were people [there]
working on neurons, and they were looking at the specific things that I had just
started becoming interested in in the glial cells, so that made it a natural choice
for me," she said. Chris and Sophia chose advisors who worked on topics that fit
with their interests in axonal pathfinding; indeed each chose as advisor someone who shared a similar orientation and focus within pathfinding. Chris chose
a lab in which molecular mechanisms of pathfinding are studied in *Drosophila*
using genetic techniques. Describing his first reaction to the lab Chris said, "I
thought it was a great system to answer some very fundamental questions about
developmental neurobiology." As described in Chapter 8, Sophia first learned
about her advisor's work at an orientation meeting where it was described with
pictures, showing axons turning and following paths, which resonated with her
own interest. She signed up to do a rotation with him — and described them,
as noted in Chapter 4, "watching growth cones" together, sharing a common
bond and interest, that cemented her decision to work with him. Takao also
chose his advisor and lab based on his interest: his advisor works on the developing visual system, and when Takao approached him was open to Takao
introducing molecular biology techniques and developing projects based on
these techniques to study the developing visual system.

   Interests were certainly not the only factor for the individuals I interviewed in
deciding about advisors. Many mentioned the importance of the interpersonal
match, practical issues such as how effective they thought their advisor would
be in helping them get a job, and many of the neuroscientists mentioned the
importance of the lab work environment. But interests were fundamental —
all of my subjects described trying to identify an advisor who they thought
shared a similarity of interests, at least at a broad level.

   A fundamental decision individuals face in creative development is what
projects to undertake. Undertaking a project and focusing energy on it marks
a fundamental transition: in undertaking a project an individual shifts away
from relatively open-ended exploration of his interests to focus on project
execution. The decision to undertake a project generally involves some degree
of commitment — of time and energy, often of resources, and in many cases,
in terms of making an agreement with someone else to collaborate on the
project. Thus the decision is meaningful — it cannot costlessly be reversed,
though in many cases individuals do modify their conception of a project in
the course of working on it.

   There are a variety of ways in which individuals come to define and undertake projects. In general individuals do not simply take on projects that are
presented to them, already defined. While this is what happens in some cases, in

many others individuals develop ideas for projects themselves. Here I describe three basic processes through which individuals come to undertake specific projects, focusing on the central role of interests and conceptions of interests in project development and decision-making: (1) developing a project out of an interest through identifying or constructing a specific problem, question, idea, or creative possibility; (2) choosing from among a set of offered projects; and (3) modifying or adapting a project that is presented or encountered into a form that fits with an underlying interest.

Developing a project through identifying or constructing a problem, question, idea, or other creative possibility within a domain of interest is a natural and common pattern of development. There are in fact two different processes for this. One is identifying a problem, question or possibility — recognizing it, seeing its importance and possibilities. In most cases in my experience when individuals do this the problem, question, or possibility they identify is one that others have not identified, or at least not seriously considered pursuing as a project. There are exceptions; for example, a mathematician may choose to work on a problem that is well known or has been identified by others before him, but not solved, at least not in the way he aims to try to solve it; but such exceptions seem to be relatively rare in most fields. In general, even when an individual tackles a seemingly well-known problem he conceives it differently, thus originally, for example transforming it in some way. A good example of this is Victoria Rayskin's definition of the problem she worked on for her dissertation, described in the next chapter. Similarly, Wilbur Wright approached the problem of building an airplane differently from the way others before him had, focusing on different aspects of flight, in particular on turning and the integration of control, stability, and lift. The other process is constructing a problem, question, or other possibility based on elements and possibilities one has encountered and learned about while exploring one's interests. This is a creative process of project generation — the question, problem, idea, or possibility that is defined is new and original. I note that these two forms of project definition are not sharply distinguished.

Hans Krebs is an example of an individual who identified — thus defined — a project in the domain of his interest that led to his first important independent discovery.

After working in Otto Warburg's lab for more than four years, Hans left the lab in the spring of 1930, first going to Altona, then moving to a research position at Freiburg in the spring of 1931. More independent, Hans began pursuing the interest he had identified some years earlier: *to apply manometric techniques with the tissue slice method to study processes of intermediary metabolism.*

At Altona he purchased the equipment he needed to pursue his interest, then began experimental investigations, initially working primarily on problems carried on from Warburg's lab, but increasingly initiating investigations focused more on intermediary metabolic processes.[1] During his first few months at Freiburg he continued the investigations he had begun at Altona. Then, about four months after arriving there, he made a break. Holmes, describing this juncture, writes that there was "a real change in the nature of his research." Krebs was at last "freer than he had been to undertake ambitious research projects," in line with his own interest, and he did so. He initiated "a new line of investigation," Holmes writes, a project which he "chose deliberately" to explore "the [application and] effectiveness of the tissue slice method in intermediary metabolism."[2]

The project Krebs chose was investigation of the formation of urea in the liver. He seems to have viewed the domain of his interest as filled with interesting problems and, in the interviews Holmes conducted with him, indicated that he did not choose the formation of urea for very strong reasons, but simply because it appeared, based on the limited amount he knew about it, a suitable system in which to attempt to apply the tissue slice method. "I think," he told Holmes, "[that] without searching very deeply, I thought this was a suitable system to study." Indeed when Holmes showed him an initial draft outlining the reasons he may have had for choosing to study this problem Krebs noted in the margin, as noted in Chapter 4, that there were "many pebbles on the beach."[3] In fact Holmes has identified a number of reasons why this particular problem may have attracted Krebs's attention and seemed a good choice to pursue: (1) two papers had recently been published in a journal Krebs regularly read about the formation of urea in liver extracts; (2) urea is a synthetic process, thus one in which being able to work with intact cells, as the tissue slice method allowed, was likely to be important; (3) the synthesis of urea appeared to be a relatively simple process, though at the time not at all well understood, as compared with other challenging problems like protein synthesis; and (4) urea is synthesized at a high rate in organisms, thus was likely to be relatively straightforward to measure, allowing the manometric method to be applied effectively. Whether some or all of these factors, or others not identified, played a role, it is evident that once Krebs gained the freedom to pursue his own investigations he was guided by his conception of his interest and moved quickly to pursue a problem that seemed important and lay clearly

[1] The projects he initiated and experiments he conducted at Altona are described in Frederic Holmes, *Hans Krebs: The Formation of a Scientific Life*, pp. 213–36.

[2] Ibid., pp. 247–48.

[3] Ibid., pp. 248–49.

within its domain. It is noteworthy that his project — to apply the manometric tissue slice method to study the formation of urea — was distinctive to him. I describe his success pursuing this project in the next chapter.

Azad developed his initial doctoral project idea through linking his two main interests. Azad developed his idea during his third year of residency training in neurology. By this time he had decided he wanted to study mechanisms of action governing gene transcription. "I felt it would be interesting to look at it [transcription] in relation to how it is regulated by outside factors," he said, a focus that fits with his interest, "rather than just knowing how it works itself," which is the focus of many researchers who study transcription. Azad had also formed an interest in nerve regeneration. Through a link with this second interest he defined a project. "I thought, 'I'm really interested in how neurotrophins would act on cells to promote nerve regeneration.' . . . And one of the molecules that people were talking about at that time was GAP-43 . . . which is found in the growth cone and is up-regulated when the nerve is regrowing. So I thought, 'I'd be interested to look at how it's regulated at the transcription level by NGF.' So that's how I brought it together." As described above, Azad contacted a professor who was enthusiastic about his idea and went to the university at which this professor taught, planning to pursue the idea for his dissertation. As it turned out, once he arrived there his thinking changed. He learned that much of the regulation of GAP-43 is post-transcriptional, hence occurs after the pathway that interests him, which made him less interested in pursuing the project. At the same time he learned that a researcher whose interests seemed to match his own whom he had thought was at a different institution had moved to his university. He switched to this individual's lab, and ended up pursuing a different, though related project, described in the next chapter.

The second process described above, creating or generating a project oneself, occurs through various pathways. A fundamental pathway is a creative response. Many of the individuals whose developments I have studied reported creative responses that were the basis of projects. Tim Berners-Lee's idea to write a computer program to describe the organizational structure at CERN is an example — his idea was a creative response defining an idea for a project. Chris developed the idea for his project as a creative response, sparked by the talk he and his advisor attended. Susan's dissertation project grew out of her insight about the different languages being portrayed as spoken in the dialogue in *Kim*.

Many ideas for projects, especially in certain fields, emerge through a collaborative process. Several of the neuroscientists I interviewed described developing ideas for projects in collaboration with their advisors or labmates.

Chris and Sophia each developed an initial dissertation project idea in collaboration with their advisor. Kelly developed the idea to study the mechanics of waste disposal systems in neurons in collaboration with her advisor, the project being a natural overlap of her interest in the "way of life" and routine activities of daily life of neurons, like shuttling materials around the cell, and her advisor's interest in microtubule structures. Roger developed a project through collaborating with a post-doc in his lab who recognized Roger's expertise in video microscopy and suggested a project they could work on together: using video microscopy to study in real time the transport of materials from the cell nucleus to distal locations in the cell where dendrites are forming. Takao also developed many of his projects in collaboration with others.

As an example of the process of project development, Jeffrey Shoulson's dissertation project, as he described it, emerged through a combination of moving away from an earlier project, together with identifying a puzzle in the domain of his interest, which was a creative insight. Jeffrey's dissertation grew out of his interest in *Paradise Lost*, in particular its connection with rabbinic literature, as well as his related interest in similarities between rabbinic interpretation and literary criticism. Jeffrey developed the idea for his dissertation in reaction against the approach he had taken in his undergraduate honors project, in which he had explored a possible source for some of Milton's ideas about the Bible. "I decided," he told me, "that I wasn't as interested in pursuing the whole question of sources — of whether or not Milton was actually indebted directly or indirectly to rabbinic literature. That was a question that might or might not be answered, but it wasn't as interesting to me, finally, as why it was that there were so many people who had thought there was a connection between Midrash and Milton. It seemed to me that it was remarkable how many people had noticed some kind of similarity, of common approach to the interpretation of the biblical story of Genesis between Midrash and Milton. . . . [Especially] because it wasn't even clear that Milton had been influenced by the rabbis. If it was clear then you could say that's why everyone thought that that's what had happened. But because the question had never fully been answered it seemed to me that there was probably some other reason why they had noticed this resemblance or tried to establish some link. I wanted to pursue what that resemblance or link was." Thus his recognizing that others had noticed a similarity between "Midrash and Milton" became the basis for his dissertation project, for which he said: "The general idea was to look into similar approaches to reading the Bible that you could find in *Paradise Lost* and in Midrash."

The second way individuals come to undertake projects is through choosing a project from among a set of projects that are offered to them or they encounter. This process of selection is especially important for individuals working in organizations, because in many cases they are not able to define their own projects freely, but rather must work on projects that are approved by their superiors and fit with the organization's needs and constraints. It is crucial in business, where many opportunities are encountered, and what is critical is seizing an opportunity with potential, guided by business criteria and one's interests. Ray Kroc's decision to pursue development of a chain of franchises of the McDonald brothers' restaurant is an outstanding example — he recognized the tremendous potential of their restaurant operation and forged an opportunity to pursue developing their restaurant as a chain.

Several of the neuroscientists I interviewed described choosing projects from among a set offered to them by their advisor or available in their lab. Teresa Nick described choosing her dissertation project from among a set of alternatives suggested by her advisor. As described above, at the time she entered her doctoral program Teresa was set on working with a specific faculty person who had collaborated with Eric Kandel. She followed this plan and joined his lab the summer after her first year. As she described it to me, during her first several months in the lab she mainly helped out other people. Wanting her own project, she spoke with her advisor and he suggested, as she recalled, five projects. One of these was to study the development of the bag cell neuron in *Aplysia*, the neuron that controls the bag cells which secrete a hormone that causes the organism to initiate egg-laying. Teresa told me when he mentioned this project she "jumped at it." She was so enthusiastic because the project fit with her interest in the link between single neuron activation and specific behaviors. "I mean they're pretty classic," she told me. "They secrete their hormone and the animal initiates egg-laying. I thought that was a pretty clean system." In discussing her project further it was clear that she was also attracted to it because it focused on the control of an evolutionarily significant behavior — hormone secretion that initiates egg-laying, thus connecting with her interest in spanning levels, from the cell to the organism to the group, seeing the evolutionary significance of a behavior.

It is important to note that the fact that an individual in an organization is constrained to choose from among a set of offered projects does not mean that this individual does not have distinctive creative interests. To the contrary, as is shown by the examples of many individuals whose development I have studied, including the neuroscientists and Hans Krebs, such individuals do form distinctive interests, independently, that, in many cases, are quite distinct from the aims of the organization for which they work. What it does mean is that such individuals are not free to define and pursue whatever projects they wish that fit with their interests, but rather are constrained by their organization. In such cases there are two main possibilities. There may be an accommodation,

in which an individual is able to identify and undertake, from among a set of offered projects, one or a few that fit with his interest — so that his project is jointly
determined by his interest and the needs of the organization. Alternatively, no
such accommodation may be possible, and the individual may be forced to
work on projects that do not fit with his interest. In this case we would expect
the individual to feel unfulfilled, and he may leave the organization in order
to be free to pursue projects that fit with his interest. Hans Krebs is an example
of someone who formed an autonomous interest, distinct from the interests of
his supervisor in the lab in which he worked, Otto Warburg, was constrained
not to pursue his interest, then broke free — setting up his own independent
lab, where he was free to define his own projects and pursue his interest.

Paul Barran, whose work on network communication systems was an important step towards the development of the Internet, is an example of an individual who switched organizations and, in the second organization, sought
out and volunteered for a project that fit with his interest. Paul described his
development and early research in an interview with *Wired*.[4] He worked as
an engineer at Hughes during 1955–59, working on airplane and missile defense systems. During his last years at Hughes he was involved in bidding on a
contract for the design of the Minuteman control system. The riskiness of the
technology evoked a strong response in him, sparking him to form an interest.
"I was scared," he said. "You had all these missiles that could go off by anyone's
stupidity." "We knew it was the most dangerous thing ever put together . . . . We
thought, 'What can we do to reduce the likelihood [of this happening]?'" "[So]
I got very interested in the subject of how the hell you build a reliable command
and control system."[5] Specifically, he formed an interest in exploring *how to
design and build a system that could withstand a nuclear strike, so that reliable
communication would be possible even if part of the system was damaged.* Exploring his interest, apparently reading fairly widely, Paul discovered early work
on neural networks, which sparked a creative response, refining his interest to
a focus on how to design a reliable system based on neural net principles. "I
got interested in the subject of neural nets. Warren McCullough in particular inspired me. He described how he could excise a part of the brain, and
the function in that part would move over to another part . . . . McCullough's
version [model] of the brain had the characteristics I felt would be important
in designing a really reliable communication system."[6] At this point, as he

[4]Paul Barran, "Founding father," originally published in *Wired*, March 2001, online
at www.wired.com, Archive 9.03.
[5]Ibid., p. 2.
[6]Ibid. Barran is referring in particular to the well-known 1943 paper of Warren
S. McCullough and Walter Pitts, "A logical calculus of ideas immanent in nervous
activity," *Bulletin of Mathematical Biophysics* 5 (1943): 115–33.

pursued his interest, Paul switched jobs, moving from Hughes to RAND. "As I worked on the communication problem, I felt that I could do better at RAND. They had more freedom than at Hughes."[7] Thus he moved to an organization in which he believed he would be able to pursue his interest more freely.

At RAND a project soon came up that fit with his interest and he volunteered for it. "A request came in on the issue of command and control communications for survivability [of a strike]. I said, 'Hey, that's something I'd like to work on.'" He was given the project. Pursuing it, he did groundbreaking work, developing the basic ideas of building a redundant network for reliability and breaking up a message into discrete packets, sending each packet independently across the network using the best route available — ideas that were fundamental to the development of the ArpaNet, the precursor of the Internet.[8]

A third process through which individuals develop a creative project is through adapting a project that they have been offered or exists in their environment to fit with their interests. An example is Jef Raskin's role in the initial idea for what became the Macintosh computer. As described in Chapter 5 Jef had developed an interest in school in the 1960s in designing computers "from the user-interface out," to make computers easy for ordinary people to use. Later, in the 1970s, Jef lived in the Bay Area and worked as a professional musician. When the first microprocessors became available he built one and began using it, and his interest in computers was rekindled. He formed a company building microcomputers. He also began writing reviews for local Bay Area magazines, which sparked his interest in documentation and manuals — fitting with and deepening his interest in designing computers for the user. Then he joined Apple. At Apple, as he describes in his interview with Alex Pang, he had a meeting with the Chairman of the Board, Mike Markkula, in which Markkula suggested he work on designing a computer for games. "I spoke to Mike pretty regularly," Jef said, and on one such occasion, "he asked me to design something he called Annie." "It was supposed to be a $400 game machine. I told him I had no interest in working on a game machine . . . . But I counter-proposed, and said, 'Well, I've been thinking about something I call Macintosh.' [I said] It would give all the power of the computer, but with greater ease of use." "So he proposed Annie, and I forget if I said it right then, or if I said, 'I'll get back to you in a couple of days,' but eventually I told him about my idea for Macintosh, and he liked it; [and] he said, 'Let's go.'"[9] Thus Jef responded to a project that was proposed with a "counterproposal" that fit

---

[7]"Founding father," pp. 3, 2.

[8]"Founding father," pp. 3–5. The initial idea for packet switching was also developed, apparently independently, by Donald Davies.

[9]Jef Raskin interview with Alex Pang, p. 3.

with and reflected his interest, indeed that he had thought of independently, which he was supported to pursue. He and the team that was assembled to work on the project developed the fundamental design for the Macintosh over the next few years.[10]

Below and in the following chapters, further kinds and examples of project generation are described. In particular, examples are given showing ways in which projects grow out of interests, as well as ideas and insights themselves based in and generated out of interests.

MANAGEMENT OF CREATIVE DEVELOPMENT

The fact that individuals make decisions during creative development seems evident, and the idea that they are guided by their interests and conceptions of interests in making these decisions is highly intuitive and seems not likely to be objected to. But in my view management of creative development, guided by creative interests, goes beyond specific, relatively narrow decisions. I believe that individuals not only make specific, narrow decisions, but also endeavor to manage the course of their development more broadly, reflecting upon it from a higher conceptual point of view, guided by their conceptions of their interests, as well as values and principles they hold to that are integral to or linked to their creative interests.

The idea that individuals manage their creative development may seem counterintuitive or implausible. By its very nature we cannot manage creativity in any direct sense, cannot fix in advance a sequence of thoughts and activities that will lead us to a creative breakthrough — creativity is inherently more spontaneous than that, and necessarily involves the unexpected, ideas and discoveries that cannot be planned in advance. But the fact that we cannot engineer creative breakthroughs in a tightly controlled manner doesn't mean we don't attempt to manage our creative development at all. In fact I believe many if not most individuals do attempt to manage their development, at least to a limited degree, recognizing that it is a loosely organized process, a balance of planning, spontaneity, and chance. Many of the individuals I have studied clearly did so, in a variety of ways, as I describe below and elsewhere in the book. My view in particular is that individuals endeavor to manage their development not only narrowly, but more broadly, reflecting upon their overall course of development and how it fits with their interests and associated values, principles, and larger aspirations.

Further, I believe an individual engaged in creative development is the only one who can truly properly manage his development. For he is exploring

[10] Many of their ideas are documented, as he describes in the interview, in the "Book of Macintosh," also in the Stanford Library "Making the Macintosh" project.

interests of his own design, following his own unique path of development. While it is certainly the case that others may give him helpful advice, they are not likely to appreciate the nuances of his interest as well as he himself does. Thus individuals must define their paths for themselves, following their intuition, using their conceptions of their interests.

The management of creative development, especially as it relates to and fits with other elements and processes of creative development, has not been studied nearly as much as it deserves to be. How do individuals think about their creative development — in what terms? How do they evaluate their course and progress in their creative development, and decide when to make shifts of direction? These are important questions that have not yet been addressed satisfactorily in the creativity literature — indeed, with a few exceptions, such as Donald Schön's discussion in *The Reflective Practitioner*, which, however, is less theoretically structured than my approach, have scarcely been raised.[11] Most accounts that I am aware of that consider management focus on decision-making and critical thinking at the level of specifics. Thus, for example, the model of creativity as cycling between convergent and divergent thinking highlights the need for us to consider ideas we have generated critically, to try to determine which are most likely to be fruitful, with the discussion couched at the level of specific ideas. This is a useful model and important. However, the analysis does not root critical judgement and decision-making in creative interests. Further, it does not concern critical thinking and reflection at a higher level, about the overall course of one's development, including discussion of critical junctures in development — kinds of reflection for which creative interests and conceptions of interests come to the fore and are central. This lack of attention to the process of management reflects the general bias towards viewing creativity, and by extension creative development, as inherently uncontrollable, and not structured — not rooted in and unfolding out of a larger scale, structured process.[12] My aim is to describe a few facets of management

[11] Donald Schön, *The Reflective Practitioner: How Professionals Think in Action* (New York: Basic Books, 1983); he is one of the few who has focused on reflection in and on the creative process. Brewster Ghiselin notes the need to manage the creative process in his introduction to *The Creative Process: A Symposium*, edited by him (see Chapter 1, footnote 26). However, his conception of management is fairly different than mine and not rooted in a well-defined theoretical model, at least not one spelled out in detail.

[12] In the literature modeling creativity as a search process, it is recognized that we should think about our search path and attempt to guide it. But the focus is a narrow context — for example, identifying or solving a problem — not creative development at large. An example of creative process as search is the algorithm-based approach presented by Pat Langley, Herbert A. Simon, Gary L. Bradshaw, and Jan M. Zytkow in *Scientific Discovery*. Douglas Hofstadter also describes the creative process as search

of creative development, and hopefully to stimulate further work investigating management processes at different levels.

The Meta-Level

In psychology meta-level processes — processes of thought at a higher level, above narrow details — have come to be recognized as important, powerful processes through which individuals plan, self-regulate, and reflect upon their lives and the contexts of their lives. Meta-cognition refers to an individual, from a higher level, seeing larger patterns of his own development and thought processes — and perhaps thus making corrections and regulating them.[13] In the study of expertise meta-level analysis is defined as a mode of thinking in which an individual rises above narrow details and concerns to see or envision the larger terrain, to identify and study larger patterns and constellations of elements — interconnected sets of problems, ideas, facts, possibilities, and issues — and think about general approaches and strategies to solve difficult problems or make key decisions.[14] I believe meta-level processes are important in creative development, more than has been recognized.

Creative interests are intermediate level conceptual structures — at least that is how I describe them in this book. Consistent with this, conceptions of creative interests are typically not focused primarily on narrow details and events — though these may form parts of individuals' conceptions — but rather are conceived more broadly and abstractly, as outlining medium-sized domains for exploration and development. Thus, many of the conceptions of

in *Fluid Concepts and Creative Analogies*. David Klahr and Keith Dunbar offer an interesting account of "dual search spaces" in the sciences in "Dual space search during scientific reasoning" — search in the space of hypotheses together with search in the space of experimental designs to test specific hypotheses. The idea of such dual search is intuitive, but again is focused more on lower down processes — searching for specific projects and even experiments within projects, and specific hypotheses or ideas — not higher level management. Mark Runco and Ivonne Chand discuss the importance of evaluative thinking in the creative process in "Problem finding, evaluative thinking, and creativity," in *Problem Finding, Problem Solving, and Creativity*, pp. 20–76. Again the context of the discussion is a focus on specific creative problems and ideas.

[13]See, for example, John Flavell, "Meta-cognition and cognitive monitoring - a new area of cognitive-developmental inquiry," *American Psychologist* 34 (1979): 906–11. A large literature has developed since Flavell's work. See also Michael Sheier and Charles Carver, *On the Self-regulation of Behavior*.

[14]There is a large literature on expertise, including on the differences between experts and novices — one important difference being that experts in a field are typically good at reasoning at the meta-level whereas novices are not. For some contributions and references see *The Nature of Expertise*, cited in Chapter 10, footnote 82.

interests described in this book can be thought of as at (or near) the meta-level.
As an example, Takao's conception of his interest is defined at the meta-level:
he thought about his creative development strategically, planning his doctoral
research career, and conceptualizing his interest in terms of a general perspective and approach he would bring to bear on a research area that had
traditionally been studied using other techniques, not focusing on a specific
question or project but leaving his options open, thinking more broadly about
possibilities. Similarly, Hans Krebs, when he first set up his own lab and began
considering projects to explore, did not have any particular project in mind,
but was thinking at a broader level about applying a general set of techniques
to a class of problems. Virginia Woolf's conception of our reflections of ourselves as the basis for literature is likewise a conception at the meta-level —
she described her interest in abstract, general terms, and could not and did not
at the time provide any technical details or definite statement about the style
through which her conception might be realized, leaving that to future exploration. Many further examples could be given. It follows that, in using their
conceptions to guide or at least attempt to guide their development, individuals
think about their development and attempt to guide it on a meta-level.

Reflection at the Meta-Level

Based on the individuals whose developments I have investigated, individuals
tend to reflect upon the course of their development at certain junctures:
when they reach an impasse and are unsure about their current work or path
forward; and when they have open time, for example when they take a break
from or complete a project and are considering what to do next. During these
times they naturally look back upon their development — reflecting upon
projects they have engaged in, evaluating the products they produced and
their feelings about the experience of engaging in them, which may be quite
different than the evaluations they made at the time. Perhaps even more they
look forward — imagining and trying to conceptualize what they are most
interested in pursuing. These processes of reflection naturally occur at the
meta-level: individuals step back from immediate, narrower concerns of the
moment, and think at the meta-level about their overall course of development.
In thus reflecting an individual may conceptualize her interest differently than
she has in the past, or imagine a new project possibility, or come back in her
mind to a radical interest or possibility which she had previously set aside. In
turn, such paths of thinking may lead her to make a radical shift in her path of
development, or plant the seed for such a shift.

Virginia Woolf's description in "The Mark on the Wall" beautifully depicts
a moment of reflection at the meta-level. Having been working on her second

368   novel *Night and Day*, she allowed herself a break, and let her mind roam free. The narrator in the story describes herself sitting in front of the fire, musing — first about the mark on the wall in front of her, but then, letting her mind roam freely and deeply, about life and what is most important in life, leading to an insight about an imagined form of literature she finds profound and compelling — a conception of a literary interest to pursue. Describing her experience of writing the story some years later Virginia wrote, "I shall never forget the day I wrote the *Mark on the Wall* — all in a flash, as if flying, after being kept stone-breaking for months."[15] This very much suggests taking a break from the daily grind of writing *Night and Day* — that is what the reference to "stone-breaking" apparently refers to, letting herself go to think and write freely, to probe and try to illuminate her true interest. Thus, although the story is a fictional representation, it is hard not to believe it describes her own reflections upon life and her interest in literature.

Other writers also describe periods of reflection triggering a clearer sense of their interests or ideas for stories that were the seeds of books. William Faulkner described the origins of *Flags in the Dust* as such a moment. As already recounted in Chapter 3, Faulkner wrote, two years later, that he was "speculating idly upon time and death," thus clearly in a reflective mood, and began to think about his childhood and the South as he had known it. Feeling thus driven, and compelled to write, he began to work to re-create that world, as he now perceived it, nostalgically, as it had been in his imagination and would never be again, possessing grandeur, moral decay, and an overhanging foreboding of doom, but also, still existing among a few, innocence and deep-seated moral conviction and courage. In his reflection and remembrance he identified — conceived — his creative interest, as described in Chapter 3. Tolstoy, Dostoevsky, and Joyce all reflected, in writings that have been preserved, upon their writing and literary interests, and set forth ideas for projects that seem to have occurred to them during such episodes of reflection upon their interests.[16]

[15]Letter to Ethel Smyth, Oct. 16, 1930, in *Collected Letters of Virginia Woolf*, Vol. IV, ed. Nigel Nicolson and Joanne Trautmann, p. 231.

[16]Tolstoy in his diaries both brilliantly critiques his writing and discusses more broadly his literary aspirations and interests, specific plans, and principles of writing. For example, he remarks in an entry on Sep. 22, 1852: "To compile a true, accurate history of Europe in this century — there's a task for a lifetime." In an entry on Dec. 17, 1853 he writes: "Every historical fact needs to be explained *in human terms* (italics in original). . . ." Both entries seem to foreshadow *War and Peace*. See *Tolstoy's Diaries*, Vol. 1, 1847–1894, ed. and trans. by R.F. Christian (New York: Charles Scribner's Sons, 1985), pp. 60, 81. For Dostoevsky writings survive in which he reflects upon his literary aspirations, essentially defining his literary creative interest and ideas for specific

A number of my research subjects described episodes of reflection during
which they thought about their overall course of development, leading them to
alter their path, either to pursue their main interest in a different vein, or switch
to a different interest. Ian Baucom grew up in southern Africa, and wrote his
master's thesis in African studies about English representations and descriptions
of Africa from the early modern period to the end of the colonial era, both
cartographic representations and narrative descriptions.[17] He told me that after
completing this project, entering a doctoral program in English, he decided
that he didn't want to remain focused on Africa, but rather wanted to broaden
his focus of interest to explore representations of empire and identity in British
imperial literature more generally. "I wasn't actually finding it compelling
enough," he said (he clarified that he meant English colonists' literature on
Africa). "I wasn't finding enough individual works that I felt would continue
to sustain my interest. I had started reading Rushdie. . . . I read some Naipaul.
I began to think I wanted to switch from a specific focus on Africa to more the
[entire] Anglophone imperial world." He thus shifted his focus of interest, to
pursue a broader, more ambitious interest.

David Johnson formed an interest in college in the biology and function
of nicotinic acetylcholine receptors. Coming to graduate school he wanted
to pursue his interest, and joined a lab in which the focus is identifying and
cloning nicotinic receptor subunits — each receptor is made up of several
subunits that fit together — and exploring the way different subunits combine
to try to identify sets that produce functional receptors. At the time he began
working in the lab, however, he became excited about a very different project —
to explore the possibility that RNA, after being made in the cell nucleus, travels
out to distant parts of the cell and is translated into protein at these distant parts
instead of in the cell body. "It was such a novel idea," he said. "It went against
the paradigm. The paradigm, in the text books, which was taught to everyone,
was that it's all done in the cell body. And here was a completely new way of
looking at it." David connected this project to his prior interest by saying that
it also involved a focus on the synapse, as he wanted to try to identify RNA
strands at synapses being made into protein. But it is clear that it was a significant
departure from his prior focus. David told me he struggled on the project for

projects, at and around the time he was leaving imprisonment in Siberia and had re-
entered Russian society. Joseph Frank describes this period in Dostoevsky's life well,
including excellent commentary on his literary reflections and plans for the future, in
Volume III of his biography, *Dostoevsky. The Stir of Liberation, 1860–1865* (Princeton,
NJ: Princeton University Press, 1986).

[17]Ian's master's thesis is *Maps and Misreadings: England Writing Africa*, African
Studies Council, Yale University, 1991.

370 nearly two years, it was technically very difficult, and he was never able to run a clean experiment and identify RNA as he had hoped. Eventually, he decided to abandon this project. He told me he decided this after "great thought," that he wanted to work on a project that was more certain to lead to some definite outcome that could be the basis for a dissertation. Thus he decided to change course, and return to his main interest, nicotinic acetylcholine receptors — a good example of reflection spurring a shift in creative direction, in his case to return to his previous interest.[18]

A few months later at a conference David happened to see a research poster presenting a partial sequence for what was described as a new nicotinic receptor subunit. He was excited, thought it was a good topic for him to pursue, thus decided to pursue trying to work out the full sequence and then match it with other subunits to create a working receptor. Over the following year he worked out the sequence, but was unable to get it to work with any other subunits. At this time, a year later, he came across a paper and at a conference saw a research poster documenting a new kind of serotonin receptor that functions like a nicotinic receptor.[19] David had not read the paper carefully, and he said he found the poster "fascinating" but did not think it was directly relevant to his work, since he thought he was working on a nicotinic receptor. But when he returned home he read the paper carefully and realized it was his receptor. "Figure two of that paper was the sequence of their clone, and I realized when I saw it, 'Wow! That's my sequence!'" From this point — having made a creative connection, rooted in his vigilance in keeping up with new developments in the domain of his interest — David's project moved forward successfully, and he contributed to the characterization of the new serotonin receptor.

As discussed in Chapter 3, a common pattern of development is for an individual to be drawn to a field initially by one or more big questions, themes, or ideas in the field, then, once he enters the field and begins to learn more about it, to form a more refined, narrower creative interest, more specific and distinctive, which he explores and seeks to develop creatively. For individuals who follow this pattern the big questions, themes, issues, or ideas that first drew them to the field generally remain important to them, and provide a valuable context of meaning in terms of which they may reflect upon their course of development. Thus, at certain junctures, thinking back over his or

[18]An additional factor in his decision to return to this interest, he said, was that the lab had great expertise in the field of nicotinic receptors, and he decided he should "apply" skills the lab does well "to a project" of his own.

[19]David said, "I am [was] still very much in the mindset of thinking about neurotransmitters and receptors, and when I see articles I copy them and read them." This shows how he was continually building up expertise in the domain of his interest.

her development, an individual may consider whether he has been headed in a direction that will prove useful for making progress towards understanding the big questions, themes, or ideas that first attracted him and that he continues to view as important in defining the ultimate aims of individuals working in the field. If he finds that he has wandered very far from them he may engage in a "midcourse correction" to get his development back on track — or, alternatively, he may simply note that his interests have evolved and continue on the path he has been pursuing.

René Marois, a neuroscientist I interviewed, is an example of someone who made a change in his focus of interest when he realized that he had been led away from the initial large topic that drew him to his field. René told me that he was initially attracted to neuroscience as a field in which human consciousness might be approached as a topic of study — neuroscience seemed to offer a way to study "how the brain creates the mind." Once he came into the field, under the influence of the specific professors who taught him and the programs he attended, he focused on neural development of invertebrate organisms. For his dissertation he investigated the hypothesis that in *Aplysia* certain cells that are important for learning and memory in the adult organism also have a role in the process of brain development during maturation. As it turned out, the project was somewhat difficult and at times frustrating, and René found only limited evidence in support of his original hypotheses. As he told me during our interview, he realized that studying invertebrates was "kind of a paradox" for him — "because, why would someone go into invertebrate science if they're interested in the mind-body problem [and human consciousness]?" Thus, after finishing his dissertation, wanting to work on a topic that fits better with this larger question that fascinates him, he shifted to a very different focus — the use of brain imaging to study human cognitive neuroscience.[20] He has been quite successful following this new focus — has published a series of papers using fMRI (functional magnetic resonance imaging) to study the neural basis of attention and has established his own lab.[21]

I am convinced that most individuals engaged in creative endeavors have moments of reflection in which they think about their creative development

---

[20]René also told me that he wanted to switch to something that he would enjoy more in terms of the process of research, and was hopeful that brain imaging would indeed be more enjoyable.

[21]A number of the neuroscientists I interviewed seem to have been successful in thus reorienting their focus, often to a clearer link with what they view as their main interest. A second example is Edward Ruthazer: I do not discuss Edward's development in the body of the book, but materials documenting his development are listed in the Appendix, and give some evidence of the shift in his focus.

more broadly, at the meta-level — perhaps forming a clear conception of an interest, or reflecting upon their interests and how they have pursued them to this point, or thinking about their future path of development. However, most such moments are never recorded. Virginia Woolf's recording of her reflections, even if in a fictionalized manner, in "The Mark on the Wall" is an unusually rich recording of such reflections. But for many historical cases in which individuals who are famous for their creative contributions formed a conception of interest, imagined a path forward to realize their interest, or made a crucial decision to shift their creative direction, there is no clear record of their thinking process, making it difficult to understand fully their developmental process. We have almost no knowledge of why Galileo turned to study the problem of free fall and specifically balls rolling down inclined planes around the time of the late 1590s — his surviving letters from this time do not discuss the matter, and we have no other primary source material describing his thinking process that led him to take up this question after a gap of several years following his completion of De Motu. In the case of Henri Matisse, we know something about his first engagement with painting with vivid, primary colors and exploring juxtapositions of colors, on Belle-Ile-en-Mer, because of letters he wrote and background information about John Russell. But we know far less about his thoughts during the ensuing years and in the summer of 1905 when, at Collioure, he made a creative break in his painting. We know frustratingly little about Picasso's thinking and conceptions leading to his painting Les Demoiselles d'Avignon. Thanks to important art historiography and the fact that much material survives we have an extensive record of his intense preparatory work developing his ultimate conception for the painting, documented in the exhaustive two volume work published by Musée Picasso. Thus we can trace the development of his composition, notably the shift in focus from a more traditional depiction of a scene to a painting directed at the spectator, as well as stylistic details he introduced; I describe his process of work on the painting in the next chapter. But we know very little about his conception of his artistic interest at the time he began his work — what his aim was, what was the basis from and out of which he conceived the painting.

In general the main sources from which we are able to learn about individuals' thinking about their creative development, giving us at least the possibility of identifying and understanding their conceptions of their interests and their broader thoughts and reflections about their development, and the importance of these in influencing their decisions and creative breaks, are interviews, diaries, letters, and personal reminiscences in which they speak of their life and work or record their thoughts. The scarcity of such information highlights the great value of interviews — in which the interviewer can elicit information from a subject about his or her conceptions of interests, thinking processes, and reflections.

Shifting Levels of Attention

One of the most remarkable features of the way in which we think about and manage our creative development is the way our attention shifts back and forth between a narrow focus on specific concerns of the moment, like project details, and a much broader, meta-level perspective, contemplating the context of meaning of our work, our broader interests, and our overall course of development. Literally we may one moment be immersed in the details of our work and the next soaring at great heights of abstraction as we consider its potential significance or other possibilities we might pursue. We can shift back and forth over the course of a day, or an hour. And as shown by examples above like Virginia Woolf's break to write "The Mark on the Wall," during certain crucial moments or periods we step back from our work to think more broadly and let our imagination and thinking processes range free, to consider alternative possibilities, explore interests we have not previously focused on, or think about possible shifts in our course as, for example, David Johnson did.[22]

Many of the individual cases in this chapter involve this kind of shifting of attention, and collectively they illustrate how pervasive a feature of our creative development it is. Ian Baucom, after completing his master's thesis, feeling that the literature on British imperial identity pertaining to Africa was too limiting, stepped back to think about the way in which he would like to pursue his interest further and made the decision to pursue it in the British colonial and postcolonial world at large, thus expanding the domain of his interest. As described in the next chapter, Andreas Walz moved from a narrow focus on specific projects to a broader, meta-level perspective, to solve a problem he and others in the lab in which he worked had encountered. Liz Yoder, as described below, went through an extended period during which she thought a great deal about her path of development, and whether to pursue the more radical topic of glial signaling in her research or stick with a safer topic, before

---

[22]I am convinced that these shifts are ubiquitous. However, in general people find it difficult to remember the momentary shifts in attention that occur frequently over the course of each day when they are interviewed or write about their creative development later. Thus we do not have a good record of such shifts. This is yet another example of how the historical record is biased in its recording and omits many of the details of creative development: people are much more likely to remember a crucial moment when they feel they had a great insight than to recall the ever present ebb and flow of their attention between specific details and general context.

374   making the decision to pursue the glial project. During this time she said she was performing experiments with glia, and doing more conventional work with neurons, thus her focus was shifting between project work and the larger question of whether to pursue glial signaling.

Mondrian's "The New Plastic in Painting," discussed below, shows the depth and richness of his conception of art, of the abstract principles he formulated to guide artistic composition, philosophically and also — to the point here — practically. Unfortunately we do not have a record of the thinking processes through which he generated ideas for compositions or that occurred during his actual painting process, thus we cannot know precisely to what extent his conception and guiding principles entered into and influenced these processes. But certainly it is possible, and we can readily imagine, that they would have flitted into his mind at certain moments, or have been present in the background, thus have influenced specific decisions he made or been a factor in triggering specific ideas. Likewise, we do not know to what extent Virginia Woolf had her conception of reflections in mind as she experimented with various literary forms in the years after she expressed the conception in "The Mark on the Wall," for example while writing "Kew Gardens," written just a short time later; but even if she were not focusing on her conception or even thinking about it consciously, it seems likely it would have been important in guiding her creative process, at least from the background, influencing chains of associations and her patterns of thinking.

These examples show the importance of shifts in attention both for decision-making and critical reflection at critical junctures, and, more speculatively, in guiding creative thinking and work. More broadly, patterns of shifting attention are important in creative development in other ways as well. The famous story of Isaac Newton sitting musing in a field near his home town, seeing an apple fall, perhaps gazing also at the Moon, and having the idea that the same gravitational force that applies to apples and objects close to the Earth's surface might extend much further, as far as the Moon, is striking in that it came at a time when he was away from Cambridge, thus not focusing so intensively on specific projects and problems as he was reportedly so apt to do when in residence. Having a break from intense project activity and thinking more broadly, a process perhaps facilitated by his environment, being away from his rooms in Cambridge, sitting in a field or orchard, letting his mind roam freely, he had a remarkable idea.[23]

[23]There is some debate as to exactly what Newton understood at this time about the forces keeping the Moon in its orbit. Also, according to later accounts Newton gave he recognized also at this time that, following Kepler's third law, gravitational force from the Sun, operating as an inverse square law, would preserve the planets in their orbits;

Epiphanies about one's life and path of development happen — sudden insights that occur in the midst of life. Gregg Crane, for example, described an epiphany he had about his life while he was in an art gallery looking at paintings. Gregg said he had been working hard as a lawyer and needed a break, so he went to Italy. "I was in the Uffizi Gallery in Florence and I was looking at the art and I was thinking about my dad and I was thinking about painting and art and poetry and writing, and I was in this room full of Botticellis . . . and I had this 'turfal' experience, I had this feeling, 'I'll kill myself if I go back to practice law, I can't do that life anymore'. . . 'I'm out of sync with myself, with what I am.' So I resolved. . . 'I'm not going to do this anymore, I'm going to do something that's more connected with my real interests, my real passions.'" His epiphany thus seems to have occurred via a sudden shift from his immediate environment, beautiful paintings in a city famed for its art, to an insight about his life and path forward — sparked, it seems, by the paintings around him.

Guiding Principles and Values

Guiding principles and values are important in creative endeavors, as in all spheres of life. In many cases guiding principles and values are integral to individuals' interests, linked with other elements, for example a focus on a particular substantive topic. Guiding principles and values are often consciously recognized and articulated by individuals, thus often form part of their conceptions of their interests. Ray Kroc's interest illustrates the importance of values — he prized as values cleanliness, hygiene, and efficiency, and a clean, modern design, and these were all integral to the nature of his interest in commercial-grade kitchens, guiding him in terms of the kinds of kitchens that caught his attention and interest. The interests of Piet Mondrian, Ian Baucom, Mara Dale, Enid Zentelis, William Faulkner, and Pierre Omidyar, discussed below, all have values and principles integral to them. In some cases guiding principles and values are more distinct, more independent of substantive interests, acting as a second source of guidance, and also often as an important source of support. The example of Liz given below fits this pattern. In many cases also the values and guiding principles an individual holds to are the basis for and underlie interests he forms and which interests he chooses to pursue. The developments of a number of individuals in this book illustrate this, two examples being Liz and Faulkner.

but there is no good independent confirmation of this. See Richard Westfall, *Never at Rest: A Biography of Isaac Newton* (New York: Cambridge University Press, 1980), pp. 141–55 for a good discussion.

Guiding principles are kindred to creative interests in being intermediate level concepts that guide us in our creative development. Values are somewhat more general principles or beliefs that define desired states of the world or ways individuals or groups should act — rules of conduct.[24] Guiding principles and values guide and support individuals in their decision-making about which interests and projects to pursue, and in their creative work, down to the level of specific details. In some cases guiding principles and values function for individuals like approaches, providing guidance for them in thinking about how to go about their work and structuring their work. In many others they define ultimate ends towards which individuals hope or intend their work to contribute, or fundamental values they want their work to reflect and thus support. They are also important in defining and giving individuals a sense of purpose. In this capacity they are important in motivating individuals, in particular to pursue actions and projects that are congruent with them.

The main distinction between guiding principles and values and creative interests as defined and described in this book — though keeping in mind that often for an individual fundamental values and principles are integral to and connected with her main interest or interests — is that guiding principles and values are generally less open-ended, less domains to be explored, more defined.

Piet Mondrian's creative development flowed from philosophical, guiding principles that were integral to and underlay his creative interest. These principles, as part of his interest, guided him in his development and seem to have been central in leading to the creative breakthrough he made in the late 1910s and early 1920s.

Mondrian linked himself with the Theosophical movement. From this movement he gained a philosophical perspective and set of principles intended to define modern life and the evolution of consciousness towards a higher spiritual state. Mondrian took as a fundamental principle the duality of spirit and matter, and, connected with this, the corresponding duality of female (matter) and male (spirit) elements. As described in Chapter 4, in the sketchbooks he kept in the period 1912 to 1914 Mondrian identified these fundamental oppositions and specified the female element in painting as the horizontal, the male as the vertical. His guiding conception, hence interest, was to find a style or approach with which to express these fundamental dualities in their unity in painting through combining both elements in a manner creating harmony, balance, and equilibrium.

[24]Milton Rokeach, in his outstanding work *The Nature of Human Values* (New York: Free Press, 1973), defines a value to be a higher level principle that organizes and guides behavior.

As he pursued his conception, guided by it, Mondrian evolved towards a style that fit it more tightly. He began to paint simpler abstractions, representing form less distinctly. Initially he continued to used curved lines and straight lines at angles, but these dropped out, and in paintings like *Composition 10 in Black and White*, 1915, shown in Figure 3(ii), the curving element is present only in defining a circular or oval boundary to the painting and all lines are strictly horizontal or vertical, thus fitting his basic conception. However, he continued to paint just with lines, with white canvas a pervasive background.

In 1917 Mondrian completed his important essay, "The New Plastic in Painting."[25] In the essay he goes beyond his earlier conception, describing a new "plastic" art form that reflects modern life and contributes to its development — thus refines his conception, forming a richer, more articulated conception of art. He emphasizes pure abstraction, as against direct naturalistic representation of natural objects, as the fundamental means of expression of the universal, through which the particular or individual is expressed most perfectly — as the direction art is evolving towards, and its ultimate end. In part, the essay seems to document his own breaking free from traditional, naturalistic art towards pure abstraction. He writes as follows, describing the shift that is occurring in the artist and art:[26]

> The universal in the artist causes him to see through the individuality that surrounds him, to see order free from everything individual. This order, however, is veiled. The natural appearance of things has evolved more or less capriciously: although reality shows a certain order in its articulation and multiplicity, this order does not often appear clearly but is obscured by the conglomeration of forms and colors. Although this natural order may not be immediately discernible to unpracticed eyes, it is nevertheless this *equilibrated order* that arouses the deepest emotion of harmony in the beholder.... When the beholder has achieved some consciousness of [this] cosmic harmony, then the artistic temperament will require a *pure expression* of harmony, a *pure expression* of equilibrated order.
>
> If he is an artist, he will no longer follow order in the *manner of nature* but will represent it in the *manner of art*: he transforms order, as we perceive it visually, with the *utmost consistency*.

Traditional painting, directly representing nature and natural objects, is inherently inadequate, because it represents the particular over the universal. Thus painting has inexorably been led to abstract style as a way to express universal harmony or spirit:

> Consistency of style in the manner of art [the development of abstract art] is a product of the experience that plastic expression in naturalistic color and form

[25]Piet Mondrian, "The New Plastic in Painting," in Piet Mondrian, *The New Art — The New Life; The Collected Writings of Piet Mondrian*, pp. 27–74.
[26]Ibid., pp. 32–34.

is unsatisfactory. From the viewpoint of the particular, naturalistic representation always remains inferior to actual appearance; from the viewpoint of the universal, naturalistic representation is always [overly focused on the] individual. No art has ever been able to express the power and grandeur of nature by imitation: all true art has made the universal more dominant than it appears to the eye in nature.

Thus, finally, there had to emerge the *exact plastic expression of the universal*. . . .

In the old art, tension of form (line), the intensity and purity of color, and natural harmony were accentuated — sometimes even exaggerated. In the new art, this exaggeration increased to the point where *form and color themselves became the means of expression*.

Mondrian's principles of artistic composition continue to be rooted in a philosophy of man and his evolution. In the opening sentence of the essay he writes that the life of modern man is "turning away from the natural: life is becoming more and more *abstract*." He describes the "changed consciousness" of modern man and writes that art is the product of this development and a reflection of it, and must of necessity, reflecting man's greater consciousness of the universal, become abstract. He describes the "new plastic" means of expression, "the style of the future," as rooted in man's evolving consciousness. He continues to view matter or nature and spirit as two elements, female and male, united in harmony; thus the last section of his essay has the title "Conclusion: Nature and Spirit as Female and Male Elements," the basic idea being that the unity of the two forces is accomplished by intensifying each through expressing it in its most elemental form — female as horizontal line element, male as vertical — and combining them compositionally.[27]

He goes, however, well beyond his previous discussion, discussing colors and the relation between colors and form, and defining principles and elements of composition for the new abstract art (he names it "abstract-real") that he imagines, to express the universal. In these details he thus sets forth his more refined, richer conception.[28] Specifically, he defines abstraction in terms of "determinate primary colors," defining rectangular panes, as well as straight lines, specifically horizontal and vertical lines, and defines the essence of the art form he imagines as the abstract union of form and color. "The new plastic . . . must be expressed by the abstraction of form and color — by means of the straight line and determinate primary color." The key property of abstract expression is "equilibrated relationship," expressed through combinations of the "straight line and rectangular (color) plane." He calls attention to "the perpendicular" as essential to expressing such purity — echoing his

[27]Ibid., pp. 64–69. All italics in these and following quotations are in the original.

[28]Mondrian views the art he is describing as both abstract and real, thus as "abstract-real" art.

earlier statements in his sketchbook — because "it expresses the relationship of extreme opposition," presumably to the horizontal, "in complete harmony," thus creating unity through opposition. Then, a few pages later, he spells out the use of primary colors in bounded rectangular planes. Abstract-real painting is based, he writes, on the principle of *"color brought to determination."*[29] He specifies how this is achieved in section 3 (quotes from pp. 36–37):

> To determine color involves, first, *the reduction of naturalistic color to primary color*; second, *the reduction of color to plane*; third, *the delimitation of color — so that it appears as a unity of rectangular planes.*

Mondrian defines the three primary colors as yellow, blue, and red.[30] He continues:

> In abstract-real painting *primary color* only signifies *color appearing in its most basic aspect.* Primary color thus appears very relative — the principal thing is that *color be free of individuality and individual sensations, and that it express only the serene emotion of the universal.*
>
> The new plastic succeeds in *universalizing* color for it not only seeks the universal *in each color-as-color,* but *unifies all through equilibrated relationships.* In this way the particularities of each color are destroyed: color is *governed* by relationship.

This conception of primary colors balanced in equilibrated relationships proved central for Mondrian in the ensuing years, as he developed his mature style: rectangular panes in primary colors carefully positioned relative to one another, with horizontal and vertical lines of demarcation, creating the harmony and unity he sought.

Mondrian began his essay in 1914, wrote a friend that it was "almost complete" in 1915, and finished it in 1917. Thus the essay in the main predates the important step forward he took in his painting, beginning in 1917, introducing rectangular colored panes into his paintings — indicating that his conceptualization of the principles to guide the construction of the new abstract-real painting really did act as a guide for him in his artistic development. This is consistent with his own views — in his essay he emphasizes modern man gaining consciousness and the importance of the artist being consciously guided by the abstract principles he sets forth. Thus he writes: "The life of *truly modern man* . . . takes the form of the autonomous life of the human spirit becoming conscious." "The truly modern artist *consciously* perceives the abstractness of

---

[29] "The New Plastic in Painting," p. 45, and previous pages for more.

[30] At this point (p. 36) he seems to backtrack, and states that at the present time, because full realization of his vision for abstract expression is not yet to be realized, the primary colors must be "supplemented by white, black, and gray."

380   the emotion of beauty; he *consciously* recognizes aesthetic emotion as cosmic, universal."[31]

In the language of this book the abstract principles Mondrian sets forth in his essay can be taken to be his conception of his artistic interest — guiding him in his creative work. Mondrian took the crucial step of introducing rectangular panes of primary colors in his paintings at about the time he completed the essay, in *Composition in Color A* and *Composition in Color B* (*Composition in Color A*, 1917 is shown in Figure 3(iv)) — so we cannot know for certain whether his conception predated his artistic development, though most likely it did. His further development clearly was guided by his conception. He focused on primary colors, and began to place the colored panes more directly in relationship with one another — searching for "equilibrated relationship," seemingly gaining courage to do so over time — until reaching his mature artistic conception in his famous paintings of 1920–21. Figure 3 exhibits some paintings from these years, illustrating his development, culminating in his classic works of 1921 and the ensuing years — illustrated by the last painting shown, *Composition with Large Blue Plane, Red, Black, Yellow, and Gray*, 1921. The fit with the principles he sets forth and the way his paintings evolve, making his conception manifest, is striking.

Pierre Omidyar is a second example of an individual whose values are central in defining his interests and have guided him in developing and realizing them. For Pierre, his values led him to take on the project of developing an Internet Website for fair trading — thus acting as an interest in sparking his idea for the project — and guided him in developing the design of the site, which became eBay. Indeed these values have contributed enormously to eBay's success.

Adam Cohen writes that it was Pierre's "pure, democratic vision" that "started it all."[32] His basic design for eBay shows his abiding faith in people, and his beliefs that individuals should all be on equal footing and responsible for their actions, and that a community can naturally develop over the Internet in which individuals will treat each other with respect and fairly, with those who do not punished by other users, with a minimum of hierarchy and authoritarian intervention. What is remarkable is the degree to which he was guided by these principles in developing the eBay site, showing how deeply he holds to them and believes in their practical validity.

Pierre was interested in computers from a young age. In college he chose to work on Apple computers, a symbol of counterculturalism, and the summer

---

[31] "The New Plastic in Painting," pp. 28–29.

[32] Adam Cohen, *The Perfect Store: Inside EBay* (Boston: Little, Brown and Company, 2002), pp. 6–7. Pierre described himself in an interview with Adam as having a "democratic, libertarian point-of-view."

after his junior year worked in Silicon Valley for a company whose employees wrote programs for the Macintosh. A short time later Pierre joined Ink Development Corporation, which was engaged in software development for a pen-based system to replace computer keyboards. "It was going to be great," Cohen quotes Pierre saying. "It was going to bring computers down to the rest of us." When the pen project failed to lead to success the company shifted to online commerce, renaming itself eShop. Pierre left eShop in 1994, joining General Magic.[33]

It was while working at General Magic that Pierre conceived and developed the original version of eBay, AuctionWeb. As Cohen tells it, presumably as Pierre described it to him, Pierre had experienced firsthand the unfairness of traditional markets, trying to buy stock in a company at its initial public offering, but finding that his order was placed late and that by the time it was placed the stock had already jumped in value, so that insiders made more money than he and other ordinary investors did. Pierre decided to build an Internet site that would allow all consumers to engage in trade on equal, fair terms: an online auction in which buyers and sellers could communicate directly, with no intermediary, and such that, when an item was posted for sale, buyers could compete for it. As Pierre conceived the site: "instead of selling products from a centralized source, it connected individuals to other individuals, so that anyone on the network could buy from or sell to anyone else." "In the market he conceived of," Cohen writes, "the playing field would be level. Buyers would all have the same information about products and prices, and sellers would all have the same opportunity to market their wares."[34] In a *Business Week* interview Pierre said: "I had the idea that I wanted to create an efficient market and a level playing field where everyone had equal access to information. I wanted to give the power of the market back to individuals, not just large corporations. That was the driving motivation for creating eBay at the start."[35] By connecting individuals to one another directly, giving users each others' email addresses, the site would also function like a community — and building and preserving community is also one of Pierre's core values. Indeed, in his commencement address at Tufts University in May 2002 with his wife, Pierre singled out community, stating, "I've come to see, in terms of my life, that community is the enduring interest in mine."[36] Thus Pierre's

[33] Ibid., pp. 16–18.
[34] Ibid., pp. 6–8, 20.
[35] *Business Week* e.biz, December 3, 2001, "Q&A with eBay's Pierre Omidyar."
[36] Pierre Omidyar and Pam Omidyar, "From Self to Society: Citizenship to Community for a World of Change," keynote address delivered by Pam and Pierre Omidyar at Tufts University's 2002 Commencement ceremonies, Sunday, May 19, 2002.

values, specifically his commitment to a fair trading environment, equality of treatment, and establishing conditions to empower individuals to control their own market and establish a community, defined his interest. His statements show he was conscious of this, that these values were and are central to his conception of his interest, which guides him forward, and which he works to realize in projects.

Once the AuctionWeb site was up and running and beginning to attract sellers and buyers, Pierre posted a list of values he wanted individuals using the site to adhere to:

> From the earliest days at eBay, I posted five core values on the site — not because they came from some business plan, but because they were values I've lived my life by — values I hoped would help govern the community.
>
> These are the five values I saw as essential: We believe people are basically good. We believe everyone has something to contribute. We believe that an honest, open environment can bring out the best in people. We recognize and respect everyone as a unique individual. We encourage you to treat others the way that you want to be treated.[37]

Pierre described his motive in posting these values as "utopian." Seeking to develop an autonomous, self-governing community — partly in the interest of pragmatism, so that he would not need to resolve disputes and educate new users, but also consistent with and rooted in his values — Pierre also added a "Feedback Forum" on which users could complain about or praise other users with whom they had interacted and a bulletin board for users to help one another. And he introduced a rating system — each user would rate the other party on each transaction, with the rule that an individual whose cumulative rating fell too low would be barred from the site. These improvements further demonstrate his being guided by his values in designing the site.[38]

Fundamental values are integral to their creative interests for a number of individuals I interviewed. Enid Zentelis's fundamental social values are the basis of both her focus of interest in terms of topics she wishes to make films

[37] Ibid.

[38] Pierre Omidyar has made other statements about his values, showing how central they are to his life and his thinking. I came across an interesting statement he made about government and civil society: "That's what government should be about: laying a foundation for the growth and development of its citizens and economy. Government should focus on creating the right kind of environment for us to make good things happen for ourselves. The most important part of that environment is access to the tools we need to reach our potential — tools like health, education, a robust economy, security, and liberty." This is from an interview Pierre held with Wesley Clark's campaign staff, January 27, 2004; cited at http://pierre.typepad.com.

about, and a basic guiding principle for her in her work. Enid is committed to raising consciousness about important social and political issues — in particular her interest focuses on depicting the lives of the poor and oppressed and individuals living in unhappy family circumstances, as a way to raise awareness of their plight, so as ultimately to create social change. This is an interest rooted in political or social values. Further, Enid has as a guiding principle, as described in Chapter 6, to raise consciousness about social and political issues through showing the details of individuals' everyday lives. Her commitment to this approach is rooted in her belief that in witnessing the details of someone's life, such as the way they brush their teeth and interact with their children, the observer gains an appreciation for their true condition of life, and thus of the way social forces and political factors shape their life, in a way that is "indelible." When she makes a film this principle is crucial in guiding her in many ways — guiding her choice of actors and venue, her development of the plotline, and the specific scenes she devises.

Among the literary scholars, two who had interests in which values were integral are Ian Baucom and Mara Dale. Ian told me that a core belief he holds is that "culture is never fixed, there are no original moments that nations can identify as a sort of golden age." He said, in particular, that the British people are wrong to imagine that there was some ideal earlier time when they were pure, and that ever since they have had to deal with the contaminating influence of other cultures. He told me, "If there is an ethic that underwrites a lot of my work, it is that:" "there is no organic self-contained past [no past ideal state of cultural purity]." This ethic is a principle root of his interest in British colonial and postcolonial literature and the way in which the British have defined their identity in terms of their relationship to their colonies and former colonies and their very different cultures. Through his work he has wanted to show that British identity has always been in flux, being fashioned and refashioned, going back to the days of British power and glory in the nineteenth century. Mara, as described in Chapter 3, is interested in playfulness in literature and in double meanings, and formed an interest in graduate school in allegory. Mara is committed to feminist values, and this played a role in her interest and conception of interest. She told me in exploring theories of allegory she realized that the theorists she read, like Paul de Man, "were not gender conscious," and that she wanted to "bring gender consciousness to the sorts of things they were talking about." She was especially interested in women characters as allegorical representations, for example in Petrarchan love sonnets — in which "the woman, the beloved, is broken up into little pieces." Mara was also interested in the representation of desire in literature. Mara approached desire also from the perspective of feminism: she was interested in the fact that in

384   most literature and film the woman is the object of the man's desire, so that man's desire is expressed but woman's is not, and she consciously sought out and focused on cases of the opposite, in which a woman is portrayed desiring a man.

In addition to Piet Mondrian and Pierre Omidyar, a number of the other individuals famous for their contributions whose development I have studied had fundamental values and guiding principles that were integral to their interests and in guiding them in their development and work. Rachel Carson was deeply committed to the conservation of nature as a value. Further, she believed that fundamental human values are rooted in nature appreciation, as she describes in *The Sense of Wonder*, and that educating people about nature is important in instilling in them an appreciation for nature and the need to preserve it. These values underlay her interest in nature writing, and her interest in the use of pesticides and the harms pesticides cause to the natural environment; and, in their depth and breadth, they shaped her conception of *Silent Spring* and its tone of moral outrage and call to action. Her case illustrates the enormous importance of values for social activists, underlying their interests and shaping their interests and conceptions of interests and the way they pursue them. Jef Raskin's interest — in designing computers for users, with the user interface integral to and at the center of the design — essentially centered on a guiding principle: to create ease of use in designing computers. In addition, this principle seems to have been rooted in a fundamental sense of egalitarianism.

Values have a further important role in creative development, in supporting individuals in their struggle to pursue their interests and develop them creatively, in pursuing interests, projects, and ideas they perceive as risky, that may take a long time to come to fruition. In our culture, perhaps many cultures, and in my experience studying individuals' statements of their values and their role in their development, values that provide such support are values that champion autonomy, individuality, the questioning of authority and convention, courage, and values that inspire effort and give a vision of ultimate success against steep odds. Believing that there is a connection between an interest, project, or idea and these values sustains individuals, gives them courage and conviction to follow a difficult, untrodden path, that may challenge convention and authority, and the work of others who are powerful and prominent.

In his Nobel Prize Address William Faulkner stated his belief that "man will not merely endure; he will prevail." He continued:

> He is immortal, not because he alone among creatures has an inexhaustible voice, but because he has a soul, a spirit capable of compassion and sacrifice and endurance.

The poet's, the writer's, duty is to write about these things. It is his privilege to help man endure by lifting his heart, by reminding him of the courage and honor and hope and pride and compassion and pity and sacrifice which have been the glory of his past. The poet's voice need not merely be the record of man, it can be one of the props, the pillars to help him endure and prevail.[39]

Faulkner spoke of the toil and struggle of man, and of the artist, and connected this struggle with the depiction and thus sustaining of the fundamental values that support man in his noble struggle. Conversely, for the artist, knowing his enterprise is in the service of supporting and sustaining these values gives him the motivation and courage to persevere, through the difficult struggle to create, so that man can ultimately prevail.

While Faulkner made these statements long after his initial great creative period, his conception and the values he sets forth as central for man's existence and struggle are a central, vital part of the literary interest he pursued in those years, as I have described it in previous chapters — his focus on depicting individuals who have moral courage and conviction fighting against the tide of corruption and depravity, degeneration, and decay. This is seen in his depictions of individual men and women — Caddy in *The Sound and the Fury*, the boy in *The Bear* — in their purity, pride, courage, and compassion. Thus Caddy, the character he called most dear to him, rebels against the moral decay and corruption and selfishness around her, showing the possibility of the human spirit, pure and uncorrupted, rising like a phoenix out of a civilization in its twilight.

Individuals who adhere to values of autonomy and individuality, challenging authority and the status quo, may well be more likely to form interests that go against the grain, against prevailing wisdom in their field, and to pursue these interests, over long, difficult periods. Albert Einstein comes to mind as such an individual: he opposed conformity, believed in individual autonomy and creativity, had a stance of challenging authority, and formed and pursued for many long years an interest that took him beyond the conventional boundaries of his field, finally making a contribution that was radical and challenged prevailing conventional views in his field and more broadly about time and space.

Among individuals I interviewed Liz Yoder is someone whose values both had a role in her formation of her interest and sustained her in pursuing it and staying with it during a difficult time. Liz's interest in glial signaling was sparked during her senior year in college, as described in Chapter 4. From the start she perceived this topic as radical, as posing a fundamental challenge to

[39]"Address upon Receiving the Nobel Prize for Literature" (10 December 1950), in William Faulkner, *Essays, Speeches & Public Letters*, p. 120.

the conventional view in neuroscience, which is that the glial cells are merely support cells for the neurons. Liz was attracted by this radicalness — the fact, for example, that the glia were scarcely discussed in her classes or textbooks made her even more interested in them. But at the same time she was unsure whether or not she wanted to pursue the topic as her primary interest given how risky and out of the mainstream it seemed to be. She struggled for more than a year with this decision, whether to pursue this radical, inherently risky, unconventional topic, or stay with a safer topic, learning and memory, focusing on neurons. "I would say that looking back at that first year [in graduate school], I was in a transition phase," she told me, "where [I was asking myself], 'do I stick with this more traditional neuronal electrophysiology approach? Or do I make this radical departure into doing this calcium glial stuff?'"

In her second year Liz made the decision to pursue glial signaling, and it was her primary focus from that point on in her doctoral research. Her decision was in part driven by data she collected, through reading and her own experiments, that convinced her that it was a real phenomenon. She told me she discovered through researching the literature that glial signaling had been observed by many labs around the world, and that she undertook some experiments herself and also observed it, which convinced her it was real.[40]

But beyond this she connected her decision to pursue a topic that poses such a radical challenge to established opinions with her fundamental values, in particular an independence of mind that she absorbed from her father and shares in common with him. She described her father and her values in our interview:

> My father grew up Old Order Amish. Of course he left and got out of that. But there were these religious undertones in my ancestry, that I always rebelled against, [and] my father rebelled against them [too].
>
> He left. And in order to do that it takes a very very strong person who's willing to say: "This is what I think, this is what I believe for myself, this is what I want to find out. And I'm going to assert my right to do it, even if it means I get shunned, even if it means all these horrible things happen to my family. It's my right — it's my right to be educated, it's my right to do this." ... The idea that you can go in, that you can take on a piece of knowledge and work at it to your own understanding of it, that was all around me.
>
> My mindset is that you are ultimately responsible for your own education and your own work. So ... I stayed on my own path ... [And] this goes back to what I had learned growing up, that, if you find something and you think it's real and you think

---

[40]Liz said she undertook "a huge collection of articles, reading things that were happening in the glial cells." She has sent me a list of many of the papers she read, dated from that time.

it's interesting, then you stick to it, even if no one else is doing it, even if other people
tell you you're crazy; if it's real for you, then you can do it.

Liz's values, rooted in her family upbringing, are clearly important to her and support her as she follows her own path of life. They have given her an outlook and independence of mind that was very likely essential in first attracting her interest to glial signaling as a radical topic, and clearly were crucial in her decision to pursue glial signaling as her main focus of research. Her values also sustained her as she pursued her research. She described going through a difficult time as she struggled to find a novel, interesting finding. "I have this quote hanging up over my desk," she told me, "it's by André Gide: 'A man cannot discover new oceans unless he has the courage to leave sight of the shore.'" Gide's statement resonates with her own values, and shows how her values, thus expressed in inspirational statements, helped her have the courage to stay the course on her chosen path.

CREATIVITY IN PROJECTS

Creative development has three fundamental phases: (1) formation of creative interests; (2) exploration of creative interests, generation of creativity rooted in interests and conceptual structures built up in interest domains, and the defining and selection of creative projects to pursue; and (3) work on projects, leading to the creation of creative works and contributions. Most individuals cycle through these phases over the course of their development.

My focus in this book is on the first two of these phases. This focus befits my main purpose, which is to demonstrate the importance of creative interests, conceptions of interests, and conceptual structures associated with interests in creative development — to show their central functions and roles in structuring the process of development, and how creative contributions and creativity are based in and grow out of interests. During the first two phases of development in particular, creative interests are at the center of development. Interests are less central in phase three, project work, thus I focus less on this phase. The project work phase is, however, extremely important for creativity. Individuals generate many ideas and insights, and make important discoveries, in the course of working on projects; and projects are essential to and the basis for creating creative works. Thus, to describe creative development as a whole it is essential to describe the project phase of development, at least in outline.

In this chapter I describe processes in creative projects, focusing on the generation of creativity during project work. This chapter thus fits with and complements the preceding three chapters, which describe processes of creativity generation during phase two; collectively, the four chapters describe core processes generative of creativity over the course of creative development.

My discussion here is brief: I scarcely touch on many aspects of project work, such as collaborative work and resource needs. Indeed my description is not primarily intended as a contribution to understanding project work in itself. In fact, much research in creativity focuses on creative processes and the generation of creativity in the context of project work, or, more accurately, in the context of short-term activities. Many creative processes have been described in the context of studies of such activities, including remote associations, creative search, perceptual shifts, and the creative use of metaphors, for example, to solve problems. Many of the processes I describe here, for example methods of problem solving, are these very processes, thus familiar. Accordingly, I do not describe them in detail.

I focus on placing creative projects in context — describing and illustrating by example how project work and processes of creativity generation in projects are embedded in the overall process of creative development. For many of the processes I describe and in the examples, I have as one focus links with underlying creative interests, which have not in general been described previously. The narrative links of the examples in this chapter with other chapters also serve to forge such links: the examples describe projects of individuals whose creative interests have been described in previous chapters, thus manifesting connections between their interests and projects.

The chapter is divided into four main sections. In the next section I describe experimentation and discovery. In the second section I describe problem solving on projects. In the third section I describe realizations, insights, and creative responses during project work. Finally, in the last section I describe revisioning.

EXPERIMENTATION AND DISCOVERY

Experimentation is integral to many creative projects. In many cases experimentation is central to the definition of a creative project. At the time we initially define a creative project we often do not have a clear view of its end product (this is a basic difference between a creative and an ordinary project, for which we often have a clearer idea and specification of the end product at the time we initiate it); rather we define it in terms of experimentation — a set of possibilities to explore through experimenting, for example experiments to test a hypothesis or to explore different styles, approaches, or materials. In addition to such relatively planned experimentation, in many other cases experimentation occurs more by happenstance in the course of working on a project.

Through experiments we acquire information and make discoveries. Many experiments end in failure. Many others generate information or discoveries that we do not view as important and do not pursue. But the few that succeed and produce information or discoveries that are important and we pursue are crucial. In general these divide into two groups: experiments that confirm a result, principle, or hypothesis; and those through which we discover a result or possibility that we had not imagined beforehand, at least not as a realistic possibility — that perhaps no one has previously discovered or imagined as a possibility. Experiments in the first group can be quite important and sometimes constitute a highly valued contribution. Also, they sometimes have a major influence on our development through giving us more confidence about a particular direction to pursue. Experiments in the second group stand out even more: the discoveries made through them are unexpected and can change the course of a field.

Just as creative projects are rooted in and grow out of creative interests, so too the experiments individuals run or try in the context of projects — scientific experiments or experiments in the sense of experimental scenarios and approaches — are in many cases rooted in their interests. When a person chooses to run a certain experiment it is often because the experiment has a connection with an interest he has, often the same interest that is the basis of the project. The interest may be the source of the idea for the experiment, and gives the experiment relevance, spurring the individual to try it. There are other paths through which individuals generate ideas for experiments of course — some are hit upon more or less at random in the course of working on a project, others are sparked by events; but for many interests are important.

Many scientific projects center on experiments, and experimentation leads to many discoveries and is a major part of many important contributions in the sciences. The philosophy and importance of experimentation, and design and practice of experimentation, are extensively studied and discussed in the literature on the history and practice of science.[1] Here I present a few examples of experiments and discoveries made by individuals whose developments I have studied for whom experimentation was a central approach they employed in their projects and led to discoveries.

Hans Krebs's method of investigation centered on experimentation. He would, on his own account, try many experiments, exploring alternative possibilities, following hunches. "I always had the habit of trying out many things and exploring just whether there was a possibility," he said. "I was, then as today, an optimist, and . . . thought if you persist and keep at it something might turn

---

[1]Two noteworthy contributions among many linking experimentation with the process of discovery, hence creativity, are: Karl R. Popper, *The Logic of Scientific Discovery* (New York: Basic Books, 1959); and Pat Langley et al., *Scientific Discovery: Computational Explorations of the Creative Process.*

up . . . [if you] do different kinds of experiments, not just doing the same."[2] The
manometric technique he used was well suited to this approach, as it allowed
multiple experiments to be run simultaneously and many experiments to be
run in the course of a single day.

Krebs's investigation of the formation of urea, as Holmes carefully recon-
structs it in his biography, illustrates his approach, and is a classic case of
discovery through experimentation.[3] Krebs began his investigation testing the
influence of a set of substances on the formation of urea in liver tissue, including ammonia (ammonium chloride), recognized to be a source of the
amine group (NH_2) needed to form urea, glucose, and the amino acid alanine,
which was known to increase formation of urea. His testing of an amino acid
and glucose shows the influence of his interest in intermediary metabolism
in guiding his experimentation from early on — for amino acids and glucose
and other sugars are main substances entering into the metabolic pathway and
broken down into end products.[4] As he continued his investigations he tested
more substances, in various combinations, concentrations, and conditions. Although he found a number of results that seemed potentially interesting, he
found nothing of major significance beyond what was already known. Among
the substances he tested was the amino acid arginine, which was known to produce urea and ornithine through a specific reaction catalyzed by the enzyme
arginase. He tested a series of other amino acids and other substances central in glycolysis and oxidative respiration. Both of these lines of investigation
again reflect his interest in intermediary metabolism, thus are an illustration
of an interest guiding a path of experimental investigation on a project. At
this point, about four months into his investigation, seemingly somewhat at
random, Krebs tested the effect of the amino acid ornithine on urea formation. Holmes writes that the notebook description of the experiment shows that
Krebs ran this experiment as part of a group of experiments, seemingly almost
as an afterthought. Krebs himself stated to Holmes that he had no special reason for trying ornithine — "it was just, without any too specific ideas, that we
tested the effects of all sorts of substances" — and that he was planning on

[2] Frederic Holmes, *Hans Krebs: The Formation of a Scientific Life*, pp. 266, 272.

[3] Ibid., pp. 249–336. Krebs gives his own account in "The discovery of the ornithine
cycle of urea synthesis," *Biochemical Education* 1 (1973). This citation is from Holmes,
footnote 24, Chapter 9; I have not been able to locate a copy of this journal.

[4] Ammonium salts were well known to promote formation of urea in liver tissue.
Löffler, whose work was among the most recent and well known in the field — and
known to Krebs — had shown that alanine and several other amino acids increased
formation of urea. See *Hans Krebs: The Formation of a Scientific Life*, pp. 249–54.
Although I write my account in terms of Krebs running experiments, in fact, as Holmes
describes, Krebs had a research assistant who did much of the bench work.

testing all or at least many of the amino acids, supporting the view that he was engaged in wide-ranging experimentation.[5] By itself ornithine did not increase urea formation. But in combination with NH_4Cl it had a dramatic effect — the highest rates of production of urea of any experimental run.

Krebs came to call his discovery "the ornithine effect." Over the following months he puzzled over its chemical basis. The fact that ornithine enhanced urea formation only when combined with ammonia indicated that it does not donate its amine groups to form urea — in fact Krebs found that ammonia donates all the nitrogen atoms used to produce urea, supporting the idea that ammonia donates all the nitrogen for the reaction. He found that even small amounts of ornithine, in combination with ammonia, generated high rates of urea formation, which led him to conclude that ornithine must be a catalyst in the formation of urea. This meant, as he stated retrospectively describing his thinking process, that as a catalyst it "must take part in the reaction and form intermediates. The reactions of the intermediates must eventually regenerate ornithine and form urea." Knowing the arginine reaction that produces ornithine and urea, it occurred to him that arginine is a natural intermediate. Working from this idea he deduced a cycle through which urea is produced: (1) ornithine plus two ammonia molecules plus carbon dioxide produces arginine plus water; (2) arginine plus water produces ornithine plus urea, via the catalytic effect of arginase. Thus he discovered the basic pathway of formation of urea in mammals.[6]

Experimentation was central for Liz Yoder in her doctoral project. Liz, pursuing her interest in glial signaling, came to focus as a project on investigating glial signaling in Schwann cells, which she described as the glia of the peripheral nervous system; in the next chapter I describe how she came to this project through combining two of her interests. She ran many experiments,

---

[5]As Holmes describes, ornithine was one of the most expensive amino acids and it seems surprising that Krebs would have tested it before testing many others that were cheaper given his tight budget. Ornithine in fact would have stood out in two ways: it has a second amino group — one of only two amino acids that does, the other being lysine, which, however, Krebs did not test beforehand or immediately afterwards as one might have expected him to; and it is the second product in the arginine reaction that produces urea, which might call attention to it, though that reaction by itself gives no reason to believe ornithine would enhance production of urea since it is produced with urea. When Holmes broached these possible explanations to Krebs he did not agree that either was the motivation for his choice, but rather that he tested ornithine more or less at random, because he obtained some. See *Hans Krebs: The Formation of a Scientific Life*, pp. 283–87.

[6]Ibid., pp. 294–334.

trying many different neurotransmitters on Schwann cells for more than a year without finding any clear response, engaging in wide-ranging experimentation. Then she found an effect for a compound she did not expect to give any effect — the neurotransmitter serotonin, thus discovering that serotonin triggers a response in Schwann cells.

Experimentation is important in many other fields, including creative writing, the arts, and fields of invention and design.

Virginia Woolf, having developed her conception of reflections as the basis for literature in "The Mark on the Wall," worked in a process that can be described as one of experimentation to find a literary form that would embody her conception in a new form of literature. Over the succeeding three years she wrote a series of four short stories in which she experimented with different methods and forms to develop a new form fitting her conception.[7]

In "Kew Gardens," begun just a few months after "The Mark on the Wall," Virginia quite deliberately sets out to present the human world as heard by — thus reflected by — the natural world, notably a creeping snail. The story is an experiment in presenting the human world from an unusual point of view, depicting it by reflection.[8] In the story a series of couples walk past, and we overhear their conversations. Meanwhile a snail makes his slow progress, butterflies flit, and we are given fragmentary views of the people as colored, blurry objects, as a snail might perceive them, and hear bits of their conversation — thus they are shown to us in a series of fragmentary vignettes and in reflection. In "The Evening Party," written most likely in mid-1918, Virginia explores conversation as a way to loosen the narrative structure and provide reflections.[9] In the story the narrator arrives at a party, and gives us her subjective impressions. There is disjointed conversation and gossip, moving from topic to topic, discussing literature, writers, death. At the end the narrator and her companion venture away through the garden onto the moor. In the story Virginia explores dialogue as a way of conveying multiple points of view. There is a quickness of tempo, including much repartee, and in the gossip about other people we see others' views of them — thus she experiments with depicting people through reflections, that is, others' opinions of them. However, unlike later works, these people, famous writers and others, are outside the story itself. In "Solid Objects," written in late 1918, Virginia experiments further with

---

[7]I note that no stories beyond these four are listed as having been written by her during these years in *The Complete Shorter Fiction of Virginia Wolf*.

[8]"Kew Gardens," in Virginia Woolf, *The Complete Shorter Fiction of Virginia Wolf*, pp. 90–95.

[9]"The Evening Party," ibid., pp. 96–101.

alternate viewpoints and reflections, representing subjectivity.[10] We first see an indeterminate "small black spot," which turns out to be a boat, then two young men digging in the sand; all is conveyed subtly, indirectly, subjectively. One of the young men finds a lump of green glass, and this discovery has a powerful effect on him, seemingly altering his whole relation to life. As the story unfolds he gives up his career and society to search for other discarded objects; we are shown him seeing life concentrated in the objects he collects, and, at the end, see him through his friend, who visits him and cannot understand his life view. Virginia shares the thoughts of the main character with us, and the view his friend and the world have of him — thus juxtaposing different views of him — but does not quite achieve a composition of him entirely through reflections, more traditional narration and description remain central to the story's creation of meaning. In "Sympathy," written in spring, 1919, Virginia explicitly focuses on a character thinking about other people. In the story the narrator learns of the death of an acquaintance, which sets him off on a train of reminiscences, thinking about the dead man and his widow, seeing them in various contexts — thus showing them to us via his reflections upon them.[11] Virginia also experiments with time: it is fluid, more so than in the previous stories, as the story shifts from present to different times in the past; and a main theme is life as a journey towards death. There is a looseness of form and sense of movement that foreshadows "An Unwritten Novel." But the narrator is more central than in "An Unwritten Novel," her grip is tight, and we are not shown characters, other than the narrator, thinking about other characters.

"An Unwritten Novel" was a further experiment, the crucial one, through which Virginia attained — and realized she had attained — a creative break-through. She makes two key steps forward in it. Characters are depicted thinking about other characters directly, without mediation by the narrator — thus making such reflections central to the construction of characters. And there is a looseness and fluidity, both in the narrative — moving rapidly from one scene to the next — and in style — informal and freewheeling — building on the stylistic development in "The Evening Party" and "Sympathy." Her unconventional stopping at points in the story to pause and consider options, as the author, highlights the sense of freedom — showing I think that she was focused on this freedom, on constructing a loose knit, fluidly moving story.

An equally important venue for experimentation for Virginia during these years, paralleling her fiction writing, was her diary. Writing just for herself, spontaneously, composing on the fly, it was relatively easy for her to let herself go: without worrying about critics or literary tradition she could more freely experiment. Indeed a striking feature of her development over these years is

---

[10]"Solid Objects," ibid., pp. 102–7.
[11]"Sympathy," ibid., pp. 108–11.

how her writing in her diary foreshadows the stylistic break to a freer, flowing, loosely connected style in "An Unwritten Novel." In the diary we often find sentences running through a series of descriptions, vivid, loosely connected, having a kind of quickness of motion, foreshadowing her later style. Virginia herself recognized a connection between her diary and her growth as a writer. In an entry in it in April 1919 she writes that her diary "loosens the ligaments" and muses about what her diary might become: "I might in the course of time learn what it is that one can make of this loose, drifting material of life; finding another use for it than the use I put it to, so much more consciously & scrupulously, in fiction. What sort of diary should I like mine to be? Something loose knit, & yet not slovenly, so elastic that it will embrace any thing, solemn, slight, or beautiful that comes into my mind." Her description resonates strikingly with the new fictional form she developed just a few months later in "An Unwritten Novel."[12]

Virginia herself seems to have viewed this time in her work, roughly 1917 to early 1920, as one of experimentation and discovery. She recognized her frequent changes of style. And in her letter to Ethel Smyth of Oct. 16, 1930, she uses the word discovery twice in describing her creative breakthrough in "An Unwritten Novel," calling it a "great discovery."[13]

There are many artists whom we can readily imagine engaged in experimentation, guided by a conception of interest or a guiding principle, for whom experimentation is likely to have been crucial in leading them to discoveries that form the basis for major contributions they made. Unfortunately in many of these cases there is little direct evidence of experimentation.

It seems logical that it was through experimenting with colors, color combinations and juxtapositions, and relationships between color and line that Matisse was able to make the steps he made in his painting, beginning with his stay on Belle-Ile-en-Mer, and culminating in his creative breakthrough at Collioure in the summer of 1905. His innovations, the effects of striking juxtapositions of colors, cutting across compositional and figural lines, seem quintessentially the result of experimentation and discovery. But there is no good record of experimentation for him. The record we have is mainly canvases he painted, as well as sketches. These show the development of his style, in steps, but do not indicate periods of formal experimentation, for example

[12]*The Diary of Virginia Woolf*, Vol. 1, 1915–1919, ed. Anne Olivier Bell (London: Harcourt Brace & Company, 1977), entry for April 20, 1919, p. 266. Quentin Bell also writes that Virginia believed her diary writing contributed to improving her fiction writing, giving it "greater force and directness." See *Virginia Woolf: A Biography*, 2, pp. 44–45.
[13]She comments on her ever-changing style, in a remark remarkable for its prescience, in her diary entry for November 15, 1919 — *The Diary of Virginia Woolf*, Vol. 1, p. 311. For her letter to Ethel Smyth see supra, Chapter 11, footnote 15.

mixing and juxtaposing colors intentionally to record their effects. Both Hilary Spurling and Pierre Schneider use the word "experiment" to describe Matisse's art and path of development, but they do so evocatively, without much in the way of direct evidence of actual experiments he made. Matisse wrote in 1904 in a letter from Saint-Tropez about his painting *The Gulf of St-Tropez*, describing his labor on the painting, "it seems to me that it was by accident I got my result" — implying a process of discovery, though not necessarily experimentation. He did not, however, give a full account of his own creative development and did not describe formally experimenting in achieving the technique of color composition he developed.[14]

PROBLEM SOLVING IN CREATIVE PROJECTS

Problems are ubiquitous in creative projects. Creative projects are by their nature novel: in a creative project we are attempting to do something that has never been done before, or create something that has never been created. Thus it seems inevitable that problems will arise as we pursue a creative project — indeed in many cases a creative solution we develop to a problem is a main contribution we make through pursuing such a project.

There are two fundamentally distinct ways in which problems arise in creative projects. One is as the basis for defining a project. A common pattern of development is for an individual, in the course of exploring a creative interest, to come to focus on solving a specific problem as a project.[15] This pattern is

[14]The quote from the Saint-Tropez letter is on p. 284 of *The Unknown Matisse* and refers to a letter Matisse wrote to Manguin. Hilary Spurling refers frequently in *The Unknown Matisse* to Matisse's experiments in painting. A few examples are pp. 159, 194. Schneider refers to Matisse's innate drive for "experimentation" on p. 192 of his *Matisse*, trans. by Michael Taylor and Bridget Strevens Romer (New York: Rizzoli, 1984). Matisse's fullest early statement of his theory of painting is in "Notes of a Painter," 1908, in *Matisse on Art*, ed. Jack D. Flam (New York: Phaidon Press, 1973), pp. 35–40. In the essay he describes his aim in painting as being one of expressing his subjective feelings evoked by a scene, and describes how he successively adds colors to a painting, creating a composition. But he does not discuss how he developed his technique more generally, thus his own creative development.

[15]As mentioned in Chapter 1, a model of creative development implicit in many studies and models of creativity is an individual entering a field, learning about various elements and open problems in the field, then picking a specific problem to pursue. The flaw in this description is that it does not incorporate the process of individuals forming and exploring creative interests. A better description, fitting accounts individuals give of their development and the description in this book, is an individual being led through exploring her interest, thus through a transitional phase of development, to focus on a particular problem.

common in many fields, for example mathematics — Victoria Rayskin, for example, described following a path of development fitting this pattern. The other way problems arise is in the course of project work. Problems arising in this manner are pervasive on creative projects. Solving and resolving problems is in fact a main part of the work individuals do on creative projects, and problems and their solutions — or lack of solution or resolution — are often central to project outcomes and end products.

The failure to solve or resolve problems is often a main cause of the failure to complete a project successfully. Many of the neuroscientists I interviewed described being unable to solve or resolve problems they encountered. David Johnson was unable to isolate RNA at synapses in order to test the hypothesis that some cell products are produced there. This failure is what led him to return to his basic interest in receptors and begin work on the novel receptor he saw a partial sequence for at a conference. Sophia was unable to build a chemotaxis chamber to study axon turning processes, her initial dissertation project, which led her to undertake a set of additional projects. Several of the mathematicians I interviewed also described being unable to solve problems, which thwarted them in their work.

A well-known model of problem solving in the creativity literature is the four-stage model: (1) identification of a problem and initial unsuccessful attempts to solve it; (2) a period of latency with no evident progress; (3) a moment of illumination in which a potential solution is conceived or identified; and (4) verification of the solution. A number of instances of problem solving my interview subjects described, for example Lisa Zhang's description of her invention of the stripe algorithm described below and Enid Zentelis's creative response described in the next section, fit with this model, suggesting that it is a useful description in some cases. It would be interesting to explore further the role of creative interests — specifically the conceptual structures encoding interests — in this process.

Cognitive Strategies for Problem Solving

I describe three cognitive strategies or approaches that have been described in the literature on problem solving that seem to have been employed by individuals whose developments I have explored in their attempts to solve problems they encountered in creative projects.

A fundamental technique for problem solving is search and trying alternative potential solutions. Search and exploration are widely discussed in the computational cognitive science literature; a main focus of research and description is combinatorics — the sheer number of alternative solutions to be explored, and the development of efficient search algorithms. Though I have not made a detailed investigation of problem solving in creative projects, it is my sense that in creative projects the search process is often more intuitively based than search methods and processes focused on in this literature. Individuals seem to use their intuition, perhaps following heuristic rules, in searching. Their conceptions of their interests are often important in this regard, helping to guide them in focusing on kinds of potential solutions that fit with their larger aims.

Chris Callahan engaged in a process of search to try to find a solution to a problem he encountered on the project that was the basis of his dissertation. As described in Chapter 8, Chris and his advisor defined as a project for Chris to build an enhancer trap screen for use with the *kinesin-lacz* reporter to identify genes involved in axonal pathfinding in *Drosophila*. Chris told me he built the screen and screened many cell lines using the reporter, but in analyzing the cell lines discovered that the reporter did not work as they had hoped — it was transported very quickly down the lengths of axons, pooled in the axon tips, and was not distributed throughout the lengths of the axons, thus did not display them in full as they had hoped it would. Chris said at this point he began searching for alternative reporters he could construct. "I did a literature search on other possible microtubule associated proteins [to link to the *beta-gal-lacz*]. [And] after I did this lit search on all the variety of ones that I could try, we sat down and decided on trying *tau*." Chris said they had two main reasons for picking *tau*: it is a relatively small gene, and so would most likely be easier to spring successfully into the genome; and its basic structure, in particular its main functional domains, had been documented, which made it more likely they could successfully isolate a region to splice and link to the *lacz* reporter. Thus Chris's search was guided by rules for what would make a gene a good candidate for a reporter.[16] The reporter Chris constructed, *tau-beta-gal-lacz*, turned out to work very well; at the time of our interview he told me he had sent his construct to more than 100 labs worldwide.

A second method of solving problems is identifying and breaking a constraint that is implicit in the way a problem is conceived but not essential to it. An example of this is Lisa Zhang's description of solving an algorithm design problem. Lisa's problem was to develop an algorithm for executing a set of computations utilizing a set of processors arrayed along a line. For a given processor i computation at step t requires — as she first thought of the problem — communication of the results for step $t-1$ obtained by the adjacent processors

[16]Chris mentioned two other candidate genes that other groups had tried, one of which he said was his second choice after *tau*; these were less successful as it turned out.

on the line, $i - 1$ and $i + 1$ (for processors on the boundaries of the line there is only one adjacent processor). The time required to communicate results from processor i to $i + 1$ is d_i, with the d_i's allowed to be different. The time required to complete the computation for this problem is bounded above by $\sqrt{d_{max}}\,T$ where there are T steps. Lisa's problem was to try to construct an algorithm to achieve a smaller bound. Define a flow for this problem to be the set of communications that are made to each processor each period. For a long time Lisa and her advisor focused on flow patterns in which the jobs move vertically on the grid — so that in each period processor i draws on the results of $i - 1$ and $i + 1$ from the previous period. Unfortunately, with this approach all processors end up relying, directly and indirectly, on computations made by all other processors in previous periods, hence the largest delay time ends up slowing down all processing steps. One day, Lisa said, while they were working on the problem, she and her advisor had the realization that a vertical flow is not necessary, that jobs can move in other patterns. Thus they recognized that they could break the vertical line constraint — and they came up with the idea of a diagonal flow, inventing what they call "the stripe algorithm." In this algorithm the line of processors is divided in half; processors on the left side move up and to the left each period — processor i draws each period on its own last period computation and the computations performed by $i - 1$ and $i - 2$; similarly, processors on the right side move up and to the right. With this approach communication flows only in one direction on each half-line — essentially processor i uses information only from processors 1, 2, ..., $i - 1$ and itself. As a result, it can be shown that the time to completion of tasks is proportional to the square-root of the average of the d's, rather than the maximum, thus the bound on computation time is lowered.[17]

A third method of solving or resolving problems is refining a proposed solution that at first fails, making improvements, until finally attaining a successful solution or resolution. This method is frequently employed for solving and re-solving problems of implementation — in getting an experiment or invention to work. Inventors famously make many small changes, resolving problems, in developing a working prototype of an invention — Thomas Edison, as his notebooks reveal, would often make dozens. Many of the neuroscientists I interviewed described having to make many alterations and improvements to get experimental preparations to work, for example to express genes in model systems or purify preparations. Refinement is also employed in the creation of works with many parts, in working to reconcile and harmonize the different elements.

[17] For details see Yihao Lisa Zhang, *An Analysis of Network Routing and Communication Latency*, diss., MIT, 1997, Chapters 2 and 3.

Other problem solving processes have been described in the literature, for example metaphoric thinking. I have not encountered these, at least have found no clear evidence of them. Such processes may well occur and simply not be revealed in the kind of data I have collected and on which I base my description.

Meta-Level Thinking and Problem Transformation

Meta-level thinking and problem redefinition and transformation are two additional approaches to solving and resolving problems in project work. Both approaches are often rooted in broader conceptualizations, very often a conception of interest or guiding principle.

In the literature on expertise meta-level thinking has been shown to be a style of thinking that experts employ effectively to solve problems in their domain of expertise.[18]

Among my interview subjects, an example of the use of meta-level thinking to solve a problem is Andreas Walz's description of how he developed a novel approach to solve a problem he and fellow lab workers had encountered. Andreas has an interest in axonal pathfinding in the developing visual system; he is specifically interested in the biochemicals that guide axons in the extracellular matrix, and in studying pathfinding *in vivo*, as a naturalistic process.[19] At an orientation Andreas attended entering his graduate program, one of the faculty described her research studying development of the visual system in *Xenopus*, the frog. As Andreas described it, it struck him as an ideal system for him: one can open up the brain of a tadpole and watch the axons of the developing visual system growing along the surface of the brain, so that it is possible to study the process directly *in vivo*. He thus applied to and was accepted into this lab for his doctoral research.

None of the initial projects Andreas worked on in the lab were successful. Thus, about six months after entering the lab, he found himself at an

---

[18] See *The Nature of Expertise*, cited in Chapter 10, footnote 82.

[19] These specifics differentiate his interest from those of Chris and Sophia. Whereas Chris was interested in the systems level — how many neurons get wired up at the same time and signals shared in common, Andreas was interested in biochemicals in the brain by which individual axons are guided. Andreas's interest was closer to Sophia's in that both were interested in the chemicals that guide axon growth cones and were fascinated by axon paths. But Andreas did not describe being interested in the complexities of individual paths or turning processes, focuses of Sophia's interest, and he wanted to study pathfinding *in vivo* whereas Sophia did not mention this and, in fact, in her original dissertation project was planning to build an artificial chamber to study pathfinding processes.

impasse. Indeed, as he described it, his whole section of the lab was somewhat at an impasse, because it had proven extremely difficult to find any way
to disrupt pathfinding in tadpoles and thus identify critical elements in that
process. Describing their approach Andreas said they "were looking at individual molecules" in the extracellular matrix, disrupting one at a time, searching
through many possibilities, and "none had any effect."

At this point, reflecting upon the failure to find any individual molecule
that disrupts the pathfinding system, Andreas shifted to thinking about the
problem at the meta-level. "I realized that this system is so robust that tinkering with a single molecule will not get you anywhere because it will just fall
back on a lot of other molecules that it uses to do its trick [guide axons along
their paths]." "It makes sense — this animal is one hundred percent dependent on its vision at this early stage — it has to see. So if you were Mother
Nature...you make it foolproof. Make it so that if one mechanism doesn't
work you have a second; if that doesn't work you have a third, a fourth, a fifth.
And you have to disturb several of those mechanisms before you make the
system go awry." "So my idea, that I developed at that point, was that another
way of going about it is not to look at [try to identify] what molecules are involved, but [instead] to find some agent which disturbs a lot of molecules at
the same time, and see if that has an effect." Once an effect was found, he
said, the plan would be then to seek to identify the molecules that had been
disrupted, which one would know as a group are important for pathfinding.
Thus stepping back from the details of individual experiments, reflecting at
the meta-level, Andreas was led to an idea for an alternative approach. Interestingly, his approach for solving the problem fits with his interest, as he
described it to me, which may have had some part in his developing it. In
particular, the approach is naturalistic, starting from the system in an intact
organism, which is what fascinates him, disrupting its functioning, and then
working backwards to identify the molecules that have been disrupted. It is less
experimental and less focused on individual mechanisms, which is the way for
example Azad and many other neuroscientists would commonly approach the
study of pathfinding.

In my study of creative development I have found that individuals sometimes
achieve success — are able to complete a project and make a contribution —
through transforming or redefining an initial problem or project focus. There
are different forms or modes of transforming and redefining problems. One is
narrowing a problem or project focus, so that it becomes more amenable to being successfully worked with and solved. Another is conceptually transforming
a problem into a form that is more amenable to solution or resolution, an
approach pioneered in Gestalt psychology approaches to problem solving.

402   Individuals often face a choice about precisely how to pose a problem defining a creative project they wish to pursue — a choice, in a sense, over a continuum of possibilities. Indeed it is surprising the degree of flexibility an individual has often in terms of how he defines a project. Further, as individuals learn more about their field their modes of defining projects and problems that are the basis of projects often change.

Victoria Rayskin is an example of an individual whose definition of the main problem she set herself in her graduate research shifted, becoming more mature and rooted in a larger sense of her field. As described in previous chapters, Victoria solved a problem in analysis concerning the construction of a linearization of a function around a point of singularity in her college thesis, out of which she formed an interest in working further on such problems. In graduate school she communicated with a faculty person, who showed her how the problem she had worked on could be reformulated as a linearization around a resonance or higher order singularity. This reformulated problem has a large literature connected to it, including in chaos theory, that she began to read. "People were trying to find bounds for the smoothness [of the linearization] in cases in which there is a resonance" she said, describing the literature. Victoria wanted to pursue working on this topic, but she now faced a critical choice — to define precisely the form of smoothness she would investigate — thus to move from a focused interest to a definite formulation for which to try to demonstrate a bound. There are various definitions of smoothness that might be explored; thus, a central issue for her was defining precisely the form of smoothness or property for which she would try to prove a result.

In preparing for her oral exams, reviewing papers on linearization, Victoria found a mistake in a paper another mathematician had written trying to prove, for a certain example of a type of resonance called hyperbolic, that a linearization can be constructed that is differentiable at the point of resonance.[20] Victoria decided she wanted to work with the same class of functions, but did not want to focus on differentiability at the point of resonance but rather on the degree of smoothness of a linearization in the neighborhood of the point — for chaos theory and dynamics, she told me, that is a more useful kind of result. There is a particularly difficult case within this class that is known not to be able to be linearized with a degree of smoothness C1, thus ruling out that degree of smoothness as a general result. Starting from this known result, Victoria said, she took one logical step to a slightly lesser degree of smoothness, Lipschitz of degree *alpha, alpha* being less than 1. "This is the next logical bound," she told

---

[20]Victoria describes this type of problem in her dissertation, for a specific, difficult example due to the mathematician Hartman. See the reference in the following footnote.

me, explaining her thinking. "If it's not C1, then, probably the next step is to think [to try to see whether] it's Lipschitz-*alpha*." Thus she defined a specific problem — and she was in fact able to prove the result, that a linearization mapping can be constructed of type Lipschitz-*alpha*.[21]

403

CREATIVE REALIZATIONS AND RESPONSES

During work on creative projects individuals have creative realizations and insights and creative responses, generating important insights and ideas and making discoveries that are crucial for their work. Creative realizations and insights are often perceptually based, "seeing" a relationship among elements or a pattern; this is a classic form of creativity, central to Gestalt models of creativity and work based on such approaches. I note that these processes are connected with the large literature on insight; I do not discuss this literature or these processes in depth, but recognize their great importance for creativity in projects.

The processes described in this section bear a family resemblance to the processes for generating ideas and insights described in Chapters 9 and 10. But the processes described in those chapters occur in the course of exploring interests, whereas the processes described here occur in the course of working on creative projects, thus center on issues and problems arising in projects. In turn, this is linked to a further difference: the realizations, insights, and responses described here are generated within the context of a narrow focus on a project, rather than in the course of broader, more open exploratory activity and thinking. Newton's discovery of the binomial theorem, for which I summarize the main steps he appears to have followed leading up to his discovery, is a good illustration of this — he came to this discovery, as far as can be determined, engaged in working out the solution to a mathematics problem he had set himself. One similarity between the processes described in this section and those described in the preceding chapters is that, in a fair number of cases, a realization or insight an individual has or response he makes on a project is rooted in or connected to the conceptual structure encoding the interest his project is based in. The examples below illustrate this. This grounding of creative realizations and responses and insights made in projects in conceptual structures of interests is a further link connecting creative interests with creativity in projects. I note, lastly, that a number of the processes

[21]The details are given in her dissertation, Victoria Rayskin, *Degenerate Homoclinic Crossings*, UC Berkeley, 1997, Chapter 4 in particular. She gives the Lipschitz-like property she uses on p. 24. She published her work in an article: "alpha-Hölder linearization," *Journal of Differential Equations* 147 (1998): 271–84.

described in the previous parts of this chapter fit with the description in this section. For example, recognizing a constraint in a problem often occurs through a perceptual shift and a relatively sudden realization — Lisa and her advisor recognizing that they could construct an algorithm with a diagonal flow is an example.

A famous historical example of a creative realization made in the course of working on a project — working to solve a problem — is Isaac Newton's discovery of the binomial theorem, which he arrived at through a pair of insights, recognizing a pattern, then deducing a general formula.

Newton came to this problem through his studies teaching himself mathematics.[22] In the course of learning in the field he read John Wallis's *Arithmetica Infinitorum,* and this sparked his interest in working out series representations of integrals as a way to compute their value. Wallis sets forth principles for creating such series and using them to intuit values. He works out in particular an infinite series representation for π(pi), computing π as the ratio of the area of one quadrant of a circle to the rectangle that bounds it: $\int_0^a \sqrt{a^2 - x^2}dx \div a^2$. He computes the value of this integral by embedding it in a series of integrals defined for the family of functions $(a^2 - x^2)^n$, for which the value of the integral for integer n can be computed directly, then deducing the value for $n = \frac{1}{2}$ from the pattern of known values. In his notebook Newton replicates Wallis's work, slightly modifying notation. He embeds the function $\sqrt{a^2 - x^2}$ within the series of functions $(a^2 - x^2)^r$, r increasing by one-half at each step, evaluating the value of the integral of this function over the range 0 to a divided by a^{2r+1} — a normalization that eliminates the dependence on a.[23] In this series, each integral for which r is an integer can be expanded as a polynomial in x and computed using standard formulas that Wallis and others before him had worked out. For terms in which r is an odd multiple of one-half, including $\sqrt{a^2 - x^2}$, the integrals cannot readily be evaluated — and Newton, following Wallis, deduces them, in particular the value for $r = \frac{1}{2}$, by intuiting them from the known values. He arranges the values in a series, with the known values and the unknown values interspersed, and switches to working with the inverse of the original series. He then writes down the

[22] My description of his path of development is drawn from a reading of Newton's early mathematics work in his Notebooks, as collected and translated in *The Mathematical Papers of Isaac Newton,* Vol. I, 1664–1666, ed. D.T. Whiteside (Cambridge: Cambridge University Press, 1967). I have also drawn on Richard S. Westfall, *Never at Rest: A Biography of Isaac Newton.* The classic biography is David Brewster, *Memoirs of the Life, Writings, and Discoveries of Sir Isaac Newton,* 2 volumes (Edinburgh: T. Constable & Co., 1885).

[23] *Mathematical Papers of Isaac Newton,* I, pp. 99–101.

sequence of known values for integer values of r: $1, 1 \times \frac{3}{2}, 1 \times \frac{3\times5}{2\times4}, 1 \times \frac{3\times5\times7}{2\times4\times6}$, et cetera. Here the second term is in the ratio $\frac{3}{2}$ to the first, the third is in the ratio $\frac{5}{4}$ to the second, and so on. Newton posits a similar form for the series generating the unknown terms, following the logic of Wallis, moving back one term, beginning with $r = -\frac{1}{2}$, and intuiting that the ratio of term 3 to term 2 in the unknown series is $\frac{4}{3}$, fitting between the ratios of terms 2 to 1 ($\frac{3}{2}$) and 3 to 2 ($\frac{5}{4}$) in the known series, the ratio of term 4 to term 3 in the unknown series is $\frac{6}{5}$ (between $\frac{5}{4}$ and $\frac{7}{6}$) and so on, with the ratio of the first two terms $\frac{2}{1}$. He thus writes the overall series, alternating terms from the known and unknown series, with a the value he is interested in (not the same as the a above):

$$\frac{1}{2}a : 1 : a : \frac{3}{2} : \frac{4a}{3} : \frac{15}{8} : \frac{8a}{5} : \frac{35}{16} \cdots$$

He then works out upper and lower bounds on a, one way based on the observation that the series is monotonically increasing, and successive terms of the known series give ever tighter bounds on the value of the unknown term between them, enabling ever tighter bounds on a to be computed.[24]

At this point Newton goes beyond Wallis. The idea of developing infinite series representations of integrals and then intuiting the patterns of such series as a way to figure out values for difficult-to-evaluate expressions had caught his interest. It thus seems, though there is no definite written evidence, that he formed a creative interest in applying the approach to other problems, perhaps to explore it generally as an approach. Immediately following the above analysis in his notebook he sets himself the following problem. Given x between zero and one, find the angle for which the sine of the angle is x; he couches the problem as a problem of integration similar to but extending the previous problem (see below).[25] Given Newton's study of classical geometry and mathematics over the preceding months it is reasonable to think that he recognized this as a classic difficult problem, worthy of tackling with the infinite series approach. Certainly there were other problems he could have chosen, for example, series of integrals in one-third or one-quarter powers — his interest defined a domain of problems — but this one fit with earlier work he had done in mathematics on trigonometric identities. He seems to have connected the approach he learned from Wallis with this earlier body of work, identifying a classic problem to try to solve with the infinite series approach. It is noteworthy that the problem he chose is more general than the one Wallis had

[24] Ibid., pp. 101–5.
[25] "Having ye signe [sine] of any angle to find ye angle or to find ye content of any segm^{nt} of a circle." Ibid., pp. 104.

406   worked out, in that he poses the problem in terms of a variable x — wanting to
find a general formula for inverting the sine function, rather than calculating
the value of a single number as Wallis did.[26] Richard Westfall stresses in his
biography that Newton consistently sought for generalization. In terms of the
framework of this book we might say that this was a defining principle for
Newton in conceptualizing his creative interests.

The angle for which the sine is x can in fact be calculated via computing
an area — the area of the wedge inside the unit circle defined by the arc
of the circle corresponding to the angle, the equation for the circle being
$y = \sqrt{1 - x^2}$. Newton's approach is to compute the area of the wedge as the
area under the curve $\int_0^x \sqrt{1 - y^2}dy$, an integral à la Wallis, minus the area of
the triangle defined by the segment of the x-axis from o to x, the vertical line
from x to $y = \sqrt{1 - x^2}$, and the line on the angle from the origin to y; see Figure
4a for his original diagram. Since the area of this triangle is straightforward to
compute, the computation of the integral yields the value of the wedge area
directly, thus Newton focuses on determining the value of this integral.[27] This is
similar to the integral he had solved following Wallis, with the one change that
whereas that integral had the fixed value a this new integral has upper bound x,
a variable, and Newton set out to solve it by generalizing the earlier method.
In particular, he considers integrals for a sequence of functions: $(1 - s^2)^0 = 1$,
$(1 - s^2)^{1/2}, (1 - s^2), (1 - s^2)^{3/2}, (1 - s^2)^2, \ldots$[28] As before, for integer powers the
value of the integral is straightforward to compute: each such integral is the
sum of odd powers of x, specifically $\frac{x^n}{n}$, n odd, multiplied by coefficients; for
example $\int_0^x (1 - s^2)ds = x - \frac{x^3}{3}$ and $\int_0^x (1 - s^2)^2 ds = x - 2\frac{x^3}{3} + \frac{x^5}{5}$.

Newton, focusing on these integer powers, writes out their series expansions
for low powers. Then, seemingly in the midst of doing so, he recognizes that they
fit a pattern, the well-known Pascal's Triangle. This was his first realization —

[26] It is also noteworthy that Newton began some of his earliest research in mechanics
around the same time as the work I am describing here, and that one of his first
focuses in mechanics was working out the laws of force for an object in circular motion.
Circles — and more broadly curving motion — were already and would continue
as a central interest for him. Newton's earlier researches on triangles, trigonometric
identities, and related propositions about circles, are on pp. 54–57 and especially pp. 72–
88 in *Mathematical Papers*, I. His early work in mechanics is described in John Herivel,
The Background to Newton's Principia (Oxford: Clarendon Press, 1965); see especially
pp. 7–13, 128–32, and (this is most likely later, but it is not known exactly when) 192–98.

[27] The notation I have given is modern and slightly different from the way Newton
states the problem. Newton makes this calculation in his notebook after working out
the first formula for the binomial expansion: *Mathematical Papers of Isaac Newton*,
I, pp. 108–10.

[28] A diagram he drew showing the curves is reproduced in *Mathematical Papers* , I,
p. 104.

a classic example of pattern recognition. In a letter written just over a decade after his discovery Newton described how his thinking developed from this first insight. Recognizing that the denominators of the coefficients for the x powers follow a simple arithmetic progression (x^n is divided by n), he focused on the numerators. He had the insight — this also was a realization, recognizing a pattern — that for integer powers these numerators are generated by the formula $(11)^m$: 1, 11, 121, 1331, et cetera. Then he states,

> I began to inquire how the remaining figures in these series [i.e., additional terms in the expansion of 11^m] could be derived from the first two given figures [which are 1 and m; e.g., 11^3 has as its first two terms 1 and 3], and I found that when the second figure m was given, the rest would be produced by continual multiplication of this series,
>
> $$\frac{m-0}{1} \times \frac{m-1}{2} \times \frac{m-2}{3} \times \frac{m-3}{4} \times \frac{m-4}{5}, \text{ etc}:$$
>
> For example, let $m = 4$, and $4 \times \frac{1}{2}(m-1)$, that is 6, will be the third term, and $6 \times \frac{1}{3}(m-2)$, that is 4 the fourth, and $4 \times \frac{1}{4}(m-3)$, that is 1 the fifth, and $1 \times \frac{1}{5}(m-4)$, that is 0, the sixth, at which term in this case the series stops [so the coefficients in this case are: 1 : 4 : 6 : 4 : 1]. Accordingly, I applied this rule . . . [to work out the series for the half-powers], and since, for the circle, the second term was $\frac{\frac{1}{2}x^3}{3}$, I put $m = \frac{1}{2}$, and the terms arising were:
>
> $$\frac{1}{2} \times \frac{\frac{1}{2}-1}{2} \text{ or } \frac{-1}{8}; \ -\frac{1}{8} \times \frac{\frac{1}{2}-2}{3} \text{ or } \frac{1}{16}; \ \frac{1}{16} \times \frac{\frac{1}{2}-3}{4} \text{ or } -\frac{5}{128};$$

and so to infinity.[29]

Thus Newton deduced a general formula for a series expansion representation for the area under a curve of the circle. The table in Figure 4b depicts the table Newton constructed, showing how he filled in the series terms.

[29] From a letter by Newton to Henry Oldenburg, 24 Oct., 1676: *The Correspondence of Isaac Newton*, Vol. II; 1676–1687, ed. H.W. Turnbull (Cambridge: University Press, 1960), pp. 130–31. Newton seems to have deduced the first two terms for the case of the $\frac{1}{2}$ power from the table he constructed. In the table the first row is all ones and the second row, for the integer powers, is simply the powers, in linear progression: 1, 2, 3, et cetera. Thus it would make sense that for the half-powers for this row the entry would simply be the power as well, which for the circle is one-half, so that the first two terms are one and one-half, as he writes. Also, the circle is defined by $(1 - x^2)$ raised to the $\frac{1}{2}$ power, thus setting $m = \frac{1}{2}$ makes sense. The formula Newton works out, with successive multiplications of terms, has a resemblance to the form of the series Newton had previously worked out based on Wallis; thus he very likely drew on this previous experience working out series in deducing this form. Westfall also notes that Newton seems to have drawn on his work based on Wallis more than he indicates in his later letter. Indeed the formula in Newton's notebook is presented slightly differently from the presentation in the letter — see *Mathematical Papers*, I, pp. 107–8.

408   Newton recognized that the approach he had developed would enable calculation of the values for many difficult-to-compute functions — that it was a general approach, which is its importance. Going forward he applied the method to compute hyperbolic functions, working out formulas for the logarithm in terms of its integral; later he developed the method further, and it was the base for further mathematical work he engaged in. It is certainly worthy of note that Newton's creative leap fit with his interest, at least as I reconstruct it. For Newton was interested not in one particular number, the way Wallis was, or even one particular function, but in seeking to work out series representations to calculate function values generally, thus seeking for a general approach. Thus the pattern and series representation he discovered was something he was attuned to look for given his interest.

Many of my interview subjects described creative realizations they had in the course of working on projects that were important for their work and contributions they made. I have mentioned Lisa Zhang's realization about diagonal flow processing above. Realizations that are insights about texts is a main form of creativity in literary analysis — many of the literary scholars I interviewed described such insights. Further, their insights were in many cases rooted in the underlying interest they had that spawned their dissertation.

Tina Brooks is an example. As described in Chapter 5 Tina is committed to crossing boundaries, disrupting conventional social categories of race and gender, and wanted to do a "cross-racial" analysis in her dissertation. This values orientation was the ground for a creative insight Tina had about *The House of Mirth*. Tina paired *The House of Mirth* with Pauline Hopkins's *Contending Forces*, a pairing fitting with her interest, analyzing them as both about fallen women alienated from conventional society and subject to harsh social pressures. Reading *The House of Mirth*, thinking about the pairing of Lily Bart with Sappho in *Contending Forces*, who is of mixed race, Tina made a creative connection: In the scene in which Lily Bart's beauty is displayed in a portrait and Lily engages in a "performance" (this word is used in *The House of Mirth*) displaying herself, Tina saw that when Wharton has Lily's cousin refer to Lily as "a girl standing there as if she was up at auction" she is, in Tina's words, "associating her [Lily] with the black slave woman" who is sold at a "slave auction" — thus creating a cross-racial "associative link" linking Lily in her alienation with a slave woman. In her dissertation Tina also connects this racial image with Lily's imagining conventional life as a "long white road."[30]

[30] Kristina Margaret Brooks, *Transgressing the Boundaries of Identity: Racial Pornography, Fallen Women, and Ethnic Others in the Works of Pauline Hopkins, Alice Dunbar-Nelson, and Edith Wharton*, diss., UC-Berkeley, 1995, Chapter 2, especially pp. 121–24.

I give as another example a creative insight Henry Chen had linking Dante's
Divine Comedy and the end of *Ulysses* in Chapter 15.

Creative Responses

Creative responses on projects are analogous, in general terms, to responses generated during exploration of interests: a link to a problem or conceptual structure in an individual's mind draws his attention to a stimulus and triggers a creative response he makes to it. A main difference between creative responses made in the context of projects and responses made while exploring interests is that responses made in projects are typically more narrowly based — typically they are linked with a specific aspect or element or issue of a project, for example resolving a problem or issue an individual has been thinking about; they typically thus have an immediate, direct relevance and application.

Individuals' creative interests, specifically the conceptual structures in their minds encoding their interests, often play an important role in their genera- tion of creative responses on projects — less central perhaps than in creative responses they make during periods when they are exploring their interests, but significant nonetheless. In some cases an interest that lies behind a project in which an individual is engaged is what draws his attention to a stimulus that sparks a creative response. In other cases an interest shapes the nature of an individual's response to an experience or element, in the context of his project.

A stunning example of a creative response in the context of a project is a response Enid Zentelis described having while in early stages of work on what became her film *Dog Race*.

Describing the origins of the film, Enid told me she began thinking about making a film about the poor in response to the statements being made about the welfare system and single mothers by members of the political Right like Newt Gingrich. As she described it she wanted to portray her own conception of the life of the poor as a rebuttal. Thus her film was rooted in her commitment to — creative interest in — making films manifesting her deeply held opinions about social conditions and issues, including poverty and social justice, and triggered by a political event that sparked a response in her.

Describing what was said, in her view, and her response she said: "The attack was largely on single mothers — [people saying] they are sucking out all this money from the government because they have too many babies. And an unending stream of political debate and controversy without ever anyone really living those lives." "And I said to myself, 'This is utter bullshit, because it doesn't matter if you have a job, you have to have something [more], it's your life, it's not just something that brings in money and feeds you, and shut up and go to sleep and keep living until you die.' I said, 'someone has to experience what it is like.'" "The other thing that they were saying is that we have to cure the poor of their multigenerational dependency on welfare. Which is not only insulting but also wrong. Because it skips over the clearest fact: that if you are born into a poor family you are by birth poor, and unless something incredible happens in your life you are going to die poor."

In these statements Enid conveys her conception of the life of the poor, both as it is and, in her view, the political Right wishes it to remain. In her conception the poor lead unfulfilling lives of monotony and repetition, earning just enough to make do and continue going through the motions of life, never breaking free from the daily grind, never getting ahead, fated to repeat the same routine over and over again. If you are a poor person you have a job that just "brings in money and feeds you," giving you no sense of fulfillment or purpose, beyond just continuing to live from day to day "until you die."[31] Enid also extends her vision across the generations: "if you are born into a poor family you are by birth poor and unless something incredible happens in your life you are going to die poor."

Thus Enid described her conception — of course she described it to me after having made the film so we cannot be sure it was present in her mind beforehand, but she certainly implied that it was. She knew she wanted to make a film in some way depicting and expressing it, but said she did not initially know what the film would be.[32] Her initial thought was to show a woman and her daughter, focusing on the woman and her daily life — fitting with her approach, described in Chapter 6, of showing the details of daily life, which is essentially a second interest that guides her in her work — with the child symbolizing the inevitable chain of poverty across the generations, and also the faint hope of escaping poverty. But no compelling idea occurred to her beyond this — in particular she did not know what the basic narrative of the film would be and did not have many specific images in mind.

It was through a crucial encounter that Enid had a creative inspiration through which she developed a specific idea for the film. "I was up visiting a friend in New Hampshire," she said, "and we drove past the dog track there.

---

[31] Enid's description of the public debate about the poor, her image of the "unending stream of political debate and controversy" that led to no greater understanding — because it occurs "without ever anyone really living those lives" — mirrors her image of the life of the poor, an unending succession of days, each one like the last, leading to no greater end.

[32] She told me her desire to make a film showing the life of the poor was "the first thing on my mind — I knew that that was somehow going to be in the next film." But she made it clear she did not have any specific ideas for a film.

And then that night I knew what the film was: that this woman works on an assembly line during the day and at night goes to bet at the dog track and doesn't get ahead. That would be shown as her only possibility... the only possibility of escaping or getting ahead or having some kind of financial upward mobility would be this long shot."[33] Enid made a creative connection recognizing that the image of dogs racing around a track could symbolize her conception of the life of the poor — the dogs are in continuous, repetitive motion that leads, around an oval, back to where they started, just like the poor in their repetitive lives, each day just like the last, leading nowhere. She also made a connection linking dogs running around a track with an assembly line — the dogs racing around the track corresponding to goods moving along the assembly line. The assembly line also resonates with her conception on another level — working on an assembly line is boring, repetitive work, reflecting the boring, repetitive life of the poor person who works on it. I asked Enid whether she recognized the connection between the dog race and the mother working on an assembly line consciously at the time and she said, "Yes. I was thinking of visual parallels with the dogs running endlessly around the track, and that [the dog track] also evoked, at a very stylistic level, the certain lines and angles that I would have [on the assembly line] for symmetry. I wanted her job to be very symmetrical and identified very quickly on a visual level [with the dogs racing around the track]."

The cinematography in *Dog Race* establishes these visual and thematic correspondences. In the film the woman is shown working on the assembly line, and the line is shown moving from left to right past her and then in an oval behind her. The woman is then shown picking up her daughter, and the two of them are shown traveling to the track and buying tickets. In the next scene, the central scene of the film, they are shown watching the race. This scene is shot in a way that unmistakably echoes the earlier scene of the woman working on the assembly line: the dogs are shown running around an oval track, the proportion of the screen taken up by the oval path of the track is similar to the proportion that was taken up by the assembly line, and the angle of the camera at which we watch the race is similar to the angle at which we viewed the assembly line.

Dog Race has several further links with Enid's conception of the life of the poor. The woman and her daughter and other people are shown gambling on the race, a metaphor for her belief that those who are born poor are fated to die poor and can only escape if "something incredible happens," for example,

[33] Enid told me her idea for the film literally occurred in a flash: "I went by that track and went in the track and I said, 'this is it' — it hit me like that." She also said that this was a track that catered to families, implying this was important in helping her make the connection with her conception.

if they gamble on a long shot and win. More profoundly, *Dog Race* establishes a correspondence between how the mother and daughter view dogs and how we the viewers view the mother and daughter. In the first scene of the film the mother and daughter are shown offering their dog some food in the cold morning. The dog doesn't eat the food and the daughter remarks, "Dumb dog. Now he'll be hungry all day." She recognizes the plight of the dog and also that the dog is incapable of recognizing its own plight. This scene is linked to the dog race — in which the dogs are shown running around the track in the service of an activity they do not understand — gambling — and the woman and her daughter are shown watching the race. Enid described this linkage this way: "The one thing that the woman loved and also witnessed is suffering, from frame one. [In turn] she [the mother] [also] has to . . . run around the track and what have you."[34] The depth of connections with her conception shows what a resonant creative response Enid made. In addition *Dog Race* beautifully links to Enid's underlying approach of showing the details of daily life: in the idea of a "dog's life," that is a life of mundane, everyday existence and hard work, with no greater end, symbolized by the dogs racing around the oval race track and the assembly line — illustrating a creative response in a project linked to an underlying approach that is essentially like an interest.

Several other of my interview subjects described making creative responses in the context of working on projects that sparked crucial ideas for their work. David Johnson's realization that the receptor he was trying to work out the full sequence for and characterize, which he thought was a new kind of nicotinic receptor, is actually a serotonin receptor was sparked by a creative response: seeing a poster at a conference describing a new kind of serotonin receptor — which in turn spurred him when he returned home to read the paper describing the receptor. His path of development and work on the project illustrate the recursive nature of creative development: going to a conference and seeing a partial sequence for a receptor sparked his idea for his project; and going to the same conference a year later sparked a critical realization about the project, enabling him to move forward and successfully complete it.

There are many accounts of creative responses made in the context of projects by individuals famous for their creative contributions. One famous example, among many, is the creative response Charles Darwin had reading Malthus's *An Essay on the Principle of Population*. I describe here Darwin's

[34]The fact that the gambling involves animals serves to emphasize the parallel with the mother and daughter and to increase the empathy the viewer feels. I asked Enid if she had considered showing some other form of gambling, such as a casino, and she said, "No, I wanted the stake to be involving some kind of living [animal]."

thinking leading up to his response. I note that his thinking had many steps and elements; I describe just a few central themes and steps.[35]

Darwin began working on transmutation of species a few months after returning on the *Beagle* to England, writing notes in a series of notebooks.[36] In his notebooks he raises many issues, sets out many ideas about transmutation and how it may operate, and states many facts and opinions from books he is reading pertaining to the topic and his reaction. He discusses variation; reproduction (in his terminology generation), which he viewed as fundamental for transmitting characteristics, focusing on the efficacy of sexual reproduction to create mixing, hence variation; the idea of several species descended from a common parent form; the need to explain extinction; the idea of gradual alteration, compounding, to create new species; the importance of understanding the gaps between species; and his recognition that hybridization across species must not be common or must typically be unfruitful, else the demarcation between species would be blurred.[37] Darwin does not initially state very precisely the source of new characteristics in species, considering many possibilities, though linking it to reproduction. He eventually uses the word chance, indicating his conception of chance or random variations occurring in offspring, joined with his conviction that most are maladaptive, but a few are adaptive, thus will be carried forward in future generations.[38]

Darwin was convinced essentially from the beginning of his thinking about transmutation (and before) of the role of adaptation, that variations that improve adaptation to the environment will be preserved. He writes and clearly thought about the implications of this — that over time species will become better adapted to their environment, that when the environment changes the species must change to again become adapted or is likely to be replaced by another, better adapted species, and that species that migrate to new environments

[35]A few notable contributions in the literature about the growth of Darwin's thought during this period are: Howard Gruber, *Darwin on Man*; Sir Gavin de Beer, *Charles Darwin: Evolution by Natural Selection*; and M.J.S. Hodge and David Kohn, "The immediate origins of natural selection," in *The Darwinian Heritage*, ed. David Kohn (Princeton, NJ: Princeton University Press, 1985), pp. 185–206.

[36]Darwin's notebooks have been edited and made available in *Charles Darwin's Notebooks, 1836–1844*, eds. Paul H. Barrett, Peter J. Gautrey, Sandra Herbert, David Kohn, and Sydney Smith (Ithaca, NY: Cornell University Press, 1987). Darwin has a few entries about transmutation in his early Red Notebook, dating from March 1837 or thereabouts. His sustained notes are in Notebooks B, C, D, and E and the "Torn Apart" Notebook. Notebook B was begun in June or July of 1837, Notebook D, which contains his notes on Malthus, dates from mid-summer 1838 through early October of that year.

[37]See *Charles Darwin's Notebooks*, Introductions to the sections on the Red Notebook and Notebooks B and C, pp. 17–20, 167–69, 237–38.

[38]Ibid., p. 258. This is Notebook C.

414   will undergo a modification in characteristics improving their adaptation to the new environment. However, throughout his early notebook entries he never spells out precisely what will generate the set of species we observe in existence, or how species interact — how it is determined which survive and flourish and which die out; he focuses on arguments at the level of individual species. He begins to consider relationships between groups and species in Notebook B. Describing the hereditary fates of human families he writes, "in looking at two fine families one with successors [for] centuries, the other will become extinct. — Who can analyze causes, dislike to marriage, hereditary disease, effects of contagions, & accidents: yet some causes are evident, as for instance one man killing another. — So it is with *varying* races of man: . . . whole races act towards each other, and are acted on, just like the two fine families. . . . May this not be extended to all animals.[39] He comes to the idea of war among organisms, writing in Notebook C, some months before reading Malthus, "Study the wars of organic being. — the fact of guavas having overrun — Tahiti. thistle. Pampas. show how nicely things adapted –." This last sentence, however, weakens the thrust of his statement and shows his preoccupation with adaptation.[40] And he does not take the step linking the idea that better adapted species replace weaker forms to a coherent theory of the generation of the set of species we observe.

It was reading Malthus, according to what Darwin states in his *Autobiography*, confirmed by entries in Notebook D, that spurred him to make a clear connection with the idea of a battle for survival, shifting the emphasis from adaptation to a struggle in which weaker forms are forced out, leading to a theoretical model able to predict the set of species.[41] During this time, in particular late summer and September of 1838, Darwin was engaged in a large-scale program of reading. He was guided at least in part by his idea of transmutation, thus forming an interest centering on it, reading in philosophy and natural science.[42] He writes in his *Autobiography* that he made a great study of domestic breeding, which was very instructive, recognizing the

[39] Ibid., p. 206.

[40] Ibid., p. 262. The reference to the thistle refers to his having seen wild varieties overrunning domesticated ones in South America. See the accompanying footnote.

[41] Darwin has a comment in an early notebook entry showing his awareness of the need to develop a theory predicting the set of species, balancing the creation of new species with the extinction of old ones — *Charles Darwin's Notebooks*, pp. 175–76. But he does not seem to have developed this much further, with the possible exception of the statement about war quoted in the main text, before reading Malthus.

[42] See Janet Browne, *Voyaging*, pp. 384–85. Darwin remarks in his *Autobiography* of his industry in reading during this time, reflected in his lists of reading (p. 119). Peter Vorzimmer has presented a list of the items Darwin read over this period — Peter J. Vorzimmer, "The Darwin reading notebooks (1838–1860)," *Journal of the History of Biology* 10 (1977): 107–53.

importance of selection in generating new species in this context. "But," he writes, "how selection could be applied to organisms living in a state of nature remained for some time a mystery to me."[43] Then, he writes: "In October, 1838, that is, fifteen months after I had begun my systematic enquiry, I happened to read for amusement Malthus on *Population*, and being well prepared to appreciate the struggle for existence which everywhere goes on from long-continued observation of the habits of animals and plants, it at once struck me that under these circumstances favourable variations would tend to be preserved, and unfavourable ones to be destroyed. The result of this would be the formation of new species. Here, then, I had at last got a theory by which to work. . . ."[44] In fact, Darwin's language is slightly misleading — though it may have been partly happenstance that he read Malthus, he was reading widely, and Malthus's book fit in the domain he was exploring. Further, Malthus's book and argument were well known and most likely, as Janet Browne details, Darwin knew of his ideas through various sources.[45] Regardless, reading Malthus was it seems very important, sparking a creative response in him. In his Notebook D, which covers this period, Darwin refers to "the warring of the species as inference from Malthus," which he recasts as a "force" in nature "forming gaps by thrusting out weaker ones [species]."[46] Thus, spurred

[43]*The Autobiograpy of Charles Darwin*, pp. 119–20. Darwin describes the nature of his ideas and thinking in his *Autobiography* slightly differently than recent scholars and I do based on reconstructing his creative activities more directly from his notebooks.

[44]*Autobiography*, p. 120.

[45]Janet Browne provides an excellent discussion of sources for Darwin to know of Malthus's work and his ideas; see *Voyaging*, pp. 385–86. Silvan Schweber gives as one possible route through which Darwin got to Malthus reading Quetelet: Silvan S. Schweber, "The origin of the *Origin* revisited," *Journal of the History of Biology* 10 (1977): 229–316.

[46]*Charles Darwin's Notebooks*, p. 375. Darwin wrote on the inside front cover, it appears many years later, "Towards close I first thought of selection owing to struggle" (p. 331). There is debate about exactly how much Darwin was thinking about selection pressures before reading Malthus and what he got from reading Malthus. De Beer's view is that Darwin got a sense of the quantitative force of a population explosion, which helped him realize how powerful even a slight adaptive advantage could be in generating intense selection. See de Beer, *Charles Darwin*, pp. 98–100. This also seems to be the view of Schweber in "The origin of the *Origin* revisited," and, in a somewhat modified form, of Sandra Herbert in "Darwin, Malthus, and selection," *Journal of the History of Biology* 4 (1971): 209–17. M.J.S. Hodge and David Kohn seem to advocate a larger importance for Malthus in triggering Darwin to think about population pressures being generative of selection in "The immediate origins of natural selection"; see especially pp. 192–96. Others argue that Darwin's idea of natural selection was at least in part a product of the broader culture he was part of, with roots in theology and principles of capitalist competition. See Robert M. Young, *Darwin's Metaphor* (Cambridge: Cambridge University Press, 1985).

by Malthus, he resolved a theoretical difficulty, developing his theory of evolution.

REVISIONING

Revisioning is a fundamental process in creative projects. By their very nature creative projects are novel, thus it is inevitable that we will make changes on them as we encounter unexpected problems and possibilities, and our thinking evolves: revisioning is thus inherent in the nature of such projects. Through revisions on a project, both in our overall conception of the project and in its details, we explore new possibilities and pathways, leading to new ideas, insights, and discoveries, in many cases going far beyond our initial conception of the project. Tracing the series of revisions an individual makes on a project is fascinating and illuminating, revealing the path of his work on the project, often carrying him far beyond his initial conception.

There are a variety of different kinds of revisions that individuals make on creative projects. These include revisions in project definition and scope, revisions to specific parts and elements of a work and in the conception of how the parts and elements fit together, and revisions changing techniques, approach, and materials. Oftentimes revisions individuals make on projects are linked to or rooted in their underlying interests, that are the basis for their project, thereby aligning the project better with their interests. Picasso's revisions for Les Demoiselles d'Avignon illustrate all of these points.

In being such a central, essential feature of creative projects revisioning deserves in-depth investigation and description. While there exist excellent sources and accounts of such processes in the context of specific projects, most notably for projects executed by individuals famous for their contributions, revisioning as a general process has not yet been described with the depth that it warrants. That, however, is beyond what is possible in this book, which is not focused on the project phase of creative development. Thus I do not attempt to describe revisioning in general terms. Rather, I describe the process of revisioning in one famous case — Pablo Picasso's process of work leading to his production of his painting Les Demoiselles d'Avignon, and two examples of revisioning by my interview subjects. My purpose is to set the process of revisioning in the context of creative development, and, in this context, convey a sense for its vital role in creative work.

Picasso's creative process developing Les Demoiselles d'Avignon provides a fascinating illustration of revisioning in creative project work. There exists an extensive catalogue of materials, published by the Musée Picasso, providing a detailed record of Picasso's work on the painting — enabling us to trace how his conception evolved over a period of months as he engaged in intensive work revising his idea for the composition and individual figures.

Picasso's initial conception for the painting, as shown in early sketches he made, is seven figures arranged across a horizontal extent: five women of a brothel and two male visitors or observers, one a sailor and the other a medical student. The painting thus appears to be rooted in his core creative interest in making paintings that express his feelings, in particular about women, his ambivalence about them and their sexuality — and by projection their feelings towards him and all men. His initial plan also exhibits cultural influences — art historians have identified a set of earlier paintings that seem to be related to and possibly a basis for his conception, such as Cezanne's paintings of bathers. As noted by many critics Picasso's initial conception was considerably more conventional than the final painting. In particular in his initial conception, as he presents it in early studies for the painting, the figures gaze at one another and interact among themselves — thus the scene is gazed at by the spectator, as in traditional art, and does not directly confront him.[47] Further, there is no sense of multiple perspectives.

As he worked on his plan for the painting Picasso made revisions both to the overall composition and individual figures, introducing more radical elements. The revisions he made can be traced within the materials presented in the volumes published by the Musée Picasso. Shown are literally hundreds of sketches, including several dozen reworkings of the basic composition, as well as dozens of sketches of individual figures, and several preliminary studies in paint.[48] Picasso made three fundamental changes in his revisioning. One was elimination of the male figures: first the medical student was transformed into a prostitute, and later the sailor was dropped. In eliminating these figures Picasso eliminated depiction of the male reaction to female sexuality — thus taking a step away from depicting his own feelings symbolically, as he had done in his past work, and towards creating painting evoking feelings directly in the spectator. The second change came about through intense work he engaged in constructing well-defined spaces for the figures, defined by planes. Examining

[47] Christopher Green summarizes this in his clear and succinct summary of Picasso's steps of development creating the painting: "The drama is to some extent contained within the curtained theatrical space. These [there] are gazes and movements that suggest encounters between the figures . . . onto which the spectator looks." *Picasso's Les Demoiselles d'Avignon*, ed. Christopher Green (New York: Cambridge University Press, 2001), Introduction, pp. 4–8.

[48] *Les Demoiselles D'Avignon*, Musée Picasso Paris (1988). As an example of Picasso's work process, eleven sketches he made of the overall composition are shown on pp. 189–92, with four more on p. 204. Making multiple preparatory sketches and full models for final paintings was something Picasso had done in earlier major paintings (paintings he viewed at the time as major works) as well. For example, for his painting *Science and Charity* he made seven known drafts; see Juan-Eduardo Cirlot, *Picasso: Birth of a Genius* (New York: Praeger Publishers, 1972), pp. 34–39.

418   his sketches it appears that he was working towards isolating each figure within her own space or plane.[49] The sketches seem to show him using curtains to define spaces via planes, separating and sorting out different spaces within the overall composition. In creating a separate space for each figure he separates the figures from one another, so that each engages primarily directly with the audience. This separation is present even initially — and more clearly in slightly later compositions — for the three women in the middle of the painting. In his revisions it comes to hold true also for the woman lifting the curtain on the left and the woman looking in on the right — who initially (with the woman on the left at that time being the medical student) had seemed to gaze at each other, and now are made not to gaze directly at one another or interact.[50] Thus, in the final painting only interaction with the spectator — defiant, enticing, blasé, disinterested, the emotions differing among the figures and depending on the viewer's response — remains. This shift fits with Picasso's interest in expressing his own feelings through paintings — he was not interested in relationships among women, but rather in his own, male feelings about them, thus was led to isolate the women from one another.

Finally, in his third set of changes Picasso refined his representations of the individual figures. He comes to depict the second woman from the left almost floating — perhaps seen as lying in bed. He made many sketches of the standing women, for example exploring how far the woman on the right leans in, and the proportions of the woman on the left. He also made many studies of the woman sitting in a crouching position and the woman in the center. In addition, he made many detailed sketches of the faces and heads of the figures, refining them. In the initial composition and throughout his main phase of work on the painting, in particular for the women figures, these are made following a primitive Iberian style he had formed an interest in and developed as a style in the preceding period — famously in his painting of Gertrude Stein. He accentuated this style as he made changes — the heads

[49]To give examples, sketches are shown in *Les Demoiselles d'Avignon* on: p. 148; bottom left of pp. 150 and 152; a series on p. 154; the previously noted sketches of the composition on pp. 189–92 and 204; sketches of the reclining figure on pp. 210, 254, 264, and elsewhere; interesting sketches of bodies on pp. 272–75 and 291–93; and an abstract sketch on p. 281. Picasso had worked and experimented with compositions with multiple persons from early in his career; see, for example, in *Picasso: Birth of a Genius*, plates 48 and 49, hagiographic paintings, 1896, his sketch "Flight," plate 62, 1896, his sketch "Street Fight," plate 129, 1897–8, sketch of invalids, plate 200, 1899–1900, his sketch for his painting *The Death of Casegmas*, plate 213, 1901.

[50]It certainly seems plausible that Picasso's use of the curtains was designed to help articulate these distinct spaces — the curtains define fairly sharp lines that set off distinct planes.

and eyes are oval, the noses and mouths pronounced, the faces as a whole somewhat stereotyped.[51] Picasso took one final, decisive creative step in his depiction of the faces, apparently through a link with African and Oceanic tribal sculptural art he saw — thus through a creative response. He made the faces of the women on left and right and the crouching woman like masks, harsh and impersonal — thus fitting better the emotions he wished to convey, and twisted the crouching woman's head completely around on her body so that she faces us even while her body is pointed away from us (he had taken an initial step towards doing this earlier), thus depicting multiple perspectives — which some critics view as a first step towards his eventual development, with Georges Braque, of cubism.[52]

Overall, although Picasso evidently had a certain fairly defined sense of what he aimed to express when he began *Les Demoiselles* it is clear that through the revisions he made he created a painting far more powerful and revolutionary than a composition based directly on his first conception would have been, and more resonant with his interest in conveying emotions, rawly and directly.

Revisioning was important for many of my interview subjects.

Karen Hadley, the literary scholar interested in exploring different ways in which meaning in language is analyzed, including linguistically and philosophically, with a focus on close linguistically based reading, came to focus in graduate school on how temporality is conveyed in language and literature, focusing on temporality in Wordsworth's *The Prelude*. I describe how she came to this focus as a point of overlap of her interests in the next chapter.

Karen located eight separate drafts of her prospectus, written over perhaps six months, and sent me the first and one of the last. These document the significant revisions she made in her project definition during this period. In the first draft of her prospectus Karen proposes analyzing temporality in *The Prelude* in terms of both its narrative structure and language. She devotes the majority of this prospectus to describing models of narrative temporality, both in general and as applied to Wordsworth. These include several analyses specific to Wordsworth's poem, Paul Ricoeur's model of temporality set forth in *Time and Narrative*, and the famous analysis of Heidegger in *Being and Time*, which she states she hopes will be a "centerpiece" of her own argument. She focuses, following Heidegger, on three basic levels: (1) the sequence of present moments, (2) time "extended" from birth to death — thus a series

---

[51] He had seen such primitive Iberian sculpture and had an interest in carrying it into his own art. See *Picasso's Les Demoiselles d'Avignon*, Introduction.

[52] Picasso had earlier painted a mask-like face in his painting *The Mask* ("The Bride of El Greco"), 1900, *Picasso: Birth of a Genius*, plate 190.

of presents joined together to form stretches of temporal duration, linked to change, history, duration, and "being-toward-death," and (3) "repetition," the unity of all moments of time, past, present, and future. Karen states that she will focus on both the "language of temporal imagery" and "the linguistic representation of time, tense, and subjectivity." She quotes from the first 19 lines of *The Prelude*, and notes the four shifts in tense in these lines: "from present, to the present perfect (which posits continuity of time between a point in the past and the present moment of speech), to the present, to the future, and finally back to the present again."[53]

In the later draft of her prospectus Karen's focus has narrowed and altered. She no longer discusses narrative temporality — this entire branch of her project has been dropped — focusing on linguistic analysis of temporality. It is noteworthy that this is consistent with her core interest in close, linguistically based reading of texts — thus she reverted to a topic fitting her interest.[54] She states that her project is to examine Wordsworth's construction of "autobiographical subjectivity by way of time and language," seeking "to translate Heidegger" into terms fitting Wordsworth's poetry. But, whereas some critics have sought to do this thematically, she seeks to do it through a linguistic approach. "I am formulating a literary critical method which posits a theory of subjectivity working at the level of language, and shows how this 'language of subjectivity' reveals itself at various levels as linguistic patterning," she writes. She then presents an analysis of the first lines of *The Prelude* that goes well beyond the earlier draft. She traces the four shifts in tense, then writes, taking a creative step beyond her earlier analysis: "Such shifting, especially in light of his choice of verbs, gives a feel of aspectual spannedness; the use of the present perfect creates (by way of aspect) an aspectualized, durative feeling which stretches beyond the mere capabilities of tense.... It relates every moment [of the past]...to the moment of speech, thereby creating a sort of spatialized temporal bridge over which the poet can travel...." Thus she makes a distinction between aspect and tense, and describes Wordsworth's language creating a "temporal bridge"

[53] Karen also discusses the closing image of the poem, Wordsworth's ascent of Mt. Snowdon, and states that she will analyze it as presenting a balanced sense of temporality between past time stretching out as the ocean does and the present, symbolized by the mountain. She also states she will analyze the famous "spots of time" in the poem.

[54] It seems that she temporarily took up Ricoeur and narrative theory, in part because she came upon critics employing this framework in analyzing Wordsworth and in part because she was taken by Ricoeur's work, but then reverted to her core interest. In this regard, a statement she made to me is interesting: she told me that early on she went through *The Prelude* underlining every verb and determining its tense and aspect — thus the linguistic focus was present for her from early on.

he can travel, a beautiful and powerful image. She goes on to describe how she will delineate the way in which Wordsworth creates his autobiographical self through language. Karen's ideas are sharper in this draft, and the analysis and approach she presents in fact carried through and are the basis of her dissertation.[55]

Revisioning was somewhat less common among the neuroscientists and mathematicians than among the literary scholars I interviewed. The revisions mathematicians described mainly took one of two forms. One was redefining a problem, as Victoria, for example, did. The other was switching approaches in trying to solve a set problem. David Metzler, for example, described trying to solve what became the main problem he worked on for his dissertation with one approach, then a few months later learning about a new method developed by individuals in his group to solve related problems, and successfully solving his problem using this new method.

Azad is an example among the neuroscientists of someone who made a revision in project work. As his first dissertation project Azad set as his objective to map out the pathway of action of NGF on the *c-fos* gene. His plan was to begin by identifying the mechanism through which NGF regulates the *c-fos* promoter site at the gene, then trace the pathway back to the receptor. At the time he began it was recognized that NGF was likely to act through a specific site in the promoter region known as the SRE element. Azad began by focusing on SRE using the conventional experimental design: placing the SRE element just upstream of the trigger, known as the TATA box, then exposing the region to growth hormone. He said he was not initially getting very exciting results. But in working on the project he came to the assessment that the experimental design was not satisfactory. "I thought it wasn't done in enough detail," he said. "All of it was done by putting this [SRE] element just upstream of the TATA box, which is [artificial] . . . [not] looking at the promoter [the SRE site] in its own context" — that is, positioned more like where it actually is, further away from the TATA box. When he did this — thus revising his protocol — it made a difference: he found that the effect of NGF was different depending on where the SRE site was positioned in relation to the TATA box. In executing this revised protocol he also made another discovery, which is that there is an interaction between the SRE site and the Calcium Response Elements that are also in the promoter region.

While revisioning occurs throughout creative development, it appears to be more common and extensive for many individuals on projects they undertake

---

[55]Karen Hadley, *'Timely Interference' in Wordsworthian Autobiography*, diss., UC-Berkeley, 1995.

relatively earlier in their development, and less common and extensive later, when they know their craft well. A good example is the difference between Picasso's extensive revisions on *Les Demoiselles*, that were so crucial for the radicalness of the painting, and the revisions he made in working out his plan for *Guernica*, which he created much later in his career. His process of conception for *Guernica* is documented in materials on display at the Modern Art Museum in Madrid and by Richard Arnheim in *The Genesis of a Painting, Picasso's Guernica* (Berkeley: University of California Press, 1962). What is striking is that Picasso developed his basic plan for the work in just a few weeks, and, while he made many revisions and the composition evolved, the changes he made were not radical in their effect like the changes he made working on *Les Demoiselles*. Similarly, Virginia Woolf engaged in extensive rewrites on *The Voyage Out*, but in writing later books, including *Jacob's Room* and *To the Lighthouse*, engaged in much less revisioning.

Expanding and Branching

In many cases a creative project grows and branches out well beyond one's initial conception for it. This is natural: as we work on a project, make discoveries, have ideas, and begin to see the project take shape, it is natural for our conception of it, our sense of its possibilities and our aim, to alter and in many cases expand, branching out to encompass new aspects and possibilities. Often a creative interest that is the root of a project we undertake is crucial to such branching out, bringing new elements or issues that fit with our interest to our attention, which we incorporate into the project. Many of my interview subjects described this kind of branching, especially the literary scholars and playwrights. To give one example, Cheryl's dissertation branched from an initial focus on guardianship in eighteenth-century women's novels to a second, parallel topic: guardianship as a historical and legal topic in the eighteenth century — fitting with her interest in important social issues relevant to women and, by extension, family life. In her dissertation she contrasts these fictional and nonfictional accounts of guardianship.

Many important, famous creative contributions seem to develop out of and be the culmination of a growing, expanding project. In particular, in a fair number of cases in which an individual comes to make an important, famous contribution through a project, he initially conceives the project through which he comes to make the contribution as relatively modest and not particularly grand. Then, as he engages in the project, his idea of it and aim for it grows, the project is transformed, leading to the famous, outstanding contribution he makes.

William Faulkner's development of what became *The Sound and the Fury* 423
is an example of this. Faulkner's initial idea for a story, and the evolution of his
conception and work, are traced by Joseph Blotner in his biography, based on
Faulkner's own later statements and manuscript drafts of Faulkner's work.[56]

Faulkner stated that the novel began as a short story called "Twilight" — "I
thought it could be done in ten pages," he stated — about children who had
been sent away from the house because they were "too young to be told what
was going on," which was the funeral of their grandmother.[57] Faulkner later
stated that as he was working on it, "the idea struck me to see how much more
I could have got out of the idea of the blind, self-centeredness of innocence,
typified by children, if one of those children had been truly innocent, that is,
an idiot." Then, he said, "I became interested in the relationship of the idiot to
the world... and just where he could get the tenderness, the help, to shield him
in his innocence.... And so the character of his sister began to emerge...." At
this point, as Blotner recounts and Faulkner later described, the story began
to open up before him — Caddy, her other brothers Quentin and Jason, and
the family tragedy, unfolding in a sweeping drama over thirty years. "I saw
that peaceful glinting of that branch was to become the dark, harsh flowing
of time sweeping her to where she could not return to comfort him [her idiot
brother Benjy], but that just separation, division, would not be enough, not far
enough. It must sweep her into dishonor and shame too...." "I saw that they
had been sent to the pasture to spend the afternoon to get them away from
the house during the grandmother's funeral in order that the three brothers
and the nigger children could look up at the muddy seat of Caddy's drawers
as she climbed the tree to look in the window at the funeral, without them
realising the symbology of the soiled drawers... [that] hers was the courage to
face later with honor the shame which she was to engender, which Quentin
and Jason could not face...." It is noteworthy — fitting the basic argument
of this book   how Faulkner's conception, both his initial idea to show the
innocence of childhood, his subsequent idea to show the innocence of the idiot,
and his richer conception, especially of Caddy — of moral courage amidst a
scene of moral rot and decay, resonates with his creative interest, described in
preceding chapters, in depicting the South, the world of his childhood, in its
moral decay and decline, together with the resilience of men and women, the
few having the courage to stand against the tide of destiny, to persevere in their

[56] Blotner traces Faulkner's work on the book on pp. 566–78 of *Faulkner: A Biography*,
Vol. 1. My account and quotations are drawn from his description.
[57] Faulkner had been portraying the contrast between the world and consciousness
of children and the adult world in a series of earlier stories, and that seems to have been
the root of this story as well.

moral goodness and struggle to overcome. Indeed his development of the story seems to flow out of and follow his interest — so that his interest, consciously or unconsciously, helped guide him in developing his richer conception of the story.

At this point, if Faulkner's description of his process is correct, the overall outline of the story took shape in his mind: arcing across time, from when the main characters are children to thirty years later when Caddy's illegitimate daughter, whom Jason has cheated out of money her mother has sent her, steals money from Jason's room — climbing down a tree, an act mirroring Caddy's climb up a tree so many years before — triggering him to go on a rampage looking for her. However, as Faulkner went forward writing the novel it evolved further. He first wrote the Benjy section, repeatedly shifting time frames; Blotner states that Faulkner's original manuscripts show that he was "constantly expanding and elaborating" in writing this section. Having come to the end of it, Faulkner stated that it was "incomprehensible . . . so I had to write another chapter. Then I decided to let Quentin tell his version of that same day, or that same occasion, so he told it." He next made a set of notes outlining the dates and main events of the story, then wrote Quentin's section, again revising and adding as he went. But then he realized he was still not done: "Then there had to be the counterpoint, which was the other brother, Jason." So he wrote a third section, giving Jason's version of events. But even then he was not done: "So I wrote Quentin's and Jason's sections, trying to clarify Benjy's." But "it was completely confusing," he said, so "then I had to write another section from the outside with an outsider, which was the writer, to tell what had happened. . . ." So he did, writing the fourth section. Thus he came to write his masterpiece, through a process of growth, with a layering of perspectives, that clearly took him well beyond his conception when he began to write.

13

Multiple Interests

The description of creative development presented in this book to this point describes creative development as essentially a linear progression. This progression is a sequence of the three basic phases of creative development, outlined at the beginning of the preceding chapter: (1) formation of creative interests; (2) exploration of interests, building up conceptual structures in interest domains, and seeking ways to develop interests creatively, generating creativity rooted in interests, and defining and selecting projects to undertake; and (3) focus on creative projects, leading to the creation of creative works and contributions. This description has the virtue of depicting the logic of creative development simply, manifesting its core structures and processes. But it is an oversimplification, at least for most individuals — in many cases a very great one. Further, it fails to convey a sense for the richness of creative development, in particular for the rich variety and complexity of patterns of development.

In this chapter and the following two chapters I describe larger patterns of creative development. This chapter focuses on constellations of interests: I describe patterns of development and creativity generation based in multiple interests. In the following two chapters I describe (1) project patterns rooted in interests, in particular pursuit of a set of projects rooted in a common core interest, and (2) patterns of development over longer time periods, in particular the evolution of interests and the formation and pursuit of sequences of linked interests, as well as interrelationships among projects, ideas, and interests. I do not describe these patterns in full detail. Rather, I outline them, presenting a variety of patterns and illustrating them with examples. My purpose is to

426 convey a sense for them, for their importance in creative development, and an appreciation for the richness of creative development and the variety of paths of development.

I also have as an aim to show that richer, more complex patterns can be incorporated into the description of creative development in the preceding chapters. The description in these chapters is meant to provide a foundation for constructing richer, more complete descriptions of creative development, building on the description in the preceding chapters: incorporating interrelationships and connections between the basic phases and core processes of development, and showing how through cycling through these core phases and processes larger patterns of development are generated. It is my hope that this description will spur further research, linking and integrating the description and approach in this book with other approaches, for example biographical approaches.

CONSTELLATIONS OF INTERESTS

A significant feature of creative development is that many individuals engaged in creative endeavors have not one creative interest but a constellation of interests. I have not focused on this feature of development in the preceding chapters in the interest of keeping my description streamlined. However, constellations of interests are important in creative development, a vital source of creativity for many individuals. Indeed most individuals form and pursue multiple interests over the course of their development — it is unusual in my experience for an individual to have and pursue just one interest over the course of his creative career.

In this chapter I focus on individuals who have formed multiple interests combining and interrelating their interests, during a given time period, creatively.[1] I describe two main processes through which individuals creatively connect, combine, or relate interests: defining a creative project; and generating an idea or insight. Both are central for many individuals in their development, as the examples illustrate. In Chapter 15 I describe patterns of development in which individuals form and pursue interests in sequence.

I note that during any particular moment or short period of time an individual generally pursues mainly one primary interest. There are exceptions to this rule — some individuals explore multiple interests almost simultaneously; Samuel Taylor Coleridge, for example, seems to have done this; however, based

[1] Interests that an individual thinks of as entirely separate and that he never connects or combines in any way — so that they remain separate over the course of his development — can be described separately, at least to a first approximation.

on the individuals whose developments I have studied this is not common, and indeed, as the time frame becomes short enough, does not seem possible. But, while an individual is pursuing one main creative interest, his other interests are still in his mind, in the background, and any one may come to the fore at any time, for example if an event or encounter calls it to mind — leading him to connect or relate it to or combine it with the primary interest he is focused on, generating an idea, insight, or project.

CREATIVE PROJECT GENERATION: COMBINING INTERESTS

Individuals who have multiple interests often develop and pursue projects that combine their interests in some way. Combining of interests can take various forms and come about through various pathways. In some cases an individual has a main creative interest, and is led, through a second interest he has, to focus on a specific aspect or topic in the domain of his main interest. Liz Yoder did this in defining her dissertation project as I describe below. Alternatively, an individual may fuse two or more interests together to define a project. Samuel Taylor Coleridge fused several of his interests in this way in creating the main plotline and theme of "The Rime of the Ancient Mariner"; I describe this fusion of interests below. Tom Stoppard, as remarked in Chapter 2, stated in an interview that his projects develop when two of his interests in his words "plait together." His language suggests a process somewhat similar to what I describe for Coleridge. As one kind of fusion, an individual may define a project in the zone of intersection of two or more of his interests.

Combining interests is natural. A project that combines two of a person's interests or falls in their zone of intersection naturally tends to catch his attention and interest — has, in a sense, a double intensity of attraction for him. Individuals often have a natural proclivity for recognizing connections between their interests — thus are able to recognize interesting project opportunities that combine their interests that others miss. In addition, individuals tend naturally to generate ideas for projects that combine or connect interests they have: their thinking, guided and generated by the conceptual structures that encode their interests, naturally is generative of associations and connections between these structures. In some cases individuals deliberately combine a set of interests in a project or define a project that is a point of intersection of two or more of their interests; Karen Hadley is an example given below. But in most cases such projects simply emerge, naturally, in the course of their development.

Karen Hadley combined several interests in defining her dissertation project. As noted previously, Karen has a core interest in detailed, linguistically based reading of language in literature — at the level of individual sentences.

In graduate school Karen attended and TA'd a course on the Romantics and was captivated by their poetry.[2] She was especially drawn to *The Prelude* and formed a focus of interest in it. Shortly after this Karen took a course on temporality in literature in which, as she described it, the professor described "different ways of conceptualizing time in language." Through the course Karen developed an interest in temporality. Thus, at this point Karen had three interests — her original interest in detailed linguistic analysis of language, an interest in the Romantics and especially *The Prelude*, and a new interest in temporality. She combined these three interests to define a research focus which became the basis of her dissertation, as discussed in the context of her dissertation prospectus drafts in the preceding chapter: an analysis of temporality in *The Prelude* as it is defined and represented linguistically. It is noteworthy that Karen seems to have combined her interests quite deliberately — she told me she wanted to "superimpose" the framework of temporality on her other interests.

Karen Kebarle, another literary scholar introduced in Chapter 4, defined a focus for her dissertation research also through combining three interests. As stated in Chapter 4 Karen has a long-standing love of and interest in beautiful, transcendent passages in literature. Karen is from Canada, and came to the United States for the first time when she entered a doctoral program. Originally, in Canada and during her first year in the U.S., she focused on British literature. But in her second year she became interested in America — in American values and social attitudes and, as she described it, "America's pride in itself" as reflected in its sense of its own history and values. This new interest led her to shift her focus to American literature and certain themes and kinds of books within the canon of American literature. During the same period of time Karen also formed a pair of further interests: in sexuality, including homosexuality, in literature; and in women as artists. She said she was interested in these topics both in the lives of authors and as themes portrayed in literature.[3] These different interests fused together for her during her second year. Karen took a class in which she wrote a paper about Willa Cather's *The Professor's House*. She made this choice fairly casually, she told me—did not at the time have

---

[2]Karen told me she is a mountaineer and that she remembered gaining the sense, reading the Romantics, of "being out there in the mountains." Karen likes to analyze language slowly and carefully, and, though she had previously not been interested in poetry, told me she realized at this point in her development that poetry, with its density of language, fits her approach.

[3]Karen described being interested in biographical material about women authors and homosexual relationships of both men and women authors. Her interest in sexuality and gender is connected with an interest she formed in college in love and personal relationships as portrayed in literature.

a strong interest in Willa Cather. At the same time she also read a Cather short story in another class, "Paul's Case." In reading *The Professor's House* she was struck by the portrayal of the American ideal of an unsettled, virginal wilderness land to be reclaimed — the sense of innocence, yet the impossibility of reclaiming the land without ruining it in the process, as she described it to me. She was struck also by the beautiful passages in which Cather describes the cliff city. "It's amazing prose," she said, "where you feel almost enraptured, it's so vital, so beautiful, she creates a kind of feeling of transcendence." In *The Professor's House* as well as "Paul's Case" and a biography about Cather that had recently been published that she read, Karen was also struck by the focus on themes of personal relationships and homosexuality, both in the works and in Cather's own life.[4] Karen presented her paper about *The Professor's House* in class, and then her professor spoke about it. She recalls her professor's comments as intensely interesting to her — "it was like it was opening up to me," she said. Thus through the confluence of three interests — the theme of American idealism, the beautiful writing conveying a sense of transcendence, and the focus on personal relationships — and inspired by her professor, Karen came to focus for her dissertation on Willa Cather, focusing on her portrayal of relationships and sexuality in her writings.

The project Liz Yoder pursued for her dissertation is at the intersection of two of her interests. As described in earlier chapters, during her senior year in college Liz became excited about the phenomenon of glial signaling. After wrestling for some time with whether or not to pursue this topic, which she viewed as radical, she made the decision to pursue it. Prior to becoming interested in neuroscience Liz had been interested in muscle mechanics. In her college honors project she used electromyography to measure anticipatory muscle movement.[5] Through her interest in muscle mechanics, studying muscle innervation, Liz gained knowledge about the peripheral nervous system. When in graduate school she decided to pursue the study of glial signaling, it occurred to her to study signaling in glial cells in the peripheral nervous system, which are called Schwann cells — thus a point of intersection with her earlier interest in muscle mechanics. She told me she realized, in the course of reviewing the literature, that "all the studies at that point had been done on central nervous system glia" — none had studied Schwann cells. "And so I thought, 'Well, if they really are a prominent feature then the peripheral glia should be doing

---

[4]The biography is Sharon O'Brien, *Willa Cather: The Emerging Voice* (Oxford: Oxford University Press, 1987).

[5]Elizabeth Yoder, *Muscle Strategies in Anticipation of a Disruptive Force: Timing, Visual Knowledge, and Activation Level Considerations*, submitted to the Honors College for the Bachelor of Science degree, Arizona State University, 1990.

this too.'" Her prior interest and knowledge base built up pursuing it seems to have played a crucial role in guiding her thinking, leading her to the idea to focus on the Schwann cells, which no one else, as far as she knew, had done, thus defining a topic at the intersection of her two interests. When the opportunity presented itself a short time later to pursue the topic, through another researcher making Schwann cells available to her, she seized it, initiating the project that became her main dissertation project — investigating effects of different neurotransmitters in triggering calcium-based responses in Schwann cells.[6]

Samuel Taylor Coleridge had numerous interests, clustered in a few broad areas. Indeed it is a striking feature of the literature on Coleridge, a reflection of the great variety and sheer number of his interests, that different scholars emphasize and focus on different sets of interests he had — so that we see the full universe, or at least an approximation to it, only in the composite of their descriptions.[7] Coleridge's great poems, most notably "The Rime of the Ancient Mariner," are based in and woven out of elements drawn from multiple interest domains. Here I describe clusters of interests described by three Coleridge scholars, then discuss the main interests he drew upon and wove together in composing "The Rime."

In *The Road to Xanadu* John Livingston Lowes, whose description of Coleridge's early "Gutch Notebook" and pattern of reading is the basis of my own discussion of Coleridge's creative process in Chapter 10, focuses on a set of interests Coleridge pursued primarily through his extensive reading.[8]

---

[6]At the time, Liz thought no one else was pursuing this topic. As it turned out, there was one other researcher at a different university who also began studying calcium activity in Schwann cells at this time. But she investigated the effects of different compounds on activity in these cells, and Liz made a discovery — that the Schwann cells respond to the neurotransmitter serotonin — that was not discovered by the other researcher, who herself discovered a response to a different compound that was not discovered by Liz.

[7]I am certainly not the first to note that the full universe of Coleridge's interests and thought seems to have escaped ready description by any one author. Kathleen Coburn discusses Coleridge's breadth of interests and accomplishments and the fact that in the received literature it is not grasped as a totality in the first few pages of *Experience into Thought: Perspectives in the Coleridge Notebooks* (Toronto: University of Toronto Press, 1979).

[8]Lowes refers to other interests Coleridge had, most notably his interest in wanderers in literature, and in the environment around him, which is in the main a different facet and modality of exploration of his interest in nature. See *The Road to Xanadu*, chap. XIV, pp. 242–60; chap. XV, pp. 286–91; he discusses Coleridge's interest in the night sky and the moon in Chapter XI, pp. 171–93, and in his local environs in Chapter XII, pp. 194–217 and elsewhere.

His primary focus is Coleridge's interests in the natural world explored through reading, in particular the exotic, extreme regions of the Earth, voyages of exploration, and sensory phenomena of nature — the interests I describe in Chapter 10. Central to his account, as evident in my discussion in that chapter, is description of Coleridge's extensive reading about voyages of exploration, in which many different kinds of sea phenomena are described — descriptions which Coleridge drew upon extensively in composing "The Rime." He describes also Coleridge's reading about the polar regions — the Arctic zone, with its icebergs, ice flows, and ice fields, and Greenland and Lapland, places of particular interest to Coleridge; and about the equatorial regions — the tropics — for which he identifies two distinct focuses of interest Coleridge had: (1) the West Indies, which Coleridge learned about while writing his Prize Greek Ode at Cambridge and which were on his mind later as he considered the possibility of establishing his planned pantisocratic society at some remote site; and (2) the African tropics — he notes a book, *Travels to Discover the Source of the Nile*, that was popular with Coleridge's circle at Cambridge and which he knew well.⁹ Lowes also describes Coleridge's deep interest and reading in mystical thought, including Neoplatonism. Coleridge himself refers to this interest in a well-known letter to John Thewall in November 1796. I quote it here as showing his conception of his interest and extensive reading — both in general and in this domain of interest:

> I am, and ever have been, a great reader, and have read almost everything — a library cormorant. I am *deep* in all out of the way books, whether of the monkish times, or of the puritanical era. I have read and digested most of the historical writers; but I do not *like* history. Metaphysics and poetry and "facts of mind," that is, accounts of all the strange phantasms that ever possessed "your philosophy"; dreamers, from Thoth the Egyptian to Taylor the English pagan [a Platonist who introduced Neoplatonic ideas in England], are my darling studies."¹⁰

A related interest Coleridge formed and explored that Lowes describes, though more briefly, is in paranormal phenomena, mental illusions, and hypnotism.

---

⁹*The Road to Xanadu*, Book II is largely about Coleridge's various interests in regions of the world. Chapter IX is "The Fields of Ice," Chapter X is "The Courts of the Sun." Lowes states that "books on the West Indies" Coleridge "had eagerly read for years" and discusses his interest in the West Indies on pp. 133–34.

¹⁰Samuel Taylor Coleridge, *Letters of Samuel Taylor Coleridge*, ed. Ernest Hartley Coleridge (London: William Heinemann, 1895), 1, pp. 178–83. Lowes quotes from the letter on p. 231, with a discussion on ensuing pages. In a postscript to the letter, Coleridge lists a series of works he wishes Thewall to purchase for him, including by Neoplatonists and one containing writings of Thoth.

432   Kathleen Coburn, having a deep knowledge of Coleridge's notebooks in their totality, which he wrote over a span of forty years, presents a different view of Coleridge and focuses on describing different interests he had in her books *The Self Conscious Imagination* and *Experience into Thought*.[11] She focuses on Coleridge's introspection and interest in psychology of mind, especially psychological observation of the self. She also discusses Coleridge's interest in dreams, madness, and unusual mental states, and in the self in relation to others and the world at large. She discusses his interest in the natural world in the context of his interest in the self, describing his sense of interrelationship, close observation, and inherently subjectivist descriptions of nature, linking his sense of the intertwining of self and nature to his core belief in the unity underlying the diversity of the world.[12]

Richard Holmes, in his biography of Coleridge, describing Coleridge's interests in the period leading up to his composition of "The Rime," focuses on his political interests and beliefs and their development — intertwined with his overall description of Coleridge's life and experiences. His narrative of this period in Coleridge's life centers in great part around Coleridge's interest in radical politics. He describes Coleridge's development with Robert Southey of pantisocracy — an idealistic vision of a pastoral, experimental society, with communal property and full equality, to be free from evil. Then he describes Coleridge's intellectual development from this point, lecturing in Bristol and elsewhere, reading widely, developing his ideas, and becoming caught up in personal disputes, which made him aware of the unpleasantness of practical politics and of the impracticality of realizing his utopian vision. He discusses Coleridge's intellectual engagement with the question of the origins of evil and the sin of not providing hospitality. And he describes, as the culmination of this period, Coleridge's withdrawal from active political life, to a cottage in the village of Stowey, where he devoted himself to introspection and, in his own words years later in his *Biographia Literaria*, to studying "the foundations of religions and morals" and "ethics and psychology."[13]

[11] Kathleen Coburn, *The Self Conscious Imagination* (London: Oxford University Press, 1974); *Experience into Thought*, cited in footnote 7 above. Coburn is the editor of Coleridge's Notebooks.

[12] She also describes his interest in individuals of the ages who were mystical seekers after knowledge and enlightenment and visionaries, including Paracelsus and Jacob Böhme, in Lecture Two of *Experience into Thought*.

[13] Samuel Taylor Coleridge, *Biographia Literaria*, in *Samuel Taylor Coleridge: The Major Works*, Book X. See for Holmes's discussion *Coleridge: Early Visions, 1772–1804*, especially Chapters 4, "Pantisocrat," and 5, "Watchman." For Coleridge's interest in the origins of evil see a letter from Charles Lamb Holmes quotes from on p. 139 of *Coleridge: Early Visions*, *The Letters of Charles and Mary Lamb*, ed. Edwin J. Marrs,

At the time Coleridge was settled at Stowey we can identify two sets of interests he had. One was his interests in voyages of exploration and the far reaches of the Earth — the extremes. In a letter he wrote at this time to his publisher Joseph Cottle describing how he would go about writing a great epic, he writes that he would first study mathematics and the sciences, then "the *mind of man*," and then, as his last topic, presumably the basis for his epic, "the *minds of men* — in all Travels, Voyages, and Histories."[14] These interests were linked also with his interests in sensory phenomena of nature and wanderers. The other set of interests, his primary focus as Holmes, for example, describes this period of his life, was ethics viewed from his own particular interest in psychology: the question of evil, man's relationship with other men, the wanderer, guilt, penitence, and redemption, commingled with his interest in mystical, spiritual, and religious experience and paranormal phenomena. Coleridge made an abortive attempt at linking the two sets of interests in "The Destiny of Nations." In a footnote to the fragment of the poem, which Holmes presents and discusses, Coleridge describes one basis of the epic as being a myth: There is an evil spirit who dwells under the polar sea and takes animals and people captive, and when she takes "Greenlanders" captive an "Angekok or Magician" must voyage "through the kingdom of souls" to her abode and by enchantment reclaim the ones taken. This myth combines many elements from Coleridge's different interests — there is a voyage, in particular through a mystical kingdom, there is the presence of evil and a theme of redemptive journey, and it is set in the polar regions and ocean. Coleridge's plan for the poem "The Brook" also seems to combine interests from his two sets of interests, but the poem is set in his immediate locale, not in the far distant regions, with the sense of voyage much reduced — features that perhaps contributed to his not pursuing it.[15]

Coleridge wrote "The Rime of the Ancient Mariner" shortly after these attempts. In "The Rime" he combines his two sets of interests in a way that is highly creative, drawing upon his years of study and exploration of them. From its first conception — as is well known, the poem originated during a walk with Wordsworth and his sister Dorothy — the poem had elements drawn from both sets of interests: a sea voyage; and a crime committed for which the mariner

Jr. (Ithaca, NY: Cornell University Press, 1975), I, pp. 95–97. For Coleridge's interest in hospitality as a virtue and the lack of it as a sin see *Coleridge: Early Visions*, p. 139.

[14]Samuel Taylor Coleridge, *Collected Letters of Samuel Taylor Coleridge* ed. Earl Leslie Griggs, 6 Vols. (Oxford: Clarendon Press, 1956–1971), 1, pp. 320–21. Quoted and discussed in *Coleridge: Early Visions*, pp. 144–45.

[15]See *Coleridge: Early Visions*, chap. 7; for the myth p. 140, for "The Brook" pp. 160–62.

434 must do penitence to gain redemption. As Coleridge developed the poem he gathered elements from both sets and wove them together.[16] In Chapter 10 I describe the way he drew upon and synthesized the vast knowledge he had built up exploring his interests in voyages of exploration, the far reaches and extreme climate zones of the Earth, and descriptions of natural phenomena — creating the brilliant imagery of the poem. Paired with this, his interests in ethics and the psychology of crime, guilt, punishment, and redemption, as well as paranormal states and spirits, are the foundation of the plot and action of the poem. The crime the mariner commits is shooting the albatross, violating the ethic of hospitality and respect for the spirit of a place, thus a crime tied to being a wanderer in a strange region and also to the footnote to "The Destiny of Nations"; this crime is the origin of evil in the poem. The poem's action is driven by the necessity for the mariner to do penitence for his crime and thus achieve redemption: the deadly calm, slimy, rotting creatures in the water around the ship and death of his fellows carry the punishment; he achieves redemption when he feels genuine love for the sea creatures — then angels carry the ship forward, the curse is broken, there is an uplifting breeze, and he makes his return to land. The poem is thus a synthesis of a Christian morality tale with a traditional myth — mirroring Coleridge's interests. Embedded in the poem, at its core, is a state of altered reality, akin to hallucination or mystical experience, with the skeleton ship, the curse of the spirit, the angels, and the strange, gothic atmosphere. The sense of its being the tale of a wanderer and the sense of altered reality are enhanced by the brilliant structural layering — the mariner telling the tale at the wedding, the tale of a wanderer who has returned from a mythic journey and altered state of being.[17]

CREATIVE CONNECTIONS BETWEEN INTERESTS

Creative connections between interests — between elements drawn from different interest domains — are a powerful source of creativity. Such connections are often highly creative and can and do lead to important projects and contributions.

[16] See *Coleridge: Early Visions*, pp. 171–73. The walk that sparked the poem occurred on November 13, 1797; Coleridge completed the poem, in its first form, in the early spring of 1798.

[17] There is one further element that was crucial for Coleridge in his poetic development from his school days: an interest in writing poetry in a plain, down-to-earth style. This is linked to his interest in nature as a subject of poetry and was quite important historically in terms of his influence and collaboration with Wordsworth and the growth of Romanticism.

As described in Chapter 10, once an individual forms a creative interest he explores it, building up a rich conceptual structure in its domain. Individuals who have multiple interests explore many or all of them: typically they explore them in sequence, so that during a given period of time they are focused on one main interest, often shifting back and forth between interests over time; alternatively, in some cases an individual explores multiple interests more or less simultaneously, as Coleridge seems to have done. Through exploring individuals build up, over time, conceptual structures in each of several interest domains. Typically individuals pursue each of their interests independently, as a distinct interest, and hence do not expect to make creative connections between them. Such connections are not inevitable and might never be — and in many cases never are — made. Indeed even when individuals pursue related interests as, for example, Coleridge did, they typically do not consciously expect to forge connections between them — don't see a connection generally until they make it (though they may at some level imagine connecting them or wish to connect them prior to this, thus in a sense anticipate a connection).[18] Thus when an individual does make a creative connection between two interests he has it is usually unexpected and exciting — and the connection is often highly creative.

There are three main processes through which individuals generate creative connections between different interests — between elements belonging to different interest domains. One is through a creative response. A second is through making a connection while thinking more broadly about their development, thus at the meta-level, a mental state naturally conducive to making connections across multiple interests. Finally, a third is identifying, while striving to develop one of their interests creatively, a link with a second interest. I describe and give examples of these in the remainder of this section; the last two seem in many cases to occur together, and are not easy to distinguish, thus I discuss them together.

I have described creative responses in Chapter 9 as a fundamental process through which individuals generate ideas and insights during creative development. The creative responses I describe in that chapter are responses in which a single creative interest mediates the response. Creative responses involving multiple interests are analogous: sparked by an element he encounters or experience he has, an individual makes a creative connection between elements belonging to two different interest conceptual structures, generating

---

[18]While individuals do not generally explore their interests from the point of view of making connections between them, nonetheless the fact that someone has multiple interests may and often does influence his path of exploration indirectly; for example, one interest may influence his attention, what he notices, as he is exploring a different interest.

an idea or insight. The most common form of such response is one in which the element or experience that catches a person's attention fits with one of his interests, so that through this first interest guiding his attention he is led to notice and focus on the element or experience, and then, through a chain of associations, or thinking, he makes a creative connection with an element in the domain of the second interest. Alternatively, an element an individual encounters or experience he has may simultaneously connect with two of his interests, thus leading him to make a connection between them, which may itself be an idea or insight, or may lead to an idea or insight through a chain of further associations. In these processes there are a number of different ways in which a stimulus may trigger an individual to make a creative connection. The stimulus may be an element that, while mainly connecting with one interest he has, has a second characteristic or aspect that connects with a second interest he has. Alternatively, it may be a new element, for example a new fact or model, that makes a connection between two interests evident which was previously not apparent to him.

Azad Bonni is an example of an individual who made a very creative response that involved two interests he had, sparked by a stimulus he encountered that was at the intersection of his interests.

In describing Azad's creative development in prior chapters I focus on his core interest, which has been at the center of his development, in mechanisms of action, specifically mapping out the pathways through which responses are triggered in cells by extracellular agents, with a particular focus on pathways of regulation of gene transcription by NGF and the neurotrophins. In fact, in the course of his development Azad formed a number of distinct interests. His development is thus richer and more complex than described in previous chapters. This is in fact true for many of the individuals whose developments are discussed in preceding chapters: their development is richer than described, in particular they developed multiple interests. Here I describe a second creative interest Azad formed and the creative response he made at the intersection of his main interest and this second interest.

Azad received medical training after college. Within medicine he was especially interested in neurology and did his internship and residency in neurology. During these years he developed interests in nerve regeneration and degenerative motor disorders. Describing the origins of these interests he said that clinical cases sparked his initial interest in degenerative motor disorders, specifically cerebellar disorders, and that there was a top researcher at the school where he did his residency training who studies nerve regeneration, which sparked his interest in that topic. He also said that at the time researchers were just beginning to study "the molecular basis" of regeneration, molecules that "may be involved" in it, which he found interesting as a topic, fitting with his general interest in studying molecules and their effects on cells. Further, he said that one reason he found NGF exciting was that "people were talking about it in terms of its involvement in ... degenerative diseases" and possible therapeutic value for treating such diseases, thus it connected with his interest in degenerative disease and nerve regeneration; early on his two interests were thus linked in his mind. He also told me he conducted original research on cerebellar degenerative disorders of movement which was never published, gaining considerable knowledge about this class of diseases.

As described in Chapter 11, at the time he was accepted into his doctoral program Azad was planning to pursue a project characterizing the pathway through which NGF regulates GAP-43, but his plans changed. He decided not to pursue GAP-43, and switched to a different lab, under a principal investigator whose interests matched his own and who had published an important paper on NGF regulation of the *c-fos* promoter. As described in the preceding chapter Azad defined as his main doctoral project the characterization of the mechanism through which NGF regulates *c-fos*. Azad said that early on work on this project progressed rather slowly and there were no exciting findings. He thus decided to expand his focus — "I decided that I needed to work on something else, too." He said that in thinking generally about his interests and possibilities — thus at the meta-level — he realized that another neurotrophin he might study is CNTF, ciliary neurotrophic factor. CNTF stood out for him, among the neurotrophins, because it is believed to be involved in nerve repair and has effects on motor neuron survival, thus fit with his interest in motor disorders and nerve regeneration. "I thought it was really interesting from a neurologic point of view," he said, "because people had found that it promotes the survival of motor neurons, and I thought that might definitely be of interest to people in neurology, because it might be useful — to figure out how it does that [exerts its effect] — for a whole group of motor neuron disorders." He also said he thought there was an opportunity — there was active research on CNTF receptor biology, "but there was nothing known about its downstream effects." As a topic the CNTF pathway thus fit nicely at the intersection of his interests in pathways of action and in motor disorders and nerve regeneration, and Azad decided to pursue it. In particular he decided to do his prelim exam on CNTF. He told me that in the course of preparing for his exam he did a comprehensive literature review — "you can't imagine how many things I read for my prelim" — thus built up an extensive knowledge base about CNTF and its biology.

Azad's creative response occurred shortly after his prelim exam. Two papers on interferon signaling were published that Azad read. The papers describe a signaling pathway for interferon, one paper, as he recalled, giving a "prediction of the secondary structure" of the interferon receptor, the spatial configuration of its main amino acid chains, which generates the tertiary structure target agents interface with, and the other describing "how interferons activate this pathway." Reading the papers, Azad made a creative connection: he realized that the CNTF receptor, which he was very familiar with from studying for his exam, has a similar structure to the one that was proposed for the interferon receptor — not at the primary level of the amino acid chains, but at the level of the secondary and tertiary structure; and thus he realized that CNTF might also activate the signaling pathway which was being proposed for interferons. In our interview Azad remembered the experience of having the insight vividly:

> This is probably the single insight... that really stands out for me [in my graduate school years]. I realized that the structures of the receptors were, based on what was written, similar — not necessarily at the primary amino acid level, but in terms of secondary and tertiary structure. And [also] I thought that it's quite possible that, since CNTF was involved in injury response in the central nervous system, which is, or teleologically may be, related to the function of interferons in other systems, it might be possible that CNTF activates the signaling pathway that people had discovered for interferon — [that] was suggested to be very specific at that point for interferons.

Azad's response and creative insight were based in and bridged his two interests in mechanisms of action and nerve regeneration and repair. Azad did not state why he noticed and read the interferon signaling papers, but it seems likely that it was because they are about a signaling pathway and an external agent triggering the pathway, thus fit with his interest in mechanisms of action. To be sure they are not about the molecules he was focused on, NGF and the neurotrophins, but nonetheless they fit with his broader interest. In addition, the interferons are important in injury repair, which is related to his interest in nerve regeneration; this connection may have contributed as a secondary factor in calling his attention to the papers, though it was probably not the primary factor, as he did not mention having had a particular interest in interferons prior to this time (but see below). In making the creative link with CNTF Azad drew on his knowledge about CNTF, which fits within his broader interest in degenerative motor disorders and nerve regeneration. It is noteworthy that he had focused on CNTF for his exam just a short time previously, and thus had extensive and up-to-date knowledge about it — thus, for example, knew its receptor primary amino acid structure and the secondary structure that had been proposed for its receptor based on this primary structure.

Further, given that he had taken his exam fairly recently, it is likely that his knowledge about CNTF was readily accessible mentally to him. The creative connection he made centers on an element — the CNTF receptor — that lies in the intersection of his two interests.

In describing his creative insight, Azad said that a further reason why he believed that CNTF might share the interferon signaling pathway was that he recognized a "teleological" connection between the two agents in terms of function — the function CNTF has in the nervous system in nerve repair and regeneration following injury is analogous to the function interferons have in response to bodily injury.[19] This second connection he made was rooted in his medical training and also probably in his interest in nerve regeneration — for, though he did not mention having any special interest in interferons, they are naturally linked, as a source of repair, to nerve regeneration, also a repair process. I believe this connection would have been less likely to have been recognized by a molecular biology researcher who had not been trained in medicine and did not share Azad's interest in nerve regeneration — thus showing the importance of this second interest Azad had, based in neurology, for his creative insight.

Approximately two months after having his insight Azad ran an initial experiment to test the hypothesis that CNTF activates the interferon pathway. "It was really exciting — there was a hint of a result there for CNTF activating STATs, these proteins that are involved in the interferon signaling pathway — that was probably the most exciting moment in my career here [in this lab, in graduate school]." He made a further discovery in subsequent experiments, and published his work as an article in *Science*.[20]

The second process of creativity generation linking multiple interests is through thinking about them, possibly at the meta-level. It is of course difficult

[19]Azad said: "The idea that CNTF may be — had been shown to be — involved in injury responses, and interferons are also involved in injury responses, so they're teleologically [related], and evolutionarily related, but in different systems, that suggests I think, in addition to the structural similarities of the receptors, that [their pathways may be related or they may share a common pathway]."

[20]A. Bonni, D.A. Frank, C. Schindler, and M.E. Greenberg, "Characterization of a pathway for ciliary neurotrophic factor signaling to the nucleus," *Science* 262 (1993): 1575–79. Two other groups also recognized that CNTF might activate the interferon pathway and published articles in *Science*, in January 1994. These articles are similar to the one published by Azad and coauthors but contain somewhat more details about the mechanism of action of CNTF on the pathway. I do not know how the individuals in these groups came to recognize the link with CNTF — undoubtedly they followed their own, different, paths of development.

440   to trace the exact path of thinking through which an individual comes to make a creative connection. But in my experience individuals who are able to recall and describe the process through which they made a creative connection between multiple interests generally depict the connection as coming about through a process of relatively open thinking — not occurring when they are narrowly focused on a specific problem or project but rather at a time when their thoughts are wandering more freely. Liz Yoder's process of thinking through which she linked her two interests seems to fit this description. Based on her description it seems that in the course of thinking generally about glial signaling, not as part of any specific focus but letting her mind wander, she was naturally led to think about the glia of the peripheral nervous system, the Schwann cells, which she was familiar with from her interest in and study of muscle mechanics. Thinking about them, she reasoned that if calcium signaling is a pervasive feature of glial cells then Schwann cells also should exhibit it, leading her to define a project at the intersection of her interests.

The third process of creativity generation — making a creative connection with a second interest while pursuing the development of a first, main interest — occurs in two somewhat different contexts. One is while first trying to find a way to develop an interest — trying to find an initial project to pursue in its domain. Liz's development illustrates this pattern: she was searching for an appropriate project on glial signaling to pursue, had not yet defined an independent project for herself, at the time she made the link to her interest in muscle activation and the Schwann cells, thereby generating a project idea that fit with both of her interests. The other is after completing one or a series of projects in the domain of an interest, reflecting in the aftermath of completing them. In this case often the connection is made through a project or completed work sparking a linkage. For example, an idea or element in a work one has produced may link to a second interest one has, sparking an idea. The examples of Alexander Calder and Thomas Edison below illustrate this pattern.[21] Like the second process, this process often seems to occur at a time when an individual's thoughts are roaming freely and relatively widely — for example, an individual may make a connection with a second interest just after completing a project, taking a break, stepping back to think broadly about his

---

[21] I note that the connection in this case is not made within the project work itself, but afterwards. I note also that in this second context there is often less of a sense of making a connection with a second interest in the course of struggling and striving to develop an interest, and more a sense of making a connection in the context of success — having already taken at least some steps towards developing the main interest one is striving to develop, thus having at least a limited sense of achievement.

interests and path forward. What distinguishes process three is that it always 441
occurs in the context of the active striving to develop an interest.[22]

Alexander Calder's process of creation for the mobile is an example of the
third process of creativity generation linking multiple interests. Calder had a
pair of core creative interests, described in Chapter 2: in the basic objects of
the universe, the solar system, notably the disc and the sphere, set in space,
as the basis for art; and in setting art in motion and motion as an integral element in art. His visit to Mondrian's studio sparked a creative response in him,
described in Chapter 9, that led him to begin creating abstract art, in particular fashioning original abstract sculptures that reflect and are rooted in his
interest in the basic objects of the universe in space as the basis for art. These
initial abstract sculptures, which he made in the months following his visit to
Mondrian's studio, original and creative as they are, are largely static. Then,
about a year after his visit to the studio, Calder began to make sculptures that
he set in motion — thus forging a connection with his second interest. At first
he used motors to generate simple repetitive motions — in a manner similar
to the way he generated motion in his circus. Later he took a further creative
step, creating mobiles in which the motion is generated by air currents, thus
through a natural, somewhat random process, that is not controlled or mech-
anized but rather spontaneous and, at least symbolically, free. Thus, through
this sequential process — creating a body of art sparked by a creative response
rooted in his first interest, then making a creative connection with his second
interest, through which he made a further innovation — Calder invented the
modern art mobile, a significant invention in the field of modern art.

Calder states in *Calder, An Autobiography with Pictures* that he suggested to
Mondrian during his visit to his studio that he "make" his "rectangles oscillate,"
thus set them in motion — thus the idea was lurking in his mind from that early
point in time.[23] But he did not initially pursue it, and it appears that it receded
from his consciousness. We do not know through what thinking process or
events it reemerged and he was led to set his sculptures in motion. He first set
mobiles in motion a full year after visiting Mondrian's studio, thus six months
after his exhibit of his initial abstract sculptures. It is certainly plausible that
he made the connection while taking something of a respite, during a period

[22]Another distinguishing feature of this process is that it is inherently asymmetrical
in terms of the roles of the two interests between which the individual makes a connection: one interest is being actively pursued by him, and while pursuing it he makes a
connection with a second interest which he was not actively pursuing and was thus in
the background.

[23]Alexander Calder and Jean Davidson, *Calder, An Autobiography with Pictures*,
p. 113.

442   of relative quiet, following his intense creative period the previous fall and his exhibit that spring. The fact that his first idea for motion was simple repetitive motion using motors, resembling motion he employed in his circus, suggests that his initial idea to set his sculptures in motion may well have been made via his circus. He may well have introduced motion in his circus because of his interest in motion as an art form; and having done so, later connected that motion, which was surely quite accessible in his mind as he often performed the circus, with his abstract art.[24]

Thomas Edison's invention of the phonograph is a second outstanding example of the third process. Edison formed an interest in telegraphy as a young adult, as described in previous chapters, working as a telegraph operator. Early in his career as an inventor he developed an interest in electromechanical devices for automated translating and transcribing of messages, one focus of his interest being automated writing systems, which spawned a number of his earliest significant inventions, notably the electric pen and stock ticker. As he matured and began to blossom as an inventor, Edison formed and explored new interests, also described previously, including in electrochemistry and the properties of different kinds of paper and other materials that might make for good writing surfaces. Sparked apparently by witnessing Elisha Gray's exhibit of a rudimentary telephone he formed an interest in acoustics and the transmission of sound. This interest became a focus of activity for him: he explored it actively, reading books and experimenting, and worked as a main project for many months on the invention of a telephone.

In a notebook entry for July 17, 1877, Edison writes that he has at last perfected a telephone: "Glorious = Telephone perfected this morning 5 am. . . ."[25] Later that very same day he wrote down an idea to record messages sent via the telephone by having the message reproduced at a slower speed at which it could be written out. This idea was a natural bridge to his long-standing interest in transcribing messages onto paper — thus linking an invention he made pursuing one interest with a second interest. Then, the next day, in a brilliant flash of creativity, Edison invented an approach for recording and playing back

[24]In the circus a number of different figures were set in motion, and various forms of motion were employed, including motorized motion on tracks, which seems closest to the first form of motion Calder used with his mobiles, and hand generated swinging motion. As far as I can ascertain the motion was predominantly planned — to produce circus tricks or specific movements. Thus the free, spontaneous, nonrepetitive motion of his mobiles seems to have been an innovation. For more on his circus, including photos, see *Calder, An Autobiography with Pictures*, pp. 72–73, 80, 82, 103–8, and Alexander Calder, *Calder*, plates 1–3.

[25]Thomas A. Edison, *The Papers of Thomas A. Edison*, Vol. 3, p. 439. Preceding entries describe multiple series of experiments and innovations leading to this point.

speech, the precursor of the phonograph. According to his account in his notebook, and Charles Batchelor's more detailed statement later in testimony, Edison was sounding notes — presumably with his voice — into his makeshift telephone and feeling with his hand the diaphragm behind it, feeling it vibrate in response (this was the mechanism through which the sound was converted into an electrical signal). He said to Batchelor, as Batchelor recalled it, "Batch, if we had a point on this [diaphragm] we could make a record on some material which we could afterwards pull under the point, and it would give us the speech back." Batchelor assembled a piece of wood covered with paper coated with a layer of paraffin wax with which they had been experimenting recording in the lab. As he stated, continuing his testimony: "I pulled it [the paper coated with paraffin] through the groove, while Mr. Edison talked to it. On pulling the paper through a second time, we both of us recognized that we had recorded the speech."[26]

Thus Edison made a pair of creative connections. Having just invented a telephone he linked this invention, rooted in his interest in sound transmission, with his interest in recording, generating the idea for a sound recording system that would work in combination with the telephone. Then, very likely spurred by this idea, he made a link with his interest in and extensive knowledge of surfaces for writing and recording — sparking the idea to try paper coated with wax — thereby inventing his recording and playback device. The striking fact that Edison had the idea for sound recording and then invented this device within a day after constructing a working telephone certainly fits with the idea that he made the connection while letting his thoughts roam freely, after weeks of intense work trying to perfect the telephone — thus fits the second process of creativity generation linking multiple interests, hence providing an example illustrating how the second and third processes naturally occur together.

---

[26]*The Papers of Thomas A. Edison*, Vol. 3, pp. 444–46 and Appendix 2. Batchelor goes on to describe a series of improvements they made. After setting it aside for some months, they returned to it and built a working device in December. See also Paul Israel, *Edison: A Life of Invention*, pp. 144–45.

PATTERNS OF CREATIVE DEVELOPMENT:
PATTERNS OF PROJECTS; PROJECTS
AND INTERESTS

Individuals engaged in creative endeavors generally pursue multiple projects over the course of their development. Further their projects are often interrelated, and in many cases projects are vital in shaping their subsequent path of development.

In this chapter I describe patterns of projects, specifically projects based in and growing out of a single root interest. I describe two main kinds of patterns of projects rooted in a common root interest: projects undertaken in series; and projects pursued simultaneously. After describing project patterns I describe a few pathways of influence of projects on subsequent development.

My description is brief — I describe a few main patterns of projects and pathways of influence, do not do justice to the rich variety of patterns and pathways. The description in the next chapter adds to my description here, describing richer patterns and processes of development. The description in this chapter, together with the descriptions in the previous chapter and next chapter, show how the core processes described in earlier chapters are repeated and link together, generating larger patterns of development.

There is considerable variation across fields in patterns of projects. In some fields individuals undertake just a few projects in the course of their creative activity, while in others individuals undertake many. Further, in some fields projects naturally link together while in others this is less common and natural. I focus on describing patterns of development in which an individual pursues a few main projects. Also, I focus on patterns that unfold over a time span of medium duration, during which an individual focuses on one main creative interest and seeks to develop this interest in multiple projects; I describe patterns of development over longer time spans in the next chapter.

The project patterns and pathways of influence I describe in some ways fit and in some ways are different than biographical accounts. In most biographies a main focus is description of different projects an individual engaged in and his successes and failures on these projects. Further, in many biographies linkages between projects are traced or suggested — for example, ways in which an early, relatively unsuccessful project was important in spawning or spurring an individual's definition of and engagement in a later, successful project. An example is Ellmann's description of how James Joyce's work on *Stephen Hero* was the basis out of which he developed A *Portrait of the Artist as a Young Man*.[1] My description fits such accounts to some degree, but I focus on the links between projects and interests, which generate linkages between projects that are less direct, running through connections to and from interests.

In the creativity field there is a small literature on patterns of projects. A notable contribution is the concept of a network of enterprise introduced by Howard Gruber — an individual engaged in a set of related projects or activities that are loosely connected or related.[2] In my experience this concept is descriptive for many individuals of their project activities during certain periods in their development, usually quite active periods. However, it describes only one kind of pattern, most similar to the project pairings I describe below. Few other theoretical concepts have been developed — for example, there is little theoretical discussion of projects influencing subsequent creative processes and paths of development.

PATTERNS OF PROJECTS BASED IN A SINGLE ROOT INTEREST

A very common pattern of creative development is engaging in a set of creative projects based in and growing out of a single root interest. This pattern has the structural form of a tree: the root interest is the trunk and projects grow out of this trunk as distinct branches. A key feature of this form is that projects are not

[1] Richard Ellmann, *James Joyce*, pp. 144–49, and chap. 18, especially pp. 295–99, and succeeding chapters. Ellmann notes in particular how Joyce refined his vision of an autobiographically based novel in the wake of *Stephen Hero*, gaining a greater sense of distance and aesthetic form; see also my discussion in Chapter 3.

[2] Howard E. Gruber, "Networks of enterprise in creative scientific work," in Barry Gholson, William Shadish, Robert Neimeyer, and Arthur Houts, eds., *Psychology of Science* (New York: Cambridge University Press, 1989), pp. 246–65.

446   directly linked; each project is rooted in and grows out of the root interest, and projects are linked only indirectly through all being rooted in the same interest.

An individual whose development fits this pattern, upon completing a project, returns to his root interest to identify and define his next project. He thus is not led to his next project directly from or through the project he has just completed — one project directly linking to the next, which defines a second pattern of development. I believe this second pattern fits more closely the common view of creative development — an individual being led to his next project through what he learns and discovers on a current project, for example a current project sparking an idea he decides to pursue further. Such chaining of projects definitely occurs and is important for many people, including, for example, Albert Einstein in his development of relativity theory. But it is certainly not the only or even the dominant pattern. In fact, for many individuals, including probably Einstein, their pattern of projects incorporates elements of both patterns. Here I emphasize the first pattern both in order to challenge the conventional view and to show that projects are rooted in interests.

There are two main variants of the tree pattern of projects. One is pursuing a series of projects, one at a time, all based in the same root interest. The other is undertaking a set of projects simultaneously that are all rooted in a common interest. I discuss each in turn.

Series of Projects

Many of the individuals I interviewed have engaged in a series of projects over time rooted in a core creative interest. For the literary scholars, a typical pattern was to engage in a senior thesis in college rooted in an interest they had formed and then develop their dissertation out of the same root interest — with their interest often having become richer conceptually, contributing to their defining their dissertation project in a richer, more mature way. For the neuroscientists, there were two main patterns: a number undertook a series of projects rooted in a single core interest in their doctoral work; and several have pursued a series of projects rooted in a common interest over a longer time, spanning their doctoral research and research they engaged in after finishing their dissertation — typically with their interest evolving over time, and sometimes combining with a second interest they form. The mathematicians had not in most cases engaged in a series of projects at the time I interviewed them; but several have since then engaged in projects and published papers rooted in the core interest that was the basis for their doctoral work.

Roger Knowles is an example of a neuroscientist who has pursued a series of projects all rooted in his core interest, "visualizing neurons developing into their shapes." As described in Chapter 9, for the project that became the first

part of his dissertation Roger set up a video microscopy system and watched
cells that had been transfected with a gene that expresses the protein tau grow
axon-like extensions; this project was clearly rooted in his interest. Roger spent
a year on the project and was reasonably successful, making several minor
discoveries and publishing a paper.[3] A major focus of the lab in which Roger
was working is the neurobiology of Alzheimer's disease, and Roger learned a lot
about Alzheimer's during his first year in the lab.[4] He learned in particular that
abnormal phosphorylation of tau is thought to be important in the formation of
the neurofibrillary tangles that are found in the brains of Alzheimer's patients
and believed to be important in the disease. After completing his first project
Roger undertook as a second project to try to extend the model system he had
used to study the growth of axon-like extensions by adding the expression of a
kinase for phosphorylation of tau — he said at the time I interviewed him that
no good system had been developed to study this process in intact cell systems,
thus this was an open area for work. This project is connected more with his
first project and the focus in the lab and less directly rooted in his interest;
but see below where I describe a link with his interest he later made. Roger
worked on the project for more than a year and a half with little success, and
eventually decided to drop it.

At this point Roger began collaborating with a post-doc in the lab who
worked on RNA translocation on a project to visualize and thus demonstrate
the existence of RNA granule translocation from the cell nucleus to distant
parts of the cell where dendritic extensions are forming, the RNA granules
being the template for production of proteins at these locations. This project
is clearly connected with Roger's interest in visualizing neurons developing
into their shapes. Indeed like his first project, defined in conversation with his
advisor, this project is in the region of overlap of his interest and the interest
of the person with whom he collaborated in defining it. The project was quite
successful; Roger and his collaborator were able to stain and visualize the RNA
granules, and also found, in Roger's words, that an entire "organizational unit"
of "different components of translational machinery" was transported out to the
growth point; and the project resulted in a publication in a main neuroscience
journal.[5]

[3]For the reference see Chapter 9, footnote 57.
[4]Roger told me that he had not been interested in Alzheimer's disease before joining
the lab and that the fact that the lab worked on this disease had not strongly influenced
his decision to join the lab.
[5]R.B. Knowles, J.H. Sabry, M.E. Martone, T.J. Deerinck, M.H. Ellisman, G.J.
Bassell, and K.S. Kosik, "Translocation of RNA granules in living neurons," *Journal
of Neuroscience* 16 (1996): 7812–20.

During follow-up interviews I conducted with Roger two years after our first interview and several years later he described the projects he has been engaged in since our original interview. His more recent projects integrate his interest in visualizing neurons developing into their shapes with his interest in Alzheimer's disease. "I'm now studying the morphology of neurons, the development of their shapes, in Alzheimer's disease, and the role of those shapes in the disease process," he told me — thus he linked his original interest with his interest in Alzheimer's, developing a project distinctive to him. He has published a series of papers on this topic since the time of our interview. It is noteworthy that his interest, which he originally formed and conceptualized in the Army, continued to be the basis for his creative work, guiding his development of projects, more than a decade later.

Teresa Faherty and Jeffrey Shoulson are two literary scholars whose developments over their last years in college and in graduate school fit the tree structure. As described in Chapter 3, Teresa formed an interest in *The Winter's Tale* in college, which remained a central focus of interest for her in her first years in graduate school. As described in Chapter 7, for her honors thesis in college Teresa developed an original interpretation of the play, focusing on the first act; she did not complete her thesis and said she left college feeling that she had "unfinished business" with the play. In graduate school Teresa took a class on pastoral, in which pastoral was described as a singing contest, and subsequently made a creative connection, described in Chapter 9 — she realized that the "flowers" scene in Act IV, Scene IV, is an evocation of pastoral as a singing contest, a model rooted, in the Renaissance, in Ovid. This insight was the starting point for her dissertation and is the basis of the first chapter. It is noteworthy, as mentioned already in Chapter 7, that the two ideas and projects she developed are about completely different parts of the play and not directly related. Thus her pair of projects fits the tree structure: both rooted in her interest, but not directly connected.[6]

Jeffrey's main literary interest in college and graduate school was *Paradise Lost*. I described the origins of his interest, his attraction to *Paradise Lost* for its

[6]A thematic link is that both ideas are about competition between characters. In describing her idea of the play as all in Leontes's mind Teresa said her idea was that he was "wrestling with" the different characters in his mind, "over who was going to have dominance or what their relationship was to each other." Her later idea is that Perdita and Florizel are engaged in a singing contest to see who can pay tribute to Ovid more eloquently and in a more sophisticated way. Thus there is a common focus on wrestling for supremacy. But Teresa did not indicate that she made any direct connection with the earlier idea in coming up with the later one. Also, the characters competing are different in the two cases.

difficultness and his sense of "familiarity" — that it seemed somehow similar or related to the rabbinic literature in which he was trained, in Chapter 4. In college Jeffrey was interested in possible sources Milton may have had that would have created a direct link with the rabbinic literature. During the summer after his junior year, at Cambridge, he discovered an early sixteenth-century figure whose work he thought might have been a source for some of Milton's knowledge of the Bible, Paul Fagius, and he pursued as the topic for his senior thesis Renaissance sources for Milton's rabbinic interpretations of Genesis.[7] In graduate school Jeffrey's interest evolved, as described in Chapter 11; in particular his focus shifted from rabbinic texts as sources for Milton to the resemblance between the rabbinic texts and *Paradise Lost*. For his dissertation he defined as his project to explore the nature of this resemblance in terms of similarities and contrasts in style, strategies of argumentation, and both specific and general themes. Thus his two main projects were both rooted in his interest in *Paradise Lost* and its relationship with the rabbinic literature, but were not directly connected.

It is noteworthy that in two of the cases above, Roger and Teresa, an individual undertook a new project because a project they had engaged in was not successful. Failure triggers individuals to search for and undertake new projects, rooted in creative interests they have which often have been the bases for earlier projects they have engaged in, but not directly linked to these earlier projects.[8]

The tree pattern of sequential projects is common among individuals famous for their creative contributions. Here I give a few examples drawn from different fields, illustrating that the pattern is common across a wide range of fields.

Hans Krebs, during his early years as an independent researcher, pursued a series of projects rooted in his interest in applying the manometric technique and related quantitative techniques to study problems of intermediary metabolism. The main project lines he pursued were relatively unconnected — thus fit the tree structure. Here I describe two main project lines he pursued drawing on the account by Frederic Holmes.

[7]Jeffrey's senior thesis is "'Who Himself Beginning Knew?' Creative Appropriation in John Milton's Account of Genesis: Books VII and VIII of *Paradise Lost*," Princeton University, Dept. of English, 1988. He discusses sources in Chapters 4, 5, and 6.

[8]A not uncommon pattern is for an individual to undertake a project not rooted in his main interest — caught up in the excitement of a new idea — not be able to develop it successfully, and then return to his main interest, generating a project based in it. This is what Roger did; it is also what David Johnson did.

450 As described in Chapters 11 and 12, soon after establishing his research laboratory at Freiburg Krebs embarked upon a project investigating the formation of urea, and through his discovery of the ornithine effect and resolution of the puzzle it raised characterized this process. This project was rooted in his interest, indeed was an initial foray into conducting research fitting with it. Nine to ten months after his creative breakthrough on the urea project, Krebs initiated what Holmes describes as "a major new line of investigation," the investigation of the effect on the rate of respiration in tissue slices of adding biochemicals thought to be important intermediaries in the oxidation of foodstuffs. This line of investigation was more broadly conceived than the urea project, and was to take far longer to come to fruition. Krebs, in discussing his initial idea for it with Holmes, stated that the "question" that initiated it was, "What are the intermediates in the oxidation of foodstuffs?" — thus a broad focus. Holmes, reviewing Krebs's development and the actual experiments he conducted, suggests that in fact Krebs had a narrower focus than this when he began. Krebs had recently written a chapter for a handbook on rates of respiration and glycolysis in living cells. In his review he writes, as recounted by Holmes, that substances that occur in the body have not "all been systematically investigated with respect to their effects on the rate of cell respiration." Further, he writes that with "more exact investigations, many other substances will be found," beyond those currently known to increase respiration.[9] Fitting with these statements his initial plan seems to have been to test the effect on respiration of a range of substances, using the manometric technique and related techniques to measure rates of respiration, hoping to open further opportunities for investigation. Krebs began his work on this project by focusing on a series of substances familiar in the literature on oxidation processes — acetate and what was known as the "succinate series."[10] He continued on the project after moving to England. He added citric acid to the set of compounds he was investigating, apparently guided by ideas he had about possible reaction pathways it might be incorporated in, and investigated the role of glucose and insulin in oxidation of various compounds. Thus his project branched out. Holmes remarks that Krebs's line of investigation studying oxidation was essentially "unrelated" with his line of work on the synthesis of urea. Further, he writes that Krebs told him that "there was, he thought, not 'any contact'

---

[9]Frederic Holmes, *Hans Krebs: The Formation of a Scientific Life*, pp. 398–422. The quote from Krebs's handbook chapter is on p. 398.

[10]Holmes suggests he was guided in his choices also by the theoretical Thunberg-Knoop-Wieland framework, which proposed a chain of reactions of decomposition. Ibid., pp. 402–7.

between the lines of investigation."[11] Thus in initiating this project Krebs did   not make a direct link with his work on urea — rather he returned to his root interest and initiated a new project to investigate a main topic in its domain, fitting the tree pattern.

Krebs worked on his oxidation project for several months in England, then dropped the project for about two years — and when he returned to it, it was to pursue it successfully, discovering the famous Krebs cycle.

Virginia Woolf's brilliant modernist novels *Jacob's Room*, *Mrs. Dalloway*, and *To the Lighthouse* essentially fit the tree structure: a series of independent projects, having distinct story lines, characters, and structures, all rooted in the approach she developed in her creative break in "An Unwritten Novel." To be sure she did carry over stylistic features from one book to another, but in a broad sense each was an independent project, conceived separately from the others. *Mrs. Dalloway* is especially distinct from the other two. In it Virginia sought to depict, as she wrote in her diary, "a study of insanity & suicide: the world seen by the sane & the insane side by side," and to show a woman's life and interior thoughts as against men's.[12] *Jacob's Room* and *To the Lighthouse* are more closely connected: both center on veiled portraits of family members — Jacob a portrayal of her brother Thoby, and Mr. and Mrs. Ramsay of her mother and father; both are in the tradition of elegy and concern the intertwining of death with life; and both center on a main character who is shown having a great influence on those around him or her and is shown to us indirectly through the thoughts others have about him or her and his or her effect on others.[13] Nonetheless Virginia's statements about their origins do not indicate any direct connection leading from the one to the other. In particular she seems to have conceived *To the Lighthouse* in thinking about her mother and father and the idea of depicting their characters, not through thinking about *Jacob's*

---

[11]*Hans Krebs: The Formation of a Scientific Life*, p. 403, see also p. 407.

[12]Virginia Woolf, *The Diary of Virginia Woolf*, Vol. 2, ed. Anne Olivier Bell (San Diego: Harcourt Brace & Company, 1978), October 14, 1922, p. 207. Virginia also states she is portraying the sane and the insane in the book in a later diary entry, June 19, 1923, Ibid., p. 248. Hermione Lee notes that Virginia also refers to depicting the two views — "Mrs. D seeing the truth. SS seeing the insane truth" — in her early notes for the book; see her *Virginia Woolf*, p. 450 and the accompanying footnote. Some view *Mrs. Dalloway* as Virginia's response to James Joyce's portrayal of the inner world of thought of a man in *Ulysses*.

[13]Mrs. Ramsay is more richly developed than Jacob in also having a rich interior life and her own thoughts woven into the narrative, a way in which *To the Lighthouse* gained from Virginia's literary development in *Mrs. Dalloway*.

Room and extending it.[14] It is important to note that in coming to write these novels Virginia had had a crucial creative breakthrough, in "An Unwritten Novel." Thus they do not fit the simplest model of a series of projects rooted in a common interest — rather they are rooted in the approach she developed exploring her earlier interest. However, fitting with the recursive nature of creative development, we can think of this approach, once she hit upon it, as in turn forming a base interest to be developed creatively.

Many filmmakers follow the tree pattern in their development, engaging in a series of film projects rooted in a common thematic interest and approach but not directly linked with one another. Ingmar Bergman fits this pattern in several different phases of his development. One example is a series of films he made in the early 1950s. Bergman has said, "At that time I was much preoccupied with the fear of death" — both actual death and dying in a spiritual sense, the idea that "every choice either leads to an access of life or else to one dying a little."[15] Linked to this he was interested in exploring and depicting the juxtaposition of the innocence of youth and young love with the adult world and a rationalist view of life — romance and its fatalistic ending and aftermath and adults, having compromised with life, looking back on their youth. He made a series of films rooted in these themes, including *Summer Interlude, Secrets of Women*, and *Summer with Monika*. In *Summer Interlude* a boy and a girl meet and have an idyllic summer experience, then the boy dies in an accident, leaving the girl alone — thus youthful love is abruptly ended by death, and the girl must cope in some way. The story is framed by the woman, now older and entering the adult world, looking back on the experience, recognizing its profound effect on her — thus juxtaposing the adult view with the youth's.[16] Slightly later, in *The Seventh Seal*, Bergman again creates a juxtaposition of life and death, and the romantic belief of childhood and realist adult world, but in a very different setting and way — a classic example of the tree structure, in which a new project is rooted in the trunk interest but not directly in previous projects. Describing part of his original conception for the film in *Images: My Life in Film*, he writes: "I placed my two opposing beliefs side by side, allowing each to state its case in its own way.

[14]See in particular her notes for the book reproduced in Appendix A of *To the Lighthouse: The Original Holograph Draft*, ed. Susan Dick (Toronto: University of Toronto Press, 1982).

[15]Ingmar Bergman, *Bergman on Bergman; Interviews with Ingmar Bergman*; by Stig Björkman, Torsten Manns, and Jonas Sima, trans. from the Swedish by Paul Austin (New York: Simon and Schuster, 1973), p. 64.

[16]For comments Bergman made on the origins of the film see Ibid., p. 72.

In this manner a virtual cease-fire could exist between my childhood piety and my newfound harsh rationalism."[17]

Enid Zentelis also has made a series of films rooted in her core interest in making films showing the poor and disadvantaged, to raise social consciousness about their plight and depict ordinary, everyday details of their lives as a way to leave an indelible mark on the viewer. Her film *Dog Race*, described in Chapter 12, fits with this interest and approach. In 2004, she had her first feature length film released, *Evergreen*, about a teenage girl from a poor family who has a relationship with a boy from a wealthy family. *Evergreen* is remarked by many reviewers for its focus on everyday details, and for Enid's mastery in showing these details of life, again fitting with her basic interest and approach. Connie Ogle of the *Miami Herald*, like a number of reviewers, points to Enid's grasp of everyday details of poverty: "Writer-director Enid Zentelis skillfully zeroes in on the sour details of poverty: plastic sheets protecting a worn chair, garbage bags substituting for raincoats." Another reviewer describes her "careful observation."[18] The movie has few dramatic events, again fitting with her interest, and Enid is quoted as stating: "To me, there are plenty of events in everyday life that don't involve crack cocaine or someone getting their head blown off that are plenty dramatic and can engage audiences."[19] Thus *Evergreen* fits strikingly with Enid's interest — both in topic and approach — as she described it to me in our interview six years before the film was released and several years before she began work on it.

Serial entrepreneurs often follow a pattern of development fitting the tree structure, engaging in a series of projects that are all rooted in a core interest they have but are not directly connected. Scott Painter has a longstanding interest in cars, including customizing cars for customers, as well as more broadly in making transportation easy. An online article about him states:

[17]Ingmar Bergman, *Images: My Life in Film*, trans. from the Swedish by Marianne Ruuth (New York: Arcade Pub., 1994), pp. 231–42. See also Egil Törnqvist, *Between Stage and Screen: Ingmar Bergman Directs* (Amsterdam: Amsterdam University Press, 1995), pp. 97–98.

[18]Review by Connie Ogle, *Miami Herald*, posted at: http://ae.freep.com/entertainment/ui/michigan/movie.html?id=165852&reviewId=16058. "Careful observation" is from a review by Stephen Whitty of the *Newark Star-Ledger*, Sep. 9, 2004, posted at: www.accessatlanta.com/news/ content/movies/news/0904/10evergreen.html. Additional reviews I read include Ty Burr, *Boston Globe*, Sep. 10, 2004, William Arnold, *Seattle Post-Intelligencer*, Sep. 10, 2004, and Kevin Thomas, *Los Angeles Times*, Sep. 10, 2004. See also the Evergreen film promotion site: www.evergreenthemovie.com.

[19]The interview is posted at: filmforce.ign.com/articles/547/547291pl.html, and dated Sep. 13, 2004. The interviewer is listed as Todd Gilchrist.

454 "Scott Painter is a car guy. At age 12, he started an auto detailing service. .... Half of the 14 businesses the serial entrepreneur has started — including Web site CarsDirect — involved automobiles." He is best known for being cofounder of CarsDirect, an Internet site for selecting and buying a car online. More recently he has been working to launch another company, Build-to-Order, based on an idea closer to his true interest — enabling customers to put together customized cars on the Internet. Describing the idea for the company he told me, "Our cars will be personal. Rather than saying, 'I'd like an LX or EX in blue or beige', you'll actually have choices that say, 'Okay, what matters to you?' And you'll be able to tweak all those choices." Scott mentioned further ideas he was interested in pursuing as business opportunities, including an idea for automating and streamlining the process of identifying and ticketing drivers for traffic light violations — a project fitting with his interest, but not directly linked to his online car purchasing business.[20]

Simultaneous Projects

The second variant of the tree project pattern is engaging in a set of projects rooted in a common interest concurrently. The most common form of this variant is engaging in a pair of projects simultaneously that branch off in different directions from a root interest. In my experience this pattern is especially common at crucial junctures in an individual's development, for example when he first begins to explore an interest he has formed — pursuing a pair of projects in a burst of excitement and energy.

A classic example of an individual launching a pair of projects at a crucial juncture in his development is William Faulkner. Faulkner, in turning in his writing to focus on exploring the world of his childhood, the rural South, its historical development and ideals and decay and moral turpitude, embarked upon two projects concurrently, *Father Abraham* and *Flags in the Dust*. As Blotner describes it he worked on them in parallel, alternating between them. *Father Abraham* is about newcomers to the rural South, epitomized by Flem Snopes, and their gaining of power and status through amoral and immoral acts and sheer energy and activity. *Flags in the Dust*, at least in its initial conception, depicts the opposite pole of the rural Southern culture of Faulkner's experience

[20]I am grateful to my colleague Fiona Scott Morton for arranging the opportunity for me to meet Scott during a visit he made to SOM. We spoke for 40–45 minutes, not enough for a detailed discussion but still an opportunity to talk about his creative development. The first quotation in the text is from baselinemag.com, "Dude, you're gettin' a car," August 1, 2003. The second is from thecarconnection.com, article 4818, 2002.

and imagination: the legacy of the Romantic, gallant old South, ineffectual, nonsensical in the modern world, courageous, and, in the aftermath of World War I, in decline, centering on the Sartoris clan and its history, the lives of its members across several generations. It is thus more strongly rooted in Faulkner's feelings of nostalgia for the world of his childhood. The two projects are thus counterbalanced — in them Faulkner was exploring distinct, even opposite facets of his interest.[21]

An interesting form of project pairing among writers is pursuing fiction and nonfiction projects rooted in the same creative interest in parallel. Nick Halpern described following this pattern: at roughly the same time that he was working on his dissertation he also wrote a novel rooted in his creative interest in prophet figures and the relationship between the prophetic and the everyday world. Describing his novel Nick said, "It's about a prophet, a prophetic figure in his family," "essentially it's about the difficulties that such a figure represents to his wife and children — that's the basic theme of it." Thus his fiction and nonfiction writing of this time are rooted in the same interest. In them he explores somewhat different facets of this interest — in his fiction he focuses on the prophet as a person living in a family, thus the relationship and tension between the prophetic and the everyday on a personal, family level.[22]

A generalization of the pairs pattern is undertaking three or more projects concurrently, all of which are rooted in a common interest. This project pattern is less common: one reason I believe is that engaging in creative projects is such an intense activity that most individuals want and are able to focus on just one or two projects at a time. The pattern seems most natural in fields in which projects extend over long periods of time with down periods during which there is little active work on the project — for example, periods waiting for results or feedback.

As an example, Takao Hensch pursued three main projects in graduate school, essentially concurrently, all rooted in his main creative interest. As

[21]See Joseph Blotner, *Faulkner: A Biography* Vol. I, pp. 531–34 and 556–57, and Chapter 3. *Flags in the Dust* proved the more compelling — at a certain point Faulkner ceased work on *Father Abraham* to focus on *Flags*, completing a draft somewhat less than a year later.

[22]In a brief follow-up interview Nick described a current project studying historical examples of father–son pairings, exploring the impact of prophet-like father figures on their children and their work — thus his interest, evolving (see the next chapter), continues to be the root of his creative work. Henry Chen described V.S. Naipaul also following the pattern of pairing fiction and nonfiction: he told me that later in his career Naipaul would often publish a novel and then later publish an essay or other work that "would be a nonfiction basis for the novel."

described in Chapter 6 Takao's interest at the time he came to graduate school was in using molecular and cellular techniques that had been developed for studying plasticity in other parts of the brain to study plasticity in the developing visual system. Coming to graduate school Takao was set on working in the lab of a well-known investigator in visual system development, as described in Chapter 11, who became his advisor. A main focus in the lab at the time was studying the effects of monocular deprivation on ocular dominance and plasticity in the developing visual system. The topic thus matched Takao's interest. However, the main approach in the lab for studying plasticity was different than Takao wanted to use, in particular less cellular and molecular. "I felt like I could bring my cellular perspective to the lab and start to address many of the questions which were hypothesized to involve certain circuits or certain pathways and look at it more concretely," he told me. "I thought I could carve a niche for myself looking at cellular aspects of the visual system and plasticity. That would be something that the lab did not have and that I could bring [to it]."

Takao's three projects grew out of his interest, as well as opportunities in the lab, and reflect the distinctiveness of his approach compared with the standard approach in the lab and the field. Takao developed his initial project in conversation with his advisor. As he described it to me, they were discussing a computational model predicting the width of ocular dominance columns that had been developed by another graduate student in the lab. The model assumes that there are both excitatory and inhibitory connections between cortical neurons, and that the distance between two neurons determines the nature of their connection. A main implication, as Takao stated it, is that "the modulation of inhibition should have effects on column spacing," in particular that increasing inhibition should decrease column width, and decreasing inhibition increase column width.[23] Takao and his advisor designed an experiment to test this implication biologically in cats: choosing at random one brain hemisphere in each cat when it is very young, injecting it with a drug

---

[23]The function relating distance to the nature of the relationship between two neurons is sometimes called a "Mexican hat" and has the following form: at small distances two neurons have a strong excitatory connection; as the distance between them increases the connection at first remains excitatory, but with diminishing intensity, and eventually a critical distance is reached at which the connection crosses zero; as distance increases beyond this critical point the connection becomes increasingly inhibitory; finally, at a second critical value a maximum level of inhibition is reached, and as distance increases beyond this point at first the connection remains inhibitory with diminishing intensity, and eventually at a third critical point it again passes through zero, so that for large distances the connection is weakly excitatory.

(benzodiazepine) that increases the level of inhibition between visual cortical neurons, then randomly selecting one eye, corresponding to either the injected or control hemisphere, and depriving it of light (monocular deprivation); then examining the cats when mature and comparing the width of ocular columns in the injected and control hemispheres, comparing results across deprivation conditions. The idea to test a theoretically based hypothesis by measuring effects at the level of local circuits and at the cellular level fit with Takao's interest; also the project focused on synaptic plasticity in the formation of dominance columns, also fitting his interest. It is noteworthy that this project had a longitudinal design with down periods, making it natural for Takao to engage in other projects concurrently.

Takao's second project was to test to see if newly developed metabotropic glutamate receptor antagonists might prevent the development of ocular dominance plasticity. This project illustrates how the originality of a project is often rooted in the distinctiveness of an interest. "This is another clear example of having a cellular perspective in a lab that didn't really do that kind of work," Takao said. "I was aware of these new antagonists that were coming out for metabotropic glutamate receptors" — which others in the lab, not sharing his molecular perspective, may well not have been. "At the same time I was aware that people in the past... had made correlations [showing a positive relationship] between glutamate stimulated phosphoinositide turnover [which is triggered by activation of metabotropic glutamate receptors and releases intracellular calcium that can trigger depolarization and make it easier for a cell to have an action potential] and the critical period [for the formation of ocular dominance columns] in kittens. And so it seemed to me natural to see if you could prevent ocular dominance plasticity by using these new metabotropic receptor antagonists." Being aware both of the new antagonists and the historical work in the ocular dominance field thus was crucial in sparking the idea for this project — a classic example of a creative connection, rooted in his distinctive interest. Takao investigated the effect of blocking the metabotropic receptors both *in vitro* and *in vivo* and found that blocking the receptors prevented long-term depression in visual cortex slices *in vitro*, but that although he was able to block the visual cortical receptors *in vivo*, this did not prevent ocular dominance plasticity in response to monocular deprivation. Thus the result indicated more work was needed exploring the molecular basis of ocular dominance plasticity in the developing visual system, a topic Takao has pursued since his dissertation.[24]

[24]T. Hensch and M.P. Stryker, "Columnar architecture sculpted by GABA circuits in developing cat visual cortex," *Science* 303 (2004): 1678–81.

Takao set up a tissue slice system for *in vitro* analysis in the lab that was important in serving as the base for much of his work, including his second project. His third project grew out of his desire to compare *in vitro* tests of visual cortical plasticity, using the system he had set up, and *in vivo* tests. Researchers in Takao's lab had traditionally worked with cats, for which "knock-out" technology — producing mutants lacking a specific gene — was not available. A fellow graduate student had developed a system for recording from the visual cortex in mice, for which "knock-out" technology is available. He and Takao designed an experiment using mice comparing ocular dominance plasticity *in vitro* and *in vivo* between normal mice and mutant mice lacking genes for specific proteins thought to play a role in plasticity. Their results were that *in vitro* the mutant mice failed to exhibit long-term depression or depotentiation that the normal mice exhibited, but that *in vivo* the mutants and normals both exhibited significant ocular dominance plasticity shifts in response to monocular deprivation. Thus again Takao found a significant difference between *in vitro* and *in vivo* effects. Takao has continued to engage in research following this line as well.

Two last comments about project patterns. One, many individuals, over the course of their development, pursue projects fitting both of the patterns described. Takao is an example: in addition to pursuing three projects concurrently in his doctoral research he pursued related projects before coming to graduate school, and has pursued further projects grounded in the same basic interest since. Two, in fields in which individuals pursue many smaller projects it is common for them to pursue clusters of related projects, both concurrently and in series. Alexander Calder, for example, executed many sculptures over relatively short periods of time, often fitting into natural groupings. This approach fits naturally with his conception of his interest — conceiving his interest as a rich domain teeming with creative possibilities, thus naturally spawning many diverse projects.

INFLUENCE OF PROJECTS: CONCEPTUAL LINKS

The description of projects rooted in a common creative interest is intuitive. However, it does not incorporate pathways through which projects individuals engage in influence their subsequent creative development. In fact such pathways are very important for many individuals in their development. Elements they learn or create, ideas they have, discoveries they make, and techniques they develop during projects often influence them in their subsequent development, in both major and minor ways.

One important pathway of influence through which work on a project influences future development is through having an idea or making a discovery working on a project that forms the basis for a subsequent project. René Marois is an example of someone who followed this pattern in his development: he had a crucial insight working on his master's thesis that became the basis for his dissertation project. Virginia Woolf's discovery of a style through which she could realize her conception of reflections writing "An Unwritten Novel" was a vital basis for the brilliant novels she wrote beginning just afterwards, as noted above, in particular sparking her conception for *Jacob's Room*, which she began directly after finishing the story.

A problem encountered on a project may also become the basis for a subsequent project. Albert Einstein's path of development shows a problem identified on a project driving further development. Having worked out the special theory of relativity Einstein went on to pursue the further development of the theory, and specifically to incorporate the effect of gravity. He writes in his "Autobiographical Notes": "That the special theory of relativity is only the first step of a necessary development became completely clear to me only in my efforts to represent gravitation in the framework of this theory."[25] He thus defined essentially as a project to extend the framework to incorporate the effect of gravity, which involved generalizing the theory, incorporating more general coordinate transformations and a more general form of coordinate system invariance. This led him ultimately, after several years, and various influences and a number of attempts, to his development of the general theory of relativity.

A second pathway of influence is using or incorporating conceptual elements that one learns or generates in the course of working on a project in subsequent projects.

Expertise gained working on a project often provides the basis for a subsequent project. Many of the neuroscientists I interviewed described learning techniques working on projects that had a role in their coming to engage in subsequent projects, including defining new projects. The expertise Roger gained setting up a video microscopy system for visualizing cells on his first doctoral project was critical in giving him the opportunity to engage in the subsequent project with a post-doc studying translocation of RNA granules. In particular he said the post-doc approached him about developing a system for visualization because he knew Roger had this expertise and Roger was the only one in the lab who did. Ted Cummings, another neuroscientist I interviewed, developed expertise in using patch clamp methods to record current flows of different ions in neurons while working as an associate research scientist in a laboratory

---

[25] "Autobiographical Notes," in *Albert Einstein: Philosopher-Scientist*, p. 63 and following, where he describes the difficulty and the approach he pursued ultimately resolving it.

460 studying sudden infant death syndrome. In turn, this expertise was crucial for him in graduate school: a principal investigator in his program, knowing of his expertise, offered him the opportunity to study the functioning of a mutant sodium channel that had been identified as a likely cause of symptoms in the rare disease hyperkalemic periodic paralysis, and this became his dissertation project. Techniques Takao Hensch learned in Japan before coming to graduate school were important in providing the base for his dissertation projects. Expertise developed in projects is important in many fields, for example in companies, in which a series of projects are engaged in. The Harvard Business School "Microsoft Opus Case" describes how expertise gained by members of the Opus team in developing Word for Windows influenced their views and approach on subsequent projects, including the decision to move to "build the code every day" and "common code" approaches.[26]

Individuals often employ specific conceptual elements they develop on one project in subsequent projects. Virginia Woolf often did so: there are numerous instances in which she constructs a specific image or setting in a work, then draws upon it creatively in later works. An example is her description of Mrs. Ramsay as imagining herself like a fish hanging suspended at the dinner party and as having a "dark wedge" at her core below the gleaming reflecting surface of her self — each is rooted in a corresponding description in "The Mark on the Wall." As another example the dinner party scene in *To the Lighthouse*, in particular with the natural world depicted as quite separate, present outside the windows, resonates with a corresponding description in "The Evening Party." This same resonance and carrying forward of stylistic elements and very specific descriptive elements can be found in the work of many writers, for example, is very evident in William Faulkner's writings — Blotner, for example, notes his fondness for twilight and an essential commonality in his description of it across different works.[27]

Thomas Edison often employed specific circuit designs and approaches he developed working on a project in subsequent projects. A good example is his use of a "bug trap" circuit — he developed this working to reduce resistance and noise on telegraph circuits, and employed it repeatedly on subsequent projects. As a second example, the idea of a diaphragm that moves in response to sound waves that he developed working on his telephone seems to have been, based on his account and that of Charles Batchelor, a crucial element in his coming to the idea for the phonograph — feeling the diaphragm move

---

[26] *Microsoft Corporation: Office Business Unit*, Harvard Business School, 1993.

[27] Blotner makes many such connections throughout his biography, both between early short stories and poetry Faulkner wrote and his later, famous novels, as well as between earlier and later novels.

when he spoke gave him the idea of having a stylus cut grooves into a soft
material to record the sound.

In some cases a project is generative of evolution in an individual's creative interest or conception of interest, or formation of a new interest. This evolution or generation of a new interest may be driven by a realization sparked by working on the project, an idea generated in the course of working on the project, a discovery made on the project, or the project outcome, including reflection upon the outcome.

This kind of project influence and pattern of development is relatively common. The experience and excitement of working on a project, success and failure achieved on it, and the learning and maturity that is gained working on it all tend to be generative of enrichment of the creative interest or interests the project is rooted in. Further, in the course of working on projects it often happens that individuals form new interests, linked to the interest that was the basis for the project. Paul Barran's work on missile systems at Hughes spurred him to form an interest in designing and building robust communication systems that could survive a missile attack. Jane Minturn said that it was while working on a project studying development of ion channel expression in glial cells in the developing visual system that she came to her "first understanding of how [during development] not only do new cells come about, but cells can change their molecular constellation of protein expression" and "initially got interested" in this topic.

A specific form of this pathway is a project exerting influence through a negative pathway. Having worked on a project, in many cases spurred by a negative outcome on the project, an individual, thinking critically about the project, comes to realize that he does not wish to pursue the interest that was the basis of the project further, or, more typically, is led to alter significantly his conception of his interest. Andreas's experience working on his college thesis convinced him that he did not want to do *in vitro* work, which he viewed as artificial and not closely enough linked to the corresponding biologic processes in living organisms, and thus he was led to refine his conception of his interest: he decided he wanted to focus on studying axonal pathfinding *in vivo*. For Ian, the experience of writing his master's thesis on representations of Africa in British literature led to a shift in his interest, again through a negative route, to broaden to a focus on what he called "the Anglophone imperial world." In some cases the influence of a project occurs mainly through its effect on motivation or through triggering an emotional response. A negative experience or outcome, for example, may disappoint an individual, and this disappointment may trigger a shift in his interest. For William Faulkner the experience of having his novel *Flags in the Dust* rejected led him to turn inwards, to "shut a door," he said, between himself and the publishing world, which seems to have freed him to pursue his interest in the rural South of his childhood and its lingering decay in a different way, thus to conceptualize it differently, at a more personal level, tapping deeply into personal feelings, memories, and images, first in short stories and then as the basis for *The Sound and the Fury* — freeing him to focus on describing this world through children's eyes, which in turn led, through a creative step, to his brilliant depiction of the world as experienced by Benjy the idiot.[28]

RECURSION

I state throughout this book that creative development is an inherently recursive process. In the context of this chapter that statement applies in particular to the interrelationships between projects and interests: linkages run from interests to projects and, conversely, from projects to interests. Thus, individuals' creative interests and conceptions of interests are the base out of which they develop, define, and select projects to pursue; and, in turn, their projects spur changes in their interests and conceptions of interests and spur them to form new interests. Such influences often alternate over the course of an individual's development; for example, an interest is the basis for a project he defines and pursues, which in turn leads to a discovery or idea which in turn is generative of evolution in the individual's interest or leads him to form a new interest. Virginia Woolf's development illustrates this pattern. Pursuing her conception of a world in which selves are shown through their reflections — which defined her literary interest, exploring its development in a series of stories, she at last discovered, writing "An Unwritten Novel," a literary form through which she could realize it. This new style in turn essentially became an interest for her, serving as the basis for *Jacob's Room* and her subsequent novels.

There are of course many further linkages and interconnections in creative development, and many further patterns of development to be described, some of which are described in the next chapter.

[28] *Faulkner: A Biography*, p. 570.

15

Patterns of Creative Development: Evolution of Interests and Sequences of Interests

In preceding chapters I depict creative interests as enduring, core structures of creative development. This is a simplification that fails to capture important dynamic features of creative development. For most individuals over the course of their development their creative interests evolve, and they form new interests, in many cases connected with a preexisting interest. This is only natural: it is natural for individuals' interests to evolve and for them to form new interests as they have new experiences, work in different environments, as their fields evolve and they pass through different life stages. Indeed individuals whose interests do not evolve and who do not form new interests are likely to be at risk of stagnating in their development.

In this chapter I describe the evolution of interests and the formation of new interests, especially new interests linked with preexisting interests. My description fits with and builds on the description in Chapter 3 of the formation of interests, showing how those processes continue to be important throughout development, albeit in different forms.

The processes described here are very important for many individuals. Indeed many outstanding contributions arise out of them. Two examples I present here of individuals for whom these processes were the basis for major contributions are Hannah Arendt and John Maynard Keynes.

Evolution of interests and conceptions of interests occurs naturally for many people in the course of their development, as they learn, in general and in the domains of their interests, explore and reflect upon their interests, and engage in projects. As individuals engage in these activities they encounter new elements — new ideas, works, facts, questions, and possibilities — in the domains of their interests or adjacent to them or connected with their interests, that catch their interest, and their perspectives change. In turn this leads naturally to evolution in their interests and conceptions of interests.

Individuals' conceptions of their interests often become richer over time as they reflect upon their interests and integrate new conceptual elements, experiences, and events into their conceptions. I note that the conceptual structures that encode interests almost always develop and become richer over time as individuals explore their interests, learn about them, and engage in projects rooted in them, as described in Chapter 10. But this progression is not what I am describing here; here I mean evolution at a higher level. The basic enrichment of the conceptual structure of an interest at the level of specific learning and building up of elements and relationships can and often does occur in the context of an established, fixed interest. Here I am referring to and describing evolution in the definition of an interest.

I use the word evolution to describe the way individuals' interests change because in most cases the change that occurs is one of increasing richness, complexity, structure, and sophistication, reflecting increasing knowledge and experience. Many of my interview subjects followed this pattern in their development. Jane Minturn's interest evolved in this way, as she described it to me looking back on her development. In high school she was interested in development as an evolutionary process. In college she formed an interest in the development of specific brain regions anatomically and, again in an evolutionary sense, linked to the emergence of specific behaviors. In graduate school her orientation became molecular and her interest evolved further, to an interest in development at the cellular level, specifically cells in the brain changing their molecular constellation of protein expression during critical phases of development. Jeffrey Shoulson's interest also evolved. Jeffrey formed an interest in *Paradise Lost* during his freshman year in college. From the start he said he recognized that there was a "resemblance" between *Paradise Lost* and rabbinic literature, which he was very familiar with, that drew his interest. In college, as described in the preceding chapter, Jeffrey's interest focused on possible rabbinic sources Milton may have known and drawn upon in developing his own ideas and approach. In graduate school Jeffrey's interest, in particular his conception of his interest, evolved, as described in Chapter 11: he decided he did not want to pursue the question of possible sources for Milton's ideas, but rather what the nature of the "resemblance" is between *Paradise Lost* and rabbinic literature, which so many critics have noticed — thus he shifted to a focus on comparative literary analysis. This evolution was driven both by his own reflection upon his interest and the critical literature on *Paradise Lost*, and also his more general learning, as he gained familiarity with modern literary analysis, which also struck him as resonant with rabbinic approaches to textual analysis, spurring his interest in comparative analysis of different traditions of textual analysis. Azad Bonni, Andreas Walz, and Ian Baucom are three further examples of individuals whose interests evolved over the period from college to early in graduate school, as described in preceding chapters. The further evolution in Azad's interest is described below.

The formation of an interest in some cases reaches back to childhood, with the interest later evolving into a mature interest. This was Walt Disney's pattern of development. He had an interest in animal characters, with personalities, in cartoon art even in childhood, which seems to have been a base out of which his later interest in making animated films with animal characters who possess rich personalities — mischievous, sentimental, maudlin, clever — developed. Charles Darwin's interest also evolved from an early childhood interest in collecting to his more mature interest in ranges of extent of species, formed during the voyage of the *Beagle*. Jane Minturn's interest also began in childhood and evolved, as described above.

In many cases individuals' interests and conceptions of interests evolve in tandem with and at least in part driven by their maturing and passing through different stages of life, in some cases as a direct result of life experiences. Often the impact of a life experience on an individual triggering an evolution or shift in focus of interest occurs in part through its emotional impact. One important kind of shift is an individual shifting his focus from one facet of an interest to a different facet that fits better with his new emotional state. While speculative, it seems very possible that Pablo Picasso experienced this kind of a shift during the crucial period of the late fall of 1906 and winter and early spring of 1907, linked to a change in the nature of his relationship with Fernande Olivier, his mistress, for whom his infatuation seems to have lessened at this time, as well as perhaps more broadly his growing older and having worked through some adolescent feelings concerning his relationship with his mother and women generally.[1] He continued to be driven by his root interest of expressing emotions

[1]This is clearly evidenced in Fernande Olivier's journal. Her journal breaks off in March of 1907, and she wrote a letter to Gertrude Stein in August 1907 stating, "Do you want to hear some important news? Picasso and I are ending our life together." Fernande Olivier, *Loving Picasso; The Private Journal of Fernande Olivier*, pp. 188, 191.

in his painting, specifically feelings about women and his relationships with them. But, reflecting and driven by the shift in his emotions, the focus of his interest shifted from expressing intimacy, loving support, sadness, and finding love apart from his mother, to expressing the harshness of women, sex without emotion, anger, challenge, thus very different feelings — rooted, if we are to believe psychoanalytic descriptions of his personality, in feelings of fear of women and anger towards women and by projection of women towards him. This shift seems an early, perhaps his first clear turn to making his paintings "subversive," which according to Françoise Gilot he described as his aim in painting (see my discussion in Chapter 3). Strikingly, his first subversiveness is in terms of challenging the viewer in his conception of women and their sex — whereas later he would take it as a more abstract creed, mainly about visual experience, here it has an emotional basis. This shift seems to be the root of the creative breakthrough he achieved in *Les Demoiselles d'Avignon*, as discussed in Chapter 12. William Faulkner's disillusionment with the publishing world after *Flags in the Dust* was rejected seems to have triggered an emotional shift in him, triggering a shift in his conceptualization and focus of interest, to focus on re-creating the world of the South of his childhood in a more personal way, as described in the previous chapter.

Nick Halpern's creative interest and conception of interest evolved over time, becoming conceptually richer, more mature, and more generative of creativity, in particular of a valued contribution in his field.

As described in Chapter 3 Nick formed a creative interest as a young adult, rooted in his family experiences growing up, in prophet figures in literature, and in particular the prophetic voice in literature. His interest had two facets: the difficulties writers have in producing this voice, in making it persuasive; and successful versions of the voice — works in which it is authoritative and convincing. After college Nick worked for several years, then returned to school in a master's program. He wrote his master's thesis on a contemporary poet, Allen Grossman.[2] He told me he has always been interested in poetry, and that after college it became his main focus. In addition he said he wanted to work on a contemporary poet, that even at that time he had decided he wanted to write about "the fate of prophecy" in our modern "post-religious world." He also said he wanted to write about contemporaries of his father.

Nick said that in critical reading of Grossman's poetry he focused on trying to understand "why some of his poems seem to be more successful than others, and what goes wrong in his poetry when it goes wrong." He told me that as

[2]David Nicholas Halpern, *The Prophet's Speech Impediments: An Introduction to the Poetry of Allen Grossman*, Master of Arts thesis, NYU, 1988.

he matured in his twenties he came to focus on this issue. "[My approach] had to do with watching my own reactions and trying to figure out why some poems... gave pleasure and some didn't.... I watched the poem sort of as a performance — it's a little bit like going to a play and... trying to figure out what goes wrong." This approach grew out of his interest in understanding why the prophetic voice is not persuasive — why it is so difficult for poets to create authentic versions of it, and a goal he had, if only dimly perceived at this time, "to save the idea of prophecy" in the modern world.[3] Allen Grossman has a prophetic tone in his poetry, which was a reason Nick was drawn to his work. In analyzing Grossman's poetry and his reactions to it Nick came to the insight that when Grossman's poetry "goes wrong" his failure, in Nick's view, "has to do with his inability to say anything about everyday life." Nick told me that in college he used the term "everyday" but was "much more interested in the prophetic," and that it was during this time that he "first started to think about the everyday" as an independent voice in literature having an important role.[4]

After completing his master's Nick enrolled in a doctoral program, and his creative interest and conception of interest evolved further. He incorporated the voice of the everyday into his interest and conception of interest, thereby expanding the scope of his interest by adding a second component, making it conceptually richer, and developed a framework in which the prophetic voice and the voice of the everyday coexist in poetry in a dynamic relationship, in tension and with many different kinds of interconnections. He told me he began "using both terms," concurrently and counterbalancing one another: "I saw that the everyday, the human, could be, would be, a really interesting counter [to the prophetic]." He also said he wanted "to do justice to both sides of the equation."

In part the evolution of Nick's interest developed out of his creative insight, which he came to reading Allen Grossman's poetry, that part of what makes

---

[3]Nick said that being older, increasingly doubtful of the value or meaning of his father's work, he was more skeptical and his mind felt sharper, making it natural for him to focus on analyzing what goes wrong in poetry.

[4]One of the striking things about Nick's insight about Grossman's poetry, linked to the evolution of his interest, is how it contrasts with his earlier idea of the "prophet as vessel." At the time when Nick was interested in the idea of the prophet as a vessel in college he imagined the prophet's ordinary everyday self being emptied out and replaced by the prophetic voice; thus he seems to have believed that the two voices cannot mix. In contrast, in analyzing Grossman's poetry, and as his interest developed going forward, he came to believe that not only can the two voices coexist, but that when "things are going right" for the prophetic voice it is in part because it is in dialogue with the voice of the everyday and there is a persuasive connection between the two.

the prophetic voice in a poem successful is the inclusion of the voice of the everyday and the establishing of a "deeply persuasive" "connection between the two voices" — and that conversely when the prophetic voice in a poem fails to be persuasive it is often because the poem fails to include the voice of the everyday, as Grossman failed to, or to establish a convincing relationship between the two voices. In part also it was linked to and, as he views it in retrospect, driven by his own maturational process, and developments in the field of literary criticism and interests of people in his program. He told me, "Having that other term [the everyday, the ordinary human world] worked well because it was interesting to me as I got older, was married and thinking about starting a family and being domestic." Further, he said: "[At the school where I went to college], in the 1970s, everyone was working on the prophetic and the sublime and those things. And when I went back to [graduate] school in the late 80s and 90s no one was interested in that — academic trends [had changed]. . . . So [adding the everyday] made my project interesting to other people who were interested in the domestic and the everyday and not in the prophetic — it offered them a term they could catch hold of."

Nick articulates his conception of the prophetic voice and the voice of the everyday as equally important and in tension with one another in his prospectus. In the opening paragraph he writes:

> Wallace Stevens wrote that "to say more than human things with human voice,/That cannot be; to say human things with more/Than human voice, that also cannot be." The reader has to be persuaded by the voice of the poem, by its rhetoric, that there can be a "more than human" or prophetic voice and that it can speak of an available reality. But the reader also needs to be persuaded of the human voice: the voice of dailiness can seem spurious as well. My dissertation will explore the complex tensions between these two voices.[5]

He describes many different versions of each voice, and various moods it can express. Next he lists similarities between the voices. "Both voices are often voices of hospitality," inviting us in, he writes. "Both voices seduce us with the possibility of no mediation." Lastly, he describes different forms of relationship between the two voices that poets and readers imagine and try to create. Some poets, he writes, "try to keep the [two] rhetorics from contaminating each other," while others "fold the [two] worlds into each other."

> For some readers the voices offer, chiefly, "meaning," and, to those readers, they do present rival claims. To readers for whom the voices offer, principally, pleasure

---

[5]Nick Halpern, Prospectus, not titled, Harvard University, 1993. The quote from Wallace Stevens is from "Chocorua to its Neighbor," pp. 296–302, p. 300, in *The Collected Poems of Wallace Stevens* (New York: Alfred A. Knopf, 1955).

one voice acts as an easing of the incitements of the other. But poets have felt that the voices can be brought into a more intimate relationship than either of these two possibilities suggests. One strategy might be to let the voices flirt with each other. A poet may mix the most shopworn terms from the one vocabulary with the most charged words from the other and hope for the best — the best being the tremendous rhetorical energy releasable by such mixtures. . . . These voices can seem to believe in, even depend on, each other and poets have tried to develop not just an "answerable style" but a style in which these two voices are answerable to each other.

In his dissertation Nick presents original critical readings, based in his framework of analysis, of the poetry of four contemporary poets, Robert Lowell, Adrienne Rich, A.R. Ammons, and James Merrill. He published a book based on his dissertation in 2003.[6]

Projects and the Evolution of Interests

The impetus triggering evolution of an individual's interest is in some cases a project.

Tim Berners-Lee is an example of an individual whose interest evolved as a result of his experience and insights he generated on a project. As described in Chapter 6 Tim formed an initial conception of his interest in high school — of representing information in nonhierarchical data structures and freely generating new links. At CERN in 1980 he wrote Enquire, a first attempt to realize his conception; I have described his idea for this program and his documentation describing it in Chapter 9. Tim writes in *Weaving the Web* that through writing and using Enquire a "larger vision" formed in his "consciousness" — thus he formed a new, evolved conception of interest. "*Suppose all the information stored on computers everywhere were linked*, I thought," he writes. "*Suppose I could program my computer to create a space in which anything could be linked to anything*."[7] He thus took the important conceptual step of conceiving linking information on many different computers together to create a web of information, through which any piece of information, stored on any computer anywhere in the world, might be linked with any other. When he returned to CERN in 1984 Tim pursued his interest in creating such a web, first writing a Remote Procedure Call (RPC) program to facilitate communication between computers, then, with the stimulating organizational environment of CERN again seeming to have been crucial, as well as technical developments in computer science, including the development

---

[6]Nick Halpern, *Everyday and Prophetic: The Poetry of Lowell, Ammons, Merrill, and Rich* (Madison, WI: University of Wisconsin Press, 2003).

[7]Tim Berners-Lee, *Weaving the Web*, p. 4. Italics in original.

of hypertext, which he had learned about, developing a project idea to realize his conception of interest more fully. "My vision," he writes, describing his initial project conception, "was to somehow combine Enquire's external links with hypertext and the interconnection schemes I had developed for RPC." "New webs could [then] be made to bind different computers together." "Plus, anyone browsing could instantly add a new node connected by a new link."[8] Tim states in his description that, consistent with his interest from early on, he wanted the web to be decentralized, with no central node; also, he wanted it to be easy for individuals to add nodes and connections. These requirements and his conception drew him to the Internet as a natural technology within which to implement his vision — and thus he embarked upon the project out of which grew the World Wide Web.[9]

Evolution in Stages

The evolution of an individual's creative interest often occurs in multiple stages.

As an example, Azad Bonni's interest has evolved in several stages. As described in Chapter 2 Azad formed an interest while in medical school in mechanisms of action in cells, pathways through which external agents trigger effects. During the ensuing years he refined his focus of interest, focusing on neurotrophins and pathways through which they regulate gene expression. This interest was the basis for his two main dissertation projects, described in previous chapters.

Azad's interest has evolved since he completed his dissertation. In particular, new elements have been added to his interest, much as occurred for Nick. He has developed a focus of interest in studying neurotrophin-based regulation of cell survival, programmed cell death (apoptosis), and axon and dendrite development during brain development. I do not have good information on how he came to form this new focus within his interest area. But a few factors seem likely to have played a role. Cell death has been a hot topic and has come to be recognized as central in development. Further, cell survival, paired with cell death, is linked to growth factors, including neurotrophins, thus fits within

[8]*Weaving the Web*, pp. 13–16, and chap. 2 generally. Tim's use of the word "browsing" seems an anachronism — this word only became popular, as far as I know, in the 1990s.

[9]For the further story of Tim's work on the project and its growth see Chapters 3 and 4 of *Weaving the Web*. See also Tim Berners-Lee, *Information Management: A Proposal*, unpublished document written at CERN, 1989. For a broad account of the development of the Internet see Janet Abbate, *Inventing the Internet* (Cambridge, MA: MIT Press, 1999). Her description of the World Wide Web, including Tim's contribution, is in Chapter 6.

the scope of his interest. In addition, factors governing cell survival, and by extension apoptosis, were the focus of a series of studies in the lab in which Azad did his doctoral work, some of which Azad participated in.

An indication of Azad's interest is the title of a talk he gave at several universities a few years after I interviewed him, "Neurotrophin Regulation of Cell Death in the Central Nervous System." He also was awarded a grant to study "Neurotrophin Regulation of Amyloid-induced Neuronal Degeneration and Cell Death."[10] Azad is first author on an important article published in *Science* in 1999 — two years after I interviewed him — entitled "Cell Survival Promoted by the Ras-MAPK Signaling Pathway by Transcription-Dependent and -Independent Mechanisms." The first sentence of the abstract states: "A mechanism by which the Ras-mitogen-activated protein kinase (MAPK) signaling pathway mediates growth factor–dependent cell survival was characterized."[11] This project clearly grew out of Azad's interest in neurotrophin regulation of pathways promoting cell survival and blocking cell death. The main focus of the article is results characterizing a specific signaling pathway, Ras-MAPK, activated by brain-derived neurotrophic factor (BDNF), involved in suppressing cell death machinery and promoting cell survival. At the time of this writing, this paper has been cited more than 500 times, thus is a significant contribution.

Azad left the lab in which he did his doctoral research a few years after finishing his dissertation and established his own lab. Since then his focus of interest and research has evolved further. His lab Web page for the summer of 2004, describing the overall focus of interest in the lab, states: "We are interested in elucidating the intracellular signal transduction pathways that regulate cell survival and differentiation in the developing mammalian brain."[12] Azad and several collaborators have been engaged in research studying regulation of granule neuron axon growth and patterning and dendrite development during development of the cerebellum. They published a paper in *Science* in 2004 describing a role for a particular intracellular signal regulation agent, Cdh1-APC,

---

[10]I found the title of his talk and a list of several places where he gave the talk on the Internet. The grant is from the American Federation for Aging Research and was given to Azad in 2000.

[11]A. Bonni, A. Brunet, A.E. West, S.R. Datta, M.A. Takasu, and M.E. Greenberg, "Cell survival promoted by the Ras-MAPK signaling pathway by transcription-dependent and -independent mechanisms," *Science* 286 (1999): 1358–62.

[12]Azad Bonni faculty Web page, Harvard University School of Medicine. The second and final sentence of the overview states: "We are also interested in determining how abnormalities of these developmental signaling pathways contribute to neurologic disorders" — connected to Azad's long-standing interest in neurologic disorders.

in controlling granule neuron axonal patterned growth in the development of the cerebellum.[13]

Describing the current focus of research and questions for research in the lab the Website states a series of questions about the role of Cdh1-APC, then states that "addressing these questions should significantly improve our understanding of the intracellular mechanisms that control axonal growth in the mammalian brain." This statement clearly reflects Azad's long-standing interest in mechanisms of action, in particular tracing the entire pathway, beginning with an external agent triggering activation, and also the evolution in his interest that has occurred.

A rich pattern of development is an interplay over time between an evolving interest and ideas and projects generated out of the interest which in turn influence its further evolution. Nick is an example of someone who seems to have followed this pattern in his development. His interest in prophet figures and the prophetic voice in literature was the basis for his college thesis and his master's thesis. In turn, in working on these projects, especially his master's thesis, he gained the insight that poetry that is only prophetic in tone is not persuasive — that to be persuasive poetry must also include the voice of the everyday world. This insight, together with his own maturing and change in life status, and his awareness of changing trends in literary studies, led to an evolution in his interest: to analyze both the prophetic voice and the voice of the everyday, with tensions and interconnections between them. He then developed this evolved interest creatively in his dissertation work.

Piet Mondrian's creative development is a further illustration of this pattern of development. Mondrian engaged in a quest to realize in painting the conception he formed of an abstract art expressing the universal and reflecting the evolving consciousness of modern man; linked with his conception were guiding principles he formulated to create this art. His conception, formulation of principles, and art evolved jointly, at least so it appears, in a remarkable, fascinating creative process of work, conceptualization, and invention, leading to his development of a fundamental modern art form. Mondrian's motto, "always further," captures the resonant dynamic of his development.

Over the period of his development I focus on in this book the interplay of Mondrian's conception and art occurred both on a large scale and a small scale. On the large scale he went through two main phases of development. In the first phase, approximately 1911 to 1915, he formed his initial conception

---

[13]See Appendix for citation. The focus on the cerebellum resonates with Azad's earlier interest in cerebellar degenerative motor disorders.

of an abstract art. His conception and its evolution are documented in his   473
sketchbooks, discussed and quoted from in Chapter 4. He formulated as a
guiding principle the idea of the fundamental duality of spirit and matter, represented as male and female, to be united in spiritual harmony, and developed
principles of art based on this — the use of abstract vertical and horizontal
line elements, representing the male-spiritual and female-material elements,
unified in composition. In his painting over this period he evolves from using lines at different angles and curves to using only horizontal and vertical
lines, thus towards realizing his conception, as described in Chapter 11. Thus,
for example, he made a series of sketches experimenting with representing
a tree (trees had been a focus of his art) with just horizontal and vertical
lines, arranged in jagged sequences. At the end of this period he was able
to realize his conception, at least to a degree, notably in his pier and ocean
series.[14]

The second phase of development of his conception occurred over the period 1914–1917, culminating in "The New Plastic in Painting," quoted from
and discussed in Chapter 11. Mondrian began composing paintings with rectangular planes in primary colors in 1917, at the time he was completing his
essay, and in the following years, guided by his conception — at least such
appears the case — he explored ways to realize it, as described in Chapter 11,
for example, experimenting with different sizes of rectangles (see, e.g., *Composition with Grid 9: Checkerboard Composition in Light Colors*, 1919 shown in
Figure 3(vi)), and different patterns, culminating in his creative breakthrough
of 1920–21. A sequence of his paintings from this period are shown in Figure 3.

On a smaller scale it seems likely that Mondrian gained specific insights
from individual paintings, leading to modification in his conception, especially principles for realizing it artistically. Evaluating a painting in relation to
his conception may have spurred his thinking. For example, such a process
may have led him ultimately to realize that the kind of "equilibrated relationship" of colors he sought required lines abutting colors and colors juxtaposed
tightly with lines between them, with far less white canvas showing. In turn, he
explored particular approaches for realizing his conception artistically in paintings. For example, he executed a set of paintings in 1918–19 employing small
equally sized squares and another set exploring diamond or lozenge designs;
he then abandoned many of these approaches, shifting to larger rectangles of

---

[14]For the trees see Piet Mondrian, *The New Art — The New Life*, images 90–92;
these are from his sketchbooks, 1913/1914. Images 94–102, 106–8, and 111–13 show his
further development. *The Sea, Pier and Ocean*, and related paintings are shown in
plates 120–26.

474 different sizes and proportions, with those on the edges seeming to extend off the canvas. Thus his conception and painting each influenced the other in an evolving process. It is important to be clear that there is no written record documenting these processes for Mondrian; nonetheless it seems likely — is consistent with the logic of creative development and his own interplay of conception and art — that they were ongoing.

SEQUENCES OF LINKED INTERESTS

Most individuals who engage in a creative endeavor — or several such endeavors — form more than one creative interest over the course of their engagement in the endeavor. It is common, as described in Chapter 13, to form and pursue multiple interests concurrently. Even more common is forming and pursuing a sequence of interests over time.

Indeed forming a series of interests is natural. Having explored a creative interest and developed it creatively over a period of time, often in several projects, it is natural that one's interest in it should wane, as it becomes less exciting and is less novel, and as one comes to believe that one has exhausted its creative possibilities, at least those that are most alluring. Further, new topics — puzzles, problems, works, possibilities, data, models, theories — are likely to catch one's attention and spark one's interest. There are bound to be new developments in one's field and the world at large, and over time one meets and gets to know new people, with different interests — and these events and people naturally tend to spur one to form new interests. It is in fact far rarer not to form a series of interests than to do so.[15]

In this section I describe a few basic patterns of sequences of interests. I focus on sequences of linked interests, in which a later interest an individual forms and pursues is linked in some way with an interest he formed previously. Such sequences are especially common, and fit with the focus in this book on creative development as an evolving process with rich conceptual structures at its core. There are of course cases in which individuals form a series of more or less unrelated interests; however, I do not consider these here. The examples I present are individuals whose main creative contributions were made through their pursuit and development of later interests in a linked sequence, paths with linkages extending over long periods of time. Two of these, Hannah Arendt and John Maynard Keynes, serve as more in-depth examples illustrating this pattern.

---

[15] Probably the most likely reason this may happen is if an individual ceases to engage in creative endeavors after a short time.

When we form a new interest via branching from a preexisting interest we do so in many instances by moving one conceptual step from the preexisting interest, or, more rarely, a few steps. Typically this means branching from one topic of interest to a conceptually adjacent, related topic. An example of branching is Henry Chen moving one conceptual step from his interest in literary geography to form an interest in journeys in literature, described below — journey is directly linked to place conceptually in a conventional conceptual map of basic concepts and links among them. Another example is Wilbur Wright branching from an interest in bicycles, including their design, construction, and principles of operation, to form an interest in flight and the design and construction of a flying machine. The link between these two topics was likely to be especially strong during the 1890s, when bicycling was a major hobby and new mode of conveyance, and flight was also a hobby, viewed as having great potential and even linked by some to bicycling. Sometimes the branching from one interest to a new interest is driven by a desire to approach a class of problems or issues or a broader topic rooted in an interest in a new way, for example with new methods. An example is John von Neumann's development of an interest in designing and building computers, specifically to solve difficult partial differential equations, described below.

Branching is natural for two reasons. We naturally tend to encounter elements, such as new ideas, facts, topics, contributions, and problems, in the zones surrounding interests we have, thus are exposed on an ongoing basis to elements linked to our interests and adjacent to their domains. Further, we are naturally likely to be drawn to and become interested in such topics, issues, concepts, problems, facts, data, and possibilities, for we are familiar with and have expertise with elements related to them, in domains adjacent to them, and have some basis for appreciating them. Wilbur Wright was undoubtedly drawn to flight due to its kinship with bicycling, and may well have read articles about it because of the link — it being also a hobby and mode of locomotion. Also, he was able to transfer his expertise from the one domain to the other, so that, from the time he first seriously turned his mind to it, in the winter and spring of 1899, he conceptualized flight and an approach for achieving it in a sophisticated manner that naturally led him forward to pursue it as a serious enterprise.

Henry Chen formed a creative interest in "literary geography" — how writers create, describe, hence define places — in college, as described in Chapter 2. He also has a longstanding interest in James Joyce's work, especially *Finnegans Wake*.

In graduate school Henry's interest in place in literature sparked an idea for a paper in a class on *Finnegans Wake*, which led to a branching of his interest. Describing the origins of the paper Henry said he knew about the references to New Ireland in the South Pacific from Roland McHugh's *Annotations for Finnegans Wake*.[16] "I had lived in the Solomon Islands, which is not too far away from New Ireland, so it had kind of a personal resonance for me." "So I said, 'I know there are these references to the South Pacific, [where] I live. And there are also these references to China and Japan. So why don't I write a paper about that.'" This idea clearly fits with his interest in place and specifically places in *Finnegans Wake*. Henry's professor taught the class that *Finnegans Wake* has the structure of going through a night to day, specifically a person who goes to sleep, sleeps through the night, then wakes up in the morning.[17] Henry recalled that his professor also presented the idea that in the course of the night the sleeper travels to the Crimea. In working on his paper Henry extended his professor's ideas, developing the idea that the book is about a journey to the southeast, not just to the Crimea, but continuing all the way to China and Japan and beyond to the South Pacific and New Ireland.[18] It is noteworthy that journey is one conceptual step from place, and that Henry's idea that there is a journey to the southeast in *Finnegans Wake* grew out of his original interest in place — thus through branching.

Henry wanted to write his dissertation on Joyce and also wanted to write about place, which continued to be central for him as a literary interest. He did not, as he described it to me, initially expect to focus on journeys in Joyce's works. Henry had formed an interest during his first few years in graduate school in depictions of the third world in Western literature. His initial idea for his dissertation fused his three interests together. The traditional approach to Joyce emphasizes that his writing derived from his own life experiences and the places he knew well, especially Dublin. Thus in regards Joyce's description of places the conventional view focuses on his description of Dublin. Henry wanted to challenge this conventional view by investigating

[16]Roland McHugh, *Annotations for Finnegans Wake* (Baltimore, MD: Johns Hopkins University Press, 1980).

[17]His professor was John Bishop. He published his ideas in *Joyce's Book of the Dark, Finnegans Wake* (Madison, WI: University of Wisconsin Press, 1986).

[18]Discussing the source of his idea Henry said "there is certainly also a lot about journeying [in *Finnegans Wake*], there's a lot of ships plying the South Pacific." It is to be noted that Henry refers to wanderers in literature in his college honors thesis, *A New Map for the Atlas of Literary Geography: V.S. Naipaul's Trinidad Novels*, pp. 69–70; and in describing works of "literary geography" in the first part of his thesis he mentions Dante and Homer, two epic journeys.

Joyce's descriptions of places and cultures he did not know well, specifically
non-European places. His initial plan was to discuss non-European places in
Dubliners and *Ulysses*, then focus on Joyce's depiction of non-European places
in *Finnegans Wake*.

But as Henry began working he made an unexpected discovery that shifted
his focus from places back to the theme of journey. He read an article by
Brewster Ghiselin describing how the different stories in *Dubliners* depict
journeys to the east.[19] Henry said he noticed that the journeys are not just to the
east, but in fact to the southeast, and made the connection with the journey to
the southeast in *Finnegans Wake*. Further, he saw that the journeys in *Dubliners*
become progressively shorter as the main characters become older, and was led
through this to an insight that "in childhood you have this longer journey to the
[south]east, and [as] you grow up, the journey is still towards the [south]east, but
it's a shorter journey." "So I developed this idea that *Finnegans Wake* was the
logical extension of *Dubliners*, a kind of going back to childhood and fulfilling
this dream of going to the east." After *Dubliners* Henry read *Ulysses*, and noticed
that at the end of that book again there is a journey to the southeast. Then he
read Michael Seidel's *Epic Geography: James Joyce's Ulysses* and was stunned,
as he described it, to find that Seidel describes *Ulysses*, up to the last chapter, as
a journey to the northwest.[20] Spurred, Henry developed an integrated theory:
that over the course of these three works Joyce traces a journey to and fro — to
the southeast in *Dubliners*, back to the northwest in *Ulysses*, then again to the
southeast, beginning at the end of *Ulysses* and continuing in *Finnegans Wake*.

Through his work on journeys across Joyce's oeuvre Henry developed an
interest in journeys more broadly in literature. This new interest is shown by
what he read later, described next. Thus his interest branched from place in
literature to journeys in literature, sparked by a discovery he made working on
a project.

Shortly after developing his theory of the axis of journeys in Joyce's work
Henry stopped working on his dissertation and took a job at Apple. A few years
later, distressed that he was drifting away from literature, he made the decision
to devote some of his time "to reading great literature." One of "the first books"
he decided to read, he said, was Dante's *Divine Comedy*. Henry did not tell me
why he chose the *Divine Comedy*, but it seems likely that he chose it because

[19]In Henry's dissertation there is a reference which I believe is the one he was
referring to: Brewster Ghiselin, "The Unity of Joyce's *Dubliners*," *Accent* 16 (1956).

[20]Michael Seidel, *Epic Geography: James Joyce's Ulysses* (Princeton, NJ: Princeton
University Press, 1976).

478   it is one of the most famous works of literature about a journey, thus fit with his new interest. In addition, he said that "Joyce's love of Dante" is well known, which may have attracted him to Dante.[21]

    This branching out to read a great work of literature about an epic journey, from a different time than the modern period and thus quite separate from James Joyce, clearly created the possibility for making creative connections. For Joyce scholarship and Dante scholarship inhabit different worlds and as Henry said, for the most part, "there haven't been Dante scholars who are also Joyce scholars." And Henry did indeed make a creative connection.

    While reading Dante, in a bookstore one day Henry decided to look for books about Dante and came upon one that has a chapter that has the word "Ulysses" in the title; his interest piqued, he decided to read the book.[22] Henry was familiar with arguments that at the end of *Ulysses* Bloom, who has been Homer's Odysseus, becomes Dante's Ulysses sailing out beyond the Pillars of Hercules to his death. But the essay he read led him to realize that this is not a satisfactory reading: "Basically he said Ulysses is the opposite of Dante, Ulysses is a bad guy and what the *Divine Comedy* is about is the alternative to Ulysses' voyage, that Ulysses is a failure, he doesn't get there — you have to follow Dante's path [to heaven] to get to where you want to get to." Henry thus realized "there's no way you can say that Bloom is the Dantean Ulysses . . . because it's someone who failed, it's not Odysseus who gets back home, who succeeds." There are many references to rocks in the last part of *Ulysses*, including a reference to "Daunt's" rock — "Dante's rock", and shipwrecks on rocks, which have been taken to confirm the interpretation that the story is showing Bloom as Dante's Ulysses, sailing through the Pillars of Hercules at the Straits of Gibraltar. Henry said the identification of Daunt's rock with Gibraltar fits the idea that Bloom is Dante's Ulysses, but that now, thinking there might be a different identification for Bloom, he felt a different interpretation was called for.

    After more than a year of puzzling, it dawned on Henry that Gibraltar — "the Rock" — is actually the mountain of Purgatory that Dante climbs with his guide Virgil on his way to heaven, and that Bloom is not Ulysses at the end of the book, but rather to be read as Dante and Virgil, his journey akin to Dante traveling to heaven, thus successfully completing his journey. With this insight he completed his dissertation; he told me he views the insight as his most creative contribution in literary analysis. Especially noteworthy is the way

    [21]As noted in footnote 18 above he also mentions Dante in his college honors thesis, thus was clearly familiar with his epic work from well before.

    [22]The book seems to have been John Freccero, *Dante: The Poetics of Conversion*, ed. Rachel Jacoff (Cambridge, MA: Harvard University Press, 1986).

the insight grew out of the branching of his interest, from place to journeys, which led him to read the *Divine Comedy*.[23]

479

Events Spurring Branching to Form New Interests

In many cases branching to a new interest is driven by events and circumstances. John von Neumann forming his interest in designing and building computers for use in solving partial differential equations is an example. When he began his career in mathematics and formed his interest in partial differential equations, computers did not even exist. He gained an appreciation for the power of computers through his consulting work with the United States Government during World War II calculating bomb charge configuration impacts and on the Manhattan project making calculations of the hydrodynamics of implosion. In his book *The Making of the Atomic Bomb* Richard Rhodes recounts Stanislaw Ulam's statement that he realized that the "ingenious shortcuts and theoretical simplifications" that had been proposed to solve the hydrodynamic equations for imploding nuclear material were not likely to give reliable answers, and pushed for solving the equations using numerical methods, which was the approach employed once an IBM computer arrived. Rhodes writes that the experience of using a computer to solve such equations "apparently set von Neumann thinking about how such machines might be improved" so as to be able to make such calculations more rapidly.[24] Von Neumann had a long-standing interest in solving partial differential equations, appreciated their practical importance in many domains, and thus through this work came to recognize the great value computers might have for solving them, sparking him to form his new interest. It is noteworthy that his interest was possible only once computers had been developed, and was spurred by his experiences on the Manhattan project.

Hannah Arendt

Hannah Arendt's creative development was marked by branching and connections from an initial interest to new interests, through a combination of personal and political events, and what is best described as a coming to

---

[23]Henry noted in our interview that other scholars have caught some of the references to the *Divine Comedy* he used. He mentioned in particular Mary Reynolds, *Joyce and Dante: The Shaping Imagination* (Princeton, NJ: Princeton University Press, 1981). Henry presents his insight in Chapter 2 of his dissertation, *The Non-European World in the Works of James Joyce*, UC-Berkeley, 1995, pp. 136–66.

[24]Richard Rhodes, *The Making of the Atomic Bomb*, pp. 479–80 and 544–45.

480 consciousness sparked by these events. Her interests evolved and tended to expand, becoming more encompassing and forging interconnections between different subdomains. Here I describe some main elements in her creative development up to the point after World War II when she formed a definite conception and plan for the book that became *The Origins of Totalitarianism*.

Hannah's first interest as a young adult was in theology and philosophy. She formed an interest in Kierkegaard as a teen, her interest sparked by lectures. Later, in a letter to Gershom Scholem, responding to his misguided view that she "came from the German Left," she replied, "If I can be said to 'have come from anywhere,' it is from the tradition of German philosophy."[25] Hannah went to the University at Marburg. There, studying theology, she fell under the spell of Heidegger and was greatly influenced by his philosophical ideas. After her love affair with Heidegger she left Marburg, and a short time later went to the University at Heidelberg, where Karl Jaspers was her teacher. Hannah wrote her dissertation during this time, *Love and Saint Augustine*.[26] There is no extant record I have seen that offers a clear statement of why she focused on Augustine and this topic, but it is certainly plausible that her choice of topic was connected with her love affair with Heidegger and its aftermath — her quest to understand her self in light of her love and loss drawing her to Augustine, the great early theorist of love and the self — exemplified in his famous statement: "I am become a question to myself" — an attitude resonant with many of Hannah's statements in her poems around this time.[27] In the wake of her love affair with Heidegger Hannah formed an interest in German Romanticism, which seems to have grown in part out of her work on Augustine, and in pursuing her interest encountered the figure of Rahel Varnhagen, who sparked her interest, as discussed in Chapter 3. While Hannah's interest in Rahel seems to have been rooted in her identification with Rahel as a Jewish woman and a woman who had a love affair of great intensity that ended, her interest was very likely also spurred by the rising tide of anti-Semitism in Germany — Hannah later dated the time of troubles for the Jews to 1929, about the time or just before she focused on Rahel.[28]

[25] Elisabeth Young-Bruehl, *For Love of the World*, pp. 34–36, 104. The letter is printed in *The Jew as Pariah: Jewish Identity and Politics in the Modern Age*, ed. Ron H. Feldman (New York: Grove Press, 1978), pp. 245–46.

[26] This is the English translation: *Love and Saint Augustine*, ed. Joanna Vecchiarelli Scott and Judith Chelius Stark.

[27] Possible pathways leading Hannah to this topic are alluded to in *Love and Saint Augustine*, pp. 115–41.

[28] See *For Love of the World*, pp. 67–68, 79, 85–92, 98. Young-Bruehl seems to imply in a statement on pp. 73–74 that a motivation for Hannah's work on love in St. Augustine was to try to understand anti-Semitism and the question of how the Jews could live side

During the years 1930–33 a decisive shift occurred in Hannah's intellectual
focus. As events unfolded in Germany, with the Nazis gaining influence and
power and anti-Semitism rising, her own Jewishness and crucially the larger
"Jewish question" took on far greater importance for her. Hannah had met Kurt
Blumenfeld, a leading Zionist, in 1926; she began spending time with him and
his circle of friends after 1930 when she moved to Berlin. Blumenfeld, as
Elisabeth Young-Bruehl puts it, believed and wanted to make all Jews realize
that they "would always be perceived by non-Jews as, first and foremost, Jews."
He and the movement he was part of wanted to bring Jews, in particular
assimilated Jews, into a Jewish cultural community, to develop a Jewish culture
which could then form the basis for emigration to Palestine.[29] This orientation
links with Hannah's work on Rahel Varnhagen: Hannah focuses in her book
precisely on Rahel's coming to the self-understanding that her fundamental
identity in the eyes of the world has been, always, that she is a Jew. As Hannah
tells it Rahel spends her entire life trying to escape from her Jewishness, to
become assimilated, only to realize at the end that it has been her truest,
deepest identity that defines her life and its meaning—as I have noted, with
a key quotation from page 1 of *Rahel Varnhagen*, in Chapter 3. There is a
clear resonance with Hannah's own experience through these years, being
ostracized by Nazi sympathizers, seeing Heidegger being a supporter of the
Nazi movement, living in circumstances in which her Jewishness was viewed
by the wider German community as her distinguishing characteristic.

Beyond her focus on Jewish identity Hannah made a fundamental shift in
her life and intellectual orientation, to a focus on political action and analysis.
Her shift is signaled, as recounted by Young-Bruehl, in a review dated 1932 of
a book on the contemporary women's movement: she focuses in her review
on the political issue, arguing that a movement that is strictly ideological and
not politically motivated will not be effective, that political action is crucial.[30]
Her political engagement intensified, on her own account, in 1933 with the
burning of the Reichstag in February and the Nazis seizing power and arresting

by side with the non-Jewish Germans. I do not find evidence in the text of Hannah's
published work on St. Augustine to support this view. It is not clear whether her focus
on neighborly love came first — the work may well have begun with a wish to explore
the horizon of being and temporality in St. Augustine as a parallel to Heidegger's work
and also to some degree Jasper's, or out of her quest to gain understanding of her self
and love affair.

[29] Ibid., pp. 70–73.

[30] "Review of Dr. Alice Rühle-Gerstel's book *Das Frauenproblem der Gegenwart*,"
Die Gesellschaft 10 (1932): 177–79. Discussed by Young-Bruehl in *For Love of the World*,
pp. 95–97.

many citizens. In her 1964 interview with Günther Gaus, as quoted by Young-Bruehl, she described the effect on her. "You see, I had been primarily occupied with academic pursuits. Given that perspective, the year 1933 made a lasting impression on me — both negatively and positively." The earlier events, she states, were political and did not affect one personally, but now things changed. "The general political realities transformed themselves into personal destiny as soon as you set foot out of the house. And, also, . . . [there was] cooperation. . . . And cooperation meant that your friends cooperated. . . . And I came to the conclusion that cooperation was, so to speak, the rule among intellectuals, but not among others. And I have never forgotten that. I left Germany guided by the resolution — a very exaggerated one — that 'Never again!' I will never have anything to do with 'the history of ideas' again." "I arrived at the conclusion which I always, at the time, expressed to myself in one sentence, a sentence which clarified it to me: 'When one is attacked as a Jew, one must defend oneself *as a Jew*.'" This insight is linked to her focus on Jewish identity, but she took it further, to an active involvement with the Jewish cause and Zionist movement. "After I realized this, I clearly intended to affiliate myself with the [Jewish] cause. For the first time." Referring back to her *Rahel Varnhagen*, of which she had completed the bulk by this time, she said, "In it, of course, the Jewish Question plays quite a part. The work signified to me that I wanted to understand." Thus she formed an intellectual interest, broadening out from her work on Rahel and branching away from her original interest in German Romanticism: in understanding the "Jewish question," including its history in Germany and Europe, and the question of what is the best way for Jews to live in the world. At the same time she formed a determination to be politically active: "I wanted to do practical work — exclusively and only Jewish work." She acted on this intention, working to help fugitives escape from the Nazis and undertaking a project for the Zionist movement at the Prussian State Library collecting materials documenting anti-Semitism, indeed being arrested for this and held in jail for eight days.[31]

Later that year Hannah left Germany and made her way to Paris. In Paris she worked for Jewish organizations, her most extensive involvement being with Youth Aliyah. She followed unfolding political events closely, with the conviction that the Jews should not be passive and keep a low profile — a position maintained by the established French Jewish community — but rather engage in political action and protest. During these years in France it is evident from Hannah's activities and later writings that she not only was politically engaged in current events but began to pursue her interest in the "Jewish question" as a

[31] *For Love of the World*, pp. 102–10; the quote from the Gaus interview is on p. 108 and citation is on p. 502, footnote 10 to Preface.

historical one. Living in France, it was natural for her to explore, as a parallel   483
branch to her interest in the history of the Jews in Germany and their place
in German society, begun with her work on Rahel, the place of the Jews in
France.[32] Hannah studied the history of the Dreyfus Affair — her article "From
the Dreyfus Affair to France Today" published in *Jewish Social Studies* in the
United States in 1942 demonstrates and draws upon her extensive researches
into the history of anti-Semitism in France, containing many references to
works in French that she undoubtedly first read in France.[33] She also followed
the activities of the Fascist group *Action Française*, gaining understanding and
knowledge about anti-Semitism in France. She became a devotee of Bernard
Lazare, who had developed the terms parvenu and pariah that were fundamental to her understanding of the choice — or lack of choice — open to
Jews; she uses these terms extensively in the last two chapters of *Rahel Varnhagen*, written in 1938. Hannah's interest in the history of anti-Semitism in
Europe and her interest in Zionism were evidently and naturally connected.
The connection is shown in her articles "Zionism Reconsidered" in *Menorah
Journal* in 1945 and "The Jewish State: Fifty Years After" in *Commentary* in
1946, a commentary on Theodor Herzl's Zionist manifesto *The Jewish State*.
Both articles evince a deep knowledge of the history of the Zionist movement,
showing that one facet of her interest in Zionism was to explore its historical
context and development; the latter article roots Herzl in his European milieu,
making an explicit link between Zionism and conditions in Europe.[34]

During these years Hannah had an estrangement from her first husband,
Günther Stern, and they were divorced. In 1936 she met Heinrich Blücher.
Blücher was a communist when they met, and influenced by him and his circle
of acquaintances Hannah's interest in the political sphere broadened out. In a
1946 letter to Karl Jaspers she wrote, describing her current orientation: "First,
thanks to my husband, I have learned to think politically and see historically;

[32]Ibid., chap. 4, pp. 115–22, 136–48. Unfortunately, the details of Hannah's intellectual
pursuits and conception of her interest during these years is not clearly documented or
traced in *For Love of the World* or any other source I have encountered.

[33]Hannah Arendt, "From the Dreyfus Affair to France Today," *Jewish Social Studies*
4 (July 1942): 195–240. Her article also contains references to works in English, many of
which she presumably read after coming to the United States.

[34]Hannah Arendt, "Zionism Reconsidered," *Menorah Journal* 33 (August 1945): 162–
96; "The Jewish State: Fifty Years After," *Commentary* 1 (May 1946): 1–8. Young-Bruehl
also describes her, Heinrich Blücher and Walter Benjamin reading Gershom Scholem's
Major Trends of Jewish Mysticism, in which he describes the Sabbatian movement,
which Arendt later labeled "the last great Jewish political activity" in "Jewish History,
Revisited," *Jewish Frontier* (March 1948): 34–38.

484 and, second, I have refused to abandon the 'Jewish question' as the focal point of my historical and political thinking."[35] This broadening is best thought of in those terms — not as a new interest unconnected with her interest in the "Jewish question," but as linked to it. Hannah read and was exposed to Marxist ideas and her knowledge of political thought expanded outside the German philosophical tradition. In the months before leaving France she read Clausewitz's *On War,* and became familiar with the life and thought of Rosa Luxemburg.[36]

The link connecting Hannah's interests in the "Jewish question" and politics is shown by her work. In her article "Why the Crémieux Decree Was Abrogated" in *Contemporary Jewish Record* in 1943 Hannah analyzes the abrogation of the decree granting French citizenship to Jews in Algeria by General Giraud in political terms, showing how different groups supported abrogation for their own interests, including the French colonials and the Arab landholders, who were opposed to the decree being expanded to extend citizenship to many Arabs.[37] Further evidence of the links she was making, albeit slightly later, is her article "Imperialism: Road to Suicide" in *Commentary* in 1946. In the section "The Bourgeois Philosophy" she outlines the philosophy of Hobbes, having clearly studied him with care. She quotes his dictum that "power must strive for more power," and develops the thesis that the pursuit of power, with imperialism its modern manifestation, must lead ultimately to nothing, for it has no other end point it can logically lead to; and she connects this with the Nazis drive for world conquest — viewing their drive for world domination as inevitably leading to annihilation.[38]

Hannah had the view, which grew only stronger over these years and her first years in America, that active political participation as a people was the best if not the only way for the Jews effectively to combat anti-Semitism and attain their rightful place among the peoples of the world. Thus her broader

[35] *Hannah Arendt Karl Jaspers Correspondence 1926–1969,* ed. Lotte Kohler and Hans Saner, letter of Jan. 29, 1946, pp. 28–33, quote on p. 31.

[36] *For Love of the World,* pp. 124, 158. Hannah has an essay on Rosa Luxemburg as one chapter in *Men in Dark Times* (New York: Harcourt Brace & Company, 1968), "Rosa Luxemburg; 1871–1919," pp. 35–56.

[37] Hannah Arendt, "Why the Crémieux Decree Was Abrogated," *Contemporary Jewish Record* 6 (2) (April 1943): 115–23. Hannah's notes for the paper on the Crémieux Decree are in the Hannah Arendt Archives at the Library of Congress, available at: http://memory.loc.gov/ammem/arendthtml/mharendtFolderP05.html — essays and lectures, in two folders.

[38] Hannah Arendt, "Imperialism: Road to suicide," *Commentary* 1 (4) (February 1946): 27–35.

political interest served her underlying interest in the place of the Jews in the world, providing an analytic base for practical policy recommendations and opinions. Ultimately Hannah forged a definite conceptual link — when is not clear, though Young-Bruehl implies this occurred at the very end of her time in France, thus 1940–41 — defining what she came to call the concept of "race-imperialism," thus made a creative connection between her two interests.[39] Thus during these years Hannah's twin interests broadened and ultimately coalesced through a creative insight she had.

Over the following decade Hannah pursued her interest, really now a single interconnected whole, increasing her knowledge, gaining deeper insight, in the midst of upheaval and sorrow and the struggle to define a way forward in the aftermath of the Holocaust. Hannah and Heinrich Blücher were married in 1940 and, after a harrowing escape, made their way to the United States in 1941.[40] In the United States Hannah was heavily involved with Zionist issues. She wrote a column for the German language newspaper *Aufbau*. She set forth her views about the formation of a Jewish state, arguing for the formation of a nation in which all would have equal rights and which would become part of a British Commonwealth if such a Commonwealth were formed.[41] She published a stream of articles in Jewish publications, including *Commentary* and *Menorah Journal*, as well as in other venues, including the *Review of Politics* and *Partisan Review*, based in and clearly generated out of the knowledge she had built up exploring her interests in their different branches. It is clear from the references in these articles, a fair number of which are to works in English, as well as her initial outline for the book that became *The Origins of Totalitarianism*, that Hannah continued to engage in extensive research, and her knowledge about the history of anti-Semitism and imperialism continued to grow. The first two parts of *Origins* are largely based on research and articles she had written by 1945.

The Holocaust was a great, terrible shock when it became known in late 1942 and 1943. Its revelation served as an event sparking a response in Hannah, crystallizing her intentions, and shaping her ideas. To understand how the Holocaust could have come about — what the forces and historical conditions were out of which Nazism could have emerged leading to this horrible outcome — became a compelling question for her, driving her determination to write a book about the history of the "Jewish question" and the emergence

[39] *For Love of the World*, p. 158. For her later terminology see the discussion of her initial outline for *The Origins of Totalitarianism* in the main text below.

[40] The story of their leaving France and coming to the United States is told in *For Love of the World*, pp. 152–63.

[41] Ibid., pp. 169–71, 180–81.

486   of imperialism and Fascism and the rise of the Nazis.[42] Her initial outline for
her book, dated 1946 (there are also outlines dated somewhat earlier), is entitled "The Elements of Shame: Antisemitism — Imperialism — Racism." In
her overview she states: "These three elements are combined in the amalgam
of race-imperialism. Nazism, the first pure type of this amalgamation, used
antisemitism as the amalgamator, took the concept of illimited expansion as
the essential aim of politics from the arsenal of imperialism and transformed
racism into a new principle for the organization of peoples."[43] Her outline
clearly shows her book rooted in her interests, that she had pursued by this
time for many years, indeed creatively tying different branches together.

Over the ensuing years, as she worked on the book, Hannah went well beyond this initial outline — following the classic pattern of work on a creative
project, generating further insights and making revisions to her initial design.
She formed a focus on the Concentration Camps, which are not mentioned
in her initial outline for the book. Her unpublished papers from these years
contain multiple proposals for research on the Camps that show the scope
of her interest, including historical research and documentation, witness accounts, and consideration of the psychological, philosophical, and political
significance of the Camps. And, crucially, she broadened and deepened her
understanding of Nazism, and forged a connection in her analysis of it with
her wider interest in political organization and theory.[44] Her initial outline lists
only one chapter on Nazism, with an outline closely based on her overview and

[42]For Hannah and Heinrich's feelings in the aftermath of revelations about the
Holocaust see Ibid., pp. 181–88.
[43]Hannah Arendt Papers, Library of Congress, http://memory.loc.gov/
ammem/arendthtml/mharendtFolderPo5.html—Miscellany—Outlines and research
memoranda—1946, n.d., two folders, folder 1. This outline runs over images 9–14, six
pages. There is also an earlier outline in English and another in German. Elisabeth
Young-Bruehl states that Hannah submitted an outline to Houghton Mifflin in late
1944 and early 1945: *For Love of the World*, p. 200.
[44]It is also of note that she came to see a direct connection between the "Jewish
question" and contemporary world politics. In a "Memo on Research" to Elliot Cohen,
editor of *Commentary*, that is not dated but Young-Bruehl estimates as having been
written in 1948 (*For Love of the World*, chap. 5, footnote 55, p. 511) she writes: "Twentieth-
century history has driven the Jewish people into the storm center of events." "The
significance of this situation is twofold. On the one hand, all purely Jewish problems . . .
cannot possibly be isolated, but must be considered within the very large framework
of general political trends and policies. On the other hand, the most central political
issues of our times, such as totalitarianism, the race question . . . have an intimate
relationship with the destiny of the Jewish people." Hannah Arendt Papers, Library
of Congress, http://memory.loc.gov/ammem/arendthtml/mharendtFolderPo5.html —
Miscellany—Outlines and research memoranda—1946, n.d., folder 2, image 37.

previous researches. She writes that she will describe how the "subterranean streams of European history" that she has traced in the previous chapters filled the "vacuum" in Europe in the wake of the first World War, and then were amalgamated by Nazism, and will describe the Nazi creed of world conquest, which she explicitly links to Hobbes's argument of power leading on and on, never-ending, to a "last war." As she learned more, and over time, her understanding and depth of analysis went well beyond this initial plan. A line in a book review, "Nightmare and Flight," published in the spring of 1945 shows the new depth and direction of her thought beginning as early as 1945: "The problem of evil will be the fundamental question of post-war intellectual life in Europe." Her use of the word "evil" is noteworthy, a new note in her thinking.[45] She connected Nazism and the Stalinist Soviet Union, viewing both as belonging to a single type, totalitarianism. And she developed an original, brilliant analysis of totalitarianism as a general form. She had the insight of a fundamental link between totalitarianism and terror, this in turn revealing a necessary connection between totalitarianism and concentration camps: "No totalitarian government can exist without terror and no terror can be effective without concentration camps."[46] And she developed her brilliant analysis of the layered organization of totalitarian regimes, isolating each layer of functionaries from external reality. Thus the last part of *The Origins of Totalitarianism*, the most famous, came to be written — a brilliant example of creativity generated in the course of work on a project.

Sequences of Linked Interests

A common pattern of development is forming a series of interests that are linked in some way. There are three basic channels through which a preexisting interest a person has and his conceptual structure associated with the interest may link to and influence a new interest he forms. These three channels naturally tend to overlap and the distinction among them is not sharp. Most fundamentally, a preexisting interest may influence the way a person conceptualizes a

[45]Hannah Arendt, "Nightmare and Flight," book review of *The Devil's Share* by Denis de Rougemont, *Partisan Review* 12 (2) (Spring 1945): 259–60. Her use of the word evil hearkens back to her work on Augustine. She discusses Augustine's concept of evil in the first part of her dissertation, "Love as Craving" — see, for example, p. 10 of *Love and Saint Augustine*. On p. 65, in the second part, discussing the importance of Plotinus for Augustine she comments that "Plotinus raises the question of the origin of evil . . . which is of compelling significance for Augustine."

[46]In the Archive folders, cited above, there are multiple research proposals for research on the Concentration Camps. The quotation is from folder 2, image 16.

488   new interest. Azad Bonni's conceptualization of his interest in the mechanisms of action through which extracellular agents trigger responses in cells is an example. As described in Chapters 2 and 3, Azad had a preexisting interest in classical mechanics at the time he formed his interest. This made it natural for him, when he became interested in biologic processes, to approach them from a perspective rooted in and fitting with this earlier interest — thus to focus on the "mechanisms of action" of biologic agents, by analogy with mechanisms of action in classical physics. A second channel is a preexisting interest a person has leading him to focus on a particular facet or subtopic of a new topic he has become interested in. A third channel is a person forming an interest in employing a particular approach, rooted in a preexisting interest, for studying a new topic he has become interested in. John Maynard Keynes's interest in the formation and role of expectations in economic processes is an example of these pathways: his focus of interest was linked to his long-standing interest in the rational grounds for action, and as an approach was conceptually rooted in the theory of probability judgements he had developed through his early interest in philosophy. Even when an individual switches to a new field of endeavor the creative interest he forms in his new field, in particular his initial interest, is often linked to a preexisting interest he had in his previous field — this was the case, for example, for Keynes.

Often when an individual forms a series of linked interests their distinctiveness grows, and his earlier interests are a source of distinctiveness of his later interests. For example, a preexisting interest an individual has may lead him to focus on an unusual aspect of a new topic he becomes interested in, so that even if it is a topic that others in his field are also interested in his interest is distinctive. Further, through forming and pursuing a series of linked interests an individual in general follows an unusual, unique path of development and exploration, leading, at least in some cases, to highly creative, original contributions.

A classic pattern of development is an interest an individual pursues sparking an idea she has which in turn becomes the basis for a new interest she forms — thus two interests linked through an idea.

Both Virginia Woolf and Susan Ferguson followed this pattern. Virginia's discovery writing "An Unwritten Novel" of a form of writing through which she could realize her conception of a world in which individual characters and selves are constructed out of reflections they see of themselves in the world around them and other characters' views of them — which, as I describe in Chapter 12, came out of her exploration of her conception in a series of short stories — in turn became the basis for her literary work going forward, thus

served her as an interest defining a style that was the basis for her work, as   489
described in the previous chapter.

Susan's interest in the use of different languages in conversation, the norms governing language usage, and language and code switching was the grounding for her insights about the way different languages are conveyed as being spoken in *Kim*, and the importance of translation in the book. In turn growing from her insight she developed an interest in exploring the "scene of dialogue" in novels, in particular the way different languages and dialects are conveyed in the dialogue in novels, through both narration and grammar, as well as the reasons authors choose to have certain characters speak in dialect. In her prospectus Susan writes that her dissertation will focus on "the role of speech in the English language novel." She continues: "Literary representations of speech referred to in discussions of fiction as 'dialect' provide a starting point for this project." "How does the novel, operating in a word of standard English, represent a variety of languages, dialects and speech styles?"[47]

Ultimately Susan connected her interest with theories of narrative and the role of narrators in novels (a body of theory linked to her interest through the pairing of narrative and dialogue as the two basic structural elements in novels), her interest evolving to a focus on exploring the relationship between the narrator and the dialogue of the characters.[48] She emphasized to me that her perspective remained different from that of most scholars working in this area — in particular most scholars focus on the narrator whereas she continued to focus on dialogue. Thus her evolved interest was distinctive and its distinctiveness was rooted in the distinctiveness of her earlier interest in the use of different languages in conversation and the norms governing language use. Going forward Susan had a number of insights about the relationship between the narrator and dialogue, including the idea of assessing the degree of convergence or divergence between the narrator and specific characters in terms of language, especially the degree to which their language is standard English versus dialect. She said that early on her focus was on the idea of the narrator using standard English versus characters speaking in dialect — looking at the conflict between them and "the control that the standard language narrator has over dialect-speaking characters." This clearly is linked with her insight about *Kim*, but whereas that concerned how the narrator translates the characters' speech, she had now shifted to a focus on the balance of power between the

---

[47]Susan's prospectus is "Speaking Volumes: The Novel in a World of Standard English," Harvard University, 1993. The quotes are from p. 1.

[48]Susan mentioned as narrative theorists who had the greatest impact on her work Dorrit Cohn, Gerard Genette, and Franz Stanzel.

narrator and dialect-speaking characters. Later, however, she came to see that often the narrator is suffused in the idiom of dialect, so that there is less of a distinction — thus recognized that there are variable degrees of convergence between narrators and dialect-speaking characters.

Beyond this pattern of interest-idea-interest there are many other possible patterns, for example forming a new interest linking two previously unconnected interests.

Linkages Extending Over Long Periods of Development

For many individuals their creative development unfolds over many years, during which time they form and pursue a sequence of linked interests, generating linkages in their development spanning decades. This pattern can be highly creative. Indeed in some cases it leads to extremely highly valued creative contributions. Several of the individuals whose developments I have studied and describe in this book made important contributions rooted in an interest itself linked to an interest they had pursued earlier. Here I present and discuss in some detail as an example John Maynard Keynes's creative development. Hannah Arendt's and Isaac Newton's developments also fit this pattern. Hannah's development is described in the preceding section. I do not describe Newton's development here for lack of space — it seems best to give one example in some depth as the pattern of sequential interests is relatively complex. As Richard Westfall describes in *Never at Rest* Newton formed and pursued a range of interests, in mathematics and physics, the study of the Bible and prophecy, and alchemy. Noteworthy, in terms of interconnections and linkages among his interests, are those between his interests in mathematics and physics. Early on there was an overlap between them in his interest in the circle: in physics one of the first problems he focused on was circular motion, and this seems to have been linked to his interest in the circle mathematically, for example in his calculation of the arc sine.[49] Later, when Newton returned to physics and

---

[49] For Newton's early work in mathematics see Richard Westfall, *Never at Rest*, pp. 107–12 and my discussion in Chapter 12. For his early work in physics see John Herivel, *The Background to Newton's Principia: A Study of Newton's Dynamical Researches in the Years 1664–84* (Oxford: Clarendon Press, 1965), pp. 2–13, and translations of Newton's work on pp. 128–82. Herivel states on p. 7: "It is worth pausing for a moment to consider how fortunate the *existence* of uniform circular motion was for Newton. . . ." There also seems to be a natural link of Newton's interest in circles and circular motion to his initial thought about the force of gravity extending to the Moon and his rough calculation of the force required to keep the Moon in its orbit, which at the time he conceived as circular.

the problem of gravity and orbital motion he drew on his method of fluxions,
naturally suited to describing trajectories, in particular curving trajectories.

John Maynard Keynes

John Maynard Keynes formed and pursued a sequence of interests having striking conceptual linkages, leading ultimately to his development of a revolutionary theory of macroeconomics set forth in the *General Theory of Employment, Interest and Money* in 1936. Keynes's initial focus of interest was not in economics, but rather philosophy and, to a degree, policy; his earliest sustained intellectual project was his development of his theory of the logic of probability judgement, published as his *Treatise on Probability*. Here I describe a long span of his development: his interests in college, early interest in economics, and later, mature creative interest in economics, out of which his further development unfolded. I describe fundamental links across these interests, thus in his ways of thinking across fields and over time. I draw upon Keynes's own writings, both his early unpublished writings and *The Collected Writings of John Maynard Keynes*. I also draw on Robert Skidelsky's biography, in particular the first two volumes: *Hopes Betrayed; 1883–1920* and *The Economist as Saviour; 1920–1937*.

The nature of the linkages between Keynes's early work, ideas, and beliefs and his later revolutionary economic theory is a central issue in the extensive literature of the past two decades discussing his intellectual development and the origins and his own understanding of the principles and framework he sets forth in the *General Theory*.[50] This literature is interesting and illuminating. However, it does not describe his development in the way I describe creative development in this book. As a result, the structure of his development and linkages between his earlier and later interests are not, in my opinion, drawn out and described clearly. A main approach is the attempt to identify and describe links from *A Treatise on Probability*, largely composed in the period 1904–08, to the *General Theory*, composed after 1930, thus spanning a period of twenty-five years, without attempting to describe Keynes's development between these two

---

[50]Some main contributions are: R.M. O'Donnell, *Keynes: Philosophy, Economics and Politics* (Basingstoke, UK: Macmillan, 1989); Anna Carabelli, *On Keynes's Method* (Basingstoke, UK: Macmillan and St. Martin's Press, 1988); John B. Davis, *Keynes's Philosophical Development* (Cambridge: Cambridge University Press, 1994); Bradley W. Bateman, *Keynes's Uncertain Revolution* (Ann Arbor, MI: University of Michigan Press, 1996). A useful recent volume that provides a range of perspectives by different contributors is Jochen Runde and Sohei Mizuhara, eds. *The Philosophy of Keynes's Economics* (London: Routledge, 2003).

492 periods.[51] This approach does violence to creative development as a process unfolding over time. Thus, while it may provide insight about linkages between ideas set forth in Keynes's different works, it is inappropriate for describing his creative development. Indeed it skips over a pivotal period of his development in the early and mid-1920s, when he formed a mature interest in economics, and his struggle wrestling with developing a theoretical framework, set forth in his *Treatise on Money*.

As an undergraduate at Cambridge, Keynes's primary intellectual interest was philosophy, with a secondary interest in statesmanship and policy-making. The focus of his life was the Apostles, the select society he belonged to.

Two factors influenced Keynes strongly in his college life. One was the values and philosophy of the Apostles. These were shaped in reaction to the preceding generation, and also seem to have been a reflection of the times. The fundamental values the younger Apostles of the time held were set forth by Desmond MacCarthy in a paper he read to the Apostles in 1900, two years before Keynes became a member, indeed before he came to Cambridge, which is quoted from and discussed by Skidelsky. As Skidelsky describes it, MacCarthy "contrasted his generation's attitude to life with that of its Apostolic predecessors. The key difference was that his generation took 'everything more *personally*' than they did." "The change was due," Skidelsky continues, "to 'all institutions, the family, the state, laws of honour, etc. . . . having failed to produce convincing proofs of their authority.'" Skidelsky then quotes this passage from MacCarthy's paper: "But there is another characteristic, which is the result of a shaken belief in rules of thumb and the usual aims in life, which also contributes directly to the greater interest taken in personal relations." "They [the previous generation] did *not* trust their immediate judgements as completely as we do."[52] This emphasis on making immediate judgements of specific cases to guide conduct and decision-making, rather than trusting to general rules and institutions, was a crucial feature of Keynes's philosophy of life, that he adopted and then explored and developed analytically. The other crucial factor in Keynes's life and development was his interest in statesmanship and

[51]O'Donnell specifically focuses first on the *Treatise on Probability* and then on the *General Theory* — it is his avowed intent to identify linkages between them. Similarly, Carabelli focuses on linkages running between these two works. Both Donald Gillies and Athol Fitzgibbons focus on comparing Keynes's views of probability in these two works in their contributions to *The Philosophy of Keynes's Economics*: Donald Gillies, "The relationship between Keynes's early and later philosophical thinking," pp. 111–29; and Athol Fitzgibbons, "Keynes's epistemology," pp. 55–67.

[52]Robert Skidelsky, *Hopes Betrayed; 1883–1920* (London: Macmillan, 1983), pp. 134–35. All italics in this and following quotations are in the original text.

policy. This interest was for the most part external to the Apostles, extending back to his school days at Eton.[53]

It is easy to imagine these two principal factors coalescing, and it seems that in fact they did — leading Keynes to form an interest, as I reconstruct it, in *the grounds for action, in probing for the reasons for action*, with a general view that generally accepted rules are often not well justified, and that it is possible, in given circumstances, to go beyond convention to identify rationally grounded, sound actions. Keynes's interest is evident in his essay on Peter Abelard, written during the winter vacation of 1902–03. In the essay he celebrates Abelard for his effort to ground faith in reason, citing Abelard's own statements that he was trying to find a way "to demonstrate by reason the dogmas of faith," and for his "systematic application... of dialectic to theology." He also celebrates Abelard's brilliance as a debater — Keynes loved debate and naturally linked it with stating grounds for action, especially policy.[54] It is shown also in his essay slightly later on Edmund Burke, his longest college paper. He writes of Burke the statesman, praising him especially for focusing on immediate consequences, never sacrificing the immediate prosperity to chimeric long-term goals, an approach he himself always favored, for his sound reasoning in identifying practical grounds for action, and for his outstanding speech-making.[55]

The great event of Keynes's undergraduate years was the publication of G.E. Moore's *Principia Ethica* in October 1903. This book was, as Keynes himself makes clear in his much later autobiographical statement "My Early Beliefs," read in 1938, the most important book in his life.[56] He states that Moore's book and the talk that "preceded and followed it, dominated, and perhaps still dominates, everything else," that it was "exciting, exhilarating, the beginning of a new renaissance...." Skidelsky quotes from a letter Keynes wrote just a few days after the book was published showing how great was his excitement and interest at the time: "It is a stupendous and entrancing work, *the greatest* on the subject." As Skidelsky describes, Moore essentially formalized as a philosophy the approach to life that the Apostles had already developed, at least to a degree,

[53] Skidelsky describes a variety of activities Keynes engaged in at Eton that fit this interest; Ibid., pp. 95–101. Keynes's interest in social welfare and active community involvement seems rooted in part in his family, in particular the values of his mother Florence.

[54] Keynes Papers, Kings College Archives, UA/16.

[55] Keynes Papers, Kings College Archives, UA/20. Written in summer and fall of 1904.

[56] "My Early Beliefs," in *The Collected Papers of John Maynard Keynes*, Volume X, *Essays in Biography* (London: Macmillan, 1972), pp. 433–51.

494   as described by MacCarthy.[57] Moore's philosophy is based on three principles:
(1) the good is a fundamental or simple property which cannot be described in
terms of other properties; (2) the ultimate good or elements of value are states
of mind — which Keynes and his circle took as being, in Keynes's later words,
"timeless, passionate states of contemplation and communion" grounded in
love and friendship, and "the creation and enjoyment of aesthetic experience,
and the pursuit of knowledge"; and (3) action is taken so as to strive to achieve
good states of mind.

Moore's book was crucial for Keynes in sparking a creative response, rooted
in his interest in identifying the grounds for action — sparking the initial idea
from which his work on probability grew. Keynes presents his ideas in a paper
he read to the Apostles on January 23, 1904, "Ethics in Relation to Conduct." It
is noteworthy that he read the paper just three months after Moore's book was
published — a classic illustration of a creative response, sparked by an event
which was one of the greatest intellectual events in his life.

In his paper Keynes takes issue with Moore's analysis and prescription of
the guides to action in his chapter "Ethics in Relation to Conduct."[58] Moore
is cautious in his argument in this chapter. In most cases, he writes, even if
we know a given action may do better than another, say a conventional rule,
in the immediate future, we have no ready way to gauge its effect in the long-
term, and for our choice of it "to be rational, we must certainly have some
reason to believe that no consequences of our action in a further future will
generally be such as to reverse the balance of good that is probable in the
future which we can foresee." Given that it is in general extremely difficult
to make such a determination we do best to follow general, conventional
rules. Moore's tone and conclusion are thus diametrically opposite to what
the young Apostles believed, as portrayed by MacCarthy: They held to their
ability to make judgements in individual cases as to the appropriate course
of action, not sharing Moore's pessimism about the impossibility of rationally
deciding for one action over another, viewing their elders' trust in rules as

[57] *Hopes Betrayed*, p. 134.

[58] G.E. Moore, *Principia Ethica* (Cambridge: Cambridge University Press, 1991 (first
published 1903)), Chapter 9. Keynes states in "My Early Beliefs" (p. 436) that he and his
circle "took not the slightest notion" of Moore's chapter "Ethics in Relation to Conduct,"
ignoring Moore's views on ethics and right conduct guided by rules. Since his response
was exactly focused on criticizing Moore's view on ethics it seems clear he meant not
that he (not stating what others did) ignored Moore's views on ethical conduct but
rather took issue with them, viewing them as not fitting the spirit of Moore's philosophy
but rather rooted in the more traditional emphasis on following rules that his circle
challenged. Further, other Apostles disagreed with Keynes's statement — Skidelsky
gives a summary of various points of view in *Hopes Betrayed*, pp. 143–47.

old-fashioned, rules as not worthy of blind obedience. It is thus not surprising that they would be driven to respond, in particular that Keynes was. It is noteworthy that Keynes was the only one of the young Apostles to be sufficiently driven to work out a response which he presented to the Apostles. It is a natural interpretation and fits with the description in this book that his focusing on this particular part of Moore's book was due to his interest in the grounds of action, especially practical action. His interest would naturally have led him to read this chapter closely in order to see what Moore argues as far as principles to guide action — and when he did he discovered Moore's conservative adherence to conventional morality which he viewed, as Skidelsky writes, as "anathema," spurring his response.[59]

Keynes begins his paper quoting Moore's passage containing the passage quoted above, then his statement that "our utter ignorance of the far future gives us no justification for saying that it is even probably right to choose the greater good within the region over which a probable forecast may extend . . . ," leading to his conclusion that "failing . . . proof" that an action will have no harmful consequences in the distant future overturning the good it causes in the immediate future, "we can certainly have no rational ground for asserting that one of two alternatives is even probably right and another wrong." Keynes then argues against this. "This conclusion does not seem to me to be justified . . . it is not obvious that any such proof is required before we are able to make judgements of probable rightness." "The crux of the matter, of course, lies in the meaning of probability, and I am not clear as to what interpretation underlies Moore's use of the word." "Any adequate definition of probability I have never seen, and I am unable to give one; but it is possible to try to refute given definitions and to find out the real questions at issue." These lines are important in showing his interest in the issue of defining probability generally. At this point he goes beyond Moore. He sets forth as the conventional view, which he believes Moore adheres to, a frequency account. He states that he believes Moore's position is this: "[to say an action] 'is probably right,' there are two necessary requirements:- firstly, so far as we can foresee, x produces the best result in the immediate future. [A]nd secondly—the certain knowledge that the doing of actions right so far as we can foresee produces a total good result more often than not" — that is, on the action being repeated many times, in

---

[59]*Hopes Betrayed*, p. 152. Another way to put this is that Keynes's interest was distinctive to him, generating his distinctive response. Many of the younger Apostles were interested more in aesthetic judgement — for example Desmond MacCarthy and Saxon Sydney-Turner. There were Apostles other than Keynes interested in action, for example Leonard Woolf, but he did not respond this way and may have been less specifically interested in rational grounds for action.

496   the majority of cases it leads to good outcomes. He continues: "I am inclined to think that [for] the statement 'x is probably right' the first requirement alone is necessary," then sketches an alternative definition: "By the statement 'A is more probable than B'. . . I mean something of this nature 'I have more evidence in favor of A than in favor of B'; I am making some statement concerning the bearing of the evidence at my disposal; I am not stating that in the long run A will happen more often than B <u>for certain</u>." Thus his definition is inherently oriented towards evaluating each individual case, based on the evidence at hand, believing that this is sufficient to form a probability judgement and thus guide action. At the end of the paper, arguing against Moore's view that an individual should always follow a general rule, he writes, "it is clear that, in any particular case, we have far more evidence by which to form our judgement than in the general case, and hence the probabilities in the general and in the special case may be different," so that we may be justified in not following a general rule in any particular case, contrary to Moore's view.[60]

In his paper Keynes thus sets forth and defends an original approach for defining probability, tailored to evaluating all available evidence in any particular case, as grounds for forming a judgement. It is noteworthy that his view clearly fits with his interest in the grounds for practical action, for example for formulating policy, and with his orientation towards evaluating policies on the basis of their foreseeable, immediate effects, as he praised Burke for doing. In the ensuing years Keynes developed his ideas, working out a theory of probability judgements and the logic of probability as an objective relationship between evidence and judgement. This was indeed his main intellectual endeavor during much of this time.[61]

Keynes's sustained interest in economics developed from 1905 when he studied economics for his tripos and the Civil Service examination. After graduation from Cambridge he took a position in the Indian Foreign Office, gaining exposure to economics in a more practical way, reviewing statistics and evaluating policies. On returning to Cambridge after two years he began teaching economics.

From early on Keynes was most interested in and learned the most about financial systems and money and banking. His main interest during this time, based on the surviving record, was in the practical workings of financial and monetary systems, and had three main facets: capital flows, including exchange

---

[60]"Ethics in Relation to Conduct," Keynes Papers, Kings College Archives, UA/16.

[61]Keynes turned in his dissertation on the subject in December 1907, and continued working on it through 1911. See *Hopes Betrayed*, pp. 182–84, 254–56, 259.

and foreign investment; the technical intricacies of financial dealings and banking; and policy-making, especially central bank policy. Collectively, these defined a rich domain: volumes of statistics and intricate details of the workings of real systems to be learned. Keynes's interest is shown in the series of memoranda and articles he wrote. In his article "Recent Economic Events in India" published in 1909 he presents data about Indian currency and prices, showing they broadly support the quantity theory of money. In "Great Britain's Foreign Investment" in the *New Quarterly* in 1910 he discusses foreign investment and factors that influence investors to invest overseas versus at home. He delivered lectures at the London School of Economics in 1910 that became the basis for "Recent Developments of the Indian Currency Question," in which he discusses currency reforms, monetary policy, and what he views as a new approach to managing currency, a modified gold standard, in which gold is held in reserve, used to pay foreign demands but not sent into domestic circulation, which he called a "gold-exchange standard."[62] His interest and work culminated in his book *Indian Currency and Finance* published in 1913 and his service on the Royal Commission on Indian Finance and Currency during 1913–14. His book shows his grasp of the intricacies of the Indian banking and monetary system. It is mainly empirical, consistent with this being the main focus of his interest at this time, with theory in the background, supporting his analysis and recommendations, most notably that the Indian Secretary of State issue credit during the busy season in India as a way to offset the high demand for money for transactions and thus reduce the interest rate, which historically had peaked at very high levels during this season.[63] Keynes lectured on monetary economics, and through his teaching developed a solid base in classical monetary theory. However, as Skidelsky notes, his lectures are based on Marshall and not very innovative, supporting the view that his main interest at this time was more the workings of real monetary systems than theory.[64]

[62]"Recent economic events in India," *Economic Journal* 19 (1909): 51–67. See *The Collected Writings of John Maynard Keynes*, Volume XV; *Activities, 1906–1914; India and Cambridge*, ed. Elizabeth Johnson (London: Macmillan and St. Martin's Press, 1971). His *New Quarterly* article is on pp. 44–59, "Recent developments of the Indian currency questions" is on pp. 67–85.

[63]For his service on the Commission and his writings for it see *Collected Writings*, XV, Chapter 2, 3, and 4. *Indian Currency and Finance* is Volume I of *Collected Writings* (London: Macmillan and St. Martin's Press, 1971). Keynes's policy prescription regarding the rate of interest in the busy period is in the last chapter (Chapter 8).

[64]*Hopes Betrayed*, pp. 207, 217–21. It is to be noted that Keynes had other interests in economics — in population, and the use of statistics and induction, but these were less central.

498   Keynes's interest in monetary and financial systems during this time was for
the most part distinct from his interest in and work on probability. It is thus
best to think of these as two distinct interests that he pursued concurrently. In
particular his interest in monetary and financial systems was empirically focused far more than theoretical, thus not likely to be strongly connected with
his more theoretical work on probability. The most obvious and most commonly described link is in his view of investment as decision-making under
uncertainty. Keynes himself made the connection with probability: Skidelsky
quotes from a letter to his father in 1908 in which he writes, "I lie in bed
for hours in the morning reading treatises on the philosophy of probability
by members of the Stock Exchange."[65] In his article on foreign investment
in which he discusses the investor's decision about whether to invest at home
or abroad, Keynes writes that in making his calculation the investor will be
"affected, as is obvious, not by the net income which he will actually receive
from his investment in the long run, but by his expectations." He writes that
the investor makes a "subjective risk" assessment dependent on "the amount
of relevant information" available to him, and that the risk is "not the real
risk as measured by the actual average yield of the class of investment over
the period of years to which the expectation refers, but the risk as it is esti-
mated, wisely or foolishly, by the investor." The connections with his theory
of probability is evident: risk is the risk perceived by the investor, not as measured by any objective long run frequencies — very close to the point he
makes in his initial paper on probability, quoted above.[66] Thus Keynes was
attuned from the start to view investment as based on subjective assessment of
probabilities attached to different outcomes. But he did not carry his thinking
about investment further, did not develop the link to his theory of probability systematically, and investment was not at this time his main focus in
economics.

        I believe a deeper link in Keynes's development is between his interest in the
rational grounds for action, linked with his view that it is possible to identify

[65] *Hopes Betrayed*, p. 208.
[66] *Collected Writings*, XV, pp. 44–47. With regard to the tradeoff between risk and
return he states "no mathematical rule can be laid down respecting the exact compro-
mise" or tradeoff that will be made — this links to his view in probability work that in
many cases no exact mathematical calculation can be made. In the context of financial
investment he seems to allow for more, or at least stresses more, individual variations in
judgement and lapses of rationality. For example, in discussing risk assessment he states
that expectations may depend upon "fashion" and "purely irrational waves of optimism
or depression" — a harbinger of his later thinking. Such issues are mentioned in the
Treatise on Probability in the notion that individuals may differ in their information and
grasp of logic, but are less emphasized.

actions better than previously accepted actions, which often were based on rules and not rationally based, and his interest in and focus on policy-making. The tenor of his own interest, and the belief of his circle of Apostles, was one of doubting the value of preconceived rules, moving to judging individual cases. This view links naturally to his confidence in the ability to formulate policies that will improve things, to challenge prevailing wisdom, which was often more passive and distrustful of intervention. This view set him apart from much of the tenor of economic thinking of the time. I believe Keynes naturally identified with the economic policy-maker as the person who, through his actions, can improve economic conditions in the same way he identified with Edmund Burke. From the start he focused on short-term policy effects, linked to his views on probability, not believing in allowing oneself to be paralyzed by the fact that one does not know for certain what the long-term consequences of a policy will be, as Moore was — believing rather that, all else equal, a policy that is likely to do good in the short-term should be pursued. His interest and orientation were given additional force by their link with his work on probability, which gave principles for making probability judgements, thus helping to guide choice among alternative policies — it was natural for him to believe that a policy-maker can gather information and apply logic to choose the best policy in given circumstances.

World War I was a crucial period of transition for Keynes. He joined the British Treasury and gained recognition and influence with his aptitude for work, intelligence, efficiency, and rhetorical skills. After the war he attended the Paris Peace Conference and, in fundamental disagreement with the heavy reparations burden placed on Germany, wrote *The Economic Consequences of the Peace*, which made him famous. He gained confidence in his voice as economist and ability to develop policy based on his understanding of the workings of economic systems and the play of events.

The period after the war was decisive for Keynes. It was during this time that he formed his mature creative interest in economics. His interest, as I reconstruct it, drawing also on Skidelsky's excellent account in *The Economist as Saviour*, may roughly be stated thus: *understanding how monetary systems are intermeshed with and may countervail the workings of the real economy of goods and services, especially through expectations of (hence probability judgements in relation to) future variables, and formulating an activist policy, especially and at first a monetary policy, to create stability for economic systems subject to basic instabilities rooted in factors linked to problems of uncertainty and adjustment, including international factors.* Thus his early interest in the workings of monetary systems and policy evolved, becoming more theoretical and conceptual, and more sophisticated. Undoubtedly, associated with this maturing

500 of his interest, he formed a richer conception of interest. As well, in becoming more conceptual and sophisticated, his interest also became — at least so it seems in retrospect — more amenable to being developed creatively.

The specific impetus to Keynes's interest evolving and his beginning to develop his interest creatively was the postwar atmosphere: the prevailing sense that the old order was destroyed and the world had entered a new, more precarious era; the recession of 1921–23; and the official British policy returning to a gold standard and attempting to generate a revaluation of the pound to its prewar level of exchange with the dollar. Keynes's sense of the change in regime is presented in *The Economic Consequences of the Peace*, in which he describes the new order as less stable and more rooted in psychology. On this Skidelsky quotes Dennis Robertson, who in his review of the book notes its turn to "psychology" and the view that "forming a rational judgement [now] becomes much more elusive and precarious."[67] The recession and monetary policy were central for Keynes. He wrote many articles decrying the deflationist monetary policy, which he was convinced exacerbated the recession, developing the general idea, building on ideas and understanding from his prewar period, of using monetary policy to make adjustment in the real economy — in particular by not pushing prices down, but rather stabilizing them, holding the pound at its current depreciated level. His statements in an article in *The Manchester Guardian* in May 1922 give a sense of his thinking at this time.

> Ultimately we make goods to exchange them for other goods; but immediately we make money. An interval of time elapses between production and sale. If therefore there is an expectation that the money price prevailing at the date of sale will be lower than the money cost during the period of production, obviously no one will produce.... [T]he productive process is bound to be brought to a standstill whenever a fall of prices is widely anticipated amongst merchants.[68]

He adds that the anticipation of such an effect, if widespread, will "turn the anticipation into effect," thus generating a cyclical movement.

Building on his work on seasonal fluctuations in India, Keynes developed the idea of using monetary policy to offset real shocks in the economy that may trigger fluctuations. He set forth his ideas in his *Tract on Monetary Reform*,

---

[67]Robert Skidelsky, *The Economist as Saviour, 1920–1937* (London: Macmillan, 1992), p. 29. D.H. Robertson, "Review of *The Economic Consequences of the Peace* by John Maynard Keynes," *Economic Journal* 30 (1920): 77–84.

[68]*Collective Writings*, Volume XVII; *Activities, 1920–1922; Treaty Reform and Reconstruction*, ed. Elizabeth Johnson (London: Macmillan and Cambridge University Press, 1977), pp. 429–31.

published in 1923.[69] A set of notes Keynes made from which he spoke in December 1923, show his thoughts at the time. In describing the workings of a monetary economy he states that the current system is a failure; then, elucidating causes, he writes a series of notes:

> Under a regime of money-control
>   Expectations are based on stability
> The investor lends in money [not in goods]
> The entrepreneur incurs liabilities in terms of money
> If money fluctuates, expectations are upset and the harmony between individual interest and social interest is destroyed.
> If prices go up investment is discouraged
>   and enterprise discredited.
> If prices go down enterprise is brought to a standstill
>   (Example in full)
> The triple evils of modern society
>   Vast enrichment of individuals out of proportion to any services rendered
>   Disappointment of expectation and difficulty of laying plans ahead — i.e. the precariousness of our economic system
>   Unemployment   Strikes
> All of these mainly due to instability of standard of value.[70]

These notes, written at the end of 1923, focus on money as the cause of fluctuations and monetary policy as the key to stabilization. In the following year Keynes's focus of interest branched to a new topic. Unemployment remained high in the United Kingdom, and this spurred him to expand his thinking about the economy and the scope for policy intervention. Keynes had already, as shown in the notes above and many other statements he made, begun to incorporate businessmen, entrepreneurs, and investors more fully into his thinking, recognizing that their expectations and investment decisions are at the crux of fluctuations in economic activity and drive activity — fitting with his underlying approach focusing on probability judgements as the grounds of action, now focused down to a specific set of economic decisions about the future. Now he came to a clearer insight that the system might be locked in a low state, with individuals holding expectations that the future state of the economy would be poor, causing them not to wish to invest, which in aggregate was preventing the system as a whole from recovering.

[69]*Collected Writings*, Volume IV (London: Macmillan and St. Martin's Press, 1971). He was also concerned about international factors, foreign investment and the value of the pound, and the inadequacy of current policies in this area. See *Collected Writings*, Volume XIX; *Activities, 1920-1929; The Return to Gold and Industrial Policy*, ed. Donald Moggridge (London: Macmillan and Cambridge University Press, 1981), Volume 1.
[70]*Collected Writings*, XIX, 1, pp. 159–60.

In an article in *The Nation and Athenaeum* in May of 1924 Keynes aligns himself with those advocating direct government expenditure on public works to create jobs. He states that "there is no place or time here for *laissez-faire*. Furthermore, we must look for succour to the principle that *prosperity is cumulative*. We have stuck in a rut. We need an impulse, a jolt, an acceleration."[71] Two years later, in notes for a speech he states: "The economic problem of England is essentially a problem of solid and economic disequilibrium." "The orthodox economics, which we have inherited from the nineteenth century, assumes a high degree of fluidity of the economic organism." But this kind of fluidity of adjustment, he writes, is "in England at least — much less than it used to be."[72] Pushed by events, exploring new ways of thinking about the problems plaguing modern economic systems, naturally aligned with his focus on decision-making under uncertainty, Keynes thus began to focus more on investment and, as time passed, the link and possible disconnect between savings and investment.

As the notes and comments I have given indicate, Keynes explored his interest and developed his ideas as he went. The volumes of his *Collected Writings* devoted to his "Activities" during these years contain dozens of newspaper articles, public letters, and speeches.[73] His observations and ideas centered on and grew out of his interest, which I have reconstructed above, as he grasped for a general theoretical approach to formalize his intuitive sense of the difficulties caused by decision-making rooted in judgements susceptible to others' decisions, creating feedback, hence an inherent possibility of instability, in the nexus of monetary and real variables, as well as a role for active policy intervention to create stability.[74]

Keynes's interest has strong connections with his preexisting interest in the grounds for action, including his optimism about the possibility of identifying good actions, better than those of the past, linked to the beliefs of his circle of Apostles and his work on probability. Indeed the links seem more fundamental than they had been to his early interest in economics before the war; thus his is a case, in this regard similar to Hannah Arendt, of an individual

[71] Ibid., pp. 219–21.
[72] Ibid., pp. 434–41.
[73] These are Volumes XVII and XIX (XIX is two volumes) of his *Collected Writings*, running to more than 1200 pages.
[74] Keynes states in a letter that a great economist needs to engage in "vigilant observation" (letter written to Roy Harrod in 1938, quoted in *The Economist as Saviour*, p. 413). See also the general discussion in *The Economist as Saving* on pp. 410–28, and Keynes's well-known essay on Malthus in *Essays on Biography*, *Collected Writings*, X, Chapter 12, "Thomas Robert Malthus," in two parts, pp. 104–8.

forging, over time, stronger links between his interests. A guiding principle of Keynes's interest in economics was his belief in the possibility of formulating an activist policy tailored to the conditions of the times that would improve upon current policy in stabilizing and reviving the postwar economy. It is hard to imagine him being and remaining so interested in economics after the war or forming and pursuing his interest in monetary systems and policy without adherence to this principle — it was a source of confidence and motivation. The principle seems clearly rooted in his interest in developing grounds for action, judging specific cases on their own merits, applying sound logic and bringing to bear all available information, confident of the possibility of identifying good actions, often going beyond historical precedent and conventional rules. Thus this earlier interest and the orientation springing from it was a root of his creative interest in economics more than fifteen years later. His focus on active policy, especially for the immediate term, fits with his initial response to Moore's arguments, which he saw as wrong-headed in sacrificing clear immediate benefits to the unknown future. Indeed it is in his *Tract on Monetary Reform*, written at this time, that he puts forth his famous dictum: "[The] *long run* is a misleading guide to current affairs. *In the long run* we are all dead."[75]

As a second link, Keynes's focus of interest on expectations formation and exploring the importance of expectations in modern economies fit naturally with his interest in probability. Given his interest and work on the formation of probability judgements it was natural for him to recognize the uncertainty inherent in economic actions, especially investment decisions, and to become interested in pursuing modeling such decision-making and expectations formation and working through the implications for economic systems. Indeed the link between his probability and his later focus on expectations formation is the one most commonly described in the literature on Keynes's intellectual development.[76] Over time, as economic conditions remained in flux, and as Keynes thought about these issues in the context of economics, he came to believe in the importance of expectations being susceptible of irrational impulses, and that expectations may differ across individuals; he did not necessarily abandon his views in the *Treatise on Probability*, but his emphasis shifted. He also came to appreciate the complexity of the modern world and

[75]*Collected Papers*, IV, p. 65.

[76]O'Donnell discusses this and gives citations to earlier discussions, in Chapter 12 of *Keynes: Philosophy, Economics and Politics*. It is noteworthy that Keynes revised and finally published his *Treatise on Probability* around the same time he began to focus on investment and expectations, suggesting there may have been a direct cognitive link.

504   the difficulties thus involved in forming sound expectations of future variables and outcomes.[77]

In the fall of 1924 Keynes began on what turned out to be the pivotal creative project of his career, rooted in and growing out of his interest as he had developed it over the preceding five years. He set himself the task to construct a theory of the monetary system enmeshed in the real economy, in particular a model of short run disequilibrium caused by shocks to the system followed by adjustment, worked out in terms of movements in prices and income, combining the monetary theory he had developed in the *Tract on Monetary Reform* with a new focus on savings and investment — his aim being to rationalize and design activist monetary policy for the short-term. He struggled with formulating a theoretical structure for nearly seven years, finally publishing his *Treatise on Money* in 1930.

He did not stop there, however. Driven, developing his ideas further, he recast his system, developing a more powerful, integrative framework. Spurred by criticism by fellow economists, and by the continuance of the Great Depression and public debate about its fundamental cause and policies to create recovery, he worked to incorporate adjustment in output into his model, to develop a better understanding of the savings and investment relations, and incorporated the idea of the multiplier. On a fundamental level — showing his depth and resilience — he extended his vision to one of economic systems as not necessarily inherently tending, without some impetus, towards full employment equilibrium. Thus developing his ideas further, he came to write his masterwork, *The General Theory of Employment, Interest and Money*.[78]

[77]There is much disagreement and different positions taken in the literature concerning the relationship of Keynes's later views of expectation formation and his earlier views. O'Donnell and Carabelli argue a basic continuity in his thinking, perhaps with a shift in focus or emphasis; see *Keynes: Philosophy, Economics and Politics*, Introduction and Chapter 12, and Anna Carabelli, *On Keynes's Method*, and "Keynes: Economics as a branch of probable logic," in *The Philosophy of Keynes's Economics*, pp. 216–26, especially pp. 224–26. Others argue that Keynes's fundamental conception shifted. Thus John Davis argues that, influenced by Ramsay's critique of his *Treatise on Probability* and Wittgenstein's later ideas, Keynes shifted to a view of "interdependent" probabilities among individuals in a society; see his *Keynes's Philosophical Development*. Gillies has put forward similar ideas.

[78]For a discussion of responses to his *Treatise*, the impetuses pushing him forward, and his development going forward, leading to the *General Theory*, see *The Economist as Saviour*, Chapter 11 and Chapter 13, section II.

DIFFICULTIES IN CREATIVE DEVELOPMENT

The description of creative development presented in this book may impart the impression that individuals are always able to be highly creative and make valued creative contributions through the process of development described. In fact, while each of us is capable of engaging in creative endeavors, and, I believe, capable of being creative and making creative contributions, that does not mean that we are guaranteed to do so or that an individual who engages in a creative endeavor will always make contributions valued by others and feel satisfied with his outcome — creative development does not inevitably lead to what may be described as a "successful" outcome. Individuals who engage in a creative endeavor do, I believe, in most cases follow a path of development that fits the description I have given. But in following such a path they are not necessarily able to generate original ideas or insights or make discoveries leading to valued contributions. The description in this book is a description of a process, and the end results vary. While throughout the book I present many examples of individuals generating creativity, I do this strictly in order to show how such creativity is generated out of and through the processes and structures I describe. The fact that I describe these end results is not to be taken to mean that development following the description leads to the generation of creativity and valued contributions in every case.

Linked to the possibility of failure are difficulties individuals experience in creative development. I have described difficulties in preceding chapters in many of the case studies, as part of describing the process of development individuals go through — thus some sense of the struggles and difficulties individuals encounter has been conveyed. But I have not described difficulties

506   in general. In fact difficulties are a pervasive feature of creative work: most individuals experience periods of difficulty in their development, even those who achieve the greatest fame and success.

In this chapter I discuss difficulties individuals experience in their creative development and approaches for possibly overcoming these difficulties, grounding my discussion in the framework of creative development set forth in this book. In grounding my discussion in this framework I approach the issue of difficulties in creative work differently than the way this issue has generally been approached in the creativity literature. My discussion is thus complementary to other approaches. I focus on two basic areas in which difficulties may arise in creative endeavors. One is in the basic cycle of creative development. The approach I follow here is to consider in turn each of the core processes of development described in the book, describing difficulties individuals may encounter at each step and in moving from one step to a following step. The second area of difficulty, discussed briefly at the end of the chapter, is fixation and difficulties in being open to and generating evolution in one's interests and forming new interests, initiating a new cycle of development.

The subject matter of this chapter is important in that through understanding the difficulties individuals encounter in creative development we can hope to find ways to help them overcome these difficulties and achieve greater success — enabling them to realize their creative potential more fully. In my view, by making individuals themselves consciously aware of the difficulties they may face we make them better able to recognize and surmount them. This fits with the view I hold, which lies behind a central part of the description in this book, that through forming conceptions of their interests individuals define their interests more clearly and thus are able to pursue them more effectively.

Many creativity books focus on overcoming difficulties to being creative. One fine example is Julia Cameron's *The Artist's Way*. More generally, techniques have been developed that are designed to foster creativity, such as brainstorming and Betty Edwards's approach to learning to draw, which she develops in her classic *Drawing on the Right Side of the Brain*.[1] In general these

---

[1] Julia Cameron, *The Artist's Way: A Spiritual Path to Higher Creativity* (New York: Jeremy P. Tarcher, 1992); Betty Edwards, *The New Drawing on the Right Side of the Brain* (New York: Jeremy P. Tarcher / Putnam, 1999). See also Michael Ray and Rochelle Myers, *Creativity in Business* (Garden City, NY: Doubleday, 1986), Edward de Bono, *Lateral Thinking: Creativity Step by Step* (New York: Harper & Row, 1970), James Adams, *Conceptual Blockbusting: A Guide to Better Ideas* (Reading, MA: Addison-Wesley Publishing, 1986), Robert Sutton, *Weird Ideas That Work* (New York: The Free Press, 2002), and Barry Nalebuff and Ian Ayres, *Why Not?* (Boston: Harvard Business School Press, 2003).

various approaches and techniques are not rooted in creative development and certainly not in the theoretical framework set forth in this book.

The subject matter of this chapter is connected with two other topics. One is the emotions individuals experience engaging in creative endeavors. Research suggests that positive affect is associated with greater creativity, at least in the short-term creative tasks in which individuals engage in experiments.[2] For creative development, which extends over long periods of time, the situation is undoubtedly more complex than this. In particular I believe positive affect and negative affect can each have both constructive and detrimental effects, with positive affect associated with creativity generation but possibly less astute judgement, and, conversely, negative affect associated with greater critical judgement, including meta-level thinking.

Individuals must be able to persevere in the face of difficulties and setbacks to continue in their development and reach a point at which their creativity flowers.[3] As an interesting case, Hannah Arendt dealt with feelings of distress throughout her life. There were two periods of deep emotional loss for her during the years of her life I describe in this book, the first the aftermath of her love affair with Martin Heidegger, the second the time when the Holocaust became known. Interestingly, each spurred her on in her creative work: it was shortly after the first that she formed her interest in Rahel Varnhagen; and the news of the Holocaust spurred her recognition of the importance of understanding Nazism and cemented her resolve to begin work on her book about the constellation of historical currents and elements out of which totalitarianism emerged. Certainly not all individuals experience periods of depression or distress, at least there is no record of them having such episodes. Among individuals whose developments are described in this book, Alexander Calder, Hans Krebs, and Albert Einstein all seem to have been able to pursue their work, at least during the periods when they made the contributions I describe, with a relatively even or cheerful emotional tone.

[2]*Creativity and Affect*, ed. Melvin P. Shaw and Mark A. Runco (Norwood, NJ: Ablex Pub. Corp., 1994); A.M. Isen, K.A. Daubman, and G.P. Nowicki, "Positive affect facilitates creative problem solving," *Journal of Personality and Social Psychology* 52 (1987): 1122–31; A.M. Isen, M.M.S. Johnson, E. Mertz, and G.F. Robinson, "The influence of positive affect on the unusualness of word associations," *Journal of Personality and Social Psychology* 48 (1985): 1413–26; T.M. Amabile, S.G. Barsade, J.S. Mueller, and B.M. Staw, "Affect and creativity at work: A daily longitudinal study," manuscript, 2004; K. Gasper, "Permission to seek freely? The effect of happy and sad moods on generating old and new ideas," *Creativity Research Journal* 16 (2004): 215–29.

[3]Extreme depression may thus be an issue. Kay Jamison discusses possible links between manic-depressive temperament and creative activity in the arts in *Touched with Fire*; his work points to rich connections between emotions and creativity.

The other topic linked to the discussion in this chapter is differences in outcomes across individuals. The great differences across individuals in both the quantity of their creative output and the influence their contributions have in their field and more broadly is a striking feature of creative work. The framework presented in this book is naturally suited to investigating these differences. For example, the framework may be used to explore whether differences in creative interests are associated with differences in outcomes, for example whether certain kinds of interests are more likely to be associated with extraordinary contributions. Likewise, the possibility that certain patterns of development are conducive to making highly valued contributions might be investigated. Of course there are many other factors, outside of the framework in this book, that are likely to be important in explaining differences in outcomes including personality, intelligence, divergent thinking aptitude, memory, and motivation — all of these have been active areas of study. But, complementary to these, I believe the framework of creative development can contribute significantly to understanding and explaining differences in outcomes.

A further issue is what the term "success" means in regards creative endeavors. There is no single clear meaning of success. Success may be defined in terms of the evaluation of creative products an individual produces by a reference group; different possible reference groups include colleagues, senior individuals in one's field, contemporaries in one's field, and society at large. Evaluation is often taken as historical — in this regard there are different frames of reference, in terms of how far out in the future beyond the time when an individual produces his work it is evaluated.[4] Separate from all of these, which are based on evaluation of an individual's works by other people, there is the individual's sense of his own success in his creative endeavors. Here again there are a variety of reference frames — individuals make both contemporaneous evaluations during development (these are like meta-level assessments), and retrospective evaluations. Individuals who hold values they wish their work to support or exemplify, as many of the individuals in this book do or did, including Pierre Omidyar, Enid Zentelis, Tina Brooks, and Rachel Carson, are likely to define the success of their work in terms of the degree to which it adheres to or advances these values. Finally, an individual may evaluate success in terms

[4]In recent years there has been work focusing on the reception of creative works, and the recognition that this is important in our definition, even much later historically, of how "successful" a particular work or individual has been. See Mihaly Csikszentmihalyi, "Society, culture, and person: A systems view of creativity," in *The Nature of Creativity*, ed. Robert J. Sternberg for one example (see Chapter 1, footnotes 31–33 for additional references).

of the experience of engaging in a creative endeavor, how much he enjoys it, how fulfilling it is, and in terms of striving to reach his potential. In focusing here on difficulties individuals encounter in their development, and ways to overcome these, I circumvent the precise definition of success.

ANALYZING DIFFICULTIES: THE THREE PHASES
OF CREATIVE DEVELOPMENT

I describe potential difficulties and bases of creativity for each of the three main phases of creative development: formation of creative interests; exploration of interests and generation of creativity rooted in conceptual structures built up in interest domains; and engagement in creative projects.

Phase 1: Formation of Creative Interests

In the basic description of this book creative development — and the generation of creativity and creative contributions — is rooted in the forming of creative interests, specifically interests having creative potential. Put in the converse form, if an individual does not form a creative interest, or if his interest is barren in the sense that it is an interest that cannot readily be developed to be generative of creative ideas and discoveries and creative contributions, this poses an enormous obstacle to him in his development.

It is my belief that essentially all individuals who engage in a creative endeavor are capable of forming a creative interest and will naturally do so. However, forming an interest takes time, and to form a conception of interest may require deliberately turning one's attention to the task. Assuming an individual does form an interest there is no way to know for certain at the time he forms it whether it will prove to be fruitful. Further, in cases in which an individual pursues an interest and is not able to be creative and productive we cannot generally know with certainty whether the interest he formed did not have creative potential, or whether in fact it did have potential but he was unable to develop it in such a way as to realize its potential — meaning he had difficulties in later phases of development, whether because of lack of motivation or ability, or simply because he was unlucky, pursuing an interest that genuinely seemed to hold potential but that turns out not to, or unlucky in the specific path of development he followed. Nonetheless it is possible, drawing on the description in this book, to describe what appear to be main sources of creative potential of interests, thus characteristics that seem likely to make an interest more likely to have creative potential or conversely relatively unlikely to have much potential.

Distinctiveness and conceptual richness are two characteristics of creative interests and conceptions of interests that appear to be sources of creative potential. The link from distinctiveness to creativity and originality of contributions is shown by many of the examples in the book. William Faulkner and Virginia Woolf each formed a highly distinctive creative interest which was a fundamental root of the originality of their work. The same is true of many of the other individuals famous for their contributions whose developments are discussed. Likewise, many of my interview subjects, such as Nick Halpern and Roger Knowles, formed distinctive interests that were the root of their creativity. Conceptual richness — often reflected in the richness of an individual's conception of interest — is also likely to be an important source of creativity. Faulkner and Mondrian both had conceptually rich interests. Robert Kaufman's conception of interest, with its layering of interrelationships, was crucial in guiding his learning, leading in turn to his main creative insights.

The failure to form an interest that is conceptually rich and distinctive, it follows, may reduce the chances of being highly creative and producing an original contribution. In fact a number of my interview subjects formed interests that were less distinctive — though still somewhat so — and this appears to have hampered them in their development. A number of the mathematicians I interviewed do not seem to have formed rich, distinctive interests in graduate school. For example, one described an interest in the mathematical theory of computation, with little further elaboration, and two others described their interest as abstract algebra, again with little elaboration. These individuals essentially relied on their advisors to provide them with the problems they worked on for their dissertations. They would presumably need to form richer, more distinctive interests going forward, as they gained more experience, in order to produce highly creative work.

It is not uncommon in fact for an individual to form a more conventional interest early in his development or when first entering a new field, then later to form a richer, more distinctive interest that becomes the base for his mature work. Charles Darwin's original interest in the variety of life-forms and collecting specimens was clearly not nearly so distinctive as his later interest in the geographic and temporal ranges of extent of species and similarities and differences in morphology and behavior between closely allied species and varieties. Thomas Edison's initial interest in telegraphy was focused on multiple telegraphy, a conventional focus for inventors at the time; but his interest branched out from there, to a more distinctive focus on peripheral devices for telegraphy, especially input, output, and writing. A number of my interview subjects also followed this pattern in their development, their interest becoming more distinctive over time, such as Jeffrey Shoulson.

Breadth, the other defining characteristic of creative interests, is also a factor in the creative potential of an interest. A pattern of development that may in some cases reduce the opportunities for making original, significant contributions is having too narrow a focus too soon, thus not forming a broader interest defining a rich domain filled with many potential avenues for development.

As described in Chapter 3, individuals' creative interests and conceptions of creative interests often form over time, becoming richer, in some cases coalescing out of fragments. These processes are important in coming to form a rich, mature interest that can be generative of creativity at a high level, leading to original contributions. Conversely, an interest that an individual does not develop into a mature, rich form may be less generative of creativity than it might be if it were so developed. Albert Einstein and Virginia Woolf are two examples of individuals who formed rich mature interests over time — interests that were then generative of creativity and creative contributions at the highest level of significance and influence. At a lower level of significance, Victoria Rayskin's interest gained in maturity over time, leading to more significant work in her field. In contrast with this pattern of development, defining an interest early on then not developing it further conceptually is more likely to be associated with less creativity and less original contributions. As an example, one of the literary scholars I interviewed had a somewhat fragmentary interest that never coalesced. This individual described his/her interest as "cognitive history" of a particular time period, and wished to tie this approach to literary analysis in some way, but seems never to have been able to do so in a compelling way, and, without a well-formed interest, generated a number of ideas that were interesting but were disconnected and did not cohere. It is an open question whether if this individual had been able to form a more coherent interest he/she would have been able to produce a more coherent contribution, but it is certainly possible.

Interests are sparked by and grow out of experiences and encounters, and a natural question is whether certain experiences and encounters are more conducive to forming interests having creative potential. Without having any clear sense for this I make two observations. Interests rooted in a puzzle or paradox, as Albert Einstein's was, or in negativity, may be relatively likely to lead to a significant contribution. Also, interests rooted in personal experiences are relatively likely to be distinctive, as for example Nick Halpern's was.

There are a number of basic kinds of creative interests, as described in Chapter 6, and it thus is a natural question whether certain kinds are more likely to have creative potential or pose special difficulties. As discussed previously relationship interests, based on the cases I have studied, seem to be associated with quite successful development. Holistic conceptions are distinguished by being rich and typically highly distinctive, thus a great potential source of creativity, as shown by the case of Virginia Woolf's brilliant creative development rooted in her conception. Further, it seems natural that they would spawn ambitious creative projects — as is illustrated in Tim Berners-Lee's development. Beyond these specific cases, I believe that in general for any interest the most important factors determining the likelihood that the interest has creative potential and can be fruitfully developed are its richness, distinctiveness, and breadth, as well as importance and openness.

I do not intend for this discussion of sources of lack of creative potential associated with certain characteristics of creative interests to be taken to mean that individuals should be pressured in their interests. Indeed my guiding principle and focus is an ideal world in which individuals are free to form their own creative interests. However, it is my view, fitting with my description in this book, that through coming to consciousness of and conceptualizing their interests individuals can contribute to their own process of creative development. This point of view suggests as practical guidance that individuals might be asked as an exercise to describe their creative interests, to think about them, define them, and articulate them. For through the very act of thinking about, thus conceptualizing, and articulating their interests, individuals may form richer, more integrated conceptions of them, pulling latent elements into consciousness and integrating them. This may well make their interests richer and more distinctive and more generative of creativity, including not only through being richer but also through being more accessible in consciousness, thus more helpful, for example in decision-making.

Individuals often form multiple interests, as described in Chapter 13. In such cases two further issues arise regarding an individual's likelihood of being able to be creative: (1) the likelihood he will make creative connections between his interests; and (2) his choice of which interest to pursue as a primary interest.

Phase II: Exploration and Creative Development of Creative Interests

I discuss in turn sources of creativity and difficulties in regards creative responses, making creative connections, having insights, and guidance.

The factors that are vital for the generation of creative responses fall into three categories: stimuli that trigger responses; attention and psychological factors that lead individuals to respond to specific stimuli; and cognitive processes through which individuals generate responses. For each factor or process there are characteristics that seem to be associated with a greater likelihood of generating a creative response, so that the lack of these characteristics may pose difficulties.

The kinds of stimuli and experiences that are most likely to spark a creative response depend critically on the nature of an individual's creative interest and the conceptual structure he has built up associated with it. But in general it seems to be the case that encountering a diverse set of stimuli is more likely, other things equal, to trigger a response. For Matisse, for example, spending summers in diverse locales, very different natural environments, was clearly important for him in sparking creative responses, culminating in his great blaze of creativity in the summer of 1905. While living a cloistered existence and having few encounters with stimuli may well be conducive to generating creativity through other pathways, for example imaginative thinking and contemplation, it is less likely to lead to the generation of a creative response. Diversity of encounters does not mean lack of focus; individuals may encounter diverse stimuli and still spend their time primarily focused on their own creative work, as seems to have been the case for Hans Krebs, who read widely even while engaged in experiments. Indeed some individuals may be especially capable of both seeking out diverse stimuli and being intensively engaged in creative work, which may be a factor in their success.

Among my interview subjects some stand out as encountering a wider range of stimuli, for example, reading widely in their field or attending conferences, or having a diverse set of interests, which would naturally lead them to encounter a diverse set of stimuli. Azad had multiple interests and read widely, and this was crucial in leading him to read the papers in *Science* that sparked his creative response recognizing the similarity between the interferon receptor and the CNTF receptor. For David Johnson reading widely in the domain of his interest and going to conferences and looking at posters was important in sparking his creative responses. Robert Kaufman arranged a learning sequence so as to read materials in a pair of distinct but, as he viewed it, connected fields, thus establishing conditions favorable to triggering creative responses relating them. In contrast, other subjects did not seem as good at arranging matters so as to encounter a diverse set of stimuli, for example did not describe reading widely in their field or related fields, attending conferences, or interacting with individuals outside their immediate circle.

As stated in Chapter 9 and shown with examples there, highly salient or unusual stimuli seem to be more likely to generate responses. Individuals who shy away from such experiences or encounters may thus reduce their chances of generating creative responses.

An individual must be sufficiently open to a stimulus in order to notice and respond to it. In part openness is a personality trait, as Frank Barron identified

514   in his work on creativity.[5] Among my interview subjects it is noteworthy that Susan, Ross, and Azad, three who generated creative responses, each formed an interest that was outside their main field or focus of research — suggesting openness to experience — that was crucial to their generation of a creative response. A person is more likely to be open to experiences and stimuli at some times than others; in particular when a person is focused on his own work he is likely to be less open. A stimulus that is sufficiently unusual or salient and has a creative connection with an individual's interest that he can readily perceive may draw his attention and spark a response even if he is relatively inwardly focused at the time. But there are undoubtedly stimuli on the border in terms of how relevant they seem, and an individual who encounters such a stimulus at a time when he is not open may not attend to it sufficiently to make the connection. It is possible an individual might be too open, thus expend his time and energy generating creative responses that turn out not to be fruitful or that he has difficulty choosing among as far as which to pursue — but I have encountered little evidence in support of this.

A number of factors seem likely to influence the possibility of an individual recognizing a connection between a stimulus and a creative interest, sparking a response. An individual will probably be more likely to recognize a connection between a stimulus and a creative interest if he has his interest in mind at the time he encounters the stimulus. Chris Callahan, for example, appears to have been actively thinking about his interest, hoping to define a project rooted in it, at the time of his creative response. A person will also be more likely to recognize or forge a connection with his interest if he has built up a conceptual structure in its domain, as for example Azad, Darwin, and Robert Kaufman had done — for this increases the chances that there will be elements in the conceptual structure associated with his interest that connect with a stimulus. Finally, an individual may be preconditioned to make a connection between his interest and a stimulus because he intuits a connection may exist — indeed this may be a factor leading him to arrange matters so as to encounter the stimulus. CERN sparked a creative response by Tim Berners-Lee because its organizational environment fit with his interest in nonhierarchical systems and connections, and it is certainly plausible that Tim was drawn to CERN, perhaps unconsciously, in part by an intuitive sense of this connection.

The third step in the generation of a creative response is the cognitive process of generating the response. A creative response is essentially a creative connection, as discussed in Chapter 9. Research in creativity suggests that certain

[5]Frank Barron, *Creativity and Personal Freedom* (Princeton, NJ: Van Nostrand, 1968).

individuals have greater propensity to make such connections. In particular divergent thinking is commonly viewed as generative of creative connections and associations, and tests designed to measure individuals' divergent thinking abilities indicate considerable variation across individuals. Individuals who do not generate creative responses may be blocked due to their lack of ability in divergent thinking. However, individuals who find it difficult to generate creative connections spontaneously may nevertheless be able to generate creative responses if they hold their interests in mind while having encounters or experiences or while thinking about them afterwards: in the juxtaposition their mind may generate a response. For responses generated through longer trains of thought other cognitive functions, notably memory and the ability to follow out a train of thought, are likely also to be important.

A final comment: Openness, seeking out diverse stimuli, and divergent thinking ability may well be linked. Further while these variables are likely to have a causal influence on diversity of stimuli encountered and the generation of creative responses, there may also be reciprocal pathways of influence, for example the experience of making a creative response to an unusual stimulus may in turn spur an individual to seek out more unusual stimuli. Thus identifying the effects of the three personality trait variables on generation of creative responses is challenging, and will require data collection of both personality factors and patterns of encounters and responses over time and a structural analysis.

The generation of creative connections and insights in interest domains rests on two fundamental steps: (1) building up a rich conceptual structure in an interest domain — creative expertise; and (2) making creative connections or having an insight, for example recognizing a pattern embedded in the conceptual structure.

There are four central factors that are crucial for an individual to build up a rich conceptual structure in an interest domain. A fundamental factor is the nature of the interest — does it define a rich domain containing a myriad of elements with rich potential interrelationships, interconnections, and patterns? A second factor is the individual's opportunity to encounter many elements and thus build up a rich structure in his interest domain. This fits with the benefit of diverse experiences and encounters for generating creative responses, but here the focus is specifically on encountering elements in the domain of one's interest. Darwin's voyage with the *Beagle* and overland journeys in South America gave him a remarkable opportunity to build up a knowledge base in his interest domain. Samuel Taylor Coleridge was an avid reader and through reading widely was able to build up rich conceptual structures in his domains of interest. As a salesman visiting many kitchens Ray Kroc had excellent opportunities to build up expertise in the domain of his interest. Luck may play a role in building up a rich conceptual structure — Darwin was clearly very fortunate to be traveling as naturalist on the *Beagle*, circumnavigating South America. Planning may also have a role, as is shown by the case of Robert Kaufman. A third factor is the motivation an individual has to build up a rich conceptual structure in the domain of his interest — to visit places, pay attention to what he encounters that fits with his interest, and internalize his observations and integrate them into the conceptual structure of his interest. Darwin, Coleridge, and Kroc all were clearly highly motivated to build up rich structures. Finally, a last factor is the individual's ability to store the many elements he internalizes in his mind. This requires a good memory — storage in an external medium such as a notebook or computer is possible, but only an imperfect substitute; as an example, Samuel Taylor Coleridge, in composing "The Rime of the Ancient Mariner," in all likelihood drew on constellations of elements in his mind, not bothering to look at notes to any great degree (as far as we know), which would most likely have disrupted his flow of composition.

For individuals who do not build up rich conceptual structures in their domains of interest any of these four factors may pose difficulty. If an individual pursues an interest that does not define a rich domain it will obviously be difficult for him to build up a rich conceptual structure associated with it. Assuming he pursues an interest that defines a rich domain, if he does not have the opportunity to encounter numerous elements in its domain he will not be able to build up a rich conceptual structure in its domain. One exception is domains of imaginative elements that a person can create somewhat independently of experience, for example color patterns for painting — but even here, as the example of Matisse visiting the south of France shows, external stimuli are likely to be important in building up a rich set of elements. Finally, assuming an individual forms an interest that defines a rich domain and does encounter many elements that fit in the domain, if he does not attend to these elements and internalize them, or is unable to store them in memory effectively, his ability to build up and maintain a rich conceptual structure will be limited. A number of the individuals I interviewed had interests in rich domains, but do not seem to have pursued learning a great deal about the elements in these domains to build up rich structures, which may have limited their creativity. A high degree of motivation, organization, and expenditure of time is required to build up a rich conceptual structure in an interest domain, and it seems that many individuals engaged in creative endeavors do not pursue doing so, which limits their ability to generate creativity through this pathway.

Making a creative connection is a classic form of creativity, as described in previous chapters. Making connections between elements embedded in a rich conceptual structure in a domain of interest is not necessarily identical to making creative connections at large, between elements not embedded in a common, integrative structure. Hence, while divergent thinking is undoubtedly relevant for making such connections, other factors, related to building up associations and structure among elements in a conceptual structure, are likely to be just as important. In particular, over time an individual integrates elements he has internalized in his interest domain into the conceptual structure associated with his interest — building up, through both conscious and unconscious processes, associations — and these in turn can be the basis for creative connections. Samuel Taylor Coleridge is a classic example of this, an individual who had great fluency in the generation of creative connections and combinations of elements in his interest domains, rooted in a rich web of associations. For individuals who have difficulty making creative connections in their interest domains, thinking about their interest domains, including calling to mind specific elements, may be helpful.

Recognizing a pattern or relationship among elements is a different process, one of having a creative insight. The ability to have such insights seems to be rooted in general intelligence, pattern recognition, and the ability to generalize. It also seems to require, at least in many cases, the ability to hold many elements in mind and sort through different possibilities.[6] Much of the literature in psychology on insight focuses on solving problems. In contrast, insights based in conceptual structures in interest domains are not in general triggered by problems, at least not well-defined ones, but rather emerge more spontaneously. They seem to occur naturally as individuals engage in thinking over elements they have encountered and internalized in the domain of their interest, sifting through elements, comparing and contrasting them. It seems indeed natural to engage in such processes given that a person is intrinsically interested in his creative interest, so that probing for such insights seems a natural part of creative development. Charles Darwin, Ian Baucom, and Cheryl Nixon all did this, generating insights rooted in conceptual structures they built up in their interest domains.

For individuals who appear to build up rich conceptual structures in the domain of an interest but do not generate creative insights based in this domain it may be because they have not actively searched for general patterns

[6]For discussion of creative insight from various perspectives see *The Nature of Insight*, ed. Robert J. Sternberg and Janet E. Davidson. For pattern recognition as a form of logical-mathematical intelligence see Howard Gardner, *Frames of Mind: The Theory of Multiple Intelligences* (New York: Basic Books, 1983), pp. 151–52.

or relationships, have not thought about their interests in ways conducive to generating such insights. Of course if a domain does not contain latent patterns and relationships then it is not possible to identify any; however, I believe that most sufficiently rich domains do contain interesting patterns and relationships to be discovered. Individuals who are not able to generate creative connections or insights in the domain of an interest may be able to increase their chances of doing so through altering their conception of their interest, for example so that it becomes conceptually richer, thus redefining the domain of their interest and the way they think about its elements.

Guidance during the second phase of creative development has three main components: decision-making about which directions to pursue and projects to undertake; project definition; and meta-level thinking. Here I describe in brief two main difficulties individuals seem to experience in these processes.

A crucial issue with regard to guidance is rooting one's activity and projects in one's interests and guiding principles and values, as for example Pierre Omidyar has done and Mondrian did. Failing to do this may lead one to undertake projects that do not fit as well with one's interests, principles, and values, creating a mental strain that may make it more difficult to engage wholeheartedly in such projects, leading to contributions with which one is not fully satisfied. Individuals must review their choices and paths in light of their interests, principles, and values, and be willing to abandon directions that are not naturally aligned with them. Likewise, in choosing among different projects it may be helpful if individuals have their conception of interest consciously in mind and use it to help them choose the project that will give them the best chance to develop their interest creatively. Hans Krebs seems to have been good at this kind of decision-making, pursuing projects that clearly fit with his interest.

A failing many individuals seem to have is not employing meta-level thinking. Meta-level thinking is very important for some individuals in helping them achieve success. For example, Andreas used such thinking effectively and it led him to an original, productive approach for studying visual system development in *Xenopus*. But many other individuals do not seem to engage in such thinking, thus do not have it available as a resource to help guide them in their development. They may not possess the natural inclination to engage in such thinking; or it simply may not occur to them to pause at certain junctures and engage in it. For individuals who do not engage spontaneously in meta-level thinking or use it effectively, describing this kind of thinking to them may help them learn to employ it.

In addition to difficulties in creativity generation, a further difficulty individuals may encounter in striving to develop their interests creatively is a failure to be supported in their endeavors. If a person's interest is unconventional with respect to her field of endeavor others, including supervisors and senior colleagues, may disapprove and discourage her pursuit of it, including through restricting resources. Several of the individuals I interviewed described meeting with resistance in pursuing their interests, which made it more difficult for them to pursue their interests and may have hampered the flourishing of their creativity.

A last source of difficulty is narrowing from an interest to define a specific project. This can be both emotionally and conceptually difficult, in needing to let go of many vague possibilities. As one example, Maria Carrig described having "the greatest difficulty" in moving from her interest to define a specific dissertation project. A number of other subjects I interviewed also described having difficulties in this transition.[7]

Phase III: Creative Projects

The most common sources of difficulty individuals seem to experience working on creative projects are (1) recognizing the need to make revisions, sometimes of a drastic nature; (2) being effective at revisioning; and (3) knowing when to abandon a project. Emotional factors seem important for all three processes and experience seems important in helping individuals become better at them.

For individuals who have difficulty recognizing the need for revisions and making revisions it is often because they are emotionally tied to their work, viewing it as a part of their creative self, thus as almost sacrilege to tamper with. Learning to be detached and overcome these feelings, thus more flexible in one's attitude towards one's work and able to recognize the need for revisions, is critical for many forms of creative work — as Faulkner said famously, you must learn to "kill your darlings." Experience undoubtedly is important in learning the value of revisioning to improve work, and others, especially those having experience and a good critical eye, can also be helpful in suggesting revisions.

It is also difficult emotionally to recognize and accept that it may be best to stop work on a project. Again experience is valuable in learning to recognize the signs that a project is likely not to turn out successfully, and others, especially those with experience, who are more detached from a project, can be helpful in making the decision to abandon a project. A number of the neuroscientists I interviewed told me their advisors helped them recognize that a project they were working on was unlikely to succeed and that they should abandon it and switch to a different project.

[7]Joy Amulya describes her subjects having difficulties with this as well, in her dissertation; see *Passionate Curiosity: A study of Research Process Experience in Doctoral Researchers*, chap. 3.

520   Finally, lack of motivation can be a major difficulty in project work — one must sometimes simply persevere on a project in order eventually to make a contribution.

FIXATION AND EXHAUSTION OF AN INTEREST; BENEFIT OF A SEQUENCE OF INTERESTS

Fixation is having a mindset and patterns of thinking that center around and cannot readily escape from a fixed set of elements, associations, and ideas.[8] With regard to creative interests, fixation is rooted in the conceptual structure that builds up in one's mind through exploring and learning about an interest and in the ideas one has and contributions one makes: these conceptual structures, ideas, and contributions naturally become the base for one's further thinking about one's interest. Thus fixation is a natural accompaniment to the development of an interest.

Exhaustion of the ability to develop an interest further creatively arises in two main ways: fixation, and, alternatively, as a result of there being, after a certain point, a paucity of new creative possibilities in a domain of interest. The paucity of possibilities may be tied to the specifics of one's conception of interest — a different conception, even slightly different, might open up further possibilities; this is thus a strategy for overcoming exhaustion. But it is often difficult to shift one's conception overly much due to fixation.

Dean Simonton has shown that many individuals in their creative careers follow what he describes as a typical life-cycle pattern: their level of contributions starts out low, rises to a peak in terms of both the quantity of contributions they are making and the impact of their contributions, then gradually falls off.[9] The description of creative development in this book, coupled with fixation and exhaustion, describes a process of development fitting this pattern. In the first phase of development an individual forms a creative interest; during this phase he is unlikely to make many contributions and they are unlikely to be of great significance. In the second phase he pursues his interest and develops it creatively. He may have a creative response at any time as he pursues his interest, thus may make contributions from early on in this phase. But the other

---

[8] Fixation has a long history of investigation and discussion in the psychology literature. An early discussion is given by Karl Duncker in *On Problem-Solving*, trans. by L.S. Lees (Washington, DC: American Psychological Association, 1945). See also Steven M. Smith, "Getting into and out of mental ruts: A theory of fixation, incubation, and insight," in *The Nature of Insight*, pp. 229–51.

[9] See Dean Simonton, "Creativity from a historiometric perspective," in *Handbook of Creativity*, ed. Robert J. Sternberg, pp. 116–33.

forms of creativity during this phase, rooted in exploration and the building up of conceptual structures in his domain of interest, tend to occur only after some period of time has gone by. Thus, typically a period beginning some time in the second phase of development is likely to be his period of peak creativity. Eventually he comes to a point at which he is unable to develop his interest much further: he has exhausted the creative potential his interest holds for him and his creativity declines.

The difficulties of fixation and exhaustion of an interest show the importance of forming and pursuing multiple interests and sequences of interests, for this is a good way of breaking fixations and generating creative potential anew in the wake of exhaustion. Unfortunately, there are a number of forces that often make it difficult for individuals to make such shifts. Having developed an interest creatively a person tends to identify himself with it and the body of work he has built up through pursuing it, which makes it difficult for him psychologically to shift to pursuing a new interest. Equally, if not more importantly, other people also tend to view him as identified with the work he has done in the past; as a result he may feel social pressure to continue to pursue the same interest. Thus others, even if they do not intend or desire to impede him from shifting and having the opportunity to make further creative contributions, may in fact do so. The more success an individual has achieved pursuing a given interest the more he and others will tend to identify him with this interest and the body of work he has done, making it that much more difficult for him to shift to pursue a new interest. Countering this, an individual who has been successful pursuing an interest may feel more confident about pursuing a new interest. However, having achieved success he may be less hungry for success than someone who has not achieved as much success, thus less motivated to pursue a new interest. An individual who has achieved more success is likely to have access to more resources due to his success, which may make it easier for him to pursue a new interest. With regard to having open time to pursue a new interest — crucial for the basic learning and exploration that occurs early in the pursuit of an interest — there are countervailing effects: success leads to more resources and support, but also tends to mean that more is asked of a person, for example reviewing the work of other people or giving lectures about previous work — which will tend to reduce free time.

There seem to be three main patterns of development tending to lead to an individual coming to be creative and make contributions over a longer time period: significant evolution in an interest, as for example was the case for Mondrian; forming and pursuing a sequence of interests, as John Maynard Keynes did; and forming an interest so rich as to be generative of a sequence of contributions over time, as was the case for Albert Einstein.

CREATIVE DEVELOPMENT AND LINKAGES OF CULTURAL TRANSMISSION: MODELING CULTURAL DEVELOPMENT

Linkages through which individuals are connected with their culture and the world around them are an integral part of the description of creative development in this book. These linkages are in fact fundamental channels of cultural transmission and influence. The description in this book is thus a basis for describing cultural transmission as it works through and is integral to creativity and the making of creative contributions. Below I describe the two main links in my description, recapitulating the description in preceding chapters. These links and channels of influence are fundamentally different from conventional descriptions of cultural transmission and its place in the creative process, as I also discuss, providing the basis for a better description. The most crucial difference is the link running through the formation of interests, which is distinctive to the description here.

Taking a further step, the description in this book provides a foundation for constructing models of cultural development. While a full development is clearly not possible here, I outline my thoughts concerning the construction of such models in the second part of the chapter.

CREATIVE INTERESTS AND CREATIVE DEVELOPMENT OF INTERESTS: CULTURAL LINKAGES AND INFLUENCES

The description of creative development in this book contains as an integral part a description of linkages through which individuals draw upon and are influenced by elements in their culture in their creative development.

These linkages of cultural transmission and influence are not what we may, on a superficial view, expect such linkages mainly to be. For this very reason, and because they are so distinctive, I believe they are among the most significant features of the description.

One of the distinctive features of these linkages is that there are two fundamental kinds of channels of transmission and influence, which occur during different phases of development, are different in nature, and have different roles. One is a channel of influence on the formation of creative interests; the other is channels of influence during exploration and creative development of interests. It is all too easy to imagine cultural influence as a single main kind of channel — the description here shows this not to be the case. I describe each channel in turn, focusing especially on the first.

Processes of formation of creative interests and conceptions of creative interests are described in Chapter 3. A theme of that description, illustrated by many examples in that chapter and other chapters, is that individuals form creative interests through their engagement with the world around them, out of and in response to elements they encounter and experiences they have. Out of the myriad of experiences an individual has and elements he encounters, a few critical ones spark his interest, triggering an initial interest, out of and around and based on which he then develops, often over a period of time, a fuller interest, and a conception of his interest.

While there are many different kinds of elements and experiences that influence individuals in the formation of their interests, the kinds having the greatest influence, far and away, are cultural — including social and political — elements and experiences — issues, events, activities, practices, traditions, and experiences, as discussed in Chapter 3. Myriad examples in this book illustrate this, including the more detailed case studies of Hannah Arendt, for whom political events were crucial factors in sparking her formation of her interests, and John Maynard Keynes, for whom economic events were crucial.

Of all the kinds of cultural elements and experiences that influence individuals in forming their interests, the kinds that most often spark interests are elements and experiences in their field of endeavor. These include specific works, and models, puzzles, hypotheses, data, events, facts, practices, techniques, and styles they encounter and learn about, as well as encounters with other people in their field. Myriad examples in the book illustrate the importance of these elements and experiences in sparking interests. Representative examples are: Teresa Nick's interest in simple learning and behavior circuits in *Aplysia*, sparked by her attending a talk by Eric Kandel; Hans Krebs's interest in intermediary metabolism, sparked by the vision presented by his professor Franz Knoop, from which he developed a more mature, focused interest while working in Warburg's lab learning the manometric techniques Warburg had developed; Liz Yoder's interest in glial signaling, sparked by the talk a classmate gave based on an article that had recently been published in *Science*; and Wilbur Wright's interest in flight, in particular his forming a serious interest in taking on the challenge of flight, sparked at least in part by his reading a book on animal locomotion and aeronautics.

Turning this basic description around, in particular viewing the formation of creative interests as a process of cultural transmission and influence, shows that the process of formation of creative interests is a central channel of cultural transmission. For in describing how an individual's interest is sparked by and grows out of particular cultural elements and experiences, we show, simultaneously, how these cultural elements and experiences serve as the basis for his creative interest — thus define a pathway of cultural transmission and influence. This is just the starting point, however, like the tip of an iceberg. For an individual's creative interest is at the core of his creative development. Cultural elements that spark and are the basis of a creative interest he forms influence his development in a deep and pervasive manner going forward, through many further pathways: influencing his patterns of exploration, his decisions about projects and paths to explore, creative responses he makes, conceptual structures he builds up in his mind that are generative of creative connections and insights he makes, and the projects he defines and pursues. In this sense our creative interests function like a conduit, carrying the influence of the cultural elements and experiences that spark them and form their basis forward through the course of our development, with their influence extending, albeit often indirectly, to contributions we make.

Because cultural elements and experiences that spark and form the basis for a creative interest an individual forms influence him so early in his development, and their influence is transmitted indirectly by and through his interest and his development of his interest, their true influence and importance is often not readily apparent in his subsequent ideas, projects, and contributions. Thus, ironically, the most pervasive, deepest cultural links in creative development lie buried. To discover these links we must examine individuals' creative developments not just in the periods when they make their most well-known and important contributions, but stretching far back in time, typically years, to identify the cultural sources of their interests. Many of the case studies described in this book show how hidden the true links are and how important it is to trace an individual's development back to discover these links. The fact that Susan's interest in the scene of dialogue grew out of an interest she formed in Kenya, sparked by her conversational experiences there, is not evident in her dissertation — Africa has no role, she focuses on dialogue in novels, not actual conversation, she does not focus on conversational norms, and she focuses on dialects, not distinct languages like English and Swahili. We would not know from David Johnson's dissertation, which is a characterization of a novel serotonin receptor, that his project grew out of an interest in acetylcholine nicotinic receptors, a completely different kind of receptor, and that his interest formed around his work in a lab in college in which the focus of study is neurotoxins. We would not know from Hans Krebs's project on the synthesis of urea or his publications documenting his findings that his work grew out of an initial interest in intermediary metabolism sparked by lectures he attended by Franz Knoop many years before. Nor would we know that he worked in Warburg's lab and that this experience and his training were crucial in his forming a conception of his creative interest that led directly to him working on the synthesis of urea — he might in fact have come to work on urea synthesis by many routes, through different possible creative interests, for example an interest in a class of medical diseases. Of course in some cases the links are more evident, for example, for William Faulkner, whose interest was rooted in his own childhood experiences, the rural South he grew up in and its cultural roots, which he set out to re-create apocryphally. But in many cases there are important links that are hidden. For Virginia Woolf, for example, though the loss of her mother and its traumatic effect on her family can be read directly in *To the Lighthouse*, her experiences traveling in southern Europe, seeing Perugino's fresco and classical sculpture fragments, and reading *Lettres à une inconnue*, which were specific sources of early fragmentary conceptions she formed of her interest, which coalesced in "The Mark on the Wall," are not evident. The importance of G.E. Moore's *Principia Ethica* for John Maynard Keynes's interest, which he formed more than a decade later, in the formation and role of expectations in economic systems is not at all evident in his economic writings.

The important general point is that cultural links, thus the process of cultural transmission, in the context of creative endeavors, are simply not what we would expect on a more superficial view of creativity, and that to identify them we must study the process of creative development extending over long time periods and focus specifically on individuals' creative interests and their process of formation. I do not believe this is the common view of cultural linkages and influences in creativity.

I make four additional comments. First, there are many different routes through which cultural elements and experiences spark the formation of creative interests. In most cases cultural elements or experiences spark an individual's interest through a positive direct route — exciting his interest, inspiring him to pursue an interest related to or based in the element or experience; this was the route of influence for many of the individuals in this book. In other cases, as described in Chapter 5, a cultural element or experience sparks an individual to form an interest through a negative route — the individual encounters a point of view, claim, or approach with which he disagrees and which he wants to challenge, perhaps through exploring an opposing approach. In yet other cases an individual is influenced by a cultural element or set of elements that act as a model for him — so that, for example, he forms an interest in pursuing a similar approach in regards a different topic.

Second, different kinds of cultural elements may influence and be incorporated in a given creative interest, creating rich patterns of cultural connectivity. As a specific, important case, broader cultural elements often influence individuals in their interests, especially in the way they conceive them, even in cases in which their interest centers on specific elements in their field. An example is Albert Einstein's interest. The initial seed of Einstein's interest was the paradox he hit upon concerning the propagation of electromagnetic radiation from a source moving relative to a reference frame; this initial interest was sparked by and focused on specific elements in the physics of moving bodies and electromagnetic radiation. But, as described in Chapter 10, it appears that over the next few years Einstein's conception of his interest and interest itself broadened, into an interest in conceptions of space, time, and motion in the Western philosophical tradition. Thus he formed his richer interest in the context of this cultural tradition — it was a vital second influence on his creative interest. A second example is Nick's interest in the prophetic voice in literature. Nick's interest was rooted in his experience growing up, his mother and father's new age beliefs, his father's book, and Nick's view of his father as viewing himself as a kind of prophet figure. As much as his interest thus has a personal basis, it is clear that the cultural notion of a "prophet," as it exists in the religious traditions of Western and Middle Eastern culture, was a crucial element around which Nick's interest crystallized, thus was central in his defining his interest. Not only was the concept of a prophet itself central, it also connected with other cultural elements that influenced and were elements in his interest, notably the tradition of literature written in the prophetic tone, including the Bible and Dante's *Divine Comedy*. Without this rich cultural tradition and the elements that are part of it, it's hard to imagine Nick forming the interest that he did.

Third, our interests and our conceptions of our interests are steeped in culture in a different way — they are encoded by concepts that are in general cultural constructs. Many of the interests — specifically descriptions of conceptions of interests — presented in this book are striking for the culturally based concepts they center on. Nick's interest in the prophetic voice is an example — as noted above the concept of a prophet is a rich cultural construct. Another is Virginia Woolf's conception of a world in which we see ourselves in our reflections in the eyes and attitudes of others and the world around us. The concept of the self that roots her conception, which she focuses on in "The Mark on the Wall" just before describing her conception, is a rich cultural construct. Also the concept of reflection of self is surely one that she learned culturally and has many cultural connotations and secondary meanings that enrich its meaning, for example the myth of Narcissus. A third example is Kelly's conception of the cell as being like a community, community being a rich cultural construct. Many of these examples, and many of the creative interests presented in the book, center on concepts that are linguistically based: language is quintessentially cultural, and thus this is a further cultural basis for our interests. However, other kinds of elements that are integral to conceptions of interests are also culturally based, such as images. Thus Alexander Calder's interest in the basic shapes of the universe set in space, which seems to have been primarily imagistic, and the images his interest centered on are culturally based, rooted in the image of the solar system as we have formed it in our culture — living in a much earlier time he would not have formed the same visual image defining his interest.[1]

Last, the examples I have used here and throughout the book show to what an extraordinary degree we draw upon the reservoir of concepts in our culture — sophisticated concepts like the self, community, prophet — in defining our interests. Our conceptions of our interests, and by association our interests as well, are thus based in this rich cultural reservoir. In turn this suggests that the richness of our conceptions, and by implication our interests, is linked to the richness of our cultural reservoir — richer cultures will spawn richer conceptions of interests, perhaps better able to be developed creatively in distinctive ways than simpler conceptions. This in turn suggests a link at the historical level between cultural development, enriching the cultural reservoir, and the creative process.

During the second phase of our development, when we are exploring our interests and seeking to develop them creatively, cultural elements we encounter and experiences we have are central. Cultural elements and experiences are crucial to two fundamental processes through which we generate creativity

[1]For work on the importance of imagery in scientific thought see Arthur I. Miller, *Imagery in Scientific Thought: Creating Twentieth Century Physics* (Boston: Birkhäuser, 1984). It is an open question to what degree our conceptions of our interests and interests are encoded linguistically versus with other forms of representation.

during this phase of development: creative responses, and the building up of rich conceptual structures in the domains of our interests which are generative of ideas and insights. These processes thus define two further channels of cultural transmission in creative development.

When we generate a creative response our response is sparked by an element we encounter or experience we have that has a connection with one of our creative interests. While all kinds of elements and experiences can and do trigger creative responses cultural elements and experiences are the primary kind that trigger responses in many fields. Examples of such responses presented in preceding chapters include Alexander Calder's creative response sparked by his visit to Mondrian's studio, Susan's insight about dialogue triggered by reading *Kim*, Tim Berners-Lee's idea to write Enquire sparked by the organizational environment at CERN, Chris Callahan's initial idea for a dissertation project triggered by a talk he attended, and John Maynard Keynes's idea about probability judgement sparked by reading G.E. Moore's *Principia Ethica*. In every case the precipitating element or event was cultural in nature. The pathway of influence here is more direct and evident than the pathway of influence of cultural elements acting through creative interests, and in many cases we recognize the influence of an element or experience that triggers a response that becomes the basis for a contribution in the contribution itself. Nonetheless, in many other cases a cultural element or experience that sparks a creative response is not readily apparent in contributions that develop out of the response — for example the initial triggering cultural experience is not readily apparent in Alexander Calder's mobiles.

Creative interests define rich domains, as described in Chapters 4 and 6 and illustrated by many examples in the book. In many cases these interest domains are cultural, meaning their basic elements are cultural elements. This is so, for example, for Cheryl's interest, the basic elements of which are literary works written by women in England in the eighteenth century, Ray Kroc's interest, the basic elements of which are commercial kitchens and kitchen organization and design, implements, and operations, and Robert Kaufman's interest, the basic elements of which are literary and critical works and theories. Even in the case of Samuel Taylor Coleridge's interest in voyages and phenomena in the far reaches and extreme climatic zones of the world the main elements in the domain of his interest, as he explored it, are descriptions other people have given of natural phenomena they encountered, thus culturally mediated descriptions. It is not true in every case of course that the elements in a domain are mainly cultural. A counterexample in this book is Charles Darwin's interest in ranges of extent of species and comparisons between closely allied species and varieties, though even in this case a number of crucial facts he learned were descriptions of ranges of extent of closely allied forms told to him by other people he encountered, thus culturally mediated. When an interest domain is cultural the conceptual structure an individual builds up in this domain of interest is thus also culturally based. In turn these structures are generative of creative connections and insights, as described in Chapter 10, thus defining another main pathway of cultural influence in creative development.

Though the cultural elements individuals internalize in the conceptual structures associated with their interests fit with their interests, nonetheless the particular elements they encounter and experiences they have are never fully determined by their interests, but rather reflect their environment, including cultural environment, in which they live and explore their interests. The information Charles Darwin gained, including for example what he was told about the ability of residents of the Galápagos Islands to distinguish which island a given tortoise came from, was not anything he could have foreseen at the time he formed his interest many months previously; thus his specific experiences, and the people he encountered, were a crucial factor determining the specific elements he internalized, which were then the basis for his insight that transmutation of species was consistent with the facts he had learned. Thus in building up rich structures in the domains of their interests the cultural environment in which individuals live and explore their interests is important in being the source of specific cultural elements they encounter and experiences they have that become part of the conceptual structures associated with their interests, which in turn are the bases of their creativity generation — thus this is another pathway of cultural influence. One last note: It is commonly the case that creative connections and insights rooted in conceptual structures in interest domains are based in a set of elements, for example a generalization is made based on a set of elements having similar characteristics — thus many cultural elements influence creativity generation in combination; this is quite different than for creative responses, for which a single element or experience may have a crucial impact.

A further channel of cultural transmission and influence that is important for creative work is cultural elements and experiences that influence individuals in their work on creative projects. For example, a specific element an individual encounters may spark a solution to or insight about a problem he has been struggling with on a project, as happened for Darwin reading Malthus's *Essay on Population*. As a second form of this channel, individuals often incorporate into projects elements they encounter at the time they are working on the project that resonate with it and fit with their overall conception for it. I do not discuss these channels of transmission in creative projects further here,

530   as I do not focus on the project phase of creative development in this book; these channels are also more widely studied and recognized than the channels of transmission and influence I focus on.

An important consequence of the fact that there are distinct channels of cultural transmission and influence operating during different phases of creative development is that cultural mixing naturally tends to occur: cultural elements and experiences that influence an individual in different phases of his development are linked in being incorporated in his development, and jointly influence his creative activity, thus generating new cultural connections and combinations. An example is Alexander Calder's mobiles. His mobiles are based in a linkage he forged between his conception of the universe and solar system, which was culturally based, and modern art, specifically as developed by Mondrian, with its simple rectangular shapes in solid, primary colors, also a cultural form. Another example is Albert Einstein's special theory of relativity. One way to view this theory as a cultural innovation is in the combining of Maxwell's equations and the problem of light propagation by a moving source, and the speed of light as a bound to absolute speed, with Hume's skeptical, constructive philosophy, questioning the definition of time and proposing that time measurement is in fact the essence of time. This same process goes on in the creative endeavors of many individuals and is reflected in their contributions. Takao Hensch, for example, has through his work brought techniques of molecular biology to bear in the study of the development of the visual cortex, thus forging a connection between these two areas.

In fact the scope for cultural mixing is even greater, for individuals follow rich, complex paths of development, as described in Chapters 14 and 15. Their interests evolve, they pursue multiple projects, and they form and pursue sequences of interests — and these rich paths make possible further rich cultural mixing. John Maynard Keynes and Hannah Arendt are two individuals whose creative developments involved cultural mixing across fields, and whose contributions reflect this, indeed are rooted in this cultural mixing. In the case of Hannah Arendt, her deep historical analysis of the basis of totalitarianism was distinctive to her, and clearly rooted in her earlier interest in the history of the "Jewish question" in Germany and France. In the case of Keynes his initial interest in probability judgement, rooted in his reaction to G.E. Moore's *Principia Ethica*, was an important conceptual basis for his approach to studying the economics of monetary policy and variables and the effects of expectations about monetary variables on other, "real" economic variables, notably investment and output. Bringing this approach into economics was a major innovation, and it is noteworthy that it was rooted in a cultural link with philosophy.

DIFFERENCES FROM STANDARD DESCRIPTIONS
OF CULTURAL TRANSMISSION

The channels of cultural transmission and cultural linkages described above are not described in standard models and descriptions of cultural transmission. The viewpoint of creative development presented in this book thus provides fresh insight into the process of cultural transmission. I discuss here a few key differences between the channels of cultural transmission in creative development described here and standard models and descriptions of cultural transmission, and, linked to these differences, failings of standard models and descriptions. I focus in particular on the crucial difference that standard descriptions of cultural transmission center on the transmission and influence of specific, typically discrete cultural elements, transmitted and exerting influence directly, not through the channels of creative development I describe in this book, especially the formation of creative interests.

Cultural transmission is often described as a kind of learning. There are two basic forms of learning that define channels of cultural transmission: imitation, and internalization of an element or complex of elements, for example a theory.[2] These two forms are not necessarily distinct but in fact linked. Imitation in general involves internalization, especially for acts repeated at a different time, and internalization has often an element of imitation, for example the inner voice repeating a statement a person is told. Vygotsky's brilliant description of stages of learning, moving from the use of external devices to full internalization, shows the importance of these linkages explicitly.[3] Inherited traditions and values, social practices, and attitudes all fit within these two forms, thus the general learning framework is quite encompassing and clearly a major conduit for cultural transmission. One specific model of learning through imitation and internalization as cultural transmission is the theory of memes. A meme is a cultural element, thus inherently a discrete element, passed on by imitation; in general the meme is internalized by the individual to whom it is passed on.[4] There is more to meme theory than this, and I discuss it further in the next

[2]Imitation is a form of social learning. See Albert Bandura, *Social Learning Theory* (Englewood Cliffs, NJ: Prentice-Hall, 1977).

[3]Lev Vygotsky, *Mind In Society: The Development of Higher Psychological Processes*, ed. Michael Cole, Vera John-Steiner, Sylvia Scribner, and Ellen Souberman (Cambridge, MA: Harvard University Press, 1978). There is a large literature on the practical conditions of learning.

[4]Memes were introduced by Richard Dawkins in *The Selfish Gene*. I draw in my discussion on Susan Blackmore, *The Meme Machine* (Oxford: Oxford University Press, 1999); and William Durham, *Coevolution: Genes, Culture, and Human Diversity* (Stanford, CA: Stanford University Press, 1991). Three other useful references are Charles J. Lumsden and Edward O. Wilson, *Genes, Mind, and Culture:*

section; the key feature for the discussion here is that the meme is defined, more or less precisely, as a basic unit of culture that is transmitted.

Learning through imitation and internalization, as typically described, has a few crucial features as a channel of cultural transmission that stand out as different from the channels of cultural transmission in creative development described above. The basic description of learning focuses on learning of discrete cultural elements, which are then directly repeated — imitated — or used in simple direct applications, typically, though not always, within the province of the context in which they are learned, for example, math symbols that are learned and then used in equations analogous to the equations in which they are learned. Linked to this, the basic learning process is generally described as the learning and internalization of discrete elements that stand alone, each learned independently and individually; learning can happen as the learning of clusters of elements — I discuss this below — but that is not the main thrust of the theory. Indeed for imitation to work as powerfully as claimed, for example in the theory of memes, the units transmitted must be relatively simple, it would seem, to enable them to be imitated fairly precisely and internalized as accurate copies. This in turn is a further feature of descriptions of learning, a focus on accurate imitation and the making of an accurate internal copy as crucial for learning; individual variation is allowed for, but within a framework focusing on the continuity of cultural elements created by accuracy of learning. These features are basic to many accounts of cultural transmission in anthropology, as well as models of the adoption of new techniques in economics.[5]

Cultural transmission in creative development, in particular in the formation of creative interests, has a different function and different features. This cultural transmission does not occur in the service of learning for the purposes of imitating or applying what is learned in a direct, straightforward, immediate way. Nor is the main issue one of forming accurate internal copies of

The Coevolutionary Process (Cambridge, MA: Harvard University Press, 1981), Luigi L. Cavalli-Sforza and Marcus W. Feldman, Cultural Transmission and Evolution: A Quantitative Approach (Princeton, NJ: Princeton University Press, 1981), and Robert Boyd and Peter J. Richerson, Culture and the Evolutionary Process (Chicago: University of Chicago Press, 1985).

[5] For a discussion of views of social learning in anthropology see J. Henrich and R. McElreath, "The evolution of cultural evolution," Evolutionary Anthropology 12 (2003): 123–35. An article discussing the importance of accuracy in imitation as a basis for cultural transmission is L. Castro and M.A. Toro, "The evolution of culture: From primate social learning to human culture," Proceedings of the National Academy of Sciences 101 (2004): 10235–40. The classic early work on adoption in economics is Z. Griliches, "Hybrid corn — An exploration in the economics of technological change," Econometrica 25 (1957): 501–22. There is a large literature since his article.

elements or being able to imitate specific actions accurately. In contrast to traditional learning models, cultural elements and experiences that contribute to sparking an individual's interest are not directly imitated, at least imitation is not integral to their function, nor does the individual necessarily form an internal copy of them with any great accuracy. These elements rather exert their influence through an indirect pathway, through sparking creative interests, thus triggering the formation of a conceptual structure, which may or may not directly incorporate them — for example, if they spark an interest through negativity they may not be directly a part of the interest, even though crucial in its formation. In cases in which elements that spark interests are internalized it is into the conceptual structure encoding the interest they spark — thus they are not internalized as isolated discrete elements, but rather as parts of a rich structure. What is striking about this pathway of cultural transmission, and dramatically different from the focus on cultural transmission via learning as direct imitation and application, is that the cultural elements and experiences being transmitted and exerting influence do so far less directly, through being a source and foundation for an individual in his creative development, not necessarily ever being directly expressed by him, certainly not imitated, but rather influencing, through indirect channels, his path of development and work and, ultimately, contributions. Related to this, there is a very substantial gap in time typically between the time of exposure to cultural elements or experiences that spark an individual to form an interest and the contributions that flow from the individual's development of his interest.

Cultural elements and experiences that influence an individual in his development during exploration and development of his interests also do so through a mode of transmission and influence different from the standard learning description, though the differences are less fundamental. These elements and experiences are linked with a creative interest the individual has, whether through sparking a creative response mediated by the interest or being internalized into the rich conceptual structure that encodes and is based in the interest. Thus they are intrinsically linked to a broader conceptual structure and not internalized as separate elements or imitated or used independently. This alternative view fits with the approach of situated learning, associated with John Dewey, Jean Lave, and others.[6] However, situated learning does not

---

[6]For John Dewey see, for example, *The Philosophy of John Dewey*, ed. John McDermott (Chicago: University of Chicago Press, 1981). For Jean Lave see *Everyday Cognition: Its Development in Social Context*, ed. Barbara Rogoff and Jean Lave (Cambridge, MA: Harvard University Press, 1984), and Jean Lave, *Cognition in Practice: Mind, Mathematics, and Culture in Everyday Life* (Cambridge: Cambridge University Press, 1988).

534 describe learning within a structured process of creative development, thus does not focus on the kind of links I describe.

Descriptions of learning do not in general embed learning in the context of creativity; indeed these two fields are surprisingly disjoint from one another. In the theory of coevolution set forth by William Durham, as well as the theory of memes as set forth, for example, by Susan Blackmore, creativity seems just an afterthought: creativity is mentioned only in a few places and no model of the creative process is set forth. In Blackmore's account creativity seems to be boiled down to "new combinations" produced seemingly at random in our minds out of memes we have been exposed to and internalized. Her view thus fits the view set forth by Donald Campbell: the creative process as the forming of random combinations of elements until a combination is hit upon that is potentially fruitful. Durham provides no model of the creative process but simply speaks of cultural innovation as occurring.[7] My description of creative development and the creative process is of course very different from Campbell's model: in my view the random combinations model, and the resulting description of cultural transmission, fails to describe the true channels of cultural transmission during creative development.

The differences between my description of cultural transmission and the description in learning models and the theory of memes is, not surprisingly, sharpest in the contrast with the simplest of these models and theories. Richer models based on memes, for example, seem to describe channels of cultural transmission and influence that more closely resemble the channels of cultural transmission and influence I describe in the context of creative development. Blackmore, following Dawkins and a substantial literature that has emerged, describes memes forming a complex and exerting their effects jointly, arguing this is a powerful force for cultural transmission of sets of memes and the formation of conceptual structures, such as a self-structure. Similarly, Durham emphasizes that a meme may be not just a small cultural unit like a word or gesture but a much larger unit like an ideology. These are important steps towards recognizing the formation of richer conceptual structures. Further, Blackmore's account seems consistent with the idea that cultural elements already internalized may be described as directing attention and organizing conceptual responses and integration of new elements — which comes closer

[7]The quote from Blackmore is from *The Meme Machine*, p. 15. She also discusses creativity on pp. 239–40. Her remarks there seem not to be a model of creativity as a process but rather an interpretation of creativity. Durham discusses innovation in *Coevolution: Genes, Culture, and Human Diversity* on p. 423 and incorporates it in a table listing important elements of his theory and a schematic diagram; he offers no true discussion or model of a process. For Campbell's article see Chapter 1, footnote 26.

to the kind of active directed process of creative development I describe. More recent articles seem to push even further in this direction.[8] There remains, however, a pair of fundamental differences. One is that cultural elements sparking interests need not ever be internalized, and certainly not precisely copied. The other is that cultural transmission during creative development need not involve a cultural element ever being imitated and thus propagated back into the world to replicate — rather, elements spark a process of development, including formation of an interest and conception of interest, leading ultimately to creative contributions which may show no evident trace of the original elements, as many examples in this book, some noted above, show.

Cultural transmission is discussed in many contexts beyond those mentioned here, for example in sociological analyses focusing on the transmission of cultural values, norms, and beliefs, and in the study of social and cultural channels of influence on learning and adoption, including network and group effects. These literatures are further from the thrust of my argument here, thus I do not discuss them.

The description of cultural transmission in creative development in this book fits most closely with descriptions of cultural linkages and the influence of cultural elements, events, and experiences in biographical studies of individuals engaged in creative endeavors — not surprisingly, given that the description in the book has been developed in part based on biographical studies and is naturally aligned with them. The main distinction is that I strive to present a general theoretical framework describing creative development — and thus describe, in a more general, systematic way than biographies do, main channels of cultural transmission and influence that operate during creative development. Notwithstanding this, the channels and modes of cultural transmission I describe certainly are described and can be recognized in biographies, autobiographies, and archival materials, including those I have drawn on in this book.

MODELING CULTURAL DEVELOPMENT

Cultural development is generated by and through the creativity of individuals. The ideas, inventions, modifications of existing practices and institutions, and cultural works that generate cultural change and development, across all fields, are generated by individuals, or in some cases groups of individuals working together. The great chains and webs of cultural works that create the cultures and civilizations of the world, spanning across so many fields, are comprised

[8] See, for example, S. Atran, "A cognitive theory of culture: An evolutionistic alternative to sociobiology and collective selection," *Homme* 166 (2003): 107–43.

of and grow out of the creative contributions made by many individuals, both those few who are famous for their contributions and countless others. Hence to describe cultural development in a satisfactory way we must root our description in a description of individual creativity, then describe how individuals in their creative activity and contributions fit together to generate large webs and chains of development. In general cultural development has not been described this way, as a process grounded in description of individual creativity. Further the logical necessity to approach its description in this way is not appreciated, at least not in the full depth of its significance.

The description of creative development in this book, including the channels of cultural transmission and influence described in the preceding section, provides a basis, or a part of one, for constructing a description of cultural development grounded in a description of individual creativity, specifically creative development. It is not my purpose here to try to construct a substantive description of cultural development of this kind — that is beyond the proper scope of this book; there are many difficulties to be confronted in developing such a description that require further investigation and both empirical and theoretical analysis. Rather I sketch an outline suggesting how the description in this book points towards the development of such a description.

To describe cultural development, the description of creative development must be extended in two fundamental ways. First, the creative developments of many individuals must be described. Ideally all individuals engaged in endeavors that may lead to contributions to their society should be included. Practically it is impossible to incorporate all individuals, even all those engaged in endeavors at any one time, let alone over time. Nonetheless, the ideal is important to hold in mind as an ultimate aim and guide in the development of models and approaches. Empirically, the best we can do is to sample many individuals working across a full spectrum of endeavors that may be the source of contributions influencing cultural development. A first step is to study a set of individuals, both working contemporaneously and over time, in a given field. In a small way, the sample of subjects interviewed about their creative development used as one main basis for the development of the description in this book fits this: in each of a few fields I identified all individuals who earned a graduate degree from a top program in a given year, thus a cohort of persons entering a field of creative endeavor at around the same time. This certainly is not a perfect design, especially in that individuals were drawn only from top programs. Further, to provide a relatively complete view of creativity activity in each field would require also interviewing and incorporating individuals who have earned degrees in preceding years and are actively engaged in work in the field.

Second, we must link individuals in their developments, thus building up a systems level description. This requires specifying channels through which individuals, through their activities and contributions, influence and are influenced by other individuals. One crucial set of channels is the channels of cultural transmission and influence described in the preceding section. Many different kinds of elements and experiences influence individuals in their developments through these channels. Of all these, especially important, in many fields, are the contributions and work of other people, especially predecessors and contemporaries in the field and in neighboring fields.

Focusing just on the influence of the works and contributions of individuals on other individuals in their field, especially those who enter the field after them, generates a core two-step recursive process of cultural development, having the following structure. Individuals, as they come of age and begin work in their chosen field of endeavor, are influenced in their formation of their creative interests by the work of others in their field, especially their immediate predecessors. In particular, they form their interests in reaction and response to specific works, practices, techniques, ideas, beliefs, and approaches in their field that catch their interest and spark a response in them. Sometimes the main influence is a direct, positive one, as, for example, Liz was excited by glial signaling and Hans Krebs by the vision of his teacher Franz Knoop. Sometimes it is negative, as, for example, Alexander Calder felt conventional art was too static to portray the modern world with all its movement and Celia Carlson fundamentally disagreed with the way William Carlos Williams's poetry was portrayed. In some cases an individual forms an interest intentionally seeking to define a new topic or approach different from that pursued by his or her predecessors, which was, for example, a motivating factor for Virginia Woolf in forming her conception of a literature of reflections. Thus there are different pathways of influence, as noted previously. Individuals entering a field at around the same time are in general less likely directly to influence one another in their interests; rather they tend to form their interests in parallel. Having formed creative interests, individuals set out to develop their interests creatively. In this process they are influenced by the work and ideas of others in their field as well as in neighboring fields. Works they encounter spark creative responses they make, as Mondrian's studio sparked a creative response Alexander Calder made, and the McDonald brothers' restaurant sparked a creative response Ray Kroc had. And they internalize elements, ideas, data, and insights of others into the conceptual structures they build up in their interest domains, which are in turn generative of creative insights they have and creative connections they make. Ultimately, through developing their interests creatively, individuals make their own creative contributions. The process then repeats. Their

538   contributions enter the pool of cultural elements, in particular in their field, to serve as the main cultural basis for the next cohort of individuals entering their field in their formation of their creative interests, and also to influence individuals in their field and neighboring fields in developing their interests creatively. Successive cohorts are thus linked together by a two-step process: (1) individuals' formation of their creative interests, influenced by the works of their predecessors; (2) individuals' creative development of their interests, influenced by work of their predecessors and contemporaries, leading to their creative contributions, which in turn enter the cultural pool forming the basis for the formation of interests for the next cohort, and influencing individuals in their creative development of their interests. The adage that individuals "build on the work of their predecessors" is thus given a more precise form, described as a richer process. I note that individuals do not merely take a fixed idea or problem from their predecessors and develop it directly, but rather form creative interests that are fashioned out of and in response to the work of their predecessors — as, for example, Albert Einstein fashioned a creative interest rooted in the paradox he identified based in Maxwell's theory, an interest having breadth and distinctive to him. Further, individuals are influenced by their predecessors at different stages in their development — in forming their interests, then, through different channels, in developing their interests creatively.

This core process is a template for describing the historical development of a field through tracing the creative developments of individuals who contribute to its development. To carry out such a description each individual's creative development is described, including influences on him in his development, leading to his creative contributions to the field. Then the development of the field is described through integrating all of these individual processes of development, showing the linkages among them. This approach stands in contrast to an approach focusing on describing each individual's contributions directly in terms of links with contributions made by other individuals, thus as a direct chain of development, without concern for tracing each individual's true path of development, an approach which is thus inherently flawed in that its linkages do not reflect the actual processes and channels of transmission of influence.

To describe cultural development more fully requires adding to the description of the channels of influence and transmission in the preceding section and the core two-step recursive process described above. I describe here three main additional sets of processes and channels. These lie beyond the theoretical description of creative development in this book, thus I only sketch them.

An important set of processes are processes of evaluation, and an important set of channels are those through which creative works, and evaluations of works, are disseminated.[9] Evaluation is important in determining what works are viewed as especially significant in a field at a given time. Works judged important are incorporated in standard accounts of the field, for example in teaching, and in lists of important contributions in the field. In turn these standard accounts and lists have a powerful effect on what new individuals entering a field are exposed to and perceive in terms of important contributions and current opportunities. Evaluations are also likely to influence individuals directly in their formation of their interests, often in an immediate positive way, sometimes in a negative way. Dissemination of creative works is critical in governing what works individuals in the field or entering it are exposed to and thus have the opportunity to learn about — thus which works are likely to influence them in their creative development, especially in their formation of interests. For example, Liz learned about glial signaling because a paper about it was thought interesting enough by *Science* editors to be published in that journal, and because one of her classmates, seeing it and finding it interesting, made a class presentation about it. Had Liz not been exposed to the research in class she might very well not have come to focus on it, and in particular not at that time, when she was perhaps especially open to forming a new creative interest.

I note that socially based processes of evaluation and channels of dissemination of works and evaluations of works by no means control absolutely access to the works of others and opinion and interest formation. An individual forms his own opinion of each work he encounters, and his opinion certainly may go against conventional received opinion. Further, individuals may and do seek out obscure works which in some cases influence them in their development. Both evaluation and dissemination are susceptible to control by individuals who have seniority and stature in a field, and by organizations and institutions — but they are not entirely thus controlled, as both also occur more informally and through social networks. Indeed informal evaluation is often important. Notwithstanding both the independence individuals have and the role of more informal social processes, formal processes and channels of evaluation and dissemination are evidently important. For example, reviewing the stories of development of the literary scholars and neuroscientists presented in this book it is clear that many formed interests based in works they were exposed to in class, thus selected by their teacher in the class.

Another important set of processes are resource allocation decisions. Resources are crucial in enabling individuals to pursue their creative interests

[9] For a related discussion see David Henry Feldman, Mihaly Csikszentmihalyi, and Howard Gardner, *Changing the World: A Framework for the Study of Creativity*.

540   and projects. For the most part individuals form their interests without much concern for future access to resources, as shown by many examples in this book. Resources come to the fore during later phases of development, when individuals are exploring their interests and seeking ways to develop them creatively, and engaging in projects. Individuals may be and undoubtedly are influenced by available resources in deciding which projects to pursue and choosing whether or not to pursue an interest further. Gatekeepers such as senior scientists or wealthy patrons who control resources thus can have an important influence on the creative activities of individuals, especially during later phases of their development. Inevitably, those making resource allocation decisions view some interests and projects as more likely to be fruitful and worthy of support than others, influencing work in the field. Their views in turn are influenced by patterns of dissemination and evaluations made by other individuals, as part of the larger network of evaluation in a field, indeed stretching beyond the field to individuals in society at large.

Resources are in fact emphasized in both economic and sociologic models of innovation and field development. The standard economic approach to modeling invention is a model in which increased resources allocated to an inventive activity such as research increases the probability of a valuable discovery, innovation, or invention being made. Sociological accounts of processes of development of fields focus on social processes involved in resource access and allocation, joined in many cases with an analysis of status and power. For example, David Hull describes such processes, together with a host of other processes that influence field development, in *Science as a Process*.[10] For the most part models and descriptions in sociology and economics do not include any substantive model or description of the creative process through which individuals who are given resources to engage in a creative activity go about engaging in their work and generate ideas and innovations. To the extent the creative process is considered at all, it is typically viewed or modeled as making creative connections, thus a short-term process — for example, more resources enable an individual or research group to screen through more combinations, or seek out more elements among which to make combinations. Thus creative development as described in this book is left out of account. In turn this suggests that combining the description of creative development in this book with models and descriptions of resource allocation from these literatures may be fruitful as an approach for developing better, richer models and descriptions of cultural and economic development.

[10] David Hull, *Science as a Process: An Evolutionary Account of the Social and Conceptual Development of Science* (Chicago: University of Chicago Press, 1988).

A third set of processes through which individuals influence one another in their creative activities are social interactions. Two main kinds of social interactions are important in creative development. One is support individuals give one another. Support takes various forms, including offering a willing ear to listen to another person voice his ideas, interests, puzzles, and difficulties, providing feedback and advice, and providing emotional support. Howard Gardner suggests that many highly successful creative persons gain emotional and intellectual support from a close friendship or mentor.[11] A number of my interview subjects described student support groups they participated in that were helpful to them in their work, including Maria and Tina. The other is collaborative creative activity, clearly important in many fields, for example jazz and popular music, the sciences, and business.[12] In the description in this book individuals form their creative interests independently. Collaboration may and often does, however, arise in the next stage: two individuals generate a collaborative project in the region of overlap of their interests. An example is Roger's discussion with his advisor, sparking the idea for the initial project Roger pursued in his doctoral research; a second example is Watson and Crick's collaboration.

A full description of cultural development must include additional processes, incorporating the effects of broader conditions of life, including social, political, and economic factors that influence individuals in their creative developments. Silvano Arieti lists a series of social–cultural conditions that are likely to foster individual creativity in *Creativity: The Magic Synthesis*, including tolerance for divergent views, openness, freedom after a period of oppression, and incentives for innovation. In *Wittgenstein's Vienna Revisited* Allan Janik speculates about the characteristics that made turn-of-the-century Vienna a center of creativity.[13] Notwithstanding these two examples, we know very little about the relationship between underlying social, economic, and political conditions and creativity — far more research is needed on this topic. Lastly, the development of new forms of communication and ways to access and disseminate information may be expected to alter the nature of creative development.[14]

[11] Howard Gardner, *Creating Minds*, especially Chapter 1.

[12] See Alfonso Montuori and Ronald Purser, Introduction, in *Social Creativity*; Stephen Nachmanovitch, *Free Play: Improvisation in Life and Art* (Los Angeles: Jeremy P. Tarcher, 1991). See also the references in Chapter 1, footnote 30.

[13] Allan Janik, *Wittgenstein's Vienna Revisited* (New Brunswick, NJ: Transaction Publishers, 2001), Introduction.

[14] A classic work showing the importance of a new technology on culture and creative work, cited in Chapter 2, footnote 14, is Elizabeth Eisenstein, *The Printing Press as an Agent of Change*.

542   One further cultural process should be incorporated in descriptions of individual creativity and cultural development. As a cultural develops, its conceptual reservoir — the pool of elements, works, ideas, images, and recorded events — grows richer. In turn, individuals thus have available a richer conceptual reservoir to draw upon in forming and conceptualizing their interests — richer language, for example, will likely enable them to form richer conceptions of their interests — and in building up conceptual structures in the domains of their interests. This enhanced richness can in turn be expected to influence them in their creative development and thus influence their creative contributions. Thus there is a nonstationarity that ideally will be represented in models and descriptions of cultural development: creative development itself is described as a process that evolves over time as culture becomes richer.

18

EPILOGUE: MODELING INDIVIDUALS
IN SOCIAL SYSTEMS

My aim in this book is to contribute towards the development of a theoretical framework describing the creative development of different individuals within a common framework — capturing and depicting in a common framework the distinctiveness of each individual in his development, leading to his distinctive contributions. To achieve this is to forge a methodology that integrates two approaches somewhat at odds with one another.

One is the description of an individual describing his life and work in its own terms, without much theoretical structure being placed on the description or used to organize it. This approach is pursued most purely and most richly developed in biographical studies. Biographies are indispensable as a source of details about individuals' lives; I have drawn upon many fine biographies in this book. A biography depicts the distinctiveness of the individual who is studied, tracing his or her life and development carefully and with subtlety of interpretation, providing insight into his or her development, including, in the best biographies, description of his or her conceptual world. But there is a failing in the biographical literature, at least from the perspective of developing a more general theoretical framework of description of creative development. Each biography makes use of its own conceptual terms and elements to describe the life and development and work of the individual who is its subject. There is thus little in the way of a common framework for describing individuals in their developments. Further, the terms used to construct descriptions and make interpretations are loosely defined, if indeed they are defined at all. For example, "interest" is used often, as noted in Chapter 2, but never defined,

544   its meaning varying considerably, with no attempt to define it as a theoretical construct.

The failing of not having a general theoretical framework for describing creative development is also apparent in studies in the history of thought, in which many individuals are juxtaposed, their ideas and works, and in some cases their developments, described individually, compared and interrelated. Such works are often outstanding in the carefulness of their discussion of ideas and works, but are far looser — and do not employ sharp theoretical definitions and structures — in describing the creative developments of the individuals whose ideas and works they focus on, falling back on loose biographical sketches.

The other approach is the construction of abstract models describing individuals in social and cultural systems. Such models are elegant and provide analytic power for describing system dynamics, comparative statics, and generating sharp predictions about relationships among variables in a model. They fit with the dominant approach and mode of analysis in the social sciences, and are widely used, and increasingly so, for modeling cultural development. There is, however, in the models that have been developed following this approach a fundamental failure to describe and model the distinctiveness of each individual, at least in a deep way. No real attempt is made to incorporate a description of the rich conceptual worlds we form in a structured, theoretical way. In the models as they have been developed, across a wide array of fields and applications, the distinctiveness of a person is collapsed to a few discrete traits or continuous variables, such that for example each individual occupies a location in a two-dimensional or somewhat higher dimensional space. In this world distinctiveness means only relative distance from someone else, which translates, through some specified functional relationship, to a slightly different behavior profile. The distinctiveness of individuals in the sense of possessing distinctive conceptual worlds, thus wholly different conceptual structures, is thus not depicted. The failing is a glaring one seen in light of the description of creative development in this book: no attempt is made to describe creative interests individuals form, thus conceptual domains they define for themselves, or the rich conceptual structures they build up in the domains of their interests, which are in turn generative of their creativity and contributions to society. Thus a vital component of individual life and development, including cultural links of transmission that run through the formation of interests, and the rich conceptual structures that are the bases of ideas and insights leading to social and cultural contributions, is not described and has no place.

The theoretical framework I envision, for which the description in this book is a first step, combines the strengths of these two approaches. It is, as I envision it, a tight modeling approach, with structural models based, for

example, in knowledge representation formalism, building on the description 545
in this book and going beyond it, in which individuals' conceptual worlds and
creative developments are described in a way that represents in an analytically
rigorous fashion the distinctiveness of each individual's conceptual world and
path of development, within a unified conceptual framework encompassing
all individuals.

This framework will represent in an integrated way both the rich inner
worlds of individuals, with their rich conceptual structures, and also the world
these individuals inhabit — their cultural world and environment, with myriads
of elements, as well as events and experiences that may be important for their
development. Crucially, it will contain processes and structures that enable
these two domains to be linked dynamically, for example in the formation of
creative interests based in cultural elements and experiences; I have remarked
on this in the concluding section of Chapter 9.

The value this framework will possess is in exhibiting clearly, in analytic
form, a social-cultural world containing many individuals in which each individual is distinctive, possesses distinctive creative interests and a distinctive
conceptual world centering on the conceptual structures that build up in his
mind associated with his interests, and follows a unique path of development,
thereby coming to make distinctive creative contributions. Models developed
based in this framework should be able to be used to calibrate the degree of
distinctiveness and breadth of interests, and to analyze and evaluate the overlap
among interests formed by different individuals, including the full constellation of interests formed by a cohort of individuals in a field. They should also
be able to be used to analyze interests in relation to the cultural environment
in which they are formed — for example, the connection between the richness of a culture and the richness, distinctiveness, and breadth of interests
individuals form. Models developed based in this framework will be useful for
investigating the nature of paths of creative development, identifying interesting patterns and relationships. They will finally be a basis for exploring cultural
development, as it is rooted in and emerges out of the creative activity of many
individuals, thus providing a theory to counter existing theories, such as theories of cultural development based on memes, which can be used to explore
the effects of social-cultural conditions on creative and cultural development.
The framework also has clear limits we must recognize. In particular, it will
not and is not designed to generate specific predictions about creative ideas
individuals will have, discoveries they will make, and specific contributions
they will make.

Developed as I believe it can be, this framework will provide a new vision of
individuals engaged in creative endeavors within social and cultural systems,

providing the foundation for a deeper understanding of cultural development described as rooted in human creativity and the process of creative development.

A further, profound challenge lies ahead of us: to redress the failing in the social sciences to depict individuals in their distinctiveness, having rich conceptual worlds; and to present an image of society as we envision our society ideally to be — a society in which each individual flourishes in his or her own distinctiveness and makes his or her own distinctive contributions. The discussion above — indeed the description in this book as a whole — points towards a methodological approach for doing this, a mode of analysis that reflects and is in greater harmony with our ideological convictions and our image of our society.

The failure in the social sciences, and the behavioral sciences generally also, to depict individuals in their distinctiveness and the richness of their conceptual worlds, is rooted in an imbalance — an overemphasis on formal modeling with ease and power of analysis at the expense of richer modeling of individuals. In economics as it has developed and is presently constituted there has been an overwhelming drive to develop formal models in the service of generating sharp predictions. There are different reasons for this, but one important one has been the desire to generate predictions for policy formulation. There has been little interest in depicting individuals in a way that is truer to the complexity of our conceptual world, to strive to develop sound descriptions of this world.[1] In sociology a tradition of focus on social conditions has been paramount and description of individuals either follows economics in being quite abstract or else is less well defined and left in the background. In reporting experiments psychologists focus on the "main effect" showing commonalities in response across individuals, as a way to reveal general, common features of processing and attributes; their experimental results contain individual variation, but that is left in the background, treated as noise, not a focus of analysis. This approach is valuable and important — but individuals as distinctive and as having rich, distinctive conceptual worlds, are not the focus. There are fields in psychology in which individuals are more a focus, for example the field of individual differences. But even in these fields the dominant approach is to search for and identify commonalities, for example, a set of attributes that characterize individuals in their differences; each individual is then placed in the space

---

[1]The recent movement towards behavioral economics, while it challenges the prevailing approach in terms of assumptions about rationality and processing, does not address this issue of the failure to describe individuals in their distinctiveness and richness of conceptual worlds. Indeed if anything it makes this failing even more glaring.

defined by these attributes, as described in the preceding section, and the higher order distinctiveness of individuals is left out of account. In all of these fields there are other traditions that survive, notably a focus on individual case studies — thus akin to the biographical approach.[2] But these are marginalized and do not have a tradition of formal modeling enabling the same kind of rigorous analysis. Thus the statements here, while perhaps too sweeping owing to the need for brevity, summarize the general state of affairs.

A principle aim I have in this book is to show that to describe creativity it is necessary to describe the rich conceptual structures individuals form in their minds, encoding and centering around their creative interests, which form the core of their creative development and are generative of their creativity. In fact there are many other human endeavors and activities in which it is necessary to depict the conceptual worlds of individuals and the distinctiveness of their conceptual worlds, built up through processes of development, to describe these endeavors and activities in a sound way. Examples include management, strategy, entrepreneurship, leadership, political action, complex judgement and decision-making in many spheres, and many forms of expert activity. The failing to describe the conceptual worlds of individuals, and the distinctiveness of their conceptual worlds, is a global one that applies to many areas of activity and life described in these fields and is relevant to them.

This failing has a second vital aspect. It is not only a failure to describe a defining feature of human life and activity, but also a failing of a social kind — a failure to meet the need and desire we have, that every society has, for our abstract theoretical descriptions of our culture and society to be in dialogue with our fundamental values, thus to reflect them back to us. A central value we hold in America, held in Western culture generally, and today in even a wider array of cultures, is individualism, the belief that individuals are the root and source of activity, ideas, discoveries, innovations, and change. A vital component of our belief in individualism is the belief that every individual can make a difference, can pursue his or her own, self-defined path of development, a unique path,

---

[2]Influences on me in this tradition include: Robert N. Bellah, William M. Sullivan, Ann Swidler, and Steven M. Tipton, *Habits of the Heart: Individualism and Commitment in American Life* (Berkeley: University of California Press, 1985); Studs Terkel's books, for example, *American Dreams: Lost and Found* (New York: Ballantine Books, 1980); and Gananath Obeyesekere, *Medusa's Hair: An Essay on Personal Symbols and Religious Experience* (Chicago: University of Chicago Press, 1981). Friedrich A. Hayek is one of the few economic thinkers I am aware of in the twentieth century who sought to define a different methodological approach apart from formal models with overly simplistic agents. In his great work, *The Constitution of Liberty*, he describes the context of a liberal society — rules and institutions — within which each individual may freely form and pursue his own individual plans.

548 make his or her own way in the world, and make his or her own distinctive contribution to our society. In failing to depict individuals as distinctive, to grapple with finding a way to depict the rich, distinctive conceptual worlds of individuals and the paths individuals follow — paths of their own design, following their distinctive interests — building up rich conceptual structures that are the root of and generative of their distinctive contributions to society, the social sciences fail to reflect — or, more profoundly, to be in dialogue with — individualism. This failing poses dangers, in driving a wedge between the practices and representations in these fields and our self-understanding and vision of our society, thus weakening our sense and understanding of this vision and core values we hold.

The challenge before us is to build a new framework of description, building on the conceptual advances that have been made in the construction of formal models: To construct models of social systems in which each individual in the model is distinctive, follows a unique path of life, building up rich conceptual structures in his mind, thus possesses a rich conceptual world, and makes distinctive, unique contributions, which in turn enter into and influence society and culture.

Appendix

INDIVIDUALS INTERVIEWED ABOUT
THEIR CREATIVE DEVELOPMENT
NAMES AND SOURCE MATERIALS

All interviews were transcribed with exception of those marked with an*, for which notes were taken. Only source materials that are the basis for or relevant to the description in the text are listed.

INDIVIDUALS WITH DOCTORATES IN ENGLISH AND AMERICAN LANGUAGE AND LITERATURE

All individuals in this group received their degree in 1995 and that is the date of their dissertation. Interviewed in Fall 1996–Winter 1997.

Ian Baucom.
> *Locating Identity: Topographies of Englishness and Empire*. Diss., Yale University.
> "Dreams of Home: Migrancy and Habitation in the Writing of English Culture," Diss. Prospectus, 1993.
> *Maps and Misreadings: England Writing Africa*. Master's Thesis, African Studies Council, Yale Center for International & Area Studies, 1991.
> *Out of Place: Englishness, Empire, and the Locations of Identity*. Princeton, NJ: Princeton University Press, 1999.

Kristina ("Tina") Brooks.
> *Transgressing the Boundaries of Identity: Racial Pornography, Fallen Women, and Ethnic Others in the Works of Pauline Hopkins, Alice Dunbar-Nelson, and Edith Wharton*." Diss., UC-Berkeley.
> "Developing a 'Woman's Place' in Turn-of-the-Century America: Comparative Readings of Pauline Hopkins, Alice Dunbar-Nelson and Edith Wharton," Diss. Prospectus, 1991.

550   "Mammies, bucks, and wenches: Minstrelsy, racial pornography, and racial politics in Pauline Hopkins's *Hagar's Daughter*," in *The Unruly Voice: Redis-
covering Pauline Elizabeth Hopkins*, ed. John Cullen Gruesser, Urbana, IL:
University of Illinois Press, 1996, pp. 119–57.

Celia Carlson.
The Innocent Mind of William Carlos Williams. Diss., UC-Berkeley.

Maria Carrig.
Skepticism and the Rhetoric of Renaissance Comedy. Diss., Yale University.
"Skepticism and Discovery in Renaissance Comedy," Diss. Prospectus, 1991.

Henry Chen.
The Non-European World in the Works of James Joyce. Diss., UC-Berkeley.
"Westerneyesing Those Poor Sunuppers: The World Beyond Ireland and Europe
in *Finnegans Wake*," Diss. Prospectus, 1986.
A New Map for the Atlas of Literary Geography: V.S. Naipaul's Trinidad Novels.
Submitted for Honors in English, Wesleyan University, 1981.

Gregg Crane.
*Fiat Justitia: American Literature and the Jurisprudence of Rights, Power, and
Community*. Diss., UC-Berkeley.
Race, Citizenship, and Law in American Literature. Cambridge: Cambridge
University Press, 2002.

Mara Dale.
Something Else: Women and Allegory. Diss., Harvard University.
"Allegory and Narratives of Female Desire," Diss. Prospectus, 1989.

Teresa Faherty.
Shakespeare's Poetics of Ravishment. Diss., UC-Berkeley.

Susan Ferguson.
Speaking Volumes: The Scene of Dialogue in the Novel. Diss., Harvard University.
"Speaking Volumes: The Novel in a World of Standard English," Diss. Prospec-
tus, 1993.
*Themes of Empowerment: Language, Time and Place in the Novels of Four
Afro-American Women*. Honors Thesis, Dep. of English, Dartmouth College,
1987.

Karen Hadley.
'Timely Interference' in Wordsworthian Autobiography. Diss., UC-Berkeley.
"Wordsworthian Temporality in *The Prelude*," Diss. Prospectus, early draft, not
dated.
"'Timely Interference' in Wordsworthian Autobiography," Diss. Prospectus, draft
IVa, 1992.

David Nicholas ("Nick") Halpern.
> *The Prophetic and the Domestic Voice in Contemporary American Poetry.* Diss., Harvard University.
> Diss. Prospectus (not titled), 1993.
> *The Prophet's Speech Impediments: An Introduction to the Poetry of Allen Grossman.* Master of Arts Thesis, NYU, 1988.
> *Everyday and Prophetic: The Poetry of Lowell, Ammons, Merrill, and Rich.* Madison, WI: University of Wisconsin Press, 2003.
> Follow-up interview*, 2005.

Ross Hamilton.
> *"And Nothing Pleaseth But Rare Accidents": A Literary History of Accident.* Diss., Yale University.
> "The Figure of Narcissus," Diss. Prospectus, 1989.

David Hirsch.
> *Brotherly Love: Revolutionary Fraternity and the Politics of Identification.* Diss., Harvard University.
> "Brotherly Love: Fraternity and the Rhetoric of Revolution," Diss. Prospectus, Nov. 1991.
> Oral Exam Document, April 1991.
> "Blood and Brotherhood: Nineteenth- and Twentieth-Century Fictions of Fraternity," manuscript (not dated; likely 1995).

Robert Kaufman.
> *Negative Romanticism: Keats, Shelley, and the Modern Aesthetic.* Diss., UC-Berkeley.
> "Negative Romanticism: Keats, Shelley, and the Modern Aesthetic," Diss. Prospectus, 1992.
> "Negatively capable dialectics: Keats, Vendler, Adorno, and the theory of the avant-garde," *Critical Inquiry* 27 (2001): 354–84.
> "Red Kant, or the persistence of the third critique in Adorno and Jameson," *Critical Inquiry* 26 (2000): 682–724.
> "The sublime as super-genre of the modern, or, Hamlet in revolution: Caleb Williams and his problems," *Studies in Romanticism* 36 (1997): 541–74.
> "Legislators of the post-everything world: Shelley's defence of Adorno," *English Literary History* 63 (1996): 707–33.

Karen Kebarle.
> *Muse and Audience in the Work of Willa Cather.* Diss., UC-Berkeley.
> Email correspondence, 1997.
> Follow-up contact, 2004.

Jennifer Nelson.
> *Fantasies of Deafness, Silence, and Speech.* Diss., UC-Berkeley.
> *Enter into the Dance: De Musset's Pierre et Camille.* Master's Thesis, Dep. of English, UC-Berkeley, 1990.

552   Cheryl Nixon.
        Fictional Families: Guardianship in Eighteenth-Century Law and Literature.
            Diss., Harvard University.
        "Teaching through Titillation: The Female Ward/Male Guardian Relationship
            in the Eighteenth-Century Popular Novel," Diss. Prospectus, November 1991.
        Oral Exam Document, March 1991.
        Interview* with Professor James Engell, Havard Dep. of English, 2004; taught
            class on eighteenth-century literature Cheryl took and supervised her inde-
            pendent study on eighteenth-century women writers.

    Anne Mette Pedersen.
        The Aesthetics of Allegory in George Santayana. Diss., Yale University.
        "The Authority of Things: An Analysis of George Santayana's Aesthetics and
            Literary Criticism," Diss. Prospectus, 1991.
        Email correspondence, 1996.

    Stephen Shapiro.
        Dread and Curious Alteration: Republican Panic and Personal Intimation in Early
            American Fiction. Diss., Yale University.
        "'Making It Work': Authorship and Hegemony in the American Cultural Econ-
            omy," Diss. Prospectus, 1989.
        Email correspondence, 1996.

    Jeffrey Shoulson.
        Interpretation in the Making: The Reading and Creation of Genesis in the Rabbis
            and in Milton. Diss., Yale University.
        "Interpretive Creativity and Creative Interpretation: Midrashic Texts, Literary
            Critics, and John Milton," Diss. Prospectus, 1991.
        "Who Himself Beginning Knew?" Creative Appropriation in John Milton's Account
            of Genesis: Books VII and VIII of Paradise Lost. Senior Thesis, Dep. of English,
            Princeton University, 1988.
        Milton and the Rabbis: Hebraism, Hellenism, and Christianity. New York:
            Columbia University Press, 2001.

    R. Clifton Spargo.
        Elegy as Narrative: The Relation to the Other in the Work of Mourning. Diss.,
            Yale University.
         "Elegy as Narrative," Diss. Prospectus, 1991.
        The Ethics of Mourning: Grief and Responsibility in Elegiac Literature. Baltimore,
            MD: Johns Hopkins University Press, 2004.

    Elizabeth ("Libby") Spiller.
        Telling Knowledge: The Facts of Empiricism and Imaginative Literature, 1560–
            1680. Diss., Harvard University.
        "Telling Knowledge: The Discursivity of Experimentalism, 1580–1670," Diss.
            Prospectus, not dated.
        Email correspondence, 1996.

All individuals in this group received their degree in 1996 and that is the date of their dissertation. Interviewed in Winter–Spring–Summer 1997.

Azad Bonni.
> *Neurotrophic Factor Regulation of Immediate Early Gene Expression.* Diss., Harvard University.
>
> "Magnetic-resonance-imaging in the diagnosis of dominantly inherited cerebello-olivary atrophy — a clinicopathological study" (with R. Delcarpio-O'Donovan, Y. Robitaille, E. Andermann, F. Andermann, and D.A. Arnold), *Canadian Association of Radiologists — Journal* 44 (1993): 194–98.
>
> "Characterization of a pathway for ciliary neurotrophic factor signaling to the nucleus" (with D.A. Frank, C. Schindler, and M.E. Greenberg), *Science* 262 (1993): 1575–79.
>
> "Serine 133-phosphorylated CREB induces transcription via a cooperative mechanism that may confer specificity to neurotrophin signals" (with D.D. Ginty, H. Dudek, and M.E. Greenberg), *Molecular and Cellular Neuroscience* 6 (1995): 168–83.
>
> "Cell survival promoted by the Ras-MAPK signaling pathway by transcription-dependent and -independent mechanisms" (with A. Brunet, A.E. West, S.R. Datta, M.A. Takasu, and M.E. Greenberg), *Science* 286 (1999): 1358–62.
>
> "Cdh1-APC controls axonal growth and patterning in the mammalian brain" (with Y. Konishi, J. Stegmüller, T. Matsuda, and S. Bonni), *Science* 303 (2004): 1026–30.
>
> Website. http://www.hms.harvard.edu/dms/neuroscience/fac_bonni.html

Giedrius Buraças.
> *Selective Information Processing in the Visual Brain.* Diss., UC-San Diego.
>
> Website. http://www.cnl.salk.edu/~giedrius/

Christopher ("Chris") Callahan.
> *Genes Controlling Axonal Pathfinding in Drosophila.* Diss., UC-San Diego.
>
> Interview* with Professor John Thomas, The Salk Institute, 2004; Chris's dissertation advisor.
>
> "Tau-beta-galactosidase, an axon-targeted fusion protein" (with J.B. Thomas), *Proceedings of the National Academy of Sciences* 91 (1994): 5972–76.
>
> "*derailed* is required for muscle attachment site selection in *Drosophila*" (with J.L. Bonkovsky, A.L. Scully, and J.B. Thomas), *Development* 122 (1996): 2761–67.

Sophia Colamarino.
> *The Role of the Floor Plate and Netrin-1 in the Unique Migration of Trochlear Motor Axons.* Diss., UC-San Francisco.
>
> Orals Proposal Document, "Characterization of growth cone response to chemoattractants," not dated.

Notes and gradesheet from course on the nervous system Sophia took as an undergraduate at Stanford University, 1989–90.

Follow-up interview*, 2004.

"The axonal chemoattractant netrin-1 is also a chemorepellent for trochlear motor axons" (with M. Tessier-Lavigne), *Cell* 81 (1995): 621–29.

Theodore ("Ted") Cummins.

Molecular Pathophysiology of a Mutant Sodium Channel. Diss., Yale University.

"Heart-rate control in normal and aborted SIDS infants" (with S.M. Pincus and G.G. Haddad), *American Journal of Physiology* 264 (1993): R638–46.

"Functional consequences of a Na^+ channel mutation causing hyperkalemic periodic paralysis" (with J. Zhou, F.J. Sigworth, C. Ukomadu, M. Stephan, L.J. Ptacek, and W.S. Agnew), *Neuron* 10 (1993): 667–68.

Takao Hensch.

Development and Plasticity of Visual Cortex: A Role for Intracortical Interactions. Diss., UC-San Francisco.

REM Sleep Generation: Afferent Projections to Behaviorally Effective Drug Injection Sites in the Mammalian Brainstem. Honors Thesis, Harvard University, 1988.

"Ocular dominance plasticity under metabotropic glutamate receptor blockade" (with M.P. Stryker), *Science* 272 (1996): 554–57.

"Comparison of plasticity *in vivo* and *in vitro* in the developing visual cortex of normal and protein kinase A RI beta-deficient mice" (with J.A. Gordon, E.P. Brandon, G.S. McKnight, R.L. Idzerda, and M.P. Stryker), *Journal of Neuroscience* 18 (1998): 2108–17.

"Local GABA circuit control of experience-dependent plasticity in developing visual cortex" (with M. Fagiolini, N. Mataga, M.P. Stryker, S. Baekkeskov, and S.F. Kash), *Science* 282 (1998): 1504–8.

"Columnar architecture sculpted by GABA circuits in developing cat visual cortex" (with M.P. Stryker), *Science* 303 (2004): 1678–81.

"Specific GABA(A) circuits for visual cortical plasticity" (with M. Fagiolini, J.M. Fritschy, K. Low, H. Mohler, and University of Rudolph), *Science* 303 (2004): 1681–83.

Emily Huang.

Estimating the Synaptic Reliability Distribution. Diss., UC-San Diego.

"Slow and incomplete inactivations of voltage-gated channels dominate the encoding in synthetic neurons" (with H. Hsu, X.Y. Yang, A. Karschin, C. Labarca, A. Figl, B. Ho, N. Davidson, and H.A. Lester), *Biophysical Journal* 65 (1993): 1196–1206.

"Synaptic plasticity: Going through phases with LTP," *Current Biology* 8 (1998): 350–52.

David Johnson.   555
The Cloning, Physiological and Anatomical Characterization of 5-HT3R-A,
a Serotonin-Gated Ion Channel in Rat. Diss., UC-San Diego.
"Crosslinking by 125I-w-conotoxin: evidence suggesting multiple neuronal cal-
cium channel subtypes" (with L.J. Cruz, J.S. Imperial, and B.M. Olivera),
Society for Neuroscience Abstracts 13 (1987): 281.5.
"Distribution of alpha 7 neuronal nicotinic receptor mRNA in the rat CNS"
(with H.M. Stroessner-Johnson, J. Boulter, D.G. Amaral, and S. Heinemann),
Society for Neuroscience Abstracts 17 (1991): 105.3.
"Cloning and expression of the rat 5HT3 receptor reveals species-specific sensitiv-
ity to curare antagonism" (with S.F. Heinemann), Society for Neuroscience
Abstracts 18 (1992): 115.13.
"Rat 5HT3 receptor expression in the central and peripheral nervous systems —
an in situ hybridization study" (with S.F. Heinemann), Society for Neuroscience Abstracts 19 (1993): 265.1.

Roger Knowles.
Translocation of RNA Granules in Living Neurons. Diss., Harvard University.
Follow-up interviews, 1999, 2005*.
"Organization of actin and microtubules during process formation in tau-
expressing SF9 cells" (with N. Leclerc and K.S. Kosik), Cell Motility and
the Cytoskeleton 28 (1994): 256–64.
"Translocation of RNA granules in living neurons" (with J.H. Sabry,
M.E. Martone, T.J. Deerinck, M.H. Ellisman, G.J. Bassell, and K.S. Kosik),
Journal of Neuroscience 16 (1996): 7812–20.
"The effect of senile plaques and neuropil threads on neurite morphology in
Alzheimer's disease" (with L. Cruz, B. Kutnjac-Urbanc, R.H. Christie, H.E.
Stanley, and B.T. Hyman), Neurology 48 (1997): Sup. 2: 3045.
"Plaque-induced neurite abnormalities: Implications for disruption of neural
networks in Alzheimer's disease" (with C. Wyart, S.V. Buldyrev, L. Cruz, B.
Urbanc, M.E. Hasselmo, H.E. Stanley, and B.T. Hyman), Proceedings of the
National Academcy of Sciences 96 (1999): 5274–79.

René Marois.
Development of Serotonergic Cells in Aplysia Californica. Diss., Yale University.
"Embryonic development of serotonin-like immunoreactivity in the central ner-
vous system of the snail Lymnaea" (with B.J. Chiasson and R.P. Croll), Society
for Neuroscience Abstracts 13 (1987): 314.11.
"Ontogeny of serotonergic neurons in Aplysia Californica" (with T.J. Carew),
Journal of Comparative Neurology 386 (1997): 477–90.
"Dissociation of visual frames of reference using fMRI" (with J. Moylan and J.C.
Gore), Journal of Cognitive Neuroscience 1998 Sup.: 77.
"Neural correlates of the attentional blink" (with M.M. Chun and J.C. Gore),
Neuron 28 (2000): 299–308.
"The cortical basis of motor planning: Does it take two to tango?" Nature Neu-
roscience 5 (2002): 1254–55.

Jane Minturn.

The Cloning and Characterization of TOAD-64: A Gene Expressed Transiently During Neuronal Differentiation in the Mammalian Nervous System. Diss., Yale University.

"Sodium-channel expression detected with antibody-7493 in A2B5+ and A2B5− astrocytes from rat optic-nerve in vitro" (with J.A. Black, K.J. Angelides, and S.G. Waxman), *Glia* 3 (1990): 358–67.

"Membrane-associated sodium-channels and cytoplasmic precursors in glial-cells — immunocytochemical, electrophysiological, and pharmacological studies" (with H. Sontheimer, J.A. Black, K.J. Angelides, B.R. Ransom, J.M. Ritchie, and S.G. Waxman), *Annals of the New York Academy of Sciences* 633 (1991): 255–71.

Teresa Nick.

Developmental Regulation of Excitability in the Bag Cell Neurons of Aplysia. Diss., Yale University.

"Patterned (single) alternation in infant rats after combined or separate lesions of hippocampus and amygdala" (with N. Lobaugh, P. Greene, M. Grant, and A. Amsel), *Behavioral Neuroscience* 103 (1989): 1159–67.

"Developmental dissociation of excitability and secretory ability in *Aplysia* bag cell neurons" (with J.E. Moreira, L.K. Kaczmarek, T.J. Carew, and N.L. Wayne), *Journal of Neurophysiology* 76 (1996): 3351–59.

"Ionic currents underlying developmental regulation of repetitive firing in *Aplysia* bag cell neurons" (with L.K. Kaczmarek and T.J. Carew), *Journal of Neuroscience* 16 (1996): 7583–98.

"Dynamic control of auditory activity during sleep: Correlation between song response and EEG" (with M. Konishi), *Proceedings of the National Academy of Sciences* 98 (2001): 14012–16.

Website. http://www2.neuroscience.umn.edu/tnick/research1.html

Barbara Niemeyer.

A Study of Photoreceptor Function in Drosophila. Diss., UC-San Diego.

"The Drosophila light-activated conductance is composed of the two channels TRP and TRPL" (with E. Suzuki, K. Scott, K. Jalink, and C.S. Zuker), *Cell* 85 (1996): 651–59.

Caroline ("Kelly") Overly.

Organelle Motility and Endocytic Pathways in Cultured Neurons. Diss., Harvard University.

"Quantitative measurement of intraorganelle pH in the endosomal-lysosomal pathway in neurons by using ratiometric imaging with pyranine" (with K.D. Lee, E. Berthiaume, and P.J. Hollenbeck), *Proceedings of the National Academy of Sciences* 92 (1995): 3156–60.

"Organelle motility and metabolism in axons vs dendrites of cultured hippocampal neurons" (with H.I. Rieff and P.J. Hollenbeck), *Journal of Cell Science* 109 (1996): 971–80.

"Dynamic organization of endocytic pathways in axons of cultured sympathetic   557
neurons" (with P.J. Hollenbeck), *Journal of Neuroscience* 16 (1996):
6056–64.

Bruce Peters.
Responses to Light of Starburst Amacrine Cells. Diss., Harvard University.
"Responses to light of starburst amacrine cells" (with R.H. Masland), *Journal of
Neurophysiology* 75 (1996): 469–80.

Seth Ramus.
*Lesions of the Perirhinal Cortex or the Parahippocampal Cortex in Monkeys:
Effects on Memory.* Diss., UC-San Diego.
"Neural correlates of olfactory recognition memory in the rat orbitofrontal cor-
tex" (with H. Eichenbaum), *Journal of Neuroscience* 20 (2000): 8199–208.
Website. http://academic.bowdoin.edu/neuroscience/labs/ramus/

Edward Ruthazer.
*Development of Ocular Dominance Bands and Long-Range Horizontal Connec-
tions in Ferret Visual Cortex.* Diss., UC-San Francisco.
Avian Song Vocalization and Perception. Senior Thesis, Dep. of Biology,
Princeton University, 1988.
"Control of axon branch dynamics by correlated activity in vivo" (with C.J.
Akerman and H.T. Cline), *Science* 301 (2003): 66–70.
Website: http://www.mni.mcgill.ca/cbet.html

Elizabeth ("Liz") Yoder.
Serotonin Receptors Expressed by Rat Schwann Cells. Diss., UC-San Diego.
Follow-up interview, 2004*.
Excerpt from Minor Prop Exam: "Pituicyte Process Retraction by GFAP Phos-
phorylation," 1992.
NRSA Application, not dated (post-dissertation).
Poem, written by Liz's father, 1983.
*Muscle Strategies in Anticipation of a Disruptive Force: Timing, Visual Knowl-
edge, and Activation Level Considerations.* Honors Thesis, Honors College in
assoc. with Dep. of P.E., Arizona State University, 1990.
Glial Cell Communication Bibliography, 1990.
Lists of readings on glial cells (various dates).
"$[Ca^{2+}]_i$ transients in cultured Schwann cells evoked by activation of nicotinic
AChRs" (with V. Lev-Ram and M.H. Ellisman), Society for Neuroscience
Abstracts 18 (1992): 626.1.
"Serotonin receptors on cultured rat Schwann cells" (with V. Lev-Ram and M.H.
Ellisman), Society for Neuroscience *Abstracts* 19 (1993): 460.18.
"5-Hydroxytryptamine(2A) receptors on cultured rat Schwann cells" (with H.
Tamir and M.H. Ellisman), *Glia* 17 (1996): 15–27.
"Serotonin receptors expressed by myelinating Schwann cells in rat sciatic nerve"
(with H. Tamir and M.H. Ellisman), *Brain Research* 753 (1997):
299–308.

"5-HT2A receptors in rat sciatic nerves and Schwann cell cultures" (with G.M. Gaietta, T. Deerinck, K. Kinder, A. Hanono, A. Han, C. Wu, and M.H. Ellisman), *Journal of Neurocytology* 32 (2003): 373–80.

Andreas Walz.

The Role of Glycosylation in the Development of the Optic Pathway in Xenopus laevis." Diss., UC-San Diego.

"Substrate-dependent interactions of leech microglial cells and neurons in culture" (with L.M. Masuda-Nagakawa, D. Brodbeck, M.D. Neely, and R.S. Grombacher), *Journal of Neurobiology* 25 (1994): 83–91.

"Heparin blocks target recognition in the developing visual system of *Xenopus*" (with S. McFarlane and C.E. Holt), Society for Neuroscience *Abstracts* 19 (1993): 450.8.

"Chondroitin sulfate interferes with retinal ganglion cell axon pathfinding in the visual system of *Xenopus*" (with C.E. Holt), Society for Neuroscience *Abstracts* 20 (1994): 449.2.

"Essential role of heparan sulfates in axon navigation and targeting in the developing visual system" (with S. McFarlane, Y.G. Brickman, V. Nurcombe, P.F. Bartlett, and C.E. Holt) *Development* 124 (1997): 2421–30.

INDIVIDUALS WITH DOCTORATES IN MATHEMATICS

All individuals in this group received their degree in 1997 and that is the date of their dissertation. Interviewed in Summer–Fall 1998.

Anna Gilbert.

Multiresolution Homogenization Schemes for Differential Equations and Applications. Diss., Princeton University.

Lecture Notes (with Ingrid Daubechies). "Harmonic Analysis, Wavelets, and Applications." Lectures given in 1995. In *Hyperbolic Equations and Frequency Interactions,* ed. Luis Caffarelli and E. Weinan, Providence, RI: American Mathematical Soc., 1999.

Website. www.research.att.com/ agilbert/

Amber Habib.

Direct Limits of Zuckerman Derived Functor Modules. Diss., UC-Berkeley.

Colin Ingalls.

Deformation of Orders. Diss., MIT.

David Metzler.

Topological Invariants of Symplectic Quotients. Diss., MIT.

"A wall-crossing formula for the signature of symplectic quotient," *Transactions of the American Mathematical Society* 352 (2000): 3495–3521.

"Presentations of non-effective orbifolds" (with Andre Henriques), *Transactions of the American Mathematical Society* 356 (2004): 2481–99.

Zhao-Hui ("Bill") Qian.
  Groupoids, Midpoints, and Quantizations. Diss., UC-Berkeley.

Victoria Rayskin.
  Degenerate Homoclinic Crossings. Diss., UC-Berkeley.
  Multidimensional Differential Equations with Unbounded Discontinuities. B.S. Thesis, Kharkov University, 1989.
  "alpha-Hölder linearization," *Journal of Differential Equations* 147 (1998): 271–84.
  "Differentiability of the Hartman-Grobman linearization" (with M. Guysinsky and B. Hasselblatt), *Discrete and Continuous Dynamical Systems* 9 (2003): 979–84.

Daniel Upper.
  Theory and Algorithms for Hidden Markov Models and Generalized Hidden Markov Models. Diss., UC-Berkeley.
  Query posted on www.mathforum.org: "Finding nonsingular submatrices [of a singular matrix]," 1995.

Japheth Wood
  On the Undecidability of the Type Set of a Variety. Diss., UC-Berkeley.

Yihao Lisa Zhang
  An Analysis of Network Routing and Communication Latency. Diss., MIT.
  Topics in Generating Functions with Applications to a Domino Problem and Regular Graphs. Honors Thesis, Dep. of Mathematics, Wellesley College, 1993.
  Topics in Parallelism: A Study of Parallel Models and Networks. Honors Thesis, Dep. of Computer Science, Wellesley College, 1993.
  Website. http://cm.bell-labs.com/who/ylz/

PLAYWRIGHTS AND FILMMAKERS

All individuals interviwed in Spring–Summer 1998.

Julius Galacki
  Resume. 1998.
  "Influences on me as a Playwright," manuscript, 1995.
  Fulbright Proposal Statement. Not dated (1997–1998).
  Tautology. Play, 1989 (Julius states in a letter play first written in 1980).
  The Plain of Memory. Play, 1996 (first draft prior to 1992; play set in 1988).
  The Master and the Magician. Play, 1996.

Roger Hedden.
  Bodies, Rest, and Motion. Play, 1988.
  Bodies, Rest & Motion. Movie (Roger wrote the screenplay), Fine Line Features, 1993.
  Been Taken. Play, 1991.

560
As Sure as You Live. Play, 1997.
Hi-Life. Film (Roger wrote the screenplay and directed the film), Lions Gate Films, 1998.

James Krouse.
Resume. Not dated (current as of 1998).
The Painted Woman. Play, 1997 (first draft 1995 or 1996).
Tale of the Fat Man. Play, not dated (written during 1996–98).
Bringing Down DaVinci. Play, not dated (written during 1996–98).

Enid Zentelis.
Dog Race. Second year film, Tisch School of the Arts, Maurice Kanbar Inst. of Film and Television, NYU, not dated (made during 1995–97). Enid was awarded the Grand Marnier Award from the Film Society of Lincoln Center in association with the New York Film Festival in 1997 for this film.
The Man with My Nose. Thesis film, Tisch School of the Arts, Maurice Kanbar Inst. of Film and Television, NYU, not dated (made during 1997–1998).
Evergreen. Film, 2004. Developed by Enid at the Sundance Institute in 2000. Enid was awarded the Best Director, Narrative Feature, at the Sonoma Valley Film Festival 2004.
Interview (interviewer listed as Todd Gilchrist) dated Sep. 13, 2004. Posted at: http://filmforce.ign.com/articles/547/547291p1.html

ENTREPRENEUR INTERVIEWED ABOUT HIS CREATIVE DEVELOPMENT

Scott Painter.
Interview, 2003*.
Information about Scott's online car venture and interview at: www.baselinemag. com. "Dude, you're gettin' a car," August 1, 2003; thecarconnection.com. Article 4818, 2002.
Scott was a cofounder and is former CEO of CarsDirect, Inc. Website: www. carsdirect.com.

STUDENTS WHO DESCRIBED THEIR CREATIVE DEVELOPMENT IN CLASS EXERCISES AND CONVERSATIONS WHOSE DESCRIPTIONS HAVE BEEN DRAWN UPON

Marcy Engler.

Channing Henry.

Alice Liu.

Markus Moberg.

Chad Troutwine.

Bibliography

A complete bibliography for this book is posted online at:
www.jonathanfeinstein.com.

Index

A

Abraham, Max, 314
Academics, 18, 21
Aesthetic appreciation, 128
Approaches, 212
   creative interests and, 175–177
   problem solving and, 397–409
Archimedes, 52
Arendt, Hannah
   breadth of creative interests and,
     205, 209
   creative connections and, 485, 487
   creative expertise and, 348
   creative interests of, 164, 480, 483
   creative projects of, 485–487
   creative responses and, 253
   cultural linkages and, 523, 530
   cumulative creative responses and, 291
   desire for enlightenment and, 130
   domain interest exploration and, 298,
     348, 483
   domains of interests and, 163
   emotions and, 507
   importance of creative interests
     and, 138
   patterns of development and, 12,
     479–487
   personal experiences sparking creative
     interests and, 84–87
   registers of meaning and, 90
   source materials for, 16
   subtopics as areas of interest and, 172
Arieti, Silvano, 33, 541
Artists, natural phenomena and, 67
Attention, scope of, 250–252
Azad. *See* Bonni, Azad

B

Barran, Paul
   creative interest of, 362
   decision-making and, 362
   patterns of development and, 461
   project development and, 363
   source materials for, 17
Barron, Frank, 513
Batchelor, Charles, 443
Baucom, Ian
   beauty and, 128
   creative interest of, 128
   decision-making and, 355
   domain interest exploration and,
     298, 517
   generalization and, 344, 347
   guiding principles and values of, 383
   importance of creative interests and, 136
   Kim and, 275
   managing development and, 369, 373
   patterns of development and, 461, 465
Beauty, 128
Bergman, Ingmar, 17, 452
Berners-Lee, Tim
   breadth of creative interests and, 207, 211
   conceptions of creative interests of, 179,
     469
   creative interests and projects of, 234
   creative responses and, 252, 256, 276–278,
     514
   cultural linkages and, 528
   domain interest exploration and, 514
   early development of creative interest of,
     178–179
   holistic conceptions and, 178
   patterns of development and, 469

project development and, 359
source materials for, 16
Besso, Michele, 289, 308, 324
Biographies, 17, 29, 543
discussed/described by individuals, 59
project patterns/pathways and, 445
Blackmore, Susan, 534
Blotner, Joseph, 17
Blücher, Heinrich, 483, 485
Blumenfeld, Kurt, 481
Bonni, Azad, 21
breadth of creative interests and, 210
creative connections and, 436–439
creative expertise and, 347
creative interests of, 42, 46, 56
creative responses and, 258, 347, 514
decision-making and, 355
distinctive creative interests and, 185
domain interest exploration and, 347, 513
importance of creative interests and, 136
multiple sources of interests and, 153
openness to experience and, 514
opportunity and, 142
project development and, 359, 437
patterns of development and, 465,
470–472, 488
registers of meaning and, 88
revisioning on projects and, 421
Branching out, 422–424
Breadth, 182, 201–223, 511
domain interest exploration and,
294, 295
factors important in, 205–217
judgements of, 213–217
Brooks, Tina, 150, 176, 408
Buraças, Giedrius, 71
Businesspeople, 21

C

Calder, Alexander
breadth of creative interests and, 202,
206, 207, 214
combining interests and, 440, 441
conceptions of creative interests and,
228, 235, 236
creative connections and, 441
creative interests of, 44–46, 56, 161

creative interests and art of, 228, 235
creative responses and, 252, 255,
260–265, 288
cultural linkages and, 527, 528, 530
distinctive creative interests and, 187
negativity and, 146
patterns of development and, 91, 458
source materials for, 16, 17
Callahan, Chris
creative interests of, 240–244
creative responses and, 252, 253, 256,
281–282, 514
cultural linkages and, 528
decision-making and, 356
patterns of development and, 95
problem solving and, 398
project development and, 359, 360
projects and, 241–244
subtopics as areas of interest and, 172
work of others/predecessors and, 281
Cameron, Julia, 506
Campbell, Donald, 31, 534
Carlson, Celia, 146
Carrig, Maria
creative connections in interest domains
and, 328–329
creative projects and, 328–329, 519
domain interest exploration and, 294,
300, 519
novelty and, 126
patterns of development and, 92
Carson, Rachel, 118, 138, 140, 384
Cezanne, Paul, 67, 130
Challenges, 119–121
Chen, Henry
creative connections and, 478
creative interests of, 42, 43, 46, 476, 477
creative responses and, 256, 476
metaphors and, 179
patterns of development and, 92,
475–479, 563
registers of meaning and, 88
Childhood interests, 102–106, 107
Chomsky, Noam, 95
Coburn, Kathleen, 17, 432
Colamarino, Sophia
beauty and, 128

564

Colamarino, Sophia (*Cont.*)
  creative interests of, 237–240, 243
  curiosity and, 112
  decision-making and, 356
  distinctive creative interests and, 194
  multiple sources of interests and, 152
  problem solving and, 397
  project development and, 360
  projects and, 238–240
  subtopics as areas of interest and, 172
  wonder and, 117
Coleridge, Samuel Taylor, 9
  combining interests and, 427, 430–434
  creative connections and, 332, 334–340,
    346, 435, 517
  creative expertise and, 346
  creative interests of, 332, 433
  cultural linkages and, 528
  domain interest exploration and, 300,
    332–340, 515, 517
  multiple interests and, 426
  source materials for, 16
Complexity, 121–125
Conceptions of creative interests, 6–8,
  36–61
  breadth of, 182, 201
  conceptual elements and, 244–247
  decision-making and, 353–364
  defined, 37, 54
  distinctiveness of, 182, 195
  evolution of, 464–474
  patterns of development and, 90–106
  specific elements and, 235–237
Conceptual structures, 7–9, 38, 515–517
  building, 321–345
  creative responses and, 248–252
  distinctiveness and, 182
Conceptual synthesis, 92
Connections, 224–247, 321–340, 434–443
  as form of creative responses, 255–257
  sources of, 252
Conrad, Joseph, 80
Constellations of interests, 425–443
Contemporaneous descriptions, 41
Context, creative responses and, 289
Conventional topics, distinctiveness and,
  183–197

Conversations, creative responses and, 286
Crane, Gregg, 285, 297, 375
Creative development
  as autonomous activity, 3
  culture and, 522–542
  difficulties in, 505–521
  managing, 364–387
  modeling, 535–542
  organization of this book and, 13, 21
  patterns of, 11, 90–106, 425, 444–504
  phases of, 4–10, 388, 425, 509–520
  sequences of interests and, 521
  unique path of, 11
Creative expertise, 9, 345–352
Creative individuals examined in this
  book, 15
Creative interests, 36–61, 62–133
  breadth of, 182, 201–223
  combining, 425–443
  conceptions of. *See* Conceptions of
    creative interests
  creative potential of, 134–145
  culture and, 522–530
  decision-making and, 353–364
  defined, 36, 54
  development of, 62–106
  discussed/described by individuals, 58–61
  distinctiveness of, 182–201
  evolution of, 464–474
  exploration of, 7–9, 293–321, 512–519
  extrinsic/strategic factors and, 134–159
  formation of, 5–7, 509–512
  importance of, 135–141
  intrinsic sources of, 107–133
  multiple sources of, 151–159, 512
  narrow, 217–223
  other countries/cultures and, 69
  patterns of development and, 90–106,
    463–504
  resonances/connections and, 224–247
  sequences of related, 474–504
  types of, 160–181
  what sparks them, 62–90
Creative potential, 134–145
Creative responses, 8, 62–90, 248–292
  creative expertise and, 347
  cumulative effects and, 290

forms of, 253–257
imperfect understanding of, 291
multiple interests and, 435–443
originality of, 259
problem solving and, 409–416
reflection and, 287–290
Crick, Francis, 200, 258, 284, 287
Crouch, Tom, 17, 122
Csikszentmihalyi, Mihaly, 29, 30, 33
Cultural context, 67–70
Cultural development literature, 34
Cultural transmission and influence, 4,
  522–535
Culture, 522–542
Cummings, Ted, 459
Curiosity, 112–117

D

Dale, Mara, 71, 383
Darrigol, Olivier, 314
Darwin, Charles, 9
  breadth of creative interests and, 203, 207
  childhood interests and, 103–106
  creative expertise and, 346, 347
  creative interest of, 103–104
  creative responses and, 412–416, 514
  cultural linkages and, 528–529
  distinctiveness and, 183, 190, 346, 510
  domain interest exploration and, 294,
    315, 317–321, 514–517
  domains of interests and, 163
  generalization and, 341–344, 347
  importance of creative interests and, 156
  intrinsic interest and, 156
  natural phenomena and, 66, 74
  patterns of development and, 465
  questions and, 113
  rich domains and, 109–111
  source materials for, 16
Data collection process/sources, 14–28,
  40–53
Dawkins, Richard, 34, 534
Decision-making, 353–364
Different direction, 149–151
Difficulties in creative development,
  505–521
Difficultness, 121–125

Discovery, 389–396
Disney, Walt
  childhood interests and, 102
  creative interest of, 102
  creative interests and films of, 233, 236
  patterns of development and, 465
Dissertations, 20
Distinctiveness, 182–201, 293, 488, 510
  domain interest exploration and, 321
  emergence of, 196
Domains of interest, 162–164
  approaches and, 175
  conceptual structures and, 321–345
  creative connections between, 434–443
  exploring, 293–321
Dostoevsky, Fyodor, 368
Duchamp, Marcel, 265
Durham, William, 534

E

Edison, Thomas
  combining interests and, 440, 442
  creative connections and, 442, 443
  creative interests of, 143, 442
  creative responses and, 286
  discussed/described by individuals, 59
  distinctive creative interests and, 191
  distinctiveness and, 510
  domains of interests and, 163
  opportunity and, 143
  patterns of development and, 460
  problem solving and, 399
  source materials for, 16
  work of others/predecessors and, 286
Edwards, Betty, 506
Einstein, Albert
  conceptual structure of interest of,
    312, 511
  creativity generation and special theory
    of relativity of, 322–328
  creative interest of, 158, 304
  creative responses and, 289
  cultural linkages and, 526, 530
  curiosity and, 112
  domain interest exploration and, 294,
    295, 303–315
  guiding principles and values of, 385

566   Einstein, Albert (*Cont.*)
importance of creative interests and,
138, 153
intrinsic interest and, 157–159
new developments in one's field and, 71
patterns of development and, 446, 459
rich domains and, 511
source materials for, 16
Ellmann, Richard, 76, 445
Emotions, 507
Encounters sparking creative interests,
62–90
Enid. *See* Zentelis, Enid
Enlightenment, quest for, 129–133
ENQUIRE documentation method, 277
Entrepreneurs, 21, 453
Environmental literature, 32
Erikson, Erik, 78
Evolving systems literature, 29
Exhaustion of interests, 520
Experiences sparking creative interests,
62–90
Experimentation, 389–396
Exploration, 7–9, 293–321
difficulties and, 512–519
patterns of, 294

F

Faherty, Teresa
creative responses and, 256, 288
narrow interests and, 218
patterns of development and, 448, 449
people sparking creative interests and, 72
Faulkner, William, 519
branching out and, 423–424
breadth of creative interests and, 203, 211
creative interest of, 67–68
creative responses and, 289
cultural linkages and, 525
cultural/social context and, 67
desire to do something different and, 151
distinctiveness and, 192, 198, 510
guiding principles and values of, 384
managing development and, 368
patterns of development and, 454, 460,
461, 466
source materials for, 17

Ferguson, Susan, 63–66, 68
breadth of creative interests and,
203, 206
creative connections and, 489
creative interest of, 65, 489
creative projects and, 359, 489
creative responses and, 252, 254, 258,
266–275
cultural linkages and, 69, 524, 528
decision-making and, 355
distinctiveness of creative interests and,
187, 489
domain interest exploration and, 294
domains of interests and, 164
openness to experience and, 514
patterns of development and, 93,
488–490
registers of meaning and, 88
rich domains and, 109
Filmmakers, 19, 21, 452
Fixation of interests, 520
Focus, scope of, 250–252
Foucault, Michel, 58
Franklin, Benjamin, 58, 59
Franklin, Rosalind, 284
Freud, Sigmund, 77

G

Galacki, Julius, 69
Galileo, 52–53, 165, 372
Gardner, Howard, 29, 541
Gedo, Mary Matthews, 78
Generalization, 340–345
Gide, André, 387
Gilbert, Anna, 284
Gilot, Françoise, 78, 466
Gingrich, Newt, 409
Goals, breadth of creative interests and,
210–212
Gray, Elisha, 286, 442
Gruber, Howard, 29, 61, 445

H

Hadley, Karen
approaches and, 176
combining interests and, 427
creative interest of, 83–84, 149

negativity and, 149
revisioning on projects and, 419–421
Halpern, Nick
  breadth of creative interests and, 212
  creative interest of, 83–84
  cultural linkages and, 526, 527
  distinctiveness and, 192, 510, 511
  patterns of development and, 197, 455,
    466–469, 472
  personal experiences sparking creative
    interests and, 82–84
  questions and, 113
Hamilton, Ross
  creative responses and, 254, 258, 278–280
  distinctive creative interests and, 187
  openness to experience and, 514
Hannah. See Arendt, Hannah
Hayek, Friedrich, 35, 547
Heidegger, Martin, 84, 480
Henry. See Chen, Henry
Hensch, Takao
  breadth of creative interests and, 208, 213
  creative interest of, 166
  cultural linkages and, 530
  decision-making and, 356
  distinctive creative interests and, 194, 199
  meta-level interests and, 367
  patterns of development and, 455–
    458, 460
  relationship interests and, 165–167
Hirsch, David, 74
Hofstadter, Douglas
  breadth of creative interests and, 203
  challenges and, 120
  creative interest of, 116
  curiosity and, 114–117
  domains of interests and, 162
  multiple sources of interests and, 152
Holistic conceptions, 177–181, 195, 246, 512
Holmes, Frederic, 17, 96, 358, 391, 449
Holmes, Richard, 17, 432
Hull, David, 540
Hume, David, 295, 307–312, 325, 327

Idea generation, creative responses and,
  255–257

Importance of creative interests,
  135–141
  breadth and, 208–210
Ingalls, Colin, 121, 122
Interest domains. See Domains of interest
Interviews, 14, 18–20
Intrinsic interest, 107–133, 153–157
Inventors, work of others/predecessors
  and, 286
Irwin, Robert, 114

J

Jamison, Kay, 79
Janik, Allan, 541
Johnson, David
  creative responses and, 412
  cultural linkages and, 525
  domain interest exploration and,
    298, 513
  managing development and, 369
  problem solving and, 397
Joyce, James, 475–478
  personal experiences sparking creative
    interests and, 76, 476
  projects and, 445
  reflection and, 368
Judson, Horace, 199

K

Kahneman, Daniel, 287
Kandel, Eric, 72, 355, 361
Kaufman, Robert, 21
  breadth of creative interests and,
    208, 211
  creative connections in interest domains
    and, 330–331, 347
  creative expertise and, 347
  creative interest of, 171
  cultural linkages and, 528
  distinctiveness and, 510
  domain interest exploration and, 315–317,
    513, 514, 516
  patterns of development and, 98
  questions and, 113
  relationship interests and, 170
Kebarle, Karen, 128, 428
Kenner, Hugh, 76

568

Keynes, John Maynard
  approaches and, 493, 498, 501, 503
  breadth of creative interests and, 210
  creative connections and, 498, 501
  creative interests of, 68, 493, 496, 499
  creative projects and, 497, 504
  creative responses and, 256, 494–496
  cultural linkages and, 523, 525, 528, 530
  cultural/social context and, 68, 500
  domain interest exploration and, 498, 502
  guiding principles and values of, 493, 494
  importance of creative interests and, 156
  patterns of development and, 12, 488,
    491–504
  source materials for, 16
Kim (Kipling character), 254, 266–275
Knoop, Franz, 96, 167
Knowles, Roger
  breadth of creative interests and, 211, 215
  conception of creative interest of, 89
  conversations and, 286
  creative interests and projects of, 227,
    287, 360, 446–448
  creative responses and, 253, 257, 286
  curiosity and, 112
  distinctiveness and, 188–190, 194,
    198, 510
  importance of creative interests and, 135
  judgements of importance and, 139
  metaphors and, 179
  patterns of development and, 94,
    446–448, 449, 459
  registers of meaning and, 89
Kosik, Ken, 286–287
Krebs, Hans
  breadth of creative interests and, 213
  creative interest of, 168, 357
  creative interests and projects of, 227
  cultural linkages and, 525
  decision-making and, 357–359, 361, 518
  development of creative interest of,
    167–168
  distinctive creative interests and, 194
  domain interest exploration and, 513
  experimentation and, 390–392
  meta-level interests and, 367
  patterns of development and, 95, 449–451

people sparking creative interests and,
    523
  project development and, 357–358,
    361, 362
  relationship interests and, 165, 167–170
  rich domains and, 111
Kroc, Ray
  creative expertise and, 348–352
  creative responses and, 9
  cultural linkages and, 528
  domain interest exploration and,
    348–352, 515
  guiding principles and values of, 375
  project development and, 361
  source materials for, 16
Kuhn, Thomas, 35

L

Language, 24
Literary scholars
  domain interest exploration and, 297
  managing development and, 383
  reflection and, 288
  work of others/predecessors and, 285
Literatures, 28–35
  exploration processes and, 295
  managing development and, 365
  patterns of projects and, 445
Liz. See Yoder, Liz
Lorentz, Hendrik, 313
Love, John, 349
Lowes, John Livingston, 17, 300, 332–340,
    430
Luria, Salvador, 200

M

MacCarthy, Desmond, 492–494
Mach, Ernst, 306, 308, 310
Madness, creativity and, 79
Managing creative development,
    364–387
Markkula, Mike, 363
Marois, René, 371, 459
Mathematicians
  beauty and, 129
  challenges and, 120
  creative interests and, 510

revisioning and, 421
work of others/predecessors and, 284
Matisse, Henri
  breadth of creative interests and, 207
  cumulative creative responses and, 290
  discussed/described by individuals, 59
  distinctive creative interests and, 198
  domain interest exploration and,
    513, 516
  domains of interests and, 164
  experimentation and, 395
  intrinsic interest and, 157
  managing development and, 372
  people sparking creative interests and, 73
  source materials for, 16
McDonald brothers, 349–352
Meaning, registers of, 87–90
Memory, 22–24, 26
Meta-level processes, 518
  managing development and, 366–373
  multiple interests and, 439
  problem solving and, 400–403
Metaphors, in conceptions of creative
  interests, 180
Metzler, David, 129, 421
Meyer, Bernard, 80
Mill, John Stuart, 35
Miller, Arthur, 17, 304, 305, 313
Minturn, Jane
  decision-making and, 355
  natural phenomena and, 66
  patterns of development and, 461,
    464, 465
Models of creative development, 535–542
Mondrian, Piet, 441
  conceptions of creative interests and,
    234, 235
  creative interests and paintings of, 235,
    472–474
  creative responses and, 255, 260–265
  distinctiveness and, 510
  early conception of creative interest of,
    132–133
  guiding principles and values of,
    376–380, 473, 518
  managing development and, 374,
    376–380

philosophical considerations
  and, 131–133
  source materials for, 16
Moore, G.E., 493–496
Movies, 20
Multiple interests, 425–443, 512
Multiplicity of elements, breadth and,
  206–208

N

Narrow interests, 183, 217–223
Natural phenomena, 66
Negativity, 146–149
Neighboring fields, 12, 74
Nelson, Jennifer, 186
Neuroscientists, 228
  creative responses and, 257
  curiosity and, 112
  decision-making and, 355, 361
  distinctive creative interests
    and, 198
  natural phenomena and, 66
  patterns of development and, 94
  projects and, 519
  revisioning and, 421
  wonder and, 117
Newton, Isaac
  conception of absolute space and time
    of, 305
  creative interests of, 405, 408
  creative realizations by, 406–407
  managing development and, 374
  patterns of development and, 490
  problem solving and, 403–408
  source materials for, 16
Nick, Teresa, 55
  decision-making and, 355, 361
  people sparking creative interests and,
    72, 523
  project development and, 361
Nixon, Cheryl
  branching out and, 422
  breadth of creative interests and, 203,
    213, 216
  conception of creative interest of, 97
  creative expertise and, 347
  creative interest of, 97

570   Nixon, Cheryl (*Cont.*)
      cultural linkages and, 528
      distinctive conceptions of creative
       interests and, 195
      domain interest exploration and, 297, 517
      domains of interests and, 162
      generalization and, 344, 347
      importance of creative interests and, 140
      multiple sources of interests and, 153
      patterns of development and, 96
      rich domains and, 111
    Novelty, 125–127

O

Olivier, Fernande, 79, 465
Omidyar, Pierre
    creative responses and, 256
    guiding principles and values of,
     380–382, 518
    managing development and, 380–382
    source materials for, 17
Opportunity, 141–145
Outcomes, differences in across
    individuals, 508
Overly, Kelly
    conceptions of creative interests of,
     181, 244
    creative interest and projects of, 245
    creative interest of, 181
    cultural linkages and, 527
    distinctiveness of creative interests
     and, 196
    holistic conceptions and, 180
    metaphors and, 180
    project development and, 360

P

Painter, Scott, 453
Pattern recognition, 340–345
Pauling, Linus, 201
Peak creative moments, 2
Pedersen, Anne Mette, 145, 302
People sparking creative interests, 70,
    280–287
Perception, creative responses and, 253–255
Personal experiences sparking creative
    interests, 75–90

Peters, Bruce, 94, 140, 189, 253, 254
Philosophical considerations, 131
Picasso, Pablo
    managing development and, 372
    patterns of development and, 465
    personal experiences sparking creative
     interests and, 78
    revisions on projects and, 416–419, 422
    source materials for, 16
Pitt-Rivers, Augustus Henry Lane-Fox, 34
Planck, Max, 311
Plays, 20
Playwrights, 19
Poincaré, Henri, 310, 311, 314
Prince, Earl, 349
Principles, 375–387
Problem literature, 30
Problem solving, 396–409
Projects, 9, 55, 388–424
    combining interests and, 427–434
    decision-making and, 356–364
    difficulties and, 519
    evolution of interests and, 469
    expanding, 422–424
    pathways of influence and, 444,
     458–462
    patterns of development and, 444–462
    problem solving and, 396–409
    resonances/connections and, 226–235
    revisioning and, 416–422
    simultaneous, 454–458
    subsequent, 237–244
Psychology, 77, 79

Q

Questions, 113, 210–212

R

Ramsay, Mrs. (Virginia Woolf character),
    229–233, 246
Randomness, 32
Raskin, Jef
    creative interest of, 148
    guiding principles and values of, 384
    negativity and, 147
    project development and, 363
    source materials for, 16, 17

Rayskin, Victoria
  breadth of creative interests and, 221–223
  challenges and, 120
  creative interests and, 511
  decision-making and, 355
  domain interest exploration and, 301
  problem definition and, 402
  problem solving and, 397, 402
  revisions and, 421
Reflection, 287–290
Registers of meaning, 87–90
Relationship interests, 165–171, 176, 208
Resonances, 224–247, 252
Retrospective descriptions, 21, 25–28, 41, 225
Revisioning, 416–422
Richness, 109–112, 141
Roger. *See* Knowles, Roger
Russell, John Peter, 73
Ruthazer, Edward, 371n

S

Schön, Donald, 365
Shapiro, Stephen, 142, 163
Shoulson, Jeffrey
  breadth of creative interests and, 219
  creative interest of, 122
  creative interests and, 510
  decision-making and, 354, 355
  difficultness and, 122
  multiple sources of interests and, 152
  patterns of development and, 448, 464
  project development and, 360
Simonton, Dean, 30, 520
Skidelsky, Robert, 17, 491, 492
Social context, 67–70
Social interactions, creative responses and, 280–287
Sophia. *See* Colamarino, Sophia
Source materials/information, 14–28, 40–53
  biographies and, 17
  contemporaneous materials and, 25
Spurling, Hilary, 17
Stachel, John, 17, 304
Statistical analyses literature, 30
Sternberg, Robert, 33

Stoppard, Tom, 58, 427
Strategic positioning, 146–151
Subtopics, as areas of interest, 171–175
Success, 508
Successful individuals, sources of interest of, 154–159
Susan. *See* Ferguson, Susan

T

Takao. *See* Hensch, Takao
Time
  creative interests/conceptions over long period of, 98–101
  creative responses and, 258, 289
Tolstoy, Leo, 368
Transmutation literature, 30
Truth, quest for, 129–133
Tversky, Amos, 287

U

Ulam, Stanislaw, 479
Understanding, quest for, 129–133
Unique path, 149–151
Upper, Daniel, 355

V

Values, 375–387
von Neumann, John
  creative interest of, 174
  distinctive creative interests and, 195
  importance of creative interests and, 138
  patterns of development and, 475, 479
  subtopics as areas of interest and, 173–175
Vygotsky, Lev, 531

W

Wallis, John, 404–406
Walz, Andreas
  beauty and, 128
  managing development and, 373
  meta-level thinking and, 400, 518
  patterns of development and, 461, 465
  problem solving and, 400
Warburg, Otto, 96, 167, 169, 357, 362

572

Watson, James
  breadth of creative interests and, 208, 220
  conversations and, 287
  creative responses and, 253, 257, 258, 282–284
  development of creative interest of, 136–137
  distinctive creative interests and, 199–201, 283
  importance of creative interests and, 136, 155
  judgements of importance and, 140
  source materials for, 16
  work of others/predecessors and, 282–284
Wilkins, Maurice, 282
Wonder, 117–119
Woolf, Virginia, 46–52, 57
  breadth of creative interests and, 212
  conceptions of creative interests and, 229–233, 246
  creative interests and projects of, 229–233, 246
  cultural linkages and, 525, 527
  distinctiveness and, 195, 196, 510
  experimentation and, 393–395
  fragmentary development and, 99–101
  holistic conceptions and, 178
  managing development and, 372, 373, 374
  meta-level interests and, 367
  metaphors and, 180
  multiple sources of interests and, 152
  patterns of development and, 99–101, 451, 459, 460, 462, 488
  personal experiences sparking creative interests and, 81
  revisioning on projects and, 422
  rich domains and, 111, 511
  source materials for, 16
Work of others/predecessors, 12, 70, 537
  creative responses and, 280–287
  Galileo and, 52
Wright, Orville, 123

Wright, Wilbur
  breadth of creative interests and, 211, 221
  creative interest of, 124, 125
  challenges and, 119, 121, 122–125
  cultural elements sparking creative interests and, 524
  opportunity and, 142
  patterns of development and, 475
  project development and, 357
  source materials for, 16

Y

Yoder, Liz
  combining interests and, 427, 429, 440
  creative interests of, 126–127, 539
  creative projects and, 386, 440
  distinctive creative interests and, 191
  domain interest exploration and, 298
  experimentation and, 392
  guiding principles and values of, 385–387
  importance of creative interests and, 135, 136
  managing development and, 373, 385–387
  multiple sources of interests and, 153
  natural phenomena and, 66
  novelty and, 126
  opportunity and, 144, 145
  people sparking creative interests and, 72, 524, 539
Young-Bruehl, Elisabeth, 17, 84

Z

Zentelis, Enid, 21
  approaches and, 176
  breadth of creative interests and, 213
  creative responses and, 257, 409–412
  guiding principles and values of, 382
  importance of creative interests and, 136
  patterns of development and, 453
  problem solving and, 397
Zhang, Lisa, 397, 398